P9-CSG-014

Time Out

Havana & the best of Cuba

timeout.com/havana

Penguin Books

PENGUIN BOOKS

Published by the Penguin Group
Penguin Books Ltd, 27 Wrights Lane, London W8 5TZ, England
Penguin Books USA Inc., 375 Hudson Street, New York, New York 10014, USA
Penguin Books Australia Ltd, Ringwood, Victoria, Australia
Penguin Books Canada Ltd, 10 Alcorn Avenue, Toronto, Ontario, Canada M4V 3B2
Penguin Books (NZ) Ltd, 182-190 Wairau Road, Auckland 10, New Zealand

Penguin Books Ltd, Registered Offices: Harmondsworth, Middlesex, England

First published 2001
10 9 8 7 6 5 4 3 2 1

Copyright © Time Out Group Ltd, 2001
All rights reserved

Colour reprographics by Westside Digital Media, 9 Bridle Lane, London W1
and Precise Litho, 34-35 Great Sutton Street, London EC1
Printed and bound by Cayfosa-Quebecor, Ctra. de Caldes, Km 3 08 130 Sta, Perpètua de Mogoda, Barcelona, Spain

Except in the United States of America, this book is sold subject to the condition that it shall not, by way of trade or
otherwise, be lent, re-sold, hired out, or otherwise circulated without the publisher's prior consent in any form of binding
or cover other than that in which it is published and without a similar condition including this condition being imposed
on the subsequent purchaser.

Edited and designed by
Time Out Guides Limited
Universal House
251 Tottenham Court Road
London W1T 7AB
Tel + 44 (0)20 7813 3000
Fax + 44 (0)20 7813 6001
Email guides@timeout.com
www.timeout.com

Editorial

Editor Lesley McCave
Consultant Editor Claudia Lightfoot
Deputy Editor Sophie Blacksell
Listings Editor Sarah Haggard
Additional consulting Juliet Barclay Machado, Rosa
Bosch, Nelson Fernández, Sarah Haggard, Martin Hactoun
Additional listings checking Frank Hill Machado
Proofreader Angela Jameson
Indexer Marion Moisy

Editorial Director Peter Fiennes
Series Editor Ruth Jarvis
Deputy Series Editor Jonathan Cox
Editorial Assistant Jenny Noden

Design

Art Director John Oakey
Art Editor Mandy Martin
Senior Designer Scott Moore
Designers Benjamin de Lotz, Lucy Grant
Scanning/Imaging Dan Conway
Picture Editor Kerri Miles
Deputy Picture Editor Olivia Duncan-Jones
Ad Make-up Glen Impey

Advertising

Group Advertisement Director Lesley Gill
Sales Director Mark Phillips
International Sales Co-ordinator Ross Canadé
Advertising Assistant Catherine Shepherd

Administration

Publisher Tony Elliott
Managing Director Mike Hardwick
Financial Director Kevin Ellis
Marketing Director Christine Cort
General Manager Nichola Coulthard
Production Manager Mark Lamond
Production Controller Samantha Furniss
Accountant Sarah Bostock

Features in this guide were written and researched by:

Introduction Lesley McCave. **History** James Mitchell (*Life is sweet* Lucy Davies). **Havana Today** Claudia Lightfoot
(*Religious life* Christine Ayorinde; *Miami nice?* Ariadna Buñuel). **Architecture** Mario Coyula. **Sounds of the City** Katrin
Hansing. **Sightseeing** Susan Hurlich (*Going green* Rami Ahmadi; *Wheel life* Lucy Davies; *Chocolate choo-choo, Club 1830,*
State of the art, The importance of being Ernesto Sophie Blacksell). **Eating & Drinking**
Catherine Bohill, Jason Lang (*Vegging out* Karen McCartney; *Drink up; No more rice and beans!* Martin Hactoun). **Shops &**
Services Nicola Lecerf (*Catering to your needs* Catherine Bohill, Jason Lang; *Rolled gold* Jean Stubbs).
By Season James Mitchell, Ariadna Buñuel, Katrin Hansing. **Children** Sarah Haggard (*Sweet 15* Sue Herrod).
Film Nick Scott (*Cuban films* Rosa Bosch). **Gay & Lesbian** Joseph Mutti. **Music & Nightlife** Katrin Hansing (*Cabaret,*
The Tropicana Ariadna Buñuel). **Performing Arts** Ariadna Buñuel. **Sport & Fitness** Martin Hactoun. **Beyond Havana** Imilla
Cabral (*Guerrilla in the midst* James Mitchell). **Directory** Sophie Blacksell, Sarah Haggard, Lesley McCave, Joseph Mutti
(*The streets of Havana* Susan Hurlich; *US travel to Cuba* Emily Wasserman, Wendy Wasserman; *Students* Catherine
Bohill, Jason Lang; additional text Karen McCartney). Additional text by Lionel Martin.

The Editor would like to thank:

Eva Tarr Kirkhope, Eugene Patron, Nick Fitzpatrick, Ian Rees, Charlie Varley, Isabel Vincente, Helga Stephenson, Lionel
Martin, Steve Buvens, Nick Rider, Naomi Peck, Emily Hatchwell, Fred Mawer, Christopher Baker, Regino Boti, Frank
Broughton, Caroline Taverne, David Adams, Tom Gibb, Steve Marshall, Phil Gunson, Sandra Levinson, Mauricio, Patrice
Merrin Best and her assistant, Nick Caistor, Pascal Fletcher, Sarah's husband, Jordan Levin, Charles Barclay Machado,
Pamela Esterson, Chino, Toti, Jane McManus, Cathy Runciman, Nick Inman, Steve Marshall, Hugo Cancio, Andy Wood,
Martin Lawson-Smith, Andrew Coulthourne, Carole Sutcliffe, Pascal Lecerf, the two Ernestos, Ester, Maritse, Sue Kay,
Moises, Jenny Noden, Caridad, Esther Whitfield, Michael White, Christine Climenhage, Emilia, José, Jorge Mark Frank,
Ariana, Mr Monzote, Christi Daugherty, Sally Davies, Richard Lines, Andy White, Ros Sales, Nicholas Royle, Nana Ocran,
Will Fulford-Jones and all the contributors.

The editor flew to Havana with British Airways (0845 7733377), which has direct flights to Havana from Gatwick Airport.

Maps by: JS Graphics 17 Beadles Lane, Old Oxted, Surrey RH8 9JG.
Maps based on material supplied by Apa Publications GmbH & Co, Verlag KG (Singapore branch).

Photography by Adam Eastland except the following: pages 6, 8, 14, 16, 63, 118 AKG London; page 13 Hulton Getty;
pages 18, 22, 25 Popperfoto/Reuters; pages 29, 109, 199, 261, 262 Rolando Pujol/South American Pictures; page 33,
187, 221, 237, 238 Neil Setchfield; page 43 Geraint Lewis/Film Four Ltd; page 167 Francesca Odell/Impact Photos;
page 179 and 180-181 The Kobal Collection; page 202 and 203 Richard Haughton/Lebrecht Collection; page 211 AP
Wirephoto; page 216 Popperfoto; page 226 Kim Naylor/Aspect Picture Library; page 227 Farzin Malaki/Impact Photos;
page 239 Jim Zipp/Ardea; Mark Cator/Impact; page 264 and 265 Tony Morrison/South American Pictures; page 267
Francois Gohier/Ardea; page 270 John Cancalosi/Ardea.
The following images were provided by the featured establishments or artists: page 44

© Copyright Time Out Group Ltd
All rights reserved

Contents

Introduction

Havana is a city that provokes powerful reactions: visitors either fall completely in love with it or are left totally unmoved. For those that fall under Havana's spell, the city's vibrant atmosphere, its friendly people and its streets lined with centuries of architecture are utterly endearing. For others, the problems that Cubans have to overcome on a daily basis (poor transportation, often below-par food, power cuts, lack of reliable information) prove to be overwhelmingly frustrating. Although strides have been taken in recent years to improve the facilities on offer, Havana is not a place to come if your idea of a holiday is all-out luxury.

Havana is, in many respects, a hidden city. At first, it might seem that, besides visiting a clutch of major sights, there is not that much to do here. In fact, nothing could be further from the truth. There is a wealth of simple pleasures to be enjoyed in Havana: walking the streets of Vedado, whizzing along the Malecón in a *cocotaxi*, braving the frenetic atmosphere of a peso bar – these are experiences that will remain in the memory for a lifetime; they are what the city is all about.

There's no doubt that Havana is attracting an increasing number of tourists and business executives from overseas. Despite the country's economic situation, foreign companies are keen to benefit from the great untapped Cuban marketplace. While clearly a good thing from the perspective of the island's future prosperity, the incursion of capitalism has its negative side, too. A rip-off culture is emerging, most visibly among *jineteros*, usually younger *habaneros*, who see it as a life's crusade to separate tourists from their dollars. The scams are pretty tame by Western standards (black market cigars at inflated prices, extras added to restaurant bills, taxi drivers claiming their meters are broken), but the relentlessness with which such tricks are attempted is breathtaking. It is worth remembering, however, that while the touts and tricksters may be overcharging you, the amounts involved are usually very small, and they almost always need the money more than you do. Indeed, after a few days, and depending on your temperament, you'll either be sick to death of the petty rip-offs or taking a connoisseur's delight in the ingenuity of the Cubans' resourceful ways of getting more Yankee dollars.

Although the US trade embargo was relaxed slightly in late 2000, this is unlikely to have much of an effect on the Cuban economy in the short term. Whether it will be lifted entirely in the near future is impossible to predict. Perhaps the more pressing question is how long Castro will last and what will happen when he is gone? Born in 1926 and ruler of Cuba for the past four decades, his will and energy seem indomitable. Indeed, much Cuban domestic policy seems to be based on the assumption of his immortality. Still, the question of how long he will survive seems to obsess visitors to the island (not to mention the Cubans themselves), and with good reason. Who knows what will happen in the next two, five, ten years.

The only thing certain about Havana's future is that there will be major change. We are in the closing years of one of the great social experiments of the last century. Whether it was a success or a failure is for history to decide. Visit Havana now, before the city is changed beyond all recognition.

ABOUT THE TIME OUT CITY GUIDES

The *Time Out Guide to Havana & the best of Cuba* is one of an expanding series of Time Out City Guides, now numbering over 30, produced by the people behind London and New York's successful listings magazines. Our guides are all written and updated by resident experts who have striven to provide you with all the most up-to-date information you'll need to explore the city or read up on its background, whether you're a local or a first-time visitor. The guide contains detailed practical information, plus features that focus on unique aspects of the city.

THE LOWDOWN ON THE LISTINGS

Above all, we've tried to make this book as useful as possible. Addresses, telephone numbers, websites, opening times, admission prices and, for hotels, credit card details, are included in our listings. And, as far as possible, we've given details of facilities, services and events. However, owners and managers can

There is an online version of this guide, as well as weekly event listings for over 30 international cities, at **www.timeout.com**.

change their arrangements at any time. Also, in Havana and the rest of Cuba, shops, bars and, in particular, *paladares*, don't keep precise opening times, and may close earlier or later than stated. Similarly, arts programmes are often finalised very late. If you're going out of your way to visit a particular venue, we'd advise you whenever possible to phone first. While every effort has been made to ensure the accuracy of the information in this guide, the publishers cannot accept any responsibility for any errors it may contain.

There are two things to remember in Havana: everything will take longer than you are expecting, and everything will cost more than you are expecting. The golden rule is to take a sense of humour with you, wherever you go.

PRICES AND PAYMENT

The prices given in this guide should be treated as guidelines, not gospel. We have listed prices in US dollars ($) throughout, and also in Cuban pesos (rather than *pesos convertibles*) where relevant. Credit cards are generally only accepted in hotels in Havana. (Although other establishments may claim to accept them, in practice, credit card machines are often broken.) We have used the following abbreviations: MC for MasterCard and V for Visa. Note that American Express and cards issued by US banks (or even its subsidiaries outside the US) are not accepted in Cuba.

THE LIE OF THE LAND

To make the book (and the city) easier to navigate, we have divided Havana into areas and assigned each one its own chapter in our **Sightseeing** section (pages 61-122). Although these areas are a simplification of Havana's geography, we hope they will give you a useful means of understanding the city's layout and finding its most interesting sights. The areas are used in addresses throughout the guide.

The oldest part of the city – where many of its main sights are concentrated – is **La Habana Vieja** on the western side of the bay. West of here, beyond the former city walls, is **Centro Habana**, a historic district with several points of interest. Head further west to reach the 19th-century neighbourhood of **Vedado**, bounded to the west by the **Río Almendares**. On the far side of the river, **Miramar & the Western Suburbs** encompass upscale and working-class communities, fishing villages and marinas. The **Eastern Bay & Coast**, on the far side of the Bahía de la Habana, offer a compelling mixture of ancient forts, modern housing developments, provincial villages and golden beaches. South of Vedado is **Cerro**, a rundown district that leads to other attractions further south.

Though distances between the areas Havana can be big, many tourists choose to avoid the hassle and crush of the city buses and opt instead for a taxi (ranging from 1950s yank tanks to air-conditioned tourist taxis), a pedal-powered *bicitaxi*, or a cheeky little orange three-wheeled *cocotaxi*.

TELEPHONE NUMBERS

Havana's phone system can be extremely frustrating and is prone to breakdown. Phone numbers within the city tend to have five or six digits. Phone codes for places outside Havana are listed in full where relevant, for example, in the **Beyond Havana** chapters (pages 222-270). To call Havana from abroad, you need to dial your international access code, then 53 for Cuba and 7 for Havana.

ESSENTIAL INFORMATION

For all the practical information you might need for visiting Havana, including emergency phone numbers and details of local transport, turn to the **Directory** chapter at the back of the guide. It starts on page 272.

MAPS

We provide a map reference for all places listed in central Havana, indicating the page and grid reference at which an address can be found on our street maps. These are located at the back of the book (pages 303-316), and include a map of Cuba (page 304), an overview map of Havana (page 305) and detailed street maps of the city (pages 309-316). To make the maps easier to navigate, there is also a street index (pages 306-8). Street maps for towns in the **Beyond Havana** section of the guide (pages 222-270) are included in the relevant chapter.

LET US KNOW WHAT YOU THINK

We hope you enjoy the *Time Out Guide to Havana & the best of Cuba*, and we'd like to know what you think of it. We welcome tips for places that you consider we should include in future editions and take note of your criticism of our choices. There's a reader's reply card at the back of this book for your feedback – or you can email us at havanaguide@timeout.com.

Advertisers

We would like to stress that no establishment has been included in this guide because it has advertised in any of our publications and no payment of any kind has influenced any review. The opinions given in this book are those of *Time Out* writers and are entirely independent.

timeout.com

The World's Living Guide

In Context

Feature boxes

Columbus is greeted by the indigenous inhabitants of the New World. Little did they know...

History

Cuba and its capital have been subjected to the extremes of foreign intervention, from the virtual extinction of its earliest inhabitants by settlers to the 40-year US embargo.

The written history of the Caribbean begins with the arrival of Christopher Columbus (Cristóbal Colón in Spanish). What we know of the people and society of Cuba prior to his arrival is inevitably derived from the writings of the Spanish explorers themselves and subsequent archaeological explorations. However rich and varied life in pre-Columbian Cuba may have been, there is no evidence that the indigenous peoples possessed a written language.

The earliest inhabitants of Cuba are thought to have been the Siboney (or Ciboney), a group that migrated (somewhat ironically) from Florida and spread throughout the Caribbean. The archaeological evidence for their existence indicates that they were hunter-gatherers, living in small groups near the shoreline or close to rivers and streams. The Siboney

disappeared from the record some time between AD 1 and AD 1000, to be replaced by the more technologically savvy Taino people. It is unclear if the Siboneys were absorbed into or replaced by their successors.

The Taino were excellent farmers, boat builders and fishermen. Consequently, their society flourished throughout the Caribbean. Their higher degree of technological sophistication led to more complex social structures with clear leaders and class hierarchies. Labour was divided based on age and sex. Men cleared and defended the village, while women cultivated crops and produced manufactured goods (such as pottery and fishing nets). Seafood was the main source of protein, with the result that most Taino settlements were located within easy reach of the sea.

TROUBLE IN PARADISE

When Christopher Columbus first set foot on
Cuban soil on 29 October 1492, life on the island
changed for ever. That day marked the official
beginning of Spanish rule on the island, which
was to last for over 400 years. Columbus left
only a handful of men on Cuba when he sailed
home to Spain early in 1493, but returned
later in the year with 17 ships, 1,500 men
and the usual cohort of missionaries, labourers,
livestock, farm equipment, stowaways, rats,
disease and bad attitude.

Spain was abetted in its imperial ambitions
by the extremely pliant Pope Alexander VI,
who, in a series of aptly named 'bulls' issued
during the ensuing decade, effectively handed
over the lion's share of territories in the New
World to Spain (at the expense of its main rival
Portugal). The Spanish conquistadors were
given a free rein to do as they pleased, and what
pleased them was conquest. There followed a
period of barbarity, genocide, hypocrisy and
mismanagement on an epic scale. Indigenous
populations were exterminated, local flora
and fauna were pushed aside to make way for
European varieties, minerals and other natural
resources were torn from the earth by slave
labour and shipped wholesale back to Spain.
But it wasn't all bad news: the Spaniards
also built some very nice churches.

Until recently, the conventional view has
been that the Spaniards totally exterminated
the Taino in Cuba through the imaginative and
diligent application of disease, cruelty (in the
form of slavery and torture) and murder.
More recent evidence, while not detracting
from the conquistadors' formidable skills as
psychopaths, indicates that a few scattered
pockets of Taino society survived, no doubt
overlooked in the general butchery. (Even
today there are numerous groups and societies
aimed at uniting the scattered modern
descendents of the Taino.)

For the first 15 years after its discovery,
Cuba was little more than a staging post
for further colonisation. Explorers busied
themselves discovering other parts of the
Caribbean and American mainland. It wasn't
until 1508 that Sebastián de Ocampo was
appointed to circumnavigate Cuba and
found that it was in fact an island. The pace
of life in Cuba changed dramatically in 1511,
when Diego Columbus (Chris's son) decided
to 'settle' the island and appointed Diego
Velázquez as its first Governor. To celebrate
the arrival of civilisation in the New World, the
new lords of Cuba quickly set about 'enslaving'
or killing all but a handful of the indigenous
Taino. After a short time, the penny dropped
that by wiping out the locals, the Spaniards

had also destroyed their only convenient source
of labour. This little gaffe was easily remedied,
however, in 1513, when the first slaves from
Africa arrived in Cuba by way of Hispaniola
(present-day Dominican Republic and Haiti).

LAYING THE FOUNDATIONS

As early as 1512 the settlement of Cuba
was progressing at a frenetic rate and it
was clear that towns were needed to provide
administrative focus and to house the island's
burgeoning class of officers, bureaucrats,
merchants and clerics. Seven small *villas* were
founded across the island during the next few
years (they were Baracoa, Santiago de Cuba,
Bayamo, Sancti Spíritus, Trinidad, San
Cristóbal de la Habana and Puerto Príncipe –
now Camagüey). Pánfilo de Narváez established
the westernmost of these in July 1515, and
named it San Cristóbal de la Habana (after a
prominent local Indian chief, Habaguanex,
though this is disputed). Havana was originally
located about 50 kilometres (31 miles) south of
its current location, near the present-day town
of Batabanó, but this region was found to be
marshy and plagued with mosquitoes, so the
city was soon relocated to the north coast.
The second site turned out to be an equally
bad choice, so the whole caboodle was uprooted
once more, coming to rest in its current home
in November 1519.

The same year, after setting off from
Santiago de Cuba, conquistador Hernán Cortés
and his fleet stopped for supplies in Havana
harbour en route to Mexico on his notorious
mission to convert the Aztecs into a historical
footnote. The expedition was deemed a huge
success back in Spain, and the knock-on
effect meant that Havana rapidly became
an important hub for Spanish activities in the
Caribbean. Its large, sheltered harbour provided
an ideal anchorage for merchant vessels en
route to Spain, laden with silver and gold
plundered from Central and South America.

When Spanish galleons opened the
Philippines for trade in 1564, Havana's fortune
was made. Goods bound for Spain were shipped
to Acapulco on Mexico's west coast, carried
overland to Veracruz on the Gulf of Mexico,
and then shipped to Havana. Once there,
the ships joined the semi-annual Armada that
completed the final perilous Atlantic crossing to
Spain. All the riches of the New World and the
Orient passed through the city. Unbelievably, in
1583, the Armada had to leave one million gold
pesos behind because they had no room left
in the holds to carry it.

For all its wealth, Havana also had the
drawbacks associated with a boom town. It was
filthy with sewage and rotten produce; drunks,

cut-throats, and whores roamed the mud streets, and during hot weather, yellow fever epidemics were frequent. Inevitably, Havana's growing prosperity attracted the attention of the less salubrious elements of Caribbean life. During its first century, the greatest threat facing the city (aside from the rapacious greed of Spain itself) came from English, Dutch and French pirates. The city was extensively plundered or burned with monotonous regularity, until in 1558, fed up with being put to the sword, the *habaneros* began the construction of the Castillo de la Real Fuerza as a defensive bastion on the edge of the bay. In 1589 they added another two fortresses – Castillo de Los Tres Reyes del Morro and Castillo San Salvador de La Punta – on either side of the harbour entrance. A heavy chain was stretched across the harbour mouth and could be lifted into place to block the entrance. The three castles and the chain at last afforded an effective defence for the city. The pirates responded by simply plundering Spanish ships

on the open seas instead of in the harbour.

By the late 16th century, Caribbean piracy had become big business and was well organised. English and French pirates were often licensed by their governments to prey on Spanish shipping, as a means of weakening Spain's hold on the New World. The destruction of the Spanish Armada in the English Channel in 1587 was a major blow to Spain's imperial ambitions and further increased the vulnerability of its colonies to piracy.

Despite these setbacks, Havana grew in power and significance throughout the 16th century. Its position as the fulcrum of Spanish exploration in the Caribbean made it the pre-eminent city of the New World (even though Mexico City and Lima were larger), and the Cuban capital was officially moved from Santiago de Cuba to Havana in 1607.

The city continued to be a key trading and administrative centre through the 17th and early 18th centuries. Slaves, coffee, tobacco and, later, sugar kept the populace fat and happy,

Life is sweet

The significance of sugar in Cuba is perhaps best illustrated by the fact that the Cuban army's second in command is the country's Minister of Sugar. If you understand the history of sugar in Cuba, you understand Cuba. Every single twist and turn of the country's history has been inextricably linked to this single crop.

Christopher Columbus brought sugar cane cuttings to Cuba on his second trip to the Indies. He understood that even if the New World wasn't full of gold, it could become rich by servicing the European sweet tooth. Land was cleared, fields were planted with cane – especially in the central plain between Havana and Trinidad and further east towards Santiago – and Cuba's indigenous population, the Taino, were forced to work on the plantations. In the 100 years that followed Columbus's discovery of the island, European diseases and hard labour combined to wipe out the Taino, compelling the Spaniards to look elsewhere for their labourers. The British trade in African slaves soon became the prime source of manual labour in Cuba. Africans were put to work in *ingenios* (sugar plantations) where they lived and worked all their lives.

Large-scale sugar production in Cuba began in the early 19th century, when French planters fleeing from the slave revolts in Haiti

settled on the island, bringing new production techniques with them. Sugar cane starts to ferment as soon as it has been cut, so most *ingenios* became factories, where the raw material could be quickly processed. Production increased rapidly during the following decades, becoming the keystone in the Cuban economy and creating a wealthy class of plantation owner known as the *sacarocracía* ('saccarocracy').

By the 1860s Cuba was supplying one third of the world's sugar. US investors moved in quickly, concentrating the ownership of land and mills in American hands, and when the Wars of Independence came to an end in 1898, they were ready to take control of the country and its sugar industry.

while trade (legal and illegal) made them rich. Like the nouveaux riches of any age, affluent *habaneros* flaunted their wealth. The miserable shacks and smelly streets of the boom town no longer suited a city whose economic prominence was on a par with many European capitals. Stonemasons and craftsmen were brought from Spain to build vast mansions (*palacios*), full of columns and arches, grand staircases and tiled courtyards. In 1674, work began on the massive walls that would take the best part of a century to build, ultimately enclosing the city within a protective ring of stone ten metres (35 feet) high.

FIRST STIRRINGS OF REVOLUTION

In 1715 Spain created a monopolistic agency known as the *Factoria*, which purchased all Cuban tobacco at a (low) fixed price and had exclusive rights to sell it abroad. The tobacco growers tried to rebel, but were brutally suppressed by the military. This little scam worked so well that in 1740 the Real

Compañia de Comercio was founded to control all imports to and exports from the port of Havana. The resulting extortionate customs duties, inflated import prices and restricted supplies of goods caused great discontent among the populace. A black economy quickly sprang up, and Havana became the smuggling centre of the Caribbean.

In June 1762 a large British expeditionary force captured Havana. The British did not expand their holdings beyond the port, and their occupation of the city lasted less than a year. The new masters removed trading restrictions, allowing Havana to trade freely with the rest of the world for the first time, and the city prospered under the brief British rule. Unfortunately, however, the British commander, the Earl of Albermarle, was just as greedy as his Spanish predecessors, and taxed the populace and the Catholic Church heavily. When the British ceded control of the city back to Spain in 1763 in return for Spanish-held territories in Florida, they were not missed.

The occupying Americans took over the island like kids raiding a sweet shop, mopping up huge tracts of land which the departing Spaniards sold at rock-bottom prices. Cuba was only 90 miles away from the US and labour was cheap. Milton Hershey, for example, bought land and built himself a sugar factory to supply his chocolate empire in Pennsylvania. Cuban infrastructure was also vastly improved to enable sugar barons to produce more efficiently the huge amounts of sugar the American market was now demanding.

When Castro came to power, the US lost its supply of Cuban sugar and Hawaii was quickly brought in by the United States to replace it. Cuba however, continued to produce the sweet stuff on a massive scale, selling it in exchange for goods from its communist allies. Until 1991 sugar was Cuba's prime currency for buying crude oil from the USSR and sugar workers were encouraged by Che Guevara to achieve a ten million-tonne harvest. (This extraordinary target has never been achieved, but is still talked about at the beginning of each year's *zafra* – sugar cane harvest.) The sugar industry became simultaneously the engine that drove the Revolution and a symbol of the Revolution's triumph.

When property began to be nationalised in 1960, thousands of wealthy Cubans left the country and began an economic exodus that

had previously been limited to the foreign inhabitants of the island. Fidel and Che made excursions into the sugar cane fields, apparently to cover the labour shortages, picked up their machetes and chopped cane by hand alongside the *macheteros* of rural Cuba.

Nowadays the industry survives, like the rest of Cuba, on the dream of the Revolution. Sugar is no longer exported and no longer buys oil – the collapse of the Soviet Union left Cuba without a market for its prime resource and without oil to power its factories, which now produce less than half the volume they achieved in the '60s. When the Helms-Burton Act (*see pxxx*) became law under Bill Clinton in 1996, alternative markets disappeared overnight.

So Cuba has had to reinvent itself as a tourist destination. Its white gold fills the little bags of Buen Día sugar that turn up in every tourist establishment throughout the island; the rest is sent to the *bodegas* (government ration shops) where pound bags of brown, semi-refined sugar are doled out along with the monthly ration of coffee, rice and beans. Unless the embargo is lifted so that the industry can renew itself with new trade partners and spare parts, it seems that it will eventually come to a bittersweet end.

Spain was back in charge and quickly reintroduced its restrictive trade policies, but Cuban landowners and merchants had got a taste of the economic potential of free trade. Things would never be the same again.

After regaining control, the Spanish undertook an extensive programme of renewal and modernisation in Havana that was to last for most of the next century: streets were cobbled and gas lighting installed; sewers and drains were built; architectural styles were harmonised; parks and grand avenues were built and a strict grid pattern was imposed on the street layout. Havana was Spain's showpiece in the New World, a great city of 55,000 inhabitants, and the Spanish wanted everyone to know it.

Havana prospered during the Napoleonic Wars (1792-1815), despite trade restrictions and punitive duties imposed by the Crown. Demand for sugar increased dramatically, and large amounts of capital poured into creating new production capacity. Trade between Cuba and the newly established United States rapidly became an important source of revenue for the island. In 1817 the British brokered an agreement with the other Caribbean colonial powers to end the slave trade, but Cuba's fast-growing economy was heavily reliant on slave labour. The trade simply moved underground and continued to grow. Between 1821 and 1831 alone, an estimated 500,000 slaves passed through Cuba.

The arrival of a period of relative peace on the European continent after the Napoleonic Wars prompted Spain to lessen the financial drain on its colonies. Discontent over crippling taxation and heavy-handed leadership had been growing for a number of years throughout the New World, but by this point the chorus of complaint had grown loud enough to be heard in Spain. In an effort to calm tensions, the *Factoria* tobacco monopoly in Cuba was abolished in 1816. The gesture was too little, too late. The fires of revolution were already burning throughout the Latin world.

HERE COMES THE USA

In the 1820s the United States began to stretch its political wings overseas. It articulated a sweeping policy concerning the Americas that would have lasting repercussions for Cuba right up to the present day. The policy, most clearly expressed as the Monroe Doctrine, claimed the Western hemisphere as a US sphere of influence and warned Europe not to interfere in the affairs of any of the newly independent American nations. While it might be tempting to interpret the Monroe Doctrine as an expression of support by the US for its post-colonial neighbours, in practice the Doctrine has been used repeatedly by the United States to justify the most shameless interference in the internal affairs of other American nations.

By 1824 all of Spain's pigeons had come home to roost. Years of poor leadership, greed, arrogance and military ineptitude had cost it the bulk of its great American empire, which at one time had spanned nearly all of South and Central America and much of what is now the western United States. All that remained were two small islands – Puerto Rico and Cuba – and the Spanish were determined to hold on to these vestiges of their former greatness. The USA, on the other hand, felt that these two islands would make a lovely addition to its young nation. The sound of heels being dug in could probably be heard on the moon.

> ## 'In 1867 Spain demonstrated its feeble grasp of political reality by imposing taxes on property, income and goods.'

The first direct US intervention in Cuban affairs occurred in 1825. Newly liberated Mexico and Venezuela intended to mount an expedition to Cuba to free the island from Spanish rule. The US, fearing independence would end Cuba's participation in the slave trade (a major source of labour for the southern United States), made it clear that it would block any such move. US policy at that time was to distance Cuba and Puerto Rico from other Latin American countries, increase their reliance on the US as a trading partner, and thereby hasten their ultimate incorporation into the US itself. The policy was very effective and, helped in no small measure by continued Spanish mismanagement (crippling taxation, capricious legislation and disenfranchisement of mixed-blood Cubans), US influence in Cuba grew quickly.

By 1842 the value of Cuban exports to the US was double that to Spain. In 1848 President Polk felt that Cuba had become a US colony in all but name and promptly offered Spain $100 million for its territory. The Spanish government turned him down. For the next 20 years the US made numerous attempts to either buy Cuba from Spain or forcibly to annex it. This cat-and-mouse game continued until the end of the US Civil War, when the abolition of slavery diminished Cuba's value to the USA.

By the mid 19th century Cuba's once relatively diversified agricultural base had been almost completely turned over to the exclusive production of a single crop: sugar.

The economics of sugar production at the time required large amounts of slave labour, but by this time the African slave trade had largely dried up. In 1849 the first Yucatán indians were brought to Havana to be used as slave labour on surrounding farms, and indentured workers also began to arrive in large numbers from China.

While the Cuban sugar industry relied heavily on slave labour – there were 600,000 slaves working on the plantations by 1867 – the Cuban economy as a whole relied almost entirely on its ability to find an export market for this single cash crop and to import all the other goods it required. By the 1860s Cuba was producing one third of the world's sugar and attracting increasing interest from US investors who began to buy up sugar mills and plantations. *See also pp8-9* **Life is sweet**.

Whatever the long-term negative economic and political ramifications of Cuba's emergence as a monocrop economy, for the average wealthy *habanero* in the 1860s it was a good thing. Increased prosperity had resulted in new affluent neighbourhoods springing up outside the city walls. The colonial city centre became a congested slum as Havana's rich fled the old city for leafy suburbs like Cerro and later Vedado. In 1863 the city walls were torn down to accommodate Havana's explosion into the surrounding countryside.

THE TEN YEARS WAR

Early in 1867 Spain once again demonstrated its uncannily feeble grasp of political reality by imposing a new suite of taxes on property, income and goods. This was in addition to the extortionate duties already being levied on imported and exported goods, which had pushed Cubans to the brink of revolt several times in the recent past. Later in the year, the Spanish government summarily dismissed a delegation sent by Havana to Madrid to request reforms. The bonfire of revolution had once again been built and this time there was a match to light it. It came in the form of a telegram between two high-ranking Spanish officers, ordering the arrest and imprisonment of Cuba's leading dissidents. The telegram was intercepted by revolutionary sympathisers and passed on to the self-same dissidents, who had no intention of waiting around to be arrested.

The revolutionary war that followed spanned the length and breadth of Cuba for a decade. The Ten Years War officially began on 10 October 1868 when Carlos Manuel de Céspedes proclaimed Cuban independence and freed his slaves (before immediately drafting them into his rebel army), and ended on 21 May 1878 when the rebels accepted Spanish peace terms.

While the war achieved little of material benefit and certainly cost many lives, it had three effects. First, it gave Cuba the homegrown leaders and revolutionary heroes it needed to rally the populace to the cause of independence. Men such as Antonio Maceo, Carlos Manuel de Céspedes and Máximo Gómez have inspired generations of Cuban freedom fighters, and are still remembered in literature, song and monument throughout the country. Secondly, the war instilled a revolutionary spirit into the Cuban people that they possess to this day. Finally, it destroyed large amounts of agricultural land and bankrupted many Cuban sugar planters, thereby opening the door to a virtual monopoly of the Cuban sugar industry by US interests. These countervailing forces would shape much of the island's later history.

The terms of the treaty that was intended to end the war in February 1878 were hardly satisfactory from the Cuban perspective. The *Pacto de Zanjón* (Treaty of Zanjón) freed any slaves who fought on either side in the war, but left the institution of slavery in place. More alarmingly, Cuba would remain subject to Spanish rule, though its people were given some limited representation in the Spanish *Cortés* (parliament). The military leaders of the revolution continued fighting in defiance of the revolutionary government for several months, but were finally forced to accept the treaty in the face of vastly superior Spanish forces. The revolutionaries were not happy with such a settlement, however; in their minds the war had not been resolved, only deferred.

Slavery in Cuba was finally abolished by Royal Decree on 7 October 1886, not due to any surge of humanitarian feeling by the Spanish Crown, but simply because of the depressed state of the world sugar market in the decade following the war. Economic realities made it more profitable to free slaves and then hire them back to work by the day, thus avoiding the expense of year-round employment.

In 1891 the US removed the tariffs on sugar imported from Cuba and negotiated trade agreements with Spain that increased imports to the US. This newly enlarged market further increased Cuban dependency on its big brother and encouraged an increase in sugar production. When the US changed its mind and reinstated the tariffs on sugar in 1894, the decision had devastating effects on the Cuban economy.

REVOLUTION REDUX

The social upheavals that resulted from the collapse of the Cuban sugar industry led directly to the 1895-98 Cuban War of Independence. The greatest leader (and martyr) to emerge from the conflict was José Martí (*see p13* **Apostle of the nation**). Martí and his rebels attempted to make Cuba 'economically viable and politically independent'. Martí was killed in the revolution but his vision remains at the centre of Cuban political life still. Unfortunately, it is yet to be achieved.

The War of Independence was brutal and bloody with atrocities committed by both sides. Once again, the shadow of US interests fell across the proceedings, with American public opinion firmly on the side of the Cuban rebels. When the battleship USS *Maine* exploded and sank in Havana harbour on 15 February 1898, it provided the pretext for the US to enter the conflict and signalled the beginning of the Spanish-American War. It must have seemed to the US the perfect opportunity to prise Cuba away from Spain. The war was relatively short, lasting three months from declaration to settlement; just enough time for Havana to be blockaded and the Spanish fleet to be defeated at Santiago de Cuba. With US help, the rebels had won. Cuba was free.

NO SUCH THING AS A FREE COUNTRY

The first hint the Cubans got that they had been conned was their exclusion from the peace table. The US and Spain negotiated terms for the withdrawal of Spanish forces and agreed the means by which control of the island would pass to the US, with no input from the Cubans themselves. When the final Spanish ship sailed out of Havana harbour in 1899, the last vestige of the Spanish Empire was gone, but Cuba was still a long way from Martí's ideal of economic viability and political independence. For the next four years the island was occupied by US troops. That was followed by 60 years of US interference in Cuban society and politics, focused less on building a sustainable platform for democracy on the island than on protecting American commercial interests.

The US occupation had two principal objectives: firstly to rebuild the physical infrastructure that had been destroyed by the war, and secondly to ensure that the new Cuban political and constitutional framework was shaped in a way favourable to US business interests. Achievement of this goal was assisted in large part by the introduction of the Platt Amendment, the first in a long and distinguished line of US laws that had the effect of making life for Cubans as unpleasant as possible.

In 1902, the Republic of Cuba was created, with Tomás Estrada Palma its first president. Estrada, a political pragmatist, was in favour of US annexation of Cuba, which put him in opposition to the more anti-American elements within Cuban political life. As a result, schisms rapidly developed between pro- and anti-American elements. Congressional elections in 1904 were marked by violence and vote-rigging. The 1906 presidential election was also a violent mess. Estrada was elected to a second term, but the process had been such a transparent sham that, again, the US stepped in and forced new elections. Estrada and his cabinet unexpectedly resigned in protest, forcing the US to return occupying forces to Cuba. The troops returned twice more (in 1912 and 1917) in response to outbreaks of unrest that the Cuban authorities were unable to control.

To repair the worsening situation, President Teddy Roosevelt appointed Charles Mangoon as Governor of Cuba. Mangoon took to his job with a passion, and within a few months was universally hated by Cubans (regardless of political stripe). He utterly failed in his attempt to codify and rationalise Cuban law, and was responsible for the creation of the Cuban Armed Forces, the highly politicised national army that was a blot on the landscape of island politics for the rest of the pre-Castro period.

Mangoon served until 1909 when, mercifully, José Gómez was elected Cuban president. He was succeeded in 1913 by Mario Menocal, who was re-elected in 1917 amid what had become virtually de rigueur allegations of fraud, and calls for US intervention. Menocal was followed by his protégé, Alfredo Zayas in 1921.

Despite the political climate, the period of the US occupation was also a time of great opportunity in Cuba. Large amounts of capital flowed into the country from the US, and thousands of Americans settled on the island. Whole industries were rebuilt and manufacturing output returned quickly to levels reached before the War of Independence. The fact that these revitalised industries were now largely American-owned was not lost on the more alert observers of the time. Renewed industrial expansion fuelled rapid growth in Havana's population (which trebled between 1900 and 1930). Massive public works projects were undertaken to create more habitable land by filling low-lying and marshy areas with millions of tonnes of earth. New beach communities sprang up. Neoclassical mansions were built along wide avenues in Miramar and other new communities west of the Almendares River. Electrification spread across the extended city and clean water became a reality in most homes. Sewage and drainage systems were modernised, and Havana at last lost its characteristic reek. The goal of all this renewal and expansion was the attraction of tourism. In the short space of 15 years, Havana

Apostle of the nation

José Martí was born in Havana to Spanish parents on 28 January 1853. A man of prodigious energy and talent, he is almost as famous for his works of poetry and prose as he is for his role in Cuban revolutionary history. He was certainly an early bloomer. While still at school, Martí worked on at least two underground newspapers dedicated to the revolutionary overthrow of the Spanish regime. He was barely 16 when he was convicted of subversion and sentenced to six years' hard labour. But the young man was exiled to Spain before the end of his sentence, a move that was to prove crucial to his intellectual development. While there he was able to attend the great universities of Madrid and Zaragoza, graduating in 1873 with a law degree, which he followed in 1874 with philosophy and literature. His education and experiences shaped his raw talent into a potent and vocal weapon against oppression.

After leaving university, Martí moved to Mexico and began his academic and literary career. Never one to temper his opinions in the face of authority, he soon came into conflict with the Mexican government and was forced to move on again. A short period in Guatemala was also curtailed by Martí's highly public opposition to government corruption, however his exposure to Latin American countries that were free of Spanish rule gave final shape to Martí's political and social convictions. He became an even more committed anticolonialist and, somewhat uniquely for the time, espoused the rights of

man regardless of race or national heritage. In 1878 he returned to Cuba as part of a general amnesty, and was soon sounding the call for revolutionary change to any who would listen. Almost as quickly, he found himself again an exile, taking up residence briefly in Venezuela and finally settling, still short of his 30th birthday, in New York. Martí remained in New York from 1881 to 1895 working as a journalist and editor (for both American and foreign publications), acting as the consul for Paraguay, Uruguay and Argentina, and teaching high-school Spanish. He formed the Cuban Revolutionary Party, and, in his spare time, churned out essays and books of poetry that are still ranked as among the finest in the Spanish language. His collected literary and journalistic works span 73 volumes.

Martí returned to Cuba for the last time in 1895 at the beginning of the War of Independence. He briefly lead a company of insurgents drawn from his Cuban Revolutionary Party, but was killed by gunfire in a skirmish with Spanish troops at Dos Ríos in Oriente province (now Granma) on 19 May 1895.

With Martí's death, the cause of Cuban nationalism had gained its first, and greatest, martyr. Known as the 'Apostle of the nation' in Cuba, his name lives on into the 21st century as a symbol of the struggle for liberty. In many ways he has become all things to all men; he is as revered and (mis)quoted by the Cuban left as he is by the Florida exile community. Havana's airport is named after him... and so is a primary school in suburban Miami.

transformed itself from a war-ravaged hellhole into an irresistible magnet for foreign visitors.

Outside of the tourist areas and affluent neighbourhoods, however, it was a different story. Housing for lower-income families was generally poor and cramped, with several families crammed into inadequate spaces. The *palacios* that had once housed the upper classes were now subdivided into dozens of dwellings. Sanitation was nonexistent and disease a

constant threat. Discontent among the poor and dispossessed, who felt that they had gained little from Cuba's independence, fuelled much of the violence and protest that became an integral part of mid 20th-century political life on the island.

World War I was a time of great prosperity in Cuba. The US and its allies bought each year's entire sugar harvest, and once again supply grew to meet demand. The industry enjoyed

Students demonstrating in Havana against Batista, 1956.

enormous profitability from 1915 until 1920 when sugar prices soared. The period was known as 'the dance of the millions'... and was predictably accompanied by a new building boom in Havana. When sugar prices collapsed in 1921, however, the economy fell to its knees and the new President Zayas found himself the leader of a crippled country. He immediately implemented an austerity programme and negotiated a large loan from JP Morgan. The economy recovered, and Zayas left office in 1925 with a personal fortune of around $15 million.

Havana's ambition to become the premier tourist destination in the Caribbean was helped immensely in 1919 when the US implemented Prohibition laws. The resulting boom in Cuban tourism even helped to insulate the island, albeit only partially, from the effects of the sugar crisis. As the Stateside moral crusade gained momentum, holidaymakers flocked to Havana, where they could sin with impunity. Twenty cruise ships sailed from the US to Havana every week, and fares were so low that virtually anyone could afford the trip. Sun, sea, sex, drink, drugs, gambling – who could ask for anything more? For those who did ask there was opera, baseball, deep-sea fishing, golf and ballroom dancing.

ALL GOOD THINGS...

As the 1920s wore on, dissatisfaction with US interference brought nationalism once again to the forefront of the Cuban political agenda. General Gerardo Machado ran for president in 1924 on a nationalist ticket and won easily (he may even have done so without vote rigging). Through manipulation of both the Cuban electorate and the US government, Machado managed to get his term of office extended from the normal four years to six. Everyone was happy. The Cubans thought they had finally elected a president who was committed

to real independence. The Americans thought that their business interests were at last in safe hands. They were both wrong.

Machado's regime set new standards in brutality and corruption. He repressed the working class, the labour unions and students, inadvertently giving the Communist Party (or rather its pre-Revolutionary form, the Partido Socialista Popular, founded by Julio Mella in 1925) and other leftist organisations their first significant measure of popular support. The public's loathing of Machado became intertwined with a more general dissatisfaction with Cuba's dependency on the US and the hated Platt Amendment. The Wall Street Crash of 1929 and the subsequent worldwide Great Depression tied a bow on the whole sorry situation.

THE RISE OF BATISTA

In 1933 the US, which had been immersed in its own Depression-related problems, returned its attention to Cuba and discovered that, in Machado, it had helped to create a monster. For once the Americans exercised restraint and eschewed intervention in favour of sending an ambassador to resolve the situation. A combination of labour unrest, political pressure from the US and crumbling support at home precipitated Machado's resignation and flight into exile. The temporary government that replaced him also soon collapsed in the face of growing popular unrest and in September 1933 a number of non-commissioned officers seized power in an action known as the 'revolt of the Sergeants'. They installed a governing committee chosen by the student movement, and chose Dr Ramón Grau San Martín (a popular professor) as president.

The new revolutionary government lasted only 100 days, but it attempted to implement major changes in Cuban society. It repealed the Platt Amendment, established fair working practices, gave the poor access to university education, granted land to peasant farmers, enfranchised women, and reduced utility prices. The US, predictably, felt that such reforms bordered on communism, and so refused to recognise the new government.

Meanwhile, one of the revolting sergeants (so to speak), Fulgencio Batista, was busy forging the personal and business relationships that were to define the shape of Cuban politics and society for the next 25 years. He formed a friendship with mobster and gambling boss Meyer Lansky, as well as with one of President Franklin Roosevelt's closest advisers, Sumner Welles, who became a stout supporter of Batista.

'Behind the scenes, it was a different story. Batista's rule was characterised by corruption and violence.'

In January 1934 Batista forced the resignation of the revolutionary government, which he quickly replaced with his own cronies. The US immediately recognised the new government and signed the Treaty on Relations, which revoked the Platt Amendment but allowed the US to continue leasing Guantánamo Bay. Although six other men held the title of president between 1934 and 1940, it was Batista who held the real power in Cuba in these years.

During the 1940s the Batista regime was concerned with creating the appearance of good government, if not its substance. After six years as the power behind the throne, Batista had himself properly elected to the post in 1940. At the same time, a Cuban constitution was adopted that was a model of social justice and the prudent exercise of governmental power. In 1943 the Communist Party was legalised. Two years later Cuba joined the United Nations. And finally, after the candidate Batista had groomed for the presidency lost to Grau in a more-or-less democratic election in 1944, Batista graciously took himself off to 'retirement' in Florida the following year.

Behind the scenes, it was a different story. Batista's rule (whether in his own name or not) was characterised by corruption and violence. Political opponents were eliminated, student and labour groups repressed and political dissent harshly punished. It would be unfair to point the finger solely at Batista, however. The two presidents in power from 1944 to 1952 (Grau and his protégé, Carlos Prío Socarrás) presided over regimes that were, if anything, more corrupt and depraved that Batista's. The

old maxim about power corrupting was elevated to the status of divine law in Cuba.

The pretence couldn't last for ever, though. When Batista's pet candidate again lost the presidential election in 1948, Batista seemingly began to grow bored with democracy and, in 1952 he seized power in a bloodless coup, ruling as dictator until he was deposed by Castro in 1959. His new government was once again immediately recognised by the US.

While showing all the outward trappings of a democrat, Batista spent most of the 1940s cosying up to US organised crime and big business interests. He effectively handed over the booming tourist industry to the mob (in return for a piece of the action, naturally). Cuba quickly became a mecca for gambling, drug trafficking, and prostitution. These businesses operated with impunity for a decade (until they were shut down after the 1959 Revolution). In 1946 notorious mobster 'Lucky' Luciano called a summit in Havana's Hotel Nacional; among the topics discussed that night was the assassination of Bugsy Siegel.

By the mid to late 1950s, tourism had done much to eliminate the reliance of the Cuban economy on sugar production. It created tens of thousands of service-sector jobs and pumped billions of dollars into the economy. Batista was beginning to plough some of this money into urban renewal projects, aimed at improving living conditions throughout Havana. Unfortunately, his time had nearly run out.

YOU SAY YOU WANT A REVOLUTION

By this point, the Cuban peasantry and working class had endured a bellyful of bad government. For more than 450 years they had been ruled by one mendacious incompetent after another. Worse, their destiny seemed to be as a perennial pawn in someone else's game, whether the Spanish, the British, the Americans, or some homegrown despot. Revolution had twice failed to secure Cuba's independence. Maybe it would be 'third time lucky'.

The revolution got off to a very bad start. On 26 July 1953, Fidel Castro, a 27-year-old lawyer and political activist, lead a revolt in which 150 people attacked the Moncada army barracks near Santiago de Cuba, 800 kilometres (500 miles) from Havana. The attack was a failure; Castro and his brother Raúl were arrested, and around 70 of his followers were killed, either during the attack or following the subsequent trial. During the trial Castro made a speech outlining his vision for a radically reformed Cuban society. His 'History Will Absolve Me' speech, together with other speeches made by the defendants during the trial, formed the basis of the Moncada Program, the foundation upon which the Cuban Revolution would be built. At the end of the trial, Castro was sentenced to 15 years in prison. He was released and exiled to Mexico less than two years later as part of an amnesty instituted by Batista to curry favour with an increasingly hostile Cuban populace.

On 2 December 1956 Batista had cause to wonder if his 'generosity' in releasing the Castro brothers had been a mistake. Like the proverbial bad penny, they were back, and this time they had brought with them an Argentinian doctor named Ernesto 'Che' Guevara (*see also p242* **Guerrilla in the midst**). On a leaky 60-foot yacht named *Granma*, in miserable weather, Fidel and Raúl Castro, Che Guevara and 82 men landed in the eastern Cuban province of Oriente (now renamed, aptly enough, Granma) and the 26th of July Movement (*Movimiento 26 de Julio* in Spanish, often shortened to M-26-7) is born. Che described the Revolutionaries' arrival as 'less of a landing, more of a shipwreck.' There was worse to come.

The invasion was supposed to be part of a general anti-Batista uprising orchestrated by leftist political parties, student activists and labour unions in Cuba. Unfortunately, the uprising failed to develop, which left Fidel and Che rather in the lurch. To add injury to insult, Batista's forces had been tipped off about the invasion and were waiting for Castro's small force when it landed. In the ensuing firefight, most of the Revolutionaries were either killed or captured, but Fidel and Raúl Castro, Che Guevara and a handful of others managed to escape to the Sierra Maestra. Sitting in the mountains in late 1956, Fidel must have wondered what he and the 11 rain-soaked men huddled around him could hope to accomplish. All things considered, the Cuban Revolution had not made the most auspicious entrance on to the world stage.

From their mountain base, the Revolutionaries began to build an army with which they would wage guerrilla war against Batista for the next two years. Their

The making of Fidel

Fidel Castro Ruz was born on 13 August 1926 on a farm near the town of Birán in Oriente province. The fifth of nine children, he received a Catholic education in Santiago de Cuba and Havana, ultimately attending a noted Jesuit boarding school, the Colegio de Belén. Castro was successful academically and excelled in sports, particularly baseball. In 1945 he enrolled at the University of Havana to study law.

It was while at university that Castro turned his prodigious energies to the political arena. Several times during this period he was arrested for his outspoken anti-government views, and numerous attempts were made on his life, allegedly by police hit squads acting under government orders. He was forced to flee abroad for extended periods when the heat at home grew too much. All this action left little time for study so, in 1950, Castro pulled the mother of all cramming sessions and, aided by his photographic memory, graduated with a fairly incredible three degrees (two in law and one in social sciences), all doctorates.

Wasting no time, the young Dr Castro immediately set up in private practice and was soon running a busy legal firm, specialising in difficult cases and pro bono work for the poor. Castro had found time to marry Mirta Diaz-Balart in 1948 and they produced a son, Fidel Castro Diaz-Balart, less than a year later (the

marriage broke down in the early 1950s, however, and the couple were divorced in 1954). None of this distracted from Castro's steady rise in political power and popularity. His many anti-government speeches were attended by adoring crowds, and he used his considerable personal magnetism to paint a picture of a Cuba free of corruption and US-sponsored repression.

In 1952, Castro was virtually certain to win election to the Cuban Chamber of Deputies, when Fulgencio Batista seized power and suspended the democratic process. Frustrated in his attempt to attain public office by democratic means, and appalled by the excesses of the Batista dictatorship, Castro began the campaign that would eventually lead to the Revolution of 1959 and the start of his epic reign.

campaign was given new momentum and hope in 1958, when the US government, as if by magic, woke up to the fact that Batista was not a beacon of democracy at all, but a murdering megalomaniac. Worse, he was bad for business. With alacrity, an embargo was placed on arms shipments to Batista's forces. Given that nearly all the Cuban government's arms came from the US, the embargo rather hampered Batista's ability to suppress the Revolution.

In a last-ditch attempt to quieten political opposition, Batista called a presidential election for November 1958. The voters stayed away in droves, the result was clearly rigged, and the US finally withdrew its support of the regime. The writing was on the wall for everyone to see. Ever the astute operator, Batista did not intend to hang around and see how it all turned out, and on 31 December 1958 he beat a hasty retreat to self-imposed exile in the Dominican Republic.

On 1 January 1959 Che Guevara and Camilo Cienfuegos led their rebel army into Havana. Castro marched his army across the island from the eastern provinces, entering the city on 7 January. Within a month, the new government had reinstated the 1940 Cuban Constitution, which had been suspended by Batista in 1952. Recognition by the US quickly followed. The Revolution was over and Cuba was finally an independent country. It was not to last.

CUBA LIBRE?

Initially, the leadership of the Revolutionary government was split between three men: Manuel Urrutia became president; José Cardona was appointed prime minister; and Castro took control of the armed forces as commander-in-chief (*comandante*). This arrangement was short-lived. Cardona soon resigned in protest at his lack of real power, Urrutia went public on the socialist nature of the Revolution and Castro skilfully manoeuvred himself into the top job. His first actions on taking office were concerned with consolidating the Revolution's power base. He increased the size of the Cuban armed forces from 50,000 to 600,000 and dispatched Che Guevara to root out supporters of the Batista regime throughout the island, who were then tried by the Revolutionary courts and executed.

Castro's next steps were aimed at making good the promises of the Revolution. If Cuba was to be a truly independent country, it would need to eliminate its almost total economic dependency on the United States. Castro's tool for achieving this was simple: he implemented a programme to nationalise key industries and services.

The reaction in the US was one of horror. They saw the new Cuban government's actions as little better than thievery. Matters were not helped by Che Guevara's first official meeting with representatives of the Soviet Union (a fellow Communist country and therefore ally) in June 1959. The US could see its Caribbean jewel, for so long just tantalisingly out of reach, suddenly disappear over the horizon. It is tempting to argue that, but for a few inflammatory actions by the Revolutionary government in 1959, and subsequent overreaction by the US, Cuban history in the second half of the 20th century might have been very different. This view, however, ignores the resentment felt by the Cuban people at 60 years of American interference, and the need for Castro's government to maintain popular support by being seen to deliver quickly on its Revolutionary promises. The result – the four decades of mistrust, antagonism, misery and deprivation that followed – were probably, quite frankly, inevitable.

By early 1960 America's increasingly hostile stance was driving Cuba firmly into the arms of the Soviet Union. In February the two countries signed a trade agreement in which the USSR agreed to purchase five million tonnes of Cuban sugar over a five-year period. The Soviets would in turn supply Cuba with oil, iron, grain, fertiliser, machinery and $100 million in low-interest loans.

The US response was immediate: Castro must go. The spectre of communism was considered the great enemy and the Monroe Doctrine was revived to justify whatever actions were necessary to defend the Western hemisphere from this threat. In an attempt to destabilise Cuba, the US government launched a large-scale propaganda campaign, stopped the importation of Cuban sugar, embargoed oil exports to the island, indefinitely extended the 1958 arms embargo, and formed a paramilitary army of Cuban exiles, ready to take the island by force. The final straw came when the US pressured Texaco, Esso and Shell (all with refineries in Cuba) not to process the crude oil that Cuba was importing from the USSR. Castro quickly nationalised the refineries, followed by all remaining US businesses and commercial property on the island. On 19 October 1960, US-Cuban relations had deteriorated to the extent that the US imposed an economic embargo on Cuba that permitted only food and medicine to be imported to the island. On 3 January 1961 Cuba and the US officially broke off diplomatic relations.

HIT AND MISSILE

What followed was a period of both open and covert warfare between the US and Cuba, in which the American government mounted a number of increasingly irrational initiatives aimed at toppling Castro from power. The open hostility culminated in the 17 April 1961 invasion of the Bay of Pigs on the Zapata peninsula by US-trained and supported Cuban exiles. Unfortunately for the exiles, President Kennedy withdrew his approval for the operation while it was underway. Denied significant air or naval support, the insurgents were easy prey for the Cuban Army and Air Force. Of the 1,400 men who landed at the Bay of Pigs, 1,197 were captured, the remainder killed in the fighting.

After the Bay of Pigs debacle, Castro realised that there was little hope of re-establishing normal relations with the increasingly paranoid US. What he urgently needed was a powerful ally who would help him resist US pressure. The obvious candidate was America's sworn enemy and Cuba's most important trading partner, the USSR. Consequently, the day after the Bay of Pigs, Castro declared that the Revolution was in fact socialist. By May, he was referring to Cuba as a socialist country and in December he became a Marxist-Leninist. Castro's transformation from vaguely left-wing nationalist to committed communist was complete. Shortly afterwards, the 26 July Movement was merged with the Cuban Communist Party. The country has been communist ever since.

The low point in the tense relations between Cuba and the US began on 14 October 1962, when US Intelligence discovered that the Soviet Union was building nuclear missile bases in Cuba capable of attacking the US. The American response was to search all ships destined for Cuba, and turn back any found to be carrying military equipment. President Kennedy further warned that any missile launched from Cuba at a target in the Western hemisphere would be viewed by the US as an attack by the Soviet Union. An intense game of brinksmanship ensued between Kennedy and Soviet Premier Khrushchev, and the two superpowers edged towards nuclear war. Finally, and without Castro's knowledge, Khrushchev agreed to dismantle the Cuban missile sites and return all weapons to the USSR on the condition that the United States would dismantle its nuclear missiles in Turkey and guarantee not to intervene militarily in Cuba. This agreement must have been galling for Castro. Once again, two foreign powers had decided Cuba's fate without having the decency to include it in

Fidel showing his strength during a speech.

the discussion. Unfortunately, the country was in no position to do anything about it. America's policy of isolating Cuba from the rest of the world was proving highly effective and the USSR was the only friend Castro had. Cuba had unwittingly replaced dependence on the US with dependence on the Soviet Union.

THE ACCIDENTAL COMMUNIST

Throughout the 1960s the US embargo deepened. All trade between Cuba and the US was banned; even goods made in other countries but containing Cuban materials could not be imported into the US. America applied pressure to its NATO partners and to Latin American countries to join its embargo, and they obediently complied. In 1963 US citizens could no longer travel to Cuba. Finally, all Cuban-owned assets in the US were frozen. While there is some evidence that President Kennedy intended restoring normal relations with Cuba (as a hedge against growing Soviet influence on the island, if for no other reason), he was assassinated before he could do anything about it. Some conspiracy theorists assert that the assassination may have been a plot by either Cuban exiles or organised crime bosses opposed to Kennedy's softening approach to the Castro government. Whatever the truth, after Kennedy's death the stalemate resumed.

Not all US attempts to overthrow Castro were as overt as economic sanctions and amphibious invasions. Between 1960 and 1965, as part of a destabilisation programme code-named Operation Mongoose, the CIA attempted to kill Castro eight times. On at least one occasion, the Mafia was hired to do the job; other attempts involved poisoned drinking glasses and exploding cigars, but none so much as injured Castro. When they failed to kill him, CIA attention turned to trying to discredit him in the eyes of the world.

Cuban economic policy during the 1960s was a disaster. In order to reduce the country's reliance on sugar, a rapid programme of industrialisation was instituted led by Che Guevara. Whatever qualities he may have possessed as a Revolutionary, he was a dismal industrialist. The programme failed, Cuba ended up more reliant on sugar (and on imports from the USSR) than ever, and the basic necessities of life grew increasingly scarce. Food rationing, which began in 1962, worsened throughout the remainder of the decade; petrol was rationed in 1968, followed by sugar in 1969. For many Cubans, the deprivation proved too much. In October 1965 an organised 'boatlift' took over 3,000 Cubans to the US. By the time the Cuban Airlift ended in 1973, it had carried 260,000 Cubans to the United States.

The impact of the 1959 Revolution on Havana was generally negative. The periodic large-scale migrations to the US deprived the city of many of its professionals. Architects, engineers, urban planners and property developers were among the first to leave. In addition, the Revolution diverted resources away from Havana towards rural areas and the city began to deteriorate. It is estimated that, at the peak of this policy of malign neglect, 150 colonial-era buildings collapsed in the city each year. They were replaced by Soviet-style concrete high-rises of poor design and unsafe construction. In recent years, steps have been taken to restore Havana's architectural heritage. The improvement is most noticeable in La Habana Vieja (a tourist hotspot), but renewal projects are under way throughout the city.

A FALSE DAWN

The 1970s were another lost opportunity for the US to patch up relations with Cuba. In 1974, the US government conducted secret normalisation talks with Cuban officials. Apparently, excellent progress was made, but the talks collapsed when Cuba became involved in the Angolan civil war later that year. Their support for the socialist MPLA was unacceptable to the Americans. It was during this period that the US began to refer to Cuba as a 'terrorist state'. Cuban foreign policy in the 1970s had shifted from the Marxist ideal of exporting their Revolution abroad to the more practical goal of supporting other third-world countries with troops and advisers. Cuban involvement in Somalia, Nicaragua, Jamaica and Grenada (always on the 'wrong' side from the US perspective) further confirmed American opinion that Castro was a loose cannon and must be stopped. Throughout the remainder of the decade, attempts by various Cuban and US politicians to relax the embargo were blocked.

Rapprochements were made from other quarters, however. In 1975 the Organisation of American States voted to end sanctions against Cuba. In 1977 the US travel ban was dropped, the two countries signed a fishing rights agreement and opened Interests Sections (an intermediate step on the way to establishing diplomatic relations) in each other's capitals. By comparison with the previous 15 years, relations were positively balmy.

In 1976 Cuba adopted a new constitution, which formally established the island as a socialist state. Later in the year, Castro was elected president of the State Council, consolidating the roles of president, prime minister and *comandante* of the armed forces.

'In 1996 the US gave Cuba another bloody nose in the form of the Helms-Burton Act.'

In 1980 the Revolution was 20 years old, but the hoped-for improvements in living standards had yet to arrive. Scarcity and rationing were still very much a fact of life and there was little prospect of the situation improving. Many Cubans had had enough and wanted out. Castro responded by allowing free emigration from the port of Mariel, west of Havana. Within days, a flood of refugees was leaving Cuba for the US in the so-called Mariel Boatlift. By September 125,000 Cubans has set up home in Florida.

The improvement in relations with the US, which had progressed glacially during the 1970s, came to an abrupt end when Ronald Reagan became President of the USA in 1981 and instituted what was probably the most hostile Cuba policy since the early 1960s. Despite conciliatory signals from Cuba, the US administration tightened the embargo, reinstituted the travel ban and allowed the 1977 fishing treaty to lapse. Around the same time, Jorge Mas Canosa founded the Cuban-American National Foundation, which quickly emerged as the most powerful anti-Castro pressure group in the US. This group's relentless political lobbying would largely determine US Cuba policy for the next decade.

SPECIAL TIMES

In 1989 the Berlin Wall fell and within two years Soviet Communism vanished from the world stage. While this was arguably a good thing for the rest of the world, it was a disaster for Cuba. At a stroke, the island lost $6 billion per year in subsidies and other monetary support it had previously received from the USSR. The Cuban economy shrank by

25 per cent between 1989 and 1991; imports fell by $8.1 billion in 1989, causing grave shortages and strict rationing. The ensuing decade of severe scarcity and deprivation was called, with an Orwellian flourish, the 'Special Period'.

Of major concern to the Cuban government was the loss of their protector. Without the Soviet Union, how would Cuba defend itself against its rapacious neighbour to the north? Sensing easy prey, the US stepped up the pressure. In 1992 Congress passed the 'Cuban Democracy Act', designed to 'wreak havoc on the island'. The Act promised sanctions against any countries found to be 'assisting' Cuba; further restricted humanitarian aid in the form of food, medicine or medical supplies; prohibited vessels that had been to Cuba within the previous 180 days from entering any US port; and banned US Cubans from making remittances to their relatives back home. It was anticipated that the Act would bring about the collapse of Castro's regime 'within weeks'. While it is certain that the CDA caused additional hardship to the Cuban people, the US had severely underestimated Castro's ability to turn a situation to his political advantage.

That is not to say that Castro was having an easy time of it. The combined effect of the Soviet collapse and the American embargo drove the Cuban people to the point of starvation (the phrase 'as rare as a fat Cuban' entered the vernacular) and for the first time since the 1959 Revolution, protesters and police clashed on the streets of Havana. The Revolutionary regime was on a knife-edge. Castro responded by introducing a programme of economic liberalisation. Markets were set up to permit the sale of agricultural and manufactured goods; the ban on the use of US dollars was lifted; middlemen and brokers were permitted to operate; and self-employment was encouraged.

In 1994, in response to riots in Havana, Castro again announced an open migration policy, giving Cubans free licence to leave the island if they wished. Almost immediately a new boatlift began and 30,000 refugees left Havana for Florida. This time however, the arms of America were not so welcoming, and the Coast Guard was dispatched to prevent the seaborne immigration. The US had learnt its lesson from the Mariel boatlift and was unwilling to allow more Cubans to arrive unimpeded into Florida. The US policy since this time has been to repatriate any Cubans found at sea or in the air, but to admit those who make it to landfall in the US (after a detailed background check).

In 1996 the US gave Cuba another bloody nose in the form of the Cuban Freedom and Democratic Solidarity Act (better known as the **Helms-Burton Act**). There were two reasons for this. First, the Cuban Air force had recently shot down two planes that were allegedly trespassing in their airspace. The planes were flown by Florida-based exiles, apparently intent on provoking a reaction. The second reason was that it was a Presidential election year in the US and Clinton needed to secure the South Florida Cuban vote. The Helms-Burton Act introduced a raft of measures aimed at tightening the embargo still further. The international reaction was immediate. The United Nations, the European Union, the Organisation of American States, and many other countries condemned it outright. Regardless of its manifest shortcomings from a human rights standpoint, the Helms-Burton Act walks all over the concept of national sovereignty and gives the United States sole authority to determine other countries' rights to trade with Cuba. Not surprisingly, most nations have chosen to do little more than pay lip service to it, and Canada and Mexico have gone so far as to enact opposing legislation, making it an offence for their residents to abide by any provision of Helms-Burton. It seems that, at long last, the US has lost international support for its relentless campaign against Cuba.

INTO THE FUTURE

In October 2000 there was another faint glimmer of hope when the US Senate approved a bill that would lift restrictions on the sale of food and medicine to Cuba, while still prohibiting the US financing of such sales (though this too can sometimes be allowed in certain 'humanitarian circumstances'). The same bill also codified a ban on US travel, getting rid of the presidential prerogative to determine travel restrictions by US citizens to Cuba.

In reality, whatever the final outcome, the American embargo has probably done more to keep Castro in power for the last 42 years than any other single factor. Indeed, there is evidence to support the view that Castro periodically thumbs his nose at the US just to make sure the embargo stays in place. Every Revolution needs something to revolt against, and the US has obligingly filled that role. Without a common enemy, ideology and rhetoric begin to grow stale. The embargo has certainly caused a lot of damage in Cuba, but it has also provided cover for a large number of home-grown mistakes. As long as the US remains the great enemy of the Cuban people, Castro's position will be secure (though his age is a further consideration). If the embargo is lifted totally, his government will be subject to the same historical forces that swept away communism in Eastern Europe a decade ago. Whether the regime can survive where others have failed remains to be seen.

Key events

AD 1-1000 Some time during this period, the Taino replace Cuba's Ciboney inhabitants.

TROUBLE IN PARADISE
1492 Christopher Columbus lands on Cuba, kicking off a period of Spanish occupation that would last for four centuries.
1513 First slaves arrive on the island.

LAYING THE FOUNDATIONS
1519 San Cristóbal de la Habana officially founded on its present site.
1558-9 Three castles are built in Havana to protect the city from attack, though this does little to reduce piracy in the harbour.
1607 Capital of Cuba moved from Santiago de Cuba to Havana.

FIRST STIRRINGS OF REVOLUTION
1762 British expeditionary force takes control of Havana, though their occupation lasts less than a year: in 1763 they hand the country back to the Spanish.

HERE COMES THE USA
1825 First direct intervention in Cuban affairs by the US, when it prevents Mexico and Venezuela from liberating Cuba from Spanish rule.
1848 US president Polk offers to sell Cuba to Spain for $100 million. The offer is rejected.

THE TEN YEARS WAR
1868-78 Ten Years War: although Cuba loses to Spain, the Cuban people have taken their first steps towards independence.
1886 Slavery formally abolished in Cuba.

REVOLUTION REDUX
1895-8 War of Independence. Spanish rule ends, only to be replaced with interference by the US, who intervene in the war when the USS *Maine* explodes in Havana harbour.

NO SUCH THING AS A FREE COUNTRY
early 1900s Havana prospers, attracting American tourists escaping Prohibition in US. Sugar becomes an increasingly lucrative crop.
1902 Republic of Cuba created. Tomás Estrada Palma is elected first president.

ALL GOOD THINGS...
1924 Regime of newly elected President Gerardo Machado represses the working classes and ignites feelings of rebellion in the Cuban population.

THE RISE OF BATISTA
1934 President Batista, endorsed by the US, begins repressive 25-year rule.

YOU SAY YOU WANT A REVOLUTION
26 July 1953 Castro and his army try unsuccessfully to storm the Moncada Barracks near Santiago de Cuba. Castro and his brother Raúl sentenced to 15 years in jail but released after less than two. They go to Mexico, where they plan to overthrow Batista.
1956 Castro, Raúl, Che Guevara and fellow Revolutionaries arrive by boat in eastern Cuba to launch another attack but are forced to hide in the mountains.
31 December 1958 Batista flees. The following day, Guevara marches into the capital, followed six days later by Castro, who declares the Triumph of the Revolution.

CUBA LIBRE?
1960 Cuba's relationship with USSR grows, and the two countries sign a trade agreement that will prove lucrative for Cuba. The US imposes a trade embargo with the island.

HIT AND MISSILE
17 April 1961 Hundreds of US-backed anti-Castro exiles die when President Kennedy aborts an invasion of Cuba at the Bay of Pigs.
14 October 1962 Kennedy discovers that Cuba has USSR-financed missiles aimed directly at USA. A nuclear war is averted at the last minute.

THE ACCIDENTAL COMMUNIST
October 1965 First official boatlift to the US takes 3,000 Cubans to Miami.

SPECIAL TIMES
1989 Fall of the Berlin wall and subsequent collapse of Soviet bloc shrivels Cuba's economy overnight. The following year, Castro declares the 'Special Period', and rationing is enforced (still in place to this day).
1994 In response to riots during the worst of the Special Period, Castro grants that people may leave for Florida. 30,000 promptly do so.
1996 Helms-Burton Act imposes rigid conditions on trade by the US with Cuba.

INTO THE FUTURE
October 2000 Senate approves the easing of certain parts of the US blockade on Cuba. Food and medicine can be traded between the two countries, but with cash, not on credit.

Havana Today

On the surface, Havana is not a pretty sight. And, deeper down, it's a complex, troubled city, full of contradictions. But above all, it's one of the most enchanting places on Earth.

Anyone visiting Havana for the first time will be shocked at the sight. Apart from the restored historic centre, much of the city looks like a bomb's hit it. But those who live here or who are frequent visitors can detect signs that Havana is on an upswing. More houses are getting coats of paint, more kids are Rollerblading around wearing (US) designer labels, and every day there are more cars on the roads with the HM number plates that indicate Cuban owners. The queues at the centres that pass for shopping malls in Havana used to go fast, but now they can drag on for hours as trolleys fill up.

Havana entered the new millennium in a state of 'Elián fever'. A new, imposing square, officially called the *tribuna abierta anti-imperialista*, went up defiantly in front of the US Interests Section and thousands were marshalled every day wearing their government-issued Elián T-shirts to protest. (It's a sad irony that in May 2000,

schoolchildren, who so rarely get their hands on decent schoolbooks, were issued with glossy picturebooks of the little lad.) The Elián González business was wonderful publicity for Fidel and the Revolution and *habaneros* dutifully went along to the square but the public rhetoric didn't capture the mood of the city. Behind the cameras, cynical Elián jokes abounded and canny schoolchildren sold their T-shirts to foreign journalists. *Habaneros* are fed up with politics, bored with protesting, longing for change and to be left alone to take advantage of some of the city's new opportunities. Disillusion set in a long time ago.

As one 60-year-old woman put it: 'The Revolution is like a child: you are indulgent with its mistakes for the first ten years; by the time it's 20, you expect it to be heading in the right direction, but when it's 40 years old and hasn't produced anything, you give up.' Not that people want Miami Cuban-style capitalism. *Habaneros* have increasing access to information via foreigners and other channels such as the Internet and are able to make more informed judgments. In October 2000, when they were all turned out on the streets again to protest, opinion was divided. The US had just agreed to allow Cuba to buy food and medicines but was insisting on cash payments when Fidel wanted credit. 'Why on earth should he get credit?' was the general feeling. People no longer subscribe to the dogma that all Cuba's economic ills are the fault of the embargo. They know that government mismanagement is at least equally to blame. But, then again, they don't automatically reject all Fidel's rhetoric.

CAPITAL PRIDE

There are 2.2 million *habaneros* spread throughout the 15 *municipios* and the one thing they all have in common is that they are passionate about Havana. They 'know' this is the best city in the world, they have complete confidence that Havana is the centre of the universe. Ex-patriot literature is full of lament for its streets and corners.

When the Revolution triumphed, Havana was marginalised for 40 years. Not only did the new government prioritise the rest of the island, putting its meagre resources into agrarian reform first, but Fidel mistrusted the capital. Despite the mass exodus of the professional middle classes, he was left with a largely Americanised city and *capitalinos* who were sharp, sophisticated and represented possible dissent. He was right: *habaneros* are feisty and intelligent. One of the few recorded public protests since 1959 took place in the capital when people rioted in 1994 and Fidel was forced to allow another exodus across the Florida Straits. The city's demographics changed fast as people were encouraged to pour in from Oriente, Fidel's natural support base. *Habaneros* became used to the sight of straw-hatted *campesinos* coming in droves to celebrate the land reforms. *Santiagüeros* preened their feathers as Santiago de Cuba was declared the Revolutionary city par excellence. The *habaneros* didn't turn a hair; they just turned their considerable wit towards the *orientales*, known derogatorily as *palestinos*, and got on with being the best. The police in Havana, in particular, are largely drawn from Oriente and are the butt of endless jokes for their supposed country-bumpkin stupidity. They say that if you ask a policeman standing in Carlos Tercero (III) what street this is, he will answer, 'Carlos One hundred and eleven'.

STATE OF THE NATION

Havana has both suffered from and been saved by neglect. Before the early 1980s, the city was left to crumble, very few buildings went up and

even fewer repairs were made. The housing stock and infrastructure rotted away while ugly new pre-fabricated workers' settlements were erected in other parts of the country. The 1982 UNESCO declaration of La Habana Vieja as a World Heritage site first alerted the authorities to the treasure they had on their hands. By the time the tourist phenomenon caught up with the city in the '90s, what was left of it had been saved from the ravages of '60s and '70s urbanisation. Though planners and architects are generally careful nowadays about what they allow, the odd horror, such as the much-maligned Golden Tulip Parque Central hotel, does occasionally slip through the net.

'In 1993, the country was at its lowest ebb of hardship and hunger.'

The importance of Havana as the capital and a tourist magnet has raised its status again in official eyes. José Martí International Airport was built with Canadian investment in 1997 and the city's telephone exchange has been vastly improved and is being slowly digitalised thanks to Italian investment. Visits from VIPs such as the Pope in 1998 and the King of Spain to the Ibero-American summit in 1999 were focused on the capital, whether Fidel liked it or not. Both occasions gave the city a facelift, at least. In the summer of 2000, official recognition of the city's importance came in a very specific form when Havana was elected to host the country's annual 26 July celebrations. The honour of marking the 1953 attack on the Moncada barracks traditionally tends to go to small towns in the east of the island. *Habaneros* needed no confirmation of their city's importance, but they were still proud of the accolade.

FULA RULES

The Cuban government responded to the crisis of the Eastern bloc collapse by stringent belt-tightening euphemistically dubbed the Special Period and a simultaneous reluctant economic liberalisation. In 1993, the US dollar was legalised, but, in the same year, the whole country was at its lowest ebb of hardship and hunger. Havana looked like a Christmas tree by night, as power cuts turned the lights on and off in different areas of the city. At the same time, its scant resources were targeted at the embryonic tourist industry in an effort to save the economy. Havana didn't have to try hard to sell itself; the problem was building enough hotels and other facilities to cater for the tourists who were all too keen to come. The policy worked and the city has changed incredibly

Local currency: *pesos*, *pesos convertibles* and dollars.

quickly over the last few years as the areas most attractive to tourists have been rapidly and beautifully restored; hotels have shot up in the western area of Miramar and new fleets of taxis seem to appear every month. The government also allowed a limited amount of free enterprise: *cuenta propistas* (self-employed people) were allowed to rent rooms, open *paladares*, and hire themselves out as taxi drivers. *Habaneros* had every advantage to make the most of the new possibilities and the city has left the rest of the country far behind economically. Apart from enclaves such as Varadero and Cayo Coco, Havana is where the tourists go. It's now commonplace to see groups being ushered around by a guide. As confidence in Cuba's economy grows, more foreign firms – most, but not all tourism-oriented – are prepared to ignore the big stick of Helms-Burton and establish bases here. The opportunities for *habaneros* to earn dollars, legally or illegally, are increasing all the time. Life in the city is largely organised around the scramble for *fula*, slang for dollars. If you're not lucky enough to land a dollar-paid job with a foreign employer, or become a legal *cuenta propista*, there are ever-more opportunities for generating dollars in the informal sector. Whole businesses are now built up around taking commission from *paladares* and *casas particulares* for delivering punters, and more tourists mean more sales of sex and cigars. There are many ways of making a quick buck out of the tourists: one *nueva trova* song tells the story of 'Johnny Babalawo', the *santería* priest who writes prayers and predictions for tourists on his laptop.

TURISTAS

From the visitor's point of view, all this is good news. It's much more comfortable to be a foreigner in Havana these days when you're not such a rarity and the tourist apartheid is nowhere near what it was a few years ago. There is more money flowing around among *habaneros*, but the government is not so happy, because – guess what? – class is back. The growing class of nouveau riche, gold chain-sporting, even mobile phone-using *habanero* to be seen at the city's pools and discos is a thorn in the official flesh. Memories of Havana as the corrupt playground city of the 1950s have not faded and the government is acutely aware of

the social consequences of tourism. They know what the lure of the dollar means for Cubans and for youth in particular. They twist and turn, trying to control the cuckoo in the nest. Measures are suddenly taken for no apparent reason when the socialist fabric seems threatened. In 1999, all the hotel discos in Havana were shut down overnight with no explanation and not reopened for months. Havana is still relatively safe, but tourism brought an increase in petty crime and prostitution. The government responded with a crackdown and increased police presence. The city's police were given an enormous pay rise, three times the income of a brain surgeon. You now see policemen on every corner of the city, often straddling huge black motorbikes. At first, the *cuenta propistas* were subject to so many restrictions and changes in regulations that they never knew where they were. Now the government seems to have pragmatically settled for levying heavy taxes and letting them get on with it. Every visitor to the city has an apocryphal story about their taxi driver who was really an economist/teacher/lawyer. Most of Havana's professionals left in 1959, but the new generations of professionals trained to replace them have also opted out in an internal brain drain, resentful at the low value placed on their skills. Obviously they would rather be engaged in the profession they were trained for than ferrying tourists round the city, but at a derisory peso salary, they can't afford to.

LA LUCHA

Not all Havana's two million-odd inhabitants have access to dollars. Life is a hard struggle for most. A common answer to the question, 'How are you?' is '*en la lucha*' – 'struggling'. *La lucha* doesn't spare any area of human activity, it is all a struggle and the struggle all boils down to two things: the shortages and the double economy. The insidious double economy gets worse as wages are virtually frozen in pesos and more goods are available only for dollars. It's no longer a question of being able to

Getting by on meagre rations with a *libreta*.

Miami nice?

Desperate times call for desperate measures: Cubans leaving from Cojímar in 1994.

The past, present and future of Havana are inextricably linked to its 'twin' sister 200 miles away. Thanks to the US embargo, thousands of Cuban families are split between Havana and Miami. Today, Cubans account for over half of Miami's 600,000 inhabitants, and they run the place: the mayor and the chief of police are Cuban-Americans. Sadly, Havana seems to get the bum deal most of the time: while Miamians are flexing their credit cards and enjoying the freedom of the press, *habaneros* have to survive on about $200 a year, less than one per cent of the average salary in Miami, and in their country the press and Internet are heavily censored. The residents of both cities share a love of baseball, music, *telenovelas* (soap operas), practise *santería*, speak Spanish and hang out at a place called Coppelia.

There is also a vocabulary of war between the two cities. In Havana, Cubans in Miami are referred to as 'impotent', 'traitor', 'worm', 'cockroach' and 'mafioso'. Miami-based insults include 'communist' and 'stooge', but their way of putting Cubans down is by asserting patronisingly that the only problem with Cuba is Fidel, and that no one outside the Council of Ministers really supports him or the Revolution. This misconception was convincingly refuted by Elián González's father, a self-defined communist. While he was sequestered outside Washington, the Cuban American National Foundation (CANF), Miami's powerful anti-Castro pressure group,

reportedly offered him $3m in cash, plus a house, car and steady job, if he stayed in the US with Elián. He refused – not because of any threat from Fidel – but because he believed in the future of the Cuban Revolution.

How will the two cities get on when *el comandante* and his appointed successor, brother Raúl, finally die? This is an unspoken question in Cuba, where the administration seems to work on the implicit assumption that Fidel is immortal. Nevertheless, the question preoccupies Cubans everywhere. The worst that could happen is that the Miami Cubans invade the island and plunge it into civil war, and then convert Havana into a suburb of Miami. In a recent newspaper poll, 30 per cent of Miami's Cuban Americans said they would move back to the island, setting in motion a demographic shift as dramatic as that of the Mariel boatlift. A more optimistic scenario for post-Castro, post-embargo Cuba would reunite thousands of families, giving them the incentive to work together to achieve a bloodless transition to social democracy. The successes of the Revolution in terms of health, education, housing and social justice would be defended, while its failures – its utopian policies of Guevarism and its unwieldy state bureaucracy – would be phased out.

Outside politics, there is little animosity between the two sets of Cubans. As writer Eliseo Alberto puts it: 'Friends on both shores have understood a truth: they could have been us, we could have been them.'

Getting around Havana, *clockwise from top right:* a *botero, cocotaxi, camello* and *bicitaxi.*

get better things in the dollar shops; it is now the only option. There are shortages of just about everything, including food, medicine, clothes and fuel. The government blames the embargo, while the *habaneros* just try to resolve the problem. The only thing that never runs out is sugar. The ration book, the *libreta,* which guarantees basic supplies, is hanging on by the skin of its teeth, but every month less seems to arrive. People talk nostalgically of the '80s as a golden age when the *libreta* even provided clothes. They reminisce about their two pairs of pyjamas a year and their Soviet socks, but today's rations are really not enough to survive on. Typically, *habaneros* can count on six pounds of rice, three pounds of split peas and six eggs a month. Apart from the *libreta,* food can only be bought at the dollar shops, the *agromercados* and on the black market. With the average monthly wage at 200 Cuban pesos, or $10, most of these options are out of the question. The *agromercado* may look cheap to a foreigner, but a pound of onions at ten pesos is 20 per cent of a monthly wage. Not surprisingly, *habaneros* are obsessed by food. They talk about it all the time, and feel constantly deprived, partly because their taste runs to enormous quantities of meat and fried foods, and both meat and cooking oil are very expensive. Beef is as rare as caviar and black marketeers caught selling it can serve long prison sentences. Funnily enough, for a city that's on a permanent war-time footing as far as

food goes, they have not developed war-time habits. *Habaneros* do not grow or conserve. You would expect every terrace to have herbs or a tomato plant growing and kitchen shelves to be full of bottled fruit out of season, but not at all.

Transport is a nightmare in Havana. Those lucky few who have earned the right to buy a car by being exemplary workers or by some other means can't afford petrol or maintenance. Fuel and spare-part shortages mean the *guaguas,* the buses, are few and far between and queues are enormous. *La cola* (queue) is another feature of the daily struggle and *habaneros* have developed it to a fine art. You just roll up and call out '*¿último?*' and when you find out who you are after, you don't have to stand in an undignified line but may just mill about. The *camellos,* the pink lorry-drawn camel-shaped trucks that have become such a familiar Havana sight, are to be avoided if at all possible. Their nickname here is '*la película del sábado*', or 'the Saturday (night) movie', because they're so full of sex, violence and bad language. There's a rumour that the government is going to remove them because they are an eyesore, not realising that tourists love them. One enterprising agency even hired one to take a group around the city. An alternative option is to take one of the fleet of old '50s cars circulating the city, the *almendrones* (big almonds), but the ten-peso charge is high on a Cuban salary. Hitching a ride at the traffic lights is a common way for *habaneros* to get around if they don't have a bicycle. Transport problems are exacerbated by the fact that *habaneros* have a general aversion to walking. Quite often you will offer a ride to someone who only wants to go a couple of blocks. They particularly don't like getting wet and go to great lengths to avoid walking in the rain.

'The state turns a blind eye if a problem it cannot resolve is being addressed.'

La vivienda (housing) is another major preoccupation. You only have to move a little out of the tourist orbit to see the appalling state of Havana's housing stock. Broken-down, dangerous, crumbling houses shored up with makeshift wooden supports abound. Houses, in particular in Centro Habana and southern Habana Vieja, collapse regularly, sometimes killing passers-by. *Habaneros* know to walk in the middle of certain streets in case falling masonry or whole balconies crash down on them. Havana has no shanty towns, but there are *solares* (slums) and *ciudadelas* (large

mansions turned into multiple dwellings). Not only do *habaneros* have to contend with the conditions themselves but the housing laws mean that there is no escape. They can't just move house, even if there were any empty. Cubans are firmly tied to their official address by the *libreta* (ration book), which is allocated to an address not just an individual. People do move, of course, but they have to leave their food ration behind if they do. Travellers will go to great lengths to have their rations sent to them. A mother taking her child for a long stay with the grandparents in Santiago de Cuba will have the child's milk ration sent down on the overnight bus. The only legal way to move house is by exchange, *la permuta*. An expanding family in a one-room apartment might find an elderly couple willing to exchange a larger one. But as ever the poorest are caught because a *permuta* to a larger place always involves a few thousand clandestine dollars as part of the deal. Also, those trapped in the worst housing never find anyone wanting to exchange. Around the city you will see notices on gates and window frames –

Man's best friend

It comes as no surprise to find '50s cars cruising Havana's streets – kings of the road in their dilapidated glory, but visitors are not usually prepared for the sight of the counterpart monarchs of the sidewalks: Havana's dogs.

Cubans are fond of animals and it's a rare household that doesn't include a caged bird, a fish tank, a turtle and almost inevitably a *perrito* (little dog) or two. Cuba has had kennel clubs and dog shows for decades and since the advent of the dollar has bought new affluence to some, many aristocratic breeds have made their appearance, including the ubiquitous Rottweilers patrolling the gates of the wealthy. But it is the street mutt of Havana that has a character like no other. This is one of the few capitals across the globe where cats are second-class citizens in the pet world; this is dog city.

And make no mistake: these street dogs are not strays, but much-loved family members. Not that you'd know it, seeing them leading their independent, busy lives. The dogs of Havana trot purposefully around the streets with not an owner or collar in sight. They clearly have places to go, appointments to keep, possibly some

It's a dog's life.

shopping to do. They weave in and out of traffic, meet their friends in the parks, far too busy to bark or sniff at strangers.

Sadly, mange is common, but on the whole the typical Havana mutt is a healthy, happy creature, usually rather small, shaggy and short-legged with a lot of terrier in the mix. They have bright, friendly eyes and pricked-up ears and tail. They've even been the subject of a documentary by film-maker Enrique Colina.

'*se permuta 1x2*'(meaning a two-bedroomed property is being offered) – and the *permuta* system has taken on arcane proportions as it has been used to bypass the property laws. The whole chain requires several hundred dollars in palm grease at every stage, but it can be done. There are constant rumours that the state will crack down at any moment and regulate this black housing market but, as in many areas of black-market activity, the state currently turns a blind eye if a problem it cannot resolve is being addressed. People unable to raise the cash are stuck and have been for years. Meanwhile, they do their best with cardboard partitions and breezeblock extensions and *barbacoas* (barbecues), platforms thrown up to create an extra floor. The housing situation has created real suffering for many families. Even in a society like this, with a tradition of extended family, the pressure on human relations is enormous. There is no privacy, no escape from unbearable in-laws or spouses. It is very common for divorced couples to go on living together for years, sometimes in tight-lipped silence, because they have no choice.

La lucha in all its manifestations occupies a large part of every day and is met with energy, resilience and an understandable dose of self-pity. Cubans think they are the hardest done-by in the world – nobody suffers like a Cuban. On the other hand, nobody rises above their circumstances with more invention and humour. Huge amounts of energy are given to problem-solving, and the phrases most often heard are '*no es fácil*' (it's not easy), followed by '*hay que inventar*' ('You've got to be inventive') or '*hay que resolver*' ('You've got to find a solution'). The skills of resolving and inventing take on surreal proportions here as people duck and dive around the black market, barter goods and services, throw up their jerry-built extensions, add two-stroke engines to their bikes, recycle spare parts or pirate CDs and videos. No self-respecting *habanero* will pay market price for anything.

HABANEROS
The *habanero* lives with paranoia, paradox, endless humour and curiosity. The paranoia comes from years of having to live in fear of the Committee for the Defence of the Revolution (CDR), part of whose job was to report on any

Religious life

Despite efforts to create a secular society, Cuba experienced a religious revival in the 1990s. The hardships of the Special Period led many to turn to religion for both spiritual consolation and material benefits. Nowadays, people openly wear crucifixes or display the attributes of *santería (see p29)*. The ceremonies of Afro-Cuban religions, long stigmatised as *brujería* (witchcraft), are now promoted as a tourist attraction by some state-run enterprises. At least two thirds of the population are religious. Most, however, are not Christians but follow one of the uniquely Cuban religions that resulted from the mixing of African and European traditions.

While Cubans were officially free to practise religion after the 1959 Revolution, this was not encouraged because of the conflict with Revolutionary ideology. When the regime was declared socialist, some church members became involved in counter-Revolutionary activities. Many others left the country and Christian denominations experienced a fall in congregations. Afro-Cuban practices, never fully accepted in society, were forced further underground. Religious holidays such as Christmas were replaced by holidays marking important dates of the Revolution.

Known religious believers experienced discrimination and were denied access to certain professions, university education and membership of the Communist Party.

A thaw in Church-state relations began in the 1980s. The example of the Revolutionary Nicaraguan Catholics and of liberation theology showed that socialism and Christianity were not incompatible. In 1991, the Communist Party abandoned its commitment to atheism and admitted believers to its ranks. Pope John Paul II visited Cuba in 1998 and in the same year Christmas was restored as a holiday.

Almost half the population of Cuba are baptised, but many are only nominal Catholics as baptism is a requirement for *santería* initiation. Catholicism, brought to the island by Columbus, never became the people's religion because it was associated with the Spanish ruling class.

Although the 1990s saw an increase in Sunday attendance, most churches have small congregations except on major feast days. Unlike the rest of Latin America, the Cuban Catholic hierarchy has neither embraced liberation theology nor attempted to woo the Afro-Cuban population.

socially deviant or dangerously liberal-thinking *compañeros* who live on their block. Some CDR officials are committed *fidelistas*, but there are countless other opportunists ready to grass on their neighbours for their own advancement. If and when this system ends, there will be some ugly score-settling in the city. The Special Period has been a great equaliser, having made unwilling law-breakers of the most devoted Revolutionaries and forced everybody on to the black market to survive. The CDR has lost its clout as its members are now illegally renting rooms or dealing on the black market but, even so, *habaneros* will lower their voices and cast anxious glances at open windows before saying anything even mildly controversial. But once they do, the humour, the *choteo criollo*, is merciless. Everything is a tragedy and a huge joke. Humour is the only way to deal with the contradictions of daily life. *Habaneros* are asked to live on a tiny peso wage, but pay out in dollars; praise the free medical service but buy medicines on the black market; despise capitalism while watching the well-heeled capitalists pass through town, and above all,

deride the US government when most of them have family in *la yuma* and long to join them. The paranoia, the juxtapositions, the politics have all been internalised into a particularly Cuban value system incomprehensible to anyone else. Just when you think you have begun to make sense of the psyche, another mask appears and you realise you haven't even begun to fathom the complicated mind-set here. Anyone judging *habaneros* by other paradigms, even Latin American ones, is heading for a fall.

Meanwhile, day to day and on the surface, the *habaneros* continue to enchant with their warmth, humour, egalitarianism and sensuality. Statistically, Havana sounds like it's as nearly perfectly racially harmonious as possible. According to the last census in 1993, Havana's population is officially 66 per cent white, 12 per cent black and 22 per cent mulatto. In fact, the mixed-race population is much higher. Havana has been a harbour town for more than five centuries and as such is used to the cocktail of North African, European, Asian blood that that entails. Nevertheless, before the Revolution, discrimination was endemic. Even Batista,

AFRO-CUBAN PRACTICES

The most widely practised religion in Cuba is *santería*, known also as the *regla de ocha* or Yoruba religion after the Orishas or gods from western Nigeria. Orishas represent forces of nature and archetypal human qualities: **Changó** is the god of thunder, **Yemayá** the goddess of the sea and motherhood, and **Ochún** the goddess of love and fresh water. Most Orishas have Catholic saint equivalents: Yemayá is also known as the Vírgen de **Regla**, Ochún is the Vírgen de la Caridad del **Cobre**, the patron saint of Cuba. Curiously, Changó, the womanising macho man, is linked with **Santa Bárbara**, the virgin martyr.

Those who wish to initiate into the *regla de ocha* must first consult a *babalawo* – an expert in divination – to discover which Orisha is their 'guardian angel'. Some devotees simply receive the *collares*, a set of beaded necklaces, colour-coded to represent different Orishas. Others are recommended to enter into a deeper relationship with one Orisha by taking an initiation called *asiento*. Those who do so must dress completely in white for a year and observe certain taboos. Initiations are costly (around two years' salary) and most people take them for health reasons or in the hope of an improvement in their material circumstances.

A *Yoruba* New Year ceremony – when food is offered to the gods.

During the ceremonies in honour of the Orishas, each Orisha is invoked by using his or her distinctive drum rhythm and dance. Some of the initiated ▶

President of the Republic though he was, had the doors of the Havana Yacht Club discreetly closed to him as a mulatto. The Revolution swept aside institutional racism at once and officially there is complete equality here. However, the reality is that de facto racism is prevalent and largely along finely defined definitions of colour. The darker your skin, the worse housing you are likely to have and the less access to legal dollar jobs. It is very rare to see a black person working at management level in tourism, for example. Conversely, it is the young black women who have become economically powerful as the most sought-after *jineteras* by foreign men looking for exoticism. Race is not polarised into divisions of black and white, a fact that can be a source of confusion for foreign visitors. Cubans refuse to be compartmentalised in that way. The poet Nicolás Guillén told a North American writer who had referred to him as 'black', 'I am mulatto, madam, mulatto.' The racism can be shocking to visitors from a more politically correct society. It is quite common for offensively racist jokes to be told in mixed race company. On the other hand, endearments like 'mi negra' and 'mi china' are used regardless of ethnic origin.

The same is true for gender. Cuba is an endemically sexist society. The Revolution quickly raised women to fully equal legal and economic status. Even the Family Code states that men must participate equally in the housework. The FMC, the Federación de Mujeres Cubanas, has done a great deal to raise the status and profile of women. And yet, Cuba is still *machista*. *Habaneras* are strong, confident, humorous women, but they are complicit in maintaining the status quo, taught as they are to be graceful and seductive from the cradle. The *quince*, the 15th-birthday party that every young girl aspires to (*see p172* **Sweet 15**), is blatantly a presentation of the girl as sex object to the world. No *habanera*, even if she works for the Ministry of the Interior, is going to set out in public without looking her best. Nothing, not even the power cuts, the lack of water or the long, exhausting

▶ ## Religious life (continued)

participants may become possessed and assume certain aspects of the Orisha's personality.

The annual festivals of the most popular Orishas draw huge crowds. On 16 December, eve of the feast of San Lázaro or Babalú Ayé, who is renowned for his healing powers, hundreds of thousands of pilgrims make their way to the sanctuary at **El Rincón** in southern Havana. Some of the more devout drag themselves along on their hands and knees, often with large stones tied to their legs.

Membership of Afro-Cuban religions crosses race and class boundaries. Even Fidel Castro is linked in the popular imagination with Changó. Many believe that this accounts for his 40-year reign and miraculous escapes from CIA-backed assassination attempts.

Widely practised throughout Cuba, the **reglas congas**, known also as *palo monte*, originated among the Bakongo peoples of West Central Africa. The term *palo* (stick) refers to the ritual use of trees and plants, which are believed to have magical powers. A *prenda* or *nganga*, normally a three-legged cauldron, is filled with natural elements such as sticks, seeds and earth. It also contains the spirit of a dead person and is used by *paleros* to control supernatural forces. Ritual written symbols called *firmas* are drawn on the ground, the walls or on cloth worn on the body to call down spirits. Because *palo* is more closely associated with magical practices than the *regla de ocha*, paleros tend to be more reticent and it is rare for outsiders to be invited to attend ceremonies.

Abakuá is an all-male secret society, which came from eastern Nigeria. Ceremonies, called *plantes*, enact the myth of the African princess Sikán, who discovered the secret of the sacred fish Tanze. A drum called *ekue* is used to re-create the mystical voice of the fish. Masked figures or *íremes* represent the ancestors. A system of writing known as *anaforuana* uses symbols to embody religious powers and mark ritual objects. *Abakuá* members' first loyalty is to their brother members and they are required to be *chébere* or brave and defiant; much is often made of the erroneous belief that a new initiate had to kill the first person who crossed his path.

JUDAISM

The first synagogue was built in Havana in 1906. From then on, the Jewish population grew in waves. Sephardic Jews arrived from Turkey in the 1910s. They were followed in the 1920s by Ashkenazi from Eastern Europe, many of whom hoped to use the island as a transit point for immigration to the US. Later, European Jews also came to escape Nazism.

journeys to work will prevent a woman from having her hair and nails done. The beauty business here is thriving, with most blocks having at least one woman making a living out of painting nails and waxing legs. The much vaunted health service includes liposuction and 'nip and tucks' on demand and even young women take full advantage. A *habanera* will feel she has one foot in the grave if she doesn't get her share of complimentary remarks as she sashays down the street.

> ## 'People's bodies are the only area of their lives over which they have any control.'

The liberation of women achieved by the Revolution has also made Cuba one of the most sexually liberated countries in the world. Although Cubans have always been sensual and seductive, in colonial society that largely meant

the young women casting smouldering looks from behind the safety of wrought-iron *rejas* (grilles). It was not until the student activity during the Machado years, in the early 1930s, that women in Havana began to share any public space with men. Nowadays, Cuba is an avowedly promiscuous society. Men and women alike slip in and out of bed with uninhibited ease. Sexual activity starts young, helped by the *escuela del campo*, the required period all secondary schoolchildren have to spend working in the fields, which are notorious sexual experimentation grounds. According to Cuba's National Centre for Sex Education, girls become sexually active on average at the age of 13 and boys at 15. Condoms are freely available but not popular, since most are cumbersome Chinese imports. Abortion is traditionally used as a contraceptive method and the rates are astronomical: many girls have had four or five abortions by the time they are 20. The government has recently become concerned about this and is trying to change the culture of abortion on demand. The exuberant pleasure

---

Schools, shops and bakeries were set up in the Jewish quarter near the port of Old Havana. After 1959, many went into exile and the population fell from 15,000 to today's 1,500. Until recently, congregations were elderly, but now more young people are attending synagogues. As there is no resident rabbi, the American Joint Distribution Committee sends seminarists to Cuba.

SPIRITISM AND FREEMASONRY

Spiritism and freemasonry became popular during the wars of independence when their anti-clericalism made them alternatives to the Catholic Church. Cuban spiritism has its origin in the doctrine of a Frenchman known as Allan Kardec, whose *Book of the Spirits* (1857) became popular in Latin America. Kardecan spiritism offers direct communication with spirits and is also used for healing. Varieties found in Cuba have been much influenced by the Afro-Cuban practices.

Many *santeros, paleros* and *Abakuá* members are also freemasons. While freemasonry is not a religion, its initiation ceremonies and procedures satisfy the Cuban love of mystery and ritual. Freemasonry reached Cuba in 1762 during the British invasion of Havana. For a long time, freemasonry was illegal and the first Cuban lodge was only founded in 1857. During the Wars of Independence, masonic lodges provided a cover for Revolutionary

activity. In fact, many of the fathers of the Cuban nation were masons, including Céspedes, Martí, Maceo and Moncada.

Many freemasons left the island after the 1959 Revolution. Since then, it has attracted membership from a broader social base and today there are an estimated 30,000 freemasons in Cuba.

PROTESTANTISM

Protestantism came to Cuba in the latter half of the 19th century. An alternative to the pro-Spanish Catholic Church, it was identified with the cause of Cuban independence. Later, it became linked to growing US political and economic domination of the island as Protestant missionaries from the southern states attempted to inculcate American values.

The 1961 embargo meant that the Protestant denominations were cut off from their US mother churches. Most of the clergy were receptive to change and encouraged their members to participate in Revolutionary activities. As a result, relations between the state and the Protestant churches were cordial. The exceptions were the Jehovah's Witnesses, who refused medical treatment and military service, and Seventh Day Adventists, who would not work on Saturdays. There are an estimated 300,000 Protestants in Cuba, belonging to around 60 denominations.

in sex and general body culture here is a combination of tropical sensuality and the fact that people's bodies are the only area of their lives over which they have any control.

HOME SWEET HOME

Much of *habaneros'* leisure time revolves around the home and the street. In the daytime, the street is an extension of the living room and people sit on steps, set up tables for domino games, play impromptu games of baseball, and conduct their business to a cacophony of shouts and music. *Habaneros*, '*hablaneros*' (talkers) as Guillermo Cabrera Infante has it, are rapid, fluent, funny conversationalists. Talking with a group of *habaneros* can be quite exhausting: they don't take conversational turns, but say what they want to, whoever may or may not be listening. Conversation revolves around anything and everything: gossip, the *telenovela*, *la lucha*, and the latest on *radio bemba*, which is what *habaneros* call rumour. Rumour tends to be very accurate here, where they have developed it into a fine art. There is no information whatsoever in the press unless it's bad news about an imperialist country. No murders in the city are reported and there could be a serial killer on the loose in Havana without anyone knowing about it, but *radio bemba* usually has all the latest details.

Inside, the typical *habanero* home is shabby but scrupulously clean. *Habaneros* are obsessively clean and house-proud, which is why the lack of water and soap is so distressing. If and when things change here, there'll be a huge market for home-improvement goods and services. The smallest, meanest dwelling does its best within the limits of overcrowding, lack of water and antiquated fittings. Cubans adorn their houses with the ornaments and plants they love. This is the only country in the world where you see queues at the artificial flower shops. They are also animal-lovers and most homes are shared with a pet, usually a much-loved *perrito* (little dog).

The higher up the *fula* scale you go, the more electronics you find but almost all have a TV and much time is spent in front of it, despite the monotony of most programmes. Some families have managed to rig aerials to get grainy images from Miami, but mostly they are condemned to reports on the sugar harvest or re-runs of *The Professionals*. Twice a week, the whole city is glued to *telenovelas* (soaps), or, at other times the late-night movie. There are usually two running, a Brazilian or Colombian import and a homegrown version. The last, long-running Cuban soap was set in Havana and, surprisingly, tackled previously taboo issues such as *jineteras* and the housing problem.

THE YOUTH OF TODAY

Havana has a big problem in the making. About 35 per cent of its population is under 16, and this looks like a generation lost to the Revolution. Cuban children are adored and it is very rare to hear a child cry in Havana or see an irate parent losing their temper. The children of the city are bright-eyed and well turned-out in their uniforms. Primary schoolchildren (*pioneros*) are dressed in red, and secondary (*alumnos de secundaria*) in mustard yellow. Schools are desperately short of resources and parents agonise as much as in any capitalist country about the state of education. Even here, there are perceived to be 'favoured' municipalities, and the schools of Plaza de la Revolución are rumoured to have the best conditions. However, the city is facing a big problem of disaffected youth. The generation born in the '80s has known nothing apart from the Revolution, but they have nothing invested in it. They did not witness the euphoria of the early years. Instead, all they see is a system that denies them the cultural icons they long for. Added to which, there are more and more foreigners passing through the city displaying all the consumer goods they want. Parents and government alike are deeply concerned about motivating young people. How can you persuade your child that it is worth studying hard to go to university when all they can look forward to is 400 pesos a month? Schools in Havana are seeing an increasing amount of truancy from teenagers more concerned with joining the scramble for dollars than studying from torn, shared books. There is a real problem of *jineterismo* (being a tout or a prostitute; the term itself has ambiguous connotations) in schools. Recently, when one school in the city carried out its usual year-nine (age 14) careers advice, it found that not one of the students wanted to go on to study for a profession; without exception, they all wanted to work as *cuenta propistas* or with tourists. The Elián hysteria, consciously or unconsciously, had a lot to do with recalling Cuba's youth into the bosom of the Revolution. All the cries of '*nuestro niño*', all the six-year-olds on the podium chanting Revolutionary slogans, were symbols of bringing children back into the ideological fold. It may have worked for some, but the youth of Havana is looking outwards to futures that will offer them the best hopes outside the Revolution.

Nobody can say which way the city will develop. At the moment, the city is in a social and economic transition largely due to the tourist phenomenon. Whatever happens, as one of Havana's prominent city planners says, 'We will have the city we deserve.'

Sunlit balcony of the neo-classical **Palacio de los Condes de Santovenia**. *See p36.*

Architecture

Havana's glorious buildings from centuries past are a main draw for tourists. With this in mind, steps are being taken to restore the city's constructions that are most in need.

Havana is different from most other major Latin American cities. Under Spanish rule for almost 80 years longer than its continental counterparts, Havana was influenced far more heavily by Spain than other colonial cities, while the proximity of the United States had a substantial effect on the city's later development. Moreover, because Havana grew predominantly by addition rather than by demolition, the different layers of its rich architectural heritage have been spared the ravages of excessive development. The street layout, a typical Spanish-American grid creating regular city blocks, but with small lots and low-rise buildings, gives Havana a special skyline, atmosphere and scale. The city's impressive colonial heritage is combined with more recent constructions to create a rich

> ▶ Many buildings highlighted in bold in this chapter are mentioned in further detail in **Sightseeing** (*pp 62-122*).

mixture of periods, styles and streetscapes. Moreover, the exceedingly low immigration levels and slow population growth rate in the last 40 years results in a low-density population with room to breath – Havana has just over 2.25 million inhabitants (one fifth of the national population) and covers an urban area of 360 square kilometres (139 square miles).

In 1982 the old core of the city within the original 143-hectare (253-acre) walled precinct, plus the 19th-century extension and the full colonial defensive system was designated a UNESCO World Heritage Site. Although Havana's historically valuable architectural heritage is most concentrated in this area, it is also spread across more than 2,000 hectares (4,942 acres) of the city and includes pre-baroque architecture from the 1600s, baroque from the 1700s and early 1800s, some neo-Gothic and neo-classical from the mid and late 1800s, plus art nouveau, eclectic, art deco, modernist and revolutionary styles from the 20th century. Smaller urban settlements, many more than 300 years old, which have been engulfed in the conurbation process, have nevertheless managed to retain a distinct local character. Regla, Casablanca, Cojímar, Guanabacoa, Santa María del Rosario, Calabazar, Boyeros, Santiago de las Vegas, El Cano, Marianao, Arroyo Arenas and Santa Fe all encircle the busy inner city with small-town life. They show simplified, but good examples of the architectural styles that appear in the central city, but also vernacular architecture, including rare wooden constructions.

'The indigenous population disappeared without leaving architectural traces.'

Another key factor in Havana's architectural development was the city's unique social structure. Whereas most other major Latin American cities consisted of a few very wealthy families against an unending background of urban poor, Havana boasted numerous affluent families who left their mark on the city in the form of increasingly fine mansions. Over time many of these mansions were turned into shops or subdivided into tenement blocks, but the buildings were not razed to the ground by speculation and the population was not expelled by gentrification. The very poor were either masked in the inner city behind classical or baroque façades, or scattered in dreary shanty towns at the periphery where they were hardly visible. More importantly, Havana's unusually large lower-middle class population has demanded dwellings with a reasonably high quality of design and construction to create a well-defined urban fabric that covers large sectors of the city. Endurance, diversity and a decadent yet lively charm are the characteristics of Havana's architecture.

EARLY ARCHITECTURE

In contrast to the pre-Columbian Andean and Meso-American peoples, the indigenous Cuban population lacked a developed material culture and disappeared without leaving architectural traces. In the 1500s the initial dwellings of the conquistadors were mostly improved versions of the local thatched-roof hut (*bohío*), or simplified vernacular constructions from southern Spain. Significant architecture in Havana at the time was reserved for military purposes. The vital port was guarded by the most impressive system of European-colonial fortresses in the Americas, including the larger **La Fortaleza de San Carlos de La Cabaña**; from 1763. The smaller **Castillo de la Real Fuerza** (1558-1577) on the Plaza de Armas has a

Renaissance plan and is the oldest European defensive structure in the New World made with durable materials (stone, which replaced a wooden defensive structure that was burned down previously). The first European water-supply system in the Americas was built by the same military engineer responsible for the two fortresses at the mouth of the Bay, the **Castillo del Morro** (1589-1630) and the **Castillo San Salvador de la Punta** (1589-c1600).

In the late 16th century Havana was granted city status. Because of its privileged position at the entrance to the Gulf of Mexico, it was designated Key to the New World and Bastion of the West Indies by the Spanish Crown. For several centuries, the port was the final meeting point for the Spanish fleets of galleons before they sailed back to Europe laden with riches, and in the early 1600s the number of sailors and soldiers sometimes more than doubled the local population of 4,000.

The walled precinct of the early 17th-century city consisted of a grid of narrow streets and small city blocks only slightly deviating from the urban grid plan decreed by Ferdinand and Isabella for all their American possessions in their *New Laws of the Indies*. Buildings were constructed side by side and ventilated mainly through inner courtyards. This very compact pattern over a slightly irregular grid supported a coherent urban fabric where squares and churches were dominant features.

Military architecture and public buildings remained fully European during the 17th century, but religious architecture and housing – especially among the poorest people – clearly showed a more popular face, combining a very simple pre-baroque design with Spanish-Moorish *mudéjar* elements. Otherwise, the imprint of African slaves who supplied most of the construction labour force is difficult to identify. Roofs were often the work of ship-builders, and resembled inverted hulls, often with tall and finely carved wooden *alfarjes* ceilings. One of the most impressive buildings from this period is the **Convento de Santa Clara** (1638-18th century), a nunnery with thick, rammed-earth walls and beautiful cloisters covering four small blocks of La Habana Vieja. The complex incorporates a church that was finished in 1643. Other good examples are the **Casa de la Obra Pía** and the **Casa de Don Luís Chacón**, though the former was later altered.

BAROQUE HAVANA

Baroque style didn't arrive in Cuba until late in the day, and the lack of skill among the local labour force, combined with the porous nature of the locally quarried limestone, which was embedded with coral fossils and seashells, handicapped its ornate style. The best example of Cuban baroque is the façade of the **Cathedral**, which was started as a Jesuit church in 1748 and finished in 1777. The cathedral façade dominates the **Plaza de la Catedral**, considered the best proportioned of all Havana's squares. The area was originally a swamp at the end of the Havana aqueduct (1592), which brought water from the Rio

Almendares to supply the Spanish fleet. Once the square had been paved and drained, buildings were constructed around the central space to create a dry *plaza* embellished with porticoes, which provide shade and shelter from tropical rainstorms. In addition to the cathedral, the square is surrounded by the façades of the former palaces of the **Marqueses de Aguas Claras** (1751-1775), the **Marqueses de Arcos** (1746), the **Condes de Casa-Bayona** (1720;

On the road to recovery

Historic preservation had been steadily recovering relevant buildings in Havana since the 1960s, with a stronger impulse in the '80s under the leadership of the Office of the City Historian and the creation of the Centre for Conservation, Restoration and Museology (CENCREM). In 1993 the Historian's Office was given the opportunity to set up a commercial division, running a wide variety of businesses within Old Havana, renting out office space in order to invest the profits from such schemes into the restoration effort. The scope of preservation initially focused on the rehabilitation of older, unique buildings such as the **Castillo de la Real Fuerza**, the **Cathedral**, the **Palacio de los Capitanes Generales** (now the Museo de la Ciudad) and churches and noble mansions, with an approach that indirectly limited the historic centre to the old colonial walled precinct. The scope widened during the 1990s into the rehabilitation of dwellings and other social programmes for the local population, especially in the poorer San Isidro neighbourhood at the southern tip of Old Havana. Rehabilitation has also reached some newer districts, like the houses on the initial 14-block strip across from the **Malecón** (*pictured*). Awareness has grown about the cultural values of contemporary architecture; and the training of workers for rehabilitation projects has helped to start a recovery of long-forgotten skills in order that high-quality restoration and new building may gather momentum. The success of these programmes has also demonstrated the economic value of preserving a relevant built heritage, as the City Historian Office is now financially self-sufficient.

A short list of recent rehabilitation projects covers the **Convento e Iglesia de San Francisco de Asís** (1998), plus the square of the same name and several surrounding projects such as Café de la Marina; the

former **Cámara de Representantes** (House of Representatives), built in 1909-1911 and restored in 1998; and three hostels: **Conde de Villanueva** (1998), **El Comendador** (1999) and **El Tejadillo** (2000). It also includes the esplanade in front of **La Punta** castle; **Hotel Florida** (1998-1999), **La Moderna Poesía** bookshop (2000) and a mid 18th-century church, **Iglesia de Paula** (2000), recycled as a concert hall and linked to the recuperation of the traditional promenade area of the Alameda de Paula. On the one hand, preservation seems to pay, not solely with the increasingly restored city attracting a rising number of visitors from overseas, but also for the local population, by getting them to work to restore their home city.

also known as the Casa de Don Luís Chacón; *see above*) and **Los Condes de Lombillo** (mid 18th century).

Although the most significant 18th-century mansions in La Habana Vieja are classified as baroque, they are quite austere in style, built in three storeys around a central courtyard and sharing common walls with their neighbours. Features include a double-height ground floor, a low mezzanine and a high-ceilinged upper floor with wide, cool galleries. The trademark curvaceous lines of Europe only appear as occasional enhancements to the main front door. (The portico from the **Casa de la Obra Pía** in Old Havana, built between 1666 and 1793, is the best example, though it was actually carved in Cádiz.) The central courtyard was the key feature of Cuban baroque palaces. Surrounded by wide, shaded galleries where the family spent most of their everyday life, it was typically embellished with a fountain or a well and aromatic plants following a tradition from southern Spain. Sometimes there was a second courtyard at the back of the building, opening to the kitchen and cooking areas. The **Palacio de los Capitanes Generales** (now the Museo de la Ciudad; 1770-1791), on the Plaza de Armas, has probably the most beautiful courtyard in Havana and rivals the Cathedral as the city's finest 18th-century building.

By the mid 1700s the 60,000-strong population covered an urban territory of 151 hectares (270 acres). The defensive walls surrounding the city's core went up slowly between 1674 and 1797, so Havana had already outgrown them by the time they were finished, stretching out into the new district of Centro Habana. (The **Paseo del Prado**, whose construction began in 1772, was originally known as the Paseo de Extramuros, or 'Road Outside the Walls'.) Urban expansion followed the roads that led out of the city inland to the west and south-west. As the surroundings altered, the roads themselves became *calzadas*: wide streets with tall porticoed pedestrian corridors that opened into stores with dwellings above, allowing citizens to walk protected from the sun and the rain right up to the outskirts of the city.

Another special feature of this period was the decorative stained-glass window, called *mediopunto*. These were often used to soften the blinding rays of the tropical sun, filling the rooms of Havana's buildings with coloured light. Among the many fine examples are those added in the early 19th century to the **Palacio de los Condes de San Juan de Jaruco** (1737) on the Plaza Vieja. Simple wooden grilles (used to protect the windows and balconies) were later replaced with more elaborate ones in iron, creating another trademark decorative

detail for colonial architecture. To this day, many anonymous buildings are given a 'Cuban' feel by the addition of iron grilles, rounded arches and coloured glass.

NEO-CLASSICAL HAVANA

By the second half of the 18th century, western Cuba had become a plantation economy driven by an enlightened, innovative Cuban-born sugar aristocracy (referred to in Cuba as the *sacarocracía*; *see also pp8-9* **Life is sweet**). As wealth slowly accumulated, there was a gradual shift in the style of upper-class dwellings. By the mid 19th century, white Cuban Creole patricians were moving out of the 18th-century palaces of the old town into *casas quintas* (detached neo-classical villas with no central court) in the new borough of El Cerro to the south-west.

Neo-classical architecture dominated the 1800s in Havana. Fine examples of the style include the huge **Palacio de los Condes de Santovenia** (c1841) in El Cerro, now a home for the elderly, and the outstanding **Palacio Aldama** (1844) facing the Plaza de la Fraternidad in Centro Habana, which is considered the best example of 19th-century colonial architecture in Cuba. The oldest remaining neo-classical building in Havana is **El Templete** (1828) on the Plaza de Armas, marking the spot where the city was founded in 1519.

> ## 'The high point for neo-classical architecture came in the mid 19th century with the construction of Vedado.'

Around 1830 Havana already had a population of almost 170,000 and the urbanised area covered 443 hectares. Many urban innovations were brought into the city during the first half of the 19th century, including the railroad in 1837 and public gas lighting in 1848. Streets were tarmacked; and fountains, monuments, theatres, hotels and cafés were built. This period also saw the contruction of a fine tree-lined boulevard, Paseo de Tacón, in Centro Habana (it was renamed Carlos III and subsequently Salvador Allende, though it is still known to all *habaneros* as Carlos Tercero).

The high point for neo-classical architecture in Havana came in the mid 19th century with the construction of Vedado, a new district close to the sea. Begun in 1859 and a contemporary of the landmark *Ensanche* plan in Barcelona, the urban design of this area is the pearl in Havana's colonial planning. The regular grid consists of 100-metre square blocks, and streets had trees on both sides, while two wider avenues (the current Calle G and Paseo) were

El Templete, the oldest neo-classical building left in the city. *See p36.*

each bisected by a central lineal park. Houses were set back from the road with gardens and porches at the front. One particularly stunning building from this era is the **Hotel Inglaterra** (1875), overlooking Parque Central.

The Wars of Independence (1895-8) practically paralysed construction in Cuba during the last 30 years of the 19th century. Neo-Gothic architecture in this period consisted mainly of additions to, or refurbishments of, older buildings, like the reconstruction and extension of the **Iglesia del Santo Angel** in La Habana Vieja, over an older building from the late 17th century. Nevertheless, some neo-Gothic and neo-romanesque elements can be found at the extraordinary **Cementerio de Colón** (Columbus Cemetery) on the southern edge of Vedado (*see p90* **City of the dead**).

'STYLE WITHOUT STYLE'

Art nouveau appeared in Havana briefly at the beginning of the 1900s, but actually had more in common with Catalan *modernisme* than the French or Belgian style. The **Casa de Crusellas** (1908) is the one of the best examples. **Palacio Cueto** (1908) on the corner of Plaza Vieja in La Habana Vieja is a whimsical building with art nouveau influences, which differs in style from the rest of the square. Most art nouveau houses, though, are located along Calzada de Reina or close to the **Railway Terminal**, a fine eclectic building dating from 1912.

During the incredible economic boom years of the early 20th century, known as *vacas gordas* ('fat cows'), Havana accumulated a very large stock of public buildings and dwellings in the eclectic style. This 'style without style', in the words of leading Cuban novelist Alejo Carpentier, covered whole neighbourhoods such as Vedado, Santos Suárez, La Víbora or Lawton, and infiltrated other areas of the inner city and even the suburbs.

Major eclectic buildings in Havana include the **Asociación de Dependientes** on Paseo del Prado (1907), **Hotel Plaza** (1908; *see p54*) near the Parque Central; the **Lonja del Comercio** on Plaza de San Francisco (1909); the **Palacio Velasco** (1912), now the Spanish Embassy; the **Casa del Marqués de Avilés** (1915), now seat of the ICAP (Instituto Cubano de Amistad con los Pueblos); and the **Palacio Presidencial** (1920), now the Museo de la Revolución. Equally outstanding are the **Cuban Telephone Company** (1927); the **Capitolio** (1929), the **Centro Gallego** on Parque Central (Paul Bellau; 1915), now the **Gran Teatro de La Habana**; and the whole campus of the **Universidad de La Habana** (1906-1940) in Vedado. This fine walled complex, approached via a monumental staircase, sits on top of a hill like an acropolis and incorporates numerous interesting buildings including a late art deco library (1937). The campus replaced the original

Spire of the **Hotel Inglaterra**, with the Capitolio in the background. *See p37.*

university in La Habana Vieja (1728), which was knocked down during Batista's presidency to make way for a helipad.

Domestic architecure also adopted the eclectic style during the first decades of the 20th century. Significant examples include the houses of Orestes Ferrara (1928), now the **Museo Napoleónico**, and José Gómez Mena (1927), now the **Museo de Artes Decorativas**; and **Estanislao del Valle** (1930), now the residence of the French Ambassador.

By 1920 Havana had achieved a monumental urban look, and, together with Buenos Aires, had become one of the most important cities in Latin America, followed closely by Mexico City and Lima.

In the 1920s a new upscale suburb was started close to the waterfront to the west of Vedado, separated by the Almendares River. **Miramar** still followed the grid pattern, but had larger lots and even more green than Vedado. It deliberately had no services, so as to discourage the less affluent from settling there. Avenida Quinta, the green backbone of the neighbourhood, continued further to the west into the ultimate upper-class district of Country Club (now **Cubanacán**), where the Spanish-American grid changes into a relaxed pattern of gently winding streets.

The Wall Street Crash of 1929 and a terrible national political crisis led to a *vacas flacas* ('lean cows') period, in which a simplified, but still well-designed, minor eclecticism dominated throughout the city. This 'style' accounts for a large proportion of the buildings in Cuban inner cities.

ART DECO AND NEO-COLONIAL ARCHITECTURE

The influence of geometric art deco was evident in the architecture of Havana as early as the late 1920s – the mansion of Catalina Lasa, built in 1927, already shows a movement away from eclecticism – but reached its apotheosis in the early 1930s with the construction of the **Edificio Bacardí** (1930) and the **Edificio López Serrano** (1932) – the first tall apartment building in Cuba. It was followed by the streamlined architecture of buildings such as the **Teatro Fausto** (1938).

The 1929 World Fair in Seville and the influence of Hollywood films that showcased the California style also affected Havana's architecture, but the impact was delayed by the political and economic crisis of the 1930s. The neo-colonial revival spread mostly during the 1940s and is characterised by single-family houses with cosy wooden grilles and clay-tile roofs. Another important trend from that decade was the monumental-modern style,

used in public buildings like the **Hospital Maternidad Obrera** (1939) and the **Plaza Finlay** complex (1944), which showed a mixture of the Palais de Chaillot Parisian art deco trend, coupled with a strong influence from the EUR in Rome and shades of earlier Italian futurism.

MODERNISM

The post-World War II period saw another spectacular building boom, following slightly modified architectural patterns from the modern movement. In terms of its extent and influence, modernism was second only to the eclectic style in the development of 20th-century Havana.

The definitive shift into modern architecture came in 1947 with the construction of the **Edificio Radiocentro**. It was the start of an astonishing development that, by the end of the following decade, would turn La Rampa into the liveliest part of the city. Modern highlights include **La Rampa** movie theatre (1955; *see p180*) and the Havana Hilton Hotel (1958), now the **Habana Libre** (*see p55*).

Elsewhere, the Plaza Cívica (designed by Enrique Luis Varela in 1953 and renamed as **Plaza de la Revolución** in 1959) features a number of monumental modern buildings including the outstanding Tribunal de Cuentas (1953). Now the Ministry of the Interior, it features a bronze sculpture by Domingo Ravenet and a ceramic mural by Amelia Peláez.

Leading Cuban architects managed to soften the fundamentalism of early modern architecture and avoid the commercialised banality of the international style. One of the best examples of the adaptation of modern architecture to suit the tropical climate and the Cuban culture is the legendary **Tropicana** nightclub (1951). Others tried to incorporate elements taken from colonial and vernacular architecture, such as projecting eaves with clay-tile roofs, wooden jalousies and stained-glass windows. Modern architecture also produced some very fine office and apartment buildings in the 1950s, among them the Retiro Odontológico (1953), now the faculty of Economy; and the Seguro Médico (1958), now the Ministry of Public Health.

The modern movement in Havana was important not only because of the work of some masters, but for the high average quality of even little-known architects, who spread the modern style into large expanses of city fabric. Unlike in the United States, modern architecture was happily embraced by the Cuban upper and middle classes for their homes. More than 30 new districts of single-family detached houses appeared. Some of the best examples of modern architecture from the late 1940s and '50s were individual dwellings, such as the prize-winning Noval house (1949), now a protocol house (where governmental guests are entertained or stay), the Borges house (1950), now a commercial firm; the Vidaña house (1953), currently the home of the Iranian Ambassador; the Pérez Farfante house (1955); or the Schulthess house (1956), now home to the Swiss Ambassador. The blooming speculative real estate business also unleashed the construction of condominiums, epitomised by one of the first self-contained condos in Latin America, the huge **Edificio Focsa** (1956).

REVOLUTIONARY ARCHITECTURE

By 1 January, 1959, the day Castro seized power, the Cuban capital housed a quarter of the country's six million population. The new government stopped land speculation, which had already begun to distort fine residential neighbourhoods like Vedado, and diverted construction to more than 300 small new rural villages and a network of provincial capitals and intermediate cities in an attempt to create a more balanced national distribution of wealth and population. In Havana, new shapeless housing compounds were built mainly at the periphery of the city, inadvertently preserving the historical character of the inner city, and creating a sharp distinction between the central area and the new housing tracts on the outskirts where hundreds of thousands found a roof.

> ## 'The worsening economic situation slowed and eventually stopped construction.'

Against conventional wisdom, modern architecture did not end in 1959 when most of the major Cuban designers left for the United States. It actually extended well into the second half of the 1960s with outstanding works in Havana like the Habana del Este neighbourhood unit (1959-1961); the Escuelas de Artes (1961-1965); the CUJAE university campus (1960-1964); **Pabellón Cuba** on La Rampa (1963); Parque-Monumento de los Mártires Universitarios (1965-1967), and CENIC (the Centre for Scientific Research; 1966). Several of these 1960s projects showed a brutalist influence and demonstrated a search for new forms of artistic expression in structure, materials and construction. Deprived of its creative approach and under heavy administrative control, architecture would evolve in the 1970s into a dull catalogue of repetitive projects that spread nationwide

and relied heavily on prefabricated concrete elements (the economic difficulties at the time played a major part in this).

Nevertheless, some projects appeared during the '70s that demonstrated that good architecture was possible even using the most rigid, fully prefabricated technology. What some people refer to as the 'lost decade' still produced the Lenin School (1974) and the Volodia School (1978). The construction of the **Jardín Botánico Nacional** in southern Havana between 1968 and 1989 is a rare case of patient teamwork that was successfully finished.

A few special projects were allowed more freedom and a larger budget. One such plan was the **Parque Lenin** (1971) in southern Havana, which included two well-designed restaurants, Las Ruinas and La Faralla. The **Palacio de Convenciones** (Convention Hall), built in 1979, and INGEBIOT (1986), a huge scientific research centre for genetic engineering and biotechnology, were two other significant projects constructed at the city's western periphery.

In the late 1980s there was a short-lived construction boom. This opportunity was used by some young architects to replace an already outdated and poorly assimilated post-modernist architecture. In spite of some shortcomings, this represented a worthy effort by designers to regain control over the city's architecture. *Microbrigadas* (microbrigades: groups of local people who voluntarily helped with construction work) had been operating since 1971 as an alternative to self-build programmes and state housing projects. Examples of the experimentation with contemporary architecture in a valuable historic context can be found in several medical surgeries built in La Habana Vieja during 1987 and 1988. In the same period, microbrigades also realised some outstanding designs by older, established architects, at Calle 1ra and Calle 10 in Vedado and at Calle 36 and 47 in Nuevo Vedado. The late '80s also saw the birth of **ExpoCuba** (1989), a large exhibition fair that attempted, rather unsuccessfully, a high-tech style.

The collapse of the Soviet Union, Cuba's main trading partner and supplier of energy, triggered an economic crisis in 1990, which instigated the so-called 'Special Period'. Nevertheless, the government's commitment to the Pan-American Games held in Havana in 1991 ensured the construction of the **Ciudad Panamericana** (also known as Villa Panamericana). For the first time, a new urban design was adopted as a reaction to the scattered building blocks of the conventional housing tracts. **Las Arboledas** (1984) was planned as a large environmentally friendly

Love it or hate it – the **Edificio Focsa** in Vedado, typical of the area's 1950s architecture. *See p40.*

La Rampa's high-rises contrast sharply with Old Havana's colonial architecture. *See p39.*

suburban housing complex, which set the apartment buildings among existing trees and greenery. Unfortunately, the worsening economic situation slowed and eventually stopped construction on this and many other projects. New construction in the city was limited almost entirely to joint ventures between Cuban and foreign companies in tourism and real estate in an attempt to bring badly needed hard currency into the country.

RECENT ARCHITECTURE

The economic crisis of the 1990s and the subsequent search for foreign currency has forced the construction of stores and hotels in former residential neighbourhoods such as Miramar and Vedado. The streetscape has also suffered from the makeshift use of former stores as dwellings and inappropriate alterations to fences, front gardens, porches and façades.

Buildings of note from the period include the **Meliá Habana** hotel (*see p58*) and Terminal Three of **José Martí International Airport**, both from 1998, which stand out from the otherwise unremarkable globalised condominium architecture. The **Centro de Negocios Miramar** (Miramar Trade Centre) is a strip of 18 office buildings, the first two finished in 1999 – a spartan architecture on a previous layout that misused the potentials of a large tract of land, Monte Barreto. This area, already disrupted by the huge **Soviet**

Embassy (Embajada Rusa; 1988), will eventually include seven hotels, among them the already finished **Meliá Habana** (*see p58*) and **Novotel Miramar** (1999; *see p59*).

The **Lonja del Comercio** on Plaza de San Francisco, designed by Tomás Mur in 1909, underwent a full renovation in 1996, including the addition of a striking upper floor with a reflective glass façade. In 2000, the Banco Financiero Internacional on Quinta Avenida in Miramar brilliantly solved the eternal question of how to blend the old and new, wrapping and crowning the classicist late-1940s bank with a new deconstructivist extension.

This feat proved unattainable for the **Golden Tulip Parque Central Hotel** (1998; *see p53*), which crassly built over a full city block of neo-classical buildings, leaving only a few stone arcades clumsily incorporated into the main façade of the hotel. Many people consider the hotel to be an abomination that fell deplorably short of the sensitivity and adaptability that such a unique urban site demanded.

More recent plans for new projects have created a greater optimism about re-establishing architecture in the cultural field. But there is not always a consensus that the proposed ideas are what the city needs, and as investment pours into the island and tourism increases, it remains to be seen what the city will get.

The **Buena Vista Social Club** in action.

Sounds of the City

Music is Havana's lifeblood. From *son* to *salsa*, *rumba* to rap, it cannot fail to capture the imagination of the visitor.

Since the outbreak of the global *salsa* bug and the international success of the *Buena Vista Social Club*, Cuban music has become a familiar sound worldwide. However, although its universal commercial success may be a recent phenomenon, its infectious beats have developed from a long-standing and rich musical heritage. Unfortunately, we know nothing of the musical history of Cuba's native inhabitants, the Taino, who were almost completely annihilated by the Spanish discoverers (*see p7*). Cuban music instead has its principal roots in colonial occupation and slavery, which forced together the people and cultures of Africa and Spain. This involuntary cultural blending extended to Spanish and African rhythms and instruments in what noted Cuban ethnologist Don Fernando Ortiz has called the 'love affair between the African drum and the Spanish guitar'. Today, the many mesmerising sounds, songs and musical styles, which collectively we define as Cuban music, are the product of this cultural union.

CUBA'S CLASSICS

During the early centuries of Spanish colonial rule, Cuba's music was predominantly religious in nature and stylistically heavily influenced by Europe. Musicians were for the most part trained in and linked to the church, as in the case of composers Esteban Salas (1725-1803) and Juan Paris (1759-1845), Santiago de Cuba's *maestros de capilla* (choirmasters). Apart from their fine choral work, these two individuals are also credited with introducing Europe's great composers to Cuba. European music was subsequently adopted and imitated by Cuban musicians, thus broadening the island's musical horizons. While the local plantation owners loved these imported tunes, the large and ethnically diverse slave population was engaged in the creation of its own new musical and dance styles. Rhythms such as the *gurumbé, congó, tumbalalá* and *yeyé* emerged to later develop into the *rumba, guaguancó, bembé* and *tumba* respectively. Although music was segregated along racial lines during this period, in practice the

In Context

That's a Moré

Beny, or Benny, Moré (1919-63) is without doubt one of Cuba's greatest and best-loved popular artists. Nicknamed 'el Bárbaro del Ritmo' (the Barbarian of Rhythm), 'el Beny' is regarded as a national hero in Cuba. During his career he sang all kinds of music – *son*, *bolero*, *mambo*, *rumba* – but was just as gifted as a musician, composer and conductor. Besides his superb voice, it was Beny's unique stage presence that delighted his audience. While conducting the orchestra he would also sing and perform original dance steps and body movements. He had a particular dress style, including his famous sombrero and cane.

Beny Moré was born Bartolomé Maximiliano Moré on 24 August 1919 in a poor district of Santa Isabel de las Lajas, Las Villas province. During his childhood he learned to sing and play the guitar and spent much of his youth performing at fiestas in and around his village. At the age of 21 he moved to Havana where he started out by singing in cafés, parks and on the streets. It was here

that he met and worked with the legendary Miguel Matamoros, who enabled him to develop his voice and musical abilities and gave him the opportunity to make his first recordings. In the early 1950s Beny moved to Mexico where he worked with the Orquesta Pérez Prado and Orquesta Oriental de Mariano Mercerón. He was also engaged in extensive recordings and appeared in several movies. In 1953 Beny returned to Cuba where he formed his own big band, the Banda Gigante, with which he enjoyed tremendous success. The highlight of Beny's career was playing at the legendary **Tropicana** nightclub.

But just as Beny was a workoholic, he was also an alcoholic, and it was the demon drink that led to his premature death in Havana on 19 February 1963. A national day of mourning was declared in Cuba, and his funeral was attended by more than 100,000 people. His immense popularity and influence on Cuban music continues to this day, and his legend is kept alive by the existence of such venues as the **Café Taberna** (aka Café Beny Moré).

boundaries were blurred. Due to the shortage of instruments and singers, the church was forced not only to include various Creole instruments such as the *güiro* (scraper) and *maracas* in its orchestras, but also to accept black singers into the church choir. In this way sacred and European-influenced classical music slowly but surely developed a more Cuban identity.

The first distinctly recognisable and acknowledged Cuban sound emerged with Manuel Saumel (1817-1870). Known as the father of Cuba's musical nationalism, he was the first to consciously incorporate Cuban rhythms and instruments into his *contradanza* and *danzón* compositions. The *contradanza* had been brought to Cuba by the French colonialists fleeing Haiti in the wake of the 1791 Revolution. It merged with local rhythms in Cuba and was taken up by all social groups (unlike in Haiti where it had predominantly been a dance of the upper classes). In the mid 19th century the *contradanza* gave rise to the *danza*, which finally developed into Cuba's national dance, the *danzón*. Created in 1879 by Miguel Failde in Matanzas, the *danzón* was the first Cuban dance in which couples actually touched each other, albeit at a healthy distance. The *danzón* remained the most popular musical

and dance genre until the early 20th century, when it was replaced by what would become Cuba's most famous and influential musical style to date: the *son*.

Simultaneous with all of these developments was the growing popularity of European, and especially Italian, opera among Cuba's upper classes. Throughout the late 19th and early 20th centuries many foreign opera companies and stars performed in Cuba. This was the time of the Wars of Independence, American intervention and the birth of the Republic. It was also a period of fierce cultural nationalism in Cuba. Influenced by these political ideas, two of Cuba's greatest musicians, Amadeo Roldán (1900-1939) and Alejandro García Caturla (1906-1940), reacted strongly against what they perceived as an increasing foreign cultural domination of Cuba's music. They made it their mission to fight against this musical colonialism and also the pseudo-exotic promotion of Cuba's own music for tourist purposes. Their own compositions, which included ballets, suites, *danzas* and waltzes, make a point of incorporating Afro-Cuban musical elements. In the spirit of José Martí they spoke of creating music that was no longer black or white, but simply Cuban. Although the Machado dictatorship killed all hopes for a more nationalist cultural project, these two men's ideas and music influenced and inspired many later musicians.

Classical music since the Revolution has enjoyed enormous governmental support. Apart from the many new conservatories, such as the Escuela Superior de Artes Escénicas and the Escuela Nacional de Arte, numerous symphony orchestras, including the National Symphony Orchestra, were created. Among many talented post-Revolutionary classical musicians, Leo Brouwer (born 1939), guitarist, composer and director of the NSO stands out from the crowd.

THE *CANCIÓN*

The Spanish-influenced *canción*, involving only a singer and guitar, developed during the 19th century in Oriente, eastern Cuba. Accompanied by their guitar, so-called *trovadores* would go from house to house singing ballads about love, women and the motherland. Most of these musicians were poor, urban folk, whose songs reflected both their own situation as well as the patriotic and rebellious spirit of the time. The *trova*, as this style of popular music came to be known, placed primary emphasis on its lyrics; its beautiful guitar melodies being viewed as simple accompaniments. Some of the earliest and best traditional *trovadores* include José (Pepe) Sánchez, Sindo Garay, Teofilito and María Teresa Vera and Manuel Corona. Their music is still loved and listened to today and has been especially influential in the creation of other *canción* styles such as the *bolero* and *filín* (feeling), as well as more modern variants of the *trova* itself.

The *nueva trova* emerged in the early 1970s. As poetical in style as the traditional *trova*, this new genre was much more political in nature. Comparable with and partly influenced by the Latin American *nueva canción* and American and British protest songs of the period, the *nueva trova* dealt mainly with social issues. Officially established as a movement in 1972, the *nueva trova* counts among its founding members Pablo Milanés, Silvio Rodríguez, Vincente Feliú, Noel Nicola, Sara González and Enrique Núñez. Current leading lights of the *trova* scene include Geraldo Alfonso, Frank Delgado, Carlos Varela and Alberto Tosca, many of whom are quite openly critical about Cuba's contemporary social reality.

FROM *SON* TO *SALSA*

Son, on which most of Cuba's contemporary popular music is based, first emerged in the late 19th century in rural Oriente. There, *campesinos* combined Spanish folk songs with African call-and-response tunes. Apart from the bongos, *güiro*, claves, guitar and double bass the *son*'s defining instrument is the *tres*. This small guitar-like instrument has three sets of double steel strings and, like the *son*, was born in the mountains of Cuba's eastern provinces. It was from here that the new sound first travelled to the nearby towns, where it took on distinct local characteristics and developed into the *guajira* (as in the famous 'Guajira Guantanamera'), *guaracha*, *nengón* and *changüí*. It was not until 1909 that the *son* finally reached Havana by way of a military band from Oriente. The new beat was soon taken up in the capital by some of the big *danzón* orchestras, but as the accompanying dance advocated lots of bodily contact it was perceived as scandalous by the middle and upper classes and was actually banned at one point by the government. Partly due to its prohibition, but mainly because of its irresistible beat, the *son* became massively popular. What had been considered the music and dance of the *solares* (urban ghettos) and the rural poor was fast becoming the new sound of Cuba.

> **'If you're expecting to hear non-stop *son* and *salsa* during your stay in Havana, watch out; Cuba is into different tunes these days.'**

Numerous *sextetos* (*son* groups using the six basic instruments mentioned above) and *septetos* (the six instruments, plus the trumpet), including Ignacio Piñero's famous Septeto Nacional, were formed in the 1920s. It was also during this decade, in 1928, that Rita Montaner rose to fame with her classic *son* tune *El Manicero*. *Septetos* were replaced in the '30s, '40s and '50s by large dance orchestras. Groups such as Arsenio Rodríguez y su Conjunto and Beny Moré y su Banda Gigante created the so-called 'big band *son*' by adding conga drums, timbales, maracas, lots of trumpets, and the piano to the traditional *septeto* set-up. Similar in size and style, but more influenced by the *danzón*, were the *charanga* bands, which included a wooden flute and string instruments. Well-known groups include the Orquesta Aragón, Orquesta Arcaño y sus Maravillas and the hot-as-ever Charanga Habanera.

Cuba's dazzling pre-Revolutionary decades also gave birth to the *mambo*, *chachachá* and others variations of the *son* such as the *bolero-son*, *guaguancó-son* and *sucu-sucu*. Many of these musical styles became internationally popular and were important catalysts in the subsequent worldwide explosion of Latin dance music. Today the *son* is still alive in the form of the *songo*, made famous by Juan Formell and José Luís Quintana, and the *timba*, created by José

Luís Cortés. These two hot rhythms are often mistakenly referred to as *salsa* and are what you will mainly hear in nightclubs, on the radio or just walking the streets of Havana. Popular groups include Los Van Van, NG La Banda, Manolín, el Médico de la Salsa and Paulito FG.

RUMBA

Just as the *son* was making its way to the capital, the very different but equally infectious *rumba* beat was emerging in the ports of Havana and Matanzas. Very African in its rhythms, the *rumba* was initially played on makeshift instruments: boxes used as drums (codfish and candle boxes seem to provide a particularly good sound) and bottles beaten with a spoon. With time these same rhythms were taken up by conga and *tumba* drums, claves and the *guagua* (a small wooden tube beaten with sticks). *Rumba* songs comment on everyday life, often incorporating Bantu rather than Spanish phrases, while the dancers mime a courtship ritual. Besides the *yambú* and *columbia*, the best known of all *rumba* styles is the highly erotic and rapid *guanguancó*. Famous *rumberos* include the great Luciano (Chano) Pozo, Florencio Calle, Pedro 'Pello el Afrokán' Izquierdo and Celeste Mendoza. Groups specialising in *rumba* also emerged, such as Los Papines, El Coro de Clave y Guanguancó, as well as the renowned Muñequitos de Matanzas.

JAZZ

Cuban jazz has its roots in the dynamic pre-Revolutionary musical exchange and fusion between American jazz and Afro-Cuban rhythms. Famous Cuban artists such as Juan Tizol, Machito, Mario Bauzá and Chano Pozo inspired the work of Dizzy Gillespie, Charlie Parker and Duke Ellington, and vice versa. Contemporary jazz in Cuba may be less US-influenced these days, but it is still well worth experiencing. Havana's biennial jazz festival is a major international event and attracts big names such as Roy Hardgrove. Among the top Cuban *jazzistas* is legendary pianist Chuchó Valdés and his Orquesta Irakere, who can sometimes be heard at the **Jazz Café**. Also look out for Gonzalo Rubalcaba, another amazing pianist, and jazz trumpeter Arturo Sandóval.

REVOLUTION

The 1959 Revolution put a dampener on things. Hotels and nightclubs lost their foreign patronage, and home-grown musicians such as Celia Cruz, the so-called 'Queen of Salsa', left for Miami and have lived there ever since. Those who chose to stay behind were faced with economic shortages and difficult conditions, and less glamorous, more 'local' venues, including *casas de la trova*, and get-togethers, such as *peñas*, took over.

MODERN SOUNDS: ROCK, RAP AND REGGAE

If you're expecting to hear non-stop *son* and *salsa* during your stay in Havana, watch out; Cuba – in particular its youth – is into slightly different tunes these days. *Roqueros*, as rockers are called here, first appeared in the 1970s and were viewed with suspicion by the authorities for their counter-cultural attitudes, unusual appearance and preference for music sung in the enemy language: English. Despite repression and lack of support, groups such as Los Dadas, Los Gens, Zeus and Los Jets appeared on the scene, playing their music where they could. They were rarely heard on the radio and certainly never given the opportunity to record, but in the last few years the stigma against Cuban rock has somewhat diminished. More commercially successful bands include Moneda Dura, Cosa Nostra, Mezcla and Síntesis, some of which have fused rock with other rhythms such as *nueva trova*, Afro-Cuban sounds and pop.

Cuba's hip hop scene is booming. What started out with a few individuals imitating North American rap stars has turned into an island-wide craze. As no instruments are needed to rap, new groups and individual *raperos* emerge daily, equipped with little more than a boom box and some provocative lyrics (although always within limits). You can hear *raperos* all over town, but the heart of Havana's hip hop scene is Alamar, where the yearly **Rap Festival** takes place (*see p168* **A load of rap**). To date the best-known groups are Orisha, Primera Base, SVS and Obsession.

Cuban reggae is a small but growing musical phenomenon. Many of the band's musicians are devout Rastafarians who, like Bob Marley, use music as a way to transmit their message of one love. Bands like Remanente, Insurrectos and 100% can be heard chanting down Babylon in Spanish in some of the major venues, but are more often found giving free open-air concerts in the more marginal *barrios* of town. Ras Mayeta, a Rasta who can nearly always be found sitting on one of the benches in Parque Central, can tell you what's on and where.

As you walk through Havana you'll hear all these sounds, and more. Musical venues abound, but, formal places aside, music throbs through the city, giving life to its people.

▶ For music venues, *see chapters* **Music & Nightlife** and **Performing Arts**. For music festivals, *see chapter* **By Season**.

▶ For suggestions about which Cuban music to buy or listen to, *see p294* **Further reference**.

Accommodation

Accommodation   **48**

Feature boxes

Accommodation

The influx of tourists to Havana has led to a massive increase in accommodation options, from huge joint-venture hotels to B&Bs with one room to rent. Here we sort the wheat from the chaff.

Tourism in Cuba – and therefore Havana – is fast becoming one of the most important money-earners for the country. The choice of hotels has widened considerably in recent years, and almost any kind of accommodation is now available. However, while it's true that joint ventures in Havana and on the rest of the island mean that you'll now find a Novotel, a clutch of Meliás and a Golden Tulip, just don't come to Havana expecting to find the luxury of a Four Seasons or Ritz-Carlton. The influx of tourists has, and will no doubt continue to have, positive effects on the standards of hotels and even *casas particulares*, but there's still a way to go. Supposedly five-star or 'business' hotels rarely match the standards of their counterparts around the world: mini-bars might have meagre contents and may not even be restocked on a regular basis; the satellite TV offered may only stretch to a few channels, and you may try to order a sandwich at 9pm to be told that the chef has knocked off early. You may even find that a hotel provides a great breakfast one day, only to dish up relative dregs the next. How you react to such annoyances is entirely up to you: you can either disregard them, knowing that Cubans generally have a hard time getting hold of adequate materials, or kick up a fuss in the (often vain) hope that every minor problem will be ironed out. The bottom line is that, as with everything else in Cuba, you need a sense of humour. The good news, however, is that Havana does boast some truly charming places to rest your head.

WHERE TO STAY

The atmosphere of **La Habana Vieja** makes it the most popular destination for visitors, with an increasing number of attractively restored colonial-style hotels. However, while you'll certainly be close to the sights and the action, remember that this part of town can be noisy and very busy, whereas other areas tend to be calmer. Sandwiched between La Habana Vieja and Vedado, **Centro Habana** does not have a great deal of accommodation on offer, which may be a good thing considering that structural safety in this part of town can leave a lot to be desired. Because **Vedado** is very much

geared towards the tourist, hotels and *casas particulares* (along with *paladares*, restaurants and nightclubs), abound. There is also a flurry of activity in **Miramar**, with the construction of new high-rise hotels. This residential neighbourhood is home to many embassies and businesses, with hotel standards that aim to match the surroundings; if you choose a hotel here you will need to use taxis or a hire car to get into Old Havana, Centro and Vedado. Handily, a couple of the more out-of-the-way hotels at the pricey end of the market (the **Meliá Habana** and **Novotel Miramar** among them) now offer shuttle services into town. There is also a tourist bus called the Vaivén ('go and come'), but these do not operate late in the evening.

As a result of the ongoing increase in the number of tourists visiting Havana, there's currently a boom in the provision of accommodation in the city, particularly in La Habana Vieja and Centro Habana: two names to look out for in the near future, in buildings that are being renovated, include the **Hostal San Miguel** (on Calle Cuba, near the cathedral in La Habana Vieja) and the **Telégrafo** hotel on Paseo de Martí (Prado) in Centro Habana.

PESO HOTELS

These budget hotels are intended for Cubans and are priced in pesos. Foreigners are sometimes allowed to stay in peso hotels too, but will usually be expected to pay in dollars. This means that if the price in dollars is given as one to one, peso hotels are not always as much of a bargain as they first appear. However, some hotels have been known to charge a fixed nightly rate of, say, $10, irrespective of the peso price. Peso hotels tend to be very basic, and some are thoroughly dilapidated and dirty, so always check the room and the facilities before agreeing to stay. Though we have not reviewed any peso hotels in this chapter, if your curiosity gets the better of you, try the popular if characterless **Hotel Deauville** (Avenida de Italia/Galiano #1, entre Malecón y San Lázaro, Centro Habana; 338812), which also takes dollar-paying guests.

CASAS PARTICULARES

Casas particulares are private homes with rooms for rent; the owners invariably live in the house, but have arranged their homes in such a way that guests have a private room or even an apartment within the house. There are hundreds of them in Havana, catering to every taste and budget. In La Habana Vieja at least, you're very likely to be approached in the street by touts (*jineteros*), who will usually receive a few dollars' commission from the proprietor for delivering guests to that particular *casa particular*. We'd suggest you choose from those in this chapter (standards vary enormously, so it is always wise to have a look at a few and then decide) before resorting to the services of a tout. Note that many *casas particulares* are known simply as 'Casa de' (house of), though you might not see such a sign on the door.

A lot of people prefer *casas particulares* to hotels because they offer the opportunity to live with a Cuban family. They can also be cheaper than some of the hotel accommodation on offer in the city (though this is changing as more tourists flock in and prices rise), but it's also true that an average double room in a hotel is likely to offer far more amenities and a great deal more privacy than the equivalent room in a *casa particular*. It is also worth noting that not all *casas* are aiming at the same market: some are geared more towards a business clientele, while others are far more relaxed and better suited to younger guests. In accordance with the law, some proprietors may have strict rules on allowing guests to receive visitors, though it varies from place to place.

Nightly rates in a *casa particular* start from around $20 (more usually $25). Very cheap accommodation in a private house is difficult to find, especially in La Habana Vieja, where the choice is particularly limited. There are many more options available in Vedado, where some homes have been completely refurbished to cater for tourists. We have not listed prices for *casas particulares* in this chapter as you'll often find that quality, not price, is the main distinguishing factor between them.

A sign with blue and white chevrons saying *arrendador inscripto* is displayed outside any house that has licensed rooms for rent. These *casas particulares* are inspected regularly by government officials and the owners are required to pay a heavy tax on each declared room – whether or not it is occupied. In addition to registered *casas particulares* there are a multitude of private places operating without licences. While it is not illegal for you to stay in an unregistered *casa particular*, you may get tied up in bureaucratic hassle if the proprietor gets found out by the authorities. By the same token, *casas particulares* constantly come and go, though the ones listed in this chapter have a better chance of standing the test of time.

Many of the best *casas particulares* have regular clientele and fill up quickly. It is sensible to book at least one to two months ahead and then reconfirm your reservation the week before your arrival. Unless you have rented a whole apartment, many owners will not allow you to use the family kitchen, but may provide (often excellent) breakfast and/or evening meals for a few dollars extra. They may also provide such services as laundry. Be sure to agree on a price for everything beforehand. Not all *casa* owners speak English, but the vast majority can get by with a few words. Try to meet them halfway by learning some Cuban phrases.

Booking a room

It's fine for you to **phone** (or **fax**) your chosen hotel or *casa particular* to reserve your accommodation, but be aware that you might not always find an English speaker (especially in the case of the latter, which also might not be able to provide you with written confirmation of your booking). All 'tourist' hotels (as opposed to peso hotels) are either joint ventures with non-Cuban companies or state-owned, and all are affiliated to **state-run agencies** such as Horizontes or Gaviota (which often appear as part of the hotel's name; *see p223 The chain gang*), where staff can book your room for you and are more likely to speak English. At present there are no agencies for *casas particulares* (though this might change in future), so you're better off arranging to stay in a hotel for your first night or two, then checking out a *casa particular* or two in person once you're in Havana. There are also agencies in non-Cuban countries that can arrange your accommodation before you go, but this can take a while to firm up, especially if your original choice is fully booked. If you do phone or fax a hotel directly, try to get them to fax or email you something in writing, or at least get the name of the person you spoke to. **Email** is another alternative; we've included email addresses for accommodation where possible, though these, as with other details, are subject to change.

Lobby life

Hotels have always featured prominently in the social life of Havana. People come to them to have business meetings, eat, chat, swim and dance. In pre-Revolutionary times the city's hotels were a magnet for Hollywood stars, and while today you're more likely to spot Kate Moss at the Golden Tulip than a mafiosi at the Nacional, it wasn't always that way...

MOB RULE

The atmosphere of the pre-Revolutionary hotels was very different from present-day ones. Most of the bigger hotels had gambling casinos that attracted their fair share of famous (more like notorious) faces – among them was actor George Raft, who allegedly ran the casino at the **Hotel Capri** (*see p57*) on behalf of his mafia chums. Ginger Rogers flew in to open the new Copa Room at the **Habana Riviera** (*see p56*), Meyer Lansky established his headquarters at the gambling hall of the **Hotel Nacional** (*see p56*), Havana's best-known hotel even today, and Al Capone rented out the whole of the sixth floor of the Hotel Seville-Biltmore (now **Hotel Sevilla**; *see p54*) for his followers.

EVERYBODY IN THE HOUSE OF LOVE

In many Spanish-speaking countries a *posada* is an inn, but in Cuba it has traditionally been a motel-type place that rents out rooms by the hour to couples, no questions asked. Because housing conditions in Havana (and elsewhere in Cuba) have always been cramped, young couples would use *posadas* as a means to escape and have some privacy. Towels and soap were provided, and post-coital food could be delivered to the rooms. However, you could never linger for a ciggie afterwards – it was a question of in and out, so to speak. Though today you might be forgiven for mistaking some crumbly-looking hotels for *posadas*, there are few still in operation.

RATES AND SEASONS

Hotel room rates go up during high season (December to April) and particularly around Christmas and Easter. Rates also tend to be higher during July and August, when Cubans are on holiday. (Variations in rates are given in this chapter where possible.) You should also book in advance if your visit is likely to coincide with a major event in the city, such as the International Film Festival (December). For details of the main events *see chapter* **By Season**. During busy periods it is wise to pay for your accommodation for up to a few days in advance to ensure it is not given to someone else – even after you've checked in!

THE OFFICIAL WORD

Visitors to Cuba are officially required to have two nights' accommodation pre-booked, though such things seem to change periodically and we've also had one and three nights quoted. It's not unheard of for foreign visitors without proof of accommodation to be forced to book and pay on the spot for accommodation chosen by the immigration officials. Always fill in the 'address in Cuba' section of your tourist card when you enter the country.

STAR RATING SYSTEMS, FACILITIES AND LISTINGS

All 'tourist' hotels in Cuba (as opposed to peso hotels, though these will sometimes let non-Cubans in too) are either state-run or joint ventures with foreign companies, and are classified on a star system from one to five, but this is no guarantee of quality. Four- and even five-star hotels in Cuba are often only equivalent to three-star hotels in other countries, although the prices are likely to be just as high. For this reason we have chosen not to indicate official star ratings; price is normally an indicator as to how many services the hotel offers. For consistency of quality and service, your best bet is often one of the upscale hotels run under licence by a foreign hotel group, such as the **Novotel Miramar** or **Golden Tulip Parque Central**.

Note that, unless otherwise stated, hotels do not charge extra for breakfast, and that most hotel rooms are en suite. In hotels where laundry services are not officially offered, you can normally come to a private arrangement with one of the maids.

Note that American credit cards (or even American Express cards issued by a bank outside the US) are not accepted in Cuban hotels and that *casas particulares* only accept cash payment (dollars at that). All the information in this chapter was correct as this guide went to press, but, this being Cuba, rates and facilities are subject to change.

SAFETY AND SECURITY

Couple Havana's status as capital with Cuba's low wages and poor living conditions, and it's no wonder the city has a high incidence of petty crime. Be as vigilant with your belongings in the place you're staying as you would be when you're out and about. Lock any valuables in your room safe (where provided), and preferably lock your suitcase whenever you go out (clothes have been known to go astray). Also watch out for a trick sometimes pulled by maids, when they 'tidy away' guests' belongings into hidden places; that way you won't miss them till after you've checked out.

Because of problems with prostitution in Havana in the past, many hotels now have security personnel patrolling the lobby. Note that Cubans are not allowed into guest rooms in most hotels and may not even be welcome in the lobby or other communal areas, so always arrange to meet Cuban friends or contacts away from your hotel. Most *casas particulares* will let your Cuban friends into your room, provided they are over 18.

A guest card (*tarjeta de huésped*) is issued to all hotel guests in order to protect guests against prostitution and robbery. Hang onto it: in more expensive hotels you'll need it not only to get into your room but also when you sign for any drinks and meals you consume in its bars or restaurants. You may also need it to operate the lift.

ETIQUETTE

You may return to your hotel room to find your towel or manky old nightie lovingly shaped into a swan or a heart. This is the maid's way of trying to impress you in the hope you'll top up their meagre wages with a tip. If you're satisfied with your stay, make their day by leaving them a small gift such as a toiletry item; hard cash (dollars, that is) is far more desirable. If you wish, you can also leave a tip for the owners of a *casa particular*.

DISABLED VISITORS

People with disabilities are strongly advised to contact their chosen hotel or *casa particular* before going to Havana to find out which, if any, disabled services are offered.

La Habana Vieja

Expensive hotels

Hotel Santa Isabel

Calle Baratillo #9, entre Obispo y Narciso López, (608201/609619/609620/fax 608560). **Rates** single $110; double $150; suite $135-$210. **Credit** MC, V. **Map** p316 E16.
At the higher end of the price range, the Santa Isabel was originally the mansion of the Count of Santovenia; his crest can be found on the plates in the discreet restaurant on the ground floor. The hotel has 27 rooms (ten of them suites, including the Santovenia suite), which exude wonderful style and are comfortably and tastefully furnished, with wrought-iron beds and pastel pink walls. Many rooms have large, if not particularly private balconies overlooking the Plaza de Armas. An atmosphere of civilised conservatism prevails, spoilt only by the security guards patrolling the hotel with their walkie-talkies. Possibly the nicest hotel in Havana, though the breakfast leaves a lot to be desired. Despite the Santa Isabel's official address, the entrance is actually on the Plaza de Armas (eastern side).
Hotel services *Babysitting. Bars (2). Business services. Car rental. Laundry. Parking (free). Restaurant. Tourist services.* **Room services** *Air-conditioning. Mini-bar. Room service (24hr). Safe. Telephone. TV (satellite).*

Mid-range hotels

Hostal el Comendador

Calle Obrapía, esquina a Baratillo (671037/ fax 335628/hostales@valcom.ohch.cu). **Rates** single $55-$69; double $85-$106; suite $100-$125. **Credit** MC, V. **Map** p316 E16.
Opened in 1999, this is in effect an extension of the Valencia (*see p53*). The 14 upgraded rooms sport original features including stained-glass decoration and reproduction antique baths, and represent excellent value in terms of comfort and style. For something completely different, check out the archaeological excavation site within the Hostal premises, which features skulls, skeletons and other gory exhibits.

Accommodation

Two faces of the **Hotel Santa Isabel**'s splendid Santovenia suite.

Hotel services *Babysitting. Bar (1). Laundry.*
Room services *Air-conditioning. Mini-bar.*
Room service (noon-11pm). Safe. Telephone
(no direct line). TV (satellite).

Hostal Conde de Villanueva

Calle Mercaderes #202, entre Lamparilla y Amargura
(629293/fax 629682). Rates (breakfast not incl)
single $67.50-$72; double $95-$105; mini suite $80-
$120; suite $115-$175. Credit MC, V. Map p316 E15.
This hotel was originally the home of the Count of
Villanueva, an 18th-century aristocrat who brought
the railways to Cuba. Its recent renovation is a
triumph of eclecticism and style. The *hostal*'s nine
rooms (three of them are suites) are particularly
interesting for cigar aficionados, as each carries
the name of a tobacco plant. The understated
rooms are conservatively decorated in masculine
colours, and feature quality furniture. (Rooms with
a view are marginally more expensive.) The suites
have Jacuzzis, but only three of the bathrooms have
showers. The central patio, with its promenading
peacocks, is charming and the excellent cigar shop
(*see p157*) doubles as a comfortable bar. There are
conference facilities for up to 70 people.
Hotel services *Bars (2). Café. Conference rooms.*
Garden. Laundry. Restaurant. Room services
Air-conditioning. Mini-bar. Room service (24hr).
Telephone. TV (satellite).

Hostal del Tejadillo

Calle Tejadillo, esquina a San Ignacio (637283/fax
638830/638883). Rates (breakfast not incl) single
$50-76; double $58-86; triple $87-114; junior suite
$106-126. Credit MC, V. Map p316 D15.
This charming 18th-century house, which opened as
a *hostal* in summer 2000, has 32 modest-sized but
comfortable rooms. Ask for one on the second
floor to get a balcony or on the third to get one with
period shutters. There is live Cuban music every day
between noon and 10pm in the Bar San Carlos.
Hotel services *Air conditioning. Babysitting. Bar.*
Laundry. Restaurant. Room services *Minibar.*
Safe. Telephone. TV (cable).

Hotel Ambos Mundos

Calle Obispo #153, esquina a Mercaderes (609530/
fax 609532). Rates (breakfast not incl) single $65-
$75; double $90-$105; triple $110-$115; junior suite
$120-$130. Credit MC, V. Map p316 E15.
Constructed at the end of the 1920s, this hotel is
famous for being the one-time home of Ernest
Hemingway. The author first visited for 48 hours in
1928 and subsequently took up permanent residence
from 1932 to 1939. Room 511 has been kept as it was
during his tenancy and is now described rather elaborately as a museum. Ernie aside, the hotel occupies
a prime position in the old town and is right in the
heart of the buzz of Obispo. The 52 rooms were
recently refurbished and there's an impressive original lift. Other attractions include the art gallery on
the second floor, which is sometimes used for
conferences. Helpful staff and competitive prices
contribute to the hotel's significant appeal.

Hotel Florida's wonderful lobby.

Hotel services *Babysitting. Bars (2). Conference*
rooms. Laundry. Parking. Restaurant. Room
services *Air-conditioning. Mini-bar. Room service*
(24hr). Telephone. TV (satellite).

Hotel Florida

Calle Obispo #252, esquina a Cuba (624127/fax
624117). Rates (breakfast not incl) single $65-$75;
double $90-$105; single suite $125-$150; double suite
$150-$175. Credit MC, V. Map p316 E15.
First inaugurated as a hotel in 1885, the Hotel Florida
is a splendid example of the restoration work going
on in Old Havana. The entrance features a lady in
marble and the staircase is over-arched by a beautiful stained-glass roof commemorating the reopening
of the hotel in May 1999. The 25 well-furnished
rooms with Italian marble floors and small balconies
demonstrate admirable attention to detail and the
bathrooms have direct-line telephones and bidets. An
attractive central colonial-style patio leads to a rather
gloomy piano and television bar where there is music
in the evening. Also off the patio is Restaurant La
Floridana. Historical artefacts lend an original colonial atmosphere to the whole place. Great value.
Hotel services *Bars (2). Business services.*
Laundry. Parking. Restaurant. Shop. Room
services *Air-conditioning. Mini-bar. Room*
service (24hr). Safe. Telephone. TV (satellite).

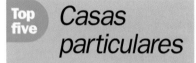

Casas particulares

Casa de Eugenio Barral García
High-class eclecticism. *See p53.*

Casa de Alexis González Lorié
Hotel facilities at *casa particular* rates.
See p60.

Casa de Huéspedes Dorys
Warm and welcoming. *See p58.*

Hospedaje Gisela Ibarra y Daniel Riviero
Guesthouse ambience and great brekkies.
See p58.

Residencias Herrero
Extras included in the price make this
a great-value choice. *See p58.*

Budget hotels

Hostal Valencia
*Calle Oficios #53, esquina a Obrapía (671037/fax
335628).* **Rates** single $40-$50; double $60-$75;
suite $75-$94. **Credit** MC, V. **Map** p316 E15.
The lack of air-conditioning and the slightly dilapidated furnishings are reflected in the cheap prices
at this old-town *hostal.* Nevertheless, the central
patio is extremely atmospheric and the location is
good for sightseeing. The architecture is Spanish-
influenced, enhanced by leather furnishings from
Spain in the 12 rooms. All in all, the bags of style at
low prices and the relaxed atmosphere mean that
the Valencia is very often fully booked. Further
incentives are provided by La Paella restaurant (*see
p128*) and half-price cocktails in the bar from 7pm
to 9pm daily.
Hotel services *Bars (2). Babysitting. Laundry.
Restaurant.* **Room services** *Ceiling fans. Mini-bar.
Safe. Telephone. TV (satellite).*

Residencia Académica
*Convento de Santa Clara, Calle Cuba #610, entre Luz
y Sol (613335/fax 335696/reaca@cencrem.cult.cu).*
Rates dormitories $25 per person; suite $35 per
person. **No credit cards. Map** p316 E15.
Santa Clara operated as a convent from 1644 to 1922,
when it lost its religious status and subsequently
passed into the hands of various ministries. The
accommodation consists mostly of four- or five-bed
dormitories, so it is used predominantly by students
or groups on a budget, although the suite offers more
privacy. Many of the Residencia's guests stay here
because of the site's historical significance, but as
there's no air-conditioning avoid staying here

between June and September unless you've prac-
tised sleeping in a sauna first.
Hotel services *Babysitting. Café. Garden. Laundry.
Parking. Payphone.* **Room services** *Telephone.*

Casas particulares

Casa de Eugenio Barral García
*Calle San Ignacio #656, entre Jesús María y Merced
(629877).* **Map** p316 F15.
This beautifully clean home is decorated in a strange
but enticing mixture of antiques and modern art.
Boisterous children would be out of place amongst
all the precious ornaments, but otherwise this place
is highly recommended. Accommodation consists of
three bedrooms and two communal bathrooms.
Services *Air-conditioning. Fans. Refrigerator.
TV room.*

Casa de Migdalia Caraballe Martín
*Calle Santa Clara #164, 1ro piso, Apto F, entre
Cuba y San Ignacio (tel/fax 617352).* **Map** p316 E15.
A very enthusiastic, helpful lady runs this pleasant
casa particular in the heart of Old Havana. The three
double rooms are light and airy with fans as well
as air-conditioning.
Services *Air-conditioning. Parking. Safe. TV room.*

Casa de Miriam Soto Delgado
*Calle Cuba #611, 2do piso, Apto 4, entre Santa
Clara y Luz (627144).* **Map** p316 E15.
One fairly basic double room with TV and adjacent
bathroom is available in this family home. Visitors
have use of the *sala* and there are panoramic views
over the Convento de Santa Clara from the roof.
Services *Air-conditioning. Telephone. TV.*

Centro Habana

Expensive hotels

Hotel Golden Tulip Parque Central
*Calle Neptuno, entre Martí (Prado) y Agramonte,
(606627/606628/606629/fax 606630/
www.goldentuliphotels.nl).* **Rates** single $115-$165;
double $165-$180; suite $250-$475. **Credit** MC, V.
Map p313 D14.
This joint venture between Cuba and the Dutch
Golden Tulip chain was criticised by some during its
conversion from the former Hotel Parque Central
(which is the name it's still known by to many
Cubans). While its blatantly new arches and stark
atrium might not be to everyone's taste, this 279-
roomer is perhaps redeemed by its uniqueness in
the city, as a centrally located hotel geared to visitors
with money. It provides what it describes as complete
business services (aka a room with two computers
offering slow but generally reliable Internet connection), boardrooms, conference facilities, plus a gym,
Jacuzzi, massage salon and a few shops in the lobby.
   The rooftop swimming pool can be stifling
in the summer months but nonetheless offers stun-

ning views over the city. Visitors and guests alike have a choice of two restaurants: the super-posh Mediterráneo and the more affordable (though still pricey by Havana standards) El Paseo; or you can simply relax at the bar or on one of the sofas in the big airy lobby decorated with plants. Refurbished rooms are already showing signs of wear and tear, but this is still an attractive hotel with facilities that approach international five-star standards. Incredibly, though perhaps because of the Dutch connection, all rooms have only 220v sockets. It also has one of the few ATMs in Havana.

Hotel services *ATM. Babysitting. Bars (3). Business services (Internet access). Car rental. Concierge. Conference rooms. Currency exchange (24hr). Gym. Jacuzzi. Laundry. Medical services (24hr). No-smoking rooms. Parking (free). Restaurants (2). Shops. Swimming pool. Tourist services.* **Room services** *Air-conditioning. Mini-bar. Room service (24hr). Telephone. TV (pay movies/satellite).*

Hotel Inglaterra

Paseo de Martí (Prado) #416, esquina a San Rafael, (608595/608596/608597/fax 608254/ reserva@gcingla.gca.cma.net). **Rates** single $75-$80; double $100-$130; triple $126-$132. **Credit** MC, V. **Map** p313 D14.

Founded in 1875, this is the oldest and one of the most atmospheric hotels in Havana. The imposing lobby is an elegant assembly of crystal chandeliers, stained glass, wrought iron, marble floors, moulded ceilings and Moroccan tilework. There are 83 rooms on four floors, the best of which have good views (some of them over Parque Central, others over the Gran Teatro). La Sevillana coffee and piano bar serves snacks and drinks, while the open-air rooftop Terraza Bar/Grill offers nightly entertainment and, again, gorgeous views. The menus and tabletops at Café El Louvre and El Colonial restaurant were designed by modern Cuban artists.

Hotel services *Babysitting. Bars (3). Car rental. Laundry. No-smoking rooms (2). Parking (free). Restaurants (2). Tourist services.* **Room services** *Air-conditioning. Mini-bar. Room service (24hr). Telephone. TV (satellite).*

Hotel Plaza

Calle Agramonte (Zulueta) #267, esquina a Neptuno (608583-9/fax 608591/reserva@plaza.gca.cma.net). **Rates** single $80; double $120; triple $171; suite $96 (1 person), $144 (2 people). **Credit** MC, V. **Map** p313 D14.

Another atmospheric haunt, the Plaza Hotel, on the corner opposite the Golden Tulip (*see p53*), has a pleasant air of bustle and an attractive lobby with a fountain and streams of coloured light pouring over the floor. Complimentary tea is served between 5pm and 6pm every day on the second-floor terrace, while other entertainment is provided by a karaoke bar and regular dance classes. The fifth-floor sun terrace has a good view of the Bacardí building, but alas no swimming pool. A useful service is the on-site 24-hour pharmacy and medical facilities available to any tourist. The beds are very soft, which may or may not be a recommendation.

The best Hotels

For atmosphere
Hotel National de Cuba. *See p56.*

For budding mafiosi
Hotel Nacional de Cuba (*see p56*) and the **Hotel Capri** (*see p57*).

For budding novelists
Hotel Ambos Mundos. *See p52.*

For business travellers (all with Internet connection)
Hotel Golden Tulip Parque Central (*see p53*); **Hotel Meliá Cohiba** (*see p56*); **Hotel Meliá Habana** (*see p58*); **Hotel Nacional de Cuba** (*see p56*) and **Hotel Novotel Miramar** (*see p59*).

For ghouls
Hostal el Comendador. *See p51.*

For originality
Hostal Conde de Villanueva. *See p52.*

For value for money
Casa del Científico. *See p55.*

Hotel services *Babysitting. Bars (3). Business services. Laundry. No-smoking rooms (10). Restaurants (3).* **Room services** *Air-conditioning. Mini-bar. Room service (24hr). Safe. Telephone. TV (satellite).*

Hotel Sevilla

Calle Trocadero #55, entre Martí (Prado) y Agramonte (608560/fax 608582/ reserva@sevilla.gca.tur.cu). **Rates** (breakfast not incl) single $100; double $130; triple $157. **Credit** MC, V. **Map** p313 D13.

Opened in 1908, this impressive Spanish/Moorish-styled hotel is currently undergoing renovation under new French management. Ask for a room on one of the higher floors, which have already been revamped and are quite delightful compared to the rather ordinary rooms lower down – and there's no difference in price. The attractive El Patio Sevillano bar off the lobby is open 24 hours should you require a *mojito* at four in the morning. The ninth floor hosts the magnificent Roof Garden restaurant with breathtaking views over the city. Breakfast is an extra $10 and there's a dinner show here for $35 at 8.30pm on Saturday and sometimes also Friday nights. Hotel staff seem very efficient, which may have something to do with the fact that the national hotelier school is based here.

Hotel services *Babysitting. Bars (2). Car rental. Business services. Guided tours. Gym. Laundry. Medical services (24hr). Parking. Restaurants (2).*

Shop. Spa. Swimming pool. Tourist services. **Room services** *Air-conditioning. Mini-bar. Room service (24hr). Telephone. TV (satellite).*

Budget hotels

Casa del Científico

Paseo de Martí (Prado) #212, esquina a Trocadero (638103/624511/633591/fax 600167). **Rates** (breakfast not incl) single $25-$45; double $31-$55; triple $37-$64; suite $70. **No credit cards.** **Map** p313 D13.

In terms of price and atmosphere, this place is hard to beat. From 1914 to 1924 it was home to José Miguel Gómez, the second president of Cuba. It is now a focal point for meetings and reunions of scientists and operates under the direction of the Ministry of Sciences. There are special rates available for groups, but the 11 rooms are often taken six months ahead, so book early. Second-floor rooms share a bathroom, but those on the first floor boast private ones (one of which is almost the size of some hotel rooms) and firmer beds. A beautiful winding marble staircase with a stained-glass roof (1914) leads up to a pleasant restaurant, Los Vitrales, while the ground floor has a café with two pool tables. Staff are extremely nice. *See also p81.*

Hotel services *Bar. Business services. Café. Laundry. Restaurant. Shuttle service. Tourist services.* **Room services** *Air-conditioning. Mini-bar. Room service (7.30am-9.30pm). Safe. TV (satellite).*

Hotel Caribbean

Paseo de Martí (Prado) #164, esquina a Colón, Centro Habana (608233/608210/608241/fax 609479). **Rates** (breakfast not incl) single $33-36; double $130-155. **Credit** MC, V. **Map** p313 D14/15.

Renovated in 1998, this hotel is a great choice for budget travellers. The rooms are done out nicely in Caribbean colours and simply furnished, and guests can make use of the small bar. The hotel is easily missed – look out for the café next door.

Hotel services *Air conditioning. Bar. Laundry. Parking.* **Room services** *Safe (free). Telephone. TV (cable).*

Hotel Lincoln

Avenida de Italia (Galiano) #164, esquina a Virtudes (338209). **Rates** single $28-$35; double $37-$42. **No credit cards.** **Map** p313 D13.

This striking pink and white building opened on 13 August 1926, the same day that Fidel Castro was born. The hotel caters for both foreign and Cuban guests and is currently undergoing refurbishment. One of the 135 guest rooms, room 810, is preserved as a museum recording the experience of Grand Prix legend Juan Manuel Fangio, who was kidnapped from the hotel by revolutionary forces for 48 hours on 23 February 1958 (racing fans can rest assured: he was released unharmed after two days). El Colonial restaurant and piano bar on the ground floor is cheap and cheerful, and retains an atmosphere of faded glory. The top floor has a roof terrace

bar and a Chinese restaurant, La Montaña de Oro. The refurbished rooms with new marble floors and nice bathrooms are decent value for money, despite the fact that the 'wardrobe' consists only of hangers on a rail.

Hotel services *Bars (2). Business services. Medical services (9am-6pm). Parking. Restaurants (3).* **Room services** *Air-conditioning. Mini-bar (some rooms). Safe. Telephone (no direct line). TV (satellite).*

Casas particulares

Casa de Amada Pérez Guelmes

Calle Lealtad #262 (altos), entre Neptuno y Concordia (tel/fax 623924). **Map** p313 D13.

This is basic accommodation in a run-down area, but the building is well secured and the family are friendly. There are four double rooms and cooking facilities are provided.

Services *Air-conditioning. Cooking facilities. Parking.*

Villa Enano Rojo

Malecón #557, entre Lealtad y Escobar (635081). **Map** p313 C13.

The Red Dwarf Villa offers one double room with a large lounge overlooking the Malecón. The accommodation is airy and the views are great. The young landlady, who has two small children, is happy to put in an extra bed for a child at no extra charge. **Services** *Air-conditioning.*

Vedado & Nuevo Vedado

Expensive hotels

Hotel Habana Libre

Calle L, entre 23 y 25 (554011/fax 553806/553141/hotel@rllibre.tryp.cma.net). **Rates** single $140; double $160; junior suite $250; presidential suite $1,350. **Credit** MC, V. **Map** p312 B11.

Opened in 1958, this well-known hotel was taken over by the Meliá group in 2000 and was slated for a revamp that would add a business centre and gym to its already extensive services. At present it has plenty of rooms (574 to be exact) and lots of facilities, but feels rather past its sell-by date. The sad lobby in particular looks like it's stuck in a time warp and is in desperate need of an overhaul. On the plus side, the glass-walled Pico Turquino on the 26th floor has great views over the city with a roof that opens and closes, and is the setting for the hotel's cabaret show and well-known disco (*see p192*). There are also several eating options, among them El Polinesio (*see p133*) and the Sierra Maestra on the 25th floor. Summing up, the hotel's many services are its only recommendation, although some visitors may be attracted by the fact that Castro stayed in the Presidential suite at the time of the Triumph.

Hotel services *Airline offices (5). Babysitting. Bars (4). Bank. Beauty salon. Business services. Café (24hr). Car rental. Gym. Laundry. Medical services.*

No-smoking floors. Parking. Restaurants (4).
Shops. Spa. Swimming pool. **Room services** *Air-conditioning. Mini-bar. Room service (24hr). Safe.*
Telephone. TV (satellite).

Hotel Habana Riviera

Malecón, esquina a Paseo (334051/fax 333739).
Rates single $72-$102; double $96-$154; triple $137-
$219; junior suite $140-$157; presidential suite $300-
$317. **Credit** MC, V. **Map** p312 A9.
Hotel Habana Riviera was constructed in the 1950s
by the mafia leader Meyer Lansky in an effort to
compete with other families operating gambling
rackets in the United States, and it received a spectacular star-studded opening. However, unlike the
Capri (*see p57*), the Riviera has adapted to the times
and is a comfortable and pleasant place to stay. The
352 rooms won't wow you with their decor but are
clean and pleasant, and have sea views (be careful
of small children near the open windows). The fresh
water swimming pool comes complete with diving
boards (a rarity in Havana), and there's musical
entertainment around it from midday to 6pm on
Friday, Saturday and Sunday nights. Guests can
also watch the show in the Copa Room (*see p192*)
every day except Tuesdays for the princely sum
of $25 (although that does include a cocktail). The
hotel plans to add a beauty salon and gym to its
facilities in the near future, but in the meantime there
are some shops on the lower ground floor, and
a business centre on the 20th floor, with its own grill
restaurant, El Mirador. All in all, a very pleasant
hotel, but lacking the spark that would make it especially memorable.
Hotel services *Babysitting. Bars (2). Business
services. Car rental. Laundry. Parking. Restaurants
(2). Swimming pool. Tourist services.* **Room
services** *Air-conditioning. Mini-bar. Room service
(24hr). Telephone. TV (satellite).*

Hotel Meliá Cohiba

*Paseo, entre 1ra y 3ra (333636/fax 334555/
dep_res_mlc@cohiba1.solmelia.cma.net).* **Rates**
(breakfast not incl) *Standard accommodation* single
$165; double $215; junior suite $250; suite $300;
senior suite $500. *Servicio real* single $215; double
$265; junior suite $350; suite $450; senior suite $650.
Credit MC, V. **Map** p312 A9.
Opened in 1995, this huge hotel with 462 rooms is
almost a village in itself. Stylish surroundings and
good service make this an appealing option for
monied visitors. The decor in the rooms is somewhat
muted but undeniably comfortable, and 12 of the
suites offer butler service. Breakfast is available for
$15 or guests can opt for a $25 buffet meal that
would be impressive anywhere in the world, let
alone in Cuba. Wealthy guests or those with an
expense account might want to take advantage of a
special 'royal' service (*servicio real*), available on four
floors of the hotel. This offers express check-in and
check-out, a running buffet (7am-11pm) and an
exclusive lift. Mere mortals will have to make do
with the hotel's other (admittedly impressive) array
of amenities: no less than five restaurants, an attrac-

The iconic, majestic **Nacional de Cuba**.

tive swimming pool, a comprehensive shopping centre and a smoking bar for cigar aficionados. The
Habana Café (whose entrance is next door though
it's part of the hotel) provides food (*see p132*) and
lively musical entertainment (*see p192*).
Hotel services *Babysitting. Bars (5). Beauty salon.
Business services (Internet access). Gym. Laundry.
Massage. No-smoking rooms. Parking ($8/day).
Restaurants (5). Shops. Squash court. Swimming
pool.* **Room services** *Air-conditioning. Dataport
(servicio real only). Mini-bar. Room service (24hr).
Safe. Telephone. Turndown (servicio real only). TV
(pay movies/satellite).*

Hotel Nacional de Cuba

Calle O, esquina a 21 (333564/fax 335054). **Rates**
Standard accommodation single $120; double $170;
triple $210; junior suite $215; senior suite $390;
special suite $400; royal suite $450; presidential suite
$1,000. *Executive floor supplement* $30 3 Jan-21 Dec;
$21 22 Dec-2 Jan. **Credit** MC, V. **Map** p312 B12.
This hotel was declared a National Monument in 1998
– and deservedly so. There's something very special
about the Nacional that cannot just be explained by
its marked sophistication, marvellous location, beautiful gardens or magnificent views. Perhaps the many
people – famous and otherwise – who have passed
through its lobby over the years have left their in-
delible mark on the hotel. The Nacional was historically very important both before and after the
Revolution and has maintained its exclusive status;
to stay here is to take part in history. The rooms aren't
the most exciting in the world, but their views over
the Malecón or the hotel gardens are impressive. The
hotel has two restaurants: La Veranda and Comedor
de Aguiar (*see p133*).
Hotel services *Babysitting. Bars (5). Beauty
salon. Business centre (Internet access). Café. Car
rental. Concierge. Garden. Gym. Laundry. Parking.
Restaurants (2). Shops. Swimming pools. Tennis
courts. Tourist services.* **Room services** *Air-
conditioning. Mini-bar. Room service (24hr).
Safe. Telephone. TV (satellite).*

Hotel Presidente

*Calzada #110, esquina a Presidentes (G) (551801-4/
fax 333753/comerc@hpdte.gca.tur.cu).* **Rates** (20%
supplement 22 Dec-2 Jan) single $90; double $140;
single suite $130; double suite $220. **Credit** MC, V.
Map p312 A10.

Fully restored in April 1999, this quiet conservative
1920s hotel has a lobby bursting with antiques
and an outdoor swimming pool that is seductively
elegant. There's no room for brashness in the calm,
muted interior, and noisy children would be out
of place, too. For a really special occasion, try to
reserve the special suite furnished in the style of
Louis XV, for which there is a $15 supplement. With
all of Havana bustling on the street outside, this 160-
room hotel seems a cool oasis in the midst of a storm.
Hotel services *Bars (3). Business services.
Concierge. Laundry. Parking (free). Restaurants (2).
Swimming pool.* **Room services** *Air-conditioning.
Mini-bar. Room service (10am-midnight). Safe.
Telephone. TV (satellite).*

Mid-range hotels

Hotel Capri

*Calle 21, entre N y O (333747/333748/fax
334750/lissette@hcapri.hor.cma.net).* **Rates** single
$65-$78; double $80-$94; triple $104-$123; junior
suite $104-$123; suite $108-$127. **Credit** MC, V.
Map p312 B12.

A 1950s hotel with heavy mob connections, the 215-
room Capri has had its day. The leafy sculptures
in the barren foyer are the only hint of its previous
position as a flagship of mafia power and gambling
activity (actor George Raft is said to have run the
Capri's casino for the mafia). All casinos closed after
the Revolution and, sadly for the Capri, this seems
to have had the effect of ripping its guts out. The top
floor has a swimming pool and restaurant, and the
ground floor boasts a cabaret in the Salón Rojo (*see
p192*), but there's little else of note.
Hotel services *Babysitting. Bars (3). Beauty salon.
Cafés (2). Conference rooms (2). Laundry. Medical
services (24hr). Restaurants (2). Swimming pool.*
Room services *Air-conditioning. Mini-bar. Room
service (24hr). Safe. Telephone. TV (satellite).*

Hotel St John's

*Calle O #206, entre 23 y 25 (333740/fax 333561/
jrecepci@stjohns2.hor.tur.cu).* **Rates** single $65-$68;
double $80-$94; junior suite $104.50-$115.70. **Credit**
MC, V. **Map** p312 B12.

Run by the same company as Hotel Vedado just next
door (*see below*), this smallish hotel has recently been
refurbished. Although it has air-conditioning that
verges on glacial, the 87 rooms are comfortable
and have showers; only the junior suite has a bath
– and a mini-bar. Other features include a spanking
new steak bar, Steak House Toro (*see p134*), where
you can select your slab of imported Canadian meat,
and the Pico Blanco terrace, which has a small swimming pool and offers nightly cabaret performances.

Hotel services *Bars (2). Business services.
Parking. Restaurant. Swimming pool.* **Room
services** *Air conditioning. Room service (24hr).
Safe. Telephone. TV (satellite).*

Hotel Victoria

*Calle 19 #101, esquina a M (333510/
fax 333109/reserva@gcvicto.gca.cma.net).*
Rates (breakfast not incl) single $80; double
$100; mini suite $105 (1 person), $130 (2 people).
Credit MC, V. **Map** p312 B11.

This intimate hotel with 28 double rooms and three
junior suites targets a business clientele. The staff
are friendly and efficient, and personal attention
is guaranteed. The hotel offers a wide range of executive business services, a reasonable restaurant and
there's a small swimming pool for when the city's
heat gets too much.
Hotel services *Bar. Business services. Currency
exchange. Laundry. Parking. Restaurant. Swimming
pool.* **Room services** *Air-conditioning. Mini-bar.
Room service (7am-midnight). Safe. Telephone.
TV (satellite).*

Budget hotels

Hotel Vedado

Calle O #244, entre 23 y 25 (334072/fax 334186).
Rates single $48-$58; double $64-$75; triple $83-$97;
suite $93-$109. **Credit** MC, V. **Map** p312 B12.

With 203 rooms, this newly refurbished hotel is
larger than the neighbouring Hotel St John's (*see
above*) and also cheaper. It's a light, bright place
with a large pool and offers free guided trips
around Havana as part of the package. The new
Spanish restaurant in the basement, El Cortijo, is
well worth a visit.
Hotel services *Bars (2). Cafés. Currency exchange.
Guided tours. Gym. Laundry. Parking. Restaurants
(2). Swimming pool. Tourist services.* **Room
services** *Air-conditioning. Room service (7am-
midnight). Safe. Telephone. TV (satellite).*

Casas particulares

Casalicia

Calle F #104 (bajos), entre 5ta y Calzada (320671).
Map p312 A10.

Casalicia is geared towards the under-30s and has a
lively liberal atmosphere. The two double bedrooms
have recently been upgraded and have upper galleries where the owner intends to install TVs and
sofas. Guests have private showers and use of the
kitchen, and smokers are welcome. Recommended.
Services *Air-conditioning. Cooking facilities. TV room.*

La Casa de Ana

*Calle F #107, entre 5ta y Calzada (322360/
312344).* **Map** p312 A10.

With ten years' experience under her belt, Ana
Victoria Lazo offers large, clean rooms with private
bathrooms, many of which tend to get booked up
two months in advance. She particularly welcomes

Accommodation

business people and diplomats and has lounges for meetings. This is certainly not the place for party animals, but is a good choice for conservative clients. There's also a roof patio.

Services *Air-conditioning. Parking. Refrigerator. Safe.*

Casa de Caridad Peñalver Martínez

Calle 3ra #557, entre 8 y 10 (36845). Map p311 A8. This roomy accommodation, provided by a pleasant, English-speaking landlady, consists of one double room, dining and lounge areas and access to the patio. Good value.

Services *Air-conditioning.*

Casa de Carlos y Nelson

Calle E #609, entre 25 y 27 (327203).
Map p312 C10.
Beautifully kept turn-of-the-century house on a quiet, tree-lined street in the heart of Vedado, with lovely floor tiling and three (small) rooms. Unfortunately, there's no food or TV, and though there's a gorgeous roof terrace with wonderful views of the city, you're not encouraged to linger on it.

Casa de Huéspedes Dorys

Calle 22 #273, entre 17 y 19 (tel/fax 304085).
Map p311 B7.
A pleasant atmosphere pervades this attractively decorated home. There are three double rooms, all with private bathroom and mini-bar, plus a pretty patio. Recommended.

Services *Air-conditioning. Mini-bar. Parking.*

Casa de Lleana Pérez Valera

Calle 30 #768, entre 41 y Kohly (811904).
Map p311 D7.
A couple of friendly university professors run this *casa* (the husband speaks English). Accommodation consists of three double rooms; two have private showers, the others share a bathroom, but could be used by disabled guests. Guests have use of the kitchen and parking is available. Families welcome.

Services *Air-conditioning. Cooking facilities. Parking.*

Casa de Marta Díaz

Calzada # 452, Apto 5, esquina a F (323891).
Map p312 A10.
This self-contained apartment has two double bedrooms, a living room and a terrace. A bonus to some (and a drawback to others) may be its position over the Turf nightclub in the basement.

Services *Air-conditioning. Parking. Refrigerators. TV.*

Casa de Mary y Tamayo

Calle 39 #1122, entre Kohly y 36 (814318/811963).
Map p311 D7.
This palatial home has four fantastic, newly refurbished double bedrooms, each with a large bathroom. Outside there's a lovely garden and a very clean swimming pool. The only downside is the lack of cooking facilities for the guests. The owner's son speaks English. Highly recommended.

Services *Air-conditioning. Parking.*

There's no place like **Hospedaje Gisela Ibarra y Daniel Riviero.**

Hospedaje Gisela Ibarra y Daniel Riviero

Calle F #104 (altos), entre 5ta y Calzada (323238).
Map p312 A10.
The charming elderly landlords of this beautifully decorated home have adopted more of a guesthouse approach, and offer three double rooms and shared bathrooms. Guests do not have use of the kitchen, but copious breakfasts are provided. The wonderful roof terraces have grand views. Recommended.

Services *Air-conditioning. Parking. Refrigerator.*

Residencias Herrero

Calle 17 #1309 and #1311, entre 22 y 24 (304919/ erasmo2000@hotmail.com). Map p311 B7.
There are two double rooms for rent (one with private bathroom) in this small house, owned by Erasmo Alfonso Machado, an ex-cultural representative for Cuba. The accommodation is clean and nicely decorated, with laundry and breakfast thrown in. Moreover, it is one of the few *casas particulares* in Havana that doesn't fall victim to power cuts, as it's on a protected section of the electrical grid. Garden and squash court at the back. A great choice.

Services *Air-conditioning. Laundry. Parking.*

Miramar & the western suburbs

Expensive hotels

Hotel Meliá Habana

Avenida 3ra, entre 76 y 80 (reservations 0800 909444/information 248500/fax 248505/ depres@habana.solmelia.cma.net). **Rates** *Standard* *accommodation* (breakfast not incl) single $165; double $215; junior suite $200. *Servicio real* single $215; double $265; junior suite $250; suite $500. **Credit** MC, V. **Map** p310 B1.

The Meliá Habana has 409 attractive bedrooms with balconies and great sea views. It may not enjoy such a central location as its sister, the Meliá Cohiba (*see p56*), but it currently offers the same efficient staff and extensive services at cheaper rates (albeit for only some rooms). The *servicio real* (royal service) includes complimentary breakfast and in-room dataports and safes. There are restaurants and bars galore, conference facilities and a business centre with Internet access on the sixth floor, plus a swimming pool that the hotel claims is the largest in Cuba. The large piano bar in the smoked-glass lobby is a pleasant venue for a cocktail. The Meliá Habana has already been visited by numerous VIPs and its position in Miramar may be an advantage if you're in Havana on business. However, it faces fairly stiff competition from the new Novotel Miramar nearby (*see below*).

Hotel services *Babysitting. Bars (5). Beauty salon. Business services (Internet access). Concierge. Garden. Gym. Laundry. No-smoking rooms. Parking (free). Restaurants (4). Shuttle bus (free). Spa. Swimming pool. Tennis court.* **Room services** *Air-conditioning. Dataport (servicio real only). Mini-bar. Room service (24hr). Safe (servicio real only). Telephone. Turndown (servicio real only). TV (pay movies/satellite).*

Hotel Novotel Miramar

Avenida 5ta, entre 72 y 76 (243584/fax 243583/ reserva@miramar.gav.tur.cu). **Rates** (breakfast not incl) single $100-$120; double $130-$155; triple $180-$205; junior suite $135 (1 person), $175 (2 people), $225 (3 people); senior suite $295 (1-3 people). **Credit** MC, V. **Map** p310 B2.

In contrast to its rather ordinary exterior, this newish hotel boasts a charming interior. It needs a bit more time to settle into its surroundings, but the first signs suggest the Novotel should be a great success: the rooms are superbly decorated in striking yellow and blue designs by a Cuban interior designer, the restaurants are of a high quality and there are loads of extra facilities, including a gym, sauna, massage parlour, squash and tennis courts and a dreamy swimming

Room with a view, **Meliá Habana**. *See p58.*

pool. Prices are competitive considering the quality. Highly recommended.

Hotel services *Babysitting. Bars (2). Beauty salon. Business services (Internet access). Car rental. Concierge. Currency exchange. Garden. Gym. Laundry. No-smoking rooms. Parking (free). Restaurants (2). Shuttle service (free). Spa. Squash courts. Swimming pool.* **Room services** *Air-conditioning. Jacuzzi (suites only). Mini-bar. Room service (24hr). Safe. Telephone. TV (satellite/VCR).*

Mid-range hotels

Hotel Comodoro

Avenida 3ra, esquina a 84 (245551/fax 242089/ reservas@comodor.cha.cyt.cu). **Rates** (breakfast not incl) *Hotel* single $65-$85; double $90-$110; triple $131-$160; suite $135-$155. *Bungalow apartments* $89-$248. **Credit** MC, V. **Map** p310 B1.

Reasons to stay at this hotel and bungalow complex include its extensive gardens, swimming pools and shopping mall (*see p150*). The sprawling dimensions mean that despite the number of guests that can be accommodated, it never feels crowded. Facilities include a business centre, which stocks international magazines, the Havana Club nightclub (*see p198*), various restaurants and snack bars, and a sea-water pool with a small beach. Service is not always as prompt as it could be, but the hotel is not without charm. The complex is frequently used by package groups and house-hunting ex-pats. The bungalows can sometimes get flooded after heavy rain storms. Rates go up by 20% over Christmas.

Hotel services *Bars (5). Business services. Concierge. Garden. Laundry. Nightclub. Parking (free). Restaurants (3). Swimming pools.* **Room services** *Air-conditioning. Kitchenette (most rooms). Mini-bar. Room service (24hr). Safe. Telephone. TV (satellite).*

Hotel Copacabana

Avenida 1ra #4404, entre 44 y 46 (241037/ fax 242846/comercio@copa.gca.cma.net). **Rates** single $75-$85; double $110-$120; triple $126-$138; junior suite $132; suite $148. **Credit** MC, V. **Map** p310 B3.

Originally built in 1946 and reopened in November 1992, the Copacabana is relaxed and informal. Conference facilities are available and Internet access is planned for 2001, but on the whole this is a family-oriented place: babies under two can stay for free and children under 12 get a discount. Long-term visitors and larger groups can easily negotiate a double room for $70. Staff are friendly and efficient, and if a relaxed ambience is what you're looking for, this would fit the bill nicely.

Hotel services *Babysitting. Bars (3). Beauty salon. Business services. Cafés (3). Car rental. Conference services. Gym. Laundry. Massage. Medical service. Parking (free). Restaurants (3). Shops. Shuttle service. Swimming pools (2). Tennis & squash courts. Tourist services.* **Room services** *Air-conditioning. Mini-bar. Room service (24hr). Telephone. TV (satellite).*

The best Hotel pools

Hotel Habana Riviera
The only swimming pool with diving boards overlooking the Malecón. Nice atmosphere. See p56.

Hotel Meliá Cohiba
Very large swimming pool with lovely views over the roofs of Havana. See p56.

Hotel Meliá Habana
Not only is it the largest swimming pool in Cuba, but it also offers great poolside service. See p58.

Hotel Nacional de Cuba
Two pools surrounded by gorgeous gardens. See p56.

Hotel Novotel Miramar
New pool with a lovely design. Separate area for children. See p59.

Budget hotels

Hotel Mirazul
Avenida 5ta #3603, entre 36 y 40 (240088/ fax 240045). **Rates** (breakfast not incl) single $45; double $60; suite $100. **Credit** MC, V. **Map** p310 B4.
An atmosphere of charm and intimacy pervades this tiny eight-roomed hotel, marked only by a blue awning on Quinta Avenida. There's no swimming pool, but the hotel is well decorated and offers a good range of services.
Hotel services *Bar. Business services. Garden. Laundry. Parking (free). Restaurant. Sauna.* **Room services** *Air-conditioning. Mini-bar. Room service (7am-midnight). Safe. Telephone. TV (satellite).*

Casas particulares

Casa de Alberto y Magda
Calle 34 #1911, entre 19 y 21 (238748). **Map** p311 C5.
This completely self-contained, secure and clean apartment is in a calm neighbourhood. Facilities include an incredibly well equipped kitchen, free parking and use of the telephone. The landlady speaks English. Very pleasant.

Casa de Alexis González Lorié
Avenida 1ra #2803, entre 28 y 30, piso 5, Apto 10 (293955). **Map** p311 A5.
This is a most impressive apartment with a wonderful sea view from the smoked-glass solarium and terrace, and private garage parking. The apartment is tastefully decorated and air-conditioned through-

out, with one double bedroom that features marble floors, quality rattan furniture and a bath with a Jacuzzi. Mercedes, the lovely maid, is on hand and also cooks on request. Highly recommended.
Services *Air-conditioning. Parking.*

Casa de Esperanza García Martínez
Calle 36 #724, entre 7ma y 17 (237178). **Map** p310 C4.
This well-decorated three-bedroom house is situated over the United Nations office in a tranquil area of Miramar. The landlady prefers to let the house as a whole, which makes it expensive for single travellers or couples. On the other hand, it's reasonable value for four or six people sharing. Two large terraces provide space to relax.
Services *Air-conditioning. Parking. Refrigerator.*

The eastern bay & coast

Hotel Club Atlántico
Avenida de las Terrazas, esquina a Calle 11, Santa María del Mar (971085/fax 961532). **Rates** single $75; double $100; triple $129. **Credit** MC, V. **Map** p314 A22.
Smart four-storey all-inclusive hotel right on the beach, with clean and pleasant rooms. For a sea view ask for a room on the second floor or higher. There's also pool, tennis and watersports if all that lazing around gets too much for you.
Hotel services *Air conditioning. Bar. Parking (free). Swimming pool.* **Room services** *Safe. Telephone. TV (cable).*

Hotel Sea Club Arenal
Lago de Boca Ciega, Santa María del Mar (971272/ fax 971287/reservas@arenal.get.cma.net). **Rates** Standard rooms: single $85-95; double $130-150; triple $190-210. Superior rooms: $20 extra per person per night. **Credit** MC, V. **Map** p314 B25.
This all-inclusive hotel, formerly known as the Hotel Itabo, consists of four two-storey blocks set around a pool. The surrounding tropical vegetation is charming, but watch out for the mossies. The ground-floor rooms have small patios. Facilities include tennis courts, archery and watersports.
Hotel services *Air-conditioning. Babysitting. Bar. Beauty salon. Garden. Laundry. Parking (free). Payphone. Restaurants. Swimming pool.* **Room services** *Safe. Telephone (no direct line). TV (cable).*

Marina Puertosol Tarará
Vía Blanca km 19, Playa Tarará (971462/fax 971333/971500). **Rates** (breakfast not incl) two-bedroom apartment $58-$174. 10% discount if only one bedroom occupied.
The apartments and houses with kitchenettes, with between two and five bedrooms, are a great choice for families.
Hotel services *Air-conditioning. Babysitting. Bar. Parking (free). Restaurant. Swimming pool.* **Room services** *Safe. Telephone. TV (cable).*

Sightseeing

Introduction

Before you take to the streets of Havana, we offer some ideas about where to go and what to see.

La Habana Vieja is the historical core of the city and the main sightseeing area. It is crammed with squares, churches and small galleries, and attracts the lion's share of the tourists. At first glance, the rest of Havana may not seem to be a sightseer's paradise. But look closer and you'll find a wealth of worthwhile attractions in all directions. Havana's sights and museums may not match the polished standards of high-class attractions in other international tourist destinations, but their diversity and charm are defining features of the city. By all means soak up the captivating atmosphere of La Habana Vieja, but make sure you also venture further afield to discover some of the city's many tourist-free gems.

TOP TIPS FOR TOURISTS

The museums in all countries are subject to rules and regulations, which can be confusing for foreign visitors. Far from being an exception to this generalisation, Havana's sights are more than usually prone to quirky opening hours, fluctuating admission prices and other tourist nightmares. Here are some general pointers to keep you one step ahead:

Tourists in **Plaza de la Catedral**. See p72.

● Generally, paying $1 or so per person over and above any admission price will secure you a guided tour. In some museums, such as the Museo de la Revolución and the Palacio del Segundo Cabo, English-speaking guides are available. In those museums that do not have official English-speaking guides, remember that Cubans are known for their willingness to try to accommodate the needs of visitors, and will make great efforts to find someone who speaks at least a few words of English. However, with few exceptions, descriptions of displayed objects in museums are written only in Spanish.

● You can take non-commercial photos in most museums, although a charge of $2 is common, and a few museums, such as the Casa-Museo Ernest Hemingway, charge $5 for every photo taken. Be sure to ask about any photography charges before you start snapping, as in many cases this information isn't posted. It often costs $5 to $10 to use a video camera.

● During summer months (July and August), the hours of many museums are slightly different to those publicised. Call to check.

● Children under 12 years of age often get into museums for free; be sure to ask as this information is not always posted.

● Guide books and other tourist resources will often give conflicting information concerning opening hours for museums. One of the quirks of Cuba is that if you call anywhere (museums, churches, theatres) for information about opening and closing times, you will often get different results with every call.

● Note that some streets have both an old and new name, and that in some instances it is the old one that is used by the locals. (This is the case with Paseo de Martí, which is more often called Paseo del Prado or El Prado.) For a full explanation of addresses in Havana, *see p277*.

● Havana is currently in the middle of a construction and restoration boom, no doubt spurred on by the increase in the number of visitors to the city. Though we have tried to include as much information as possible for affected venues, you may find that details change once they reopen. Remember that schedules are nebulous at the best of times. Many churches, in particular, are not always open, because of a lack of staff.

Art attack

Until the 1800s, artists in Cuba were concerned with keeping their colonial rulers happy, and therefore tended to copy Spanish styles of the time. The first painters considered to be truly Cuban are **Nicolás de la Escalera** and **Vincente Escobar**, both mulattos and 19th-century contemporaries. In 1817 the French painter Vermay, responsible for the tryptich in El Templete, provided the impetus for further development of the visual arts in Cuba when he founded the San Alejandro Arts School, which still trains painters today.

During the early years of the 20th century, influences from Europe began to reach painters in Cuba. **Victor Manuel**, whose most famous work is *Gitana Tropical*, was followed by **Carlos Enríquez**, **Antonio Gattorno**, and later, **René Portocarrero**, **Mariano Rodríguez**, **Amelia Peláez** and **Wifredo Lam** (1902-82). Born to a Chinese father and Afro-Cuban mother, Lam combined European techniques with themes drawn from his Cuban roots. His oil painting, *The Third World*, is pictured here.

Cuban post-Revolutionary art has passed through several phases, including the growing international reputation of exiled artists in Miami, such as **Tomás Sánchez**. The artists remaining on the island have tended to develop Afro-Cuban themes. Painters such as **Miguel Mendive** and **Nelson Domínguez** work Afro-Cuban mythologies into an idiosyncratic, primitive style.

WHERE TO FIND ART IN HAVANA

Havana's art venues are scattered throughout the city. For the best art in La Habana Vieja, *see p77*. In Vedado you'll find interesting work by young Cuban artists at the office of the magazine **Revolución y Cultura** (Calle 4 #205, entre Línea y 11, Vedado; 303665/309766; closed Sat, Sun). Exhibitions are not held here year-round, but it's worth seeking out to find out what's on. Also in the area, **UNEAC** (the Cuban writers' and artists' union; *see p92*) recently opened a new gallery aimed at showing the best of contemporary Cuban painting, sculpture, and engraving.

Further west, in Miramar, the **Hotel Meliá Habana** (*see p58*) has a changing collection of paintings, antiques, and handicrafts on show in the vast lobby area. The collection is curated under the auspices of the **Fondo Cubano de Bienes Culturales**, one of several state organisations that runs galleries in the city.

EXPO-VENTAS

Expo-ventas are private homes that act as commercial galleries for art graduates and members of the national art union, UNEAC. One *expo-venta* may represent many artists, but the home owner must register with the Fundo Cubano de Bienes Culturales. In return for providing exhibition space for an artist's work, the home owner is entitled to a percentage of the sales. When you buy a work from an *expo-venta*, the vendor will arrange authorisation with the Registro Nacional de Bienes Culturales for the works to leave the country. (Authorisation costs $1 for a small object and $2 for large object.)

To ensure that culture is at the heart of the restored city, the City Historian's Office is also making places available in Havana for well-known artists to use as studio-galleries, where they can produce, exhibit and sell their work. In return for gallery and work space, artists pay 20 per cent of their sales to the Historian's Office.

Calle Obispo is full of small *expo-ventas*. For other places selling art in Havana, as well as further information on art export, *see p150*.

Sightseeing

La Habana Vieja

The heart of the colonial city, La Habana Vieja boasts bustling street life, five centuries of architecture and a monthly lottery for a 50-year-old bottle of rum.

A UNESCO World Heritage Site since 1982 (along with the city's fortresses), La Habana Vieja, or Old Havana, is the part of the city that tourists flock to. It's easy to see why: with its buzzing atmosphere, street life, crammed-to-bursting-point housing and the lion's share of the city's sights, it's where the action never ceases. On the down side, it's the area most heaving with *jineteros* (literally 'jockeys', or touts), eager to make a buck by selling cut-price cigars, take you to a *paladar* (for a commission from the owner) or become your driver for the day. *See p281* **Jockeying for attention**.

Though the presence of police on street corners has more or less rid the area of prostitution (or at least obvious signs of it) and reduced the incidences of petty theft and bag snatching, you should still take care of your belongings when out and about in Old Havana, and don't wear masses of jewellery – flaunting your wealth is asking for trouble.

Plaza de Armas

A logical enough place to begin a day in Old Havana, and the hub of the colonial town, **Plaza de Armas** is the oldest square in La Habana Vieja and the site where the city is thought to have been founded. Impressively, and uniquely in Havana, the square is surrounded by 500 years of architecture, spanning the 16th to the 20th centuries.

On the north-east side of the square is the neoclassical 19th-century **El Templete** (*listings p65*). The temple marks the spot where, under a legendary ceiba tree, Havana is said to have been founded on 16 November 1519, with the first mass and the first town assembly. Two paintings – each of El Templete – represent the mass and *cabildo* (town council); the huge middle one shows the inauguration of the Templete. Each year, on 16 November, a procession headed by the city's 16th-century maces – normally kept in the Museo de la Ciudad (*see p65*) – makes its way around the Plaza de Armas to a ceiba (not the original) to commemorate the city's founding.

In fact, the city had been first founded as San Cristóbal de La Habana several years earlier at a different spot on the south coast of the sland, but moved later to the strategically stronger location at the mouth of the Gulf of Mexico. *See also p7*.

To the north-east, the Renaissance **Castillo de la Real Fuerza** (1558-1577; *listings p65*), the first bastion fortress in the Americas, remained the home of the Spanish captain general in Havana for the next 200 years, until a new palace was built across the square. Crowning the tower of the castle is a small bronze weathervane in the shape of a woman. Although it's not much to look at, 'La Giraldilla' has become the undisputed symbol of the city (*see p74* **First lady of Havana**).

Inside the castle you will find the **Museo Nacional de la Cerámica Cubana** (*listings p65*), with permanent collections (and some sales) by Cuban ceramicists and international artists. In the little square in front is a monument to Cubans who died in World War II. Don't be surprised by the small number of names – Cuba helped the war effort mainly with sugar and chocolate.

Parque Céspedes, at the centre of the *plaza*, has a white marble statue of Carlos Manuel de Céspedes, Cuban patriot and 'Father of the Nation'. This replaced a statue of Spanish King Fernando VII, which stood in the park until 1955. Six days a week (daily except Sunday and rainy days), Havana's largest and best second-hand book market (*see p152*) takes place around the park. Most books are in Spanish, but a few English-language titles are also available. Should you be tempted to buy, remember that older books are considered part of Cuba's literary heritage and to take them out of the country requires special permission. Ask the vendor for an export certificate or go to the Patrimonia Nacional office in Vedado (*see p150*).

Originally the royal post office responsible for all postal communication within Spain's Ibero-American colonies, the **Palacio del Segundo Cabo** (1791; *listings p65*) later became the official residence of the Vice-Captain General of Cuba. It was the first civilian building designed in the Cuban baroque style (*see p34*), with elaborate entrances, arches and windows. The palace now houses the **Instituto Cubano del Libro** (a state-run institution responsible for promoting literature; *listings below*) and three bookstores: Librería Grialbo-Mondadori (general interest), Librería Bella Habana (culture) and Librería Fallad Jamís (Cuban). The mezzanine floor of the palace is occupied by **Galería Raúl Martínez**, which exhibits and sells works by famous Cuban painters. Explanations are in Spanish, though there's sometimes an English-speaking guide on hand.

Between 1791 and 1898 more than 60 representatives of the Spanish crown lived in the baroque Palacio de los Capitanes Generales, on the west side of the square. Today it is the **Museo de la Ciudad** (*listings below*), which boasts a beautiful inner courtyard with plants and royal palms, and houses historical exhibitions; displays of old horse-drawn vehicles, artillery, funeral and religious art; and rooms furnished in the style of their epoch. El Cabildo (the room where the town council used to sit) has a portrait of Columbus.

The east side of the square is dominated by the 18th-century Casa del Conde de Santovenia, renovated in 1867 as a hotel, and again in 1998 as the upmarket (for Havana) **Hotel Santa Isabel** (*see p51*). On the south side, the former US Embassy – whose services are not (officially) needed these days – is now the cumbersomely named **Biblioteca Pública Provincial Rubén Martínez Villena** (*see p283*), the most sophisticated and modern library in the country.

Next door is **Galería Villena**, which sells books, and the entrance to **Cafetería Mirador de La Bahía** (open 11am-midnight daily), which offers a splendid panoramic view of the eastern side of the bay from its rooftop. Also on the south side is the **Museo Nacional de Historia Natural** (*listings below*), which has mammal, bird and reptile exhibitions. The museum was recently renovated to include a sophisticated video

system, so the exhibits are now accompanied by animal sounds, and displays about the origin of life on Earth and Cuban fauna (only Cuban flora awaits renovation of the top two floors). The children's room has educational toys and activities related to nature and prehistory. Several doors up Obispo, the **Museo de la Orfebrería** (*listings below*) has gold and silverwork (*orfebrería*) on display and a tempting little shop at the back selling contemporary jewellery.

Castillo de la Real Fuerza/Museo Nacional de la Cerámica Cubana
Calle O'Reilly #2 (616130). **Open** 9am-7pm daily. **Admission** $1; free under-12s. **Map** p316 D16.

Museo de la Ciudad
Palacio de los Capitanes Generales, Calle Tacón #1, entre Obispo y O'Reilly (612876/615001). **Open** 9am-6pm (last entry 5pm) daily. **Admission** $3; $4 guided tour in English; free under-12s. **Map** p316 E15.

Museo Nacional de Historia Natural
Calle Obispo #61, entre Oficios y Baratillo (639361/629402). **Open** 10.30am-5pm Tue-Sun; closed Mon. **Admission** $3; free under-12s. **Map** p316 E16.

Museo de la Orfebrería
Calle Obispo #113, entre Oficios y Mercaderes (639861). **Open** 9am-5pm Tue-Sat; 9am-1pm Sun; closed Mon. **Admission** $1; free under-12s. **Map** p316 E16.

Palacio del Segundo Cabo/ Instituto Cubano del Libro
Calle O'Reilly #4, esquina a Oficios (switchboard 628091-4/bookshops 632244/gallery 616863). **Open** *Instituto* 8am-4.30pm Mon-Fri; closed Sat, Sun. *Bookshops* 10am-5.30pm daily. *Gallery* 10am-5pm Mon-Fri; 10am-3pm Sat; closed Sun. **Admission** free. **Map** p316 E15.

El Templete
Calle Baratillo, esquina a O'Reilly (no phone). **Open** 9am-6pm daily. **Admission** $1; free under-12s. **Map** p316 E16.

From Calle Oficios to Plaza de San Francisco

In the south-west corner of Plaza de Armas, where it meets Calle Oficios, is **La Mina**, a popular restaurant (*see p128*) and **Casa de los Artistas** (*listings p66*), where four well-known Cuban artists have their studio-galleries: Zaida del Río and Roberto Favelo on the first floor; and Ernesto Rancaño Vieites and Pedro Paulo Oliva under the roof. This artists' house is part of the *expo-venta* scheme, devised by the Historian's Office, which enables artists to

Inside the **Museo de la Ciudad**.

create, display and sell their work from a single location. Though the restaurant faces the Plaza de Armas, to get to the galleries you should enter from Oficios No.6 and go up the stairs on the left.

Next door, the **Museo Numismático** (*listings below*) has a recently restored exhibition of coins dating from the conquest to the present day – including an early 20-peso coin, the only one still existing of ten ever produced. Across the street, the **Museo del Autmóvil** (*listings below*) has cars dating back to 1898. Don't expect too much: considering the phenomenon of big old decrepit cars in Havana, there isn't that much to see here. Halfway down Jústiz, between Calle Baratillo and Calle Oficios, is one of Havana's surprises. The **Caserón del Tango** (*see p188*) is the seat of the Asociación Nacional Promotora del Tango, where you can receive dance classes (with a *mojito* or ten to loosen you up) and see lively tango dancing by Havana's best.

Back on Oficios is the former Colegio de San Ambrosio, which provided ecclesiastical studies for children from 1689 to 1774. The building is now the **Casa de los Árabes** (*listings below*), the country's only functioning public mosque,

and also houses modest exhibitions on Islamic textiles, carpets, clothing, weapons, ceramics and furniture.

Casa de los Árabes

Calle Oficios #16, entre Obispo y Obrapía (615868). **Open** 9am-4.30pm Tue-Sat; 9am-1pm Sun; closed Mon. **Admission** $1; free under-12s. **Map** p316 E15.

Casa de los Artistas

Calle Oficios #6, entre Obispo y Obrapía (639981; Ernesto Rancaño Vieites 626521; Pedro Pablo Oliva 636243). **Open** *Zaida del Río* 10am-4pm Mon-Sat; closed Sun. *Roberto Favelo* 11am-5pm Mon-Sat; closed Sun. *Ernesto Rancaño Vieites* 11am-6pm Mon-Sat; closed Sun. **Pedro Pablo Oliva** times vary. **Admission** phone for details. **Map** p316 E15.

Museo del Automóvil

Calle Oficios #13, esquina a Jústiz (no phone). **Open** 9am-7pm daily. **Admission** $1; free under-12s. **Map** p316 E16.

Museo Numismático

Calle Oficios #8, entre Obispo y Obrapía (615811). **Open** 9am-5pm Tue-Sat; 9am-1pm Sun; closed Mon except shop. **Admission** $1; free under-12s. **Map** p316 E15.

Nifty wheels at the **Museo del Automóvil**.

Plaza de San Francisco

Formerly a small inlet covered by the waters of the bay, **Plaza de San Francisco** dates from 1628. From the start the square was a commercial centre, and during the colonial period a fair took place here every October with coin and card games, lotteries and cock fights – perhaps an early sign of Havana's future role as a gambling mecca.

Today, the square is dominated by the 18th-century basilica on the south side, the Lonja del Comercio (1909) on the north side, and the Aduana (1914) and Sierra Maestra cruise ship terminal on the east side. Other modern additions include Benetton (*see p155*), restaurants – whose tables, chairs and umbrellas are gradually, and somewhat controversially, creeping into the treeless square – and the Agencia de Viajes San Cristóbal, which specialises in tourism in La Habana Vieja. The **Fuente de los Leones** in the centre of the square was sculpted in 1836 by Italian artist Giuseppe Gaggini.

Built in 1738, the baroque **Convento e Iglesia de San Francisco de Asís** (*listings p68*) has a 42-metre tower, the tallest colonial structure in Cuba after Trinidad's Iznaga Tower. Recently renovated, it gives one of the best views of Old Havana. In 1846, a hurricane destroyed the cupola and knocked the head off the tower-top statue of San Francisco. The wall

Catedral de La Habana – Havana's finest example of 18th-century 'Cuban baroque'. *See p72.*

of the central nave now boasts an amazing *trompe l'oeil* mural. Today, the main hall of the church, with its excellent acoustics, is one of Havana's finest concert chambers (when it is more commonly called the Basílica Menor de San Francisco de Asís; *see p204*). The crypt of the church is the final resting place of numerous 17th- and 18th-century aristocrats. The convent, with its beautiful storeyed cloisters, houses the **Museo de Arte Religioso** (*listings p68*), with paintings by José Nicolás de la Escalera and Vicente Escobar, missals with tortoiseshell, ivory and hammered silver covers, polychrome wooden images, and early marriage registries (one for whites and the other for *mestizos* and blacks).

The armchairs and lectern used by Fidel Castro and Pope John Paul II during the latter's January 1998 visit to the island are also here. Accessible only via the church is the small **Jardín de Madre Teresa de Calcuta**, planted in memory of Mother Teresa, who visited Cuba three times in the 1980s.

Gobbling a huge chunk out of the square, the **Lonja del Comercio** (Commercial Exchange; *listings p68*), was renovated in 1996 to provide profitable office space for rent. The added glass box on top of the building obstructs the view of the beautiful golden dome, but you can still admire it by going into the building during working hours. Exit at the back of the Lonja to see the **Jardín Diana de Gales** (*listings p68*), a garden planted in memory of Princess Diana,

whose humanitarian work endeared her to the citizens of Cuba. Inaugurated in 1997, this intimate park has two abstract sculptures by Cuban artists and an engraved Welsh slate plaque donated by the British Ambassador. Stamp lovers might be able to find the Princess Diana commemorative stamps in one of the stationery stores around town.

On the eastern side of the square, beside the bay, is the **Aduana** (Customs House). This early 20th-century building has been beautifully incorporated into the ultra-modern **Terminal de Sierra Maestra** (*see p272*), which welcomes cruise-ship passengers directly into the heart of Old Havana. Future plans include further remodelling of the dock to provide more room for cruise ships.

Across from the Basílica on Calle Oficios are several restored colonial buildings, some of which have been beautifully converted into *expo-ventas*. The lovely 18th-century façade at No.162 shelters the **Galería Carmen Montilla Tinoco** (*listings p68*). This studio and gallery was created for the Venezuelan artist in 1994. On the rear patio wall is an immense abstract mural by Cuban ceramicist Alfredo Sosabravo, depicting Caribbean flora and fauna. Next door is **Estudio-Galería Los Oficios** (*listings p68*), where work by contemporary Cuban artist Nelson Domínguez and others is exhibited and sold.

A short way up Brasil (Teniente Rey) from Oficios is the **Aqvarivm** (*listings p68*), a community project set up by the Historian's Office aimed at extending the *habanero* habit of keeping fish tanks at home and also to provide a calming space in the middle of the bustle of the old city; unlike the Acuario Nacional in Miramar (*see p103*), this aquarium has freshwater fish. Back on Oficios, between the short street Churruca and Muralla is the **Palacio de Gobierno** (Governor's Palace; *listings below*).

Until it moved to the Capitolio (*see p79*) in 1929, the Republican Chamber of Representatives was housed here. More recently the palace was home to the Ministry of Education. In May 2000, the Palacio opened as a museum, with furniture and documents from the Republican period (1902-1959) and is due to become the new home of the **Museo de la Educación** in 2001.

Adjacent to the palace is **Parque Alexander von Humboldt**, named after the German naturalist, considered by many to be Cuba's 'second discoverer' after Columbus. Across the street is the house where Humboldt installed his instruments and botany and mineral collections during his first stay in Havana from 1800 to 1801. Restored as a museum, the **Casa Alejandro de Humboldt** (*listings below*) has more than 250 scientific instruments, books, maps and works of art detailing Humboldt's work in Cuba.

One block south-east on Sol is the **Fundación Havana Club** (*listings below*). Opened in March 2000, this promotional centre houses a museum (Museo del Ron) showing the stages of traditional rum production. Displays cover sugar cane harvesting, sugar mills (with a tiny working model of a mill and distillery that children will love) and the processes of fermentation, distillation, filtration, ageing, blending and bottling. The museum provides obligatory guided tours (Spanish, English, Italian, French and German) of the museum, which happily end in the tasting room; you can also buy a liquid souvenir in the gift shop.

The museum holds a lottery each month for a 50-year-old bottle of rum, based on the numbers on the backs of the admission tickets. Write your name on the back of your ticket to secure your place in the draw. The Fundación is also becoming one of the best venues in Havana for contemporary art; its second-floor art gallery has exhibitions mainly by established Cuban artists.

Aqvarivm

Calle Brasil (Teniente Rey) #9, entre Oficios y Mercaderes (639493). **Open** 9am-5pm Tue-Sat; 9am-1pm Sun; closed Mon. **Admission** $1; free under-12s. **Map** p316 E15.

It's a rum do at the **Fundación Havana Club**.

Convento e Iglesia de San Francisco de Asís/Museo de Arte Religioso

Calle Oficios, entre Amargura y Brasil (Teniente Rey) (629683). **Open** 9am-6pm daily. **Admission** *church* $2; *tower* $1; free under-12s. **Map** p316 E15.

Casa Alejandro de Humboldt

Calle Oficios #254, esquina a Muralla (639850). **Open** 9am-5pm Tue-Sat; 9am-noon Sun; closed Mon. **Admission** free. **Map** p316 E15.

Estudio-Galería Los Oficios

Calle Oficios #166, entre Amargura y Brasil (Teniente Rey) (630497/339804). **Open** 10am-5pm Mon-Sat; closed Sun. **Admission** free. **Map** p316 E15.

Fundación Havana Club (Museo del Ron)

Calle San Pedro #262, esquina a Sol (618051/623832). **Open** *Museum & gallery* 9am-5.30pm Mon-Sat; closed Sun. *Bar* 10am-midnight daily. *Shop* 10am-9pm daily. **Admission** *Museum* $5; free under-16s. **Map** p316 E15.

Galería Carmen Montilla Tinoco

Calle Oficios #162, entre Brasil (Teniente Rey) y Amargura (338768). **Open** 9am-5pm Mon-Sat; closed Sun. **Admission** free. **Map** p316 E15.

Jardín Diana de Gales

Calle Baratillo, behind the Lonja del Comercio (no phone). **Open** 9am-6pm daily. **Admission** free. **Map** p316 E15.

Lonja del Comercio

Calle Amargura #2, esquina a Oficios (669587/669588). **Open** 9am-6pm daily. **Admission** free. **Map** p316 E15.

Palacio de Gobierno/ Museo de la Educación

Calle Oficios #211, entre Churruca y Muralla (624076). **Open** 9am-5pm Tue-Sat; 9am-noon Sun; closed Mon. **Admission** free. **Map** p316 E15.

Plaza Vieja

One block west of Oficios along Muralla is the 16th-century Plaza Vieja. The square has always been a civil rather than military space, and today it is surrounded by mainly 18th-century baroque residences and other eclectic early 20th-century buildings. Over the past century, the square has been home to an open-air food market, a park, an underground car park (now demolished) and an amphitheatre.

However, recent restoration is re-establishing the Plaza Vieja's original atmosphere. The white Carrara showpiece fountain at the centre of the square is a restored version of an original 18th-century one by Italian sculptor Giorgio Massari; in addition, the 18th-century residences around the *plaza* are being restored with housing on the top floors and commercial establishments, including several museums on the ground floor. When finished in 2002, the renovated square will have a cinema, a photo gallery, a *camera obscura*, a museum, a hotel and a school for local children.

The oldest, most luxurious and best-preserved structure in the Plaza Vieja is the 1737 **Casa del Conde de San Juan de Jaruco** (*listings p70*) on the south side. Restored in 1979, it has striking stained-glass windows in the Salón de los Vitrales and interior decorative friezes. Known today as 'La Casona', it houses two *expo-venta* art

galleries run by the Fondo Cubano de Bienes Culturales: **Galería Roberto Diago** and **Galería Plaza Vieja** (also known as **Complejos de Galerías La Casona**), with works by contemporary Cuban artists and glassware. There's also a small shop selling handicrafts.

Also look out for the original small frescoes on the front of the mid 18th-century **Casa del Conde de Casa Lombillo** (No.364), restored in 1989. The exquisite baroque woodwork of the 1805 Casa de las Hermanas Cárdenas, on the *plaza*'s north-west corner, was also restored at this time, and is now the **Centro de Desarrollo de las Artes Visuales** (*listings p70*), with visual art on display. One of the *plaza*'s least opulent buildings is the Casa de Beatriz Pérez Barroto. This mid 18th-century building was renovated in 1986 with a ceramic mural designed by Amelia Peláez and crafted by Marta Arjona. Inside is the headquarters of **Fototeca de Cuba**, the state photography agency, which holds exhibitions of international photography. In the same building is **Galería Joaquín Blez** (*listings for both see p70*).

On the south-east corner is the mid 18th-century Casa de los Franchi Alfaro (which houses a peso-only café) and the art nouveau **Palacio Cueto**. Constructed as a hotel in 1908, the building was later converted into apartments, but is now being restored to its original role as a five-star hotel. In 1988 its façade featured in the Cuban movie *Vals Para*

The **Plaza Vieja**, currently being restored.

Sightseeing

La Habana as the background to a 'coming out' party for a girl's 15th birthday (*see p172* **Sweet 15**). On the south side of the square, the former home of historian Martín Félix de Arrate (No.101) is being restored as the future **Museo del Naipe** (Museum of Playing Cards).

Cuba's only silkscreen workshop is located one block west of Plaza Vieja on Calle Cuba. Inside the **Taller de Serigrafía Rene Portocarrero** (*listings below*) is a small gallery selling items by workshop artists. A block north on Calle Cuba is the former Iglesia y Convento de San Augustín, now the **Iglesia de San Francisco de Asís** (*listings below*; not to be confused with the Convento e Iglesia de San Francisco de Asís; *see p68*). Built in 1633 by the Augustinians, it was later transferred to the Franciscans, who renamed it. The convent has assumed numerous identities over the years. In 1818 it became a school of painting, where many of Cuba's major artists were trained, before becoming the Academy of Medical, Physical and Natural Sciences in 1851. It was here on 14 August 1881 that Cuban scientist Dr Carlos J Finlay presented his ground-breaking work, naming the *Aedes aegipti* mosquito as the transmitter of yellow fever. The former convent is now the **Museo Nacional de Historia de las Ciencias Carlos J Finlay** (*listings below*) and exhibits paintings, busts and portraits of erudite scientists from around the world; a panorama of medicine in Cuba; and a display of Finlay's work. There is a charming reconstruction of a old pharmacy on the third floor, which is currently undergoing restoration.

Casa del Conde de San Juan de Jaruco ('La Casona')

Calle Muralla #107, esquina a San Ignacio (623577/622633). **Open** 10am-5pm Mon-Fri; 10am-2pm Sat; closed Sun. **Admission** free. **Map** p316 E15.

Centro de Desarrollo de las Artes Visuales

Casa de las Hermanas Cárdenas, Calle San Ignacio #352, esquina a Brasil (Teniente Rey) (623533). **Open** 10am-5pm Tue-Sat; closed Mon, Sun. **Admission** free. **Map** p316 E15.

Fototeca de Cuba/ Galería Joaquín Blez

Casa de Beatriz Pérez Barroto, Calle Mercaderes #307, entre Muralla y Brasil (Teniente Rey) (622530). **Open** 10am-5pm Tue-Sat; closed Mon, Sun. **Admission** free. **Map** p316 E15.

Iglesia de San Francisco de Asís

Calle Cuba, esquina a Amargura (618490). **Open** 9am-6pm Mon-Thur; 8am-1pm Sun (Mass 10am); closed Fri, Sat. **Admission** free. **Map** p316 E15.

Art deco **Edificio Bacardí**. *See p76.*

Museo Nacional de Historia de las Ciencias Carlos J Finlay

Calle Cuba #460, entre Amargura y Brasil (Teniente Rey) (634823/634824). **Open** 8.30am-5pm Mon-Fri; 9am-3pm Sat; closed Sun. **Admission** $2; free under-12s. **Map** p316 E15.

Taller de Serigrafía Rene Portocarrero

Calle Cuba #513, entre Brasil (Teniente Rey) y Muralla (623276). **Open** 9am-5pm Mon-Fri; closed Sat, Sun. **Admission** free. **Map** p316 E15.

Calle Mercaderes

North of Plaza Vieja, the corner of Amargura and Mercaderes is known as the Cruz Verde (Green Cross). During the 18th and 19th centuries, this was the first stop for the Procession of the Cross (*Via Crucis*) on Good Friday, which progressed from the Convento e Iglesia de San Francisco de Asís (*see p68*) to the Iglesia del Santo Cristo del Buen Viaje (*see p77*). Opposite, an 18th-century residence is being restored as the future **Museo de Arte Ceremonial Africano**.

Further north, on the corner of Mercaderes and Lamparilla, sits tiny **Parque Rumiñahui**. The centrepiece of the park is a sculpture of the Indian Rumiñahui that was given to Fidel Castro by Ecuadorean artist Oswaldo

Guayasamín. On 17 May 1890, a serious fire occurred in a hardware store on the opposite side of the street at Mercaderes No.162. Undeclared explosives in the store detonated from the heat, killing 28 volunteer firemen. The firemen are buried in a stunning vault in the Cementerio de Colón (*see p90*).

Around the Parque de Simón Bolívar

Continuing north on Mercaderes, you'll reach Parque Simón Bolívar on the corner of Calle Obrapía. The park is a good starting point from which to visit the area's many museums and art galleries. In addition to a statue of 'El Libertador' himself, the park has a ceramic mural (1998) by Venezuelan artist Carmen Montilla.

South of the park is the **Casa-Museo Simón Bolívar** (*listings p72*), inaugurated in 1993 to commemorate the 210th anniversary of the liberator's birth. Bolívar stayed here when he visited Havana in March 1799. The ground floor has displays on Bolívar's life and three art galleries with works by Cuban and international artists. The floor above, with its splendid tinted-glass windows and curved iron and marble banister, has contemporary art donated by Venezuelan artists and an exhibition on Manuela Saenz, Bolívar's companion, nurse and secretary.

Across the street is a small gunsmith's shop, Compañía Armera de Cuba, which played a significant, if unwilling, part in the Revolution. Young revolutionaries stormed the shop on 9 April 1958 in order to get weapons for the guerrillas in the Sierra Maestra. The shop now houses a museum – the **Sala 9 de Abril**, though it's currently closed for restoration. Next door, **Terracota 4** (*listings p72*) is the *expo-venta* studio-gallery of three ceramicists: Amelia Carballo, José Ramón González and Ángel Norniella.

Facing the park on Obrapía is the Casa de Benito Juárez, popularly called the **Casa de México** (*listings p72*). It has permanent displays on the Aztecs, and collections of silver and copper work, ceramics, textiles and pre-Columbian and popular handicrafts from Mexico. Two rooms feature rotating exhibitions by contemporary Mexican and Cuban artists. Further along Obrapía to the east, between Mercaderes and Oficios, is the 1796 Casa de Mariano Carbó. It is now known as the **Casa Oswaldo Guayasamín** (*listings p72*) after the 'artist of the Americas', who died in 1999. Along with work by Guayasamín, the upper floor has murals painted by renowned 18th-century Cuban painters José Nicolás de la Escalera and

José Andrés Sánchez. A small shop sells Guayasamín silkscreens, lithographs, reproductions and jewellery. A little further towards Oficios is the **Casa del Abanico** (*see p159*), where you can buy fans of all kinds – cheap and cheerful or expensive and luxurious.

To the north-west of the Parque is the **Casa de La Obra Pía** (*listings p72*), built in 1665 by former solicitor general Captain Martín Calvo de la Puerta y Arrieta. The house (and street) assumed the name Obra Pía (meaning 'good or pious work') in 1669, when the owner began providing subsistence dowries for orphan girls. The *casa* has a large courtyard, coloured decorative friezes and a uniquely designed baroque portal made in 1686 in Cádiz, Spain. It was restored as a museum in 1983, and its interior features colonial furniture and linen goods typical of 18th-century Havana nobility. A permanent collection of objects belonging to famous Cuban novelist Alejo Carpentier is also housed here, including the blue Volkswagen he used when he was Cuban ambassador to UNESCO in Paris.

On the opposite side of Obrapía, the **Casa de África** (*listings p72*) has a large collection of gifts received by Fidel Castro from African countries during the last 40 years and a collection of *santería* icons belonging to famous Cuban ethnographer Fernando Ortiz, the expert *par excellence* on Afro-Cuban culture. As with many museums in Cuba, the Casa de África is a 'living museum' with classrooms for primary schoolchildren. The building is currently undergoing extensive restoration work, during which one half of the museum stays open, while the other half is being repaired. The work is unlikely to be completed before the end of 2001.

Further west, at the corner of Obrapía and San Ignacio, Casa Quitrín houses the **Estudio-Galería Yanes** (*listings p72*), which has portraits by Orlando Hernández Yanes and flower paintings by Isabel 'Casiguaya' Rodríguez Jardines.

A visit to Havana wouldn't be complete without buying cigars. Though the **Museo del Tabaco** (*listings p72*) in Casa de Puerto Rico on Mercaderes offers only a modest display of lithographic prints, old pipes and lighters, early cigar boxes and ashtrays, its ground-floor **La Casa del Habano** (*see p157*) has a good selection of cigars. A few doors up is the **Maqueta de La Habana Vieja** (*listings p72*), a scale model (1:500) showing some 3,500 buildings located within the 2.14 square kilometres (one square mile) that make up the old city. The model took three years to build, and is enlivened by an evocative sound and light show. Opposite is the relatively new **Casa** de Asia (*listings below*), which displays collections from different Asiatic cultures. Although the museum is still in development, its present exhibitions are worth a visit; silver work, mother-of-pearl and ivory objects, a carved rock from Hiroshima, a stone from the Great Wall of China and numerous Persian rugs are all on display.

Casa de África
Calle Obrapía #157, entre Mercaderes y San Ignacio (615798). **Open** 9.30am-4.30pm Tue-Sat; 9.30am-12.30pm Sun; closed Mon. **Admission** $2; free under-12s. **Map** p316 E15.

Casa de Asia
Calle Mercaderes #111, entre Obispo y Obrapía (639740). **Open** 9am-5pm Tue-Sat; 9am-1pm Sun; closed Mon. **Admission** $1; free under-12s. **Map** p316 E15.

Casa de México
Calle Obrapía #116, esquina a Mercaderes (618166). **Open** 9.30am-5pm Tue-Sat; 9.30am-12.30pm Sun; closed Mon. **Admission** $1; free under-12s. **Map** p316 E15.

Casa-Museo Simón Bolívar
Calle Mercaderes #160, entre Obrapía y Lamparilla (613988). **Open** 9am-5pm Tue-Sat; 9am-1pm Sun; closed Mon. **Admission** $1; free under-12s. **Map** p316 E15.

Casa de la Obra Pía
Calle Obrapía #158, esquina a Mercaderes (613097). **Open** 9am-5pm Tue-Sat; 9am-1pm Sun; closed Mon. **Admission** $1; free under-12s. **Map** p316 E15.

Casa Oswaldo Guayasamín
Calle Obrapía #112, entre Oficios y Mercaderes (613843). **Open** 9.30am-4.45pm Tue-Sat; 9am-12.30pm Sun; closed Mon. **Admission** $1; free under-12s. **Map** p316 E15.

Estudio-Galería Yanes
Casa Quitrín, Calle Obrapía, esquina a San Ignacio (626195). **Open** *Gallery* 10am-5pm Tue-Sat; 9am-1pm Sun; closed Mon. *Casa* 7.30am-3.15pm Mon-Fri; closed Sat, Sun. **Admission** free. **Map** p316 E15.

Maqueta de La Habana Vieja
Calle Mercaderes #114, entre Obispo y Obrapía (no phone). **Open** 9am-6pm daily. **Admission** $1. **Map** p316 E15.

Museo del Tabaco
Casa de Puerto Rico, Calle Mercaderes #120, entre Obispo y Obrapía (615795). **Open** 9am-5pm Mon-Sat; 9am-1pm Sun; closed Mon. **Admission** free. **Map** p316 E15.

Terracota 4
Calle Mercaderes #156, entre Obrapía y Lamparilla (669417). **Open** 10am-6pm Mon-Fri; sometimes also Sat, Sun. **Admission** free. **Map** p316 E15.

Plaza de la Catedral & around

Originally named Plaza de la Ciénaga (Swamp Square) because of its muddy terrain, with time **Plaza de la Catedral** became one of Havana's most important squares. Here, the main conduit of the Zanja Real, the city's first aqueduct constructed in 1592, entered a cistern supplying all vessels docking in Havana. The Cathedral, though, is what gives the square its definitive appearance, with the other three sides taken up by 18th-century aristocratic baroque mansions, all built within a 40-year period and maintaining a strong architectural harmony.

The **Catedral de La Habana** (1777; *listings p73*) – officially the Catedral de la Virgen María de la Concepción Inmaculada – is Havana's finest example of 18th-century 'Cuban baroque', with its curves and flourishes above doors and windows. The two towers, which are different in size, continue to puzzle scholars: some say one is larger to accommodate the small interior staircase, while others argue that the other is narrower to prevent closing the street. Construction of the church began in 1748 by the Jesuits, and though they were expelled from Cuba in 1767, work continued on the building for a further 20 years. In 1787, the Diocese of Havana was established and the church was consecrated as a cathedral.

The interior of the cathedral dates from the early 19th century, when the original baroque altars were replaced with neoclassical ones and the the original wood ceilings plastered over. The eight large paintings by Jean Baptiste Vermay are copied from originals by Rubens and Murillo. Note that despite the official opening times, the cathedral is often locked, though you can sometimes gain access just before Mass.

On the south side of the square, across from the cathedral, is the Casa del Conde de Casa Bayona, or Casa de Don Luis Chacón, the oldest house in the area (dating in 1721). The house once accommodated the Havana Club rum company, but became the **Museo de Arte Colonial** (*listings p73*) in 1969. Panelled ceilings with elaborate designs complement the collections of opulent colonial decorative art, furniture, glasswork and European porcelain.

The 18th-century **Casa del Conde de Casa Lombillo**, on the eastern side of the square, is unusual in having three façades: the main one on Empedrado and the other two facing Mercaderes and the *plaza*. Next door is the **Casa del Marqués de Arcos** (1746).

Sightseeing

Centro de Arte Contemporáneo Wifredo Lam.

The mansion became a post office in the mid 19th century; a role it maintains to this day (look out for the unusual stone mask mailbox in the wall). Part of the building is currently closed for restoration work, which will create retail spaces on the ground floor. The mansion's imposing main entrance is on Calle Mercedes; stand here to get a good view of the (incomplete) mural by Cuban artist Andrés Carillo on the opposite wall, depicting important artistic, literary and intellectual figures from 19th-century Cuba.

Facing these two houses across the *plaza* is the Casa del Marqués de Aguas Claras, now **El Patio** restaurant (*see p129*). Built in 1775, it boasts an exquisite inner courtyard and elegantly simple original 18th-century stained glass on its upper-storey windows. Next door, the commercial **Galería Victor Manuel** (*listings below*) occupies the former Casa de Baños (public bath house), which was built over the square's cistern in the 19th century. A commemorative stone slab on the tiny Callejón del Chorro to the south-west of the *plaza* commemorates the construction of the Zanja Real. At the end of the Callejón is the **Taller Experimental de Gráfica** (*listings below*), Havana's only engraving workshop. Although engraving in Cuba began in the 19th century, this workshop was created in 1962 by Cuban artist Orlando Suárez. Ask permission to enter the workshop and you'll find the small **Galería del Grabado** up the stairs to the right. The gallery displays and sells excellent non-touristy prints of just about every sort – etching, lithographs, woodblocks and so on.

The north-west corner of the *plaza* is occupied by the **Centro de Arte Contemporáneo Wifredo Lam** (*listings below*), one of Havana's better art galleries, with both permanent and rotating exhibitions by contemporary Cuban and international artists. A Cuban of Chinese and African parentage and

one of Cuba's leading modern painters, Wifredo Lam was strongly influenced by his friend Pablo Picasso.

Half a block west up Empedrado is **La Bodeguita del Medio** (*see p127*), the renowned Hemingway haunt that today is more likely to be full of tourists than gravelly writers. A few doors further along is the **Fundación Alejo Carpentier** (*listings below*), which promotes the work of one of Cuba's most important 20th-century writers.

Catedral de La Habana
Calle Empedrado #158 (617771). **Open** 10.30am-2pm Mon-Sat; 9am-noon Sun. *Mass* 8pm Mon, Tue, Thur, Fri; 5.30pm Sat; 10.30am Sun. **Admission** free. **Map** p316 D15.

Centro de Arte Contemporáneo Wifredo Lam
Calle San Ignacio #22 esquina a Empedrado (612096/639781). **Open** 10am-5pm Mon-Sat; closed Sun. **Admission** $2; free under-12s. **Map** p316 D15.

Fundación Alejo Carpentier
Calle Empredrado #215, entre Cuba y San Ignacio (615506). **Open** 8.30am-4.30pm Mon-Fri; closed Sat, Sun. **Admission** free. **Map** p316 D15.

Galería Victor Manuel
Calle San Ignacio #56, entre Callejón del Chorro y Empedrado (612955). **Open** 9.30am-9pm daily. **Admission** free. **Map** p316 D15.

Museo de Arte Colonial
Casa del Conde de Casa Bayona, Calle San Ignacio #61 (626440). **Open** 9am-7pm daily. **Admission** $2; free under-12s. **Map** p316 D15.

Taller Experimental de Gráfica
Callejón del Chorro #62 (620979). **Open** 9am-4pm Mon-Fri; closed Sat, Sun. **Admission** free. **Map** p316 D15.

Calle Tacón & northern Habana Vieja

To the east of Plaza de la Catedral, on the right-hand side of Empedrado, are several adjoining houses of note. The first, No.4, built in 1759, is where the Havana Architectural Association was founded in 1916. It was restored in 1988 as **Restaurante Don Giovanni** (*see p128*). The interior boasts 17th-century decorative wall friezes, painted by anonymous Italian artists. These are currently 'protected' by a layer of whitewash, awaiting possible restoration in the future; also look out for the large ceramic mural (a copy of Klimt). For the moment, some traces can still be seen in the upstairs café. The oldest house on this stretch is the **Casa de Juana Carvajal** at No.12, dating from the early 17th century. It is named after a liberated slave who

Sightseeing

Sightseeing

First lady of Havana

As you get stuck into your nth bottle of
Havana Club rum, your eyes may wander to
the small figure at the top of the label.
Standing in a peremptory manner, with one
hand on her hip and the other holding a
cross, this apparently insignificant image is
in fact a potent symbol of the city.

The image is a representation of La
Giradilla, the bronze weathervane that tops
the tower of the Castillo de Real Fuerza
(pictured; see also p65) in La Habana Vieja.
The original – which fell off in a hurricane and
is now in the Museo de la Ciudad (see p65) –
was cast in 1632 by Cuban artist Jerónimo
Martín Pinzón and is believed to represent
Doña Inés de Bobadilla, the first and only
governess of Cuba. Bobadilla was the wife of
Hernando de Soto, governor and explorer,
who sailed from Havana on 18 May 1539 on

an ultimately fatal expedition to Florida.
Bobadilla became governess in his absence,
climbing the tower of the castle every day to
scan the horizon for signs of his return. De
Soto died somewhere in the southern US in
1542 and – the story goes – Bobadilla died
of a broken heart soon afterwards.

was given this building as an inheritance by
her former owner, Lorenza Carvajal. Juana
enlarged the house in 1725, and decorated the
interior with friezes. In 1988, it was restored
as the headquarters of the **Gabinete de
Arqueología** (archeology office; listings p75),
dedicated to archaeological studies in La
Habana Vieja. Inside is a fascinating, and often-
overlooked exhibition of pre-Columbian art,
vessels and textiles, household objects from
the 16th to the 19th centuries, and glass and
ceramics from early shipwrecks in the bay.
One of the rooms, closed to the public for
restoration for the time being (though sadly
funding is a major problem), has 12 unique
floor-to-ceiling murals with scenes painted by
an anonymous 18th-century artist.

Looking towards the port from the houses,
the coloured umbrellas of the daily bustling
Feria Artesanal (handicraft fair; see p163)
are an instant eye-catcher. Across from the fair
on Calle Tacón is the large and sombre baroque
**Seminario de San Carlos y San
Ambrosio**. It was built in 1774 as a Jesuit
seminary – renowned Cuban intellectuals José
de la Luz y Caballero and Félix Varela were
among its alumni – and still functions as such.
The seminary boasts one of the most tranquil
courtyards in Havana and a magnificent
library. Visitors are welcome to visit the
courtyard at any time – just ring the bell to
the right of the main entrance to be let in –
but for a more behind-the-scenes look at the
building, you have to wait for the first Sunday
in October, when the seminary opens its doors

to the public to mark its inauguration. On the
other side of Calle Tacón is **Parque José de
la Luz y Caballero**, where little ones can
enjoy pony rides (see p171). Cross through
the park to reach the bay and the **Fuente de
Neptuno** (Neptune Fountain), which dates
from 1838. Just south is a small dock called
Embarcación La Niña, the starting point
for 45-minute trips around the bay and beyond.
Boats depart between 10am and 1am every day
and passengers are charged 5 pesos each.
However, if you're tempted by the prospect of
a romantic cruise, note that the boat is an old
clunker and the music's loud.

To the north-west, the neighbouring **Parque
de Anfiteatro** contains a small children's
amusement area (see p171). Inland from the
park, the **Palacio de la Artesanía** (see p161)
is a popular stop for handicrafts – though it
lacks the delights and surprises of the fair – as
well as books, music and light refreshments.
The palacio is housed in the late 18th-century
Casa de Mateo Pedroso y Florencia and shows a
typical arrangement of shops and warehouses
on the ground floor, slave quarters on the
mezzanine and master's quarters on the third
floor. The house was named after a former
mayor and slave trader, who was one of the
richest men in Havana at the time.

North-west of here is the **Museo Nacional
de la Música** (listings p75), with its
wonderful collection of African drums, string
instruments, music boxes, old American
phonographs, a Chinese organ and one of the
first gramophones (1904) made by the Victor

Talking Machine Company. Head a couple of blocks south to reach the beautiful **Iglesia del Santo Ángel Custodio** (*listings below*), opposite the Palacio Presidencial/Museo de la Revolución. The church's present wedding-cake appearance is due to a mixture of 17th-century Gothic and 19th-century neo-Gothic styles. The tower was reconstructed in 1846 after being destroyed by a hurricane. Two of Havana's most outstanding sons, Félix Varela and José Martí, were baptised in the church, and renowned 19th-century Cuban writer Cirilo Villaverde used it as the setting for the main scene of his famous romantic novel, *Cecilia Valdás*, when the heroine has her lover stabbed on the steps of the church as he is about to marry another woman.

Gabinete de Arqueología

Calle Tacón #12, entre O'Reilly y Empedrado (614469). **Open** 9am-5pm Tue-Sat; 9am-1pm Sun; closed Mon. **Admission** $1; free under-12s. **Map** p316 D15.

Iglesia del Santo Ángel Custodio

Calle Compostela #2, esquina a Cuarteles (610469). **Open** 5-7pm Tue-Sat; 8-10am, 5-7pm Sun; closed Mon. *Mass* 6pm Tue-Sat; 9am, 6pm Sun. **Admission** free. **Map** p316 D15.

Museo Nacional de la Música

Calle Capdevila #1, entre Habana y Aguiar (619846). **Open** 10am-6pm Mon-Sat; closed Sun. **Admission** $2; free under-12s. **Map** p316 D15.

Calle Obispo & around

One of the most animated streets in La Habana Vieja, **Calle Obispo** runs from Plaza de Armas almost as far as Parque Central (for which, *see p80*). This street is perfect for walking and it bustles with life – courtesy of a blend of tourists, *jineteros* and *habaneros*. It is lined with shops offering handicrafts, art and books, plus bars, restaurants and holes in the wall selling pizzas and ice-cream. The Historian's Office is doing all it can to restore Obispo to the glory it enjoyed in its halcyon days of the 19th century, when it was the principal shopping street of the city.

The dignified **Hotel Ambos Mundos** (*listings p76; see also p52*) occupies the intersection of Obispo and Mercaderes. Ernest Hemingway stayed here off and on during the 1930s, and began writing *For Whom the Bell Tolls* in room 511. The room has been restored as a mini-museum featuring Hemingway's desk and authentic furniture from the period. Across the street is a late 1950s building, notable for being out of character with the surrounding area. An old Dominican convent, which became the Universidad de La Habana in 1728, originally stood on this site, but was knocked down to make room for the new building; all that remains is the bell, which is rung each year on the anniversary of the university's founding.

Stunning interior of the renovated **Farmacia Taquechel**. *See p76.*

The **Farmacia Taquechel** at No.155 (*see p162*), with its floor-to-ceiling cedar and mahogany shelves and 19th-century French porcelain apothecary jars, is definitely worth a quick peek. Also check out **Droguería Escolapio** (*listings below*), two blocks up the street. Recently renovated, it boasts tall shelves and original mahogany counters, though is a peso-only pharmacy for Cubans.

On the corner of Obispo and Cuba is the 1907 Banco Nacional de Cuba, one of the first buildings constructed after the Republic was formed in 1902. The Ministerio de Finanzas y Precios and the **Museo de las Finanzas** (pretty modest, but check out the magnificent old round vault door; *listings below*) are now located here. In the early 20th century, this area was known as Havana's Wall Street because of the banks located here. You needn't go far to take a look: the 1915 Banco de la Habana (Cuba #314, entre Obispo y Obrapía), today the **Compañía de Seguros Internacionales**, was founded by rich Cubans at a time when American capital dominated practically all banking investment in the country; the 1929 Mexican baroque **Banco del Comercio** (Aguiar #402) was designed by Mexican architect Rafael Goyeneche; the 1910 Banco de Narciso Gelats (Aguiar #456, entre Lamparilla y Amargura) is today the **Banco Nacional de Cuba**; and the much older 1832 Bank of Nova Scotia (on the corner of Cuba and O'Reilly) was restored in December 1998 as the **Banco Popular de Ahorro**.

Back on Obispo heading west, just past the junction with Cuba, is the state-owned **Galería Forma** (*listings below*). Across the street is the **Hotel Florida** (*see p53*), built in 1836 and a hotel since 1885. Recently renovated, the hotel has retained its attractions, namely its beautiful inner patio and arches.

At the corner of Obispo and Aguacate, a little park has been developed in a previously vacant lot to help increase the number of green zones in La Habana Vieja. A couple of doors along Obispo is the **Casa Natal de Félix Varela** (birthplace of Félix Varela), currently under restoration. At the end of Obispo, where it widens out a bit at the Plazuela de Albear, is a cluster of good bookstores such as **La Moderna Poesía** and **La Librería Internacional** (for both, *see p153*). Beyond a kink in the road is **El Floridita** (*see p128*), where the daiquiri, king of cocktails, was born. Hemingway drank them here served by the Catalonian barman, Constante Ribalaigua, who is said to have invented the drink. Inside are photographs and a bust of the Floridita's most famous client; his ghost is said to haunt the premises. On the *plazuela* itself is a life-size

Carrara marble statue of engineer Francisco de Albear y Lara sculpted in 1895 by Cuban artist José Vilalta de Saavedra. Albear built an aqueduct, which was awarded the Gold Medal for technical and aesthetic excellence at the Paris Exhibition in 1878.

If your trawl down Obispo has left you in need of refreshment, head a couple of blocks north along Bélgica (the western boundary of Old Havana; the western boundary of the street was formerly called Egido, the section north of Muralla was Monserrate). At No.26 is the opulent art deco **Edificio Bacardí**. Built in 1930 for the Bacardí Rum company and topped by the company's bat emblem, it is a working office building that is not officially open to tourists (although the guard may let you in if you ask nicely). Luckily, however, there's nothing to stop you having a drink in the small intimate bar on the ground floor (*see p144*).

Droguería Escolapio

Calle Obispo #260, esquina a Aguiar (620311). **Open** 24hrs daily. **Admission** free. **Map** p316 E15.

Galería Forma

Calle Obispo #255, entre Cuba y Aguiar (620123). **Open** 9am-9pm daily. **Admission** free. **Map** p316 E15.

Hotel Ambos Mundos

Calle Obispo #153, esquina a Mercaderes (609529/609530). **Open** *Hemingway's Room* 10am-5pm Mon-Sat; closed Sun. **Admission** $2; free under-12s. **Map** p316 E15.

Museo de las Finanzas

Banco Nacional de Cuba, Calle Obispo #211, esquina a Cuba (573000 ext. 2468). **Open** 10am-3pm Mon-Fri; 10am-noon Sat; closed Sun. **Admission** free. **Map** p316 E15.

Plaza del Cristo

A sleepy little park three blocks south of Obispo on Bernaza, **Plaza del Cristo** was created in 1640 around the Ermita del Humilladero. The hermitage was the final station on the *Vía Crucis* (procession of the cross), which took place every year during Lent, starting from the Convento e Iglesia de San Francisco de Asís (*see p68*). The baroque **Iglesia del Santo Cristo del Buen Viaje** (*listings p77*) now covers the site of the old hermitage on the north-eastern side of the *plaza*. Of the original building, only the enclosure and painted wood-panelled ceiling still remain.

A couple of blocks east on Calle Brasil (Teniente Rey) is **Farmacia Sarrá** (*listings p77*), the most beautiful of the old colonial

Top five | Art venues

Centro de Arte Contemporáneo Wifredo Lam
See p73.

Centro de Desarrollo de las Artes Visuales
See p69.

Estudio-Galería Los Oficios
See p69.

Fototeca de Cuba
See p79.

Fundación Havana Club
See p68.

pharmacies in La Habana Vieja. Though it's a wonderful sight – with a patterned ceiling, elaborately carved floor-to-ceiling shelves, porcelain apothecary jars, old lamps and a wall clock – its location means it doesn't attract as many tourists as the other pharmacies in Old Havana. It originally occupied almost the entire block, with a laboratory at the back where medications were made – the original water steriliser still works. In late 2000, the Historian's Office began restoring the pharmacy to its former glory; work is due to be completed in May 2001. If you get the chance, ask to see the back rooms.

Farmacia Sarrá
Calle Brasil (Teniente Rey), entre Compostela y Habana (610969). **Open** 8am-5pm Mon-Fri; 8am-noon Sat; closed Sun. **Admission** free. **Map** p316 E15.

Iglesia del Santo Cristo del Buen Viaje
Calle Villegas, entre Amargura y Lamparilla (631767). **Open** 9am-noon, 7-9pm Mon-Fri; 6.30-8pm Sat; 8am-1pm Sun. **Mass** 7.30pm Mon-Fri; 8am Wed; 8am, 11am Sun. **Admission** free. **Map** p316 E14.

Southern Habana Vieja

A poorer area less frequented by tourists, southern Habana Vieja offers visitors the chance to enjoy the more natural pace of normal daily life, and to visit some stunning churches and convents. Three blocks south of Farmacia Sarrá, where Calle Compostela crosses Calle Luz, is the baroque **Convento e Iglesia de Nuestra Señora de Belén**. It was built in 1720 as a Franciscan convent, church and

hospital for the poor, but was taken over by the Jesuits in the mid 19th century. The church's present appearance is the result of over two centuries of successive renovation and expansion. The unusual vaulted arch, built in 1775, over Calle Acosta to the south, connects the convent with its neighbouring buildings. From 1854 to 1925, the Jesuit-run **Colegio de Belén** (Bethlehem School) was located here until it moved to a new building constructed in Marianao, western Havana. Later, the *colegio* became the Instituto Técnico Militar, which cannot be visited by tourists. Although the future use of the original church in La Habana Vieja is still uncertain, the two cloisters are being restored as an old people's home and a hostel for elder tourists. Most extraordinary is the **Real Observatorio** (Royal Observatory), built in 1858, on top of the tower of the school, and used continuously until 1925. The Jesuits were Cuba's first official weather forecasters and used the observatory for the study of hurricanes and other tropical weather patterns. It was the first of its kind in the Caribbean and, over time, became one of the most important weather stations in the Americas.

Along Calle Acosta one block to the west of Calle Compostela is the orthodox **Sinagoga Adath Israel de Cuba** (*listings p78*). While the synagogue is being renovated, services are held in the room downstairs. From Calle Compostela, two blocks east on Calle Luz is the **Convento e Iglesia de Santa Clara** (*listings p78*), founded in 1643 as the first nunnery in the city. Its first arrivals were from Cartagena de Indias in Colombia, and it remained a working nunnery until 1922, when the nuns sold the church and convent and moved to a new site. Apparently, for the next 40 days, people visited the convent continuously to see what was behind its formerly impenetrable walls. The simple, stark exterior of the building belies the surprising richness of the interior, which features ornately carved wooden ceilings and beautiful leafy patios, and can be visited on a tour. Two of the three cloisters are now fully restored: one houses the headquarters of the Centro Nacional de Conservación, Restauración y Museología (CENCREM), the organisation in charge of restoring most of Cuba (the Historian's Office deals with Havana); the other has become a Moorish-style hostel.

South of here, on the corner of Calle Cuba and Calle Acosta is the **Iglesia del Espíritu Santo** (*listings p78*), which claims to be the oldest church in Havana, although the original hermitage, built in 1638 for freed slaves, no longer exists. Elegant and dignified, this simple church contains murals, stained glass and a wooden ceiling. Funeral crypts for aristocratic

La Catedral de La Habana
Showpiece of Cuban baroque architecture. *See p72.*

Convento e Iglesia de San Francisco de Asís
Wonderful cloisters, also houses the Museo de Arte Religioso. *See p66.*

Museo de la Ciudad
Housed in the former Palacio de los Capitanes Generales, the City Museum boasts a wonderful shaded inner courtyard. *See p65.*

Plaza de Armas
Five centuries of architecture around one of the city's best-known squares. *See p64.*

Iglesia del Santo Ángel Custodio
Often-ignored but beautiful church on the edge of La Habana Vieja. *See p75.*

burials have been discovered under the church floor, and the 1729 sculpted tomb of Asturian-born Friar Gerónimo de Valdés is on display.

Two blocks further south is the baroque **Convento e Iglesia de La Merced** (*listings below*). Built in 1755, its plain exterior contrasts sharply with its magnificently lavish interior. With high arches and frescoes covering the chapel and cupola, it is well worth a lingering visit. Inaugurated in 1876, the Capilla de Lourdes (Lourdes Chapel) has an outstanding collection of religious paintings by renowned Cuban artists: Esteban Chartrand, Miguel Melero, Pidier Petit, Juan Crosa, among others. The frescoes date from 1904. The convent's serene courtyard has interesting statuary and sometimes you can hear guitar players practising religious songs.

West of here you enter the old working-class neighbourhood of San Isidro, one of Old Havana's poorest areas. On the corner of Calle Leonor Pérez (Paula) and Avenida de la Bélgica (Egido) is the **Casa Natal de José Martí** (*listings below*). This modest dwelling, which dates from 1810, was where José Martí was born on 28 January 1853. The Martí family rented the upper storey from the owner who lived on the floor below. Inside are objects relating to Martí's life and work, including family belongings, original manuscripts, photographs, and furniture.

At the opposite (eastern) end of Calle Leonor Pérez (Paula), overlooking the bay, is the baroque **Iglesia de San Francisco de Paula**. Unusual for its isolated location in the middle of a busy portside road, the church was built in 1745 on the site of a former hospital for women and a hermitage. In the 1940s, despite public protest, the hospital and part of the church were torn down. It was recently restored as a concert hall; the ashes of famous Cuban violinist Claudio José Domingo Brindis de Salas are said to be preserved here.

The walkway at the front of the church has been renovated so that it leads to the dockside **Alameda de Paula**, the first promenade to be constructed in La Habana Vieja. Created in 1771, it was originally a dirt track stretching three blocks and bordered by two lines of poplars. In 1805 a tiled pavement and stone seats were added; later, a fountain with a commemorative column was built in honour of the Spanish navy (only the column survives). To the north-west of the Alameda on the corner of Oficios and Luz is the Casa del Conde de Casa Barreto (1732). The owners lived on the second storey with marble floors and mahogany woodwork, while servants' quarters were on the small, low-ceilinged mezzanine. Today, the *casa* is home to the **Centro Provincial de Artes Plásticas y Diseño** (*listings below*), which develops visual arts in the city.

Casa Natal de José Martí
Calle Leonor Pérez (Paula) #314, esquina a Avenida de Bélgica (Egido) (613778). **Open** 9am-5pm Tue-Sat; 9am-2pm Sun; closed Mon. **Admission** $1; free under-12s. **Map** 316 F14.

Centro Provincial de Artes Plásticas y Diseño
Calle Oficios #362, esquina a Luz (623295). **Open** 9am-5pm Mon-Sat; closed Sun. **Admission** free. **Map** p316 E15.

Convento e Iglesia de La Merced
Calle Cuba #806, esquina a Merced (638873). **Open** 8am-noon, 3-5pm daily. *Mass* 9am Mon-Sat; 9am, noon Sun. **Admission** free. **Map** p316 F15.

Convento e Iglesia de Santa Clara
Calle Cuba #610, entre Sol y Luz (615043/613775). **Open** 8.30am-4.30pm Mon-Fri; closed Sat, Sun. **Admission** (including tour) $2; free under-12s. **Map** p316 E15.

Iglesia del Espíritu Santo
Calle Acosta #161, esquina a Cuba (623410). **Open** 8am-noon, 3-6pm daily. *Mass* 6pm Mon, Wed-Sun; no mass Tue. **Admission** free. **Map** p316 F15.

Sinagoga Adath Israel de Cuba
Calle Acosta, esquina a Picota (613495). **Open** 8am-noon, 5-8pm daily. *Services* 8am, 6pm Mon-Fri; 9am, 6pm Sat; 9am Sun. **Admission** free. **Map** p316 E14.

Centro Habana

Visitors who ignore this generally shabby-looking part of town in favour of neighbouring La Habana Vieja are missing out on some of the city's best sights.

Centro Habana is a part of the city caught between two periods, the old and the modern, with a juxtaposition of different activities, social classes and architectural styles. The most densely populated district of the capital, Centro Habana, unlike most other parts of Havana, is virtually devoid of green areas.

Much of Centro Habana's history is related to that of the city walls (*las murallas*). The walls were built between 1674 and 1797, encircling the city in an egg shape along the bay to the east and along Avenida Bélgica (Egido and Montserrate) and Calle Agramonte (Zulueta) to the west. On completion they were ten metres (33 feet) high and 1.4 metres (4.5 feet) wide. Shortly after the walls were finished, a grid pattern was superimposed over an earlier haphazard urban development of Centro Habana, with the wealthy moving into the 'better' streets (Reina and Carlos III, today Avenidas Simón Bolivar and Salvador Allende respectively) and workers settling elsewhere in apartment blocks. However, by 1863 the city had become so overcrowded that the walls began to be demolished to open up land speculation in the bordering areas. From 1880, a huge amount of building was undertaken, with construction controlled by urban ordinances. This was generally a time of effervescence and growth in Havana: Spanish regional societies built sumptuous palaces; nightlife and culture developed; and the leisured classes displayed their wealth by promenading along the new thoroughfares such as El Prado (now Paseo de Martí). Centro Habana's new look was completed in the 1920s, when French urbanist Jean Claude Nicholas Forestier was contracted to landscape the area.

Later, as the area became full of traffic and pedestrians, and shops, theatres, cinemas, bars, cafés and restaurants were constructed, Centro Habana became the city's commercial centre. Today it is also the location of the city's *barrio chino* (Chinatown), inhabited by descendants of the Chinese indentured labourers who came to work on the sugar plantations in the 1800s.

From the Capitolio north along El Prado

Surrounded by gardens designed by Forestier, the neoclassical **Capitolio** (*listings below*), built between 1926 and 1929, is a symbol of Cuba and

a prominent feature of the Havana skyline. It was designed as a smaller-scale version of the Capitol building in Washington – a potent (not to say ironic) reminder of the power and influence the United States exerted over early 20th-century Cuba – and has a similarly impressive central dome. (At 62 metres or 203 feet, the dome was the highest point in the city until 1958, when it was surpassed by the José Martí Monument in Plaza de la Revolución; *see p90*.) The three front doors are made of bronze and feature 30 reliefs showing important moments in Cuban history. They are reached via an immense flight of steps, flanked by bronze statues by Italian sculptor Angelo Zanelli, representing work and virtue. Inside is another Zanelli sculpture, the bronze 'La República', which, at 17.7 metres (58 feet) is the world's third largest indoor statue. A replica 24-carat diamond embedded in the floor in front of the statue marks point 0 of Cuba's Carretera Central (central highway network). Above the statue is the gilt-covered, carved cupola. Just as ornate is the immense Salón de los Pasos Perdidos (Hall of the Lost Steps), which is made almost exclusively of marble, with bronze and copper detailing. The hall takes its name from its unique acoustics – as you walk through it, you'll notice that your footsteps appear to be walking off in the opposite direction behind you. The wings on either side of the entrance hall house the ornate Senate and Chamber of the House of Representatives. Other rooms lavishly reflect different styles from Italian Renaissance to neoclassical, and friezes by Cuban artists Juan José Sicre, Esteban Betancourt and Alberto Sabas and international artists León Drouker and Remuzzi can be found throughout the building. The exquisite library has mahogany walls and floor-to-ceiling shelves holding 300,000 volumes. Today, the Capitolio is open daily for guided tours.

Across the street from the Capitolio to the east is the **Sala Polivalente 'Kid Chocolate'** (*see p214*), an indoor sports arena named after Cuba's finest-ever amateur boxer and winner of two world titles.

Capitolio

Paseo de Martí (Prado), entre San Martín (San José) y Dragones (603411/610261). **Open** 9am-7pm daily. **Admission** $1 (incl guided tours in English); free under-12s. **Map** p313 E14.

Parque Central & around

One block north is **Parque Central**, a natural hub for the city's social life – not to mention its transport network – since the park's creation in 1877. The centrepiece of the park is the Carrara marble statue of José Martí by José Vilalta de Saavedra. Completed in 1905, it was the first monument dedicated to the poet, writer, lawyer and fighter for Cuban independence, in the country. The area next to the statue has become an *esquina caliente* (literally, 'hot corner'), where sports fans argue about the latest baseball game.

Running along the western side of the park and on to the waterfront to the north is the **Paseo de Martí** (more commonly known by its old name, Paseo del Prado, or simply El Prado). El Prado opened in 1772 as the first promenade outside the city walls, providing welcome access to the sea along a tree-lined avenue. Originally designed for horse-drawn carriages, it quickly became Havana's favourite promenade, providing the chance to leave the sweltering city at the end of the day to enjoy the late afternoon breeze. In 1834, El Prado was remodelled, and prominent buildings sprang up along its sides; in 1928 Forestier's designs introduced bronze lions, lamp posts and marble benches to the street.

Surrounding Parque Central are some of the best-known hotels, stores and cinemas from the colonial period. The eclectic **Hotel Inglaterra** (*see p54*), built in 1856 on the western side of the park, is one of the city's most attractive. It started life in 1843 as the pavement café, El Louvre, which became a popular meeting point for youthful *habaneros* rebelling against the Spanish regime. The café still exists, and is a good place to the watch action on Paseo de Martí. Opposite the north-east corner of the park is the **Hotel Plaza** (*see p54*) and the 1910 Cuartel de Bomberos, which is currently being turned into the **Museo de los Bomberos** (Firemen's Museum; *listings below*); it should be open some time in 2001. Facing the Plaza across Agramonte (Zulueta) is the high-class **Golden Tulip Parque Central** hotel (*see p53*); its renovation a couple of years ago was criticised by some as unsympathetic to the rest of colonial Havana.

The eye-catcher at the south-western end of Parque Central is the extravagant neo-baroque **Gran Teatro de La Habana** (*listings below; see also p201*), with its magnificent interior monumental staircase and stunning exterior decoration. *Expo-venta* **Galería Orígenes** (*listings below*) is located at the front of the building, while around the corner on Calle San Martín, *expo-venta* **Galería La Acacia** (*listings below*) has art, silverwork and handicrafts.

South-east of the park is the stunning Spanish Renaissance-style **Centro Asturiano**,

The **Capitolio**, emblem of the city. *See p79.*

designed in 1927 by Spanish architect Manuel del Busto. Its rich decoration used 1,250 tonnes of marble imported from Italy, Spain and the US. Ceiling paintings by Mariano Miguel González depict Asturian history, and above the Escalera de Honor staircase is a leaded glass representation of the three caravels used by Christopher Columbus. The centre is currently closed for restoration, and will reopen in 2001 as part of the Museo Nacional de Bellas Artes (*see p81*).

Galería La Acacia

Calle San Martín (San José) #114, entre Industria y Consulado (639364). **Open** 10am-4pm Mon-Fri; closed Sat, Sun. **Admission** free. **Map** p313 D14.

Galería Orígenes

Paseo de Martí (Prado) #458, entre San Rafael y San Martín (San Juan) (636690). **Open** 9.30am-5.30pm Mon-Sat; closed Sun. **Admission** free. **Map** p313 D14.

Gran Teatro de La Habana

Paseo de Martí (Prado) #452, entre San Rafael y San Martín (San Juan) (613077-9). **Open** 9am-5pm daily. **Admission** (incl tour) $2; free under-12s. **Map** p313 D14.

Museo de los Bomberos

Calle Agramonte (Zulueta) #257, entre Neptuno y Animas (627762). **Open** closed for restoration until 2001; phone for details. **Map** p313 D14.

The northern stretch of El Prado

Beyond the park along El Prado to the north is the **Palacio de los Matrimonios** (*listings below*), one of the most popular places to get married in Havana. The 1914 building at the corner of Prado and Calle Ánimas is the former Casino Español (Spanish Social Club), and its entire upper floor is covered in deliciously ostentatious ornament.

Where Prado meets Trocadero is the Casa de José Miguel Gómez (1915), once home of the Republic's first president, and now the **Casa del Científico** guesthouse and restaurant (*listings below; see also p55*) run by the Ministry of the Environment. Its proximity to the Sevilla means this enchanting building is often overlooked, despite boasting a strikingly beautiful stained-glass window, one of the loveliest bay windows in the city and an observation tower overlooking El Prado.

East along Trocadero is the stunning Moorish-style **Hotel Sevilla** (*see p54*), built in 1908. The Sevilla is an early example of a building in Havana that was designed specifically as a hotel, and became a fashionable hang-out for celebrity guests in the early decades of the 20th century; Al Capone and his bodyguards are reputed to have taken over the entire sixth floor on a visit here. Even more famously, the hotel provides the setting for Graham Greene's *Our Man in Havana*.

Casa del Científico

Paseo de Martí (Prado) #212, esquina a Trocadero (624511/638103). **Open** 9am-9pm daily. **Admission** free. **Map** p313 D14.

Palacio de los Matrimonios

Paseo de Martí (Prado) #306, esquina a Animas (625781). **Open** 10am-5.30pm Tue-Fri; 4-5.30pm Sat, Sun; closed Mon. **Admission** free. **Map** p313 D14.

Museo de Bellas Artes & around

Built in 1954 on the grounds of an old market, the **Museo Nacional de Bellas Artes** (*listings p82*) incorporated the most advanced techniques then available to display, preserve and restore art works. Sculptures on the façades of the building and inside are by Cuban artists Rita Longa and Mateo Torriente Becker; the murals are by Jesús Casagrán and Enrique Caravia. The museum has been closed for renovation since 1998, and is due to reopen in mid 2001 as part of an expanded fine arts complex that will include three buildings: Bellas Artes (Cuban art, sculpture, engraving and drawing from the 17th

century to the present); the Centro Asturiano (ancient art of Egypt, Rome and Greece and European and Latin American art and prints); and the Cuartel de Milicias, an 18th-century barracks, which will house the museum administration. If all goes according to plan (which is by no means a certainty), the museum will also boast a café, a proper museum shop (a novelty in Cuba) and a 300-seater concert auditorium.

Facing the Bellas Artes is the **Memorial Granma**. The centrepiece of the memorial is the yacht, *Granma*, in which Fidel and 81 others sailed from Tuxpán, Mexico to Cuba in December 1956 to launch the Revolution. The boat, which is displayed under glass, is surprisingly small, and is surrounded by planes, vehicles and arms used during the Revolutionary wars against Batista and in the battle of Playa Girón (Bay of Pigs). Access to the memorial is only possible from the **Museo de la Revolución** (*listings p82*) and is included in the ticket price. The museum occupies the elegant Palacio Presidencial, official residence of 21 Cuban presidents between 1920 and 1965. The Revolutionary government announced its first new laws here in 1959 and continued to use the palace until 1965 when its headquarters moved to the Plaza de la Revolución. The building was turned into the museum of the Revolution in 1974.

The palace was designed by Cuban Carlos Maruri and Belgian Paul Belau with the interior decoration entrusted to Tiffany of New York. Highlights of the interior include the Salón de los Espejos, which is a replica of the Hall of Mirrors in the Palace of Versailles, and has paintings by Armando Menocal and Antonio Rodríguez Morey. The Salón Dorado (Golden Hall) is made of yellow marble with gold embossing on the walls and a triptych by Leopoldo Romañach. Below the intricately decorated dome are *Las Pechinas*, four canvases by Esteban Valderrama and Mariano Miguel González mounted on 18-carat gold sheets. Permanent exhibitions in the museum include weapons, maps, models, photographs and documents on the history of Cuban struggles from the 15th century to the present. Che Guevara's pipe is here, as is the uniform of Cuban cosmonaut Arnaldo Tamayo. The garden in front of the Palacio, originally designed by Forestier, is now called **Plaza 13 de Marzo** to honour the group of young revolutionaries who assaulted the palace on 13 March 1957, in a failed attempt to bring down the Batista government. Batista escaped through a secret door in his office, but bullet holes are still visible in the main stairway in the vestibule.

West of the Palacio is the **Real Fábrica de Tabacos La Corona** (*listings below*). The factory was built in 1888 by the American Tobacco Company and now offers a behind-the-scenes look at cigar making. The final products are sold in its on-site shop (*see p157* **Rolled gold**). East of the Palacio, just inside Avenida de las Misiones, which marks the edge of La Habana Vieja, is the stunning **Iglesia del Santo Ángel Custodio** (*see p74*).

Museo Nacional de Bellas Artes

Palacio de Bellas Artes, Calle Trocadero, entre Agramonte (Zulueta) y Avenida de las Misiones. **Map** p313 D15.
Centro Asturiano, Paseo de Martí (Prado), esquina a San Rafael. (639042/620140). **Open** 10am-7pm Mon-Sat; 10am-1pm Sun. **Admission** 1 gallery $3; both galleries $5; free under-12s. **Map** p313 D14.

Museo de la Revolución/ Memorial Granma

Palacio Presidencial, Calle Refugio #1, entre Avenida de las Misiones y Agramonte (Zulueta) (624091). **Open** 10am-5pm daily. **Admission** $3; tour in English $2; free under-12s.

Real Fábrica de Tabacos La Corona

Calle Agramonte (Zulueta) #106, entre Refugio y Colón (626173). **Open** 9am-3pm Mon-Fri; closed Sat, Sun. **Admission** (incl tour) $10; free under-12s.

Around La Punta

Built in 1589, the Renaissance-style **Castillo de San Salvador de la Punta**, at the north-east tip of the old walled city protected the entrance to the bay. Every night a chain was stretched across the 250-metre (820-foot) stretch of water between La Punta and El Morro on the opposite side (*see p110*), closing the harbour mouth to unauthorised vessels. The area around La Punta is currently under restoration: the first phase of work, almost completed, is to repair the moat, gardens and the eastern end of the seafront drive, **Malecón** (*see p86* **On the waterfront**); the second stage will restore the fortress itself.

South of La Punto in Parque Mártires is the **Memorial a los Estudiantes de Medicina** The memorial is based around the remains of a wall of the old Engineer Corps building that was used by colonial firing squads. On 27 November 1871 eight medical students were shot here by loyalist soldiers, after being falsely accused of desecrating the tomb of Gonzalo Castañón, a Spanish journalist who was opposed to Cuba's independence. A further reminder of Havana's brutal colonial past are the remains of the **Cárcel de La Habana** (Havana jail; *listings below*) to the south-east. Many Cuban revolutionaries who fought against Spanish colonialism, including José Martí, were imprisoned here. In the early 20th century the original building was demolished except for four cells and the chapel, which today hosts modest art exhibitions. The jail sits in **Parque de los Enamorados** (Lovers' Park), which has a powerful statue of an Indian couple. The richly decorated building on the south-east corner of the park is from 1912 and houses the Spanish Embassy; look out for the sculpted figure, which appears to be holding up the large balcony.

Presiding over the bay to the east, is the massive marble and bronze **Monumento a Máximo Gómez**. Designed by sculptor Aldo Gamba and inaugurated in 1935, the monument honours the Dominican Commander-in-Chief of Cuba's Liberation Army. It is under this roundabout that the road joins up with the tunnel under the bay, linking central Havana with the eastern suburbs. Note that the tunnel is closed for restoration until spring 2001.

Cárcel de La Habana

Avenida de los Estudiantes, entre Paseo de Martí y Agramonte (Zulueta). **Open** 9am-5pm daily. **Admission** free.

South from the Capitolio

The land immediately south of the Capitolio was originally Campo de Marte, an 18th-century drill square. In 1892 it was renamed Parque Cristóbal Colón to commemorate the fourth centennial of the discovery of America, and in 1928 became the **Parque de la Fraternidad**. The new park was designed, in accordance with Forestier's plans, for the sixth Pan-American Conference. A ceiba tree, the so-called 'Tree of American Fraternity', was planted in the centre of the park with soil from 21 countries of the Americas, and busts were erected of North and South American independence heroes: Abraham Lincoln, Simón Bolívar, Benito Juárez and others. The streets around the park are some of the best spots to see Havana's 'mobile museum' – American cars from the late 1940s and early '50s, which now are mostly privately operated taxis.

The south-west corner is overlooked by the impressive neoclassical **Palacio de Domingo Aldama** (*listings p84*). Built in 1844 by prestigious architect Manuel José Carrera, it is actually two large mansions built together to appear as one grand structure; visitors are welcome to see the staircases, ironwork, marble floors, original furniture and the refined courtyard with its ornamental fountains.

North of here on Calle Industria is the stunning neo-baroque **Real Fábrica de Tabacos Partagás** (*listings p84*), which has been producing fine cigars for more than 150

years. Don't miss the chance to tour the factory
and see Partagás cigars being hand-rolled.
Tours take place every ten to 15 minutes daily
and an English-speaking guide is always
available. The cigar shop (see p157 **Rolled
gold**) is one of the most popular in the city.

Walk along Calle Dragones to reach **Teatro
Martí**. Built in 1884 as Teatro Irijoa, the theatre
achieved great popularity because of its excellent
acoustics and central location. In 1901 it served
as the venue for the Constitutional Convention
for the new Republic, and in 1903 was renamed
after the hero of the independence movement.
The theatre is currently being restored, and is
due to be reopened in 2003 to mark its centenary.

Just south of here at the foot of Paseo de
Martí is the neoclassical **Fuente de la India o
Noble Habana**. The fountain was erected
in 1837 as the axis around which horse-drawn
carriages could either go north on El Prado or
west along the new Paseo Militar (later called
Calle Reina and now the Avenida Simón
Bolívar). The white Carrara marble fountain
portrays a young Indian girl sitting above four

dolphins; it was created by Italian sculptor José
Gaggini and is today a symbol of the city.
Longer and wider than Paseo de Martí, Avenida
Simón Bolívar leads to the slopes of Castillo
del Príncipe in Vedado (see p89), becoming
Avenida Salvador Allende (Carlos III), as it
crosses Calle Padre Varela (Belascoaín).

Across from the Fuente de la India is the
Asociación Cultural Yoruba de Cuba, which
runs the **Museo de los Orishas** (listings p84).
Opened in 2000, this is the first museum in the
world dedicated to the *orishas* (gods) of the
Yoruba Pantheon and their place in Afro-Cuban
religions. Its 31 life-size *orishas* – made of clay
by Cuban artist Lázaro Valdés – have large
painted backdrops showing the natural
environment and attributes connected with each
orisha. Descriptions are in Spanish, English and
French. Although informative, the museum is
pricey and its exhibitions seem rather hurried.
Visitors may be left with the impression that
the pressures of tourism in Havana have even
subjected religion to commercialisation. For
more on Afro-Cuban religion, see pp28-31.

Wheel life

If you fancy being chauffeured around
Havana in a red convertible Chevy, stroll
down to Parque Central in front of the Hotel
Inglaterra. The cars are parked waiting for
business; just take your pick (though the
better your Spanish, the more likely you
are to get a reasonable price).

In theory, tourists are directed towards
the state-run dollar taxis. These wait in ranks
outside the principal hotels and have meters;
although sometimes drivers will claim the
meter is broken, don't fall for it – it's invariably
their way of trying to make a few extra bucks –
always insist they turn on the meter.

Tourist taxis are good for the first couple
of days while you're finding your feet in the
city, but after a few days you start to realise
that everyone else is spending a tenth of
what you are on getting about. That's when
you ditch the tourist taxis in favour of privately
owned taxis, often Ladas belching out a
potent brew of Cuban/Soviet exhaust.
Officially these do not have the license to
transport tourists or to charge in dollars
but the PNR (Policía Nacional Revolucionaria)
seem more interested in checking Cuban
identity cards than bothering tourists trying
to save a buck (though they seem to change
their minds like the wind). Prices need to be
negotiated before the beginning of the journey

and it's useful to know the tourist taxi prices
so that you can negotiate a lower fee. Most
journeys within central Havana shouldn't
cost more than a few dollars.

Most visitors to Havana eventually fall in
love with the *boteros*. Grand old American
cars swan around town stopping to pick up
passengers... these taxis are communal
and for $0.50 or ten Cuban pesos you can
be picked up and dropped off anywhere along
the specified route. Again, these are officially
for Cubans only, but as long as your Spanish
is okay and you don't look too obviously
foreign, you'll generally be able to catch a
ride. They're a great way of meeting people
and definitely worth trying on Friday and
Saturday nights when everyone is dressed
to kill and flirting with each other... a moving
singles bar. Stand on one of the city's main
arteries and flag down any old American car
that has a taxi sign attached to it.

Museo de los Orishas

Paseo de Martí (Prado) #615, entre Máximo Gómez (Monte) y Dragones (635953). **Open** 9am-5pm daily. **Admission** $10; free under-12s. **Map** p313 E14.

Palacio de Domingo Aldama

Calle Amistad #510, entre Reina y Estrella (622076-9). **Open** 8am-4.30pm Mon-Fri; closed Sat, Sun. **Admission** phone to check. **Map** p313 E14.

Real Fábrica de Tabacos Partagás

Calle Industria #520, entre Dragones y Barcelona (620086-9). **Open** 9.30am-11am, 12.30-3pm Mon-Fri; closed Sat, Sun. **Admission** (incl tour) $10; free under-12s. **Map** p313 E14.

Southern Centro Habana

It might seem an unlikely tourist attraction, and indeed most people who come here are on their way somewhere else, but the yellow-tiled Renaissance-style **Estación Central de Ferrocarriles** (central train station; where Bélgica/Egido meets Arsenal) is worth a detour. Built in 1912, it has two 37-metre (121-foot) towers showing the shield of Cuba (left) and Havana (right). The first stretch of railway track was laid in Cuba in 1837, mainly to service the sugar industry; *La Junta*, the oldest steam locomotive in the country and one of the oldest in the world, is kept in the station's main hall and is clearly visible through the gates. The locomotive inaugurated the Matanzas-Sabanilla line in 1843. If you want a closer look at *La Junta*, ask the *jefe de turno* (duty guard) inside the main entrance.

Immediately to the north of the train station is **Parque de los Agrimensores** (Land Surveyors' Park) and the remains of *el Arsenal*, the Spanish naval shipyard. To the south, Avenida de Bélgica (Egido) is lined with remains of the original city walls, culminating in **La Puerta de la Tenaza**, the single remaining gate to the old city. A relief map on the gate shows the entire walled city with its eight entrances.

If you want to walk a little further, turn right at the bottom of Avenida de Bélgica (Egido) where, after about 500 metres (a third of a mile), you will be rewarded with a fine view of the **Castillo de Santo Domingo de Atarés**. Along with the bayside Castillo de La Cabaña (*see p110*) and Castillo del Príncipe in Vedado (*see p89*), this 1767 fortress on top of Soto hill completed the town's defensive network at its weak points after the 1762 English invasion. The castle cannot be visited by the public.

Inland from here to the north-west you'll reach **Cuatro Caminos** (Four Roads), the country's largest indoor agricultural market since 1920 (*listings below*). Officially part of the Cerro district (*see chapter* **Cerro & further south**), the market occupies an entire block at the juncture of four of Havana's most densely inhabited areas (La Habana Vieja, Centro Habana, Cerro and Diez de Octubre). Full of bustle, excitement and smells, the market is a part of everyday life for *habaneros*, who come here to buy live goats and hens, takeaway meals and a tantalising array of tropical fruit and veg, including sweet potatoes (*boniatos*), guavas (*guayabas*), papaya and yams (*óames*).

Mercado Cuatro Caminos

Calle Máximo Gómez (Monte), entre Arroyo (Manglar) y Matadero (705934). **Open** 7am-6.30pm Tue-Sat; 7am-2pm Sun; closed Mon. **Map** p312 F12.

El barrio chino

Cuba's Chinese community was once the largest, richest and most economically important in Latin America. The first 'yellow slaves' from Canton Province arrived in 1847 to work in the sugar industry, but were later joined by Chinese immigrants – enterprising traders and entrepreneurs – who came to Cuba to escape discrimination in California; at its height, Havana's Chinese community numbered 130,000 people. At one point, the district, with its opium dens and sex shows, was the focus of the city's reputation as the illicit pleasure capital of the Caribbean.

Many Chinese Cubans left the country after 1959, when private business was nationalised, but the remaining native-born Chinese (about 400 to 500 people) and their descendants still maintain a distinct community centred around Calles Zanja and Dragones in the heart of Centro Habana. Today, Chinatown (*el barrio chino*) is home to numerous traditional Chinese associations, a Chinese-language newspaper, restaurants (*see p131*) and a pharmacy with natural medicines. Chinese New Year is celebrated here every year on the 26 January,

Chinatown (*el barrio chino*) by day.

with traditional dragon and lion dances. Since the mid-1990s the area has been undergoing much-needed restoration work.

Compared to other Chinatowns, Havana's *barrio chino* is identified more by its social and cultural presence than by its architectural features. Built in 1999 as the eastern gate leading into the *barrio* from Calle Zanja, **Pórtico Chino** caters more to international images of Chinatown than to Havana's traditional Chinese community. Nonetheless – weighing 18 tonnes and with supporting posts that descend 13 metres (42 feet) into the ground – it is the largest gate of its type in the world and certainly impressive.

Two blocks east off Calle Zanja is **Cuchillo de Zanja**, a small pedestrian boulevard full of restaurants and sidewalk food stands, and lit at night by dozens of glowing Chinese lanterns. Also here is a small open food market selling what some consider the best fruit and vegetables in the city. At the end of Cuchillo on Calle San Nicolás is the office of Cuba's only remaining weekly Chinese newspaper, *Kong Wah Po*. Go inside for a peek at the 100-year-old printing presses (daily except Sunday). Back on Calle Zanja is **Farmacia Chung Wah**, which has provided homeopathic medicines to the Chinese community since 1920.

A worthwhile stop on a visit to Chinatown is the **Sociedad Lung Kong Cun Sol** at Casa Abuelo Lung Kong (*listings below*). One of 13 Chinese associations still existing in Cuba, this ancient society dates from 4 April 208 when three kings and a prince swore eternal brotherhood between their four families. The Cuban association was founded in 1900 to care for Chinese elders in the community, and today has some 800 members. Visitors are usually welcome at the *casa*, but should ask permission before entering. A special treat is the Templo San Fan Kong on the third floor, with an exquisitely carved and gold-plated mahogany altar, made in Canton over 100 years ago.

On the south-western edge of the *barrio* is the **Casa de Artes y Tradiciones Chinas (CATCH)**, a centre dedicated to promoting Chinese culture through conferences, language courses, dance, tai chi and visual arts; it also has a small gallery, which sometimes has Chinese art exhibitions (*listings below*).

Near to the *barrio chino* are two delightful churches that are often overlooked by tourists. On Calle Manrique you'll find the **Iglesia Nuestra Señora Caridad del Cobre**, which was built in 1802 and completely restored in the early 1950s. It has a gold-plated altar, lovely statuary, beautiful stained-glass windows and several grottoes (*listings below*). Flower vendors sit at the four corners of Salud and Manrique for those who want to offer blossoms to their

saint. To the west on Avenida Simón Bolívar (Reina) is the neo-gothic **Convento e Iglesia del Sagrado Corazón de Jesús** (*listings below*), built in 1922 and one of the most magnificent churches in the city. Its 77-metre (253-foot) tower is topped by a bronze cross, 32 gargoyles and a variety of statuettes and sculptures representing Christian allegories, music and human knowledge. The inside is lit by spectacular stained glass.

Casa de Artes y Tradiciones Chinas (CATCH)

Calle Salud #313, entre Gervasio y Escobar (639632). **Open** 8.30am-5.30pm Mon-Fri; 8.30am-noon Sat; closed Sun. **Map** p313 D13.

Convento e Iglesia del Sagrado Corazón de Jesús

Avenida Simón Bolívar (Reina), entre Padre Varela (Belascoaín) y Gervasio (624979/622149/635061). **Open** 8am-noon, 4pm-7pm daily. *Mass* 8am, 4.30pm Mon-Sat; 8am, 9.30am, 4.30pm Sun. **Admission** free. **Map** p312 D12.

Iglesia Nuestra Señora Caridad del Cobre

Calle Manrique #570, esquina a Salud (610945). **Open** 7.30am-6pm Tue-Fri; 7.30am-noon Sat; 7.30am-noon, 4-6pm Sun; closed Mon. **Admission** free. **Map** p313 D13.

Sociedad Lung Kong Cun Sol

Calle Dragones #364, entre Manrique y San Nicolás (625388/632061). **Open** noon-midnight daily. **Admission** free. **Map** p313 D13.

Along the Malecón & Calle San Lázaro

Parque Maceo by the waterfront at the northern end of Calle Padre Varela (Belascoaín) gives a good view of the profile of the Malecón (*see p86* **On the waterfront**) but suffers from a lack of vegetation and shade. Created in 1916 and overlooked by the Hospital Hermanos Ameijeiras, the park is dominated by a bronze, marble and granite monument to Lieutenant-General Antonio Maceo, the Liberation Army's second in command under Máximo Gómez. Maceo was known as the Bronze Titan and incredibly survived 24 bullet wounds, before he was finally killed in action in 1896. At the western end of the park is the **Torreón de San Lázaro**, a little circular watchtower built in 1665 to overlook the former cove of San Lázaro, a frequent landing site for pirates.

The 1874 **Convento y Capilla de la Inmaculada Concepción** (*listings p86*), a private school for girls until 1961, is located to the south-west of the park. The nuns who occupy this convent are slowly restoring the

On the waterfront

The **Malecón** is Havana's seaside promenade, stretching seven kilometres (4.3 miles) from the eastern, northern border of Centro Habana westwards to the mouth of Río Almendares. Constructed between 1901 and 1954 to maximise the access to the seafront provided by the Paseo de Martí (El Prado), the Malecón was developed in three stages from east to west.

In rough weather, waves often sweep over the sea wall, diverting traffic and gradually destroying the façades of the buildings across the street from the Malecón. Since 1995, the city Historian's Office has been slowly repairing the damage caused to

the seaside buildings by salt water, starting with the façades along the oldest and most traditional part of the seafront from La Punta.

Today the Malecón acts as the front porch for local residents wanting to escape the suffocating heat of the city. A walk along part of its length will bring you into contact with fishermen, late-afternoon romancers and people of every age taking a leisurely stroll.

But it is more than that. It is the city's focal point and breathing space, where people come to chill out, hang out, fish, swim, play music and make love, and faces Miami as if in a stand-off against the enemy.

building and visitors are welcome into the patio and chapel. The latter has a delicate wooden ceiling, stained-glass windows and a painted altar. Ring the bell on the front entrance at San Lázaro No.805 to gain admission.

Search the streets south-west of the convent to find another Havana surprise: **Callejón de Hamel**. This passageway is lined with houses and apartment buildings covered in murals depicting Afro-Cuban *orishas*, phrases and allegories. The murals are the work of renowned Cuban artist Salvador González Escalona. Today, Callejón de Hamel is a participatory artistic project offering numerous community arts events, including a *rumba peña* every Sunday (*see p194*). Also on Callejón de Hamel are **Estudio-Galería Fambá** (*listings below*), which has González Escalona's work for sale, and **El Yerbero del Hamel 'Ilé Osain'**, a little stand selling medicinal herbs at weekends.

Head west from Hamel to reach the boundary of Centro Habana and Vedado, marked by Calzada de Infanta. Between Calle Neptuno and Calle Concordia lies the baroque **Convento e Iglesia del Carmen** (*listings below*), one of the most beautiful churches in the city. Its 60.5-metre (195-foot) tower is topped by a striking nine-tonne, 7.5 metre (24-foot) sculpture of Our Lady of Carmen, made in Naples in 1886.

Two blocks north is the **Parque de los Mártires Universitarios**, created in 1967 to honour university students involved in Cuba's struggles for independence. Nearby

on Aramburu is the only remaining wall of the **Cementerio Espada**, Havana's first cemetery, which dates from 1806. The outlines of the coffins in the wall niches are still clear. Also in the area are the remains of the old San Lázaro quarry, where adolescent José Martí did forced labour as a political prisoner. On his release, he had a ring made out of his shackles, which he wore the rest of his life. The small **Museo Fragua Martiana** (*listings below*) has objects and books relating to his life and work.

Convento y Capilla de la Inmaculada Concepción

Calle San Lázaro #805, entre Oquendo y Marqués González (788404/700315). **Open** Mass 7am, 5pm Mon, Wed; 5pm Thur; 7am, 5pm Fri; 5pm Sat; 9am Sun. **Map** p313 C13.

Convento e Iglesia del Carmen

Calle Infanta, entre Neptuno y Concordia (785168). **Open** 8-10am, 4-7pm Mon-Sat; 7.30am-12.30pm, 4.30-7.30pm Sun. *Mass* 8am & 6.30pm Mon-Sat; 8.30am, 11.30am & 6.30pm Sun. **Admission** free. **Map** p312 C12.

Estudio-Galería Fambá

Callejón de Hamel, entre Aramburu y Hospital (781661). **Open** 10am-6pm Mon-Sat; 9am-3pm Sun. **Admission** free. **Map** p312 C12.

Museo Fragua Martiana

Calle Principe #108, esquina a Hospital (707338). **Open** 10am-4pm Mon-Fri; closed Sat, Sun. **Admission** free. **Map** p312 C12.

Vedado

Vedado is Havana's showpiece neighbourhood. Its wide leafy boulevards and 1950s hotels make it a welcome change from the crush of La Habana Vieja.

In the 17th century, Vedado (officially El Vedado, meaning 'prohibited area') was a military zone closed to civilians, but with the growth of the city in the 19th century, it became the neo-classical showpiece of the city. Vedado was the first part of Havana to be constructed according to an urban plan (*see p36*). It was laid out on a grid of measured blocks, with its main streets orientated to catch cooling ocean breezes; leafy boulevards and parks were incorporated into the design. With its artistic institutions, museums and theatres, Vedado is today one of Havana's social and cultural hubs. However, despite its numerous attractions, it is often overlooked by tourists (at least during the day), who aim straight for La Habana Vieja, missing the 'neighbourhood' feel of Vedado. The two areas couldn't be more different – Old Havana is packed tight, while Vedado boasts wide leafy boulevards and grand houses with spacious balconies.

Many streets in Vedado are laid out on a grid, making the area easy to navigate. Its wide boulevards are, heading north to south, Paseo (formerly Avenida de los Alcaldes) and Avenida de los Presidentes (also known as Calle G); the main ones running east to west are Calzada, Línea and 23.

Calle 23

Calle 23 stretches across Vedado from east to west, defining the geography and character of the district. It starts among the modern-day buzz and '50s high-rises of **La Rampa**, before morphing into a mixture of low apartment buildings intermingled with parks and commercial areas along its central stretch. The intersection with Calle 12 marks the street's second vibrating nerve centre, with restaurants, cafés, peso shops, art galleries, cinemas and the headquarters of the **Instituto Cubano del Arte e Industria Cinematográficos (ICAIC**; *see p177* and *p178*). One block to the south is the main entrance to the **Cementerio de Colón** (*see p90* **City of the dead**). The quieter western end is a residential neighbourhood of large individual properties, which extends as far as Río Almendares.

La Rampa & around

The steep stretch of Avenida 23 between Calle L and the Malecón is known as **La Rampa** and is a good place to start an exploration of Vedado. An electric wire of activity, these five blocks were the centre of pre-Revolutionary Havana high life and are still full of bars, discos, cinemas and hotels. La Rampa is also home to an excellent jazz club, **La Zorra y el Cuervo** (*see p197*), and the city's largest and most popular ice-cream parlour, **Coppelia** (*see p132* **Scream for ice-cream**). Designed by architect Mario Girona in 1966 and having a personality and reputation of its own, it was featured in the opening scenes of Tomás Gutiérrez Alea's film *Fresa y Chocolate*. Nearby is the 27-storey landmark **Habana Libre** hotel (*see p55*), built in 1958 by an American firm as the Havana Hilton. The hotel was nationalised

Leafy green **Avenida de los Presidentes**.

and renamed in 1960. Over the front entrance is an immense abstract mural by Cuban artist Amelia Peláez. On the south side of La Rampa, you'll find business offices, ministries and international airline agencies, plus a *feria artesanal* between L and M, selling handicrafts. Opposite is the **Pabellón Cuba**, an exhibition hall fronted by a wonderful statue of Sancho Panza. (To find *Don Quixote,* Cervantes fans should head four blocks west, where you'll find an unusual nude and skinny statue of the man himself mounted on his rail-thin steed Rocinante.) Towards the bottom of La Rampa is one of the most celebrated hotels in the city, the **Nacional** (*see p56*). Built in 1930 to accommodate American tourists attracted by Cuba's gambling, it was once the preferred lodging for distinguished guests, such as Winston Churchill. The hotel occupies a commanding position on the site of the 18th-century Santa Clara Gun Battery. Two cannons – a German Krupp and an immense Ordonez, once the largest in the world, with a ten-kilometre range – are still here.

South of La Rampa on Calle 25 is the **Casa-Museo Abel Santamaría**. Inside apartment #604 (on the sixth floor, though thankfully there's a lift), Fidel Castro and Abel Santamaría spent 14 months planning the 26 July 1953 assault on the Moncada Barracks in Santiago de Cuba. The small apartment with its original furnishings seems an unlikely starting point for events that would shape the history of a nation.

Casa-Museo Abel Santamaría

Calle 25 #164, entre O y Infanta (700417).
Open 9am-5pm Mon-Fri; 9am-1pm Sat; closed Sun. **Admission** free. **Map** p312 B12.

The University & around

On the corner of Calle L, three blocks south of La Rampa is the impressive 88-step *escalinata* (staircase) leading up to the Universidad de La Habana. The welcoming *Alma Mater* sculpture halfway up the stairs was made in 1919 by Czech artist Mario Korbel. Facing the base of the *escalinata*, is the small **Memorial a Julio Antonio Mella**, honouring the young student leader and founder of the University Student Federation (1923) and the Communist Party of Cuba (1925). In 1929, Mella was assassinated while in exile in Mexico.

Founded in 1728 in a Dominican convent in La Habana Vieja (*see p64*), the **Universidad de La Habana** (*listings p90*) was transferred to its present site on Aróstegui hill in 1902. The majestic and magnificent neo-classical campus was built between 1906 and 1940 around a central quadrant. The tranquillity of the

shady campus today provides a haven of peace from the bustle of the city. Note, however, that the campus is closed at weekends and throughout August.

The Escuela de Ciencias (Science Department) has a magnificent inner leafy courtyard and inside, two unusual museums. Downstairs is the **Museo de Ciencias Naturales Felipe Poey** (*listings p89*), named after an eminent 19th-century naturalist. It is the oldest museum in the country (dating from 1874) and displays Cuban flora and fauna and a fine collection of endemic multicoloured Polymita snail shells. Upstairs, the **Museo Antropológico Montane** (1903) has a rich collection of pre-Columbian pottery and idols, including a tenth-century Taíno Ídolo del Tabaco, used in religious ceremonies in Guantánamo Province. The Aula Magna (Main Hall) – open mainly during important events – has exquisite murals painted in 1910 by Armando Menocal. Note that you can't get into the museum by the front stairs; go around the northern side to the car entrance.

Two blocks south of the university steps is the former Casa de Orestes Ferrara (1928). Since 1961 this buildings has housed the **Museo Napoleónico**, considered the finest collection of Napoleonic and French Revolutionary memorabilia outside France (*listings p89*). The collection was assembled by Orestes Ferrara, adviser to President Gerardo Machado and ambassador to Washington, DC, and Rome, and includes the emperor's death mask, his gold-handled toothbrush, a lock of hair and a farewell note written by Marie Antoinette to her children on the day of her execution.

Continuing south of here past the large **Estadio Universitario Juan Abrahantes** and on to Calle Zapata, you are rewarded with a splendid view to the west of the white chalk sides and shady old jagüeye trees of Aróstegui hill. On the far side of the hill is the small 18th-century **Castillo del Príncipe**,

Death mask in **Museo Napoleónico**.

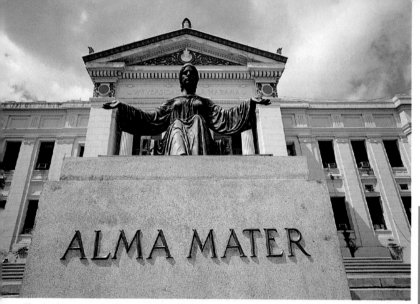

You looking at me? **Universidad de La Habana**.

built after the British invasion of 1762. This fort is unique in Cuba for its partially vaulted tunnel, which allowed the inmates of the castle to move around in safety. The fortress is off-limits to the public. Next to the castle on Avenida de los Presidentes (formerly Calle G) is the semicircular Italian marble **Monumento a José Miguel Gómez** (1936). The monument was designed by Italian artist Giovanni Nicolini, and its bas-reliefs show important moments in the life of Gómez, who was Republican president from 1909 to 1913.

Further south in a little park at the intersection of Avenida de los Presidentes and Calle Zapata is the often-missed **Memorial a Ethel y Julius Rosenberg**, sculpted by Cuban artist José Delarra. It commemorates the American couple who died in the electric chair in Sing Sing prison, New York in 1953, after being falsely accused of giving the Russians the secret of the atom bomb. Every year, on 19 June, the day of their execution, Cubans gather here for a modest remembrance ceremony.

East of the castle along Avenida Salvador Allende (formerly Avenida Carlos III) is Quinta de los Molinos, the summer residence of the Captains General of Cuba from 1837. Máximo Gómez, General-in-Chief of the Liberation Army, also stayed here in 1895. The house is named after the two tobacco mills (*molinos*) that used to occupy the site and today houses the **Casa-Museo Máximo Gómez** (*listings below*) and the Instituto Superior de Ciencias y Tecnología Nucleares.

The museum is closed for restoration (due to be completed at the end of 2001), but in the meantime visitors can enter the grounds to look around. The ornamental tropical gardens that surround the house were transplanted from an earlier site on El Prado and contain fountains, artificial hillocks, small waterfalls, pergolas, grottos and summer houses. One of Havana's main music venues, **La Madriguera**, is also to be found here (*see p191*). It is home to the Asociación Hermanos Saíz, which represents young musicians, writers, artists and poets. Musicians often can be heard practising in the gardens.

Casa-Museo Máximo Gómez

Quinta de los Molinos, Avenida Salvador Allende (Carlos III), entre Infanta y Luaces (798850).
Open *Gardens* 7am-7pm Tue-Sun; closed Mon. *Museum* (from end 2001) 10am-6pm Tue-Sun; closed Mon. **Admission** *Gardens* free. *Museum* $1; free under-12s. **Map** p312 D11.

Museo de Historia Natural Montané & Museo Antropológico Felipe Poey

Escuela de Ciencias, Universidad de La Habana, Avenida de la Universidad, esquina a J (793488).
Open 9am-noon, 1-4pm Mon-Fri; closed Sat, Sun. Closed Aug. **Admission** $1; free under-12s. **Map** p312 C11.

Museo Napoleónico

Calle San Miguel #1159, entre Ronda y Masón (791412). **Open** 10am-5.30pm Mon-Sat; closed Sun. **Admission** $3; $2 tour; free under-12s. **Map** p312 C11.

Universidad de La Habana

Main entrance: Avenida de la Universidad, esquina a J (783231/authorisation for photos 329844). **Open** 8am-5.30pm Mon-Fri; closed Sat, Sun. Closed Aug. **Admission** free. **Map** p312 C11.

Plaza de la Revolución

Rising above the city on Catalanes hill and measuring one kilometre in length, **Plaza de la Revolución** is the political centre of the country. The square is an unattractive space; a huge asphalt wasteland in need of trees for shade, but is nevertheless an essential stop on any sightseeing itinerary. The *plaza* is a key location for May Day marches and other festivities, and was also, significantly, where the Pope celebrated a mass during his first visit to Cuba in January 1998.

The first buildings were constructed around the square in the early 1950s under Batista. With the notable exception of the **Teatro Nacional** (*see p203*) and the **Biblioteca Nacional** (*see p283*), they are government buildings, including the ministeries of the Interior (1953), Communications (1954), Defence (1960) and Economy and Planning (1960). Most important is the **Palacio Presidencial**, on the south-west side of the *plaza*. This 1958 building houses the Council of State, the Council of Ministers, the headquarters of the Cuban Communist Party and Fidel Castro's Presidential Office.

The centrepiece of the square is the awesome **Memorial y Museo a José Martí** (also called Monumento a José Martí) (*listings p92*), constructed during the 1950s to designs by

City of the dead

A stunning miniature city of creamy marble, glittering bronze, angels, crosses and rich symbolism, Columbus Cemetery was designed by Spanish architect Calixto de Loira and built between 1871 and 1886 on 55 hectares of former farm land. Ironically, de Loira became the cemetery's first resident on his death in 1872. The cemetery is laid out in a grid divided by *calles* and *avenidas*, with the octagonal **Capilla Central** (central chapel) at its heart, and contains monuments, tombs and statues by some of the most outstanding artists of the 19th and 20th centuries. Plots were assigned according to social class, and soon became a means for patrician families to display their wealth and power with ever-more elaborate tombs and mausoleums, creating a superabundant hotch-potch of architectural styles. A huge number of famous Cubans have found their final resting place in the cemetery, including General Maximo Gómez, the novelist Alejo Carpentier, the composer Hubert de Blanck and countless martyrs to the revolutionary cause.

The main entrance is on the corner of Calle Zapata and Calle 12 and is marked by a suitably grandiose gateway decorated with biblical reliefs and topped by a marble sculpture by José Vilalta de Saavedra,

depicting *Faith, Hope and Charity*. Some of the most important and elaborate tombs lie between the main gate and the Capilla Central. Also look out for the modern rendition of Michelangelo's **Pietà**.

The cemetery is open 8am to 5pm daily and admission (including an optional tour) is $1 or free for children under 12. Head into the information office (34196/321050) to the right of the main entrance for a cemetery map or to enlist the services of one of the excellent English-speaking guides.

Capilla del Amor (Chapel of Love)

Panteon de la Familia Baró, Avenida Cristóbal Colón, entre Plaza Cristóbal Colón y Capilla Central.

Inside the Baró mausoleum is a burial chapel built by Juan Pedro Baró for his wife Catalina Laza. Catalina was one of the most beautiful women in Havana, but she was also the wife of the vice-president's son. Divorce was not legal in Cuba in the early 20th century, so Don Pedro and Catalina had to flee to Paris to be married. When divorce was finally legalised in Cuba in 1917, Catalina became the first beneficiary of the new laws. In 1926, Don Pedro built a mansion in Vedado (*see p92*) in honour of his wife and planted a special yellow rose – the Catalina – in the grounds. However, their

Aquiles Maza and Juan José Sicre. The monument consists of a gleaming white, 18-metre (58-foot) marble sculpture of Martí in contemplative mood, which was carved on site by Sicre. The statue sits on a vast base that spreads across the width of the square and provides an impressive podium for political rallies. Behind the statue – its top ominously circled by vultures – is a soaring grey marble tower, 109 metres (350 feet) high, in the shape of a five-point star. The *mirador* at the top of this startling and formidable structure is the highest viewing point in Havana and allows visitors to gaze on an unrivalled panorama of the city. Inside the base of the tower is a museum devoted to Martí and the achievements of the Revolution. The exhibitions display a large collection of photographic material on

Martí's life, plus information and resources on the construction of the Plaza, and the historical events that occurred here. Although the tone of the exhibitions sometimes strays into self-congratulation, the museum is undeniably impressive and interesting. Tours of the museum are available in English. The fourth room has rotating exhibitions by Cuban artists, and there is also a small concert chamber in the building.

Attracting as much attention as Martí's memorial is the steel silhouette of **Ernesto 'Che' Guevara** on the façade of the Ministry of the Interior on the north-west side of the square. The image is taken from the iconographic photograph of the Revolutionary by Alberto 'Korda' Gutiérrez, known around the world today.

happiness was to be shortlived. Catalina became seriously ill and died in 1931; her rose, too, languished and died. The chapel, with a Rosa Catalina carved on its entrance, also houses the remains of Don Pedro, who was buried here in 1941, in eternal vigilance over his beloved.

Tumba de Eduardo Chibás (Tomb of Eduardo Chibás)
Calle 8, entre F y G.
A tireless campaigner against corruption in Cuban politics, Eduardo Chibas was the leader of the Orthodox Party during the 1940s and '50s. In a dramatic gesture he committed suicide during a radio broadcast in 1951, only to be upstaged at his burial service by a young party member called Fidel Castro. Castro lept onto Chibas' tomb during the service to deliver an empassioned anti-establishment speech.

Monumento a los Bomberos (Firemen's Monument)
Avenida Cristóbal Colón, entre Plaza Cristóbal Colón y Capilla Central.
This stunning monument (*pictured above*) by Spanish sculptor Agustín Querol and architect Julio M Zapata commemorates the 28 firemen who died when a hardware shop in La Habana Vieja caught fire in 1890 (*see p71*).

La Milagrosa (The Miraculous One)
Calle 3, esquina a F.
This flower-covered tomb has become the centre of a popular myth and is by far the most visited grave in the cemetery. It is the final resting place of Amelia Goryi de Hoz, who died in childbirth in 1901 and was buried here with her stillborn baby at her feet. When her tomb was opened some years later, the dead child was found in Amelia's arms. Ever since, the mother has been celebrated as *La Milagrosa* (the Miraculous One) and has come to symbolise eternal hope. Cubans – particularly childless women – come here in droves to lay flowers on the tomb and to ask for good luck by knocking three times on the tomb with the brass ring – for the wish to come true, you must leave without turning your back on the tomb.

Mausoleo a los Estudiantes de Medicina (Mausoleum of the Medical Students)
Calle C, esquina a 1.
This tomb commemorates the eight medical students who were executed by the Spanish in 1871. *See p82.*

Nearby is **Teatro Nacional de Cuba** (*see p90 and p203*), one of the city's most important, if underused, venues. The stark, imposing façade conceals three performance spaces, a piano bar and the animated Café Cantante. The theatre is surrounded by abundant gardens, decorated with ponds, winding paths and sculptures by outstanding Cuban artists.

In the otherwise monotonous Ministerio de la Informática y las Comunicaciones on the north-east side of the square is the fabulous **Museo Postal Cubano José Luis Guerra Aguiar** (*listings below*), a little-known gem for philately lovers. Displays, with written explanations in Spanish and English, cover Cuba's postal history from 1648 to the present day. Highlights include an earthenware tablet from 2,300 BC showing the earliest known writing; examples of the rare English 'penny black' from 1850; first stamp circulated in Cuba from 1855; the First Day Cover stamped in space during the 1980 flight of cosmonauts Arnaldo Tamayo (Cuban) and Yuri Romanenko (Russian), plus examples of every Cuban stamp ever printed. The museum's shop sells a wide variety of Cuban stamps. Just north is the **Sala Polivalente Ramón Fonst**, a sports centre that houses the **Museo del Deporte** (*listings below*). The sports museum is closed for repairs until summer 2001, but the *sala* is open for basketball matches and other events (*see p213*).

Memorial y Museo José Martí

Plaza de la Revolución (820906). **Open** 9.30am-5pm Mon-Sat; closed Sun. **Admission** *Museum* (incl optional tour) $2. *Mirador* $3. **Map** p312 D9.

Museo del Deporte

Sala Polivalente Ramon Fonst, Avenida de la Independencia (Rancho Boyeros), entre Bruzón y 19 de Mayo (814696/820157). **Open** (from summer 2001) phone for details. **Admission** phone for details.

Museo Postal Cubano José Luis Guerra Aguiar

Avenida de la Independencia (Rancho Boyeros), esquina a 19 de Mayo (815551). **Open** 9am-5pm Mon-Fri; closed Sat, Sun. **Admission** $1 ($4 with tour in Spanish); free under-12s. **Map** p312 D10.

Central Vedado

Avenida de los Presidentes and Paseo run south through the heart of Vedado from the Malecón. Wider than many other thoroughfares in the city, these avenues are like linear parks with large trees on both sides and down the middle, bordered by some of the most beautiful mansions in the area. Cutting across the avenues are important east-west streets such as Calles 17, 23, 25 and Línea.

Stark architecture of the **Teatro Nacional**.

Cuban writer Alejo Carpentier called Calle 17 'the gallery of sumptuous residences' and it's easy to see why. Check out the grandiose residence at #301, now part of the Instituto Cubano de Amistad con los Pueblos (ICAP), which was designed by American architect Thomas Hastings in the early 20th century. Pompeii-style frescoes once adorned the walls of the large columned porch behind the house. Immediately west at #354 is the former residence of banker Juan Gelats. This 1920 building, with its white marble spiral staircase and lovely stained-glass window, is now the base of the **National Union of Writers and Artists of Cuba (UNEAC)**; its small bookstore is the city's best source for magazines and periodicals on Cuban literature, art and music (*listings p93*).

Further west on the corner of Calle 17 and Calle E is the **Museo Nacional de Artes Decorativas** (*listings p93*). The museum is housed in the beautiful 1927 Casa de José Gómez Mena, and boasts interior decoration by Jansen of Paris and French mahogany carpentry. The first floor has rococo Louis XV period furniture, tapestries, paintings, a Regency-style dining room with walls covered in Italian marble and paintings by Hubert Robert, among others. The second floor has collections of Chantilly and Meissen porcelain and crystal and decorative panels from China. The whole place is a luxurious treat.

Galería Mariano is located north-west of here on Calle 15. Part of Casa de las Americas (*see p93*), the gallery exhibits and sells Latin American and Caribbean art and handicrafts.

Just south of the junction of Calle 17 and Paseo, is Cuba's equivalent of the Taj Mahal: the Casa de Juan Pedro Baró, built by Don Pedro Baró for his beloved wife Catalina. The mansion was constructed in 1926 to designs by Cuban architects Govantes and Cabarrocas, and combines an Italian Renaissance exterior with a modern art deco interior. Sand from the banks of the Nile, crystal from France, and Carrara marble from Italy were used in its construction, and skilled French workers from Dominique were imported to carry out the building work. In 1995, the house became the **Casa de la Amistad**, used for cultural and recreational activities (*listings below; see also p195*). The former library is now a cigar shop.

Casa de la Amistad
Casa de Juan Pedro Baró, Paseo #406, entre 17 y 19 (303114/303115/shop 553270). **Open** *Casa* noon-midnight Mon-Fri; noon-2am Sat; noon-6pm Sun. *Shop* 10am-6pm Mon-Sat; closed Sun. **Admission** $5 Tue eve, Sat eve; otherwise free. **Map** p312 B9.

Galería Mariano
Calle 15 #607, entre B y C (552702). **Open** 10am-5pm Tue-Fri; 10am-3pm Sat; closed Mon, Sun. **Admission** $2. **Map** p312 B10.

Museo Nacional de Artes Decorativas
Calle 17 #502, esquina a E (309848/308037/320924). **Open** 11am-6pm Tue-Sat; closed Mon, Sun. **Admission** $2; $3 tour; free under-12s. **Map** p312 B10.

UNEAC
Casa de Juan Gelats, Calle 17 #354, esquina a H (324551). **Open** 8am-5pm daily. **Admission** free. **Map** p312 B11.

Along the Malecón

On the waterfront in front of the Hotel Nacional (*see p56*) is the **Memorial a las Víctimas del Maine** (also called the Memorial al Maine)

dedicated to the sailors who died when the USS Maine exploded in Havana harbour (*see p95* **The two iron eagles**; *see also p12*). Three blocks further along the Malécon is the **United States Interest Section** (USINT), the closest Cuba comes to having an American embassy. The American-designed building, constructed in 1952, is of little interest architecturally. However, as a representation of what Cuba considers to be hostile American policies, its presence is hugely significant. East of USINT, facing it in defiant confrontation, is the **Tribuna Anti-Imperialista**, a public square built specifically for protests against American imperialism. On the south side of the Plaza is the much-photographed colourful caricature of a Cuban revolutionary yelling at Uncle Sam: *Señores Imperialistas, ¡no les tenemos absolutamente ningún miedo!* ('Imperialists, we are not scared of you at all!'). For more on the Malecón, *see p86*

On the waterfront.

North-west around the headland, at the foot of Avenida de los Presidentes, is the **Monumento a Calixto García**, the 19th-century rebel leader of the liberation army in Oriente province. Made of black granite, its 24 bronze friezes depict scenes from the Wars of Independence.

One block south of here in a beautiful building on Calle 3ra is the **Casa de las Américas** (*listings p94*), a cultural centre founded in 1959 to promote, investigate and

Sightseeing

Symbol of the city: the imposing **Memorial y Museo a José Martí**. See p90.

The unwelcoming **Tribuna Anti-Imperialista**. *See p93.*

exhibit Latin American and Caribbean literature and art. International literary figures such as Gabriel García Márquez (who has a house in Miramar) are regular visitors. The collection of over 6,000 works are displayed in three locations in Vedado. The main building houses the Galería Latinoamericana, which has rotating exhibitions; the Sala Contemporánea, where Cuban and Latin American photographs and engravings are exhibited and sold; and Librería Rayuela, which sells books in Spanish and English, records and cassettes (*see p153*). The second venue is the **Galería Haydee Santamaría** (*listings below*), named after the revolutionary who founded the cultural centre, and located one block south. The gallery displays rotating exhibitions and a permanent graphics show. The final part of the collection is housed in the **Galería Mariano** (*listings p93*).

A few blocks west along the Malecón are the eye-catching, multicoloured umbrellas of the handicraft fair (*see p94*). Beyond is the 22-storey **Hotel Meliá Cohiba** (*see p56*), a Spanish-built stripey monster of a hotel. Built in 1994, the hotel is a startlingly contemporary structure that looks out of place in the traditional architectural surroundings of Paseo. The Cohiba dwarfs the nearby '50s **Hotel Riviera** (*see p56*), once the biggest casino hotel in the world outside Las Vegas. Another kilometre west is the mouth of Río Almendares and the tunnel to Miramar.

Casa de las Américas

Calle 3ra, esquina a Avenida de los Presidentes (G) (552706-9). **Open** *Casa* 8am-4.45pm Mon-Fri, closed Sat, Sun. *Galería Latinoamericana and Sala Contemporánea* 10am-4.45pm Mon-Fri; closed Sat, Sun. **Admission** *Casa* free. *Galería & Sala* $2; free under-12s. **Map** p312 A10.

Galería Haydee Santamaría

Calle G, esquina a 5 (552706). **Open** 10am-5pm Tue-Fri; 10am-3pm Sat; closed Sun. **Admission** $2; free under-12s. **Map** p312 A10.

Around Calle Línea

Calle Línea was the first east-west thoroughfare through Vedado and one of the main axes along which this part of the city was urbanised.

Starting at the eastern end of Calle Línea, one block south is the striking **Edificio Focsa**, which used to house Russian bureaucrats in the years following the Revolution. When it was built in 1956, the Focsa building was among the largest structures in the world. Now, the reinforced concrete building, with its 30-plus floors and 375 apartments, is a visual nightmare and much of it is in a sorry state of decay. (There was a fatal lift accident in the building in autumn 2000.) The tower, which adds another five storeys to the height of the building, was formerly the exclusive Club La Torre for wealthy owners of large companies.

Today, La Torre restaurant (*see p134*) occupies these lofty heights, offering a sensational view of the city (diners and drinkers are welcome to take photos).

Back on the ground and west on Linea, a little plaza with an eight-metre-high memorial honours thousands of Chinese who participated in Cuba's independence wars. At the column's base is written, to the eternal pride of Chinese-Cubans, 'not one Chinese was a deserter, not one Chinese was a traitor'. Two blocks further west, close to the Centro Cultural Bertolt Brecht (*see p204*) is **Casa de la Comunidad Hebrea** (*listings p97*), a centre for religious worship, education, social work and recreation for Havana's Jewish community.

At the corner of Calle Linea and Avenida de los Presidentes you'll find the wonderful **Museo Nacional de la Danza** (*listings p97*), opened in October 1998 to coincide with the 50th anniversary of the National Ballet of Cuba (BNC). Its displays are taken mainly from the private collection of Alicia Alonso, Cuba's prima ballerina and the founder of the BNC (*see p210* **Pointes means prizes**). They tell the story of ballet in Cuba through photos, costumes, prints, awards, sculptures and music sheets. Among the museum's treasures is a

The two iron eagles

On 15 February 1898, 266 crew members of the US battleship *Maine* died when their ship mysteriously exploded off the shores of Havana. The ship had been despatched to Cuba two months earlier to protect US interests during the war of independence with Spain. At the time, the Americans blamed Spain; a hasty US enquiry settled on 'unknown conspirators' as the perpetrators, and used the incident as the pretext for the US to enter the conflict. The slogan

'Remember the *Maine*' became a rallying war cry. However, the possibility that the US sabotaged its own ship in order to enter the war cannot be ruled out.

In 1925, the US government erected the **Memorial a las Víctimas del Maine** (*pictured*) on the waterfront in Havana. The memorial is an impressive sight, consisting of two tall marble Corinthian columns, two great cannons clad in iron chains from the ship's anchor, sombre female figures and bas-relief sea monsters and griffons. Originally the monument was topped with a heavy iron eagle, but this was knocked down by jubilant crowds immediately after the 1959 revolution, who carried the pieces triumphantly through the streets. Today, the fractured and distorted segments of the body are on permanent display in the **Museo de la Revolución** (*see p81*), while the head is in the Eagle Bar of the **US Interests Section** (*see p93*), open for lunch and drinks only to American and Cuban staff.

In fact, this was the second eagle to have perched imperiously on top of the Maine memorial. The first eagle was in danger of being knocked down by high winds due to its outstretched wings, so it was dismantled and replaced by a bird with folded wings. The original eagle today dominates the garden residence of the American Ambassador to Cuba.

But the story of the multiple eagles does not end there. In the **Museo Postal Cubano** (*see p91*) is an interesting display of first-day covers printed in the US during 1898-9 showing propaganda about North American plans for Cuba. One shows a red, white and blue eagle perched on top of a half-submerged anchor of the Maine, with the inscription 'The New Bird in Havana Harbour'.

signed autobiography of Isadora Duncan that she gave to Alonso in 1947 and a black fur cape belonging to Anna Pavlova.

Inaugurated in 1962, **Galería Habana** (*listings p97*) was the first of a national network of galleries for disseminating and promoting Cuban artists. Works by famous artists such as Wifredo Lam, René Portocarrero, Mariano Rodríguez and Amelia Peláez, among others, have been exhibited here. Today, the gallery at Calle Línea #460 promotes and markets works by young contemporary Cuban artists, established and unknown. Should you buy a piece of art here, the gallery will organise tax and export certification. (For details of Cuba's strict art export laws, *see p150.*)

Two blocks west is the Iglesia del Salgrado Corazón de Jesus, more commonly known as the **Parroquia del Vedado** (Vedado Parish Church; *listings p97*), conspicuous for the wide shaded park running along its side. Built more than 100 years ago as the first church in the district, it still retains almost all its original features, including the wooden altar, stained-glass windows and the carved wooden pulpit. One of the smaller stained-glass windows was commissioned by María Teresa Bances – wife of José Martí's son. Her former home is nearby on Calzada and is now the **Centro de Estudios Martianos** (*listings p97*), devoted to the study of Martí. The house has wide shaded balconies and a side patio opening onto a small palm garden, only spoilt by the shell of an abandoned car. Although it's not a museum, visitors are allowed into the centre during work hours, and sometimes there are a few books about Martí for sale. Phone first, before making the trip.

Other sights on Calzada include the recently restored **Teatro Amadeo Roldán** (*see p204*), one of the city's finest classical music venues and the home of the National Symphony Orchestra. Next door is **Parque Gonzalo de Quesada y Aróstegui**, created in 1915 to honour the secretary of the Cuban Revolutionary Party.

Going green

Looking west from the top of the Jose Martí Memorial in the Plaza de la Revolución, you can see **Plaza Organopónico** (*pictured*), a mini-farm with rows of neat raised beds in shades of green. Just a few blocks from the looming monument to the national hero and the Cuban government headquarters, manure and worm compost are dug into beds, spring onions, lettuce and swiss chard are systematically transplanted, roosters crow, herbs are dried in the tropical sun and city residents line up to buy the day's harvests. The farm manager, Gilberto Navarro, proudly shows off his garden to the many visitors who arrive at this urban oasis.

You don't have to leave the city to see farming and gardening in Cuba. Havana boasts thriving urban agriculture programmes, putting to use otherwise vacant, rubble-strewn land to provide affordable fresh vegetables, create lucrative work and beautify neighbourhoods. Only about ten years old, the urban agriculture movement grew out of the economic crisis of the Special Period, when hunger became an issue for the city's inhabitants for the first time since the Revolution. Today, *habaneros* are eating more vegetables than ever and the urban landscape is much greener, the result of a highly effective national strategy to grow food where people live. Havana, home to one fifth of the country's population, has more than 8,000 sites in production, ranging from informal community gardens producing fruit and veg for family consumption to intensive mini-farm co-operatives (*organopónicos*). Thanks to the scarcity of chemical fertilisers and pesticides during the Special Period, city produce is largely organically grown.

Keep an eye out for Cuba's innovative urban agriculture as you move around the capital. (Another accessible site is the beautifully lush Organopónico de Gastronomía on Avenida 5ta between Calles 60 and 62 in Miramar.) Gardeners will be eager to show off the fruits (literally) of their labour and you'll get a chance to witness the triumph of Havana's green revolution.

Plaza Organopónico
Calle Colón, esquina a Hidalgo, Nuevo Vedado (810461). **Open** 8am-5pm Mon-Fri; closed Sat, Sun. **Map** p312 D9.

Sleek tower of the **Casa de las Américas** cultural centre. *See p93.*

Casa de la Comunidad Hebrea

Calle I #241, entre 13 y 15 (328953). **Open** 9.30am-5pm Mon-Sat; closed Sun. *Services* May-Sept 7pm Fri; 10am Sat; Oct-Apr 6pm Fri; 10am Sat. **Admission** free. **Map** p312 B11.

Centro de Estudios Martianos

Calzada #807, esquina a 4 (552297/8). **Open** 8.30am-4.30pm Mon-Fri (phone first to check); closed Sat, Sun. **Admission** free. **Map** p312 A9.

Galería Habana

Calle Línea #460, entre E y F (327101). **Open** 10am-4pm Mon-Fri; 10am-1pm Sat; closed Sun. **Admission** free. **Map** p312 A10.

Museo Nacional de la Danza

Calle Línea #365, esquina a de los Presidentes (G) (312198). **Open** 11am-6.30pm Tue-Sat; closed Mon, Sun. **Admission** $2; free under-12s. **Map** p312 A10.

Parroquia del Vedado

Calle Línea, entre C y D (326807). **Open** *Mass* 8.30am Mon-Fri; 8.30am, 5pm Sat; 9.30am, 6pm Sun. **Map** p312 A10.

Nuevo Vedado

Nuevo Vedado – the area west of Avenidas Independencia and Cedspedes, and south of Calle 23 – developed in the '50s mainly along Avenida 26. It has the natural beauty of the Río Almendares on its western edge, the city zoo, abundant gardens, parks and open green areas, and winding roads skirting natural outcrops. However, sprawling post-Revolutionary apartment blocks have diminished the area's appeal.

Located just west of Cementerio de Colón (*see p90* **City of the dead**) on Avenida 26 is the **Cementerio Chino** (Chinese cemetery; *listings below*), dating from the 19th-century Qing Dynasty. Although it is designed in Asian style, with Chinese lion statues and brightly coloured burial chapels, it also shows Western classical and Christian influences. The cemetery is not usually open to the public, but visits can be arranged by contacting the offices of the Chinese newspaper, *Kong Wah Po* (*see p85*).

The most visited attraction in Nuevo Vedado is the **Jardín Zoológico de La Habana** (*listings below*), popularly called Zoológico de 26 due to its address. Founded in 1939 as Cuba's first zoo, it was ranked as one of the ten best urban zoos in the world in the late 1970s by the International Zoological Association, and attracts some 630,000 Cuban visitors each year. In these animal-friendly days, international visitors may find the animals' sparse and often cramped surroundings rather depressing, however the zoo has some interesting inmates, including the oldest chimp collection in captivity – six generations since 1946 when the first one arrived. Diverse species of Cuban fauna, exotic birds and exuberant vegetation are also well represented, and there's a large children's playground with immense seesaws in the grounds. At the main entrance are two sculptures by Cuban artists Rita Longa and Jilma Madera.

Cementerio Chino

Calle 26, entre 28 y 33. Information: Abel Fung Way Man (administrator), Periodico Kong Wah Po, Calle San Nicolás #520-522, entre Zanja y Dragones (633286). **Admission** free. **Map** p311 D7.

Jardín Zoológico de La Habana

Avenida 26 y Avenida del Zoológico (818015). **Open** 9.30am-5.30pm Tue-Sun; closed Mon. **Admission** $2.

Sightseeing

Along Río Almendares

Its sights may not be plentiful, but this stretch of land, hugging the river between Vedado and Miramar, should not be overlooked.

Sightseeing

In the 17th century, when Bishop Almendáriz arrived in Cuba bothered by rheumatism, it was the healing waters of the Río Casigüagüas that cured him. The local name for the river was duly changed to the Río Almendares. The Zanja Real (Royal Trench) and the Presa de El Husillo dam had been bringing water from the river to the city since 1592, and by the 18th century, settlements had sprung up along its banks. In the 1920s, French landscapist Forestier suggested creating a Gran Parque Nacional, including the entrance to the bay, the coast and the greenbelt along Río Almendares. The idea of a park on a smaller scale was proposed again in 1963, but it wasn't until 1989 that the Parque Metropolitano de la Habana (PMH) project began turning plans into action.

No longer a water source for Havana, Río Almendares remains the most important green lung of the city. Over the years, it has suffered deforestation and pollution caused by domestic waste and by the factories along its banks. The Embalse Ejercito Rebelde, a dam built in 1974 to control the flow of water, also affects the river's ability to clean itself naturally.

The Parque Metropolitano de la Habana covers an area of seven square kilometres (2.7 square miles) along a 9.5-kilometre (six-mile) stretch of the river, starting at its mouth. Its 30-year project is to clean up the river, revitalise agriculture and recreational facilities, and carry out reforestation. The 15,000-strong population of the municipalities affected (Cerro, Playa, Plaza de la Revolución, Marianao) will be involved and will receive environmental education. The project is a new experience for Cuba, but results can already be seen: the ceramics factory and limestone quarries are closed; the carbonic gas factory has begun to recycle its water; trees have been planted and communities have received natural water treatment plants. The long-term objective is to create a sustainable city park that is ecologically and socially viable.

The mouth of the Almendares

On a tongue of land on the eastern side of the mouth of the Río Almendares is the **Torreón de Santa Dorotea de Luna de**

La Chorrera, a tower built in 1762 to replace an earlier fort that had been destroyed by the British. The fort had been part of the island's coastal defence network with the additional task of protecting Havana's water supply. The complex is now something of a gastronomic destination, with a restaurant (553090/553092), café and bar all housed in the tower itself, and the **Restaurant 1830** in the mansion next door (*see p99* **Club 1830**). You can get a good view of the Torreón, the gardens of 1830, the Malecón and beyond from La Puntilla peninsula on the western side of the rivermouth.

From the mansion, a little road runs west along the river to **Puente de Hierro**, an old iron bridge that is the only means for cyclists to cross the Almendares (6am to 7pm daily). On the opposite bank is the tiny **Parque de los Paticos**, named after the ducklings that used to wander around here. Across the street at Calle 7 #205 is a 1950s mansion built by Chinese merchant Li Kim as a replica of his father's home in Beijing. Kim left Cuba after 1959, and the home became **Restaurante Pavo Real** in the early 1990s. The restaurant (242315) is due to reopen after extensive restoration some time in 2001 and will serve Chinese and international food. The second-floor cupola with stained-glass windows depicting graceful Chinese scenes is best seen from inside the house.

Parque Almendares & Bosque de la Habana

Parque Almendares is located on the western banks of the river at the point where it is crossed by Calle 23. The park was developed in the late 1950s to provide a recreational area for the city and at the weekend is popular with local families who enjoy its outdoor picnic areas, children's play area and nature trails. Although the park is currently being regenerated and improved, it's still a little shabby round the edges; the river here is being suffocated by *malangueta*, a voracious aquatic plant that could easily be cleared out. The best time to visit the park is on Monday, Wednesday and Friday evenings between 6pm and 9pm, when the Haitian music and dance troupe La Bann Soléy are practising. Immediately south of

Club 1830

The small peninsula at the mouth of the Almendares looks set to become one of the city's top tourist destinations. But before you get excited by the prospect of wet T-shirt competitions and booze-induced orgies, note that this 1830 is not some youth holiday resort, but rather a high-class restaurant and cabaret complex housed in a beautiful 1920s mansion overlooking its own miniature bay.

The mansion was built for Carlos Miguel de Céspedes, the Secretary of Public Works and the son of Carlos Manuel de Céspedes, and was later rented by the Currais family, who turned it into a restaurant and cabaret. Surrounding the mansion are unusual features, including the charming Isla Japonesa, a tiny island designed by Japanese engineer Nagasade, with bridges, bowers, walkways and bird cages, all constructed from stone and shells. Nearby, on a land spit jutting into the river's mouth,

is an exquisitely decorated cupola. Sadly, the complex has been closed for restoration for some considerable time.

At the time of going to press, the 1830 looked rather like a building site, but – if the PR spiel is to be believed – it will once again boast a cabaret and restaurant, and future diners will be able to choose from a series of colour-coded dining rooms, each offering a different international cuisine. Rumour has it that the (genuine) French chef from La Torre (*see p134*) will also be adding his Gallic flair to the mix. It would seem that this place is not to be missed – whatever your age.

Restaurante 1830

Malecon, esquina a 20 (334521).
Open *Restaurant* noon-midnight daily.
Cabaret 10pm-4am daily. **Main courses**
phone for details. **Tickets** *Cabaret* $10.
Map p311 A/B7.

Parque Almendares is the wilder **Bosque de La Habana** (Havana forest), where small footpaths wind through abundant vegetation and climbing plants drape from the branches of trees that are up to 200 years old. This forest in the middle of the city shelters migratory and Cuban birds, reptiles (mainly lizards) and various types of insects. Robberies, though rare, are not unheard of in the forest, so it is best not to explore on your own.

In the early 20th century, two beer factories near the river created gardens in order to promote their prized product. **Jardines de La Tropical** (*listings below*) at the end of Calle Rizo was designed by the Tropical brewing company in 1912. It is an astonishing garden with luscious vegetation, grottoes, mazes, cascades, pavilions, kiosks, riverside benches, an unusual open ballroom and a miniature Swiss chalet where the gardener once lived. The

The 25-hectare **Ciudad Deportiva** sports complex on the edge of Cerro district.

fantasy design is reminiscent of Gaudí's Parc Güell in Barcelona, and the air of neglect that hangs over it only serves to intensify the garden's other-worldly atmosphere. Located on a natural terrace overlooking the garden is the mansion of the former brewers, which is now a peso restaurant. The building combines a stark castle-like exterior with lush Moorish interior decoration inspired by the pavilions in Granada's Alhambra. East of here, Avenida Zoológica takes you to the front entrance of the **Jardín Zoológico de La Habana** (see p97).

The smaller **Jardines de La Polar**, created by the Polar brewing company, are located between Río Almendares and its tributary Río Mordazo, just off Calzada de Puentes Grandes. These gardens have recreational areas, a football stadium and a circus amphitheatre (no longer used). From here a foot and bicycle path across Río Mordazo leads to the **Aula Ecológica** (listings below), the PMH visitors' centre, where there is a scale model (1:2,000) of the project. (To reach the centre by car, turn west off Calle 26.) Behind the centre is the old Parque Florestal, an early 20th-century botanical garden with picnic and other facilities. You are welcome to walk around, but don't go unaccompanied. The *ciclovía* (cycle path) continues east as far as a large traffic roundabout (the intersection of Calle 26, Avenida de la Independencia, Vía Blanca and Avenida de Rancho Boyeros) and the 25-hectare **Ciudad Deportiva** (sports complex; see p213) on the edge of Cerro district.

Aula Ecológica

Ciclovía, off Calzada de Puentes Grandes, west of 26 (819979). **Open** 8.30am-5.30pm Mon-Fri; closed Sat, Sun. **Admission** free.

Jardines de La Tropical

end of Calle Rizo (818767). **Open** 9am-6pm Tue-Sun; closed Mon. **Admission** free. **Map** p311 F5/6.

Around Loma de Husillo

South of Calzada de Puentes Grandes and west of the river, Husillo is a distinct rural district within Havana's urban sprawl. Calle 44 and the Carretera de Husillo lead to the 65-metre (213-foot) **Loma de Husillo**, the tallest hill in the city, which is crowned by a military base. Further south are the ruins of the old **Presa de El Husillo**, which provided water for Havana for almost 300 years. Hidden behind weeds and forgetfulness, the dam was built in 1592 to channel water from Río Almendares into the Zanja Real (Royal Trench) – an open, paved aqueduct that terminated in the Plaza de la Catedral (see p72). The Presa was the earliest European-made hydraulic construction in the New World, and walking around the dam gives a powerful sense of its size and sophistication. Despite the intervention of city historians, the dam was destroyed in 1989 to prevent flooding, but what remains is impressive, including part of the original iron outlet mechanism and the first 100 metres of the Zanja Real.

To reach the Presa turn off the Carretera de Husillo to the east (an abandoned paper mill marks the turning) and continue as far as the bridge; then walk south along the eastern river bank. On the way you may see followers of the Afro-Cuban religion Regla de Ocha performing their rites in the river waters near the dam.

Unless the city's waste-recycling plant is of interest, there's not much else to keep visitors in Husillo. If you do venture into this part of town, note that the Carretera de Husillo has some bad ruts and the roads are usually badly littered.

Miramar & the Western Suburbs

Plenty of visitors make it to the grandiose embassies and marinas of Miramar and beyond; not so many bother to take in the earthier charms of Marianao.

By the early 20th century, Havana's beautiful western shores were enticing the rich out of the city. With the construction of a drawbridge in 1924, the obstacle of Río Almendares was overcome and rapid development of Miramar began. Later, this bridge was replaced by the first tunnel under the river connecting the Malecón in Vedado with Quinta Avenida, and the construction of a second tunnel, one block south, soon followed. Along with elegant mansions, gardens full of fountains and wide tree-lined streets and avenues, the area bordering the western shore became a popular location for clubs, casinos and restaurants. Westward expansion reached the Biltmore district (today Siboney and Atabey) and spread into the Country Club Park area, where eclectic country estates were built along winding streets to create the most exclusive townscape of private residences in the country.

Following the Revolution in 1959, many wealthy *habaneros* fled the country for the United States. It is estimated that some 320 residences were abandoned almost overnight, turning Miramar into a phantom neighbourhood with a glut of unused property. Some empty mansions became residential schools for youth from the countryside, others have since been converted into embassies. Today, Miramar is inhabited by professionals and workers; it is Havana's main area for embassies, entrepreneurs, protocol guesthouses and coastal hotels, as well as scientific

institutes and public buildings. More recently, and lamentably, small neighbourhood parks have been crammed with three- and four-storey condominiums with apartments sold in hard cash – part of Cuba's attempts to get quick dollars, although recent changes in the law have attempted to put a stop to this.

Note that the street system in Havana's western neighbourhoods can be rather confusing to visitors; the northern part of Miramar is a fairly straightforward grid, with even-numbered *Calles* and odd-numbered *Avenidas*, but the roads to the south and west, especially out towards Cubanacán, are winding and the numbering system is harder to follow. Even taxi drivers sometimes have trouble in lesser-visited parts of town. In view of this, it's always best to take a detailed map with you.

Miramar

There are four ways to enter Miramar: via the two tunnels under Río Almendares at Avenida 5ta (or Quinta Avenida as it is often called colloquially) and Calle Línea; over the Puente de Hierro (*see p98*); or via Avenida 23 and Puente Almendares. Unlike the Malecón, Miramar's coastal road (Avenida Primera) gives little public access to the shore – except for a few rocky swimming areas at the ends of Calles 16 and around 66 – as private houses and buildings reserve this area for their own use. However, this is also the location of **Teatro Karl Marx** (*see p199*), which is used for concerts, cultural activities and conferences.

The most interesting way through Miramar is Avenida 5ta, one of Havana's most beautiful roadways. Heading west at the junction with Calle 10, is the 1924 **Reloj de Quinta Avenida**, located in the tree-lined median. The official symbol of Miramar, it is the only freestanding clocktower in Havana. Two blocks west of here is the **Museo del Ministerio del Interior** (*listings p103*), one of the few museums of its type in the world. Photos, armaments and other objects show the history of intelligence in Cuba, from Carlos Manuel de

The **Museo del Ministerio del Interior**.

Banyan trees spread their roots across the parks of **Quinta Avenida**.

Céspedes' creation of a systematised apparatus in 1868 to the present day. (The involvement of women as intelligence agents is a noteworthy aspect of the exhibition.) Other displays show the history of terrorist actions against Cuba since 1959, with exhibits including cans of Quaker Oats used to smuggle explosives and drugs into Cuba, and information on the 637 known plans and attempts (all unsuccessful) to assassinate Fidel between 1961 and 1999. (One plot involved impregnating cigars with poison and somehow persuading him to smoke them.) Further along Quinta Avenida, at the junction with Calle 16, is the **Casa del Habano** (*see p157*) – identifiable by its large stained-glass window depicting tobacco leaves. It is one of the best places in Miramar to buy cigars, rum and coffee, and also boasts a pleasant bar-restaurant.

Four blocks further west is a lushly wooded park of ancient *jagüeyes* (banyan trees), distinguished by their overgrown roots. The park is split into two by Quinta Avenida; northern **Parque Prado** boasts a Roman-style temple at its centre and a small bust of Mahatma Gandhi; southern **Parque Emiliano Zapata** has a statue of this important early 20th-century Mexican freedom fighter. To the west of the park is the **Iglesia Santa Rita de Casia**. Though the church itself is unremarkable, it is known for its controversial statue of the 14th-century saint.

Heading north of Avenida 5ta on Calle 28, between Avenidas 1ra and 3ra, is **La Maqueta**

de La Habana (*listings p103*), a tinker-toy perfect scale model of Havana. Used for city planning and as an educational tool for students, this fascinating model is made from recycled cigar boxes, cardboard and sponges and will eventually reproduce the main metropolitan area of the city (144 square kilometres) at a scale of 1:1000. Buildings are colour-coded for different historical periods: ochre for the colonial era (16th to 19th centuries); yellow for the Republic (1900-1958); cream for post-Revolutionary developments; and white for proposed new projects and national monuments. A ramp with telescopes gives a better view of the model's detail and extent. La Maqueta is a project of the Grupo para el Desarrollo Integral de la Capital (Group for Integral Development of the Capital; GDIC), which has advised city officials on building policy and urban planning since 1987. It also runs neighbourhood workshops to help local communities identify and solve local problems.

A 15-minute walk west from the Maqueta along Avenida 3ra will take you to the recently renovated **Acuario Nacional de Cuba** (*listings p103*). Founded 40 years ago as Cuba's first aquarium, it has built up a collection of almost 4,000 sea creatures representing over 350 tropical water species. Along with exhibition tanks featuring sea life from Cuba's coral reefs – organised by sea depth – are large new dolphin and sea lion display areas, which will be completed by summer 2001. Sadly, a virus in

May 2000 killed all five trained dolphins, but the new dolphins should be ready to wow the crowds by the time construction work is completed. Phone to find out the times of the live shows.

South of the aquarium on Calle 60 is the Romanesque **Iglesia de San Antonio de Padua** (1949; *see below*), Cuba's only church dedicated to St Anthony of Padua, the Portuguese saint of the poor and of true love. This church has what was once considered the finest organ in Latin America. Although lack of maintenance has left the organ unplayable, it remains a majestic work of art. Until the **Russian Embassy** (Embajada Rusa, on the corner of Avenida 5ta and Calle 62) was built at the end of the 1980s, the belfry on this church was the tallest building in the area. Now the embassy's enormous stark tower dominates the surrounding countryside for miles around.

Several blocks further west, at the corner of Avenida 5ta and Calle 82, is the Romanesque-Byzantine **Iglesia de Jesús de Miramar** (*see below*), squatting like a toad in an otherwise open area. Built in 1953, it is Cuba's second largest church and houses 14 large oil paintings of the Stations of the Cross by Spanish artist César Hombrados Oñativia. Some of the 266 depicted figures are portraits of real people: in one station, the artist appears as one of the executioners derobing Jesus; in another, his wife is shown as the Virgin Mary. The impressive pipe organ, silenced by termites, has 5,000 Spanish pipes.

Behind the church is Monte Barreto, a partially wooded hillock covering 36 city blocks. It was once used for pasturing cattle and goats, but the arrival of foreign investment in the 1990s gobbled up part of this area for **Hotel Novotel Miramar** (*see p59*), the newest addition to the clutch of large coastal tourist hotels in this area.

Along with the construction of 18 rental office blocks to create the Miramar Trade Centre, this zone is acquiring an increasingly well-heeled, foreign look through an influx of foreign dollars. Local residents view the changes with mixed emotions, arguing that it would make more environmental (and social) sense to convert abandoned mansions into guest inns rather than altering the whole aspect of the area.

On the south side of Monte Barreto is a nursery (entrance at the corner of Avenida 9na and Calle 78) selling small trees and bushes primarily to state projects. (It's also open to visitors between 7am and 7pm.) Future plans include turning the nursery and the area behind the hotel and church into a protected ecological park.

Acuario Nacional de Cuba

Avenida 3ra, esquina a 62 (225872). **Open** 10am-6pm Tue-Sun; closed Mon. **Admission** $5; $3 under-12s. **Map** p310 B3.

Iglesia de Jesús de Miramar

Avenida 5ta #8003, entre 80 y 82 (235301). **Open** 8am-noon, 4-6pm daily. *Mass* 8.30am Tue-Fri; 5pm Sat; 9am, 5pm Sun. **Admission** free. **Map** p310 B1.

Iglesia de San Antonio de Padua

Calle 60 #316, esquina a 5ta (235045). **Open** *Mass* 5pm Mon, Tue, Thur, Sat; 8.30am Wed, Fri; 10am, 5pm Sun. To visit at other times, enter via the sacristy. **Admission** free. **Map** p310 B3.

Iglesia Santa Rita de Casia

Avenida 5ta, esquina a 26 (242001). **Open** *Mass* 5.30pm Tue, Thur, Sat; 10.30am Wed, Fri; 8am Sun. **Admission** free. **Map** p311 B5.

Maqueta de La Habana

Calle 28, entre 1ra y 3ra (227303/227322). **Open** 9.30am-5.30pm Tue-Sat; closed Mon, Sun. **Admission** $3; $1 concessions. *Guides* $20-$40. **Map** p311 A5.

Museo del Ministerio del Interior

Avenida 5ta, esquina a 14 (234432/307805). **Open** 9am-5pm Tue-Fri; 9am-4pm Sat; closed Mon, Sun. **Admission** $2 or $3 with guide; free under-12s. *Permission to photograph* $1 per photo. **Map** p311 B6.

Cubanacán & Siboney

Cubanacán is home to several important buildings. Built on the site of the old Havana Country Club, the **Instituto Superior de Arte** (ISA; *see p106* **State of the art**), Cuba's leading art academy, is one of the most beautiful constructions in the country.

Slightly west of here, meanwhile, is the most important convention centre in Cuba. The **Palacio de las Convenciones** on Calle 146 was built for the Sixth Summit of the Non-Aligned Countries in 1979. A modern architectural structure surrounded by trees and vegetation, it hosts a National Assembly meeting twice a year. The Hotel Palco is connected to the convention centre by a walkway. Right next door to the palacio is the upmarket **Rancho Palco** (*see p139*), one of the best restaurants in the city. Nearby is **PABEXPO** (1987), a large complex consisting of four interconnecting pavilions used for national and international trade fairs – such as the annual Tourism Fair in May – and scientific exhibitions.

To the west of Cubanacán is the district of **Siboney** and a complex of over 30 buildings for scientific research, pharmaceutical industries and training, imaginatively called

Remember us this way; the deeply unsubtle **Russian Embassy**. See p103.

Ciudad Científica (Scientific City). This is the site where, over the past 15 years, Cuba has developed some 200 new biotechnology products including recombinant interferon, meningitis and hepatitis B vaccines. All the buildings where this impressive work is carried out are closed to the public.

Back on Quinta Avenida north of Cubanacán, the contaminated Río Quibú – the second most important river in Havana after the Almendares – empties into the Gulf Stream. West of this, the city becomes a series of isolated buildings with large open spaces and less traffic. About two kilometres west is the old Havana Biltmore Yacht and Country Club, today **Club Habana**. Opened in 1928 for the recreation of 'jet set' *habaneros* and expats, it had such a restrictive door policy that even President Fulgencio Batista didn't manage to make the grade. After the Revolution, the State

opened the doors of all 'aristocratic' clubs to the people, turning many into workers' social centres. The dock area of the 65-hectare Havana Biltmore went to the Marines, while the main clubhouse and its grounds are now run by the International Conference Centre as a business venue, social club and sports facility for diplomats, executives and entrepreneurs. Non-members pay an admission fee to use the facilities. For further details of the sports on offer here, *see p217*.

Club Habana
Avenida 5ta, entre 188 y 192 (245700). **Open** 7.30am-1am daily. **Admission** *Non-members* $10 Mon-Fri; $15 Sat, Sun.

PABEXPO
Avenida 17, entre 174 y 190 (215513). **Open** (only during fairs) phone for details. **Admission** varies; phone for details.

Palacio de las Convenciones

Calle 146, entre 11 y 13 (226011). **Open**
normally 8am-5pm Mon-Fri; closed Sat, Sun.
Hours vary during conventions; phone for details.
Admission varies; phone for details.

Further west

Jaimanitas

A little way west of Club Habana is
Jaimanitas, a sleepy fishing village with a
provincial air. Local residents moor their boats
in the mouth of Río Jaimanitas, which forms the
village's western border, and there is also a tiny
malecón (sea wall) and beach. If you make it
this far west, don't miss the **Casa-Estudio de
José Fuster**. Fuster is an internationally
recognised painter, engraver and ceramicist (he
had an exhibition in Manchester, UK in July
2000), but his most important work is his studio
and home in Jaimanitas. The house is littered
with ceramics and paintings, which are
ingeniously incorporated into the furniture.
Look out for *La Puerta de Fuster* (Fuster's
Door); the *Banco de Amor* (Love Seat); *la piscina*
(pool), with its large ceramic mermaid
surrounded by tropical fish; and the four-metre
high *La Torre del Gallo* (Cock's Tower), a
homage to Latin American machismo, complete
with a *parrilla* (oven) for making *puerco asado*
(roast pork). If you're lucky, you may be able to
arrange to eat a meal at *La Mesa de los*

Cubanos, an oval table with ceramics of key
figures from each of Cuba's 14 provinces ($8-$9
per person for a group of ten to 15). Fuster sells
his work from his ground-floor gallery, but you
can also go up to the first-floor ceramics studio
to see *La Santa Bárbara*, a two-metre fibro-
cement and ceramic statue. The second-floor
studio is for painting, and above this is *el
mirador*, a lookout decorated with miniature
ceramic works and offering a splendid,
panoramic view of leafy Jaimanitas. Visitors are
welcome at the studio, and Fuster's son and
agent Alex speaks English.

Casa-Estudio de José Fuster

*Calle 226, esquina a 3A, Jaimanitas (213048/
www.geocities.com/jfuster99).* **Open** 10am-6pm Mon-
Fri; closed Sat, Sun. **Admission** free.

Marina Hemingway & beyond

Just west of Río Jaimanitas, at the corner
of Avenida 5ta and Calle 248, is Marina
Hemingway, Havana's main tourist harbour.
The marina provides mooring for up to
100 yachts in four parallel canals, each one
kilometre long, 15 metres wide and six metres
deep. Along with several restaurants (*see p139
and p140*) and a shopping centre, the Marina
offers scuba diving trips to 30 sites from
its **Centro de Buceo 'La Aguja'** (*listings
p107*). For details of the courses on offer,
see p219. The Marina is also known for its

Marina Hemingway is home to the Big Man's annual fishing competition.

Sightseeing

State of the art

Brainchild of Che Guevara, the Higher Institute of Arts is the jewel in the beret of Revolutionary architecture. Built between 1961 and 1965 on the old Country Club golf course, ISA's five schools, set amid a woody landscape, feature splendid Catalan vaulted arches, cupolas, curved passageways and domed halls. Project team coordinator, Cuban architect Ricardo Porro, designed the visual arts and modern dance schools, while other schools were the work of two Italians: Vittorio Garatti (ballet and music) and Roberto Gottardi (dramatic arts). The music school occupies the original country clubhouse; the visual arts school has abundant symbols of feminine and masculine sexuality representing earth, nature and fecundity; and the dramatic arts school, with its narrow passageways and inner courtyards, recalls the canals of Venice. Unfortunately, three of the schools are still incomplete and the wooded grounds and campus river desperately need a good clean-up. The good news, though, is that in 2000, the government arranged a meeting of all three architects to plan the project's completion.

Instituto Superior de Artes (ISA)
Calle 120 #1110, esquina a 9na, Cubanacán (enquiries 288075/isa@cubarte.cult.cu).

catch-and-release **Ernest Hemingway International Fishing Tournament** dating from the 1950s, for which the novelist himself elaborated many of the regulations, and for the spring-time sailing regatta **Corona Internacional**, held along the waters in front of the Malecón. For further details, *see p219*. The woody complex across the street from the Marina's entrance is the **Escuela Superior del Partido Nico López**.

Several kilometres west of the Marina is the **Escuela Latinoamericana de Ciencias Médicas**, which opened in November 1999. Conceived in the aftermath of Hurricane Mitch, which devastated Central America and the Caribbean in 1998, the former coastal Naval Academy teaches medicine to some 4,800 students from 20 countries in Latin America, the Caribbean and Africa.

Another 15 kilometres (9.5 miles) west will bring you to **Baracoa**, a quaint fishing village. When you get here, ask directions to the **Casa de Petrona**. This home is completely covered in shells, and although Petrona herself is now deceased, the extended family continues the tradition. Beyond Baracoa, at the rubbish-strewn and otherwise unrecommendable El Salado beach, is **Hotel Villa Cocomar**, which offers scuba diving and snorkelling, including equipment rental, at its diving centre (Centro de

Buceo 'Blue Reef'). It also has a one-kilometre go-cart track – one of the few in the country – built to international specifications (minimum age eight, with parental permission).

Centro de Buceo 'La Aguja'

Avenida 5ta, esquina a 248, Santa Fé (246848). **Open** *Centre* 10am-4pm daily; dives at 10.30am and some afternoons. **Rates** (incl equipment, instructor & boat) $32-$38 1 immersion; $49-$54 2 immersions.

Hotel Villa Cocomar

Playa El Salado, Carretera Panamericana, km 23.5, Caimito (0680 8293). **Open** *Diving centre* 8am-4pm daily. *Go-cart track* 8am-5pm daily. **Rates** *Diving* (incl equipment, instructor & boat) $30 1 immersion. *Snorkel hire* $5 per half day. *Snorkel & boat hire* $20 per half day. *Carting* $5 for 10min.

Marianao

The word 'Marianao' comes from the Indian word 'Mayanabo', meaning 'land between the waters'; it was the former name of the Río Quibú. In 1976, administrative districts were redrawn and Marianao was divided into three municipalities: Playa, La Lisa and Marianao. The old track joining the district to eastern Puentes Grandes and western Vuelta Abajo is today's Avenida 51, a narrow, winding road that is ill-suited to modern traffic. The old road formed the backbone for the original settlements, which developed here at the end of the 18th century. In the 19th century, local shops and services appeared in Marianao among the homes of the working class and the summer villas of the rich, and with the opening of the railway between Havana and Marianao in 1863, development of the district leapt forward.

Marianao is a part of the city rarely visited by tourists. With its shortage of services, low-quality buildings and deficient street network, the area has suffered from severe urban decay. Yet it offers interesting and important sites that can be reached relatively easily from Avenida 51.

Pogolotti, Havana's first working-class community, was founded here in 1911. It is named after the Italian architect Dino Pogolotti, who built the community's first house. For those interested in medical history, on a little side street is tiny **Finlay Parque**, where the American Walter Reed carried out experiments in 1900, verifying Dr Carlos J Finlay's identification of the transmitting agent for yellow fever. One of two little hut-like labs (Caseta #1) still exists. To get here, take Avenida 51 west to 92, go south six blocks to 59A, then east one block. The roads are very rutted, so take care.

For more of Finlay, take bumpy Avenida 61 one kilometre west to Calle 100 and go north one kilometre to **Plaza Finlay**, actually a

traffic roundabout (at Avenida 31 y Calle 100) with a 32-metre syringe-like obelisk. It was originally constructed in 1944 as a beacon for planes using the military airport at the Columbia Military Camp immediately to the north, but a 1948 medical convention in Havana suggested it should be redesigned with a needle on top as a monument to Finlay. Four classical buildings, housing schools, give the square a harmonious air.

After 1959, the barracks at the Columbia Military Camp – home to dictator Fulgencio Batista from 1953 to 1959 – were turned into Ciudad Escolar Libertad, an educational complex for 12,000 students, and in 1961 they became the headquarters of Cuba's year-long national literacy campaign. Two doors along is the **Museo Nacional de la Campaña de Alfabetización**, which has registers, photos, clothing and books belonging to the 100,000 literacy *brigadistas*, ranging in age from 12 to 19, who took part in the campaign. To reach the museum, enter via the gate at the corner of Calle 76 (to the east) and 29E, then go straight ahead for two blocks.

Back on Avenida 51, a couple of blocks west of Calle 100 is the neoclassical **Iglesia de San Francisco Javier de Los Quemados** (1747). The simple exterior hides a main wooden altar, thought to have originally belonged to the Convento e Iglesia de San Francisco de Asis in La Habana Vieja (*see p66*), plus a pulpit with baroque carvings, a wooden ceiling, original carved pews and some beautiful glass light fixtures. The church serves a neighbourhood, founded in 1720 for indigenous, Spanish and French residents and takes its name – Los Quemados ('the burnt') – from a serious fire in the district, which burned everything except the church.

Several blocks further west and two kilometres south on Calle 114 is a sugar mill, **Central Manuel Martínez Prieto** (1875). The mill originally provided refined sugar to a nearby caramel factory, but today produces sugar for the city, surrounding areas and for export. Although the mill is closed to visitors, parts of it can be seen from the outside, and the adjacent small leafy community of Toledo, with its 1920s wooden bungalows is a delight. Toledo is home to 3,000 people, many of whom once worked in the mill, and celebrates the traditional Fiesta Toledana every May to mark the end of the sugar harvest. Across the road from the mill is the **Instituto Superior Politécnico 'José Antonio Echevarría'** (ISPJAE), built in 1964 on land formerly planted with sugar cane. It's Cuba's main university for engineers and architects, with over 5,000 students, including some from Latin American and Africa.

West on Avenida 51 and one block south on Calle 128B is the former Casa de José Morada (1880), a *casa quinta* with fine ironwork and stained-glass decorative windows that today houses the **Museo Municipal de Marianao** (*see below*). This good local museum houses period furniture, decorative arts, arms and documents. Notable are two letters about an 1845 slave sale, and the colonial kitchen, which is reputed to be one of the best conserved of its kind. The museum has a small art gallery with rotating exhibitions by local artists. Phone first before you head off to the museum as it was planning to close for renovations in early 2001.

Four blocks west on Avenida 57 is the **Fábrica de Tabaco 'Héroes del Moncada'** (*see below*). Occupying a mid-19th-century building, the factory has 471 workers (63 per cent of them women), who produce 18,000 cigars a day for export, including the famous Cohiba. The entire process, from leaf classification to boxing, is done here. Visits to this non-tourist factory must be arranged through CATEC (*see below*), which provides a receipt showing time and date. As tobacco factories are production sites rather than museums, English-speaking guides cannot be guaranteed.

Fábrica de Tabaco 'Héroes del Moncada'

Avenida 57 #13402, entre 134 y 136 (209006). Tickets from: CATEC, Calle 148 #905, entre 9 y 9A, Cubanacán (282064/282164). **Open** *Factory* (only for 45 min tours) 10am, 11am Mon-Fri; closed Sat, Sun. *CATEC* 8.30am-5.30pm Mon-Fri; closed Sat, Sun. **Admission** $10.

Iglesia de San Francisco Javier de Los Quemados

Avenida 51 #10620 (207598). **Open** *Mass* 6pm Tue, Thur; 9am Wed, Fri; 9am, 6pm Sat, Sun; closed Mon. **Admission** free.

Museo de Alfabetización

Avenida 29E, esquina a 76 (208054). **Open** 8am-5pm Mon-Fri; 8am-noon Sat; closed Sun. **Admission** free. **Map** p310 F3.

Museo Municipal de Marianao

Calle 128B #5704, esquina a 57 (209706). **Open** 8.30am-noon, 1-4pm Mon-Sat; closed Sun. **Admission** free.

La Lisa

For an art gallery outside the usual tourist areas, **Galería de Arte Domingo Ravenet** (*see below*) on Avenida 51 is a good stop. It has been promoting applied arts (ceramics, papier mâché, carvings, silverwork and works in skins, metals, glass and textiles) since 1985, and

encourages two important artistic traditions in La Lisa municipality: ceramics from El Cano (*see below*) and artistic glass works. (Cuba's only centre producing such pieces is in La Lisa.) Works from other parts of Havana and by foreign artists are sometimes shown here too.

Located in the woody neighbourhood of La Coronela is the **Museo del Aire**, created in 1986 on a former military base. Anyone interested in aeroplanes will enjoy this out-of-the-way museum. The exhibition halls have displays of historic photos, documents, uniforms and objects, and the large outdoor park has 48 fighter and transport planes, helicopters, anti-aircraft missile batteries and radars. Gems include the blue Cessna piloted by Che Guevara, a rare AT6 from World War II, a P-51 Mustang fighter plane, and samples of Soviet MIG fighters. Note that visitors are charged for any photos or video footage they take in the museum. To get here, take Avenida 51 north to 39, then north again on Calle 212. La Coronela is also home to the **Fundación del Nuevo Cine Latinoamericano** (*see p181*), an old country house where films are shown year round and which is also a major venue for the festival of the same name (*see p182*).

Founded in 1723, **El Cano** is a tiny rural town unengulfed by modern suburbs, and well-known for its pottery (*alfarería*). Pottery-making in the area dates from the 1840s, when artisans from Majorca and the Canary Islands were attracted to the rich red clays found around El Cano. Today 120 potters (*alfareros*) in the village continue to use foot-operated wheels and wood kilns. Since 1945, a three-day Fiesta de los Alfareros has taken place every September to celebrate the potter's craft. Events include street displays, sales and a traditional potters' banquet. Local potters and ceramicists are now developing a community project to help promote their work. Future plans include creating a local Museo Popular de Alfarería. To meet these artisans, contact Rigoberto Gómez Sulimán (tel. 288163), president of the community project. To reach El Cano, take Avenida 51 west to the marked turn-off. For Sulimán's house, take 91 to the end of the tarmac; his house is on the right.

Galería de Arte Domingo Ravenet

Avenida 51 #16001, esquina a 160 (no phone). **Open** 10am-2pm Mon; 10am-6pm Tue-Sat; closed Sun.

Museo del Aire

Avenida 212, entre 29 y 31, La Coronela (217753). **Open** 10am-5pm Tue-Sun; closed Mon. **Admission** $2-$3; free under-12s.

The Eastern Bay & Coast

Two castles and glorious sandy beaches are the outstanding attractions in this part of Havana; but take a closer look and you'll find a whole host of other things worth crossing the bay for.

The most obvious reason for venturing across the bay is to visit the two vast fortresses that stand watch over the harbour channel. But the bayside also shelters the former villages of Casablanca, Regla and Guanabacao, each of which retains its own unique identity, while further east is the Hemingway haunt of Cojimar and the white sands of the Playas del Este.

GETTING THERE

The easiest way to reach the eastern side of the bay is by car or cab, via the road tunnel off Avenida Céspedes just south of La Punta (*see p82*). The tunnel was constructed in 1958, forming the first land link between the two sides of the Bahía de la Habana. From the tunnel exit, you can either follow the clear signs directing traffic to the fortresses, or continue along the Vía Monumental highway towards the eastern suburbs and the Playas del Este. Note that except for tour buses and other authorised transport, the bay tunnel is **closed**

for repair until spring 2001. Alternatively, it is possible to take a ferry from La Habana Vieja across the bay to Casablanca and Regla. The ferry service was established in 1911, and today departs every 15 to 20 minutes (or every hour between midnight and 5am) from the **Muelle de Luz** (map p313 15F). The journey costs ten centavos each way. You can park your car in the nearby lot across the street from the Fundación Havana Club (a tip for the parking attendant is appreciated).

Parque Histórico Militar Morro-Cabaña

Dominating the north-eastern side of the harbour, overlooking La Habana Vieja, are the two fortresses of the **Parque Histórico Militar Morro-Cabaña**. Key players in the defence of the colonial city, these fortresses are now among Havana's most impressive sights.

Serious firepower at the **Castillo de los Tres Reyes del Morro**. *See p110*.

Sightseeing

Castillo de los Tres Reyes del Morro

The earlier of the two structures is the **Castillo de los Tres Reyes del Morro** ('El Morro') at the western tip of Havana bay's entrance. Designed by Italian military engineer Juan Bautista Antonelli and built between 1589 and 1630, this fortress and La Punta (*see p82*) on the other side were built in response to the constant threat of pirates. El Morro sits on a steep rocky outcrop, which serves as its base and part of its walls, and helped it to withstand siege by the British for several weeks in 1762; the fortress only succumbed when a mine was set off beneath its walls.

Along with a deep moat and two batteries, additional defence was originally provided by an ocean-side tower, which was replaced in 1844 by a 45-metre (148-foot) lighthouse, the **Faro del Morro**. The lighthouse has since become a symbol of Havana and offers one of the finest views of the city, especially at sunset. On top of the castle is the **Estación Semafórica** (semaphore station), which has been regulating ship movement in and out of the harbour since 1888 through the use of coloured flags. Other interesting features of the *castillo* include the prisons, which have holes in them through which prisoners were fed to the sharks. Today, as well as wandering through the complex, visitors can see a scale model of El Morro and a display about the history of the bay in the **Sala de Historia del Faro y Castillo**, while the **Sala de Cristóbal Colón** has fascinating displays about Spanish colonial sea voyages to the Americas.

Castillo de los Tres Reyes del Morro

Parque Histórico Militar Morro-Cabaña, Carretera de La Cabaña, Habana del Este (Castillo 637941; Faro 613635). **Open** *Castillo* 8am-8pm daily. *Faro* 10am-8pm daily. **Admission** *Castillo* $2. *Castillo & Faro* $4; free under-12s. **Map** p313 C15/16.

Fortaleza de San Carlos de La Cabaña

In 1763, at the end of the British occupation, construction began on the **Fortaleza de San Carlos de La Cabaña**. Built on ten hectares of ground east of El Morro, this 700-metre-long fortress is the largest in the Americas and has never been attacked. However, the cost of building it was so high (14 million duros) that King Carlos III is reputed to have asked for a spyglass, claiming that such an expensive work could surely be seen from Madrid. La Cabaña is no doubt a luxurious fortress, with a rich

monumental entrance leading to ramps, a covered road, cobbled streets, gardens, a chapel and numerous military structures. Many of the former soldiers' and officers' houses are now restaurants, workshops or boutiques. Museums also abound. The **Museo Monográfico de la Fortaleza** tells the fort's history, with a display of gruesome-looking torture devices and a collection of colonial military paraphernalia; while the **Museo de Fortificaciones y Armas** traces the history of military weaponry through the ages. The **Comandancia del Che Guevara** displays objects used by Che Guevara when he set up his military headquarters in the fortress just after the triumph of the Revolution. Nearby is the baroque **Capilla de San Carlos**, a beautiful chapel where soldiers worshipped San Carlos, patron of the fort, as well as Santa Bárbara and the Virgen del Pilar, a favourite with sea-faring men.

On the eastern side of the complex, most easily accessed from Casablanca (*see p111*) is a part of the fortress that few tourists discover: the **Foso de los Laureles** (Moat of the Laurels). This wide fortified moat has an affecting stillness that is underscored by the immense walls of the bastion. During the 19th century and under the Batista regime in the 20th, dozens of Cuban patriots, who had been incarcerated in La Cabaña, faced firing squads here. A plaque in the wall commemorates their deaths. (The tables were turned after the Revolution, with the execution of counter-Revolutionaries ordered by Che Guevara.) The area of the fortress just beyond the moat is where Soviet missiles were stored during the missile crisis of October 1962 (*see p18*). Examples (thankfully, disarmed) are still on display.

In the early colonial period, a flagship in the harbour fired regular cannon blasts in the morning and at night to signal the opening or closing of the city gates. After La Cabaña was built, the cannon blast was fired from the harbour-side walls of the fortress instead. Today, a squad attired in 19th-century scarlet uniforms continues the **Ceremonia del Cañonazo** (canon-firing ceremony) at 9pm every evening. It is well worth timing your visit to coincide with this evening attraction. Note that visitors are charged for using a camera ($2) or video camera ($5) within La Cabaña.

Fortaleza de San Carlos de La Cabaña

Parque Histórico Militar Morro-Cabaña, Carretera de La Cabaña, Habana del Este (620617/19). **Open** 10am-10pm daily. **Admission** $3 before 6pm; $5 after 6pm; free under-12s. **Map** p313 D/E16.

Bayside Havana

As Havana spread out in concentric circles, it swallowed surrounding villages such as **Casablanca**, **Regla** and **Guanabacoa**. The first two communities have always had a close link with the industrial area of eastern and south-eastern Havana Bay, and been inhabited by less well-off *habaneros* dependent on the sea and harbour for their living.

Casablanca

South-east of La Cabaña is the striking topography of Casablanca. Named after its white-painted 16th-century warehouses, the settlement climbs up a steep hill with the waters of the *bahía* licking at its base. Merchants from Majorca and Catalonia were the first to settle on the southern slopes here, bestowing Casablanca with strong Hispanic roots. During the colonial period, people went from Havana to Casablanca to buy fresh fish, but this trade eventually ceased due to contamination of the bay. Today most visitors come to Casablanca by ferry (*see p109*) to reach La Cabaña fortress, to climb to the Christ statue, or to board the Hershey electric train to Matanzas (*see below* **Chocolate choo-choo**).

Estatua Cristo de La Habana. *See p112.*

Chocolate choo-choo

The picturesque **Tren Eléctrico de Hershey**, Cuba's only electric train, has its western terminus in Casablanca. Built in 1920 by the Hershey Chocolate Company of Pennsylvania, this line linked Havana to the Hershey sugar mill in Matanzas. The mill was part of the Hershey estates, which covered a huge tract of land in Matanzas province, providing sugar cane for chocolate production in the US. For more on the history of the sugar industry in Cuba, *see pp8-9* **Life is sweet**.

The dinky trains still depart from Casablanca at 4.10am, 8.30am and 9.10pm daily for the pleasant 90-kilometre (56-mile) trip through scenic farming communities to Matanzas, returning to Casablanca at 4am, 4.20pm and 9pm. The journey takes about three hours, although the 8.30am train is slightly quicker and makes fewer stops. Tickets are sold in pesos only and should be bought at the station – to your left as you exit the ferry wharf – one hour before departure.

Since 1999, there has also been a passenger service between central Havana and Matanzas from the new La Coubre terminal just south of the central train station (*see p184*). Two trains, combining electric and diesel locomotives, depart at noon and 4pm daily, and travel directly to Matanzas without passing Casablanca. The journey takes two hours and tickets must be purchased at least one hour before departure from the LADIS ticket office at the north-western end of the central train station. Take your passport.

Estación de Casablanca

Carretera de los Cocos, Casablanca (624888). **Tickets** 2.80 pesos; free under-2s.

Terminal La Coubre

Estación Central de Ferrocarriles, Avenida de Bélgica (Egido), esquina a Desamparados, Centro Habana.
Ticket office: LADIS, Calle Arsenal, esquina a Cienfuegos, Centro Habana (614259). **Open** 8am-8pm daily. **Tickets** $3; free under-3s. **Map** p313 F14.

At the top of the hill on Carretera del Asilo, the landmark **Estatua Cristo de La Habana** dominates the surrounding area and offers a sensational view of the city and the bay. This gigantic marble statue – 20 metres (66 feet) high – was sculpted in 1958 by Cuban artist Jilma Madera, and dubbed by some 'the Christ of the sensuous lips'. The statue is supposed to bring good luck, but this seems to depend on who you are – only eight days after it was erected, Batista's regime collapsed. If the sun gets too much for you up here, take refuge at the small kiosk serving light refreshments.

Although you can reach the statue by car (by taking the tunnel to Vía Monumental, then turning on to Carretera del Anilla), the 20-minute walk from the **Muelle de Casablanca** ferry dock is more interesting. One hundred metres north of the dock is a little park, from which you can either climb a staircase to the statue – the views along the way are stunning if you ignore the litter – or follow the road that winds up the hill to the west. This road takes you past a large red gate, usually open, which leads to the south-eastern end of La Cabaña fortress (*see p110*).

Regla

The old town of Regla on the south-eastern side of the bay has always been a major fishing, boat repair and port for Havana, as well as one of the first suburbs outside the city walls. It was founded in 1687, and by the mid 19th century was Havana's most important economic centre, with the largest warehouses (mainly for sugar) in the Caribbean. The many slaves who settled here bequeathed to the area a strong Afro-Cuban religious culture, including the all-male secret society of Abakúa (*see p30*). Regla has a unique atmosphere, very distinct from the city of Havana, and its inhabitants, known for their strong sense of place and identity, call themselves *reglanos* rather than *habaneros*.

As you exit the ferry at **Muelle Regla** on to Calle Santuario, you'll see the neoclassical **Iglesia de Nuestra Señora de Regla** (1818; *listings below*), with its mudéjar panelled ceiling inside. The black Virgen de Regla, housed in this church, is Havana's patron saint and is also associated with Yemayá, goddess of the ocean in the Yoruba pantheon (*see p29*). A couple of blocks up Calle Martí is the **Museo Municipal de Regla** (*listings below*), a small, interesting museum with exhibitions on the history of Regla and a display on the most important gods in Afro-Cuban religions. The museum's archive has a computerised database on the history of the area, including its connections with *santería*. Unfortunately, the exhibits are poorly

explained (if at all) and so risk being virtually meaningless to foreign visitors. The museum plans to open two further gallery spaces in 2001 for its collection of paintings by 20th-century Cuban artists, and may also renovate the astronomical observatory, founded in the building in 1921. Around the corner from the museum is **Galería Taller**, a workshop and exhibition space for the artist engraver Antonio Canet. The gallery can be visited as part of the museum and is well worth a peek.

Further along Calle Martí is the central park, **Parque Guaycanamar**, where you might catch a practice session by the **Guaracheros de Regla** – one of the most famous *comparsas* (dance troupes) in the Havana carnival (*see p168*). A short walk south-west of the park on Calle 24 de Febrero is a high metal staircase, which provides the quickest access to **Colina Lenin** (Lenin Hill; *listings below*), one of the first memorials outside the USSR to the communist leader. A bronze statue of Lenin's face is carved into the hillside surrounded by cement figures and an olive tree planted by the workers of Regla in 1924. A tiny exhibition displays photographs of Lenin, and a commemorative ceremony is held here every year on 21 January, the day of Lenin's death. In the morning light, the view from Colina Lenin provides an unusual perspective of the harbour.

Colina Lenin
Calzada Vieja, entre Enlace y Rotaria (976899). **Open** *Exhibition* 9am-6pm Tue-Sat; 9am-noon Sun; closed Mon. **Admission** free.

Iglesia de Nuestra Señora de Regla
Calle Santuario #11, entre Máximo Gómez y Litoral (976228). **Open** 7.30am-5.30pm Tue-Sun; closed Mon. **Admission** free.

Museo Municipal de Regla y Galería Taller
Calle Martí #158, entre Facciolo y la Piedra (976989). **Open** 9am-6pm Mon-Sat; 9am-1pm Sun. **Admission** $2; free under-12s.

Guanabacoa

Inland from Regla is Guanabacoa, the site where the few surviving native Indians were kept in the 1550s, and which later became the centre of the slave trade. Today Guanabacoa is a lively, colourful town and the heart of Havana's Afro-Cuban religions: Regla de Ocha, Palo Monte and Abakúa (*see p30*). The town's historical urban centre, declared in 1990 by the National Monuments Commission as one of the most important in the capital, has some of the most splendid churches in the region. Guanabacoa is about ten kilometres (six miles) south-east of central Havana and is best reached via the Vía Blanca and the Carretera Vieja de Guanabacoa.

Along the *carretera*, on the land of the old Guanabacoa cemetery, is the **Ermita del Potosí** (1675; *listings below*), the oldest church in Cuba. It has a mudéjar panelled wood ceiling and an original stone floor. A tombstone inside the church, dating from 1747, belongs to frigate Captain Don Juan de Acosta, who wrote his own charming epitaph: 'Traveller, you who treads on me today, stop to think, you will eventually be as I am: ashes.'

Guanabacoa also has two **Jewish cemeteries** (Ashkenazi and Sephardic; *listings below*), located along the old highway about three kilometres south-east of Potosí. Built in 1910 and 1942 respectively, each has a memorial to the six million Jews who died during World War II; inside the memorials are cakes of soap made by the Nazis from the fat of Jews.

Using **Parque Martí**, Guanabacoa's main square, as a reference point, it is an easy walk to visit the most interesting sights. On one side of the park is the 1721 **Iglesia de Nuestra Señora de la Asunción** (locally called Iglesia Parroquial Mayor; *listings below*), with its original ceilings of richly decorated panels and an exquisitely carved, golden-painted altar covered with artwork. The 14 carved and painted Stations of the Cross are among the most beautiful found in any church in Havana. Except for Sunday mass, when the front entrance is open, visitors must enter from the side doors, one of which opens onto the **Plaza Cadena**, where local artisans sell jewellery and handicrafts on the street (9am-5pm daily). Half a block from the *parque* on Calle Pepe Antonio is **Teatro Carral**, which has a lovely large Moorish arch over the entrance. North-east of Parque Martí, the 1748 **Iglesia de Nuestra Señora de la Candelaria** (*listings below*) in the Convento de Santo Domingo is arguably one of the most beautiful churches in Cuba. It has a magnificent panelled ceiling and a striking baroque altar painted in blue with gold decoration. There are no regular visiting hours, but if you call in advance you should be able to look around.

One block west of Parque Martí is the 19th-century Casa de Rosario Lima y Rente, which today houses the **Museo Histórico de Guanabacoa** (*listings below*). Inside are rich displays detailing Guanabacoa's colonial past, plus one of the most important ethnographic collections of ritual objects of Yoruba, Mandinga and Lucumí origin. The museum has been closed for a long time for major restoration, but, with luck, part of it will reopen in early 2001. Meanwhile, there is a tiny display

of Afro-Cuban religious objects in the **Bazar de los Orishas** two blocks further west (*listings below*). Here, handicrafts (paintings and other objects) made by local artists and reflecting the country's Afro-Cuban roots are displayed and sold. El Palenque restaurant is located next door.

One block south on Lamas is the **Convento e Iglesia de San Antonio**, known as 'Los Escolapios' for its dedication to education (*listings below*). Built between 1720 and 1806, the church has lovely mudéjar-style carved wooden ceilings with delicate decorations. Phone in advance to arrange a visit.

Bazar de los Orishas

Calle Martí #175, esquina a Lamas (979510). **Open** 9.30am-5pm Mon-Fri; 10am-2pm Sat; closed Sun. **Admission** *Bazar* free. *Museum* $1.

Cementerio de la Comunidad Religiosa Ebrea Adath Israel (Ashkenazi)

Avenida de la Independencia Este, entre Obelisco y Puente (976644). **Open** 8-11am, 2-5pm Mon-Fri, Sun; closed Sat. **Admission** free.

Cementerio de la Unión Hebrea Chevet Ahim (Sephardic)

Calle G, entre 5ta y Final (975866). **Open** 7am-5pm daily. **Admission** free.

Convento e Iglesia de San Antonio 'Los Escolapios'

Calle Máximo Gómez, esquina a San Antonio (977241). **Open** *Mass* 5pm Tue-Sun; closed Mon. **Admission** free.

Ermita del Potosí

Cementerio Viejo de Guanabacoa, Carretera Vieja de Guanabacoa, esquina a Potosí (information 979867). **Open** *Cemetery* 8am-5pm daily. *Hermitage* 8am-noon Mon-Sat; 8-10am Sun. *Mass* 8.30am Sun. **Admission** free.

Iglesia de Nuestra Señora de la Asunción

Calle División (Guiral) #331, entre Martí y Cadenas (977368). **Open** 8.30am-noon Mon-Fri; 8.30am-11.30am Sat; closed Sat. *Mass* 8pm Tue-Thur; 9.15am Sun. **Admission** free.

Iglesia de Nuestra Señora de la Candelaria

Convento de Santo Domingo, Calle Santo Domingo #407, esquina a Lebredo (977376). **Open** *Convento* 8am-noon, 3-5pm Tue-Sun, closed Mon. *Church* (for Mass only) 8am Tue-Sat; 10am Sun. **Admission** free.

Museo Histórico de Guanabacoa

Calle Martí #108, entre Valenzuela (Versalles) y Bandera (979117). **Open** 10am-6pm Mon, Wed-Sat; 9am-1pm Sun; closed Tue. **Admission** $2; free under-12s.

Sightseeing

Habana del Este

Bounded by the bay on the east, Havana grew towards the west until it reached Río Almendares – a watery barrier, but one that was easy to overcome. More difficult was the creation of a land link between the city and the eastern shore, with its wide beaches and endemic vegetation. With the construction of the bay tunnel and the Vía Monumental highway, however, this was finally achieved.

In the early 1960s, construction along the eastern shore began with a coastal urban complex called **Ciudad Camilo Cienfuegos**. Occupying 28 hectares and built for 8,000 people, the complex has houses and apartments intermingled with gardens, squares and parking lots. Unfortunately, the quality of planning and construction was not maintained in **Alamar** and other areas along the coast, where, in the 1970s, voluntary teams of amateur construction workers known as *microbrigadas* produced monotonous dormitory communities of prefabricated apartment blocks lacking parks, public areas, road signs, proper services or social life. Despite these disadvantages, Alamar has developed a strong youth culture; it is the home of Cuba's annual rap festival (*see p168* **A load of rap**), an event that attracts acts from the US, as well as local talent.

Located between the bay and Ciudad Camilo Cienfuegos is a fascinating archaeological park, the location of the last fortress constructed by the Spanish Crown in the Americas. Built in 1897, **Fuerte No.1** is a noteworthy example of modern military architecture, with an ingenious system of trenches and underground constructions and walkways. It is possible to reach Fuerte No.1 by taking the (unmarked) road west from Ciudad Camilo Cienfuegos and then the first right, but this trip should not be attempted by lone travellers. To the east is the run-down **Estadio Panamericano**, built for the 11th Pan-American Games, which were held in Cuba in 1991. The stadium is still the largest sports complex in the city, but many of the facilities are in a rather sorry state (*see p219*). Neighbouring **Ciudad Panamericana** was built at the same time to house the athletes, and later given to the workers who undertook its construction. The complex has a central avenue leading towards the coast, lined with dilapidated low-rise apartment buildings and small ground-floor shops.

Further along the coast to the east is **Cojímar**, a small traditional fishing community set in a little cove at the mouth of the Río Cojímar. Tropical trees grow along the steep western banks, the only zone in this area with examples of its original vegetation. Although it has its own special charms, Cojímar – a popular spot for catching swordfish – was made famous by the fact that Hemingway docked his boat *Pilar* here and often drank and ate in **La Terraza**, his favourite local restaurant (*listings p115*). Located on the western river bank, the restaurant is full of black and white photos of Hemingway – many shot by famous Cuban photographers Raúl Corrales and Alberto 'Korda' Gutiérrez – accompanied by captain Gregorio Fuentes and various fish. Fuentes was the model for the fisherman in *The Old Man and the Sea*, and was still in fine fettle in 2000, aged 103. If you eat at the restaurant, try Paella Terraza de Cojímar ($7.20) or a whole lobster ($29.95). Reservations are recommended to avoid losing your table to a coach tour group.

In 1962, local residents erected the **Monumento a Ernest Hemingway** in honour of their most famous visitor. The monument is down the street from the restaurant and consists of a pseudo-Greek rotundo, sheltering a bronze bust of the author, grinning and gazing out to sea. Across the street is the **Fuerte de Cojímar** (known as El Torreón), a mini fort built on the north-west spit of land at the river's mouth. Allegedly, it was a lapse of attention at the fort that enabled the British to land at the river here before marching on Havana in 1762. Although the inside of the fort is still in military use and inaccessible to the public, you can walk near it without hindrance.

East of the Río Cojímar are the soul-destroying high-rises of Alamar, which extend as far as the Río Bacuranao. On the western side of the river's mouth is a Spanish watchtower, **Torreón de Bacuranao**, which houses a military academy, while stretching away to the east is the **Playa Bacuranao**. Because it is the closest

Uninspired housing in Alamar.

Following in Ernie's footsteps at **La Terraza**.

beach to Havana, Bacuranao – a gravelly stretch of sand separated from the other beaches of the Playas del Este (*see below*) by reefs – is inevitably the most crowded.

Bar-Restaurante La Terraza

Calle Real #161, esquina a Candelara, Cojímar (559232). **Open** *Bar* 10.30am-11pm daily. *Restaurant* noon-11pm daily. **Main courses** $6-$29.95.

Playas del Este

Just 20 minutes east of Havana, the Playas del Este are the main recreational beach area for the city. To reach them, follow the (sometimes confusing) signs from Via Monumental and Via Blanca. The pine- and coconut-fringed beaches are really a single eight-kilometre stretch with changing names: Tarará, El Mégano, Santa María del Mar, Boca Ciega and Guanabo. About a dozen large resort hotels, mainly ghastly structures built in the 1960s and '70s, are scattered between Tarará and Guanabo, with the majority in Santa María del Mar. This part of the strip is the also the most heavily patrolled by uniformed security guards to control prostitution and *jineteros*.

Tarará is a spacious, partially woody complex with two beaches. Since March 1990, nearly 16,000 radiation-affected children and over 2,800 adults from the 1986 Chernobyl disaster in the Ukraine have received free medical treatment at the hospital here. The eastern beach has grainy sand and is the true start of the Playas del Este beach strip.

The western beach, located in a protected cove at the mouth of Río Tarará, is postage-stamp size and perfect for small children. Here, **Marina Puertosol Tarará** (Via Blanca km 18; 971462) provides mooring for up to 50 yachts and rents out equipment for various aquatic activities: scuba diving, snorkelling, deep sea fishing and yachting (*see also p219*). Other facilities available include accommodation (*see p60*), a swimming pool,

a discotheque, restaurant and bar. The Marina also organises international blue marlin fishing tournaments each year.

East is **Playa Mégano**, which has coarser sand but is still a pleasant enough base for swimming and sunning. The beach is backed by trees and pines, and a 50-cabin tourist complex built in the 1960s as part of a national plan to develop beaches for popular use.

The next beaches to the east are Santa María del Mar, Boca Ciega and Guanabo, a trio of creamy sands and crystalline turquoise blue waters, backed by coconut trees, pines and bluffs reaching to 80 metres. **Santa María** is the most beautiful beach in the area and an attractive alternative to Varadero, however, it is also the most touristy, with beer cans and other litter spread along its sands. Throughout the entire zone are restaurants, lodgings, grocery stores (mainly at Santa María) street-side cafés and watersports centres hiring out equipment. Horses and motorbikes can also be hired.

Just inland from the coast to the east of Santa María is **Laguna Itabo**, a lagoon with shallow estuaries, dense vegetation and several tiny islands, at the mouth of Río Itabo. The lagoon is a breeding ground for marine animals, reef fish and freshwater fish, while thick mangroves provide a rest stop for migratory herons, ducks and pelicans from the Florida Straits, and a nesting area for Cuban doves. Half-hour tours around the lagoon ($10 per person) are accompanied by English-speaking biologist Alberto Quilez, a native of the area and an estuary specialist. On the largest of the lagoon's lakes is **Mi Cayito** (*listings p116*), a small lush islet with a restaurant, cafeteria, and water bikes, kayaks and speedboats for hire. On the northerly (beach side) of the island you can rent sun loungers and sun umbrellas, catamarans and snorkelling equipment during the day.

East of the lagoon is a narrow wooden bridge across Río Itabo, which divides Santa María from **Playa Boca Ciega**. With white sand, palm-edged dunes and a gradual sandy incline into the water, this is a good beach for young children and is often crowded with Cuban families. For a fancy meal in a homely atmosphere, **La Casa del Pescador** (*listings p116*) offers good medium-priced seafood, while around the corner (Calle 444) are several snack bars and motorcycle and bicycle rental outlets.

After Boca Ciega is wee **Playa Hermosa** (blink and you'll miss it), and then **Playa Guanabo**, whose sun-faded wooden houses and seaside atmosphere make up for the slightly poorer-quality sand. With more Cubans and no big hotels, Guanabo is more laid back

Take it easy at **Santa María del Mar**, one of the area's most popular beaches. *See p115.*

than Santa María; Avenida 5ta-C is full of snack bars, restaurants and shops, with easy-to-find *paladares* on side streets and a local farmer's vegetable market daily except Monday (between Calles 5B and 5C). One of Guanabo's most charming restaurants is **El Brocal** (*see p141*), located in a 1930s wooden house.

If you need a culture injection after lazing on the beach, head to the **Museo Municipal de Habana del Este** in Guanabo (*listings below*). Occupying an enchanting old yellow wooden house, the museum has displays on the region's aboriginal history, the story of Guanabo's first house, plus an unusual salt-water fish tank. One block east is **Nuestra Señora de Carmen**, the oldest church in Guanabo and interesting mainly for its delightful front entrance. At the eastern end of Guanabo, is **Rincón de Guanabo**, a tiny cove with local flora and fauna that, in the future, will become an ecological park.

During July and August only, electric trains from Casablanca (*see p111*) stop once a day at Guanabo's **Estación Playas del Este** (off Vía Blanca), several blocks from the beach. Alternatively, bus No.400 to Guanabo leaves every hour or so from **Taya Piedra** park, two blocks east of Estación Cristina in Havana.

La Casa del Pescador

Avenida 5 #44005, esquina a 442, Playa Boca Ciega (963653). **Open** noon-11pm daily. **Map** p315 B26.

Mi Cayito

Avenida Las Terrazas, Laguna Itabo, Santa María del Mar (971339). **Open** *Sept-June* 10am-6pm daily. *July, Aug* 10am-10pm daily. **Map** p314 A/B24.

Museo Municipal de Habana del Este

Calle 504 #5B12, esquina a 5C, Guanabo (964184). **Open** 9am-4pm Mon-Fri; 9am-noon Sat; closed Sun. **Admission** free. **Map** p315 B31.

Inland

South of Guanabo is the turn-off to **Mirador de Bellomonte**, a hilltop café and bar (*listings below*). Its shady patio offers a fine view north to the coast and south to the lovely palm-studded Valle de Jústiz and Campo Florido. From the Mirador, an easy walk takes you to the ruins of Guanabo's earliest residence – a 17th-century mansion, which still retains its original slave chains in the basement.

Four kilometres south of the intersection of Vía Blanca and Calle 462 on Calzadea de Jústiz (follow the turn-off to 'La Finca') are adjacent tourist haciendas: **La Finca Guanabita** and **Rancho Mi Hacienda** (*listings below*). Covering 25 hectares of the beautiful Campo Florido area, they offer accommodation in seven basic but comfortable cabins, with cribs available upon request. Facilities include swimming pools (microscopic at the Rancho), snack bars, restaurants (traditional Cuban dishes and seafood for modest prices) and a range of activities: riding, boating, motorcycling and fishing. A rather overgrown tributary of Río Itabu flows through the Rancho, a short stretch of which is navigable in rowing boats. Unfortunately, very loud music disturbs the pastoral peace and quiet, and the mosquitoes are terrible during the rainy season.

La Finca Guanabita/ Rancho Mi Hacienda

Calzada de Jústiz km 4, Campo Florido (Finca 964610/Rancho 964711/964712). **Open** *Finca* 9am-6pm daily. *Rancho* 9am-9pm daily. **Rates** *Cabins* $25 per day. **Map** p315 D27.

Mirador de Bellomonte

Vía Blanca km 24.5, Altura Bellomonte (963431). **Open** 2pm-2am daily. **Map** p315 D29.

Cerro & Further South

Southern Havana's green spaces offer some respite from its populated *barrios*. But it's worth making the trip down this way to see its lesser-known sights too.

Cerro

If La Habana Vieja did not exist, Cerro – meaning hill – would be the city's historic centre. Here, 18th-century aristocrats escaping the congestion and pollution of Old Havana built their neo-classical *casas quintas* (summer houses). Little by little, stylish and splendid haciendas were built on both sides of Calzada del Cerro – the main artery to this area. But the poor always lived amid the palaces, and later, many mansions became tenement houses, which are now in a bad state of repair.

Located along Calzada de Cerro is the most elegant and luxurious of the 19th-century summer villas, the neo-classical **Quinta del Conde de Santovenia** (Calzada de Cerro #1424, entre Auditor y Patria, tel. 706449). Built in 1845, it was formerly the social meeting place of Havana's aristocracy, but has been a home for the elderly (Hogar de Ancianos) since 1896. The house is usually closed to tourists, but you may be able to arrange a visit by telephone. Additions to the original building include an imposing neo-gothic chapel (1929), which occupies most of the large courtyard.

Directly across the street from Santovenia is the **Fábrica de Ron Bocoy** (*see below*), the only rum factory in the city still using traditional methods and materials. Here, 40 workers produce 6,000 bottles of rum, liquors, spirits and wines each day. Built in the late 19th century, the residence has been a rum factory since 1937 and is known locally as La Casa de Culebras (House of Snakes) after the carved snakes that curl around the wooden swans on the front porch. Upstairs is a small museum with old rum-making equipment, and there's also a shop selling factory brands (Legendario and Bocoy) and others, plus tobacco and coffee.

Despite the continued operation of the 1592 Zanja Real and Fernando VII's 1827 aqueduct (*for both, see p72*) carrying water from the Río Almendares to the city, by the mid 19th century Havana was facing a water shortage. In 1856 engineer Francisco de Albear y Lara proposed and oversaw the construction of a new aqueduct based on gravity-fed water from the Vento springs ten kilometres (six miles) to

the south. The neo-classical **Pabellón de los Depósitos del Acueducto de Albear** (Calle Fomento, off Calzada de Palatino, between Chaple and Recreo) is a masterpiece of architecture and hydro-engineering, and won awards in International Expositions in Philadelphia (1876) and Paris (1878). Today, it still provides 20 per cent of Havana's water.

At the southern end of Calzada Palatino is the delightful **Quinta Las Delicias** (1905; *listings p119*). Designed by Charles Brun, this French-style mansion with its castellated parapet is surrounded by beautiful gardens with fountains, pergolas, woods and a small neo-gothic family chapel. The former home of Rosalia Abreu, it is popularly known as the Finca de los Monos (Monkeys' Villa) after the 180 monkeys that Rosalia allowed to roam free in the grounds. The interior has elaborately decorated ceilings and there's a mural by Cuban artist Armando Merucal in the vestibule. Today, part of the grounds is used as a youth centre under the administration of the Union de los Pioneros de Cuba (UPC). To visit, contact Hector Cristóbal, the organisation's director of international relations.

Two kilometres south-east of the Finca de los Monos is the exquisite **Iglesia de los Pasionistas** (officially the Parroquia del Sagrado Corazón de Jesús y San Pablo de la Cruz; *listings p119*). Hidden away down Calle Vista Alegre Este, this treasure has two tall towers and a magnificent interior with a stunning gilded altar, stained-glass windows and a pretty organ. The topography of the surrounding area is defined by *lomas* (hillocks), which once afforded panoramic views of the city. (An example is the Jesús del Monte, which is topped by a small 19th-century church and chapel.) Unfortunately the views from the *lomas* are now blocked by buildings and the access roads are in poor condition.

One of Havana's best *agromercados*, **Cuatro Caminos** (*see p84*), is officially within Cerro district, though it's actually just on the edge of – and easier to enter from – Centro Habana.

Fábrica de Ron Bocoy

Calzada del Cerro #1416, entre Auditor y Patria (705642). **Open** 9am-5pm Mon-Sat; 9am-1pm Sun. **Admission** free.

The importance of being Ernest

Ernest Hemingway (1899-1961) spent more than 20 years of his life in Cuba, and many of his best (and best-loved works) are based on the island. He was first drawn to Cuba by the promise of big game fishing in the 'great blue river' of the Gulf Stream and remained a keen fisherman throughout his life. But his relationship with the island ultimately ran far deeper than the marlin he loved to catch. Although his attitude to the Revolution has never been wholly established, Hemingway's writings depict the repression of pre-Revolutionary Havana and seem to support a central premise of social and moral justice. He is still revered among *habaneros* as a faithful friend, and his connection with the island is an undoubted lure for many literary tourists. A visit to Cuba would not be complete without checking out some of Papa's favourite places.

Basílica de Nuestra Señora del Cobre

The author donated his 1954 Nobel Prize to the home of the patron saint of Cuba in El Cobre in the province of Santiago de Cuba. Unfortunately the medal is now stored in a vault away from light-fingered visitors. *See p260* **Virgin on the fanatical**.

La Bodeguita del Medio

As the chalkboard at the bar testifies, Papa came to this restaurant in La Habana Vieja to drink *mojito*, before popping down the road for a daiquiri at El Floridita. *See p127.*

Cojímar

Hemingway's beloved boat *El Pilar* was moored in the harbour of this coastal village to the east of Havana. The writer would come to the village to eat at one of his favourite restaurants, **La Terraza** (*see p147*), and to chat with his old friend Gregorio Fuentes, the model for the fisherman in Nobel Prize-winning *The Old Man and the Sea* (1952). In 1962 the citizens of Cojímar erected the **Monumento a Ernest Hemingway** in honour of their most famous visitor (*see p114*).

El Floridita

Hemingway's daiquiri drinking den is now packed with visitors hoping to capture that quintessential Hemingway moment. *See p128.*

La Finca Vigía

This house, with its beautiful views, was Hemingway's home from 1939 to 1960 and has been carefully preserved as the Museo Ernest Hemingway. The author wrote *The Old Man and the Sea* here in 1952. *See p119.*

Hotel Ambos Mundos

During his visits to Havana in the 1930s, Hemingway stayed in Room 511. The room has been recreated as it was when he wrote his account of the Spanish Civil War, *For Whom the Bell Tolls* in 1940. *See p119.*

Jardines del Rey

Islands in the Stream is based on Hemingway's own experience of hunting German U-boats off the northern coast of Cuba during World War II.

Marina Hemingway

Since 1950 the marina has hosted the Ernest Hemingway Marlin Fishing Tournament. Many of the rules and regulations for the big catch were compiled by the author. *See p105.*

Iglesia de los Pasionistas

Vista Alegre Este, esquina a Buenaventura (990464). **Open** 7.30-11am, 3-7pm Mon-Sat; 7.30am-noon, 3-7pm Sun. *Mass* 8am, 6pm Mon-Sat; 8am, 9.30am, 11am and 6pm Sun. **Admission** free.

Quinta Las Delicias (Finca de los Monos)

Calle Santa Catalina, esquina a Palatino (information 670205/670258). **Open** by appointment only; phone to arrange a visit. **Admission** free.

South-eastern Havana

San Miguel del Padrón

Located south of the bay, San Miguel del Padrón is an old working-class neighbourhood that is often overlooked by tourists; however, it is an area with several sights that merit a visit. Across the street from the junction of Calzada de Luyanó and Carretera Central is the **Fuente de la Virgen del Camino** (Fountain of the Virgin of the Way), which features a statue of the Virgin by sculptress Rita Longa. The donations tossed into the fountain are given to the city's orphans, poor and invalids. East of here, in a shady neighbourhood park on Calle Balear, is a little-known monument to the mother of José Martí. **Monumento a Doña Leonor Pérez** depicts a dignified Doña Leonor sitting on a marble pedestal holding a book, while around the base, three bronze reliefs show José Martí at key moments in his life: giving a public talk; doing forced labour at the San Lázaro quarry (*see p86*); and receiving his mortal battle wound at Dos Ríos.

One of San Miguel del Padron's best-kept secrets are the papier mâché artisans working in the **Juanelo** neighbourhood. In 1970, local artist Antonia Eiriz began teaching children how to make papier mâché puppets as part of a national programme to disseminate art within local communities. Today, around 15 families (amounting to almost 50 people) dedicate themselves to this art form. To see local artisans in action and have a chance to buy their work, head for the **Trabajo Comunitario del Reparto Juanel Silvia Fernández Rodríguez** (*see below*). Silvia, a former student of Eiriz, works from home with her entire family to produce papier mâché fans, children's toys, masks, jewellery, and mobiles. Silvia and her mother also make papier mâché furniture, usually to order: chairs, sofas, screens, picture frames, tables, lamps and more. The Rodríguez workshop and home is located on Pasaje 2, just off Calle Piedra to the west of Calzada de Güines.

Trabajo Comunitario del Reparto Juanelo Silvia Fernández Rodríguez

Pasaje 2 #5, entre Piedra y Soto, Juanelo (916752 neighbour). Phone first to arrange a visit. **Admission** free.

La Finca Vigía

Located in San Francisco de Paula, 15 kilometres (9.5 miles) south-east of the city centre, La Finca Vigía was the home of Ernest Hemingway from 1939 until he returned to the US in 1960. It is the place where he wrote *The Old Man and the Sea*, which won him the Nobel Prize for Literature in 1952. The 19th-century country house sits on top of a hill and has such splendid views of the surrounding landscape that Hemingway's wife persuaded him to build an observation tower next to the house. On his departure from Cuba, Hemingway left his estate to the Cuban people; the house has been meticulously preserved as the **Museo Ernest Hemingway** (*listings p120*). Inside the house are Hemingway's African safari hunting trophies, shoes, clothing, guns, glasses, correspondence, his old Royal typewriter and half-drunk bottles – everything exactly as he left it. Entrance to the house is prohibited unless accompanied by an

Jardín Botánico Nacional. *See p121.*

Sightseeing

official guide – English-speaking guides are available – however, the interior can be seen clearly through the windows and visitors can look around the grounds unaccompanied. There is also a charge for taking photos ($5 each) or using a video camera ($50 per hour). To reach La Finca Vigía, take Calzada de Güines as far as Calle Vigía and go east up the hill, alternatively you can brave the M-7 *camello* bus from Parque de la Fraternidad (*see p82*) in Centro Habana. Note that the museum closes when it rains.

Museo Ernest Hemingway
La Finca Vigía, off Calzada de Güines, San Francisco de Paula (910809). **Open** 9am-4pm Mon, Wed-Sat; 9am-12.30pm Sun; closed Tue. **Admission** $3; free under-12s.

Santa María del Rosario

Santa María del Rosario, 15 kilometres (9.5 miles) south-east of the capital, is a charming old colonial town founded in 1732 by José Bayona y Chacón, the first Count of Casa Bayona. The count, bedridden with rheumatism, was cured by an old slave using healing waters from a secret spring. In return, the slave was freed. The count is the subject of the Gutiérrez Alea film *La Última Cena* (*The Last Supper*; 1976), a complex indictment of religious hypocrisy and cultural colonisation in late 18th-century Havana.

The central square of this village is shady and well maintained. On one side is the **Iglesia de Santa María del Rosario** (1766), locally known as the Catedral de los Campos de Cuba (Cathedral of the Fields of Cuba). Inside are the original baroque altars and pulpit carved of precious gilded woods, a rough-carved stone floor, a ceiling made of *jigüi* (indigo) wood and religious artworks, including four large pechinas (art works hanging from a cross beam) painted by José Nicolás de Escalera, Cuba's first important artist. One of them shows the Count, his family, and the slave who cured him, and is the first pictorial representation in Cuba of a black man. The pechinas are currently undergoing restoration at the National Centre for Preservation, Conservation and Museology in Old Havana.

The Casa del Conde Bayona, the Count's ancestral manor house, is also on the square. Since 1985, the **Bar El Mesón** (*see below*), has been serving beer, soft drinks and occasionally a few snacks (pesos only) on its shaded side patio. The Count's coach house, located to the side of the church, is divided into three homes, one of which can be visited (Calle 33, #2404) to see the stable's original thick walls and

Parque Lenin or bust. *See p121.*

cistern for catching rainwater. Nearby is the **Casa de la cultura** (*see below*), which has a faded but captivating mural by local artist Manuel Mendive. Local musicians get together here every Sunday evening at 8.30pm for a *peña* called Descarga en mi terraza (Unwind on my Terrace).

Behind El Mesón is the **Loma 'La Cruz** (Hill of the Cross), which gives a splendid view of the palm tree-studded fields surrounding the town and of distant Havana. The hill takes its name from the large cross erected here by the Count in memory of those that died in Cuba's first slave uprising. At the base of the *loma* in a small wooded valley off Calle 31 is the **Balneario de Santa María del Rosario** (*see below*), a spa consisting of four or five natural springs and two modest skin clinics.

The town has neither restaurants nor *paladares*, but fruit and vegetables are available at its small agricultural market on Calle 20 (on the corner with 31), open from 7am to 6pm Tuesday to Sunday. To reach Santa María del Rosario by bus, take the M-7 from Havana to Cotorro and change on to bus No.97.

Balneario Santa María del Rosario
Calle 30, esquina a Final (06820 2734). **Open** 8am-4pm Mon-Fri; closed Sat, Sun. **Admission** free.

Bar El Mesón
Avenida 31, entre 24 y 26 (06820 3510). **Open** noon-10pm daily.

Casa de la cultura
Avenida 33 #202, esquina a 24 (06820 4259). **Open** 7am-10pm daily. **Admission** free.

Iglesia de Santa María del Rosario
Calle 24, entre 31 y 33 (06820 2183). **Open** 8am-noon Tue-Sat; 3.30-7pm Sun; closed Mon. *Mass* 8am Thur; 5pm Sun.

South central Havana

Urbanised Havana spreads out like five fingers from the port, with green areas in between. A few scattered factories, warehouses and industrial workshops are interspersed with semi-rural settlements surrounded by fertile agricultural lands. Southern Havana is best known for its four vast areas of parkland: Parque Lenin, Parque Zoológico Nacional, Jardín Botánico Nacional and ExpoCuba. On your way south, you might also want to check out **Casa-Museo Hurón Azul** ('Blue Ferret' Museum; *listings p122*). The only museum in Arroyo Naranjo (Párraga district), it consists of the house and leafy grounds where Cuban painter Carlos Enríquez (1900-1957) spent the last 18 years of his life.

Located 20 kilometres from central Havana, **Parque Lenin** incorporates 6.7 square kilometres (2.6 square miles) of natural landscape (*listings p122*). The dream of Sierra Maestra heroine Celia Sánchez Manduley and designed by lead architect Antonio Quintana, it was created in 1969 as the first park of the Revolution. Soil was added to improve the eroded land and 160,000 trees, including oak, carob, silk-cotton, linden, pine, cedar, palm and rubber were planted. The nine-metre (30-foot) marble bust to Lenin, carved in 1982 by Soviet sculptor L E Kerbel, was the first such monument in the Americas. Also inside the confines of the park are a nine-kilometre (5.5-mile) narrow-gauge railway, an amusement park, several cafeterias and restaurants (notably Las Ruinas, built around old ruins; *see p143*), the Centro Ecuestre riding stables, a freshwater aquarium (closed for general repair), an amphitheatre, an artificial lake and more. A couple of houses in the park have been turned into Galería Amelia Peláez and Taller Cerámica, which exhibit art and ceramics. Every other Sunday (from 9am to 5pm), the small Rodeo Nacional is held in the park, featuring horse riding, rowing, children's activities and an evening disco in Café del Rodeo. Immediately to the west of Parque Lenin is **Calabazar**, a small village with an 18th-century square and church and a community of potters and ceramicists.

Easily accessible from Parque Lenin is **Parque Zoológico Nacional**, created in 1984 from 11 abandoned farms (*listings p122*). On its 343 hectares are almost 1,000 animals representing more than 110 species. Tour buses (included in the cost of entry) trawl through an African prairie habitat for giraffes, zebras, antelopes and rhinoceroses, with lakes for the hippopotamuses, and a large open area with trees, rocks and caves for the lions. The Área de Reproducción leaves nothing to the imagination,

with over 30 endangered species reproducing in small cages. In the Zoo Infantil, children can get close to young animals born in the zoo and ride ponies. The zoo is very large and has little shade, so it would be impossible to see it all on foot; car passengers are charged $3 per person including the optional hire of a guide.

The best thing about the **Jardín Botánico Nacional** (*listings p122*) are the three large exhibition pavilions near the main entrance with collections of cacti, desert plants and tropical mountain vegetation. Two of the pavilions have (bumpy) wheelchair access and one has a shady little café serving drinks. Located south of Parque Lenin, the rest of the 600-hectare garden is divided into open-air geographic zones – Cuba, America, Africa, Asia and Oceania – featuring 150,000 examples of 4,000 species of trees. The variety of palms is wonderful. You can mosey around on foot (make sure you take a sun hat), by car with an obligatory guide or in bus-tractors at no extra cost. Note, however, that the garden lacks written information identifying the species, and English-speaking guides tend to be mainly for larger groups. The beautiful Jardín Japonés, designed with the help of Japanese specialists, has the finest (indeed, only) vegetarian restaurant in Havana – **El Bambú** (also uniquely, it has wheelchair access; *see p142* **Vegging out**). Elsewhere in the gardens are several other restaurants and small (but infrequent) booths selling a few snacks and botanical literature (in Spanish).

Across the road from the Botanical Gardens is **ExpoCuba**, Cuba's largest exhibition fair (*listings p122*). Its 25 pavilions feature self-congratulatory and, frankly, tedious displays on the main achievements of the Revolution in terms of health, education, culture, sports, geology and mining, chemistry, the economy, energy, tourism, light industry, fishing and defence. ExpoCuba also has a 500-seat open-air amphitheatre, a small decorative waterfall, an amusement park and a restaurant-observatory with a view of the entire complex. An international trade fair takes place here every November, so the site is closed to visitors between September and December.

Just north of the turn off to Terminal 1 of the José Martí Airport is the **Feria Agropecuaria**, famous for its summer rodeo, which takes place on the last weekend of August (*listings p122; see also p214*). The rodeo is the real deal, with horse competitions, bull riding and roping, rodeo clowns, music, dancing and even sales of cowboy hats, and is so popular that it may be held monthly in the future. Parking is available across the street at the Mexican-style Escuela Técnico Industrial Julio A Mella.

Casa-Museo Hurón Azul

*Calle Paz, entre Constancia y Lindero, Párraga
(578246).* **Open** 9am-noon, 1-5pm Tue-Sat; 9am-1pm
Sun; closed Mon. **Admission** $2; no concessions.

ExpoCuba

Carretera del Rocío km 3.5, Calabazar (578284).
Open *Jan-Aug* 9am-5pm Tue-Sun; closed Mon.
Sept-Dec closed. **Admission** $1.

Feria Agropecuaria

*Avenida de la Independencia (Rancho Boyeros)
#31108, Boyeros (06 834536).* **Open** phone for
details. **Admission** $5.

Jardín Botánico Nacional

Carretera del Rocío km 3.5, Calabazar (544102).
Open 8.30am-4.30pm (last entry 3.30pm) daily. *El
Ranchón* 11am-3pm daily. **Admission** *Pedestrians*
$1; $0.50 concessions. *Car passengers* (accompanied
by a guide) $3; $1.50 concessions. *Parking* free if
accompanied by guide, otherwise $2.

Parque Lenin

*Calle 100, esquina a Cortina de la Presa, Arroyo
Naranjo (443026/Centro Ecuestre 441058/442819/
Rodeo 578893).* **Open** *Park* 24hrs daily. *All venues
within the park* 9am-5pm Tue-Sun; closed Mon.
Admission *Park* free. *Galería Amelia Peláez* $1.
Horse riding/classes $10/hr.

Parque Zoológico Nacional

*Entrance 1: Avenida de la Independencia
(Rancho Boyeros), esquina a 243, Fontanar.
Entrance 2: Avenida Soto, esquina a Zoo-Lenin,
Boyeros (578063/578054).* **Open** 9.30am-3.30pm
Wed-Sun; closed Mon, Tue. **Admission** $3; $2
concessions.

Around Santiago de las Vegas

Two kilometres south of José Martí Airport
is **Santiago de las Vegas**, a laid-back
provincial town. Near the charming central
square is the **Iglesia Parroquial de
Santiago de las Vegas** (*see below*), built in
1694. A 1944 renovation added a cupola of
coloured tiles that contrasts with the rest of
the ancient building. A few blocks south-west is
the **Vivero de Begonia**, a privately owned
nursery that welcomes visitors (*see below*). On
three hectares of land, flowers and ornamental
plants are cultivated for sale to La Habana
Vieja through the Historian's Office. Notable is
the striking 50-year-old *Corupita giyanensi*, a
large species of tree from Guyana with flowers
on stalks growing out of the trunk. Less than 20
such trees exist in Cuba. Six kilometres (3.5
miles) south of Santiago is **El Cacahual**, an
open-air hilltop mausoleum built in 1944 to
honour Antonio Maceo, Lieutenant-General of
the Liberation Army and Francisco Gómez Toro
('Panchito'), son of Máximo Gómez, both of
whom died in the battle of Punta Brava in 1896.

Room to roam at the **Parque
Zoológico Nacional**. *See p121.*

South-west of Santiago de las Vegas is
one of Cuba's most important pilgrimage
destinations, the **Santuario de San Lázaro**,
known as El Rincón after the tiny village
where it is located (*see below*). Every 17
December, this tranquil village is inundated
with thousands of Cubans from all around the
country who come to venerate Saint Lazarus
(San Lázaro), who is associated with Babalú
Ayé, the Yoruba god of smallpox, leprosy and
other skin diseases in Afro-Cuban religions.
Pope John Paul II also made a visit to El
Rincón during his January 1998 trip to Cuba.
Adjacent to the lovingly cared-for sanctuary
is an old lepers' hospital, reflecting the area's
long-standing association with disease and
healing, while a little way north of El Rincón
is a sanatorium, which provides high-quality
medical and housing facilities for AIDS
sufferers. When the sanatorium first opened
in 1986, HIV-positive Cubans were obliged to
live here (effectively in quarantine), but the
rules governing AIDS and HIV are now more
relaxed (*see p185* **Positive attitudes**).

Iglesia Parroquial de Santiago
de las Vegas

*Calle 190 (Calle 4), entre 409 (13) y 411 (15) (0683
3233).* **Open** 9.30am-1pm; 7-8.30pm Tue-Fri;
10.30am-1pm Sun; closed Mon, Sat. *Mass* 7.30am
Tue-Fri; 11am Sun. **Admission** free.

Santuario de San Lázaro

*Carretera de San Antonio de los Baños, El Rincón
(0683 2396).* **Open** 7am-6pm daily. **Admission** free.

Vivero de Begonia

Calle 188, esquina a 413 (0683 2184). **Open** 7am-
5pm daily. **Admission** free.

Eat, Drink, Shop

Eating & Drinking

Cuba and cocktails go hand in hand, but, contrary to popular belief, you can get a decent meal here, too. True, bad ones are ten a penny – you just need a little guidance.

Widespread provision of culinary delights isn't Cuba's forte. All the rumours you may have heard about the dismal offering can too often be true. The Michelin man hasn't been here to leave his mark and it is not surprising, since most of the restaurants are light years away from the culinary standards that a capital city like Havana should aspire to. Unless you're at a top-dollar, all-inclusive oasis, finding a bearable bite to eat can become a daily problem. The Cubans cannot be wholly blamed; despite its sophistication in the arts and sciences, Cuba is a poor country; battling with shortages, trade restraints and a dismal distribution infrastructure is a difficult task that most restaurants choose not to tackle. Instead of admiring the ability of Cuban chefs to reflect the country's extensive economic problems in one meal, leave your pessimism aside and replace it with a plan. There are great places to eat; it's just that choosing a restaurant on a whim is not recommended. With a little premeditation, that tasty Creole flavour of Havana can be discovered. You'll probably find you start lowering your standards after a couple of days here – you'll have to unless you want to starve – and will end up, by the time you leave the city, commenting on how your meal is 'not bad *for Cuba/relatively* good/quite nice, *considering'*.

STATE RESTAURANTS

The standard of quality and service varies greatly in these government-run establishments. The average waiter earns about $10 per month so has little to be enthusiastic about. Many rely on tourists' good will to secure themselves a tip, rather than bending over backwards to earn one. However, the personal touch more usually found in a *paladar* can also be experienced in a select few state restaurants, particularly in the suburbs – **El Tocororo** (*see p140*) is a good example. If you come across appalling service (or food) in a state-run restaurant ask to speak to *el gerente* (the boss).

PESO RESTAURANTS

These are eateries where you can join the locals and pay in local currency. Eating in such establishments may confirm your worst

suspicions about Cuban cuisine, but they're worth trying for the experience, if not for the food. Some peso restaurant proprietors will claim it is illegal for them to serve tourists. In fact, if the restaurant doesn't have a specific dollar menu, you should by rights be charged in pesos like the locals; however, the restaurants often get around this obstacle by offering a tailor-made menu priced in dollars ('just for you'). If you're not strapped for cash, pay the few extra dollars with a smile; the food served to you will usually be better than the peso fare and you'll be helping the waiters supplement their pitiful wages. If you're on a tight budget, stand your ground, agree on a peso price and check the bill carefully before you pay.

PALADARES

The rise of the *paladar* as a feature of the Havana eating scene exemplifies the huge impact of TV culture on Cuban society. In the late '80s, in the Brazilian-made soap opera *Vale Todo* (*Anything Goes*), Raquel, one of the main characters, opened a chain of restaurants, which she called *Paladares* (meaning palates). Cubans followed Raquel's lead and began welcoming paying guests into their houses to enjoy home-cooked food.

Along with the *casas particulares* (Cuban-style B&Bs; *see chapter* **Accommodation**), *paladares* are one of the few signs of individualistic free trade in Cuba and also a chance for foreign visitors to mix with Cubans in their homes. The owner of the *paladar* (*el dueño*) will either be strutting around like a peacock while the rest of the family does the work, or deep in the centre of all the activity, making sure everything runs smoothly. Family members are the only employees, so there are plenty of domestic outbursts for you to watch and enjoy while you eat. More importantly, at the best *paladares* the food is homegrown, home-made, tasty, filling and fresh.

Try to give a healthy tip if you have a good meal at a *paladar*; as with *casas particulares*, the owners have to contend with high taxes (up to US$1,500 per month) and constant monitoring from Big Brother, so your contribution will be gratefully received. However, these high taxes

Super dupers

Cubans love – and need – dollars, and will do anything to wheedle a few more out of their unsuspecting customers. Here are just some of the scams we've come across.

ADDITIONAL ITEMS

If the odd beer, bread and butter or coffee (that you haven't had) miraculously appears on your bill, don't be embarrassed to question it – you won't be the first!

OVERPRICED ITEMS

Right bill, wrong prices. The current record is to find seven mistakes on one bill, although, surprisingly, undercharging never seems to be a problem.

WRONG CHANGE

You get the correct bill and for a moment your faith in Cuban honesty is restored, then you get the change. A sneaky $1-$5 can easily go astray.

THE TOUT

If you are led to a restaurant (particularly a *paladar*) by a *jinetero*, his commission will inflate the price of your meal. Finding places to eat independently gives you more bargaining power and the satisfaction of knowing that the majority of your money is going to whoever's cooking the dinner.

FLUCTUATING PRICES

Depending how touristy you look, prices will escalate. Always ask for a menu with prices, even if there is only one thing on it.

'SORRY, NO CRISTAL'

The *habanero* next to you is happily drinking a Cristal, but you are offered only imported beer, which, of course, is more expensive. If this happens, you can ask for a Cristal by all means, but you have a 97 per cent chance of being told 'there are no cold ones'.

THE REAL THING

Similar to the Cristal scam. Asking for a cola will yield a $2 Coke instead of a perfectly good, albeit sweet, local 50¢ TuKola or Tropicola.

THE SET MENU

Even when there is one set price for a whole meal, some waiters will try to charge for items individually, claiming that 'that was the afternoon menu' or any other imaginable excuse.

CURRENCY CONS

If you are in a peso restaurant and pay in dollars, double check the maths ($1 = 20 pesos). And if you're given peso change in a dollar restaurant make sure it's *pesos convertibles*; otherwise you're being robbed.

'OPEN 24/7'

You're desperate for a drink at 4am, but the 24-hour bar is closed. This is an all-too-familiar scene in Havana, particularly around Obispo. If you want to be sure you can get an early-morning drink, stick to the hotel bars.

also mean that *paladares* come and go all the time, either by their own choice or because they are closed down. *Paladares* are only allowed to serve 12 customers at a time – the government wants to make sure that the state restaurants don't totally lose out – and they are not officially allowed to serve shellfish. Some owners ignore these rules (this is Cuba, after all), but as a customer you should not demand shellfish as you will be putting the owners at risk of fines of up to US$1,500 (the equivalent of five years' wages for the average Cuban).

WATCH THIS SPACE

Though restrictions on the sale of food and medicine to Cuba by the US were eased towards the end of 2000, don't get your hopes up: instead of being able to get credit for such supplies, Cuba has to pay cash – which Castro says his country cannot afford. It's

unlikely, therefore, that this will have much of an effect on the supply of better food to restaurants, at least in the short term.

In terms of new openings, look out for the no-doubt very pricey **Restaurant 1830** at the mouth of the Rio Almendares (*see p99* **Club 1830**). As this guide went to press it was yet to open, but there was talk of the chef from La Torre relocating there. Ask around.

JINETEROS

A phenomenon that has grown in line with the increase in the number of visitors to Havana is that of the *jinetero/a*. Literally jockeys, they make their dollars in a variety of ways, from

▶ For tips on self-catering in Havana, *see p160* **Catering to your needs**.

prostitution (usually women), to 'helping out' tourists by taking them to *casas particulares* (Cuban-style B&Bs, *see p49*) and 'guiding' tourists to *paladares* for the 'best meal in Havana'. *Jineteros* operating in this way will have made a previous arrangement with the *paladar* owners (often their relations), in return for commission. You may get a surprisingly good meal in this way, but if you do decide to risk it, always agree on prices first: many an innocent tourist has parted with $40 per person for rice and beans in granny's kitchen. Use your common sense and never give a *jinetero* the benefit of the doubt. *See also p281* **Jockeying for attention**.

OPENING TIMES

Opening times and days, like other listings information in Havana, should be taken with a large pinch of salt. Though the city is becoming more and more used to the demands of overseas visitors, *paladares* in particular sometimes close on a whim. Therefore, if you're likely to be going out of your way to any of the places listed in this chapter, do try to phone ahead first to check there's at least a good chance they'll be open. Given the nightmarish Cuban phone system (including changeable phone numbers), however, this is often easier said than done. So when you head out to eat, make sure you go armed with a sense of humour as well as an appetite!

PRICES

Most restaurants and *paladares* charge in dollars. The golden rule is to check the menu first. Be wary of those mystery menus with prices that alter as if by magic as soon as a foreigner enters the room. If anything on the menu is unclear, or there isn't a menu at all, clarify all the prices in person (unless you like paying $6 for bread and butter). Ultimately, though, only the bill will tell you whether you've been ripped off, so scrutinise it carefully. Note that service charges are beginning to creep into the most tourist-frequented places as Cubans catch on to the idea.

Once you've negotiated these pitfalls (*see also p125* **Super dupers**), dinner can be a relatively inexpensive outing. Food, when palatable, is usually a good deal and main meal prices don't tend to vary very much. Drinks, however, are a different story. Apply the 'Cristal test' to give you a quick indication of how hard the bill will bite. In a cheap restaurant a local Cristal beer should cost about $1, rising to $2 in reasonably priced places, and higher if it's an expensive restaurant. We have listed the price of an average main course (including a side dish) for every restaurant and *paladar* in this chapter.

For animal lovers
Marpoly. *See p136.*

For a colonial kitchen
Calle 10. *See p135.*

For a feast by the beach
Paladar Piccolo. *See p143.*

For film buffs
La Guarida. *See p131.*

For the Garden of Eden
La Cocina de Lilliam. *See p140.*

For intrepid diners
El Recanto. *See p136.*

For a kitschfest
La Julia. *See p129.*

For a meal beside the Malecón
El Bistrot. *See p134.*

For Mexico City meets Milan
Mi Jardín. *See p140.*

For pop star baroque
Amor. *See p134.*

Note: confusingly, pesos are sometimes designated by the $ sign; you can assume that virtually every bar, restaurant and *paladar* will charge tourists in dollars (and will often try to even in supposedly peso places). The exceptions to the rule are the Chinatown restaurants (where the prices in $ on the menu mean pesos), and street stalls. In both cases they'll accept your dollars with glee, but you're likely to get ripped off as the change will usually be given in pesos.

DRESS CODES

Havana is a relaxed place; although men should not wear shorts, dressing up for dinner in a restaurant is not necessary. Reservations are not usually required unless the restaurant or *paladar* is particularly popular.

CREDIT WHERE CREDIT'S DUE

Towards the end of your stay in Havana you will probably notice that you have spent far more than you anticipated. So when you've spent your wad of dollars you may need to stick some stuff on your credit card. Cash (that'll be dollars) is king in Cuba and only the top hotels and the top government-run restaurants will have the wherewithal to accept your cards (but even then they'll still prefer greenbacks). However, even in these establishments you should always double check before you consume anything. Although many places display the usual MasterCard and Visa stickers, the waiter may still go into a coma if actually asked to settle a bill with a credit card. And, even if he does say 'that will do nicely', you may have to wait for 30 minutes while the telecommunication lines deal with your plastic. Therefore, always take enough dollars with you to cover the cost of your meal, and remember that no US credit cards, even those issued by a bank associated with a US bank, are accepted in Cuba, due to the embargo.

La Habana Vieja

At the centre of Havana's tourist trade, the restaurants of La Habana Vieja suffer to a large extent from the constant flow of dollar-paying customers. This, of course, affects the standard of service, which succeeds time and time again in reminding you that you are merely a source of income. Generally, your only choice in this part of town is between cheap restaurants with bad food and expensive restaurants with reasonable food. Fortunately, there are always exceptions and the atmosphere and cooking of those listed below generally make the grade. If it's a *paladar* you're after, though, just be aware that, unlike in Vedado, you won't have a great deal of places to choose from.

Restaurants

Al Medina
Calle Oficios #12, entre Obispo y Obrapía (671041). **Open** noon-11pm daily. **Main courses** $8-$15. **Map** p316 E15.
More upmarket than most, this restaurant succeeds in providing a break from the Cuban norm. The Arabian menu is limited but good. Don't order anything less than the *Gran Plato*, which, though not cheap at $15, will stimulate your tastebuds – something you'll learn to appreciate after three days in Cuba. The courtyard is pleasant, the music great and if drinks were just a bit cheaper (beer costs $2.50) you'd be tempted to spend hours and hours here. *Air-conditioning. Outside tables.*

Bar Cabaña
Calle Cuba #12, esquina a Peña Pobre (605670). **Open** 24hrs daily. **Main courses** $5.50-$20. **Map** p316 D15.
Not far from where the Malecón meets the harbour mouth and two minutes from Havana's largest market, this restaurant (despite the name) enjoys a prime tourist location. Unfortunately, though, this means it doesn't have to try very hard to pull in the punters:

the starters are shabby; the waiters shady and its infamous for scamming innocent tourists. Still, if you've a persistent temperament and an accountant's brain, you'll get proper Creole dishes at reasonable prices here. Upstairs is lifeless and a touch smelly, so head straight for the seating al fresco. *Air-conditioning (upstairs only). Outside tables.*

La Bodeguita del Medio
Calle Empedrado #207, entre San Ignacio y Cuba (338857). **Open** *Bar* 10.30am-1am daily. *Restaurant* noon-midnight daily. **Main courses** $7.50-$10.90. **Map** p316 D15.
With its Hemingway history, La Bodeguita is a fix for tourists. Bus-loads of interested visitors make their way here to taste that famous *mojito* so well liked by Big Ern. And you should to do the same. In the restaurant, however, food isn't always as fresh as it could be, and sometimes seems to sit around until the next busload of hungry tourists arrives. Although it has won several international prizes and played host to many celebrities, who have left their designer graffiti on the walls (including Hemingway himself, whose lines are now chalked on a board at the bar), La Bodeguita is a place to look at and leave, taking the light-headedness of a good, though expensive, *mojito* with you. *Outside tables (balcony).*

Café Mercurio
Calle Oficios, esquina a Plaza de San Francisco (606118). **Open** 24hrs daily. **Main courses** $8-$25. **Map** p316 E15.
Overlooking Plaza de San Francisco, Café Mercurio can be a good alternative to nearby Café del Oriente (*see p144*), particularly if you're going to indulge in an ice-cream. Beer prices are inflated, but you'd probably do the same if you were managing such a terrific location. Go for a *mojito*, a steal at $1.50. *Air-conditioning. Outside tables.*

Café Taberna
Calle Mercaderes #531, esquina a Brasil (Teniente Rey) (611937). **Open** 11am-midnight daily. **Main courses** $5-$10. **Map** p316 E15.
Though the service is weak, this restaurant, which is also known as Café Beny Moré, provides a genuine *habanero* feeling at decent prices. The nine-piece granddad band are truly talented *son* and *bolero* specialists and fit in well with the stylish surroundings. As the music gets going, 'Mutton chops' Willi and his imaginatively dressed wife Adelaide take to the floor for a spectacular performance of *bolero* steps and style. To enjoy a charming meal here, choose pork, check your bill and tip the entertainers. The (relatively) decent milkshakes are a bonus. *Air-conditioning.*

El Castillo de Farnés
Avenida de Bélgica (Monserrate), esquina a Obrapía (671030). **Open** *Bar* 24hrs daily. *Restaurant* noon-midnight daily. **Main courses** $4.50-$15. **Map** p316 E14.
This 24-hour drinking den and restaurant claims to have hosted Fidel, his brother Raúl and Che back in

Eat, Drink, Shop

1959. Photographic proof can be seen on the wall, although judging by the picture they didn't have a great meal here. Luckily, things have changed at the Castillo and the Spanish cuisine that the kitchen now belts out is great. The bowls of hearty potatoes and chorizo, or chickpeas and ham are mouthwatering, and the chips are the best in Havana. If you fancy seafood, lobster stew at $15 is a good deal. When the band sets up, Castillo has been known to erupt with spontaneous dancing by both customers and staff (including the toilet attendants). Normally, though, it is a quiet air-conditioned haven set behind a more popular bar out front. At night, a mix of long-term travellers and Cubans sit on the pavement outside knocking back the well-priced drinks (cocktails $1.50; beer $1). Highly recommended.
Air-conditioning.

La Dominica

Calle O'Reilly, esquina a Mercaderes (602918). **Open** noon-midnight daily. **Main courses** $8.50-$25. **Map** p316 E15.
La Dominica is home to the best pizzas in Havana, with yummy starters and a better-than-average wine list. The patio provides a charming setting and the musicians are veritably enthusiastic. In fact, the only problem is that Dominica can easily seduce you into spending the whole evening watching the world and your holiday money go by. There are definitely cheaper options around, but if you've got the cash, you might as well spend it at this first-class joint. As always, checking the bill is recommended.
Air-conditioning. Outside tables.

Don Giovanni

Calle Tacón #4, entre Empedrado y O'Reilly (671036/335979). **Open** noon-midnight daily. **Main courses** $4.45-$16. **Map** p316 D15.
It's bizarre that the best dish this Italian restaurant (also known as D'Giovanni) has to offer is kebab and chips, but what a great kebab! The normal Italian fare is average, although the Princess Diana pizza (Pizza Diana de Gales), which includes lobster, garlic, mushrooms and four olives (yes, it says it on the menu!), is recommended. While you muse on how Lady Di made an impact in Cuba (there's also a garden in her memory, *see p67*), enjoy the view of the Morro, lighthouse and entrance to Havana harbour. As a bonus, from the balcony (women, don't wear a skirt), you can watch the crowds gather for *Caramelo Azúcar*, Cuba's answer to the Spice Girls, who often play from 10.30pm onwards. Avoid the red wine list: the choice is sometimes limited to three overpriced bottles.
Outside tables.

El Floridita

Avenida de Bélgica (Monserrate), esquina a Obispo (671300). **Open** *Bar* noon-1am daily. *Restaurant* noon-11pm daily. **Main courses** $11-$42. **Map** p316 D14.
This hyped-up Hemingway haunt attracts zillions of tourists paying homage to the great man. It is

difficult to believe that this place would still be Ernest's 'favourite', particularly with daiquiris at $6. Even if you decide to splurge on a cocktail, or even an over-priced beer at $3, don't try the restaurant, unless, of course, you enjoy the company of braying foreign businessmen and like being served over-priced food by miserable waiting staff. Nuff said.
Air-conditioning.

Hanoi

Calle Brasil (Teniente Rey), esquina a Bernaza (671029). **Open** noon-11pm daily. **Main courses** $3-$8. **Map** p316 E14.
The ultimate marketing scam. Full of eastern promise, Hanoi succeeds in luring tourists looking forward to an escape from ubiquitous beans and rice, when in fact the menu consists of just one semi-Vietnamese rice dish and loads of standard Cuban fare. On the up side, Hanoi is professionally run and the food is cheap and tasty. It's worth a visit, if only to taste the $1 *mojitos*, the cheapest in town.
Outside tables (patio).

El Mesón de la Flota

Calle Mercaderes, entre Amargura y Brasil (Teniente Rey) (633838/29281). **Open** *Bar* 24hrs daily. *Restaurant* 11am-11pm daily. **Main courses** $3-$18. **Map** p316 E15.
This newish bar and eaterie (which also has rooms for rent) is open 24 hours – if it looks closed just knock on the door to be let in – and is the best option for snacking in La Habana Vieja. The interior is themed on Spanish sailors and the menu offers decent Spanish wines (from $1.50 a glass) and almost *Castellano*-like tapas. The service is excellent and if you do want a full meal, not a bad plate of *cerdo* (pork) and chips is available for $3. Beer is on tap, a first for this part of town and a bargain at $1. All in all, a cheap and very cheerful place.

La Mina/Al Cappuccino

Calle Obispo #109, entre Oficios y Mercaderes (620216). **Open** *Bar* 24hrs daily. *Restaurant* noon-midnight daily. **Main courses** $4-$12. **Map** p316 E15.
Next to each other on the Plaza de Armas, these popular, busy restaurants share the same waiters, bands and, to an extent, the same menu. Music is the priority at both restaurants, and with plants encircling the patio, an agreeable setting is ensured. In their quest to lure tourists, the waiters are unusually energetic and although this place is right on the tourist track, the atmosphere and scrumptious *tamal* (corn paste) will make up for the lack of Cubans. Your best bet is to try La Mina for dinner and Al Cappuccino for lunch.
Air-conditioning. Outside tables.

La Paella

Hostal Valencia, Calle Oficios #53, esquina a Obrapía (671037). **Open** noon-11pm daily. **Main courses** $8-$30. **Map** p316 E15.
Often touted as the place with the best paella in Havana (La Fiesta provides stiff competition, *see p139*), this restaurant could be right on the Costa.

Eat, Drink, Shop

No one does rice 'n' beans like **La Julia**.

Considering the seemingly authentic Spanish surroundings, the prices aren't bad, with paella for two and a bottle of *vino tinto* coming to around $30. The house speciality is recommended, but the meat paellas are not as good (no meat!). For details of the Hostal Valencia, *see p53*.

El Patio

Plaza de la Catedral (671035). **Open** noon-midnight daily. **Main courses** $12-$25. **Map** p316 D15.
One of the most picturesque restaurants in Havana, this 1790 colonial palace is a must for a quick drink at least. Choose between the quiet, air-conditioned interior, an exquisite inner courtyard (complete with one of Cuba's only working fountains) or the busier outer patio, for a relaxed view of the Cathedral. Resident bands play inside and out to give this place a magnetic energy. The very Cuban food doesn't live up to the setting, despite its claim to international cuisine. The set menus – chicken, pork or fish with starter, dessert and a cocktail for $16 – are your best bet. El Patio gets zero points for its vegetarian menu, which, amusingly, includes a non-alcoholic cocktail. *Air-conditioning. Outside tables.*

La Torre de Marfil

Calle Mercaderes #115, entre Obispo y Obrapía (671038). **Open** noon-10pm Mon-Thur; noon-10.30pm Fri-Sun. **Main courses** $1.50-$15. **Map** p316 E15.
Although more expensive than the eateries in *barrio chino* and not as good as Tien Tan (*see p131* **Chinatown**), the Ivory Tower gets the thumbs up for value for money, edible food (the spring rolls are particularly good) and excellent service. Unfortunately the management has neglected the atmosphere factor and even when it's full, this restaurant is a bit of a vault. If, however, you are with a lively group of friends, go for the Pagoda seats at the back and enjoy the service.

La Zaragozana

Avenida de Bélgica (Monserrate) #352, entre Obispo y Obrapía (671033). **Open** 24hrs daily. **Main courses** $8-$25. **Map** p316 D14.

Billed as the oldest established restaurant in Havana (1830), La Zaragozana is either empty or chock a block. Go only on cabaret nights (Thursday and Saturday), otherwise you'll be chilled by the vacuum. The entertainment nights are loud, but they do give you a bargain whirlwind tour of Cuban music, with *rumba, son, salsa, bolero* and flamenco shows. Besides the entertainment, the food and decor is completely Spanish, with FC Barcelona and Real Madrid memorabilia giving the place an authentic feel. Prices are over the top for what you get, but the menu is varied: steak, fish, lobster, casseroles and spaghetti.
Air-conditioning.

Paladares

Don Lorenzo

Calle Acosta #260, entre Habana y Compostela (616733). **Open** noon-midnight daily. **Main courses** $5-$18. **Map** p316 E15.
Great service, a wide menu and tasteful surroundings, which means the only catch is the price. Although this is very much a family-owned joint (four relations running around madly), Don Lorenzo is more like a state restaurant, with matching tableware to prove it. Don't be put off by the walk to this place – the road is dirty and in need of repair – but once you enter, all is forgiven. For the novelty factor, try the crocodile; it's very bland, but makes a good story for your friends.

La Julia

Calle O'Reilly #506, entre Bernaza y Villegas (627438). **Open** noon-midnight daily. **Main courses** $7-$9. **Map** p316 D15.
Beans, tasty beans and lots of them. This is one of the few *paladares* in La Habana Vieja that hasn't let success go to its head. The service is quick and friendly and the helpings are substantial. Julia and her family ensure a true taste of Creole food at decent prices in kitsch surroundings. Unmissable.

La Moneda Cubana

San Ignacio #77, entre O'Reilly y Empedrado (673852). **Open** noon-11pm Mon-Thur, Sat; closed Sun. **Main courses** $8-$10. **Map** p316 D15.
Despite its tourist-trap location, La Moneda Cubana avoids all temptation to serve any ole rubbish to one-time visitors and always succeeds in delivering a good-value, filling meal. The menu features the usual suspects of chicken, pork, rice and beans, plus a better-than-average salad (for Cuba). The most distinct feature of this *paladar* are the cash notes glued to the wall (hence the name). All nationalities are invited to leave their mark, contributing perhaps to that rainy day when brothers Rafael and Antonio cash it all in.

El Rincón de Elegguá

Calle Aguacate #257, entre Obispo y Obrapía (672367/628488). **Main courses** $8-$15. **Map** p316 E15.

Breathtaking views over the city are what the **Roof Garden** does best.

This is one of those *paladares* that has tremendous connections. Clearly defying the 12-seater rule, El Rincón is a tourist magnet. One wonders, how the two policemen permanently stationed on the corner of Obispo don't seem to notice the 25-strong German tour group entering the establishment. All that aside, the food is average, but quick and pleasant service makes up for the somewhat chewy fish. The prices are a little higher than at other *paladares*, but you are paying for the location. Make sure you order an extra salad (the salad included in the price of most dishes is a piece of lettuce and a slice of cucumber) and black beans (otherwise you may end up drinking ten beers as the food is very dry). The rooms have low ceilings and a fairly clinical design, but the bamboo furniture and tasteful art give the place some character.

Centro Habana

The choice of eateries in **Centro Habana** is rather limited. Not because there is a lack of establishments here, but rather because to eat in this crumbling part of Havana is to risk being victim to a falling brick. The places listed here are special for their architecture, location and, of course, their food. For something different, try a chinese restaurant (*see p131* **Chinatown**).

Restaurants

Roof Garden

Hotel Sevilla, Calle Trocadero #55, entre Martí (Prado) y Agramonte (608560). **Open** 6.30-10pm daily. **Main courses** $7.50-$29. **Map** p313 D13.
At least once during your stay in Havana, cancel what you're doing and spoil yourself in this room with a view. With its Florentine panelled ceilings and immaculately dressed tables, this restaurant offers elegance at bargain prices. Huge windows with views give this restaurant a serenity and charm unsurpassed in Havana. All is perfect, apart from the unfortunately average food. OK, so the French chef

must be commended for his imaginative menu, but not all dishes (nor the sometimes stingy portions) live up to expectations. On the plus side, the goose is a notable exception, desserts are worth ordering, and interesting dressings (aniseed, aged rum, balsamic and ginger), a rarity in Havana, add a little pzazz to proceedings. All in all, it's the silver service and the amazing surroundings that justify the price. If you arrive early, relax at the roof-top bar for happy-hour cocktails between 6.30 and 8pm, and then nab a table facing the harbour for a view of the 9pm *cañonazo* (canon-firing ceremony) at La Cabaña.

Paladares

Bellomar

Calle Virtudes #169, esquina a Amistad (610023). **Open** noon-midnight daily. **Main courses** $1.25-$1.75. **Map** p313 D14.
This *paladar* nestles like an Aladdin's cave in the crumbling surroundings of central Havana. The decor and the friendly service give the place an authentic *paladar* atmosphere. Meat and fish lovers are well taken care of, but the sides of *congrí* (black beans and white rice), salad and chips are somewhat disappointing. Still, Bellomar is not a bad option. It's immaculately clean, too (for a *paladar*).

Doña Blanquita

Paseo de Martí (Prado) #158 (primero piso), entre Colón y Refugio (674958). **Open** noon-3am daily. **Main courses** $5-$10. **Map** p313 D15.
Blanquita is Queen of Kitsch and her pink *paladar* is crammed with 3-D images of Jesus, Chinese Buddhas, Indian chiefs, white horses and cuckoo clocks. The best table in the house is on the balcony, which offers a streetwatcher's dream view over the Prado. Blanquita and her children provide a wider menu than usual, but you'll still be able to guess the main components: rice, beans, chicken or pork. If you haven't already overdosed on the whole Creole thing, go for the pork; Blanquita has it down to a fine art. *Outside tables.*

La Guarida

Calle Concordia #418, entre Gervasaio y Escobar (624940). **Open** 7pm-midnight daily; reservation required. **Main courses** $15-$20. **Map** p313 D13.
Perhaps the best-known *paladar* of them all, La Guarida owes its fame to *Fresa y Chocolate*, the successful 1993 Cuban movie, which was filmed on the premises (*see p179*). Finding this place among the Havana rubble is a rewarding experience; the surrounding buildings are near to collapse, but the restaurant has been restored beautifully. The prices here are a little higher than at the average *paladar*, but the choice and quality of the international food justify this. Although the normal 12-covers rule doesn't apply (the owners must be well connected), it is still necessary to make an advance booking to secure a table.

Vedado

The bustling, leafy green suburb of Vedado has plenty on offer to replenish lost calories. Some of the best street vendors in the city (*see p138* **Street treats**) are to be found here,

particularly along La Rampa (the end of Calle 23 nearest the Malecón). The restaurants and *paladares* in this part of Havana tend to be slightly more costly than in other areas of the city, but the surroundings are smarter, cleaner and generally more worthwhile.

Restaurants

La Casona de 17

Calle 17, entre M y N (334529). **Open** noon-midnight daily. **Main courses** $4-$10. **Map** p312 B11.
If this bright, airy converted house was on the Malecón rather than overlooking the hideous Focsa building (*see p94*), it would be immeasurably better. According to the management, Fidel's godparents lived here in the '40s and the man himself, of course, came to stay. Whatever its history, this painted, peach-coloured 1920s mansion is well worth a visit. Choose from two indoor dining rooms (which are air-conditioned) and a recently opened outdoor barbecue-grill. Private dining rooms are available for groups, and contemporary paintings hang on the

Chinatown

If you want to sample some of the exquisite tastes of traditional Chinese cooking in authentic Chinese surroundings, book a flight to Beijing, 'cos you ain't gonna find it here. What you will get though is a good night out and food that is remarkably tasty compared to the normal Cuban fare.

Havana's Chinatown is located on Bulevar del Barrio Chino in Centro Habana (about three blocks behind the Capitolio) and consists of a 50-metre (160-foot) strip known as Cuchillo (knife), populated on both sides by numerous restaurants. The waiters are dressed up in all the garb, but tend to look more Camagüey than Canton, and will endeavour to drag you into their restaurants for the 'best food in Chinatown'. This, however, can only be found at **Tien Tan**, where the spare ribs, duck, frog and anything sweet and sour are recommended. This restaurant is pricier than the rest – a full meal should set you back around $10, including drinks – but the extra expense is justified. As with all the restaurants here, the prices on the menu are marked in Cuban pesos but dollars are readily accepted.

For a cheaper option choose **Tong Po Laug**, two doors along, where you can have a tasty chicken chop suey for $1.50. Alternatively, choose something from the bewilderingly

large menu; all the dishes are under a fiver and pork with honey and lemon ($2.50) is a not-very-Chinese favourite. Feel free to carve your name on the table or scribble your lover's name on the wall – it appears to be the done thing here.

There's not much to choose between the other restaurants in Chinatown, all of which sell bargain chop sueys and beers for about $1. Stay away from sweet and sour dishes, though – Tien Tan is the only place that can make them.

If you decide to sit outside when you dine in Chinatown be prepared for the attention of numerous street hustlers, ranging from musicians, flower sellers and artists to magicians, prostitutes and a bloke juggling an oil drum. These guys (and gals) can quickly get on your nerves, but if it all gets too much, most of the restaurants have air-conditioned interiors.

Tien Tan

Bulevar del Barrio Chino, Centro Habana (615478). **Open** 11am-midnight daily. **Main courses** $5-$18. **Map** p313 D13.

Tong Po Laug

Bulevar del Barrio Chino, Centro Habana (no phone). **Open** noon-midnight daily. **Main courses** $1.50-$6. **Map** p313 D13.

walls (allow the proud, friendly staff to point them out to you). Healthy-sized traditional Creole dishes such as beef with garlic, grilled lobster, fish and even paella grace the menu, but the best deal is the house speciality: half a chicken with rice and beans for $7. With lobster at $10 and cocktails from $1.50, eating out at La Casona de 17 really is an interesting, affordable experience.
Air-conditioning. Outside tables.

El Conejito
Calle M, entre 17 y 19 (324671). **Open** noon-midnight daily. **Main courses** $1-$18.50.
Map p312 B11.
Bugs Bunny would be seen dead here. The house speciality is rabbit, served with a variety of different sauces. Particulary recommended is a tasty, mushroom-clad rodent called Conejo Financiera ($8.40). Better value is the Pollo Gordon Blue for $2, or bargain spaghetti and pizza dishes starting at $1. The mixed salad, comprising a plate of cabbage and five slices of carrot, takes the term 'rabbit food' to a whole

new level. All in all, considering the well-priced food, attentive service and lively adjoining bar (particularly for the student night on a Wednesday, and at weekends), this place is recommended.
Air-conditioning.

Hotel Melía Cohiba
Paseo, entre 1ra y 3ra (333636). **Open** *La Piazza* 1pm-2am daily. *El Gran Añejo* 7am-11.30pm daily. *Habana Café* noon-4am daily. **Main courses** *La Piazza* $7.50-$12. *El Gran Añejo* $6-$15. *Habana Café* $11 minimum. **Map** p312 A9.
This huge imposing hotel offers a range of eating options, the best of which are the following. **La Piazza** offers standard Italian menu, with the usual suspects – pastas, meat, fish and pretty good pizzas, which are served in 17 different ways. The ground-floor **El Gran Añejo** does breakfasts and sarnies, a firm favourite being the sandwich criollo, with pork, ham, cheese and salad. Not cheap at $11, but decent service and surroundings make up for it. Next door (but part of the hotel) is **Habana Café**

Scream for ice-cream

Grannies, desperate-looking mothers, anxious fathers, whole families, in fact, all queue, queue and queue some more, while their little ones, along with any foreigners around, wonder why on earth it can take three hours to get an ice-cream. **Coppelia** in Vedado is the ice-cream and queueing mecca of the world and it's no wonder, since Cubans are nearly as good at making ice-cream as they are at queueing.

This open-air ice-cream parlour was built in 1966 as a post-Revolutionary monument to socialism. In sharp contrast to the preceding decade, when only the rich could enjoy the fancy ice-cream outlets of Vedado, Coppelia was championed by the Revolution as the 'ice-cream parlour of the people'. Regardless of colour, creed and social background, a sundae could be had by all. How liberating!

Coppelia's architecture will excite those with a penchant for 1960s design, otherwise you may think it looks like a moon station from a bad sci-fi movie. Nonetheless, it is always packed and no one every complains about the ice-cream or the prices – a huge ice-cream salad (actually a mixture of whichever flavours are on offer) costs just 25¢. The choice, on the other hand, is less than satisfactory, with typically only one or two flavours available. (We recomment the orange and pineapple varieties if you can get them.) If you're fretting about your waistline go for the Varadero brand, which is lower in fat.

If you want to say you've been to Coppelia but don't want to queue for three days, walk upstairs to the dollar section for a wider choice and a higher bill (around $4), or buy from the kiosk outside.

Or, if your craving for ice-cream strikes on a Monday, when the great temple is closed, try one of the numerous street stalls, which will sell you a quick chocolate or strawberry cone for three pesos. You'll find these stalls located everywhere throughout Havana; they can usually be identified by a sign saying '*helado*' (ice-cream). Bear in mind, however, that hygiene at these places may leave something to be desired and the milk is not always pasteurised.

Coppelia
Calle 23, esquina a L, Vedado (326149).
Open *Parlour* 11am-11pm Tue-Sun; closed Mon. *Kiosk* 24hrs daily. **Map** p312 B11.

Doña Blanquita – Centro Habana's kitsch kitchen. *See p130.*

(*see also p196*), a wannabe Hard Rock-style place (though don't get your hopes up – the food is overpriced and not great, but then again even bad nachos might be a welcome change to beans and rice).

Hotel Nacional

Calle O, esquina a 21 (333564/333567). **Open** *Comedor de Aguiar* noon-4pm, 7pm-midnight daily. *Buffet Veranda* 7-10am, 11.30am-3pm, 7-10pm daily. *Cafetería El Rincón del Cine* 24hrs daily. **Main courses** *Comedor de Aguiar* $11-$36. *Buffet Veranda* $13 (set breakfast); $15 (set lunch); $25 (set dinner). *Cafetería El Rincón del Cine* $6-$10. **Map** p312 B12.
This remarkable building epitomises all that Havana used to be. Grand, elegant and swanky, it's a great place to swan around and pretend to be wealthy. There are three restaurants here, offering food in varying price brackets, but note that drinks prices are in keeping with the surroundings ($2.50 for a Cristal). For details of the Hotel Nacional, *see p56*.

The **Comedor de Aguiar** is built on the site where Don Luis José Aguiar kicked the Brits' butts during the 1762 occupation. It's so elite that there's hardly ever anyone in it; possibly something to do with the intimidating, immaculately dressed waiters guarding the doors. Starters, such as smoked salmon with capers and onion, cost $6 to $11; main courses (butterfly lobster, for example) are up to $36, and the drinks add a further ouch factor. The quality is good (for Cuba) and the service is second to none. You get the drift. Downstairs is the more relaxed, all-you-can-eat, self-service **Buffet Veranda**. (On the way down, look out for the cheesy photo of South London's finest: 'Naomi Campbell. Top Model'.) Equally top quality and self-confident is the food, including a good selection of fruits, salad and nine sorts of bread. The buffet gains extra points for three different potato dishes (unbelievably

rare in Cuba). Round the corner from the buffet is the cinema-themed, American diner-style **Cafetería El Rincón del Cine.** Here you can scoff down a full American brekky for $9.50, or choose from a selection of well-prepared and moderately priced burgers, pizzas and sandwiches.
Air-conditioning. Outside tables.

El Polinesio

Hotel Habana Libre, Calle L, entre 23 y 25 (334011). **Open** noon-3.30pm, 7.30-11pm daily. **Main courses** $9.50-$35. **Set menu** $14. **Map** p312 B11.
The decor may be Polynesian, but the food is Chinese/Cuban. Among the bamboo and lobster pots look for the glass-screened smoking room built to cook the house speciality, barbecued chicken. Special wood is brought in from Pinar del Río to fire the barrel-like stone stoves and all this effort results in a tasty dish of pleasant, smoky flavours. Prices are steep, but for the atmosphere it may be worth it. Set meals ($14) include a starter (dodgy cheese balls), a main course (barbecued chicken) and a not-very-Thai ice-cream dessert; add another $3 to $5 to the bill for a side order of rice. Most recommended is the hard-to-leave comfy bar, with large value-for-money cocktails ($3.25) served up in 'genuine', British-made Polynesian goblets.
Air-conditioning.

La Roca

Calle 21, entre L y M (334501). **Open** noon-midnight daily. **Main courses** $3-$25. **Map** p312 B11.
Founded in 1956, this restaurant has recently been renovated to its original art deco dinginess. With multi-coloured glass windows and an ornamental flame, you can almost imagine the gangsters of old pouring in from the nearby Capri casino (now closed). An abbreviation of Roberto Carnival (its founder), La Roca stands out from other state restau-

rants due to its excellent service and spotless interior – although the automatic 10% surcharge means you do pay for these privileges. If you can brave the ice-cold air-conditioning, you'll find the food is tasty and well cooked, although portions are a bit skimpy. Sample dishes include spaghetti, salmon and steak. Enjoy a bottle from the plentiful wine list and a cigar from the *humidor* (surprisingly rare in Cuban restaurants). Roast beef is another option, although the sea bass (*cherna*) is a safer, local bet. The neon-lit bar alongside the restaurant is a great spot for cocktails (see *p147*).
Air-conditioning.

Toro

Calle O #206, entre 23 y 25 (333740). **Open** noon-midnight daily. **Main courses** $10.50-$38. **Map** p312 B12.

Not for veggies this one. This first-floor, mirror-walled steakhouse in the Hotel St John's (see *p57*) imports all its meat from Canada, and is embarrassingly proud of the fact that it doesn't use Cuban beef. Prices range from $5 for a burger to $18 for a 12-oz ribsteak to $25 for a T-bone, and higher still; each main dish comes with a jacket spud or rice with veg. If you're feeling carnivorous go for the all-you-can-eat roast beef special for $9.90. This will also get you a free beer or a glass of wine. A good choice of fish and a healthy wine list keeps everyone happy (well, except the veggies.)
Air-conditioning.

The best Restaurants

For celebrity class
Roof Garden at Hotel Sevilla. See *p130*.

For a country club atmosphere
La Giraldilla. See *p139*.

For dainty deco
La Roca. See *p133*.

For faux US burgers
Habana Café at the **Hotel Meliá Cohiba**. See *p132*.

For flush & plush
El Tocororo. See *p140*.

For a perfect pizza (almost)
La Dominica. See *p128*.

For proximity to the beer
El Castillo de Farnés. See *p127*.

For sizzling steak
El Rancho Palco. See *p139*.

For sophistication, Soviet-style
La Torre. See *p134*.

La Torre

Edificio Focsa, Calle 17, entre M y N (553089). **Open** noon-midnight daily. **Main courses** $16-$24. **Map** p312 B11.

It's hard to believe that such an ugly building can house such a sumptuous restaurant. The 36-storey Focsa structure was once called home to thousands of Russian bureaucrats, who were stationed here in the post-Revolutionary years. Now the Russians are gone, its claims to fame are the expensive top-floor restaurant, the national TV studios and the biggest supermarket in the area (on the ground floor). Stunning views and Havana's best French chef (who, as this guide went to press, was due to move to 1830; see *p99* **Club 1830**) have kept the expense account punters coming back to The Tower time and again. Expect to blow $50 per head, as you won't want to miss either the starters or the wine. The menu includes a variety of imported meats to ensure a high-quality meal. If you want the views without emptying your wallet, the adjoining bar does excellent cocktails from $3 a shot. A word of warning: in late 2000 a lift in the building fell 28 floors killing four people, including the proprietress of La Torre; it was unclear at press time how this would ultimately affect the restaurant.
Air-conditioning.

Paladares

Amor

Calle 23 #759, entre B y C (38150). **Open** noon-midnight daily. **Main courses** $8-$12. **Map** p312 C10.

You'll literally love Amor. This is one of the best restaurants in Havana, not just because of its great food, but also because it's one of the best-kept houses in the city. Exquisite furniture and decor from the '20s to the '50s adorns this huge, top-floor apartment, giving diners a real eat-in-a-museum experience. As a bonus, this *paladar* actually has everything that's on the menu; great chunks of pork, sizzling chicken in peanut sauce and fantastic fresh fish are served with genuine care and attention. You can even get stuck into a smashing plate of spuds. And, as the icing on the cake, Amor hosts a *peña* (informal musical get-together) called La Azotea de Elda on the first Sunday of each month, with free wine and soft drinks (see *p194*). What a find!

El Bistrot

Calle K #12, entre 7ma y Malecón (322708). **Open** noon-midnight daily. **Main courses** $8-$10. **Map** p312 A11.

This *paladar* sells itself as a French restaurant, but even the cook readily admits that after experimenting with the virtues of French cuisine for a while, he has now gone back to tried-and-tested Cuban fare. Cuban cuisine is apparently more 'manageable' (believable) and more 'popular' (less believable). Despite the lack of French flair, though, this *paladar*

Fast food

Limited access to snacks and junk food can have its benefits. Rarely does a tourist gain weight in Cuba, but you could be the first. If you really do get the munchies and desire a (fairly) quick snack, one place to head for is **Burgui**. This is Cuba's answer to Maccie D's but without the golden arches. There are a few scattered around town, but the best one is on Calle 23 next to the Riviera cinema just past Coppelia. Here you can get cheeseburgers and fries along with the ubiquitous fried chicken. The burgers (from $1) are surprisingly good, and even come in sesame seed-topped baps. Unfortunately, the fries ($1) let the Burgui phenomenon down. Cold, small and in tiny portions, they make you long for a bag of Harry Ramsden's finest.

Another fast food chain you'll find peppered around Havana is **El Rápido** (*rápido* means fast). This red-and-white-canopied franchise has little style and deserves vilifying for dressing all its waitresses, regardless of age or size, in mini dresses. If you can overcome this fashion faux-pas, El Rápido will flog you a piece of fried chicken, or a ham and cheese sandwich and a drink for less than $2. Once again the fries – fatty, crisp-like objects – are not worthy of the name.

You'll find **Rumbos** caféterias (*pictured*) all over the place. They're similar to El Rápido joints, but are more indoor and air-conditioned affairs, serving a variety of food depending on their location. Typically

a Rumbos outside the city serves up more homegrown-type food, while the slickers make do with greasy chicken and plasticky cheesy pizzas. Most operate 24 hours a day and charge less than $3 for a 'meal'.

Going more upmarket (or downmarket, depending on your luck) is **Doña Yulla**. This 'mini restaurant' chain charges in pesos but will happily take your dollars – a dual currency system whereby tourists don't exactly get a great deal. The Cuban *chico* next to you will be getting a cola and a *cerveza* for 20 pesos ($1), while you may be asked to fork out $2. Don't fall for it, particularly as the prices will be marked clearly behind the counter. Occasionally Doña Yulla can turn up trumps with a menu, waitress service and tablecloths. Most of the time, though, expect nothing but fried chicken and pineapple juice. Oh, and another thing – fast food places, in particular Doña Yulla, often run out of what's advertised on the menu, though perhaps that's a blessing in disguise.

is excellent and serves substantially scrumptious food. (It's a good sign when you actually look forward to eating your doggy bag the next day.) The great location in front of the Malecón is at its best at night, when there's less traffic. *Outside tables.*

Calle 10
Calle 10 #314, entre 3ra y 5ta (296702).
Open noon-midnight daily. **Main courses** $8.
Map p311 A8.
Another excellent *paladar* showing off the warmth of Cuban country cooking within the exquisiteness of a Miramar mansion. The service is excellent and the food, while being very Cuban, is cooked with a minimum amount of grease and the maximum amount of vegetables. A welcome break! The fish with Russian salad is especially recommended.

Casa Sarasua
Apartamento #1, Calle 25 #510, entre H y I (322114). **Open** noon-11pm Mon-Sat; closed Sun.
Main courses $3-$5. **Map** p312 B11.

This peso eaterie just near the university on leafy Calle 25 specialises in huge chunks of meat. The owner, the last of his family left on this side of the Florida Straits, takes great pride in showing off his weaponry collection and is happy to recount his entire family history, before and after the Revolution. There are tables in his mini-museum and on the balcony, making this *paladar* ideal for a low-key, low-budget educational evening.

Le Chansonnier
Calle J #257, entre 15 y Línea (321576).
Open 1pm-1am daily. **Main courses** $5-10.
Map p312 B11.
This old colonial house, which also offers accommodation, boasts a lovely front porch. The food is simple but tasty – anything from lamb to rabbit to a huge fruit-and-veg salad for vegetarians – and is enlivened by French-style use of sauces. Service is friendly and the wine selection, though a bit limited, is good.
Outside tables.

La Roca, restored to its art deco former self. *See p133.*

La Esperanza

Calle 16 #105, entre 1ra y 3ra (224361).
Open 7-11pm Mon-Wed, Fri-Sun; closed Thur.
Main courses $5-$10. **Map** p311 A8.
A well-appointed, pretty house with a front room
rather like a lounge. Food is prepared with care, and
tastes good, dammit. There's a decent wine list,
although you can never rely on it due to Cuba's general supply problems. Reservations advised.

Marpoly

Calle K #154 (322471). **Open** noon-midnight daily.
Main courses $6-$10. **Map** p312 A11.
Monkeys, tortoises, parrots, dogs and cats can be
viewed, but not eaten in Marpoly's private zoo out
the back, while at the front of the house, Santa
Barbara protects the household from bad spirits
(usually government inspectors). Sit in the inside
dining room – the garden tends to smell like a pet
shop – and tuck into generous portions of well
cooked typically Creole food. Marpoly is difficult to
find – go one block north of Línea and look out for
the terracotta red pillars.
Air-conditioning. Outside dining.

Las Mercedes

*Calle 18 #204, entre 15 y 17 (no phone/
neighbour 37512).* **Open** noon-midnight daily.
Main courses $8-$14. **Map** p311 B8.
This place is delightful to look at, fun to be in, not
exactly cheap, but worth every cent. Situated in
the leafy streets of Vedado it offers a winning combination of great charm and great food. When you

enter this subtly lit den, be careful not to tread on
the house turtle that roams free. Cuban dishes are
cooked superbly and with imagination. You can
order set menus starting at $15 or pick from the à la
carte choices. The *brocheta* (kebab) is particularly
recommended, but for a real treat go for the Pescado
à la Mercedes (two types of fish in a cheesy sauce).
Outside tables.

Nerei

Calle 19, esquina a L (327860). **Open** noon-
midnight Mon-Fri; 6pm-midnight Sat, Sun.
Main courses $6.80-$8.50. **Map** p312 B11.
There's not even a stool to sit on inside Nerei, so the
outdoor tables, set back from the street by a narrow
leafy garden, are particularly inviting. Perhaps the
family sold off their furniture to invest in their
restaurant; if so, it paid off. The food is above average and includes an excellent duck dish – a welcome
surprise on a *paladar* menu. Chaos seems to reign in
the kitchen, but the service at table is excellent, and
most of the family speak good English. Standards
of cleanliness in the toilet can vary, but it was looking OK the last time we popped in. For a scam-free
evening, this place is recommended.
Outside tables.

El Recanto

Calle 17 #957, entre 8 y 10 (304396).
Open noon-6am Mon, Tue, Thur-Sun; closed
Wed. **Main courses** 25-40 pesos. **Map** p311 B8.
Don't lose confidence on the approach to this hidden
gem. Secreted in a crumbling 1930s house in a

once-affluent area of Vedado, this place offers just about the best value in Havana, but only the intrepid get to enjoy it. Enter through a battered doorway, climb to the first floor (minding the decaying steps), walk down the darkened passageway and enter through an iron barred door. Ignore the people watching telly as you traipse across their living room through to the kitchen. Eventually you will pop out onto the roof, where you'll find a charming palmleaf-lined eating area, kitschly lit for that authentic Cuban atmosphere. Choose the house specialities and avoid anything adventurous such as chop suey. The portions are huge and the food is homegrown and tasty. The bill will be in pesos, but dollars are welcome, and it will be so cheap you won't believe it. That is, until you've seen the state of the toilet.

Outside tables.

Las Tres Bs

Calle 21, entre K y L (329276). **Open** until 11pm daily. **Main courses** $8. **Map** p312 B11.

It's shabby rather than pretty, but in other respects this cosy *paladar* (situated opposite the Coppelia ice-cream parlour in Vedado) lives up to its strap line, 'Bueno, Bonito y Barato' (good, pretty and cheap). Here, the Alfonso family serves up generous helpings of Creole food washed down with a couple of cold ones for the negotiable price of $10 a head. Bad-taste pictures and a mad caged parrot add to the ambience.

Air-conditioning.

Miramar & the western suburbs

A suburb full of diplomats, politicians and expatriates, it's not surprising that Miramar's restaurants seem to have been groomed to satisfy wealthy locals, with service to match.

Restaurants

El Aljibe

Avenida 7ta, entre 24 y 26 (241583). **Open** noon-midnight daily. **Main courses** $12-$24. **Map** p311 B5.

Another one of those restaurants catering for diplomats, business people and nouveau riche Cubans, El Aljibe is very popular, and is certainly the best state restaurant for Creole food. A chicken dish ($12) is the house speciality, but the beef *brocheta* (kebab; $18) far surpasses it. Considering it's one of the largest restaurants in Havana, El Aljibe manages to create an intimate atmosphere. This is mainly due to the palm-leaf bamboo design and the well-placed lighting and fans. Service is good – staff even come around with seconds of rice – but can be slow when the restaurant gets full. The only slight downer is the presence of Top Cat and friends hanging around the tables waiting for scraps. All dishes include rice, beans (of course), salad, fried bananas and potatoes.

Outside tables.

Let them eat cake

Cubans go mad for it. Sickly sweet, large and kitsch, '*kek*' or '*ke*', as the Cubans call it, is an integral part of Cuban life. Brought out for any occasion: birthdays, Mother's Day, International Day of the Woman (huge in Cuba), Children's Day, Father's Day, weddings, Elián González coming home, whatever... It's not unusual to see a *habanero* cycling through the back streets precariously balancing a three-foot cake on his handlebars. For *quince años* celebrations (a girl's 15th birthday/coming of age party; *see p172* **Sweet 15**) and weddings, the government allows citizens to buy cake, beer and rum in pesos. All the other cakes that you see will have been bought illegally (which gives you an idea of the extent of the black market). Unfortunately, the cakes don't taste as good as they look: the pastel-coloured, creamy coverings are more reminiscent of shaving foam than icing and, to ensure a maximum gorge factor, they are often enhanced with coconut and sugar syrup.

Eat, Drink, Shop

Street treats

Whether or not you eat from a Cuban
street stall will be directly related to the
strength of your stomach. Quite often the
kitchens at these places are clean and use
purified water, but where food is concerned
'quite often' is not good enough. Many
street stalls can been visited several times
with no ill effects, but if you are prone to
stomach upsets when abroad it is best to
proceed with caution.

Street stalls sell an array of calorie-
packed snacks: pizzas; sandwiches of
malanga (a root vegetable similar to taro);
Cuban pasties (disappointing); every
type of fritter you can imagine; pasta
sandwiches; pork sarnies (very fatty) and
cakes to add some sugar to the grease
intake. Pizzas are the most common
offering, and although they're a far cry
from the Neapolitan originals, they're
cheap, filling and actually quite enjoyable.

If you're in need of a nibble, take
advantage of individual vendors selling
maní (nuts), *pan con guava* (jam sandwich),
tamal (a corn paste that takes a bit of
getting used to) and popcorn (chewy).

All produce from street vendors is sold
in pesos and is therefore extremely cheap
(less than 20 pesos or $1 for a meal). If
you've got the stomach for it and a sense
of adventure, street food is an integral part
of the Havana experience. For some of the
best snacks in town, follow the queues to
the **Doña Laura** kiosk on Calle H in Vedado.

La Cecilia

Avenida 5ta, entre 110 y 112 (241562). **Open**
noon-midnight daily. **Main courses** $15-$30.
La Cecilia has it all: air-conditioning, outdoor eating,
indoor eating, top points for being virtually the
only place in Havana to serve *ajiaco*, which is
supposed to be the national dish. The waiters are
very friendly, remaining so even when a group of
60 or so drunk businessmen descend upon them.
Recommended is the *Especialidad de la Casa*, which
is a huge meal to share, with all the Creole specialities you could imagine: corn paste, sweet potato,
pork scratchings, *moros y cristianos*, plantains,
yucca, chicken, pork and *ropa vieja*. At weekends a
cabaret entertains with dancing going on till the
early hours.
Air-conditioning. Outside tables.

Dos Gardenias

Avenida 7ma, esquina a 26 (249662). **Open**
noon-midnight daily. **Main courses** from $10.
Map p311 B5.
Absurdly called a 'Cultural Tourist Complex', Dos
Gardenias is just a dolled-up shopping mall, with
three restaurants to chose from: Shanghai (Chinese),
Gambinas (Italian) and El Criollo (Creole).

Go local, as the food at **El Criollo** is tasty, plentiful and reasonably priced. For $9.90, you can get as
much roast beef as you like, with chips, salad, bread
and rice – it's probably as near that you will get to
the likes of a Sunday roast while you're in Cuba. The
usual suspects of chicken, pork and lobster offer
some choice, but go for the beef while you've got the
chance. Vegetarians are, as usual, very under-catered
for. Located in the covered patio of the complex, El
Criollo also provides the most pleasant atmosphere
of the three. Both the **Shanghai** and **Gambinas**,
while nicely air-conditioned, are slightly sterile.

At the side of the complex on Calle 26 is the open-
air **Palmares** garden, which serves fast food and
drinks. To end the night, the **Salón Bolero** provides music and entertainment from 7pm till 4am.
*Air-conditioning (Shanghai, Gambinas only). Outside
tables (El Criollo, Palmares only).*

La Ferminia

*Avenida 5ta #18207, entre 182 y 184, Siboney
(336555/336786).* **Open** noon-midnight daily.
Main courses $12-$30.
Reputedly one of Havana's best restaurants, La
Ferminia doesn't quite achieve those dizzy heights,
but is certainly pleasurable to look at. The doormen
are immaculately dressed, the interior is crystal-lit
and the gardens are well manicured. Unfortunately
less time and care has been spent on the food.
Although wide in variety, it is thin on quality. Dishes
are sometimes served up cold, and overcharging is
not unknown. Nonetheless, since the main clientele
are on expense accounts, most enjoy an evening here.
Of the dishes, peppered salmon with garlic (sweet and
sour, for some strange reason) and the *filet mignon*
with bacon and (tinned) mushrooms are recommended. The musicians are talented and soothingly

No more rice and beans!

Cuban cooking has been the brunt of jokes for many years. Yet, at its best, the country's essentially peasant cuisine is distinctive, hearty and uncomplicated; not as spicily hot as a lot of other Latin American and Caribbean fare, but certainly not lacking in flavour and taste. Ingredients such as lime juice, orange juice, olives, peppers, cumin, marjoram, bay leaves, garlic and lots of onion are evidence of the mix of Spanish, African and Chinese influences that have created this vibrant, earthy and sensuous cuisine. Today, you might be forgiven for thinking that Cuban

cooking consists solely of rice and beans, with the odd bit of chicken or pork thrown in. While you can certainly overdose on these staples within a few days of being in Havana, if you look hard, you might find the occasional, more traditional Cuban dish hidden away on the menu. Dishes to keep an eye out for include *ajíaco* (a Creole stew) and *tasajo* (dried cured beef). Typically Cuban ingredients, meanwhile, include *yuca* (cassava, often shaved or as fritters) and *plátano* (plantain, often served fried). Amazingly, for an island, seafood (good or otherwise) is hard to come by.

un-*Guantanamera*. The service is attentive, if not a little intrusive (it's a training school for upcoming waiters) and if you don't mind paying for the water and bread that you didn't ask for, you may well have as pleasurable an evening as the ambience promises. A 10% service change is added automatically.
Air-conditioning. Outside tables.

La Fiesta
Avenida 5ta #248, Marina Hemingway, Santa Fe (241150). **Open** 1-9pm Tue-Sun; closed Mon. **Main courses** $15. **Main courses** $6-$20.
La Fiesta combines good food, professional service and great wine (well, for Cuba), and although the size of the main courses can be slightly disappointing, this can be pleasantly overcome by indulging in a tasty tuna salad or *brocheta* (kebab) for starters. Paella and calamari are the house specialities, but the real reason to make a beeline for this place is the music. If the resident band has not been poached by the time you come to Havana, you're in for a real treat from the four talented and musicians, two of whom are blind. The music is loud, but you really won't mind leaving the conversation till later.
Air-conditioning.

La Giraldilla
Calle 222, esquina a 39, La Coronela, La Lisa (246062). **Open** noon-midnight daily. **Main courses** $5.60-$29.
It's worth every penny of the cab fare ($12 or so from Vedado) to reach Havana's trendiest scene. By day, a palm tree-surrounded pool and tapas bar attract foreigners and locals alike. By night, La Giraldilla's Macumba cabaret awakens and Havana's elite dines in complete un-Cuban luxury. Between noon and midnight you can choose to dine in several restaurants at the complex. Particularly recommended is the wine cellar, **La Bodega del Vino** (*see also p158*). It's cool and cosy and serves a pared-down version of the menu offered in the three restaurants of **El Patio Los Naranjos**. The white, red or green room of the latter serves the best food in the complex.

Try a $10 bottle of French merlot with your duck ($15) or a $300 bottle of Château Mouton-Rothschild (1993) with your grilled lobster in Ricard sauce ($20). The gazpacho ($4.50) and the shrimps in sweet and sour sauce ($18) will leave your taste buds watering for weeks. If you spend $25 in the restaurant (and you will) you can get into the nightclub for free (otherwise the cover charge is $10 to $15).
Air-conditioning. Outside tables.

La Maison
Avenida 7ma, esquina a 16 (241543/241546). **Open** 10am-12.45am daily. *Dinner shows* 8pm-1am daily. *La Maison en Verano* 10am-4pm daily. **Set menus** *Dinner shows* $30. *La Maison en Verano* $2.50-$5.50. **Map** p311 B6.
La Maison is supposed to be a fashion, shopping and eating extravaganza, but it doesn't quite make it. Set in a spectacular building that could double as an Embassy, you need to walk through the (messy) air-conditioned shopping section (*see p149*) to arrive at the rear courtyard, catwalk and dining area. From Monday to Thursday there are evening events such as fashion shows, concerts and dancing. Fridays and Saturdays are billed as 'Spectaculars' and include all sorts of musical madness and fashion festivities. A $30 cover will get you in and pay for your Creole dinner; the usual Cuban mix of chicken, pork, rice and the ever-disappointing Cuban salad. Also check out **La Maison en Verano**, the café next to the pool at the back. Here you can watch kids tire themselves out jumping in and out of the pool, while you sip your *mojito* in the jacuzzi. Set prices range from $2.50 for chicken and chips to $5.50 for grilled fish with rice. All options come with a drink.
Air-conditioning. Outside tables.

El Rancho Palco
Calle 140, esquina a 19, Cubanacán (289346). **Open** noon-midnight daily. Main courses $15-$35.
Without doubt one of Havana's best restaurants, El Rancho Palco (also known as El Ranchón) will blow away any negative feelings about Cuban food (well,

for the duration of the meal anyway). Super, juicy steaks, beautifully cooked fish, a basket of, shock! horror!, different types of fresh bread, and elaborate desserts all feature, though you will pay through the nose and the waiters will seemingly make up the prices as they go along. The restaurant is set amid lovely tropical gardens and a lake, with ceiling fans, and signs and fake parrots hanging from the ceiling. Say hello to the (real) parrots before you leave.
Air-conditioning.

El Tocororo
Avenida 3ra, esquina a 18 (242209/242998).
Open noon-midnight daily. **Main courses** $20-$30. **Map** p311 B6.
Money no object? Then Tocororo (named after the Trogon, Cuba's national bird) may be the place for you. The service is excellent but the fact that there is no menu means you have to engage in conversation with the waiters whether you like it or not, though thankfully here they're pleasant and accommodate less wealthy customers by lowering their voice when it comes to the question of prices. (Though they'll still flog the most expensive stuff to tourists.) Try asking for pork and the waiter will look sympathetic and explain that 'pork is peso currency food.' Negatives aside, Tocororo has a beautiful dining room with lanterns speckled among the plants, their musicians are top class and the food, including Cuban classics such as *tasajo*, is delicious. *Air-conditioning.*

Paladares

La Cocina de Lilliam
Calle 48 #1311, entre 13 y 15, Playa (296514).
Open noon-3pm, 7-10pm Mon-Fri, Sun; closed Sat. Closed 1st 2wks Aug & all Dec. **Main courses** $8.50-$10. **Map** p310 C4.
La Cocina de Lilliam offers the best cooking in Havana and has earned a deserved reputation among expatriates for well prepared, well presented and tasty food. The chickpeas, fish and the *ropa vieja* are especially recommended. Dining in the garden is a delight and service is quick and unobtrusive. This place is something of a trek from the main tourist scene, but it's totally worth the taxi fare as La Cocina de Lilliam represents the best value for money in Havana. Note the unusual opening times.
Air-conditioning. Outside tables.

Mi Jardín
Calle 66 #517, esquina a 5B (224627). **Open** noon-midnight daily. **Main courses** $6.50-$9.50. **Map** p310 C3.
This place should be called '*Sí, como no?*' (Yes, why not?) in honour of the Mexican proprietor's favourite expression. The owner knows what service is about and his Neapolitan wife and two children, the chefs, certainly know how to cook. Mi Jardín offers a refreshingly unusual menu combining Mexican, Italian and Creole food, and although the pitiful state

of Cuban food distribution hurts the Mexican side of the menu by denying it beef and great dollops of cheese, the food is still recommended. The *topopas* (nachos), *enchiladas*, *brocheta* (kebab) and the *papas fritas con mojo* (chips with garlic and lemon-seasoned salsa) are especially excellent. After all this, make sure you also sample the house speciality, *helado caliente* (hot ice-cream). Don't be surprised if Señor takes a shine to you and asks if he can take your photo to adorn his walls. Top class.
Air-conditioning. Outside tables.

Pizza Nova
Marina Hemingway (all branches 246969).
Open *Restaurant* 11am-1am daily. *Takeaway* 11.30am-midnight daily.
Not a bad little set-up, tucked neatly into the quay just before the yacht club. For sunny days and calm nights, the leafy green, red-bricked garden is a charming place to sit. The air-conditioned interior, which looks onto the garden, provides a safe haven if the weather plays up. And, if you fancy a frame, there's a pool room out the front. Eating-wise, pizzas, pastas and salad are available. Stick to the pizza (pasta is inevitably overcooked in Cuba). You design your own pizza by adding toppings to a small, large or family-sized cheese and tomato base; toppings range from $1 for basic things like garlic, to around $10 if you want lobster on your family-sized. The tasty creations will arrive worryingly quickly (especially considering they look slightly overcooked). Telephone orders are accepted and ready in 45 minutes (or so they claim), but bizarrely there's no delivery service.
Air-conditioning. Outside tables.
Branches: Avenida de Italia (Galiano), esquina a Concordia, Centro Habana; Calle 17, esquina a 10, Vedado.

The eastern bay & coast

If you're spending a day at the **Playas de Este**, there are plenty of places to grab a bite. The best ones, **Paladar Piccolo, Villas Los Pinos** and **El Brocal**, are reviewed below. In **Guanabo**, **Cafetería La Cocinita**, on Avenida 5ta, is another good option, or, if it's ice-cream you're after, try **Cremería Betty** or its better nextdoor neighbour, **Los Almendros**.

Restaurants

Los XII Apóstoles
Vía Monumental, Castillo de los Tres Reyes del Morro, Parque Militar Morro-Cabaña (638295).
Open noon-2am daily. **Main courses** $2-$28.
For pure Criollo and an excellent view of the Malecón, the Twelve Apostles at the foot of the lighthouse in Casablanca has to be tried. A terrific meat plate (it's even got a piece of beef on it) can be yours for $12, and after 11pm locals start to gather for

dancing. You will be expected to join in the rum-swilling action. To cap it all, Los XII Apóstoles has the cleanest toilets in Cuba, although this claim is unlikely to be sustainable.
Outside tables.

El Brocal

Avenida 5ta, esquina a 498, Guanabo (962892).
Open noon-midnight daily. **Main courses** $2-$19.
Map p315 B30.
This 1930s house has a calmness about it. The Mexican-laid wooden tables may remind you of a low-key, Key West Margaritaville. With cocktails and beer from 85¢ up, the charm comes cheap. The brave attempts at Mexican food is substantiated by the ultimate treat for a Cuban, a bottle of shop-bought salsa. No complaints though: where else in Havana can you get tacos for US$1.50? El Brocal does offer what it knows best, the trusted Cuban pork steak and the more appropriate – for the visitor – seafood dish. Set menus available from $7.50, though beers and nachos (*a la cubana*) are most recommended.
Outside tables.

La Divina Pastora

near the Fortaleza de la Cabaña, Parque Militar Morro-Cabaña (338341). **Open** noon-11pm daily.
Main courses $15-$25.
Fancy fish, fancy service, fantastic views. Like its neighbour, the cheaper Los XII Apóstoles (*see p140*), this place is protected from the hectic mayhem of La Habana Vieja by the beautiful (if sometimes smelly) entrance to Havana harbour. Dominated by the splendid fortress directly behind, its palm tree and cannon-lined waterfront makes the hassle of finding it worthwhile. Moreover, the superb cooking and generous portions almost warrant the hefty pricing. Touches like an ice bucket for your Cristal and a quality eight-piece band tip this place into the top ten list. Though, with over 100 (often empty) seats, those of you seeking an intimate experience should look elsewhere.
Air-conditioning. Outside tables.

Villas Los Pinos

Avenida de las Terrazas, Santa María del Mar (971361). **Open** *La Parrillada Costarenas Bar* noon-5pm daily. *Restaurant* noon-6pm daily.
Cafetería Pinomar 7am-10pm daily. **Main courses** *La Parrillada Costarenas* $2.50-$22.50.
Cafetería Pinomar $1-$3. **Map** p314 A20.
This tourist complex has several eateries; the best is the grill-restaurant **La Parrillada Costarenas**, with clean, glossy tiles and plastic double-glazing. Choose from the simplest piece of chicken ($2.50), or go upmarket with the lobster. Service is friendly, but the best thing is being able to sip beers on the balcony. There's a pool table upstairs.
For morning coffees and cheap snack food, walk 100m inland. The extra few paces from the beach are worth it. Snack bar **Cafetería Pinomar** has an extensive, inexpensive menu (a burger for $1.20, a 'super' burger for $1.95 should give you the gist). The fried

Eat, Drink, Shop

If music be the food of love…

During your first few days in Havana, you will fall in love with the constant sound of musicians serenading you as you eat. By the fourth day, however, when you begin to recognise all the songs, you may find yourself searching desperately for seats in the background to avoid unnecessary attention. At this point it is worth remembering that the limited repertoire you keep on hearing is designed to appeal to package tourists; if you ask the musicians for something other than tunes from the *Buena Vista Social Club*, you are likely to be dazzled by their talent and virtuosity. The excellent musicianship on show is poorly reflected in a miserable salary of $10 per month, so be generous with the tips (anything from one dollar up will be graciously accepted), but don't give anything if the band approaches you as soon as you sit down (it does happen). The band will invariably have a tape ($4-$5) to flog to you, and some of the more inventive groups organise raffles, too. It is surprising how successful they are in drumming

up enthusiasm, considering the tickets are sold for $3 and the grand prize is usually a $3 bottle of rum.

OTHER ENTERTAINMENT

Dancing, Cuba's national pastime, is to be found in cabarets, restaurants, bars and clubs throughout the city. The impromptu dances are the most fun, particularly when the locals grab tourists to join in. Cubans take great pleasure in most foreigners' inability to dance, but that won't stop them trying to teach you. Often you will go out for a quiet meal or a drink and find yourself immersed in a *salsa* set – throw caution to the winds, drink lots of rum and enjoy!

A few magicians stroll the streets of La Habana Vieja and Chinatown and will be happy to amaze you in return for 'whatever you'd like to give'. One chap, Felipe, who haunts Café Taberna (*see p127*) and Chinatown, is particularly excellent.

For the bars and restaurants with the best musicians, including ones also mentioned in this chapter, *see chapter* **Music & Nightlife**.

Vegging out

Vegetarians will go hungry in Cuba. Due to a long Spanish occupation and the mandatory no-meat eating during the Special Period, the Cubans love meat and naturally assume that tourists do too. Many of the *paladares* are excellent for a good meat feast, but are unlikely to be able to rustle up anything flesh-free, besides the odd omelette. Once you've exhausted the hotel salad bars, **El Bambú** (officially Eco-Restorán El Bambú), in the appropriate setting of the Jardín Botánico way down in southern Havana, is really the only solution. Good job, then, that it's worth the trek (whether you're veggie or not).

Not just a restaurant but an inspired and inspiring project, El Bambú offers around 25 different dishes created using organic produce grown on the adjacent plot of land or in the *organopónico* (market garden). As you walk into the main area check out the herb beds boasting healthy crops of basil, coriander, mint, linden and rosemary, used for flavouring and for Bambú's delicious herbal tea. Even the honey comes from the restaurant's own hives located at the rear of the building.

Both the existence of El Bambú and its growing popularity are a virtual miracle in a country where the staple diet is notoriously unhealthy (starchy, fatty and lacking in vitamins, being as it is based on rice and pork, plus the occasional overboiled vegetable and an insipid salad of white cabbage and cucumber). It was with the ambitious aim of reversing these deeply ingrained habits that Bambú was established in 1992. The wide selection of cooked and raw dishes, based on Cuban and foreign recipes, is an attempt to lure locals away from a starch-, sugar- and salt-heavy diet. When groups from workplaces, schools and senior citizens' homes visit El Bambú, they are often welcomed with an introductory talk about the benefits of healthy eating. The social aspect of El Bambú's work means that this is one of the few restaurants in Havana where both foreign visitors and local Cubans eat together, enjoying food of the same quality from the same menu.

Admittedly, as a visitor you will pay $10 for the privilege, as opposed to the 40 pesos paid by local diners, but this still represents excellent value for money. The meal is an extended buffet consisting of soup, rice and pasta dishes, exotic vegetables such as taro and cassava (*yuca*), as well as pumpkin,

French beans, Swiss chard, beetroot, *tamal*, spinach, aubergine cooked in a cheese sauce, *fufo* (mashed boiled green banana with a garlic seasoning) and a good selection of salads and salad dressings. Since the produce is not imported, the menu varies according to the season and, as long as there is still food on the buffet table, you can fill your plate as often as you wish. The price includes natural fruit juice, but beer, bottled water and other beverages are sold separately in recyclable containers. Coffee and herbal teas are available on a self-serve basis from large urns. For an extra $2 you can get a dessert – usually a version of ice-cream made on the premises with non-dairy produce.

To get to El Bambú from the centre of Havana you will either need to take a taxi (about $15) or brave a bus ride (40 centavos) from the corner of Presidentes (G) and 27 in Vedado. Once there, you pay a $1 entrance fee to the Gardens, and take a ten-minute 'train' ride (wagons pulled by a tractor) to the restaurant, which is located beside magnificent Japanese gardens and a lake. The train departs every 15 minutes (in theory). However, like all public transport in Cuba, it fills to capacity very quickly, so you may be forced to wait for some time before you are able to board.

The restaurant has a seating capacity of around 60 and is usually fully booked, particularly at weekends. It is always worth reserving a table, either by telephone in advance or by arriving early (well before 11am) and collecting a reservation voucher at the entrance to the Botanic Gardens.

El Bambú

Jardín Botánico, Carretera El Rocío 3.5km, Calabazar, Boyeros (544106/reservations 547278/fax 544184). **Open** 1-5pm Wed-Sun; closed Mon, Tue. **Set lunch** (incl dessert) $12; 40 pesos.

chicken and toasted *bocaditos* are dependable (if you aren't already sick of them). With a bar atmosphere and cold tinnies at 85¢ a piece, it's not a bad place. Like all joints in this area, Pinomar shuts early.

Paladares

Paladar Piccolo

Avenida 5ta, entre 502 y 504, Guanabo (964300).
Open noon-midnight daily. **Main courses** $6-$10.
Map p315 B31.

With Pinocchio standing guard, this *paladar* is painted nearly as brightly as it deserves. The garden is full of vegetation – healthy lettuce and bright red tomatoes. Guests wait on the yellow chairs for one of the 12 well-used seats inside (as required by law).The decor just about manages not to be kitsch, while at the same time maintaining the *casa*'s colour. The food is excellent: very Italian (even though the owners are of Greek origin), very comforting (fresh food, big salad) and very surprising (it's such good value). Piccolo is the perfect place to answer those hunger pangs when you're at the beach, which is only 150m away. Other recommended eateries in the area, all near the corner of Avenida 5ta and Calle 482 are **Don Peppo**, **Italnova** and **Restaurante Menabel**, which has a nice balcony.
Outside tables.

Cerro & further south

Paradiso

next door to Terminal 3, Aeropuerto Internacional José Martí (558864). **Open** 11am-11pm daily.
Main courses $2.65-$35.

If you get to the airport early and find your Cubana flight has been delayed till next Tuesday (which is always a distinct possibility), you'll be glad of the new, purpose-built Paradiso. This restaurant is not only convenient (three minutes' walk from the terminal), but unbelievably cheap and well stocked and serviced. Or, as the restaurant's flyer puts it: 'You can dine or get together in a tranquil ambience without having to worry about being in a herry since we have the privilege of being a restaurant with its own airport.' (sic) Paradiso is comfortably away from the airport hustle and bustle and, with bargain meals such as pork steak with chips and veg for $3, you really can't go wrong. If you've got holiday money to get rid of, the menu also has lobster and beef. If you fancy the novelty of eating in a converted Russian Ilyshin 62 plane, head to El Avión, in the terminal building, which serves cheap, light meals.
Air-conditioning.

Las Ruinas

Parque Lenin, southern Havana (578286/578523). **Open** noon-9pm Tue-Sun; closed Mon.
Main courses $15-$20.

Las Ruinas is a 1972 concrete, Meccano-like structure suspended over the ruins of the 19th-century residence of Countess Paso Seco. This contradictory design provides an enchanting atmosphere, only slightly compromised by the mosquitoes. The stained-glass art work is by the Cuban Ponsocarrero, probably of equal interest to art enthusiasts as the building is to architects. The food is less appealing, though it's filling and fairly cheap. The service is prompt and efficient and worth the 10% charge (unusually, this is not added automatically). Combine the specialties of the house with plenty of *mojitos* and you're laughing. This place is recommend if you're on your way back from the Botanical Gardens, PABEXPO or Parque Lenin, but otherwise it's hard to justify the taxi fare.
Outside tables.

Bars

Most visitors are surprised to find that the bar life in Havana does not meet their high, Hemingway- or Graham Greene-inspired expectations. You will not find unshaven, linen-suited drunks being kicked out of one neon-lit cocktail joint only to stumble next door for another *mojito* – far from it. The packed, noisy and lively bars and brothels of pre-1959 days are long gone. Today, you have to search quite hard to find a reasonable oasis to while away the hours. Most of the bars follow a tried-and-trusted formula of watery *mojitos*, Cristal beer, and four- or five-piece bands churning out the same old *salsa* songs. Shame. That's not to say you cannot recapture some of that swinging pre-Revolutionary bar life in 21st-century Havana, you just have to look harder for it.

The flashy hotels have great bars, each with their unique character and ambience. **Hotel Sevilla** in Centro Habana and **Hotel Nacional** in Vedado are particularly good examples. To find a genuine independent bar is tougher. Even the Hemingway haunts of **La Bodeguita del Medio** and **El Floridita** have lost their former quality. If you fancy a bit of a bar crawl it's best to head to the Obispo area, in La Habana Vieja, where you'll find the densest concentration of drinking holes. Bars here have been refurbished to cater for tourists and are therefore cleaner, hipper and of better quality.

If you fancy something grittier and Cuban, try any of the peso bars around Neptuno in Centro Habana, immediately identifiable by the absence of cans of Cristal. If beer is served at all in these joints, it will be in one-and-a-half-litre brown bottles at ten pesos (50¢) a go. You may even come across bars charging three pesos (15¢) for a rum from an unmarked, old plastic bottle served up in a sawn-off beer bottle. Although these bars are a great experience and are full of interesting characters, after a few drinks here the average holidaymaker is likely to gravitate back to the tourist bars, if only to find a toilet that works.

Eat, Drink, Shop

Most bars serve cheap food such as fried chicken and toasted sandwiches, though you get what you pay for. Notable exceptions, reviewed in the eating section of this chapter, include **El Castillo de Farnés** (*see p127*), **El Patio** (*see p129*), **La Torre** (*see p134*), **Hotel Meliá Cohiba** (*see p132*), **El Polinesio** (*see p133*), **El Conejito** (*see p132*), **La Roca** (*see p133*) and the **Roof Garden** at the Hotel Sevilla (*see p130*).

La Habana Vieja

Bacardí Bar
Edificio Bacardí, Avenida de Bélgica (Monserrate), entre Progreso (San Juan de Dios) y Empedrado (629271/629208). **Open** 8am-8pm Mon-Sat; closed Sun. **Map** p316 D15.
Nice little snug with leather upholstered seats and mirrored walls. The decor is exactly the same as it was in the 1930s, this time though, in contrast to most of Havana, it is shiny and new. Prices are reasonable and with a friendly tip, you will be shown to the *mirador* (lookout) at the top of the building for a wonderful view of old Havana. Recommended for a *mojito* out of the sun.
Air-conditioning.

Bar Monserrate
Avenida de Bélgica (Monserrate), esquina a Obrapía (no phone). **Open** 8.30am-3am daily. **Map** p316 D14.
The Monserrate has the kind of cheap, but not so cheerful food that seems a great answer to those one o'clock in the morning hunger pangs. Otherwise, just enjoy the beer ($1) and the cocktails ($2.50), the resident band and the other tourists. This place is lively, teaming with born-again *salsa* dancers, and the service is always terrific – until they rip you off. Watch your change – they'd do your granny off here.

Café O'Reilly
Calle O'Reilly #203, entre Cuba y San Ignacio (no phone). **Open** 24hrs daily. **Map** p316 E15.
Don't go here expecting Guinness and a good old Irish fry, as tragically they are both unknown substances in Havana. Split between two floors joined by a cast-iron spiral staircase, Café O'Reilly is a relaxing place to stop in the middle of an Old Town tour. Sit on the balcony sipping a cocktail or a beer and listen to the caged birds sing over the bustle below. Food is basic – sandwiches, chicken and pizza – but well priced.
A few doors further along O'Reilly heading east, on the corner of San Ignacio, is a terrace area with barbecue that seems to be connected with O'Reilly. Often a band will sing to you while you munch barbecue platters and sarnies on offer. Wash it down with a cool Cristal.

Café del Oriente
Calle Oficios, esquina a Amargura (602917). **Open** *Bar* 24hrs daily. *Restaurant* noon-midnight daily. **Main courses** $12-$30. **Map** p316 E15.

Also overlooking Plaza de San Francisco, Café del Oriente is a chill-out favourite. For some strange reason *jineteros* don't seem to descend on this place, so the pleasures of sipping a *mojito* and watching the *plaza* go by can be savoured in peace. Quality bands entertain both inside and out. The swish surroundings of the interior are the excuse for relatively expensive food. Service is excellent.
Air-conditioning. Outside tables.

Café de París
San Ignacio, esquina a Obispo (no phone). **Open** 24hrs daily. **Map** p316 E15.
One of the more popular bars in this part of Old Havana, Café de París is always a hive of activity. It attracts the punters with the live Latin music, filling up till there's standing room only inside and hordes of locals without the means to drink outside. If hunger strikes, avoid the greasy fried chicken and grab some pizza from the adjoining street window. Cocktails ($2.50) are average. The music is from noon to midnight daily. About as Parisian as Middlesbrough.

Casa del Escabeche
Calle Obrapía, esquina a Villegas (632660). **Open** 8am-2am daily. **Map** p316 E15.
With no more than 20 seats, Casa del Escabeche only has room for the six-piece band and a small group of tourists to squeeze in. Everybody else waits outside to enjoy the beats. If you can be among the lucky sardine group inside, try it; when the band are playing Casa del Escabeche has the best atmosphere on Obispo. Cocktails cost $2.50; beers are $1.

El Castillo de la Real Fuerza
Plaza de Armas, esquina a Avenida del Puerto (612876). **Open** 9am-midnight daily. **Map** p316 E16.
The roof terrace of the castle (*see p64*) is the most peaceful and pleasant place in Havana to sip a cocktail or a beer. The entrance is through the armour museum, which deters most punters, leaving you to enjoy the wonderful view of Casablanca in splendid isolation. Once you've climbed to the top, you'll be rewarded with a first-class view, wrought-iron furniture and a great *mojito*. It's fully worth the $1 admission charge to enjoy this place and a tour of La Giraldilla's statue (tip the waiter).
Outside tables.

Dos Hermanos
Calle San Pedro #304, esquina a y Sol (no phone). **Open** 24hrs daily. **Map** p316 E15.
As befits its location, this is a port-style bar, with the hookers around the back to prove it. It tends to be empty as it's just off the beaten track, but don't let this dissuade you from giving the Two Brothers a go. There's a good selection of reasonably priced cocktails ($2.50) and the cheap food is actually rather good. A better-than-average band provides entertainment – shame their ridiculously loud microphones ruin the show. Visitors hoping for a conversation will be leaving at 10.30pm.

Useful vocabulary and phrases

PHRASES

Are you open tonight?
¿Están abiertos esta noche?
Sorry, but we ordered an hour ago
Disculpe, pero hace una hora que ordenamos
The coffee is cold
El café está frío
The beer is warm
La cerveza está caliente
Waiter, can we have a menu?
Camarero, ¿Nos podría dar el menú?
Do you have anything besides chicken and pork?
¿Hay algo más en lugar de pollo y cerdo?
Could you check the bill, we think it's wrong
¿Podría revisar la cuenta?, parece que está mal

MISCELLANEOUS

aceite y vinagre oil and vinegar; **agua** water; **con gas** fizzy; **sin gas** still; **autoservicio** self-service café; **bocadito, bocadillo** sandwich; **cerveza** beer; **combinación/menú** set meal; **cremería** ice-cream parlour; **pan** bread; **primer plato/entrante** first course; **mojo** seasoned gravy; **propina** tip; **segundo plato** second or main course; **servicio incluído** service included; **vino** wine

COOKING STYLES AND TECHNIQUES

adobado marinated; **al ajillo** with olive oil and garlic; **a la parilla** charcoal-grilled; **a la plancha** grilled; **asado (al horno de leña)** roasted (in a wood oven); **cocinado** cooked **crudo** raw; **en salsa** in a sauce or gravy; **en escabeche** marinated in vinegar; **estofado** braised; **frito** fried; **guisado** stewed; **hervido** boiled; **relleno** stuffed

HUEVOS (EGGS)

huevos fritos fried eggs; **revuelto** scrambled eggs; **tortilla de papas** potato omelette

SOPAS Y POTAJES (SOUPS AND STEWS)

ajíaco traditional Cuban stew; **caldo** broth; **fabada** white kidney bean soup

PESCADO Y MARISCOS (FISH AND SHELLFISH)

almejas clams; **atún/bonito** tuna; **bacalao** salty cod; **calamares** squid; **camarones** small shrimps; **cangrejo** crab; **cherna** grouper (sea bass); **gambas** prawns; **langosta** lobster; **langostinos** langoustines; **macarela** mackerel; **mejillones** mussels;

ostras oysters; **pargo** red snapper; **pulpo** octopus; **rodaballo** turbot; **salmón** red mullet; **sardinas** sardines; **trucha** trout

CARNE, AVES (MEAT, POULTRY)

bistec steak; **cerdo/lechón** pork/pig; **chivo** goat; **conejo** rabbit; **cordero** lamb; **costillas** ribs; **chuletas**, chops; **cuarto de pollo** chicken leg quarter; **estofado de ternera** veal stew; **faisán** pheasant; **gallina** hen; **hígado** liver; **jamón** ham; **lacón** gammon ham; **lomo (de cerdo)** loin of pork; **pato** duck; **pavo** turkey; **pechuga** breast; **picadillo** mince; **pollo** chicken; **riñones** kidneys; **ropa vieja** (literally old clothes) dish of shredded beef and tomato; **salchichas** sausages; **sesos** brains; **tasajo** dried cured beef; **ternera** veal

ARROZ Y LEGUMBRES (RICE AND PULSES)

congrí/arroz congrí/moros y cristianos rice and black beans cooked together; **fríjoles colorados** red kidney beans; **fríjoles negros** black beans; **garbanzos** chickpeas; **judías** white beans; **lentejas** lentils;

VERDURAS/VEGETALES (VEGETABLES)

acelga Swiss chard; **aguacate** avocado; **berenjena** aubergine/eggplant; **berzas** collard greens; **boniato** sweet potato; **calabaza** squash; **champiñones** mushrooms; **col** cabbage; **ensalada** salad; **habichuela** garden beans; **lechuga** lettuce; **mariquitas** plantain chips; **nabo** turnip; **lechuga** lettuce; **malanga** a root vegetable similar to taro; **papas** potatoes; **pepino** cucumber; **pimientos** sweet peppers; **plátano** plantain, always cooked for eating, either fried (ripe or green) or boiled; **quimbombó** okra; **rabano** radish; **remolacha** beetroot; **tomate** tomato; **vegetales hervidos**, **viviandas hervidas** cooked vegetables; **yuca** cassava; **zanahoria** carrot

FRUTAS (FRUITS)

cerezas cherries; **ciruelas** plums; **fresas** strawberries; **fruta bomba** papaya; **guayaba** guava; **limón** lemon; **manzana** apple; **melocotón** peach; **melón** watermelon; **naranja** orange; **pera** pear; **piña** pineapple; **plátano de fruta** banana; **uvas** grapes.

POSTRES (DESSERTS)

arroz con leche rice pudding; **flan** crème caramel, baked custard; **helado** ice-cream

Eat, Drink, Shop

Drink up

Daiquiri, *mojito* and Cuba Libre are the drinks that are most commonly associated with Cuba. Sure, you'll see plenty of others on offer, such as Ron Collins, but these are the three biggies. Refreshing and easy to throw together, they've been the inspiration for parties and bar menus for more than a century.

For ideas on where to buy rum in Havana, *see p158*.

MOJITO ▶

First drunk by slaves on the island, the *mojito* achieved its current popularity in the 1940s thanks to Ángel Martínez, founder of **La Bodeguita del Medio** restaurant and bar in La Habana Vieja (*see p127*). Artists, musicians and writers (most famously Ernest Hemingway) gathered at the Bodeguita for a glass of the stuff. Check out the chalked-up quote attributed to Hemingway at the bar of the Bodeguita: 'My mojito in La Bodeguita, my daiquiri in El Floridita'.

Where to drink *mojito* in Havana: For the real McCoy it's got to be the **Bodeguita del Medio**.

Recipe: In a tall 8-oz glass mix ½ teaspoon sugar and 15ml lemon juice in a small amount of soda water. Add a couple of mint leaves and crush their stems. Then, add ice cubes and 45ml rum. Fill with soda water and stir. Add 7ml angostura and adorn the drink with a small sprig of mint.

DAIQUIRI ▶

Named after the mining town in eastern Cuba where it was first drunk, the daiquiri's 'home' is **El Floridita** (*see p128*), where barman

Fundación Havana Club (Museo del Ron)

Avenida San Pedro, entre Sol y Muralla (no phone). **Open** 9am-midnight daily. **Map** p316 E15.
The Rum Museum in the Fundación Havana Club is a grand setting for a bar, but the location and the prices render it a vacuum. The excellent resident singer deserves a far bigger, more appreciative audience than the cruise-ship passengers who dock across the road once a month. When there's no cruise ship in town, she stands and sings to a near-empty bar, so make the most of a private concert and drop in after the last museum tour at 4.30pm.
Outside tables.

La Lluvia de Oro

Calle Obispo #316, esquina a Habana (629870). **Open** 8am-1am Mon-Thur; 8am-3am Fri-Sun. **Map** p316 E15.
Prop yourself up against the elegant wooden bar in this large and airy hang-out on Obispo for a beer ($1) or a cocktail ($2.50) – the *mojitos* at the Golden Rain have a definite kick. Lluvia deserves a visit when the band is in full swing, otherwise it's a tad quiet. Recommended as a one-drink stop-off.

Roof Garden Bar

Hotel Ambos Mundos, Calle Obispo, esquina a Mercaderes (609529/609530/609531). **Open** 7am-11pm daily. **Map** p316 E15.
Forget the rather dead lobby bar at this historical hotel and head upstairs to the rooftop bar. Very convenient: close to the action down below on Obispo, but far enough away for you to enjoy your drink in peace. *Outside tables.*

Centro Habana

Roof Garden Bar

Hotel Inglaterra, Paseo de Martí (Prado), esquina a San Rafael (608595). **Open** 6pm-2am Mon, Wed-Sun; closed Tue. **Map** p313 D14.
Overlooking the Parque Central is the hidden rooftop bar of Hotel Inglaterra. It's not the prettiest of bars, but the views (particularly the rooftop of the Gran Teatro) make it worth a visit. Generous cocktails and plenty of Cristal mean that it's not long before people loose their inhibitions and get up to dance on the catwalk-type stage. Only the resident band is capable of emptying the place with its over-enthusiastic use of a dangerously loud microphones.
Air-conditioning.

Vedado

Cafetería Sofía

Calle 23 #202, esquina a O (320540). **Open** 24hrs daily. **Map** p312 B12.
Apart from having a good atmosphere (it's always packed), there's not much to recommend this place. The '50s building is a turn-off for some visitors and the resident band, though very good, is also exceedingly loud. During the course of the Sofía's 24-hour day, however, all sorts drift in and out, which makes it a great place to people-watch. The atmosphere is further enhanced by open-plan terrace seating. Average snack food is available and prices (cocktails $3; beer $1) are pretty much normal for this part of town.

Constantino Ribalaigua Veri gave the daiquiri its current look by adding crushed ice and five drops of Maraschino to the original recipe. **Where to drink a daiquiri in Havana**: Today, any Cuban bartender will whip up a masterful daiquiri, but, in addition to El Floridita, try **El Castillo de Farnés** (*see p127*), **Café de Paris** (*see p144*), **El Patio** (*see p129*) and **El Tocororo** (*see p140*). **Recipe:** mix 45ml rum with two cups of crushed ice, 15ml lemon juice, ½ teaspoon sugar and a few drops of maraschino, and serve it in ready-chilled glasses. For a Hemingway daiquiri, or Papa Doble, omit the sugar in favour of a double shot of rum or whisky.

CUBA LIBRE ▶ Named after the war cry of Cuban independence fighters, the Cuba Libre celebrated its 100th birthday in 1998. **Where to drink a Cuba Libre in Havana:** The bar at the **Museo del Ron** (*see p146*) is recommended. **Recipe:** Fill a tall glass with cola, 45ml rum and 20ml lemon juice, then add ice cubes and decorate with a thin slice of lemon.

Eat, Drink, Shop

Casa de la Amistad

Paseo #406, entre 17 y 19, Vedado (303114/5). Open 11am-midnight Mon-Fri; 11am-2am Sat; 11am-6pm Sun. **Admission** $5 Tue, Sat only. **Map** p312 B9.

This magnificent place should be the British Ambassador's local as his residency is only a couple of doors down on Paseo. Strangely, though, you never see him propping up the bar or staggering home with a carry-out. It's his bad luck, for this converted mansion, with a luscious green garden, hosts great entertainment in the evenings (for details, *see p195*). The food consists of basic snacks, including pizzas and chicken, but to be fair Amistad's real pulling power is its music and happy atmosphere, rather than its grub. Despite the cover charge ($5), this place is highly recommended. *Outside tables.*

Casa del Coctel

Calle 23, esquina a Presidentes (G) (309375). Open 24hrs daily. **Map** p312 C10.

Hidden behind a rickety wooden fence and tall potted plants, this place does bargain cocktails ($1 each) and should be visited only for that reason. If your stomach rumbles enough, you may be tempted to try the bargain $1.30 chicken and chips, but sticking to the booze is more advisable. *Outside tables.*

La Fuente

Calle 13, esquina a Presidentes (G) (662514). Open 8.30am-11.30pm daily. **Map** p312 B10.

La Fuente is a secret little garden hideaway tucked around the corner from the busy Avenida de los

Presidentes (Calle G). A pleasant pond is the focal point of this very cheap yet dignified open-air café/bar. Spirits start at 30¢ a shot (the same price as a coffee), beers are just 85¢ and cocktails just $2. *Outside tables.*

La Roca

Calle 21, entre L y M (334501). Open noon-midnight daily. **Map** p312 B11.

Forget the peso-looking exterior and venture into the bar for a quiet drink, where the low lighting and blue-glowing decor really capture the essence of '50s Havana. Cool, swanky and overflowing with character, La Roca should be a definite pit-stop on a bar crawl of Vedado. And if you need any more persuading, drink prices are more than decent. *Air-conditioning.*

La Terraza del Hotel Nacional

Calle O, esquina a 21 (333564/333567). Open 24hrs daily. **Map** p312 B12.

Stroll up the palm tree-lined, spotlit driveway; breeze past the fancily dressed doormen; strut straight through the glorious lobby and you'll pop out onto the Nacional's magnificent terrace; settle into a sofa and within a minute you can order that cocktail ($3.50) – can't be bad. This is definitely the place to smoke your latest black market purchases, but it's not at all pretentious and is *the* place in Havana to chill out. With music comfortably in the background and seats throughout the grounds, this place should not be missed. As a bonus you'll be rewarded with the best sea view in Havana. For details of the hotel itself, *see p56.* *Outside tables.*

Shops & Services

No one comes to Havana to shop. Years of shortages have left their mark on the city. As dollars flood in, however, things are beginning to change, and if you look carefully you can find most things you need, if not everything you'd like.

Shopping in Havana is quite a complex process. Despite the US embargo, there are shopping opportunities in the city, but it is necessary to keep an open mind about what's on offer and not judge the quality and choice of goods in terms of other, more advanced markets. The golden rule is: if you see something you want, buy it immediately, as it may not be there next time you pass by. Likewise, basic provisions come and go – even staples like milk have been known to run out – so stock up on any favourite food items.

WHERE TO GO

Not surprisingly, Havana has no Rodeo Drive or Bond Street. In terms of shopping areas as such, there are some good shops in **La Habana Vieja**, particularly in and around **Calle Obispo**, while **Avenida de Italia** (Galiano) in **Centro Habana** is where you'll find the Cuban **peso shops** (see p152). If you really want to see some of the more interesting shops you'll need a car to travel out of the centre. A lot of the best-stocked shops are to be found in the shopping malls, in particular those in hotels, and those concentrated in the **Miramar** residential area and spreading out towards **Marina Hemingway**. **General stores** that sell a bit of everything are far more common in Havana than specialist shops and, on the whole, **department stores** provide the most comprehensive range of goods. Many shops in both department stores and hotel complexes are targeted exclusively at foreigners, with prices that may not seem that over the top to Westerners, but are out of the reach of the average Cuban, whose monthly salary rarely tops $20.

Given the increasing numbers of tourists visiting Havana, is not unreasonable to expect substantial developments in the retail sector in Cuba in the near future. Although changes have been slow in previous years, the precedents have now been set for a significant increase in foreign investment and joint ventures.

PRACTICALITIES AND ETIQUETTE

You are not allowed to enter most of the bigger stores with any sort of bag (including a handbag). Instead, shoppers deposit their bags at the *guardabolsas* for the duration of their shopping trip. (Always take your money and identification papers out of the bag before you hand it over.) When you leave the shop, any products you have bought will be checked against your receipt by the security guard.

If you drive to a shop, it is normal to pay a *parqueo* (car park attendant) 25 cents to watch your vehicle; around the bigger hotels a $1 charge is more usual.

Most shops in Havana don't close for a summer break, but do close for national holidays such as 1 May and New Year. Shops that are very popular with tourists may stay open even then, though.

Credit cards are accepted in more 'gifty' shops and international ones, provided they're not issued by a US bank. However, you're wise to try to pay in cash (generally dollars) at all times, as credit card machines in Havana have a habit of breaking down.

Habaneros are desperate for dollars, so you will be able to barter successfully in the city's **markets** (see p162), especially if you show appreciation for an object's craftsmanship or quality. Bear in mind, however, that prices are already likely to be more than reasonable, so don't get carried away trying to reach the lowest possible price. Always be aware of the lure of the dollar: even widely travelled people can get ripped off in Havana (but at least it's always done with a smile).

One-stop

Also look out for **Tiendas Panamericanas**, small department stores catering particularly to tourists, found all over Havana.

Department stores

Many of the following are also recommended for particular items elsewhere in this chapter.

Casa Blanca

Avenida 1ra, esquina a 36, Miramar (243941/2).
Open 10am-6pm Mon-Sat; 9am-1pm Sun.
Map p310 B4.
Another department store housed in a beautifully decorated mansion. There are electronic goods on the second floor, while shoes, clothes, food and drinks complete the picture.

Try **La Época** for an epic Havana shopfest.

La Época
Avenida de Italia (Galiano), esquina a Neptuno, Centro Habana (669414/669419). **Open** 9.30am-7pm Mon-Sat; 9.30am-2pm Sun. **Map** p313 D14.
This department store, one of the TRD chain of shops found all over town, is particularly good for children's clothes and for fabrics. There are also some French-label fashions on the first floor.

Harris Brothers
Avenida de Bélgica (Monserrate) #305, entre O'Reilly y Progreso (San Juan de Dios), La Habana Vieja (611644/611615/612045). **Open** 9am-9pm daily. **Map** p313 D14.
This well-known department store stocks a reasonable range of fashions, including Benetton, a range of kids' clothes and toys and a good selection of sportswear. The first floor has decent (for Havana) provisions and toiletries.

La Maison
Calle 16 #701, esquina a 7ma, Miramar (241546/241548). **Open** 10am-6.45pm Mon-Sat; closed Sun. *Hairdresser* noon-7pm Mon-Sat; closed Sun. **Map** p311 B6.
This collection of shops, housed in a beautifully decorated colonial building, is most famous for its fashion shows and events, held every night in its attractive garden. Inside you'll find jewellers selling antique tableware; collectors' coins; a wide range of watches and modern and antique jewellery; a perfumery with Havana's widest selection of cosmetics and La Preferencia cigar shop. Upstairs are children's toys and clothes, baby items, male and female fashions, shoes, luggage, household goods by Baccarat and tableware and bed linen. Other attractions include a pool, Jacuzzi, bar, restaurant, sauna, piano bar, beauty salon and a hairdressing salon.

Le Select
Avenida 5ta, esquina a 30, Miramar (247410/247411). **Open** 10am-8pm Mon-Sat; 10am-2pm Sun. *Hairdresser* noon-8pm Mon-Sat; closed Sun. **Map** p311 B5.

Housed in a beautiful mansion, this upscale department store has a fantastic entrance hall, with sparkling chandeliers, marble statues and a stained-glass window as you go upstairs. It's one of those places where there are more staff than clientele and is arguably the best shop in town for service. You may be forgiven for thinking you're in Beverly Hills as staff park your car and load your shopping.

On the ground floor is a delicatessen – the only one in Havana worthy of the name – stocking a variety of products including caviar, smoked salmon, cheese, salami, pâté, dried fruits and nuts, pastas and freshly baked bread. Upstairs are various boutiques selling men's and women's fashions, jewellery, shoes, bags, accessories, lingerie, swimwear and beauty products. There's also a bridal hire shop, an outdoor restaurant, a hair and beauty salon and a present-wrapping service. The boutiques are sometimes locked, but can be opened on request by the ever-present, hovering sales staff.

Shopping centres

5ta y 42
Avenida 5ta, esquina a 42, Miramar (247070). **Open** 10am-6pm Mon-Sat; 9am-1pm Sun. **Map** p310 B4.
Belongs to the Cubalse chain, of which there are branches throughout the city. There's quite a large array of shops at this shopping centre, and it's especially recommended for kids' stuff, shoes and leather goods, oh, and the decent pizzas sold in the car park.

Centro Comercial Náutico
Avenida 5ta, esquina a 152, Náutico (286212). **Open** 10am-6pm Mon-Sat; 9am-1pm Sun.
Stores include a mini-supermarket, cafeteria, dollar shop and perfumery. Electronic goods, furniture and poor-quality fashions are also sold.

Centro Comercial La Vigía
Avenida 5ta, esquina a 248, Marina Hemingway, Jaimanitas (241151/56). **Open** 10am-7pm Mon-Sat; 10am-2pm Sun.
Security is quite tight at the Marina, with Cubans not allowed to enter alone unless they work here. The supermarket stocks some good but fairly expensive wines, plus obscure products such as Angostura bitters that can't be found elsewhere. The complex also includes a perfumery, cigar shop, souvenir shop and two restaurants. Sports and electrical goods, shoes and T-shirts are also sold. Quality is generally high.

Centro de Negocios Miramar
Avenida 3ra, entre 76 y 80, Miramar (244437/8). **Open** 10am-6pm Mon-Sat; 10am-1pm Sun. **Map** p310 B2.
Shops in the Miramar Trade Centre include Ofimática, an offshoot of Dita (*see p154*), which sells computer equipment, a photo-processing outlet and stores selling sports equipment. Clothes, shoes and jewellery are also available.

Harris Brothers – an old-time Old Havana favourite. *See p149.*

Galerías Amazonas

*Calle 12, entre 23 y 25, Vedado (662438/
662437).* **Open** 10am-7pm Mon-Sat; 10am-2pm
Sun. **Map** p311 C8.
This shopping mall is devoted mainly to fashion, but
also has a delicatessen called Delicatessen (!) that's
worth a look (*see p158*). The two most interesting
shops are Tienda Brava (*see p155*) for men's fashion and Peletería Claudia (*see p155*), one of the best-
quality shoe shops in Havana.There is also a fairly
well-stocked sports shop.

Galerías Cohiba

*Hotel Meliá Cohiba, Paseo, entre 1ra y 3ra Vedado
(333636).* **Open** 10am-7pm Mon-Sat; 10am-2pm
Sun. **Map** p312 A9.
The Hotel Meliá Cohiba has a good range of shops,
including a deli, cigar shop El Corojo (*see p157*) and
a number of fashion outlets selling reasonable
clothes, shoes and sports equipment. The beauty
salon is also recommended.

Galerías Paseo

Calle 1ra, entre Paseo y A, Vedado (553475).
Open 10am-6pm Mon-Sat; 9am-1pm Sun.
Map p312 A9.
Lots of stores, including an interesting furniture
outlet, a real and artificial flower shop (*see p156*), a
delicatessen (*see p160*) and a pet shop. When you're
done with shopping you can relax in the Jazz Café
on the top floor (*see p196*).

Hotel Comodoro

Avenida 3ra, esquina a 84, Miramar (245551).
Open 10am-7.30pm Mon-Sat; 10am-2pm Sun.
Hairdresser noon-7pm daily. **Map** p310 B1.
A good hotel shopping complex (whose official name
is Complejo Comercial Comodoro) selling quality
products. Stores include a mini supermarket, per-

fumery, jewellers and two photo service outlets, plus
shops selling children's clothes (*see p153*), electronic
goods, sports equipment (*see p164*), shoes, bags and
toys. Fashion concessions include Mango, Benetton
(*see p155*) and Versace. There's also a cigar shop
across the road (look out for the crocodile statue), a
good T-shirt selection in the hotel lobby and a range
of international magazines in the business centre. For
further details of the hotel, *see p59.*

Plaza de Carlos III

*Avenida Salvador Allende (Carlos III), esquina
a Árbol Seco, Centro Habana (666370).*
Open 10am-7pm Mon-Sat; 10am-3pm Sun.
Map p312 D12.
This well-known shopping centre in Centro Habana
features, among other things, a pet shop, a sports
shop, a hairdresser's, a supermarket and a food court.

Art & antiques

Art galleries selling original work and antiques
shops stuffed with curios abound in Havana,
and many visitors are tempted to buy a
little piece as a memento of their stay.
However, there are strict Cuban laws
governing the export of items considered
to be of national and historical interest, so
if you want your treasures to make it further
than the airport (there's a room there
bursting with confiscated items), make sure
you buy from authorised sources, which
can provide you with the necessary export
certificate. If you're not given an export
certificate when you buy the item, take it
(or a photo if it's too large) to the Patrimonia
Nacional office (Calle 17 #1009, entre 10 y 12,

Vedado) between 8.30 and 11.30am from Monday to Friday, where, for a small fee, officials will assess and authorise it. To give you an idea, many items over 40 years old may be subject to export regulations. Classic cars and paintings are the most strictly controlled, but furniture, stamp collections, coins, books and porcelain are also affected.

In addition to the places listed here, **La Maison** (*see p149*) sells antique tableware and jewellery and collectors' items. **La Habanera** (*see p155*) also sells antique jewellery. *See also p153* **Design & household goods**

Antiques shops

Eurl Trium
Zona Franca, Wajay Nave 11, Boyeros (540120). **Open** 8am-5pm Mon-Fri; closed Sat, Sun.
The proprietor of this shop, Germain Delgado, is an expert in French antiques, and sells a wide selection of Cuban and French antiques. He will also give advice to visitors who are searching for a particular piece. His English is limited.

Galería Kohly/ Casa de Antigüedades
Calle 36 #4704, esquina a Ave 47, Kohly (242776). **Open** 10am-3.30pm Mon-Fri; closed Sat, Sun. **Map** p311 E5.

Dollar shops

Though foreigners buy nigh on everything in Havana with dollars, many tourist-oriented shops are still out of the reach of Cubans. But so-called dollar shops are hugely popular with the locals. Selling a variety of products for $1, $3, $5 or $10, these stores are often surrounded by queues of Cubans waiting to get their hands on the goods. The items on offer are always changing, which makes for an interesting if unpredictable shopping experience. Much of the stuff is tat in the eyes of the seasoned traveller, but there are also some nifty bargains to be had and the atmosphere is invariably entertaining. And they can sometimes be a life-saver if you've run out of a basic toiletry item, or are hankering after a well-known brand of chocolate. Dollar shops can found throughout the city in branches of the shopping chain **Tiendas Panamericanas** and in many of the shopping malls, such as **Centro Comercial Náutico** (*see p149*).

This is a real Aladdin's cave for anyone even remotely interested in antiques, with some fantastic finds for those in the know. There's an array of crystal chandeliers and art nouveau and art deco pieces. All of the items have been deposited here by Cuban owners and they are sold at negotiable prices. It's a shame this place is so far out and difficult to find, but it's well worth the trip (preferably by taxi).

La Vajilla
Avenida de Italia (Galiano), esquina a Zanja, Centro Habana (624751). **Open** 10am-5pm Mon-Sat; closed Sun. **Map** p313 D13.
La Vajilla is an official antiques shop, meaning that everything it sells has to have a certificate of export. Stock seems to be quite erratic – sometimes there are some excellent finds, at other times it seems to be a bunch of old tat. Either way, it's a good way of spending half an hour. Payment officially in pesos.

Art galleries

In addition to regular shops and galleries, there are masses of paintings on sale at the crafts market on **Plaza de la Catedral** (*see p163*).

Grupo Peregrino Talleres Galería
Calle Mercaderes #207, entre Lamparilla y Amargura, La Habana Vieja (673993). **Open** 9am-11pm daily. **Map** p316 E15.
This gallery sells paintings that are a cut above the tourist market collection.
Branch: Calle Obispo 209, entre San Ignacio y Cuba, La Habana Vieja (no phone).

Taller Experimental de Gráfica
Plaza de la Catedral #62, at end of Callejón del Chorro, La Habana Vieja (620979). **Open** 9am-4pm Mon-Fri; closed Sat, Sun. **Map** p316 D15.
During the week this active workshop is open to visitors, who can observe the process of lithograph production and buy the results (for dollars, of course). However, those in the know turn up on the last Wednesday of every month, when you can buy the same lithographs in Cuban pesos, which works out considerably cheaper. The workshop also runs printmaking courses of one, two and three months' duration, costing between $250 and $500.

Picture framing

La Exposición (*see p159*) and Papelería O'Reilly (*see p164*) also offer a picture-framing service.

Arte Cuadro
Calle Ayestarán #210, entre 19 de Mayo y 20 de Mayo, Cerro (666229). **Open** 9am-1pm, 2-5pm Mon-Fri; 9am-1pm Sat; closed Sun. **Map** p313 E10.
A Cuban-Spanish enterprise offering a wide variety of frames and a good-quality framing service.

Eat, Drink, Shop

Arte Real

Calle 42 #310, entre 3ra y 5a, Miramar (249443).
Open 10am-6pm Mon-Fri; 10am-2pm Sat; closed
Sun. **Map** p310 B4.

Arte Real offers a highly recommended professional
service at reasonable rates and is often used by artists.
There are various frames to choose from.

Books

Antique & second-hand

Look out for antique books among the goodies
on offer at the **crafts market** on the Malecón
in Vedado (*see p162*). You're required to obtain
special permission to take some older books
out of the country; be sure to check with the
vendor whether you need to do so. Note that
international press is very hard to get hold
of; you'll sometimes find Italian or Spanish
newspapers in the **Meliá Cohiba** (*see p56*) and
other business hotels.

Librería Anticuaria 'El Navío'

*Calle Obispo #119, entre Oficios y Mercaderes,
La Habana Vieja (no phone).* **Open** 9am-7pm daily.
Map p316 E15.

El Navío sells antique, rare, new, second-hand
and collectable books; first editions, stamp collections, ancient photos, postcards and a collection
of cigar bands. The shop itself is of enormous interest; it was constructed in the middle of the 16th century, and a portion of the original wall is now
displayed under glass.

Plaza de Armas book market

Plaza de Armas, La Habana Vieja (no phone).
Open 9am-7pm Mon-Sat; closed Sun and when
raining/overcast. **Map** p316 E16.

This book market (*mercado de libros*) has numerous
political tracts, books on Che Guevara and the
Cuban Revolution, original Gabriel García Márquez
novels, plus atlases, encyclopedias and the odd
book in English. Also wonderful 19th-century
illustrated books and some great bindings. Well
worth a browse.

Peso shops

All Cubans who work for the government are
paid in pesos and it is only since 1993 that
Cubans have been allowed to possess and
use dollars, too. One dollar is equal to 20
ordinary pesos or one convertible peso but,
confusingly, the dollar sign is often used
to denote the peso. If you buy ice-creams or
food from vendors in the street, be aware that
a sign saying $3 means three pesos and not
three dollars (though of course vendors are
very happy to relieve you of your greenbacks).

Away from the hotels and upscale
department stores, you'll find numerous
shops catering for peso customers. They
may not be temples of consumerism but it is
enlightening to see how Cubans without
access to dollars cope: for starters,
there's not much choice. All of the food
markets (*agromercados*, or simply *agros;
see p160* **Catering to your needs**) sell
items in pesos, as do an array of shops,
restaurants and bars on Calle 23 between
Calles 10 and 12 in Vedado. Not surprisingly,
they're not the most luxurious of premises,
and can be downright grim, but you can
often spot some real bargains in among
the goods. Expect to find very cheap food
and drink; lots of hardware items; old vinyl
discs; party paraphernalia; baby clothes
for 100 pesos; musical clown toys for
125 pesos; and handmade leather shoes
for around 300 pesos.

At the same time, you'll also find plenty
of very poor-quality second-hand clothes,
naff domed glass ornaments decorated
with flowers and sparkles (typical Cuban
taste), and fantasy jewellery.

Bazar Inglés

*Avenida de Italia (Galiano) #352, esquina
a San Miguel, Centro Habana (632242/
631940).* **Open** 10am-5pm Mon-Sat;
9am-1pm Sun. **Map** p313 D14.

This peso second-hand clothing shop in
Centro Habana is a bit like an old Oxfam.
The quality is not brilliant, but you may find
something interesting. Worth a peek if you
enjoy rooting around charity shops.

Flogar

*Avenida de Italia (Galiano) #402, esquina
a San Rafael, Centro Habana (626006/
631668).* **Open** 10am-5pm Mon-Sat;
9am-1pm Sun. **Map** p313 D14.

This place sells second-hand clothes and
spare parts for electrical domestic items.

Pinochín – Casa de Fiesta

*Casa de Fiesta, Calle Reina #313, entre
Lealtad y Campanario, Centro Habana
(633023).* **Open** 10am-6pm Mon-Sat;
10am-2pm Sun. **Map** p313 D13.

A shop entirely devoted to children's birthday
parties, selling all the necessary goodies at
extremely cheap prices

La Maison: shopping heaven. *See p149.*

General

Casa de Las Américas

Calle 3ra, esquina a Avenida de los Presidentes (G), Vedado (552707-09). **Open** 8am-4.30pm Mon-Fri; closed Sat, Sun. **Map** p312 A10.
There are two bookshops on this site. On the right-hand side is a peso bookshop selling general literature and poetry books, while the larger shop on the left sells art books, international literature, cassettes and CDs for dollar prices.

Centro Cultural Cinematográfico ICAIC

Calle 23 #1155, entre 10 y 12, Vedado (36430). **Open** 9am-5pm Mon-Sat; closed Sun. **Map** p311 C8.
If you don't make it to the cinema while you're in Havana, you might want at least to stop by the Cuban Film Institute, ICAIC, for Cuban films on video, plus silkscreen prints and T-shirts.

Instituto Cubano del Libro

Calle O'Reilly #4, esquina a Tacón, La Habana Vieja (628091). **Open** 10.30am-6pm daily. **Map** p316 E15.
The Cuban Book Institute houses three bookshops. One stocks encyclopedias and modern fiction; one covers the tourist market with guidebooks and postcards; and the other sells Cuban editions.

Librería La Internacional

Calle Obispo #526, esquina a Bernaza, La Habana Vieja (613283). **Open** 9am-5pm daily. **Map** p316 D14.
A fairly wide range of books, CDs, cassettes, office supplies and postcards but, despite the name, very little in non-Spanish languages. Still, it's worth passing by if only to see the great mosaic inlay in the floor of the entrance.

La Moderna Poesía

Calle Obispo #527, esquina a Bernaza, La Habana Vieja (616983). **Open** 10am-8pm daily. **Map** p316 D14.
This shop specialises in Cuban editions, posters, pens, paints, music, videos and items for children.

In terms of non-Spanish books, you might find speeches by Fidel, the odd book of Cuban short stories and erotica and a few English novels.

Specialist

Librería Cervantes

Calle Bernaza #9, esquina a Obispo, La Habana Vieja (622580). **Open** 10am-5pm Mon-Sat; closed Sun. **Map** p316 D14.
Second-hand books (some in English), including conversation guides and books on *santería* and Cuban poetry. Also some old magazines.

El Navegante

Mercaderes #115, entre Obispo y Obrapía, La Habana Vieja (613625/623466). **Open** 8am-5pm Mon-Fri; 8am-1pm Sat; closed Sun. **Map** p316 E15.
A wonderland of nautical charts, yachting chart kits and detailed tourist maps, plus old postcards, T-shirts and telephone cards.

Children's clothes & toys

Crafts markets (*ferias*) often stock interesting handmade toys (*see p162*). The department stores are also a good bet, in particular **Harris Brothers** (*see p149*), whose third floor sells lots of products for babies and smaller children, including cuddly toys, bicycles, Chinese toys (admittedly of poor quality) and art products. Options in Miramar include **5ta y 42** (*see p149*), which sells children's clothes and shoes, and **La Época** (*see p149*) and **La Maison** (*see p149*). **Hotel Comodoro** (*see p150*), has shops selling good-quality children's clothing and shoes; it's also home to a reasonable toyshop, **La Juguetería**, although quality can vary.

Casita de Piedra

Avenida 5ta, esquina a 248, Marina Hemingway, Jaimanitas (241150 ext 147). **Open** 9.30am-6.45pm Mon-Sat; 9.30am-2pm Sun.
Three shops in the complex cater for children – one has toys and swimming pool accessories; another sells children's clothes and the third has baby accessories.

Design & household goods

With a bit of luck it is possible to find some good-quality household goods in Havana, but it's unusual to find much in the way of designer items. Much more common are craft products, which are often well made and good value. Of the department stores, **La Maison** (*see p149*) has the best selection of housewares. For fabrics and soft furnishings, *see p154.*

Casa del Mueble La Flora

Calle 6, entre 11 y 14, Miramar (225543). **Open** 9am-5pm Mon-Sat; closed Sun. **Map** p311 B6.

Eat, Drink, Shop

A variety of fairly ordinary furniture is on sale here, but there's also some quite nice stained-glass craftwork and original stained-glass pictures. Its distance from the centre of town means it's not worth a special visit unless you happen to be dropping in on the Casa de Antigüedades (*see p151*) at the same time.

Colección Habana
Calle Mercaderes #13, entre O'Reilly y Empredrado, La Habana Vieja (613388). **Open** 9pm-6pm daily. **Map** p316 D15.
There is a wide variety of reproduction items in this tastefully decorated shop. Choose from china, glass, furniture, jewellery, materials, Cuban pottery, repro pistols, silk scarves, screens, mugs, dinner services and much more. Fabrics include designs from Old Havana that have been produced in Spain. There's also a great garden with a fountain, home to three huge turtles. Well worth a peek.

Galería Victor Manuel
Calle San Ignacio #56, entre Callejón del Chorro y Empedrado, Plaza de la Catedral, La Habana Vieja (612955). **Open** 9.30am-9pm daily. **Map** p316 D15.
This gallery stocks a wide variety of crafts, jewellery, paintings and sculptures, to suit all tastes.

Galerías La Casona
Casa del Conde de San Juan de Jaruco, Calle Muralla #107, esquina a San Ignacio, La Habana Vieja (622633/623577). **Open** 10am-5pm Mon-Fri; 10am-2pm Sat; closed Sun. **Map** p316 E15.
Situated around a beautiful colonial patio are two art galleries – Roberto Diago and Plaza Vieja – and La Boutique, selling crafts. *See also p162.*

Electronics

Many of the items for sale in electronics outlets are not available to Cubans. These include microwaves, computers, air-conditioners, rice cookers, freezers, VCRs and video cameras. Cubans who desire these items are obliged to buy them second-hand. There are also electronics outlets at the **Hotel Comodoro** (*see p150*), and **Náutico** (*see p149*) and **La Vigía** (*see p149*) shopping complexes.

Centro Video
Avenida 3ra, entre 12 y 14, Miramar (242469). **Open** 10am-6pm Mon-Sat; closed Sun. **Map** p311 B6.
This chain, with branches across Havana, sells electrical equipment and videos, plus sweets, snacks, drinks and toys. There's also a dollar shop and a repair service on site.
Branches: Calle 23, entre L y M, Vedado, (662321); Avenida 5ta, esquina a 86, Miramar (244919).

Dita
Calle 84, entre 7ma y 9na, Playa (245119). **Open** 10am-6pm Mon-Sat; 9am-1pm Sun. **Map** p310 C1.
Dita offers two floors of electronic products including kitchen items, lighting, hi-fis, televisions, computers, computer components, electronic protection

Top chocs at **Galerías Amazonias**. *See p150.*

systems and spare parts. Some of the stock is only available to diplomats or foreigners with special permission, but there's quite a wide choice nonetheless. There's also a repair service on site. **Ofimática**, in the Miramar Trade Centre (*see p149*), is a branch.

Tecún
Avenida 42, esquina a 7ma, Miramar (249364/247689). **Open** 9.30am-noon, 1-4.30pm Mon-Fri; closed Sat, Sun. **Map** p310 B4.
Tecún sells mainly computer products and components. It also offers a computer repair service.

Fabrics & trimmings

Colección Habana (*see above* stocks some beautiful fabrics and other trimmings. Try also **La Maison** (*see p149*).

Mercado del Oriente
Calle Mercaderes #111, entre Obispo y Obrapía, La Habana Vieja (639740). **Open** 9am-5pm Tue-Sat; 9am-1pm Sun; closed Mon. **Map** p316 E15.
Situated next to the Museo de Asia, the Mercado del Oriente has a limited stock of good-quality, attractive material for curtains or furniture coverings. It also stocks craft goods from Asia.

La Muñequita Azul
Calle Obispo, esquina a Mercaderes, La Habana Vieja (no phone). **Open** 9am-7pm daily. **Map** p316 E15.
Don't miss this little gem. There's not much in the way of material, but the Little Blue Doll has plenty of broderie trimmings, satins, zips, cotton thread and sewing machine needles. It also houses an 1886 Singer sewing machine and some 19th-century sewing utensils.

Fashion

Necessity is the mother of invention, and the Cubans' marvellous ability to improvise is most apparent when it comes to their fashion sense. Despite tight budgets, most *habaneros* are well turned out and women in particular love dressing up in Lycra, sequins and transparent clothing, whatever their size or shape.

Fashion houses are few and far between in Havana, although **Benetton** has its foot in the door with three shopping outlets in the city. A selection of labels can also be hunted down in the department stores and shopping malls, such as **Le Select** (*see p149*), **Harris Brothers** (*see p149*) and **Galerías Cohiba** (*see p150*). The **Hotel Comodoro** (*see p150*) has possibly the most contemporary fashion outlets in Havana, including Benetton, Mango, Guess, Versace, Givenchy and YSL, and an attractive shoe store with accessories. **La Época** (*see p149*) has some French labels at bargain prices, but otherwise you'll have to search hard to find anything of quality. However, way out in front as the focal point for *la moda* in Cuba is **La Maison** (*see p149*), which holds regular fashion shows and is frequented by designers and *fashionistas*. A good place to pick up traditional clothing, hats and crocheted pieces, meanwhile, is the **crafts market** on the Plaza de la Catedral (*see p163*).

Benetton

Calle Amargura, esquina a Oficios, La Habana Vieja (622480). **Open** 10am-6.30pm Mon-Sat; 10am-1pm Sun. **Map** p316 E15.
The world-famous Italian brand also has concessions in **Harris Brothers** department store (*see p149*) and the **Comodoro** hotel (*see p150*).

Casa de Exclusividad de Verano

Calle 18, entre 41 y 43, Miramar (241982). **Open** 10am-6pm Mon-Sat; 9am-1pm Sun. **Map** p311 D6.
Hidden away behind the Clínica Cira Garcia, this store has a selection of good-quality female fashions, perfume and jewellery downstairs. Upstairs, you'll find male fashions and a wide range of shoes, including some funky denim platforms.

El Quitrín

Calle Obispo #163, entre San Ignacio y Mercaderes, La Habana Vieja (620810). **Open** 9am-5pm daily. **Map** p316 E15.
El Quitrín sells very beautiful handmade Cuban clothing. The quality is better than you'll find at the markets and this is reflected in the higher prices. The fabulous *guayaberas* are a must for men and there are some very chic dresses for women and girls. Tablecloths and shawls are also sold and the staff will make curtains to order.

Tienda Brava

Galerías Amazonas, Calle 12, entre 23 y 25, Vedado (no phone). **Open** 10am-7pm Mon-Sat; 10am-2pm Sun. **Map** p311 C8.
Follow the smell of leather towards Tienda Brava, with a saddle in the door, for possibly the widest selection of men's fashions in Havana. The shop stocks Lacoste, Levi's, Givenchy, Calvin Klein and Guess, plus hats, backpacks, belts, trainers and sunglasses.

Jewellery

Look out for fine handmade jewellery in most hotel **Caracol** shops (*see p158*). There are also very cheap handmade pieces to be found at the city's crafts markets (*see p162*).

La Habanera

Calle 12 #505, entre 5ta y 7ma, Miramar (242546/242648). **Open** 10am-6pm Mon-Fri; 10am-2pm Sat; closed Sun. **Map** p311 B6.
A well-kept secret, this very private antique jewellery store has fantastic pieces including watches, pendants, rings, cameos, bracelets and tableware. The setting is hush-hush and conservative, which is rare in Cuba. Prices from $50 to exceedingly expensive.

Shoes & leather goods

The best selection of shoes and leather items can be found in the **Hotel Comodoro** (*see p150*), **Galerías Amazonas** (*see p150*), **Galerías Cohiba** (*see p150*), **La Vigía** (*see p149*) and **5ta y 42** (*see p149*) shopping centres. All of these have some very tempting shoes for women; the choice for men is more limited. For handmade leather accessories, head to the crafts market near the Plaza de la Catedral.

Shoe repairers can be found in the streets in La Habana Vieja; otherwise there are state-run repair shops opposite Frankfurt's at the corner of Calle 16 and Calle 23 in Vedado; at La Infancia, Calle 23, esquina a 16, Vedado; and at at Calle 35, entre La Torre y 26, Nuevo Vedado.

La Habana

Calle Obispo, esquina a Aguacate, La Habana Vieja (no phone). **Open** 10am-7pm Mon-Sat; 10am-5pm Sun. **Map** p316 D15.
La Habana stocks shoes, bags and belts. The Novator branch has women's and men's hats.
Branch: Novator, Calle Obispo, entre Habana y Compostela, La Habana Vieja (615292).

Peletería Claudia

Calle 12, entre 23 y 25, Vedado (662437/8). **Open** 10am-7pm Mon-Sat; 10am-2pm Sun. **Map** p311 C8.
This shop has some of the most beautiful shoes in the city, plus good-quality luggage by Delsey.

Flowers & plants

It is only in the last few years that flowers have been widely available in Havana. After the Revolution, having flowers in the home

Rolled gold

The Cubans know cigars. When they spin a long yarn, they're said to be '*contando la historia del tabaco en dos tomos*' – telling the two-volume story of tobacco. Tobacco is that important to the island and its people, and, of all tobacco products, the cigar has reached mythical proportions: long considered the best in the world, and long imitated elsewhere.

The early cigar belonged to the Amerindians, but, from the conquest of Columbus in 1492, the story became a swashbuckling one of piracy, contraband and uprisings against Spanish colonial monopoly. Highly lucrative, the cigar was prey to German, British, French and North American capital, part of a 19th- and 20th-century world cigar tobacco economy whose tobacco blends were produced as far afield as Cameroon, Turkey, Java and Sumatra, and whose key markets were London, Amsterdam, Bremen and New York. The cigar was also at the heart of major political upheavals, exile communities and rival economies, from 1868, with the outbreak of Cuba's first War of Independence from Spain, through the Cuban Revolution of 1959, to the cigar hype of the 1990s.

For the neophyte, what better than a trip to Cuba for the real thing? The complete cigar experience would be in January or February, to take in the green rolling fields of sun-grown tobacco or the sea of white cheesecloth over shade-grown tobacco in the mecca of Cuban cigar industry, Vuelta Arriba, in western Pinar

del Río, or Vuelta Abajo, in central Villa Clara and Sancti Spíritus. Havana, however, is cigar city, the home of the *habano*, the place for that ultimate Cuban fashion accessory, which brings in over $10 million from tourists alone, avid to buy at a fraction of the cost abroad. However, the undiscerning should beware. The cigar fever of the 1990s brought the paradox of quantity versus quality, as cigar tobacco was grown in substandard areas; young workers were crash-trained, and quality

was considered undesirably bourgeois, so Cubans had to make do with artificial flowers and plants. Nowadays peso flower stalls and flower carts (*floreros*) are a common sight on the streets of Havana. For a range of flowers and arrangements, try the stall opposite Galerías Amazonas on the corner of Calle 23 and Calle 12 near the Cementerio de Colón (*see p90* **City of the dead**).

There are also fantastic flower arrangements (including vase) available for around $6 or so at the **Cuatro Caminos market** (*see p160*). Garden centres in the European sense do not exist in Cuba, but there are a few outlets selling plants.

Floralia

Galerías Paseo, Calle 1ra, entre Paseo y A, Vedado (553266). **Open** 10am-6pm Mon-Sat; 9am-1pm Sun. **Map** p312 A9.
This shop is entirely devoted to artificial and natural flowers. Even if you don't want any your-

self, it's worth coming here to see the long queues of Cubans patiently waiting up to an hour to get in to this palace of plastic.

Jardín Wagner

Calle Mercaderes #113, entre Obispo y Obrapía, La Habana Vieja (669017). **Open** 9am-5pm daily. **Map** p316 E15.
If you're walking along Mercaderes, you're unlikely to miss the window at Jardín Wagner, which has water cascading down it. The shop stocks beautiful imported roses, fresh flowers and houseplants, plus artificial flowers. It also offers an Interflora service.

Tropiflora

Calle 12 #156, entre Calzada y Línea, Vedado (662332/303869). **Open** 8am-8pm Mon-Sat; closed Sun. **Map** p311 B8.
This shop stocks a wide variety of flowers, including many tropical varieties. It is responsible for the fantasy arrangements that decorate the world-famous Tropicana cabaret (*see p193*), and also

export cigars were made in non-export factories outside Havana. So, when you're buying a brand type – Cohiba Siglo III, Hoyo de Monterrey Double Corona, Montecristo A, Partagás, Ramón Allones Gigantes – check the factory it was made in (a code on the box) and its year rating, and choose carefully where you buy; if you don't have bona fide proof of purchase, you might have your booty confiscated at the airport.

In Havana, there are plenty of places for visitors to indulge their desire to learn about, buy and smoke cigars. For $10, you can take a factory tour: **Real Fábrica de Tabacos Partagás** (see also p82) and **La Corona** (see also p82), near the Capitol, are the favourites. Both have their own stores. Or slip into the fantasy of Old Havana's newly created 'cigar hotel': **Hostal Conde de Villanueva/Hostal del Habano** (pictured), the decadence of the splendid 1920s **Hotel Nacional**, with its **Casa del Habano**, or the modern appeal of the 1990s **Hotel Meliá Cohiba**, with **El Corojo**. If you're going the whole hog and want to buy a humidor for your treasures, **La Escogida**, with its friendly staff, is recommended.

Casa del Habano

Hotel Nacional, Calle O, esquina a 21, Vedado (333562/333564). **Open** 9am-5pm daily. **Map** p312 B12. **Branch**: Calle 5ta #1407, esquina a 16, Miramar (247974).

El Corojo

Hotel Meliá Cohiba, Paseo, entre 1ra y 3ra, Vedado (333636). **Open** 9am-8.30pm Mon-Fri; 9am-2pm Sat; closed Sun. **Map** p312 A9.

La Escogida

Hotel Comodoro, Avenida 3ra, esquina a 84, Miramar (247646). **Open** 10am-7.30pm Mon-Sat; 10am-2pm Sun. **Map** p310 B1.

Hostal Conde de Villanueva/ Hostal del Habano

Calle Mercaderes #202, entre Lamparilla y Amargura, La Habana Vieja (629293/4). **Open** 10.30am-7pm daily. **Map** p316 E15.

El Palacio del Tabaco

Real Fábrica de Tabacos La Corona, Calle Agramonte (Zulueta) #106, entre Refugio y Colón (626173). **Open** Tours 9am-3pm Mon-Fri; closed Sat, Sun. Shop 9am-6pm Mon-Sat; closed Sun **Admission** (tour only) $10; free under-12s. **Map** p313 D15.

Real Fábrica de Tabacos Partagás

Calle Industria #520, entre Dragones y Barcelona, Centro Habana (338060). **Open** Tours 9.30-11am, 12.30-2pm Mon-Fri; closed Sat, Sun. Shop 9am-7pm Mon-Fri; 9am-5pm Sat; closed Sun. **Admission** (tour only) $10; free under-12s. **Map** p313 E14.

provides flowers for many hotels and embassies. Tropiflora sells artificial plants and flowers and can provide arrangements for all kinds of special occasions and private events. Interflora service available.

Food & drink

Most of the department stores and shopping complexes found across Havana house small supermarkets for emergency provisions. There are also small grocery shops in all **Servi-Cupet** petrol stations selling food, drinks and sweets. For fresh fruit and veg, meat, supermarkets and delis, see p160 **Catering to your needs**.

Bread & cakes

Bread is generally not very good in Cuba, and tends to go rock hard within a day, but there are a few worthwhile outlets in Havana.

Bosque de La Habana

Hotel Meliá Habana, Avenida 3ra, entre 78 y 80, Miramar (248500). **Open** 24 hrs daily. **Map** p310 B1.
This ice-cream parlour on the lower ground floor of this hotel sells the best cakes and pastries in town.

La Francesa del Pan

Calle 42, esquina a 19, Miramar (242211). **Open** 8am-8pm daily. **Map** p310 C4.
This boulangerie sells very good bread, including one variety made with seven grains.

Pain de Paris

Calle 25, entre Infanta y O, Vedado (333347). **Open** 24hrs daily. **Map** p312 B12.
The Pain de Paris chain is pretty expensive and can be disappointing if you expect too much from it. Still, at least there are branches across town (not all are open 24 hours, though). **Branches**: Calle Linea, entre Paseo y A, Vedado (no phone); Avenida 26, esquina a Kohly (555125).

Panadería San José

Calle Obispo #161, entre Mercaderes y San Ignacio, La Habana Vieja (609326). **Open** 24hrs daily. **Map** p316 E15.

This bakery in the heart of La Habana Vieja is open 24 hours daily. Look out for the beautiful fresco above the shop entrance.

Pastelería Francesa

Paseo de Martí (Prado) #410, entre Neptuno y San Rafael, Centro Habana (620739). **Open** 8am-11pm daily. **Map** p313 D14.

Good bread, croissants and cakes can be had at this bakery-cum-café next to the Hotel Inglaterra.

Coffee

Casa del Café

Calle Baratillo, esquina a Obispo, La Habana Vieja (338061). **Open** 10am-6pm Mon-Sat; 10am-3pm Sun. **Map** p316 E16.

Cuban coffee of all sorts of roasts and grinds, plus every imaginable coffee accessory. There is an original bar from the 1900s and a variety of tourist souvenirs and coffees on sale.

Luxury items

La Bodega del Vino

Complejo Turístico La Giraldilla, Calle 222, esquina a 37, La Coronela, La Lisa (330568/330569). **Open** 10am-5am daily.

This tourist complex is rather a long way out of town, but you may be tempted to make the trip in order to visit the wine-cellar, which, with over 200 wines, represents the largest choice in Havana. It's also a good place to purchase rum and cigars.

Delicatessen

Galerías Amazonas, Calle 12, entre 23 y 25, Vedado (no phone). **Open** 10am-7pm Mon-Sat; 10am-2pm Sun. **Map** p311 C8.

A large stock of rums and handmade chocolates from Spain.

Rum

Aside from Bacardi, which was first made in Cuba but is now produced in the Bahamas, the most famous brand of Cuban rum is Havana Club, which, along with the many other varieties, is sold all over Havana. Mathusalem is often recommended by connoisseurs. White three-year-old rum is used for the famous *mojito* and Cuba Libre cocktails, while *añejo* is a great digestif with a smooth rounded taste. To learn more about the art and history of rum making in Cuba, visit the **Fundación Havana Club (Museo del Ron)** or the **Taberna del Galeón/Casa del Ron.**

Plaza de Armas book market. *See p152.*

Fundación Havana Club (Museo del Ron)

Calle San Pedro #262, esquina a Sol (618051/623832). **Open** *Museum & gallery* 9am-5.30pm Mon-Sat; closed Sun. *Bar* 10am-midnight daily. *Shop* 10am-9pm daily. **Map** p316 E15.

The newly refurbished museum has a colonial-style bar and a shop next door decorated in 1930s style. It stocks only Havana Club products, including cocktail sets, T-shirts, caps and gift sets. *See also p68.*

Taberna del Galeón/Casa del Ron

Calle Baratillo, esquina a Obispo, La Habana Vieja (338476). **Open** 9am-5pm Mon-Sat; 9am-3pm Sun. **Map** p316 E16.

A brass galleon hanging in the entrance welcomes visitors into this old beamed building for free rum tasting and a good selection of rums for sale.

Gifts

While cigars and rum are cheap, handy fallbacks in terms of gifts to take back home, they're hardly the most groundbreakingly original souvenirs. The shops below offer some alternative ideas.

There are dozens of good gift shops in the shopping complexes of the major hotels in Havana, and unique bargains to be had at the city's crafts markets (*see p162*). Also, branches of the **Tiendas Caracol** chain can be found in the major hotels, and sell everyday items such as toiletries, swimwear, cigarettes along with souvenirs such as rum, jewellery, T-shirts, posters and postcards. Though they can be a bit bland, they're good places to know about in case you run out of a basic item.

Casa del Abanico
Calle Obrapía #107, entre Mercaderes y Oficios, La Habana Vieja (634452). **Open** 10am-5pm Mon-Sat; closed Sun. **Map** p316 E15.

This is a beautiful shop full of fans, where you can have a fan hand-painted to order with images or your own messages by the team of specialist skilled fan-painters.

La Exposición
Calle San Rafael #12, entre Bélgica (Monserrate) y Agramonte (Zulueta), Centro Habana (638364). **Open** 9am-6pm Mon-Sat; 9am-1pm Sun. **Map** p313 D14.

Upstairs at La Exposición you'll find stationery, postcards, maps, *guayaberas* (traditional Cuban shirts for men) and pretty fans. Hidden away downstairs, meanwhile, and not even signposted, is a vast array of reproduction prints of Cuban artwork and posters at fantastically cheap prices. A framing service is available and there are poster tubes for transport home available for just $1.

Shopping by area

LA HABANA VIEJA
Artex (Music, *p163*); **Benetton** (Fashion, *p155*); **Casa del Abanico** (Gifts, *p159*); **Casa del Café** (Coffee, *p158*); **Colección Habana** (Household, *p154*); **Farmacia Taquechel** (Pharmacies, *p162*); **Fotografía Luz Habana** (Photographic, *p163*); **Fundación Havana Club** (Rum, *p158*); **Galerías La Casona** (Household, *p154*); **Galería Victor Manuel** (Household, *p154*); **Grupo Peregrino Talleres Galería** (Galleries, *p151*); **La Habana** (Shoes, *p155*); **Habana 1791** (Perfumes, *p161*); **Harris Brothers** (Department stores, *p149*); **Hostal Conde de Villanueva/Hostal del Habano** (Cigars, *p157*); **Instituto Cubano del Libro** (Books, *p153*); **Jardín Wagner** (Flowers, *p156*); **Langwith** (Pets, *p164*); **Librería Anticuaria 'El Navío'** (Books, *p152*); **Librería Cervantes** (Books, *p153*); **Librería La Internacional** (Books, *p153*); **Longina** (Music, *p163*); **Market near the Plaza de la Catedral** (Crafts markets, *p163*); **Mercado del Oriente** (Fabrics, *p154*); **La Moderna Poesía** (Books, *p153*); **La Muñequita Azul** (Fabrics, *p154*); **El Navegante** (Books, *p153*); **Palacio de la Artesanía** (Gifts, *p161*); **Panadería San José** (Baker, *p158*); **Papelería O'Reilly** (Stationery, *p164*); **Papelería San Francisco** (Stationery, *p164*); **Plaza de Armas book market** (Books, *p152*); **El Quitrín** (Fashion, *p155*); **Taberna del Galeón** (Rum, *p158*); **Taller Experimental de Gráfica** (Galleries, *p151*).

CENTRO HABANA
Adidas (Sports, *p164*); **La Época** (Department stores, *p149*); **La Exposición** (Gifts, *p159*); **Foto Prado** (Photographic, *p163*); **ORBE** (Gifts, *p161*); **El Palacio del Tabaco** (Cigars, *p157*); **Pastelería Francesa** (Baker, *p158*); **Plaza de Carlos III** (Shopping centres, *p150*); **Real Fábrica de Tabacos Partagás** (Cigars, *p157*); **La Vajilla** (Antiques, *p151*).

VEDADO
Casa de Las Américas (Books, *p153*); **Casa del Habano** (Cigars, *p157*); **Centro Cultural Cinematográfico ICAIC** (Books, *p153*); **El Corojo** (Cigars, *p157*); **Delicatessen** (Luxury foods, *p158*); **Feria del Malecón** (Crafts market, *p162*); **Floralia** (Flowers, *p156*); **Galerías Amazonas** (Shopping centres, *p150*); **Galerías Cohiba** (Shopping centres, *p150*); **Galerías Paseo** (Shopping centres, *p150*); **Pain de Paris** (Baker, *p157*); **Peletería Claudia** (Shoes & leather, *p155*); **Primavera** (Salons, *p161*); **Suchel** (Salons, *p161*); **Tienda Brava** (Fashion, *p155*); **Tropiflora** (Flowers, *p156*).

MIRAMAR & THE WESTERN SUBURBS
5ta y 42 (Shopping centres, *p149*); **Almiquí** (Pets, *p164*); **Arte Real** (Picture framing, *p152*); **Aster Lavandería** (Launderette, *p162*); **La Bodega del Vino** (Wine, *p158*); **Bosque de la Habana** (Baker, *p157*); **Casa Blanca** (Department stores, *p148*); **Casa de Exclusividad de Verano** (Fashion, *p155*); **Casa de la Música de la EGREM** (Music, *p163*); **Casa del Mueble La Flora** (Household, *p153*); **Casita de Piedra** (Children, *p153*); **Centro Comercial Náutico** (Shopping centres, *p149*); **Centro Comercial La Vigía** (Shopping centres, *p149*); **Centro de Negocios Miramar** (Shopping centres, *p149*); **Centro Video** (Electronics, *p154*); **Dita** (Electronics, *p154*); **La Escogida** (Cigars, *p157*); **Farmacia Internacional** (Pharmacies, *p162*); **Galería Kohly/Casa de Antigüedades** (Antiques, *p151*); **La Francesa del Pan** (Baker, *p157*); **La Habanera** (Jewellery, *p155*); **Hotel Comodoro** (Shopping centres, *p150*); **La Maison** (Department stores, *p149*); **Óptica Miramar** (Opticians, *p161*); **Le Select** (Department stores, *p149*); **Tecún** (Electronics, *p154*); **Tienda Tecmusic** (Music, *p163*).

Eat, Drink, Shop

Catering to your needs

Havana's food markets and supermarkets might not be the best stocked in the world, but if you're trying to save a bit of cash, they're a godsend. *See also p174* **Food & drink**. For tips on how to cater for children, *see p174* **Feeding time**.

FRUIT AND VEG

A great place to start is one of the many *agromercados*, where bags of fresh produce can be yours for only vendors will accept your dollars, but having some pesos on you will ensure a better deal). Everything is clearly priced, but be aware of the difference between paying per pound (marked 'lb') or paying for each item separately (marked 'c/u'). You can sometimes buy fresh produce in the dollar supermarkets, but you'll pay tons more than at the *agro* for the privilege.

The quality of the produce varies drastically, but depending on the time of year, you may find fresh onions, garlic, lettuce, tomatoes, peppers, cucumbers, beansprouts, avocados, oranges, lemons, papaya, pineapples and melons. If you're in Cuba between May and September, congratulations – you're smack in the middle of the mango season. Those of you looking for more exotic Caribbean fruits and veg, however, will need to get a taxi to José Martí International Airport and a flight to one of the other islands – remember, this is Cuba.

Surprisingly, one thing you can't get in the *agro* markets are spuds. These are grown in the country, but are exclusively reserved for Cubans with *libretas* (ration books). If don't want to go without, ask a Cuban to buy you some – $1 should get you a huge bag.

One of Havana's best agricultural markets is the one at **Cuatro Caminos** (*see p84*). Other addresses include Plaza Mariano, Plaza de la Revolución (a mammoth market held every first Sunday of the month; *see also p96* **Going green**), and at the following addresses: Calle 19 y 68; Calle 42 y 19; Calle 19 y B; Calle 15 y 24; Calle 17 y K. Most, with the exception of the one at Plaza de la Revolución, are open from 9am to 6pm Tuesday to Saturday, and 9am to noon Sunday (closed Monday).

'TREAT' YOURSELF TO SOME MEAT

Due to its high price and unavailability, meat is a real treat for the average Cuban. At big family get-togethers, affluent citizens bring out a pig on a spit. Just don't ask where they got it from (it's not available in the shops and

hence illegally purchased on the black market). Packaged chicken and pork are sold in the larger dollar shops, but forget about buying beef (or anything else for that matter). If you're desperate for some steak and willing to push the boat out, the butcher's at the **Centro Comercial La Vigía** at Marina Hemingway (*see p149*) can save the day with a nicely cut, albeit expensive, piece of beef. Pork can be purchased at the *agromercado*, but you'll soon realise hygiene is not a priority, so beware. Frankfurters made out of chicken meat are available everywhere and although they're highly processed, the 'made in Canada' sticker is somewhat reassuring.

NOT SO SUPERMARKETS

For most foodstuffs you'll need to visit the 'dollar shops'. Here you can get basic provisions like pastas ($1), sauces (invariably tomato), eggs, meat, oil, butter, herbs and spices (expensive) and bread. You might even find some cheese, but be aware that it's like goldust in Cuba. In contrast, mayonnaise is available by the bucketload. Cubans eat as much of it as they can get, thickly spread on bread or crackers.

The mother of all Cuban supermarkets is the imaginatively named **Supermercado** on Avenida 5ta, between Calles 68 and 70 in Miramar. Not far from the daunting Russian Embassy and in the heart of ambassador territory, it was until recently called the Diplomercado for obvious reasons. This place resembles a shop back home (well, nearly): wide aisles and large choices (relatively). There are discounts if you buy beer by the crate, but the fruit and vegetables are ridiculously overpriced: onions, for example, cost ten times what you'd expect to pay in the *agro* markets. Further west, at the **La Vigía** complex (*see p149*), is another upscale supermarket.

Another decent supermarket with a wide variety of goods is **Galerías Paseo** (*see p150*) opposite the Meliá Cohiba hotel. The supermarket in the **Fosca** building (*see p94*) on Calle 17 offers a similar choice. **Harris Brothers** (*see p149*), meanwhile, has homely extras like Heinz tinned soups.

DELI GOOD

For the best-quality delicatessen items head to the deli in **Le Select** (*see p149*), **Galerías Paseo** (*see p150*), **Hotel Meliá Cohiba** (*see p56*) or **Delicatessen** (*see p158*).

Making fans at **Casa del Abanico**. See p159.

ORBE

Calle Monserrate #304, entre San Rafael y Neptuno, Centro Habana (no phone). **Open** 9am-9pm Mon-Sat; 9am-1pm Sun. **Map** p313 D14/15.

This newish gift shop sells a variety of interesting souvenirs, including T-shirts of decent quality, *santería* objects, books, postcards, fans and hats.

Palacio de la Artesanía

Calle Cuba #64, esquina a Tacón, La Habana Vieja (671118/9/338072). **Open** 9am-7pm daily. **Map** p316 D15.

A good one-stop shop for gifts. It sells a large selection of quality T-shirts, plus craft objects such as glass, ceramics, watches, fans and books.

Health & beauty

Beauty salons

Cuban women are very aware of their appearance and pay particular attention to their hands and feet. Apparently, if your nails are not varnished you are considered dirty, so manicures and pedicures are big business here. There are peso beauty salons throughout Havana, offering a range of services, including hairdressing, facials, manicures, epilation and massage. Most salons also cater for men, and they are all ridiculously cheap, charging one to two pesos for a manicure. If you want a wider range of treatments, head for the salons at **La Maison** (*see p149*), **Le Select** (*see p149*) or at one of the larger hotels. Among the best are those at the **Nacional** (*see p56*), **Meliá Cohiba** (*see p56*), **Meliá Habana** (*see p57*) and **Habana Libre** (*see p55*).

Primavera

Calle Línea #459 entre E y F, Vedado (320159). **Open** 8.30am-8.30pm daily. **Map** p312 A10.

In addition to a temperamental sauna, this place has hairdressing, massage and cellulite treatment.

Suchel

Calle Calzada #709, entre A y B, Vedado (38332). **Open** 8.30am-8pm daily. **Map** p312 A9.

Gym, second-hand clothes shop, massages, steam bath, snacks, hairdressers, facials, mud massages and 'green' medicines (ie with herbal ingredients).

Cosmetics & perfumes

Cosmetics are sold in all the large hotels and perfumeries can be found in all the shopping centres, including **Comodoro** (*see p150*), **La Vigía** (*see p149*) and **Náutico** (*see p149*). If you are looking for something special, **La Maison** (*see p149*) has the widest selection of perfumes and cosmetics, while **Le Select** (*see p149*) has a very good range of hair products.

Habana 1791 (Aromas Coloniales de la Isla de Cuba)

Calle Mercaderes #156, entre Obrapía y Lamparilla, La Habana Vieja (no phone). **Open** 10am-6pm daily. **Map** p316 E15.

This recently opened, beautiful shop is breathtaking. It makes and sells about ten varieties of original cologne, including a tobacco fragrance made from marinated tobacco leaves; customers are welcome to try out the ready-made colognes or you can ask Yanelda, whose official title is the Alchemist of Old Havana, to make up a personal mixture. The finished product is packed into a glass or ceramic bottle, sealed with wax and sold in an attractive linen bag at very reasonable prices. The shop also sells original silver pendants containing perfume, pot pourri and dried flowers, while next door is an array of toiletries imported from Europe. Olfactory satisfaction guaranteed.

Opticians

Óptica Miramar/Casa Matriz

Avenida 7ma, entre 24 y 26, Miramar (242269/242990). **Open** 10am-6pm Mon-Fri, 9am-5pm Sat; closed Sun. **Map** p311 B5.

Óptica Miramar sells contact lens fluids, sunglasses and children's frames. It also stocks some lenses, but doesn't always have a wide variety available. No appointment is required for the on-site optician. **Branch**: Calle Neptuno #411, entre San Nicolás y Manrique, Centro Habana (632161).

Pharmacies

It's sad and ironic that although training standards for doctors in Cuba are high, the embargo has put a stranglehold on supplies, so pharmacies do not a offer a great choice and are often not fully stocked. (Though restrictions on such supplies were recently lifted, the effects on the Cuban populations have yet to be seen). Mosquito repellent, for instance, is not always

Eat, Drink, Shop

readily available. Provisions have improved, but don't be surprised to be sold a different antibiotic to the one that you were prescribed.

There is a 24-hour pharmacy in the lobby of the **Hotel Plaza** (see p54) and a small but fairly well-stocked outlet in the **Hotel Comodoro** (see p150). In addition to the standard outlets, there are two homeopathic pharmacies in Vedado; on the corner of Calles 23 and M, and on the corner of Calles Linea and 14.

Farmacia Internacional
Avenida 41, esquina a 20, Miramar (244350/242051). **Open** 9am-9pm daily. **Map** p311 C16.
Only foreigners are allowed to buy medicines at this pharmacy, so it tends to have a fairly comprehensive stock. It also sells toiletries and perfumes. The unfriendly staff and security guard at the entrance are rather off putting, though.

Farmacia Taquechel
Calle Obispo #155, entre Mercaderes y San Ignacio, La Habana Vieja (629286). **Open** 9am-6.30pm daily. **Map** p316 E15.
Farmacia Taquechel is effectively a museum. Initially opened as a pharmacy in 1898 by Francisco Taquechel, it re-opened in 1995, completely restored to its original glory. The interior is beautifully decorated with intriguing gadgets, such as a century-

1791's super scents. *See p161.*

old French porcelain water filter, a solar microscope, antique measuring pots, a skeleton and 'Los ojos del botánico' – two glass containers originally filled with amber or blue fluid which reflected the light to allow the pharmacist to spy on his employees at all times. Nowadays, the shop sells a selection of natural products, including sponges, infusions, shark's cartilage, face creams, honey wine, Spirulina (a fortifier made from algae), ginseng and some essential oils. A brass flask hanging outside the pharmacy indicates the presence of this treasure trove.

Don't miss Shops

Casa del Abanico
Hand-made fans to order. *See p159.*

Farmacia Taquechel
Lotions and potions galore in this restored pharmacy. *See p162.*

Galería Kohly/ Casa de Antigüedades
A rummager's paradise. *See p151.*

Habana 1791 (Aromas Coloniales de la Isla de Cuba)
Perfumes mixed to your own personal recipe. *See p161.*

La Habanera
Antique jewellery in appropriate surroundings. *See p155.*

Langwith
All manner of supplies to keep your animals in top-notch nick. *See p164.*

Libreria Anticuaria 'El Navío'
Books, stamps and postcards in a 16th-century setting. *See p152.*

Laundry & dry-cleaning

Most hotels offer dry-cleaning and laundry services, although these can be expensive and unreliable. To do it yourself head to one of the numerous launderettes around the city. The **Aster Lavandería** in Miramar is particularly recommended.

Aster Lavandería
Calle 34 #314, entre 3ra y 5ta, Miramar (241622). **Open** 8am-5pm Mon-Fri; 8am-2pm Sat; closed Sun. **Map** p310 B4.
Offers a very good, cheap and efficient dry-cleaning service. There are also self-service washing and drying machines available at three dollars each.

Markets

Crafts markets

Feria del Malecón
Malecón, esquina a D, Vedado (no phone). **Open** 8.30am-6pm Tue-Sun; closed Mon. **Map** p312 A10.
Smaller than the crafts market (*feria*) near the Plaza de la Catedral (*see p163*), this one near the Meliá Cohiba in Vedado tends to offer more original products, including antique books, coins and stamp collections. One old lady sells unique jewellery made out of antique silver spoons and forks. This is a favourite place for locals to buy presents.

Eat, Drink, Shop

Market near the Plaza de la Catedral

Calle Tacón, La Habana Vieja (no phone).
Open 8.30am-7pm daily. **Map** p316 E15.
The largest crafts market is held in a beautiful setting, close to the cathedral in La Habana Vieja. During the day it is a hub of activity and bustle, and is the ideal place to find tourist souvenirs. Clothing items include a huge array of hats, from berets adorned with images of Che Guevara or a Revolutionary red star, to straw hats and crocheted pieces. Crochet items, including sexy transparent dresses and more sophisticated shawls, are a big draw throughout the market. Other highlights include handwoven hammocks; musical instruments; papier mâché toys, mobiles and masks; hardwood and cow-horn sculptures; maquettes; hundreds of paintings and very cheap handmade jewellery. Also look out for *guayaberas* (traditional cotton shirts worn as evening wear to replace a shirt and tie); lovely outfits in embroidered cotton for little girls and babies; and a variety of leather shoes and accessories at reasonable prices. In short, there's something here for everyone.

Food markets

See p160 **Catering to your needs**.

Music

Cuban music has smashed through all frontiers and is now enjoying worldwide popularity. Internationally, the best-known Cuban music is salsa, but in the country itself you'll have access to other typical musical styles, such as *son, danzón, cha-cha-chá* and *folclórico*. Try **Centro Video** (*see p154*) for cassettes, music systems

Browsing at the **Feria del Malecón**.
See p162.

and electrical repairs. You might also be offered a tape or CD by a band at a restaurant: go ahead and buy – the quality can't be guaranteed and the price may not always be as low as you'd expect but, what the heck, it may just buy a few luxuries for these often-talented musicians.

Artex

Calle Oficios 362, entre Luz y Santa Clara, La Habana Vieja (623228/95/635392). **Open** 9am-5pm Tue-Sat; closed Sun. **Map** p316 E15.
These shops sell musical instruments, CDs and cassettes, handicrafts, souvenirs and publications. There are about 25 branches around the city.

Casa de la Música de la EGREM

Calle 20 #3308, entre 33 y 35, Miramar (240447).
Open 10am-12.30am daily. **Map** p311 C6.
Musical instruments, sound systems and a wide variety of Cuban music in the form of CDs, tapes and sheet music. The Casa also houses a club where you can listen and dance to live music (*see p198*). There's a pleasant café next door.

Longina

Calle Obispo #360, La Habana Vieja (628371).
Open 10am-7pm Mon-Sat; 10am-1pm Sun.
Map p316 E15.
A beautiful shop with an art nouveau exterior and stained-glass features. Percussion instruments, cassettes and gifts all feature.

Tienda Tecmusic

Avenida 5ta, esquina a 88, Miramar (248759).
Open 9am-6pm Mon-Sat; closed Sun. **Map** p310 C1.
A wide range of musical instruments, CDs and tapes.

Photographic services

Many hotels offer photo developing services, among them the **Nacional** (*see p56*), **Habana Riviera** (*see p55*) and **Comodoro** (*see p150*). Other outlets can be found in the **Centro de Negocios Miramar** (Miramar Trade Centre, *see p149*); and at the shops on the corner of Calle 23 and Calle O in Vedado (335031) and at Avenida de Italia (Galiano) #527, entre Reina y Salud, in Centro Habana (338141).

Foto Prado

Paseo de Martí (Prado), esquina a Virtudes, Centro Habana (634186). **Open** 9am-7pm Mon-Sat; 9am-1pm Sun. **Map** p313 D14.
Sells films and offers a developing and photocopying service.

Fotografía Luz Habana

Calle Tacón #22, entre O'Reilly y Empredrado, La Habana Vieja (634263). **Open** 9am-7pm daily. **Map** p316 E16.
An attractive shop near the Cathedral selling a good variety of cameras and films. Also check out the antique cameras on view.

Eat, Drink, Shop

Our man in Havana

Cubans are ingenious at making ends meet – they have no choice but to. As you walk through the streets of Havana you'll pass by people making a living by refilling lighters (*pictured*) or repairing bicycles. Then there are the *jineteros* or *jineteras* – male and female touts (or sometimes prostitutes, depending on the context – the term has come to mean both). In addition to trying their luck at persuading hapless tourists into taking a room in a *casa particular* or eating a meal at a *paladar* (they work on commission from the owner) they'll often try to sell you something – anything. This being Havana, in many cases it's cut-rate

cigars, but we've also seen people offering, among other things, cabbages, fish (whether fresh or decidely green), or their services as a hair braider. If you're not interested, a polite 'no' should do the trick. After all, they'll soon latch onto someone else.

Eat, Drink, Shop

Pet services & supplies

Cubans are nuts about animals, and know how to take care of them.

Almiquí
Centro Veterinario, Calle 164 #506, entre 5ta y 17A, Playa (286127). **Open** 8.30am-4.45pm Mon-Sat; closed Sun.
This centre has a range of supplies, including medication, for birds, fish, cats and dogs.

Langwith
Calle Obispo #410, entre Compostela y Aguacate, La Habana Vieja (no phone). **Open** 10am-7pm Mon-Sat; 10am-1pm Sun. **Map** p316 D15.
Cubans love animals but can't always afford to keep them properly. Therefore, it's somewhat of an anomaly to find this pets' hairdressing service in Havana. In addition to pampering your pooch, the staff sell pet food, accessories, aquarium products and birds.

Sports

Don't worry if you forget to bring your running shoes to Havana (mind you, you'd be mad to jog in this heat): you can buy everything from a pair of Nike trainers to a pool table here – you just have to know where to look. In addition to the places below, try the city's department stores and shopping centres (especially **Harris Brothers**, **Galerías Carlos III**, **Galerías Meliá Cohiba**, **La Vigía** and the **Centro de**

Negocios Miramar). The **Deporte** shop in Hotel Comodoro (*see p150*) is a small but well-stocked option. Also check out the sportswear on offer at **Benetton** (*see p155*). There's also a sports shop at the back of the **Estadio Latinoamericano** (*see p213*).

Adidas
Calle Neptuno, entre Campanario y Manrique, Centro Habana (625178). **Open** 9.30am-7.30pm Mon-Sat; 9.30am-1.30pm Sun. **Map** p313 D13.
The three-striped brand has a well-stocked two-storey shop. The ample range includes men and women's sportswear and jackets; gym wear; running shoes and sandals; football boots; sunglasses; bags; towels; swimming hats and baseball caps.

Stationery & supplies

Papelería O'Reilly
Calle O'Reilly #102, esquina a Tacón, La Habana Vieja (634263). **Open** 9am-7pm daily. **Map** p316 E15.
O'Reilly's has some decent-quality pens, office equipment, wrapping paper, puzzles, stationery products and children's books and offers picture framing and photocopying services. Briefcases and luggage also sold.

Papelería San Francisco
Calle Oficios #52, entre Amargura y Brasil (Teniente Rey), La Habana Vieja (no phone). **Open** 9am-5pm Mon-Fri; Sat 9am-1pm, closed Sun. **Map** p316 E15.
Office equipment and stationery supplies.

Arts & Entertainment

By Season

From carnivals to book fairs, there's always something going on in Havana. You just might wear yourself out trying to get hold of reliable information.

It's an amusing if rather frustrating fact that many people living in Havana do not find out about events taking place in the city until after they're over. You may see a fraying poster on the wall outside a venue the very day of the performance it's advertising, but you're more likely to hear nothing at all until it's all over. And, although *Cartelera*, Havana and Varadero's so-called listings magazine, does advertise the major cultural festivals, the information it carries isn't always full or accurate. You'll have to rely on word of mouth once you get to Havana: ask other people, at your hotel reception or the owners of the *casa particular* you're staying in. Just don't expect to see flyers or posters.

That said, though, it should be pointed out that Havana is a melting pot of celebrations of dance, theatre, film and sport; but don't plan a trip around a specific event unless you can confirm the dates with a trusted and reliable source. Cubans are notoriously laid back when it comes to providing concrete, reliable information (and may even tell you the first thing that comes into their head just to get rid of you). A lack of money and other resources is another factor, too.

Some events do get more coverage. Major cultural festivals are well advertised on TV on programmes such as *Hurón Azul*, the UNEAC's cultural round-up on a Thursday, as well as on radio and in *Granma*. But most aren't, and so, with the exception of the *cañonazo* and the **Carnaval** (though you never know in Havana), the following information should be treated with caution. Unless otherwise stated, all events are annual. In theory, anyway…

There aren't many – or any – websites that have particularly exhaustive information about festivals in Havana. One that is sometimes worth trying, however, is www.cubarte.cult.cu, which has information in both English and Spanish, even if it's not particularly exhaustive. If you're likely to be attending a music festival, speak to the Instituto Cubano de la Música (ICM) about a reduced-price pass. The ICM office is located on Calle 15, esquina a F, Vedado (328298/323503) or you can email them at icm@cubarte.cult.cu.

With the exception of May Day, public holidays in Cuba don't tend to have public celebrations of a festive nature. For a list of public holidays, *see chapter* **Directory**. And in addition to the following events, the Casa de las Américas also stages literary events throughout the year, including an annual competition. However, they're usually of little interest to the casual visitor.

Regular events

Every year, each of Havana's municipalities hosts its own **cultural festival**. Live concerts are a major component of these local celebrations, which take place mainly in parks, plazas and other open-air spaces. Although dates vary, no two festivals ever overlap. Ask around for specific dates and venues. The Ministerio de Cultura, Calle 2, entre 11 y 13, Vedado, can sometimes provide information about such festivals.

Also keep an eye out for **Noches en la Plaza de la Catedral**, consisting of an upmarket cabaret performed in Cathedral Square, with food provided by El Patio (*see p129*). It's meant to be a monthly event, but this hasn't always been the case recently.

Cañonazo

Time: Every night at 9pm. **Venue**: Fortaleza de San Carlos de La Cabaña castle. **Map** p313 D/E16.
At 9pm every night a cannon is fired from the ramparts of the Cabaña castle (*see p110*) across the bay from Old Havana by soldiers dressed in 18th-century costume. This recalls the curfew from the days when all citizens were supposed to be inside the (now-demolished) city walls before the gates were closed for the night. It's a very good and popular show, so try to get there early, both to get a seat and to see the sun set over the city across the bay. You can also get good views from Havana itself – try to get a windowside table at the Hotel Sevilla's Roof Garden restaurant (*see p130*).

Spring

Festival de Música Electroacústica 'Primavera en La Habana'

Information: ICM, Calle 15, esquina a F, Vedado (328298/323503). **Venues** all over La Habana Vieja. **Date** Mar, even-numbered years.
Every two years, the museums, cafés and cultural centres of the old town play host to this festival of electro-acoustic music.

Arts & Entertainment

The shy and retiring come out for **Primero de Mayo** celebrations.

Día de los Niños

Venues all over Havana. **Date** Apr, annual.

April 4 is a special day set aside for kids and known as the Day of the Children, with child-centric events and attractions throughout the city.

Feria Internacional del Disco 'Cubadisco'

Information: ICM, Calle 15, esquina a F, Vedado (328298/323503). **Venues** Pabexpo; Teatro América; Teatro Nacional; Teatro Roldán. **Date** May, annual.

Part fair, part festival, Cubadisco is Cuba's biggest and commercially most significant musical event. During the annual week-long festival, all the Cuban albums released in the preceding 12 months compete for the title of best album of the year. The main event is held at the huge exhibition hall, Pabexpo, but concerts by many of Cuba's best known musicians take place in most of Havana's major theatres.

> ▶ Many of these events are covered in greater detail in chapters **Film**, **Music & Nightlife**, **Performing Arts** and **Sport & Fitness**.
> ▶ For festivals outside Havana, *see* pp222-270 **Beyond Havana**.

Festival Internacional de Guitarra

Information: ICM, Calle 15, esquina a F, Vedado (328298/323503). **Venue** Teatro Roldán. **Date** May, even-numbered years.

Presided over by Leo Brouwer, this biennial classical guitar festival attracts musicians, fans and aficionados from all over the world.

Primero de Mayo

Date May 1, annual.

No socialist country worth its salt could go without commemorating May Day (Primero de Mayo), the International Day of the Worker, and Cuba is no exception. That said, Cuba's May Day is a tightly choreographed demonstration of revolutionary fervour and loyalty to Fidel, involving the chanting of party slogans and the waving of banners by about 20,000 carefully chosen party faithful who line the parade route. Still, it's worth a look, if only for a last glimpse at the fading trappings of state communism.

Summer

Festival Boleros de Oro

Information: UNEAC, Calle 17 #351, entre G y H, Vedado (324152). **Venues** Teatro América; Teatro Mella. **Date** June, annual.

Bolero singers, trios and larger groups from all over Cuba, Latin America and Spain attend this annual week-long festival in order to compete for several prizes. In addition to all the wonderful live music, there is also a conference on bolero music, held at the UNEAC.

Encuentro Internacional de Bandas de Conciertos
Venues across Havana. **Date** June, odd-numbered years.
The International Concert Band Festival is a fascinating trip back in time, with music from the 1940s, '50s and '60s – as well as some more contemporary works – played by some of the best concert bands in the world.

Havana Cup Yacht Race
Venue Marina Hemingway. **Date** June, annual.
A revival from the decadent '30s, this annual race from Tampa, Florida to Marina Hemingway in Havana was suspended between 1960 and 1994. However, since its resurrection, it's become bigger than ever, and now boasts some 250 competitors.

Festival Nacional del Humor
Venues Teatro Mella, Teatro Nacional. **Date** July, annual.
The National Comedy Festival aims to bring a smile to the faces of Cubans and visitors alike. Your (Cuban) Spanish will have to be excellent, though, to get the jokes.

Coloquio Internacional Hemingway
Venue varies. **Date** July, odd-numbered years.
The International Hemingway Colloquium offers the chance to discuss the importance of being Ernest

with Hemingway experts from around the world. The event is a moveable feast, with the venue announced shortly before the event begins.

Cuba Danza
Venue various. **Date** Aug, even-numbered years.
A festival of modern dance classes, workshops and performances organised by Danza Contemporánea.

Carnaval de La Habana
Venue all over Havana. **Date** last two weekends of July, first two weekends of Aug.
Havana's Carnival is a non-stop pageant of parades and street parties. The centrepiece of the festivities is a massive parade in which processions of musicians, singers and dancers march through Havana, dressed in colourful costumes representing the various *barrios* (neighbourhoods) of the city. Elsewhere, the Malecón becomes a stage for the island's hottest musical groups, and this and other events contribute to the whole carnival. A word of warning, though: be careful with your belongings, and don't flash wallets or jewellery around.

Autumn

Festival Internacional de Teatro
Venue across Havana. **Date** Sept, odd-numbered years.
The ten-day Havana Theatre Festival – sponsored by the Consejo Nacional de Artes Escénicas (the National Council of Scenic Arts) – features the best in contemporary and classical Cuban and international (mainly Latin American) theatre. Performances cover classical and contemporary drama, street theatre, musical theatre and dance.

A load of rap

Hip hop, complete with all the trimmings of gold chains and baggy trousers, has spread to Cuba, and nowhere is this more evident than in the annual **Festival de rap de Alamar**. One of Havana's most exciting festivals, the increasingly popular event draws together rap groups from all over the island – as well as from the United States and, occasionally, Europe – to celebrate hip hop culture. If you're into rap or just interested in checking out the contemporary Cuban youth scene, the menacing towerblocks of Alamar, in Havana's eastern suburbs, is where it all goes off.

Festival de rap de Alamar
Information: Asociación Hermanos Saíz, La Madriguera, Quinta de los Molinos, entre Infanta y Salvador Allende, Vedado (798175).
Venues Casa de la cultura de Alamar; Anfiteatro de Alamar. **Date** late Aug.

Carnaval de La Habana:
quiet it ain't. *See p168*.

writers, artists and poets in Cuba. Cuban rock, rap, *nueva trova* and Afro-Cuban music are especially well represented.

Festival de La Habana de Música Contemporánea

Information: UNEAC, Calle 17 #351, esquina a H, Vedado (324152). **Venue** phone for information. **Date** Sept/Oct.
This annual festival features a wild mix of musical genres, ranging from electro-acoustic to classical.

Festival Internacional de Ballet

Venue various theatres, including the Gran Teatro. **Date** late Oct, even-numbered years.
This festival is held under the aegis of the Ballet Nacional de Cuba and, if nothing else, is a great chance to see the often-touring BNC themselves. Other companies from around the world – and particularly Latin America – round out the line-ups.

Bienal de La Habana

Venue Centro de Arte Contemporáneao Wifredo Lam, *Calle San Ignacio #22 esquina a Empedrado (612096/639781)*. **Date** Nov, even-numbered years. **Map** p316 D15.
This ever-expanding art festival is held at the Wifredo Lam centre, though expect to be frustrated in your quest for information: until the day, the staff can only tell you which venues are being used, but not which artists are exhibititing where.

Festival de Raíces Africanas 'El Wemilere'

Information: Casa de la cultura de Guanabacoa (no phone). **Venue** Casa de la cultura de Guanabacoa. **Date** late Nov, annual.
El Wemilere is a celebration of Afro-Cuban culture and takes place in Guanabacoa, a municipality in Havana with strongest historical links to the city's Afro-Cuban religions. There's a wide range of cultural activities, including art exhibitions, dance shows, theatre productions and lots of live Afro-Cuban music.

Winter

Festival Internacional de Jazz

Information: ICM, Calle 15, esquina a F, Vedado (328298/323503). **Venues** Casa de la cultura de Plaza; Club Imágenes; Jazz Café; Teatro Nacional; La Zorra y el Cuervo. **Date** Dec, even-numbered years.
Internationally speaking, Havana's biennial Jazz Festival is probably its most famous music event. Presided over by Chuchó Valdés, it always attracts first-rate local and foreign jazz artists and bands.

Festival del Nuevo Cine Latinoamericano

Venues: various cinemas. **Date** early Dec, annual.
This high-profile festival is a glamorous, swanky affair. Social activities and networking are centred around the Nacional hotel, while the films (which is what it's about, after all) are shown at venues across town, but these are often not announced beforehand.

Los Días de la Música

Information: Asociación Hermanos Saíz, La Madriguera, Quinta de los Molinos, entre Infanta y Salvador Allende, Vedado (798175). **Venue** La Madriguera. **Date** Sept, annual. **Map** p312 D11.
The purpose of this annual festival – whose name translates as 'the days of music' – is to introduce and promote unknown, young musicians and bands affiliated to the Asociación Hermanos Saíz, the youth wing of UNEAC, which represents musicians,

Children

Havana lacks the theme parks and obvious children's attractions found in other cities across the world, but this may be a blessing in disguise – a chance for families to explore the city's lesser-known child-friendly sights.

It's still relatively unusual to find tourists with children outside the resort areas, so families visiting Havana will be met with extra – generally friendly – attention and interest. While many of the child-orientated conveniences found in other countries do not exist in Cuba, Cubans love children and you'll probably find that your holiday will go very smoothly if you have a youngster in your party.

ACCOMMODATION
In hotels, children under 12 often have to pay half the adult room rate, but if no extra bed is required they can sometimes stay for free. Ask for a *triple* or get an extra bed put in a double room. Larger families might manage to get two rooms adjoining, although this is sometimes promised but rarely achieved. One of the hotel chambermaids can usually babysit if you want to go out for a child-free evening.

TRANSPORT
Trying to get on one of Havana's cramped pink buses (*guaguas*) is not a good idea at any time, let alone if you've got children in tow: you're better off choosing an alternative method of getting about. Infant car seats are non-existent so bring one with you and make sure your hire car has seat-belts in the back (many don't). If you decide not to rent a car, and choose instead to hire a private car and driver, be aware that safety regulations for private vehicles are way below international standards and seat-belts are usually non-existent. Note too that there are sporadic crack-downs on the hiring of Cuban drivers by foreign tourists (*see p274*).

For a special treat, hire a vintage car off the street or from **Gran Caribe** (*see p274*); children (and adults) will get a kick from cruising the streets in a classic open-top car from the 1920s.

ADMISSION
Under-12s pay little or nothing to get into museums and other sights. Children are usually allowed into bars with their parents, but clubs and discos are a no-no.

RISKS AND PRECAUTIONS
The heat in Havana at any time of the year can be hard on children more used to temperate climates and the usual precautions should be taken even more rigorously with them than with adults. Bring really light, open-weave clothes – even normal-weight T-shirts can be too heavy in the summer months – and avoid synthetic fabrics. Unlike the rest of Latin America, Cubans do not take a siesta during the working day, but it's not a bad idea to adopt the custom with children anyway. Try to do your active sightseeing in the morning and have some down-time in the afternoon when the sun is at its fiercest. You won't see many Cuban kids with hats on, but make sure your offspring wears them whenever they go out. Apply sunblock every day, whatever the weather, and make sure everyone gets lots to drink.

There are very few public toilets in Havana and those that exist are grim in the extreme, so if you're caught short with a desperate child, head for the most upmarket hotel or bar you can find. Toilet paper is now easy to buy, but always carry some with you as many lavatories do not have it.

Diarrhoea and other stomach complaints are not a particular problem in Cuba compared with other parts of Latin America, but children should avoid eating uncooked food and food sold on the street. (Peanuts sold by *maniceros* are an exception to this rule; *see p138* **Street treats**.) Try to remember to pack some oral rehydration sachets just in case.

WHAT TO BRING
You can buy basic baby kit in Havana, but save yourself the challenge of tracking it down by packing nappies and baby wipes. As well as taking precautions against the heat by bringing plenty of sunblock, you should also be prepared for sudden torrential downpours, especially between May and October. Bring a brolly and lightweight waterproofs with you, as you'll struggle to find them in Havana. It's also a good idea to bring books, small toys, crayons and even paper with you to keep the little ones entertained in the hotel room or at restaurants; these things are surprisingly hard to find in Havana and often poor quality. If you're likely to be buying food from *agromercados* (*see p160* **Catering to your needs**) be sure to pack (deep in your luggage) a knife and a teaspoon or two. For general tips on what to bring, *see p290*.

Days out

While some of the splendours and excitements of Havana will be lost on younger visitors, they will find something fun to do in almost all areas of the city. Most museums and sights provide explanations in Spanish only, so below we have tried to pick out places where guidance is not essential, or where tours are offered in English.

La Habana Vieja

Thanks to recent efforts to improve the lot of Cuban children living in the area, the old city has a growing number of diversions suitable for the young. The area can easily be covered on foot, but if your team starts to wilt, hail a *bicitaxi* (*see p274*) and complete your tour in comfort for a couple of dollars or so. Many of the drivers of these passenger tricycles have an intimate knowledge of the old city and will be happy to point out the major sights as you ride by. Alternatively, you could hire a horse-drawn carriage from the stand at the corner of Calles Tacón and Empedrado. Finally, the **Tren Turístico Bella Época** (tel. 662476) is another fun way of seeing the sights without tiring little legs. This road train runs from 10am to 1am every day from the Terminal Sierra Maestra, opposite Plaza de San Francisco de Asís, to Hotel Meliá Cohiba in Vedado and costs $1 per person each way. It travels along a slightly different route in each direction,

passing major sights such as the Capitolio, the university, Coppelia and the Hotel Nacional.

If you decide to tackle the old town on foot, start in the Plaza de Armas at the **Castillo de la Real Fuerza** (*see p64*). There are good views from the tower and you can try a sustaining glass of *guarapo* (sugar cane juice) in the snack bar on the terrace. The displays of armour on the ground floor include a magnificent helmet made for a horse. On the south side of the square, the recently modernised **Museo Nacional de Historia Natural** (*see p65*) has child-friendly displays on the plants and wildlife of Cuba. You might also want to check out what's on offer in the games and video rooms, but bear in mind that everything is in Spanish.

North of the museum, along Calle Tacón, is the **crafts market** (*see p163*). Rummage through this junky and colourful handicraft market to find hats and pretty bead necklaces. In nearby **Parque José de la Luz y Caballero** between Calle Tacón and Avenida Céspedes, there are some small but peppy ponies, which can be hired for 3 pesos for a saunter round the grounds. The ponies are in action from 11am to 6pm on Saturdays and Sundays and daily during the school holidays. Further along Tacón, in the **Parque del Anfiteatro**, is the **Parque Infantil la Maestranza** (*see p74*), a great favourite with local children. It has low-key fairground rides, for which you'll need to buy strips of tickets at the kiosk by the entrance.

The immense **Parque Lenin**. *See p174.*

Arts & Entertainment

Sweet 15

Think young but maturing girls decked out in long frilly frocks, with big hairdos, plenty of mascara, bright lipstick and blue eye-shadow. Add lashings of soft drinks, ice-cream, enormous pink and blue meringue-iced cake and plates of cold titbits. Mix in the sweet sounds of *merengue*, a Strauss waltz, a little *salsa* and a few Backstreet Boys hits. Capture the moment with a phenomenal number of photos – photos with friends, parents, family; Lolita-like in front of mirrors; photos as the girl changes from Sultana to cowgirl – and you have one of the most enduringly kitsch events in the Cuban calendar – a girl's 15th birthday party, known as a *fiesta de quince*.

The early *quince* celebrations were Spanish in origin and exclusive to the upper classes. Similar to the old British 'coming out' party, they were an opportunity for a girl of 16 or 17 to enter into adult society for the first time and signified her transition from girl to woman. Moreover, it was an appropriate place for young women to meet potential, hopefully rich, suitors.

In the 1940s the age at which girls were accepted into adult society was lowered to 15 and the name '*los quince*' was adopted, but the show remained pretty much the same. Families continued to hire big houses or exclusive sports clubs to which they invited 14 young couples. Much dancing, eating, meeting and mating took place and the party closed with the young girl and her boyfriend or close male friend dancing.

The Revolution put an end to the excess of the *quince* celebrations. The values of 1959 were deemed incompatible with the elitism of this white, bourgeois celebration and the *quince* all but disappeared from view. Then, during the 1970s and '80s, it re-emerged in a more popular form. The influence and dollars of Miami-based Cubans saw the return of those puffy-sleeved frocks. Stories of daughters in Florida descending in helicopters or parading on carnival floats encouraged many families in Cuba to reinstate the tradition. Preparations for the big day would begin three or four years beforehand in order to finance the festivities, despite crippling economic hardships.

Nowadays, the tradition remains, but it is changing again. Some families still go the whole hog with frocks, photos and all the trimmings, but others choose instead to eat out with friends or to hold a small party at home. Some parents proudly describe '*los quince*' simply as a happy celebration of their daughter's coming of age; others as '*un grand show*' – a vulgar and competitive spectacular that is, at best, simply old-fashioned and inappropriate and at worst a huge political contradiction in these harsh economic times. Whatever you make of *los quince* it is, in one form or another, an enduring part of many Cuban lives.

A final note: if you get the chance to go to a *fiesta de los quince* take plenty of photographs and try to make sure you send copies to the family. While some people here have money and contacts, most don't, and photos are very, very precious. So, put on your lippy and your dancing shoes, get out your camera and – ¡*Quince*!

Don't miss the new and magnificent **Fundación Havana Club** (*see p68*) in Calle San Pedro, opposite the Aduana (Customs House). The most entertaining bit for children is the Museo del Ron (within the Foundation), with its rum-barrel lift and working scale model of a sugar distillery. A short video and guided tour are available in English, although the strong Cuban accents can be hard to follow. Nearby, the **Iglesia de San Francisco de Asís** (*see p66*) has a 42-metre (140-foot) tower, which kids love to climb: the view of Old Havana from the top is one of the best.

In an attempt to bring the delights of marine life to urban kids, the city has opened the tiny **Aqvarivm** (*see p67*). There are plans to expand the site, but for the time being the exquisite and highly colourful sea creatures are displayed in half a dozen tanks in a single aqua-tinted room. The fish are easy to spot, but the information panels are in Spanish only. Films and puppet shows relating to the exhibits are shown at 3pm on Tuesdays.

The other two museums worth taking in are the **Museo del Automóvil** (*see p66*), with its collection of vintage cars, and the **Maqueta de La Habana Vieja** (Scale Model of Old Havana; *see p71*). Of the many places to hang out over a cold drink in La Habana Vieja, **El Patio** restaurant (*see p129*) in the Plaza de la Catedral provides the most entertaining pageant of street performers and passers-by.

Centro Habana

Even parents with a fierce anti-smoking policy should overcome any qualms and take their children to the **Real Fábrica de Tabacos Partagás** or the **Real Fábrica de Tabacos La Corona** (*for both, see p82*) to learn how a cigar is produced. The tours are fascinating and the workers are particularly responsive to young visitors. Close to La Corona is the **Museo de la Revolución** (*see p82*), where older children and teenagers might be interested to learn something about Cuba's extraordinary recent history.

European children are unlikely to have seen a traditional agricultural market such as the large *agromercado* at **Cuatro Caminos** (*see p83*).

Vedado

Energetic offspring can stride along the **Malecón** from Centro Habana to Vedado or alternatively run about in the lovely park that surrounds the **Quinta de los Molinos** (*see p89*). Here you may be lucky and catch young musicians rehearsing in **La Madriguera**, the

headquarters of the youth wing of UNEAC, the Union of Writers and Artists (*see p89*).

If you're in town on 1 May (Labour Day) or 26 July (National Rebellion Celebrations) join the huge gatherings that take place in the gigantic **Plaza de la Revolución**, which can hold nearly a million people. On other days take the lift to the top of the **Memorial y Museo José Martí** (*see p91*) for superb views of the city.

Nuevo Vedado to the west is the home of the **Jardín Zoológico de La Habana** (*see p97*). If your children are accustomed to the highly educational and environmentally friendly zoos of more prosperous countries, this place might come as a bit of a shock. The animals are confined to small cages in some rather inauthentic habitats and the sparse information plaques are in Spanish only. On the other hand, many of the inmates look surprisingly sleek and content – and it is a treat to be able to see them at such close quarters. The landscaping is attractive, with plentiful shade trees, and facilities include two large but scruffy playgrounds and several modest cafés. There are few tourists but lots of Cubans making a day of it, so bring a picnic and join in.

Río Almendares

Opposite the entrance to the zoo (*see above*), Avenida Zoológico leads down to a bridge over the Río Almendares. Cross this to enter the **Bosque de La Habana** (*see p99*), a densely wooded park that stretches in both directions along the river. The occasional pillared shelters are sadly run down, but nothing could detract from the exotic appeal of the tangle of jungle vegetation and the magnificence of the *jagüey* (banyan or Indian) trees with their hanging aerial roots. The banyan near the bridge between Kohly and Calle 23, for example, forms a canopy the size of a circus tent.

Miramar & the western suburbs

La Maqueta de La Habana (*see p102*), a vast and detailed scale model of Havana, gives a great sense of the growth and layout of the city. Buildings are colour-coded by period so you can trace the development since colonial times and there is always someone on hand to answer questions in English. A mezzanine affords a bird's-eye view – useful for smaller children.

Nearby, the recently refurbished **Acuario Nacional** (*see p102*) boasts a fine display of tropical fish and has regular dolphin and seal shows throughout the day. It's very popular with Cuban families but note that the cafés accept *moneda nacional* rather than dollars so make sure you have some pesos with you.

Arts & Entertainment

Feeding time

EATING OUT

Cubans are very indulgent with their own children and take them everywhere, so you won't find many restaurants in Havana where yours will be unwelcome. On the other hand, service can be slow and menus are not often geared to picky eaters. (In a nation where food rationing is still in force, it's no wonder.) *Criollo* food won't faze most children but, if you want to steer clear of the hunks of pork and piles of chips, you can usually get a side order of *moros y cristianos* (black beans and rice) or a *tortilla* (omelette), even if they don't appear on the menu. *Tostones* (fried banana chips) are a tasty though rather high-calorie finger food that goes down well with kids. Pizza and spaghetti are familiar fall-backs but can be tasteless and stodgy. Salads, often the only fresh vegetable on offer, are generally safe but may be no more than undressed slices of cucumber (or whatever vegetable is in season). Cuban ice-cream is consistently good – although there is no predicting what flavours you'll find (*see p132* **Scream for ice-cream**). Children's meals per se are not generally offered, but it is acceptable to order one meal for two children or for an adult and a child to share – just remind the waiter to bring you an extra (empty) plate.

In terms of liquids, all the usual soft drinks are available – you will probably offered imported brands, which are more expensive and, as a result, often forced upon tourists, although local varieties are always available – and every café and restaurant stocks Tropical Island fruit juices in a few flavours. A freshly made *limonada natural* or bottled water make good, refreshing alternatives. Tap water is normally good quality within the pricier hotels.

GOING IT ALONE

You can put together a passable picnic in Havana, especially if you're prepared to venture to a supermarket or an *agromercado* (*see p160* **Catering to your needs**).

South-west of Miramar in La Coronela is the **Museo del Aire** (*see p108*), an aviation graveyard where you can climb up into obsolete helicopters and fighter jets.

The eastern bay & coast

THE FORTRESSES

Don't be put off by what looks like an awkward hop across Havana Bay to the **Parque Histórico Militar Morro-Cabaña**. This vast military construction is a great place to set Havana's historical scene for children of all ages and it's only a short ride through the tunnel by taxi. The obvious highlights are the lighthouse (**Faro del Morro**) and maritime displays at the **Castillo de los Tres Reyes del Morro** and the moats, ramparts, and display of weaponry at the **Fortaleza de San Carlos de la Cabaña**. There are several places to get a meal (*see p139*), so you can easily spend the best part of a day on this side of the bay. Alternatively, come in the late afternoon and then stay on for the **Ceremonia del Cañonazo**, which takes place at 9pm every night. It's well worth keeping the younger ones up for this traditional ceremony, in which soldiers dressed in the colours of the Spanish colonial army fire a cannon from the battlements of La Cabaña.

THE BEACHES

The beach is the obvious place to go for a jaunt out of town with children and there is no shortage of them near Havana. Of the ones detailed on *pp109-116*, **Tarará** is perhaps one of the best suited to young swimmers, with its shallow waters.

Cerro & further south

If everyone's had enough of city sightseeing and you have a car at your disposal, consider spending a day in the huge parks on the south-western outskirts of Havana. You can get a taxi to take you there from more central parts of the city, though it's not always easy to get one back into town. The immense **Parque Lenin**, about 20 kilometres (12.5 miles) from the old city, is open seven days a week and offers a range of amusements from Tuesday to Sunday. If you come to the rodeos (*see p214*) at the weekend you'll see some pretty macho cowboys wrangling steer and calf-roping. (If you don't make it to Parque Lenin there is another, larger rodeo held a couple of times a month at the **Feria Agropecuaria** just south of José Martí Airport; *see p214*). Very near the Parque Lenin rodeo you can rent six-person boats on the Embalse Paso Saquito, an artificial lake. The park's freshwater aquarium is closed for renovation at time of writing but is due to

Most shops have a good range of natural (but long-life) Tropical Island juices in small cartons. Note that some of the drinks are 100 per cent juice and can be identified by the word *jugo*: *jugo de naranja* (orange juice); *jugo de piña* (pineapple juice); *jugo de mango* (mango juice) etc. A fruit drink with added sugar is known as a *néctar*: *néctar de manzana* (apple juice); *néctar de guayaba* (guava juice) etc.

In terms of milk, only UHT is available commercially (La Niña brand). It's actually made from reconstituted milk powder and tastes pretty dire, so if you are concerned about your child's dairy intake you could try the rather runny yoghurt instead, sold in one-litre plastic bags in various flavours – the coconut one is delicious. Jars of baby food, for some reason, are sold in even the smallest of supermarkets.

Decent bread is not easy to find in the supermarkets but oddly the rolls are usually OK. You should be able to find at least one basic variety of cheese and maybe some ham

or salami for sandwiches. There is never any shortage of sweet biscuits, though they often come in strange artificial-looking colours. The **Pain de Paris** bakeries (*see p157*) are a better source of bread and pastries than the supermarkets.

Havana has a large number of *mercados agropecuarios* (farmers' markets) commonly known as *agros*. They are fun to visit and are really the only source of seasonal fresh fruit and vegetables (bananas and avocados are good choices). Most markets also have someone selling *turrón* – brittle bars made of peanut (*maní*) or sesame seeds (*ajonjolí*) that are worth having on hand. These vendors (*maniceros*), who rove the street on foot or by bicycle, also sell packs of delicious mango and guava paste and twists or cones (*cucuruchos*) of freshly roasted peanuts (*maní tostado*).

For further details of *agros* and other self-sufficiency options, *see p160* **Catering to your needs**.

re-open some time in 2001. The park also encompasses a real old-fashioned fairground (*parque de diversiones*) with merry-go-rounds, candy floss and a miniature train. There are pony rides of the quick-canter-round-the-nearest-tree variety, so perhaps best reserved for older kids with some idea of how to stay in the saddle. The riding school (Centro Ecuestre, also known as the Club Hípico) can arrange riding lessons for children and also cross-country jaunts within the park. For further details of all the attractions to be found within Parque Lenin, *see p121*.

South of the park is the **Jardín Botánico Nacional** (*see p121*), which has a variety of tropical and sub-tropical plants, many in glass houses, and a Japanese garden. Get the most out of your visit by having one of the English-speaking guides accompany you in your car.

To the west of Parque Lenin, the **Parque Zoológico Nacional** (*see p121*) is more of a safari park than a zoo, and will give you a good couple of hours of surprisingly unsupervised contact with the animals. Watch out for the kleptomaniac elephant!

Sport & fitness

Don't despair if there is no pool at your hotel, since other hotels offer non-guests access to their pools for about $5 per person. The best

ones for children are the **Deauville** in Centro Habana; the **Habana Libre**, **Capri**, and **Meliá Cohiba** in Vedado; and the **Novotel** and **Comodoro** in Miramar, both of which have separate pool areas for children. (For details of these hotels, *see chapter* **Accommodation**). Try also the **Complejo Turístico La Giraldilla shopping centre** at Calle 222, esquina a 37.

Under-13s have free admission to the beach and pool at the hotel at **Club Habana** (*see p104*) and can hire jet-skis, kayaks or dinghies for a small charge. **Hotel Copacabana** (*see p59*) hires out pedal boats and canoes for a few dollars an hour, but they can be used only in the saltwater pool. At **Marina Hemingway** (*see p217*) diving courses for non-resident children over 11 and sailing courses for younger ones are sometimes held. Ask to be put through to the pool at the Hotel Acuario (tel. 247628) and they will tell you what is currently on offer for short-term visitors.

Entertainment

Musical shows, dance, films, puppets, clowns, magicians, story-telling and art classes are presented in theatres, cultural centres and museums all over the city at weekends (usually at 10am and 5pm) and often in the afternoons on other days, too. None of the

Arts & Entertainment

A big hand for **Teatro Nacional de Guiñol**.

Shops

You can buy a limited range of children's clothes, shoes and toys in Havana, but don't expect to see anything that you wouldn't rather buy at home. Most of the shops are located in shopping centres, often within hotel complexes; prices are reasonable, but quality tends to be mediocre at best. For full details of shops in Havana, *see chapter* **Shops & Services**.

Trips out of town

Many of the excursions described within the **Beyond Havana** section (*pp222-270*) would also appeal to children, though remember that journeys by public transport often take much longer than scheduled. We particularly recommend **Las Terrazas** (*see p224*) and **Soroa** (*see p225*), which can be combined to make a really good day out, taking in the coffee plantation at the **Hotel Moka**, a swim at the **Baños de San Juan**, and lunch by the waterfalls at **Soroa**.

Viñales (*see p228*) is a magical place, good for walks and horse rides in the valley. Don't miss the boat ride through the vast **Cueva de los Indios** (*see p228*) and a tour of the **Jardín Botánico de Caridad**, the private garden developed by two sisters. There is usually someone there who speaks English and it is a great way of learning more about all those tropical fruits and flowers that you see around. If you go during the week, try and stay at **Hotel Los Jazmines** (*see p228*), which has a games room and a co-ordinator who organises children's activities. The pool at **Hotel La Ermita** (*see p229*) has a shallow end for kids.

About 45 kilometres (28 miles) east of Havana in the **Parque Escaleras de Jaruco** you can see the stair-like rock formations and get a good view of the surrounding countryside. Combine **Jaruco** with a visit to **Matanzas** and the **Cuevas de Bellamar**. These impressive caves deep underground are not for the claustrophobic, but tours are conducted on foot and are available in English.

Some 35 kilometres (22 miles) south-west of Havana, just before you reach **San Antonio de los Baños**, is the **Hotel Las Yagrumas**, where you can rent a rowing boat or motor boat and explore ten kilometres (six miles) of the Río Ariguanabo.

You can get the best out of the **Península de Zapata** (*see p235*) in a day if you stick to the *criadero de cocodrilos* (crocodile farm) at Boca de Guamá and a boat trip across the **Laguna del Tesoro** to the re-created Taino Indian village at Guamá (*see p235*).

events are geared towards tourists, but if your children understand some Spanish or are relaxed about not being able to follow everything, it's worth seeing what's on. *Cartelera* sometimes prints a schedule of activities, but programme details are best obtained from the venues: **Teatro Nacional de Guiñol** for puppet shows (*see p205*); **Centro Cultural Bertolt Brecht** (*see p204*), **Teatro Fausto** (*see p204*), **Teatro Mella** (*see p205*) and **Museo de Arte Colonial** (*see p72*) for shows of all kinds; **Maqueta de La Habana** (*see p102*) for story-telling and art workshops; and the **Basílica de San Francisco de Asís** (*see p204*) for ventriloquists, clowns, and magicians on Tuesdays. Older children will enjoy the Afrocuban ballet at the **Conjunto Folclórico de Cuba** (*see p208*) and shows by **La Colmenita**, a young dance troupe that sometimes performs around town.)

The following cinemas show films for children: **Cinecito**, **Charles Chaplin**, **Charlot**, **23 y 12**, and the **Fundación del Nuevo Cine Latinoamericano**. For more details, *see chapter* **Film**.

Film

Cineastes will have a hard time in Havana. The city boasts no multiplexes, but instead a good number of charming (and not-so-charming) cinemas and video rooms showing US hits and home-grown classics.

Despite – or maybe because of – the US embargo, Cubans are one of the most knowledgeable cinema audiences in the world. Not only have the latest US blockbuster films managed to slip through the net and make their way to Cuban ears but the blockade itself has resulted in Cubans being exposed to a multitude of non-Hollywood movies: everything from Eisenstein to Sam Mendes to Almodóvar.

Cuban cinema-going has a long and varied history. In the pre-Revolutionary years, American stars reigned supreme in the swanky film theatres of Havana, especially in Vedado, where the largest and newest cinemas were located. The Revolution inevitably brought about a change in the political orientation of films available to Cuba: virtually no American films made it across, and this was counteracted by an increase in availability of Latin American, and, because of the island's ties with the Soviet Union, Eastern European films. Over the following years, the Cuban public hungered

Catch the big screen at **Payret**. See p180.

for something more relevant and entertaining than the often dull, patriotic and propaganda-filled Soviet films, and, come the 1980s, their wishes were granted when more films from outside the Soviet bloc were allowed to arrive on the island. The 1990s saw a continuation of this process, with the result that now big blockbuster hits from the previous year are shown on video projectors in some of Havana's cinemas and in most of the special video rooms (*salas de video*) of the capital. Unfortunately the majority of cinemas in Havana still rely on old film-roll projectors that are as much in need of repair as the cinemas and buildings themselves. It is still very difficult to get rolls of film for the latest movies into Cuba, as most major and many minor distributors are based in the USA. So don't expect to find North American or European films until at least a couple of years after their original release date.

If your knowledge of Spanish is poor then you're going to have to rely on good luck to find a film in its original English. Cubans in general dislike dubbed films, but with very little to choose from, the **ICAIC** (Instituto Cubano del Arte e Industria Cinematográficos) has to accept whatever comes its way. Created at the dawn of the Revolution, ICAIC is in charge of the exhibition, production and distribution of films in Cuba as well as international affairs; it also publishes the well-respected but hard-to-get-hold-of *Revista Cine Cubano* magazine, sometimes available at ICAIC itself, or, more likely, second-hand book markets. Despite many political and financial problems through the years, the Institute has been a great success and has produced some very highly regarded, award-winning films.

But things may be moving forward as the use of video projectors becomes more prevalent in cinemas and *salas de video*, allowing many of the latest films (with Spanish subtitles) to be seen as pirate videos recorded off Mexican and Miami satellite television. Unfortunately, as is the case with most pirate films around the world, the quality can be rather dubious.

It's worth checking out the surprisingly good range of films on Cuban television. There are two films on Saturday night at around 10.30pm and midnight, another two on Sunday at about

The well known and popular **Yara**. *See p180.*

2.30pm and 11pm, and others dotted throughout the week (particularly Latin American films, late at night). Films shown include standard and often pretty up-to-date Hollywood action movies, plus some older but nonetheless enjoyable films, especially in the Sunday afternoon slot.

Even if your Spanish is poor it is definitely worth going to a large screening of a major Cuban or foreign film just for the experience. On these occasions, cinemas are packed and huge queues can develop. Inside the cinema you will find a noisy but very lively audience that laughs en masse, claps the end of good films and generally demonstrates a high level of critical appreciation for the direction, subject matter and comedy, not just the special effects.

CINEMAS, SCREENINGS, PRICES & OTHER INFORMATION

Cinemas in Havana tend to be a bit down-trodden and in need of repair. This is truest in La Habana Vieja and Centro Habana, while Vedado hosts a few nice cinemas in relatively good condition – check what's on at **La Rampa** or the **Riviera**, for example. There are no multiplexes in Cuba and all the cinemas you visit will be showing one film at a time. While this helps to get the large audiences and special atmosphere at big films, it has the effect of making it hard to classify Havana cinemas by Western categories of 'art-house' or 'multiplex'. That is not to say, however, that the same types of films are screened at all cinemas.

The cinema industry in Cuba is based around the intersection of Calle 23 and Calle 12 in Vedado, where ICAIC is located. The three movie theatres in this area are by far the most diverse and 'arty' of all Havana cinemas. The **Chaplin** cinema, on the street level of the ICAIC building, offers a varied schedule, including some major previews and good foreign films; the **Centro Cultural Cinematográfico ICAIC** video room shows less common, more cultish films and is a favourite with resident film buffs; while the **Sala de Video Charlot** in the same building

as the Chaplin specialises in seasons focusing on different directors, such as, in the past, Pedro Almodóvar.

For the big showings of the latest releases to Cuba, the **Yara** in Vedado and **Payret** in La Habana Vieja are two favourites. These are very busy places (especially Yara, which is situated directly opposite Coppelia ice-cream parlour; *see p132* **Scream for ice-cream**) and queues are not infrequent for the newest films.

Screening schedules are shown on the front of every cinema and change every Thursday. The addresses and schedules of some cinemas are found in Spanish and English in the weekly *Cartelera*, available free from hotels (most reliably the Nacional; *see p56*) or for 50 centavos at *correos* (street kiosks) around the city. Spanish speakers can try calling ICAIC direct (552841/9). Cinema buffs may be interested in the website (**www.cinecubano.com**), which details the history of Cuban cinema (in Spanish only), and also has information about film festivals.

Note that most cinemas and video rooms have air-conditioning or fans. We have noted the exceptions where possible. Also, most venues charge in pesos and do not accept credit cards or advance bookings. Performances in cinemas tend to start between 4.30pm and 9pm (exceptions are noted below), with some late shows at the weekend and children's films also on Saturday and/or Sunday mornings. Many cinemas and salas de video charge in pesos or centavos, with others such as the Payret normally charging in dollars. Most venues are open seven days a week unless otherwise stated. And, one final tip: you might want to choose a cinema or *sala de video* in Vedado: being a major tourist hub, it is subject to fewer power cuts than other parts of town.

Major cinemas

23 y 12

Calle 23 #1212, entre 12 y 14, Vedado (36906). **Map** p311 C8.
A nice smallish cinema that specialises in children's films in the afternoon, although there are often good screenings for the older cinema-goer at 8pm.

Chaplin (Cinemateca de Cuba)

Calle 23 #1155, entre 10 y 12, Vedado (311101). **Closed** Tue. **Map** p311 C8.
Housed in the ICAIC building, this large, well-kept cinema shows some of the best films in Havana. It specialises in arty offerings, although major pre-mières have also been held here. The foyer has an exhibition of posters advertising some of the great Cuban films from the decades since the Revolution. Posters and videos of the best Cuban films of the last 40 years are on sale on the fourth floor.

Arts & Entertainment

Cuban films

Cuba was one of the major leaders in the new wave of Latin American film-making from the mid-1950s and beyond and still retains a great film-making tradition.Though it has had to be scaled down over the years of the Special Period due to shortages, visitors are always guaranteed the chance to see at least a handful of Cuban films in the various Havana cinemas. A good way to get hold of Cuban film videos, including the following, is to visit the website of LAVA (Latin American Video Archive) at www.latinamericanvideo.org.

Here, **Rosa Bosch**, one of the producers of *Buena Vista Social Club*, picks out some of the most memorable Cuban films.

Name: *Fresa y chocolate (Strawberry and Chocolate), 1993; pictured*
Directors: Tomás Gutiérrez Alea and Juan Carlos Tabío
The gist: The trials and tribulations of a young homophobic Revolutionary student, David, who befriends an older gay intellectual, Diego, who has had problems with the Cuban authorities. There were huge queues in Cuba to see the film, which included a harsh critique of some of the country's social and political problems. On the plus side, the screening of the film (impossible without government support) suggested a growing acceptance of being able to portray some of the drawbacks of the system. By the way, the name of the film comes from the two most popular flavours of ice-cream at Coppelia, which features in the opening scenes of the film. The only Cuban film since the Revolution that received a wide release in the US, by Miramax, under a clause of cultural exception.

Name: *Buena Vista Social Club, 1998*
Director: Wim Wenders
The gist: Focusing on the elderly stars of the album of the same name, Wenders' internationally successful documentary offers an insight into Cuban music of a past era when Havana was among the nightclub capitals of the world. You won't find this film shown much in Havana; the Cuban public has failed to catch the bug for a music that it left behind 50 years ago and shows little desire to return to it – except as a means of extracting tourist dollars, of course.

Name: *La muerte de un burócrata (Death of a Bureaucrat), 1966*
Director: Tomás Gutiérrez Alea
The gist: In this black comedy, an exemplary labourer dies in an industrial accident and is buried with his worker's booklet, the symbol of his proletarian status. His widow discovers that she needs the booklet to be able to claim her widow's pension, and, furthermore, that bodies are not allowed to be exhumed for two years after burial. There follows a series of hilarious – sometimes almost surreal – episodes that illustrate Cuba's often absurd bureaucracy.

Name: *Lista de espera (Waiting List), 1999*
Director: Juan Carlos Tabío
The gist: The directorial début of Tabío, this comedy drama follows a group of travellers waiting at a run-down Cuban transit station for the next bus, as it slowly starts to dawn on them that it's not going to come (a familiar tale in Cuba). There's a love story going on between Emilio and Jacqueline, while most of the rest of the characters start to conjure up a plan to revamp the dilapidated bus station.

Name: *Memorias del subdesarollo (Memories of Underdevelopment), 1968*
Director: Tomás Gutiérrez Alea
The gist: When his family flees Cuba for Miami in 1961, intellectual but neurotic Sergio chooses to stay behind. The film, based on a novel by Edmundo Desnoes, follows Sergio's thoughts on pre- and post-Revolutionary Cuba; interspersed are clips of documentary footage of hugely important events of the time (the Bay of Pigs invasion, the Cuban Missile Crisis, speeches by Kennedy). The resulting film is a moving piece of work that became the seminal reference point within the Latin American and Spanish world.

Reel life story

When Cuba's most revered director of recent years died in 1996, thousands came to his funeral. Born in Havana in 1928, **Tomás Gutiérrez Alea** (or Titón as he was affectionately known) studied law at university, but, having shot several shorts, was already showing an interest in film-making by the time he graduated. Alea headed to the Centro Sperimentale film school in Rome, where he befriended two other students who would later figure prominently in the Latin American film world: Fernando Birri and Julio García Espinosa. The neo-realism movement, prevalent in Italy at the time, was to heavily influence Alea's work, though he also counted Buñuel and Godard, as well as the Italian great Rossellini, and Zavattini, as his influences.

In 1953, when Alea returned to Cuba, he became involved in the new political ideas of Revolutionary Cuba, and two years later he co-directed (with García Espinosa) *El Megano*, about the kidnapping of a coal worker by police. With the Triumph of the Revolution in 1959, Titón was instrumental

in the founding of ICAIC, the Cuban Film Institute. His next few years were prolific, with *Historias de la revolución* (Stories from the Revolution, 1961), *Las doce sillas* (The Twelve Chairs, 1962), *Cumbite* (1964) and *La muerte de un burócrata* (Death of a Bureaucrat, 1966; *pictured*). But it was in 1968 with *Memorias del subdesarollo* (Memories of Underdevelopment) that he achieved international recognition. The film even made it onto the *New York Times* top ten films for that year.

Payret

Paseo de Martí (Prado) #503, esquina a San José, Centro Habana (633163). **Map** p313 D14.
The Payret, situated across from the Capitolio, is the largest cinema in the area and, along with the Yara, screens the most popular films in Havana at any time. As a result, there are often long queues. In December it is one of the main venues for the New Latin American Film Festival. As with nearly all cinemas in Old and Central Havana, Payret is dingy and dark, but the interior decor and the bar below the main entrance point to an era of luxury before the Revolution. Showings from 12.30pm. Late shows at midnight on Friday, Saturday and Sunday.

La Rampa

Calle 23, entre O y P, Vedado (786146). **Closed** Wed. **Map** p312 B12.
A comfortable and plush cinema (plenty of '50s leather here), specialising in Latin American and Cuban films, though a fair clutch of US films are also shown. As a member of the Cinemateca de Cuba, La Rampa often shows more obscure films, in addition to the latest and greatest from the US (none of those blockbusters, mind).

Yara

Calle L #363, esquina a 23, Vedado (329430). **Map** p312 B11.

The most famous cinema in Havana is situated on one of the city's most famous street corners, right across from Coppelia (*see p132* **Scream for ice-cream**). People queuing for ice-cream have been known to pop into the cinema to catch a film while they're waiting. The Yara is not as dingy as many other cinemas in Havana, though it does have its share of broken seats. It's definitely worth checking out any major films here, as the large audiences tend to have a great laugh. At night the doorsteps of the Yara become a haunt for the city's gay population (*see p185*). Showings from 12.30pm, with late shows at midnight on Friday, Saturday and Sunday.

Other cinemas

Actualidades

Avenida de Bélgica (Monserrate) #262, entre Ánimas y Neptuno, Centro Habana (615193). **Map** p313 D14.
Calling itself the 'Cinema of Cinematografic Genres', Cine Actualidades is located right opposite the beautiful Bacardí building. In great contrast to its neighbour, however, the cinema is small, ugly, uncomfortable and noisy. If you really have to use the toilet, go to one of the nearby hotels. Nevertheless, the films are worth the discomfort, since this cinema is one of the more diverse in

Alea was one of the best intellectual critics of the Revolutionary process in Cuba and was never afraid to tackle taboo subjects. In 1993, his *Fresa y chocolate* (Strawberry and Chocolate) sparked a national debate about homosexuality. Significantly, it was Cuba's first submission to the Oscars' foreign film category. Even Alea's last movie, *Guantanamera* (1995), took a swipe at Cuban bureaucracy, at a time when many intellectuals left the island and the Revolutionary ideas were waning.

Havana, showing international films of all genres. Every day of the week is dedicated to a different genre, with the itinerary changed each month. The full schedule is shown on the door of the cinema.

Águila de Oro

Calle Rayo #108, entre Zanja y Dragones, Centro Habana (633386). **Map** p313 D13.
The 'Golden Eagle' specialises in action, kung-fu and Japanese manga films, but watching is an unpleasant experience, as the cinema is both uncomfortable and noisy, due to the huge fans blowing air at you from beside the screen. No air-conditioning.

América

Avenida de Italia (Galiano) #253, entre Concordia y Neptuno, Centro Habana (625416). **Map** p313 D13.
Though the América rarely shows films, it's worth a trip just to sneak a look at the interior, a masterpiece of art deco. The man on the door will usually let you in for a dollar or two.

Astral

Calzada de Infanta (Menocal) #501, Centro Habana (781054). **Map** p312 C12.
The Astral was recently renovated and so now stands out from the other cinema halls on the street. At the time of writing the cinema was still not open, so little is known about the films that will be shown

here, although renovations suggest it will be used for larger films. A small art gallery in the foyer shows paintings by lesser-known Cuban artists.

Cervantes

Calle Lamparilla #312, entre Aguacate y Compostela, La Habana Vieja (630026). **Closed** Mon. **Map** p316 E15.
Hidden in the run-down back streets of Old Havana, the Cervantes is particularly hard to find and differs little from its surroundings. It is dark, dingy and uncomfortable, with more than its fair share of broken seats. The films, too, are low quality and are mainly for children. No air-conditioning.

Cinecito

Calle San Rafael #68, esquina a Consulado, Centro Habana (638051). **Map** p313 D14.
The Cinecito (Little Cinema) specialises in children's films, although it also shows more adult fare at 8pm (like the much better 23 y 12). Children's shows begin at 2.30pm on Saturdays and Sundays. Unfortunately, there's no air-conditioning.

Fundación del Nuevo Cine Latinoamericano

Quinta Santa Bárbara, Calle 212, esquina a 31, La Coronela, Marianao (218967/218141). **Open** 11am-8pm Tue-Fri; 9.30am-8pm Sat; closed Sun, Mon. **Admission** $2; $1 concessions.
Located out in a leafy western suburb of Havana, this former country house with its comfortable auditorium, Sala Glauber Rocha, is a secondary venue for the Festival del Nuevo Cine Latinoamericano (*see p182*). The emphasis is on Latin American films all year round but they give reasonable prominence to other regions, too. Outside the festival, showings are at 3pm and 5.30pm, with a children's film at 10am every Saturday.

Riviera

Calle 23 #507, entre Presidentes (G) y H, Vedado (309564). **Map** p312 B11.
The blue-fronted Riviera is well placed in the heart of Vedado, though its programming is generally disappointing (showing, as it does, either US action films from a few years ago or whatever ex-premiere has just finished its run at the Yara up the street; *see p180*). The air-conditioning is prone to breaking down, with the result that the audience is often forced to sit and wilt in the heat. The only recompense for the discomfort is the price of the tickets (just one peso).

Trianón

Calle Línea #706, entre Paseo y A, Vedado (309648). **Map** p312 B9.
The Trianón doubles as a theatre and, as such, is not always the most reliable place to see a film in the evening as sometimes there's a live performance on. Apart from that, it's a nice venue, well placed and close to the Meliá Cohiba and Habana Riviera hotels (for both, *see p56*). It generally shows older action or suspense films from Spain and the US.

Arts & Entertainment

Salas de video

They're hot. They're sweaty. *Salas de video* (video rooms) are specially built rooms for watching all the films that can't be obtained on normal film rolls. Since the 1980s Cubans have found these small communal television rooms the only way to see the latest and greatest foreign films. Most are attached to cinemas and are generally in the place of the old bar or shop. A particularly interesting example is the Alhambra (*see below*) in the Payret where it is actually in the still-intact bar from the '50s. You have been warned.

Águila de Oro

Calle Rayo #108, entre Zanja y Dragones, Centro Habana (633386). **Map** p313 D13.
The video room tends to show the same types of films – action and kung-fu – as the main cinema (*see p181*), but has the advantage of air-conditioning. Another advantage is that it's not quite as noisy or in such a state of disrepair as the cinema.

Alhambra

Paseo de Martí (Prado) #503, esquina a San José, Centro Habana (633163). **Map** p313 D14.
Situated in the bar of the Payret cinema (*see p180*), this is one of the more obviously improvised video rooms. Thirty or so red leather stools face two video screens and noise from the foyer makes it hard to hear. But if atmosphere is what you're looking for, you'll find it hard to beat the '50s bar with all trimmings intact. No air-conditioning.

Centro Cultural Cinematográfico ICAIC

Calle 23 #1155, entre 10 y 12, Vedado (information 552841/9). **Map** p311 C8.
Along with the Charlot video room and the Chaplin cinema, the Centro Cultural Cinematográfico ICAIC is responsible for screening arty, obscure or older films in Havana. Hidden in an entrance next to the 23 y 12 restaurant, opposite the Chaplin cinema, it is by far the nicest video hall in Havana, with just over 30 plush and comfortable seats. The area outside the hall is used for meetings, special exhibitions and sales of posters and videos. Screening information is posted in front of the building. There are also special children's showings during school holidays.

Charlot

Calle 23 #1155, entre 10 y 12, Vedado (311101). **Closed** Tue. **Map** p311 C8.
Attached to the Chaplin cinema, the Charlot shows films devoted to famous directors or periods in history, and also has special and children's showings.

Yara A, B, C

Calle L #363, esquina a 23, Vedado (329430). **Map** p312 B11.
These are the city's three principal video rooms, and as such the 30 or so seats can fill up quickly. To ensure entry into the small, dark rooms you should turn up about 15 minutes before a screening and ask the other people which one of them is '*el último para la sala de video*' – the last in queue for the video room.

Festivals

Since 1979 this often-represented film-making continent has been celebrated during the annual **Festival del Nuevo Cine Latinoamericano** (Festival of New Latin American Cinema). In the post-Revolution years Latin American films were some of the only films that made it through the Soviet bloc stranglehold on the Cuban film market. This competitive festival was designed to showcase the production of cinema in any Latin American country. It also shows some international films, including ones from the US and Latin America. The festival attracts a fair share of interest from Hollywood and Europe (Ken Loach, Jonathan Demme, Francis Ford Coppola, Robert de Niro, Helen Mirren and Taylor Hackford, to name but a few), though the Cuban public is also keen to take advantage of its presence.

The festival offers a chance for Cubans to see many different films and genres at cheap prices, and its popularity demonstrates Cubans' appreciation of the medium. It is one of the only events in the Cuban calendar to bring people to Havana from all over the island; no doubt the festival's home-grown version of the Oscars, the Premio Coral, is a further attraction. A schedule for that day's and the following day's films is available from the Hotel Nacional (*see p56*), which is also a great place to hang out during the Festival, being as it is the hub of the action, as it caters to the press.

Tickets are available from the cinemas on the day (and usually the day before), or you can buy a pass, usually for around $25. As with everything else in Havana, though, timings, prices of tickets and even the films themselves are subject to change. The closing and opening ceremonies for the festival are held at suitably impressive **Teatro Karl Marx** (*see p199*). With rare exceptions, most films are shows in Spanish (without English subtitles) or with Spanish subtitles.

Other, lower-profile film festivals, including a French and a European one, have been held in Havana in the past, but these are extremely erratic. Some cultural centres such as the Instituto Cervantes sometimes hold festivals, too. They are normally advertised in *Cartelera*.

For exact dates and information on all these festivals, contact ICAIC (*see p177*), though bear in mind that dates and programmes are often not finalised until the last minute.

Gay & Lesbian

It's hard to say where Havana's gay and lesbian scene is going: while Cubans themselves adore sex of any kind, Havana's non-straight haunts are prone to closure at a moment's notice.

Once they've satisfied their initial curiosity, Cubans are notoriously unconcerned about each other's sexual identity. It is of little importance if your neighbour is married or not, gay, lesbian, straight, bi-, trans- or asexual (although the latter is hard to believe, given the Cuban libido). Saved from the most excessive rigours of Spanish religious morality by its heavy African cultural mix, the island's population is sure of one thing: sex is fun and they're determined to have lots of it. Foreigners are often shocked by the overt sexuality in Cuban dress, from tight and very explicit jeans to clinging Lycra that exposes every bodily crease and bulge. Never mind the heat, Cuban men and women look, and indeed, are hot.

In the 1960s, homosexuals were sent to work camps euphemistically called Unidades Militares de Ayuda a la Producción (UMAPs, Military Production Aid Units) – as well as being removed from government and teaching posts. During the following two decades, persecution was rife and many gays – including some high-profile ones in the arts world – left the country as a result. Yet, in spite of its past record, Cuba is now probably the most easy-going of all Latin American and Caribbean countries in terms of its acceptance of gay culture and lifestyle. There are openly gay couples (especially male) on the streets of Havana and Santa Clara, as well as in most other major cities, but those looking for a 'scene' as such might come away disappointed as folks just generally hang out on the street – not even in cafés or bars, just the street corner – before going on to parties. Holding hands in public might be frowned upon, but a little kiss on the cheek no longer turns heads. Even transvestites and cross-dressers can now be seen on the streets in full regalia. This is a marked change from the old days, when they were confined to cabarets, including street cabarets in working-class districts. One of the odd and contradictory aspects of macho culture in Cuba is its immense enjoyment of cross-dressing or transvestite shows (see p184 **Castropol**, and p192 **Sociedad Cultural Rosalia de Castro**), though these are subject to periodic police closures.

The international success of Tomás Guttierez Alea's 1993 film *Fresa y Chocolate* (*Strawberry and Chocolate*), about the attraction of an openly gay man for a young straight revolutionary (see p179), did more for gay liberation in Cuba than anything else. Sonja de Vries's 1994 documentary *Gay Cuba* recorded the ecstatic reactions of Cubans pouring out of the Yara cinema after watching the film ('What a friendship! I would love to have a friend like that!' – 'Are you gay?' – 'What me? No way! Straight! Pure macho!').

The **Yara** (see p180) is now the night-time rendezvous point for gay men before they party into the small hours. On Fridays and Saturdays there is almost always a gay fiesta going on somewhere; just show up at the Yara around 10pm and ask. There'll be cars ready to take you to the action for $5 or so. You could end up at anything from an old mansion in the middle of a wood, to a pre-Revolutionary open-air fantasy temple, to a 1950s beachside club. The entrance fee is usually $2 or 20 pesos, the music is a mixture of house and *salsa*, and beer, rum and soft drinks are served for reasonable prices. It's invariably hot, smoky and sexy, with gorgeous, shiny bodies everywhere (one advantage of Cuba's economic crisis is that people are in good shape as they're rarely able to overeat). Most of the party-goers will be gay men, but you'll find a good sprinkling of lesbian, bi, tranny and straight types, too.

On Friday nights there are regular lesbian-oriented parties for a smaller 'in' crowd. These *fiestas de diez pesos* (ten-peso parties) take place at people's houses and feature house and *salsa* music and a very mixed crowd. Cubans don't make a big deal about who is what at these parties; everyone is welcome. Again, your best bet is to ask at the Yara cinema.

LISTINGS AND LINGO

As with many things in Cuba, the gay scene is prone to sudden change for no apparent reason; you should therefore be prepared for any of the following to be closed at short notice and for other information, such as admission prices, to vary (these are nebulous at the best of times for any venue in Havana, let alone gay ones). Note also that some, but not all, venues have air-conditioning and that even this is prone to break down.

As well as the straightforward *homosexual*, to denote either a gay or lesbian, you might also hear the terms *maricón* or *cherna* (poof), *loca* (queen) and *tortillera* (dyke).

Bars & cafés

Many bars and cafés attract gay crowds without necessarily advertising themselves as gay. As always in Cuba, everyone's welcome, although there are specific nights at the places below that have become primarily gay. Bars come and go quickly, especially as the gay population asserts its presence more and more, so keep your ears to the ground for the latest haunts.

Castropol
Malecón #107, esquina a Genios, Centro Habana (614864). **Open** noon-midnight daily. **Admission** $1 and minimum one drink. **Map** p313 C15.
A drag-show cabaret (which starts at 11.30pm), with tables and chairs crowded together in small, close environment. Castropol combines a fun atmosphere with respect for the artists, who often put on a very good show. This is a rather upscale hangout for a gay and lesbian crowd of all ages – including well-known Cuban TV, theatre and film personalities. Decent snack food adds to the appeal.

Club Tropical
Calle Línea, esquina a F, Vedado (327361). **Open** 10am-4pm daily. **Admission** $2. **Map** p312 A10.
A small, hot cellar joint offering different nights for different patrons. Club Tropical attracts the young, gay fashion victims that can also be found at the Saturn (*see below*), and their intentions are usually the same. The place is under new ownership, so there may be changes afoot that could alter its feel: find out before paying the cover charge. As this guide went to press, there was karaoke every night at midnight.

Cubalse/Fiat Café
Malecón, esquina a Marina, Centro Habana (335827). **Open** 24 hours daily. **Admission** free. **Map** p313 C13.
This café, next to the Fiat car showroom, is an after-hours place to relax and chat until dawn. Just as the Yara is the pre-party hangout, so the Fiat is the post-party venue, and it's also a good place to go during the week when things are quiet. A large crowd gathers along the seafront opposite the café, but it's also a major hangout for hustlers, so be warned.

La Pampa
Calle Marina #102, esquina a Vapor, Centro Habana (783426). **Open** 24 hours daily. *Disco* 10am-4pm daily. **Admission** $2. **Map** p313 C13.
This dive attracts a mixed, rather than specifically gay crowd. There's a smoky, clubby atmosphere

Hanging around outside the **Yara**. *See p183*.

and a full bar selling snacks. Varied disco music (little of it Cuban) is played Monday to Thursday, and there's reggae from Friday to Sunday.

El Saturno
Calle Línea, entre 10 y 12, Vedado (no phone). **Map** p311 B8.
Still referred to by its old name, the Joker, this is a small, very hot cellar bar that is frequented by a young, fashionably dressed male crowd looking for a good time. It's fun to be around these stunning guys for a drink or two, but remember it isn't always your gorgeous body that's attracted them. If they're after the bulge in your trousers, it's likely to be the one made by your wallet. Ask among the local gay scene for details of opening times.

Cruising

Cuba's public scandal laws seek to dissuade prostitutes and those looking for casual public sex. Although they do not employ vice squads to lure and entrap people into lewd conduct (as in Britain or the United States), individual police officers have ample room to interpret these laws in whichever way they see fit. Thus, the simple act of picking someone up in a park may lead to hassle. This is especially true for any Cuban involved, who is likely to be regarded and treated as a hustler (which is often the case). It is certainly not illegal to meet and talk with someone in the street, but if you do this behind the bushes – even if your clothes are intact when a police torch lights up your evening – you will probably be taken down to the station and given a warning. Having said this, police intervention is rare and it is highly unlikely you will be booked unless you've done something particularly kinky. So, despite public scandal laws, cruising action abounds in the locales below. And, believe it or not, Christmas midnight mass at the Cathedral is another cruising opportunity – check it out.

Arts & Entertainment

At the ballet

Any good ballet (and in Cuba it's always good) attracts a large percentage of Havana's gay male population. You can find in full force them at the Sala García Lorca at the Gran Teatro in Centro Habana (see p201) and the intermissions offer great cruising opportunities. Just lounge in the curve of the grand piano in the foyer, look gorgeous and disinterested, and wait...

At the beach

Playa Mi Cayito, some 30 minutes from Havana along the Playas del Este (see p115), offers a perfect backdrop – palm trees; blue, calm, warm, clear water lapping on the shore; hour-glass fine sand – and plenty of same-sex couples worshipping the sun, with a plethora of bods to choose from at the weekend. The easiest way to get to the beaches is to take a taxi for about $10 to $15 each way from anywhere in Havana.

At the cinema

Cine Payret (see p180), opposite the Capitolio building in Centro Habana, offers the chance for old-fashioned back-row snogging. The film can be quite good, too.

In the park

Parque Maceo (see p85), situated in front of the Almeijeiras Hospital along the Malecón, is especially active during Carnaval in July. At other times of year, try the small **Parque de la Fraternidad** (see p82), next to the Capitolio in Centro Habana.

On the street

It may not have the most romantic setting, but there's plenty of action along **Calle G** (from Calle Línea to Calle 23, and from the circular monument to Calle José Miguel Gómez and on towards the School of Dentistry). Try also the stretch of seafront in front of the Hotel Tritón at the corner of Avenida 3ra and Calle 72 in Miramar.

Where to stay & eat

Most establishments in Cuba are gay friendly, but we'd especially recommend *paladares* **Le Chansonnier** (see p135), **La Esperanza** (see p136), **La Guarida** (see p131), **Las Mercedes** (see p136) and **El Recanto** (see p136). If you're looking for a gay-friendly place to stay, try **Casa de Carlos y Nelson** (see p58) in Vedado.

Positive attitudes

Cuba's controversial AIDS policy has been the brunt of much international criticism in the past. The island's system of sanatoria, set up in the late 1980s to combat the HIV virus by effectively quarantining HIV-positive Cubans, was seen as repressive and despotic. But to understand the state of mind of the health authorities at the time, one has to understand the nation's approach to public healthcare in general.

The system's primary focus is on preventative rather than curative medicine. The health rights of the community dominate those of the individual. Thus, when the virus hit the island in 1986 (borne by soldiers returning from service in Africa), and while the world was still determining where the infection may have come from and how it was transmitted, Cuba wasted no time in destroying every unit of blood in the country and seeking out those who may have been infected. A dozen or so sanatoria were quickly built across the nation to contain the virus and enable residents to be close to the important support of their families.

The sanatoria provided housing units where same-sex infected partners could live together as couples; where psychological and medical counselling was available around the clock;

food was much better than most people could get at home; and residents were taught not only to look after their own health, but also that of the community. By 1993, the health authorities realised that a modified approach to containing the virus was now necessary, and people in the sanatoria living with HIV and AIDS were allowed to come and go freely.

Whatever one may think of the methods, the results of the public health authority's initial rapid response has been effective; Cuba currently has the fifth-lowest HIV-infection rate of any nation on the planet – a remarkable feat for a developing country with a highly sexually active population and very limited resources.

The island now has labour legislation protecting HIV/AIDS carriers; an AIDS hotline; STD education in schools; public notices about condom use on billboards, radio and television ('No Condom? No Way!'); and outreach programmes that distribute information and condoms across the country. The sanatoria still provide optional housing for people living with HIV and AIDS, but also operate as outpatient units and educational support centres for the recently diagnosed.

For contact details and further information about HIV and AIDS, *see chapter* **Directory**.

Arts & Entertainment

Music & Nightlife

Havana is renowned for its *vida nocturna*. Whether you want a (relatively) quiet drink in a bar or a full-on cabaret extravaganza, this city has the lot.

Havana is alive and kicking with music. Whether you are into traditional *son*, the more upbeat *timba* or the classical *danzón*, the island's capital has it all. Big names, small names and no-names can all be heard in the many theatres, clubs and cafés, and long before you go looking for the music, *la música cubana* will have probably already found you. Walking around town you will be bombarded with different musical sounds: people's pumped-up radios, in-house *rumbas*, groups of amateur *trovadores* (troubadours) hanging out in the parks, or even a lone trumpeter in La Quinta de los Molinos. And, if you like this kind of impromptu musical fare then you'll love the Malecón after sunset, when Havana's famous seashore road (*see p86* **On the waterfront**) turns into the city's largest communal living room.

INFORMATION

Whatever kind of music and atmosphere you fancy, you're bound to find it in Havana. However, we encourage you to go beyond the tourist spots and discover the real riches of Cuba's many different rhythms. To keep your finger firmly on the pulse of Havana's multifarious music scene, either call in at the venues listed in this chapter or try to get a hold of the tourist newspaper *Cartelera*, published every Thursday (but sometimes not available until the following Wednesday, the day it ceases to be useful). Try to pick up a free copy at any hotel or from the paper's office at Calle 15 #602, esquina a C, Vedado. If you have access to a radio, **Radio Taíno**, the self-proclaimed tourist station (FM 93.3), gives frequent entertainment news updates, as does the weekly TV programme **Hurón Azul** (Thursdays at 10pm).

As with most venues in Cuba, opening times of the places listed in this chapter are subject to change at short notice, so if you're

▶ For classical music, *zarzuela*, comedy and dance tuition, see chapter **Performing Arts**.
▶ For the history of music in Cuba, *see* chapter **Sounds of the City**.
▶ For other restaurants and bars with music, *see* chapter **Eating & Drinking**.

intent on listening to a certain sound on a certain night, you are best advised to call ahead to check it's definitely on.

In this chapter, we have listed most of the city's day and nightlife venues that offer some form of musical entertainment, be it live dance or recorded club tunes, or a mixture of both. Because many places tend to play a range of different rhythms, venues are classified by area rather than by type of music. *See pp188-189* **Facing the music** and *p190* **The best Music & Nightlife venues** for more details and for our pick of the bunch.

In theory, all admission prices for foreigners are in dollars, although some venues still charge in pesos (even if their prices are officially quoted in dollars) and others seem to make up the prices from one night to the next. We have tried to make our listings as accurate as possible, but in Cuba things can change overnight. It is worth noting that only very few places (the most expensive, including the Tropicana) accept credit cards, but never US cards such as American Express (not even if issued in a country other than the United States).

Despite the economic hardships faced by Cubans on a daily basis, they always make an effort to look good. So, while there's never been a need to enforce dress codes at venues, bear in mind that most nightclubs prefer you not to wear shorts and that cabaret venues go one step further by not allowing shorts, sleeveless T-shirts or sandals.

A final word of warning: many, but by no means all, venues have air-conditioning, so don't rely on it.

La Habana Vieja

Barco Havana Princess

Avenida Carlos Manuel de Céspedes; look for the medium-sized white cruiser opposite the craft market near the cathedral, by the Neptune Fountain. **Open** for lunch noon-3pm daily; for shows 7pm-3am daily. **Admission** *see below.* **Map** p316 D16.

This ship is home to a nightclub and restaurant. It's open for lunch and dinner every day, but at 7pm every night it cruises along the coast beside the Malecón for two hours, after which people can stay on board and dine and dance until 5am. Admission to the club is $10 ($15 Fri-Sun), or you can enjoy the surroundings of the Pano Bar for $10 (with two free

In Havana the streets are alive with the sound of music.

drinks). Alternatively you can choose not to pay admission and to pay for every drink separately. This is a tourist-only venue, allegedly to prevent Cubans from hijacking the boat and heading off to you-know-where.

Bar Monserrate
Avenida de Bélgica (Monserrate) #401, esquina a Obrapía, (669751). **Open** 8am-3am daily. **Admission** free. **Map** p316 E14.
You'll find this tranquil open-air bar just off the main drag, around the corner from Obispo and El Floridita (*see p128*). The decor is 1920s and there's music from 1pm to 1am.

La Bodeguita del Medio
Calle Empedrado #207, entre San Ignacio y Cuba (671375). **Open** noon-midnight daily. **Admission** free. **Map** p316 D15.
Hemingway's most famous haunt is always crowded, but the *mojitos* are worth the wait. Live *trova* is played in the bar and restaurant. *See also p127.*

Café de París
Calle San Ignacio #202, esquina a Obispo (no phone). **Open** 24 hrs daily. **Map** p316 E15.
Lots of punters, lots of *jineteros* and lots of live music (11am-11pm). *See also p144.*

Café Taberna
Calle Mercaderes #531, esquina a Brasil (Teniente Rey) (611937). **Open** 11am-midnight daily. **Admission** free. **Map** p316 E15.

Café Taberna is also known as 'el Rincón de Beny Moré' (Beny's corner), because the whole place is dedicated to the man and his music (*see p44* **That's a Moré**). Full of new jukeboxes and old pictures of pre-Revolutionary celebrities, the airy bar/restaurant has a 1950s feel to it. El Septeto Matamoros and the Septeto Son de Trópico play *son* and *bolero* music here daily from 11am to 5pm and from 7pm to 11pm. Watch out: the waiters will rip you off in a flash. *See also p127.*

Casa de la cultura de La Habana Vieja
Calle Aguiar #509, entre Amargura y Brasil (Teniente Rey) (634860). **Open** Tue-Sun (performance times vary); closed Mon. **Admission** $1. **Map** p316 E15.
This very active *casa* features live gigs almost every night at around 8pm (6pm on Sunday), many of which are staged in the *casa*'s beautiful old theatre or outside in the church courtyard. Young and old Cubans from the local neighbourhood come here to dance and listen to *bolero* on Tuesday, a Caribbean night on Wednesday, *son* on Thursday, Afro-Cuban music or reggae on Saturday and a varied programme on Fridays and Sundays. Phone the *casa* on Monday for details of the coming week's programme and then take your pick.

Casa del Escabeche
Calle Obispo #505, esquina a Villegas (632660). **Open** 24hrs daily. **Admission** free. **Map** p316 D15.

A cosy but often packed little bar, which serves very good *mojitos*, with live *son* music from noon to 5pm every day.

Casa de las Infusiones
Calle Mercaderes, entre Obispo y Obrapía (620216). **Open** 10am-10pm daily. **Admission** free. **Map** p316 E15.
An all-female *son* group and a classical string quartet play on alternate days from noon to 5pm, and there's also often a *son* or *salsa* group (at 7pm Tuesday to Saturday, and from noon on Sundays). The Casa de las Infusiones is also known as La Columnata Egipciana (Egyptian Colonnade).

Caserón del Tango
Calle Jústiz #21, entre Baratillo y Oficios (610822). **Open** 8am-midnight Mon-Sat; 8am-2am Sun. **Admission** $2-$5. **Map** p316 E16.
Located in a beautiful colonial mansion just around the corner from the Plaza de Armas in Old Havana, the Caserón del Tango is another of the city's musical treasure chests. Run by the Asociación Nacional Promotora del Tango, the venue aims to preserve and promote this music and dance form in Cuba. A wide range of activities are offered in the mansion's grounds, including informal tango *peñas* from 5pm to 7pm on Wednesdays and Fridays,

Facing the music

Visitors to Havana are often overwhelmed by the range of entertainment venues the city has to offer. Here we deconstruct the various types of spaces, though you should bear in mind that there is still some overlap between many of them.

Bars, cafés & restaurants
In addition to the city's dedicated music venues, many bars, cafés and restaurants offer live performances several times a week. Bands usually play standard tourist fare (*see p141* **If music be the food of love...**), which is fine if you just want some accompaniment while you drink, but it's certainly not the best music Havana has to offer. Some bars are worthy of a mention as a music venue as well as an eating or drinking place; for this reason we have listed them both in this chapter and in **Eating & Drinking** (*pp124-147*).

Hotel bars and terraces, including those at the Nacional, the Inglaterra, the Sevilla and the Plaza (*see chapter* **Accommodation**) offer a similar set-up-cum-tourist music, plus a drink and light snack. You might want to take along some extra dollars to tip the musicians for their music – either that or you'll virtually have to be rude to them to make it clear you don't want to shell out anything.

Casas de la cultura
After the Revolution, *casas de la cultura* (literally, 'houses of culture') were established in each municipality across the country, with the aim of providing each community with a cultural space for the teaching and performance of various art forms. Most *casas* offer drawing, painting, dance and music classes during the day and turn into lively theatres and concert halls at night. The *casas* have played an especially

important role in the social life of their communities since the beginning of the Special Period, as they constitute some of the few remaining venues that Cubans can afford to visit. Amateurs and young up-and-coming artists, as well as well-known bands, give concerts in the *casas* on a regular basis, and the atmosphere is always relaxed and welcoming. We have listed some of the most musically active *casas* in Havana. Phone or drop in for a detailed calendar of events.

Casas de la trova
These are venues specialising in performances of *trova*. The *casas* of Santiago, Trinidad and Centro Habana date back to the 19th century and are among the oldest and finest examples on the island, but there are also more modern *casas*, created since the Revolution in order to preserve the genre.

Cultural centres
There are numerous state-sponsored cultural associations, institutes and centres in Havana that offer a variety of musical activities. Most do not have a particular fixed programme, so you will need to call ahead or check the weekly *Cartelera* for concert information.

Discos
There are basically two types of nightclub in Havana. The first type caters mainly to tourists and usually has high admission charges. These discos are similar in decor and ambience to any standard Western nightclub and play a mixture of pop, rock and Latin tunes. Other standard club comforts such air-conditioning and a decent bar are also usually available. Beware, though, drinks can be ludicrously expensive at these venues and *jineteras* are a standard feature.

and a music and dance show starting at 10pm on Saturday. The bar is the venue for discussions and impromptu performances from 9.30pm to 2am on Sunday. Tango classes (which cost $5) are held from 4pm to 6pm Thursday and from 2pm to 4pm on Saturday. Even if you can't make it for one of the scheduled events, be sure to stop by for a swift drink and a little tango music in the charming peso bar out the back.

La Lluvia de Oro
Calle Obispo #316, esquina a Habana (629870).
Open 8am-1am Mon-Thur; 8am-3am Fri-Sun.
Admission free. **Map** p316 E15.

Old-fashioned drinking den with a long wooden bar and overhead fans. There's live *son* music 11am to 10pm daily. *See also p146.*

La Mina
Calle Obispo #109, entre Oficios y Mercaderes (620216). **Open** 24hrs daily. **Admission** free.
Map p316 E15.
La Mina has a restaurant and two cafés; waiters and bands are shared with Al Cappuccino next door. The patios, located on Plaza de Armas, are a great spot to relax and listen to live *son* until 11pm followed by *boleros* until the early hours. The downside is that they can be rather touristy, though. *See also p128.*

The Cuban clubs mainly attract a local clientele for the simple reason that they are cheaper to get into. Generally speaking, most of these places are pretty run-down and often don't have air-conditioning (although this is changing as places receive a much-needed facelift). The pre-Revolutionary, dilapidated decor, however, has a quirky charm of its own, plus the music is great, mostly *salsa* and *merengue*, although some pop and techno is also played. The atmosphere is totally unpretentious and the experience of dancing and hanging out with Cubans is loads of fun.

At most such venues there's a pre-disco, usually hour-long, late-night show, which tends to be a pale imitation of the **Tropicana** (*see p193*).

Live Cuban dance music venues
A number of large venues cater for visitors who've caught the worldwide *salsa* bug or just want to check out some of the big-name Cuban bands such as Los Van Van, El Médico, Isaac Delgado and others. With few exceptions, most of these places have high admission charges, and thus mainly cater to tourists and nouveaux riches Cubans. If you are looking for a more 'authentic' Cuban venue head straight for the **Salón Rosado Beny Moré** (*see p199*). In addition to *salsa* clubs, other venues cater specifically for *bolero*, *filin* and jazz aficionados. Music is of a high quality and you will often find there's a minimum drinks charge.

Peñas
In Cuba, any type of gig, whether large or small, is known as a *peña*. There are, however, also private gigs (*peñas particulares*) made up of amateur and professional musicians who get together in

private homes to *descargar* or jam. Often these sessions turn into fixed weekly or monthly events and are open to anyone who wants to join in. During the early years of the Special Period, when many nightclubs had to close down and increasing numbers of musicians found themselves out of work, the number of private *peñas* increased dramatically. Nowadays it is the commercialisation of Havana's more established nightlife that keeps these *peñas* alive. The *peñas* listed in this chapter have a fixed schedule, but there are dozens of others popping up around the city all the time. Ask around for a *peña particular* and you will be treated to some fantastic Cuban music.

Where the Cubans go
Habaneros go to the Malecón to *coger aire* (catch a little air), chat with friends, meet their lovers or... hassle tourists. Many bring along their guitar or ghettoblaster and a bottle of rum to transform their little coastal spot into an open-air fiesta.

Since Havana's nightlife entered the dollar zone, this kind of impromptu get-together is how most *habaneros* now socialise. You'll soon realise that the more expensive a venue is, the fewer Cubans you will encounter there (apart from *jineteras* and the increasing number of nouveaux riches Cubans, who seem to have a particular liking for glitzy five-star hotel discos). The few places that are still affordable to Cubans are, however, also some of the most interesting, lively and fun venues in town. These especially include the **casas de la cultura** and **casas de la trova** as well as the non-hotel clubs. And, if you really want to party with Cubans, don't miss the carnival in July/August.

El Patio

Plaza de la Catedral (671035). **Open** noon-midnight daily. **Admission** free. **Map** p316 D15.
Located in front of the cathedral, this café-restaurant occupies one of the most beautiful spots in Havana and features live *son* music from 10am to midnight daily. Sadly, the roof-garden bar is now closed to the public, although it can be hired out for special events. Choose between the quiet, air-conditioned interior, an exquisite inner courtyard or the busier outer patio, for a relaxed view of the Cathedral. *See also p129.*

Roof Garden Bar

Hotel Ambos Mundos, Calle Obispo #153, esquina a Mercaderes (609529/609530/609531).
Open 7am-11pm daily. **Admission** free.
Map p316 E15.
If you're looking for a place with a great view of Old Havana and the bay, a lush garden-like atmosphere and live traditional music (11am-6pm, except Monday and Wednesday), then the rooftop bar of this near-legendary hotel is it. Light meals are available. *See also p75 and p146.*

Yola en Familia

Calle Cuba, entre Brasil (Teniente Rey) y Muralla (no phone). **Open** 4-7pm 3rd Sat of month only.
Admission free. **Map** p316 E15.
For the past seven years this wonderful street event has brought together amateur and professional musicians from all over Havana as well as other parts of Cuba. It was set up by Yolanda Torres, an ex-Navy woman who now dedicates all of her time to cultural work in the local community. Torres believes strongly in the power of music and other art forms, and her *peñas* aim to unite and inspire people, especially in these economic hard times. Her vision and enthusiasm have made this one of the most popular events in town. Don't miss it.

Yola en la Comunidad

Calle Muralla, esquina a Compostela. **Open** 3-5pm Thur only. **Admission** free. **Map** p316 E15.
Another one of Yolanda's community projects, this *peña* takes place in a senior citizens' cafeteria in the old town, but is certainly not only for the elderly. *Bolero* music seems to dominate the activities, but other musical genres also crop up.

The best Music & Nightlife venues

For an all-round good time
Check out any of the city's *peñas particulares*, especially **Yola en Familia** (*see above*) and **La Azotea de Elda** (*see p194*).

For *bolero*
There's a double bill of romantic music nightly at **El Bolero** in Miramar (*see p198*), from 10pm to midnight and 12.15 to 3am.

For disco *a la cubana*
Head down to **Disco Chang** on a Saturday night (*see p191*) for an experience that's uniquely Cuban.

For disco (Western-style)
Club Ipanema (*see p198*) has air-conditioning *and* good music.

For *filin*
You can enjoy live music and a fantastic view at **El Pico Blanco** (*see p197*).

For jazz
La Zorra y el Cuervo in Vedado (*see p197*) is a near-legendary jazz venue featuring well-known local and foreign musicians.

For rap (Cuban)
The *casa de la cultura* in Alamar (*see p199*) is the centre of the Cuban rap and hip hop scene; a little out of the way, but worth the trip.

For reggae
Check with Rasta Mayeta, permanently based on one of the benches in Parque Central. He knows when and where bands are playing.

For rock (Cuban)
Havana's *roqueros* flock to **Patio de María** (*see p197*) on a Saturday night.

For *rumba*
Don't miss the incredible live show by Conjunto Folclórico at **El Gran Palenque** (*see p196*) every Saturday afternoon.

For *salsa*
Enjoy great music in a beautiful setting at the **Casa de la Música** (*see p198*).

For *son*
Check out the lively *casa de la cultura* in La Habana Vieja on Thursday and Friday nights (*see p187*).

For tango
Live shows, impromptu gigs and dance lessons are on offer at the beautiful **Caserón del Tango** in La Habana Vieja (*see p188*).

For traditional *trova*
Listen to the real sound of *trova* in a packed atmosphere at the **Casa de la trova** in Centro Habana on Friday evenings (*see p191*).

Arts & Entertainment

Rumba at **Callejón de Hamel**. *See p194.*

Centro Habana

Casa de la cultura de Centro Habana

Avenida Salvador Allende (Carlos III) #720, entre Soledad y Castillejo (784727). **Open** phone for details. **Map** p312 D12.
This very popular venue usually hosts a variety of nightly musical activities. At the time of going to press, it was closed for repairs and due to reopen early in 2001. Call ahead to check out what's on.

Caserón del Tango

Calle Neptuno #309, entre Águila y Italia (Galiano) (630097). **Open** 10am-8pm daily. **Admission** free. **Map** p313 D14.
This museum-cum-cultural centre dedicated to the tango was founded by Edmundo Daubal in 1980 as a showpiece for his collection of tango sheet music, records, tapes, trophies and other memorabilia, amassed over half a century. The tango was very popular in Cuba during the 1930s and '40s, as evidenced by the grey-haired regulars who now flock to the *casa*'s weekly events. Join them for fantastic music, dance and a very welcoming atmosphere. The main attraction for visitors is the live tango music and dance on Mondays from 5pm to 8pm. Although formal tango classes are not currently on offer, the *casa* should be able to put you in touch with a private teacher.

Casa de la trova de Centro Habana

Calle San Lázaro #661, entre Padre Varela (Belascoaín) y Gervasio (793373). **Open** from 5pm daily. **Admission** $5. **Map** p313 C13.
Live *trova* music is played here most evenings, but Fridays from 6pm is the time to stop by. This cultural gem is usually crowded with locals and can be highly recommended.

Centro Andaluz en Cuba

Paseo de Martí (Prado) #104, entre Genios y Refugio (636745/666901). **Open** noon-8pm Tue-Thur; noon-midnight Fri-Sun; closed Mon. **Admission** $1. **Map** p313 D15.
This is one of Havana's many Spanish cultural centres. Dedicated to keeping the city's Andalusian roots alive, the centre offers a show with live flamenco music on Fridays (9pm), Saturdays (10pm) and Sundays (9pm) followed by dancing. There are also flamenco classes from 9am to 11am Tuesday to Thursday at $15 per hour.

Disco Chang

Calle San Nicolás #517, entre Dragones y Zanja, Centro Habana (621490). **Open** 10.30pm-3am Fri-Sun only. **Admission** *men* $5; *women* $1. **Map** p313 D13.
Chang's is a privately owned club housed in a first-floor flat in the heart of *Barrio Chino* (Chinatown), which makes for a rather peculiar but unique ambience. It's popular with both Cubans and foreigners; many people start out here and then move on to nearby Los Tres Chinitos (*see p194*), which stays open until dawn. Watch out for the long queues of heavily made-up girls who wait impatiently at the bottom of Chang's stairway entrance on most Friday and Saturday nights. Women get in for less than men, which might explain it.

Disco Ribera Azul

Hotel Deauville, Avenida de Italia (Galiano), entre San Lázaro y Malecón (338813). **Open** 10pm-3am daily. **Admission** $3 incl one free drink. **Map** p313 C14.
Recently refurbished basement club that caters to both Cubans and foreigners with a variety of Cuban and international music. There is a reasonable show on Fridays to Sundays starting at around 11pm, and affordable drinks and light snacks are also available.

La Madriguera

Quinta de los Molinos, entre Infanta y Salvador Allende (Carlos III) (798175). **Open** 9am-7pm Mon-Wed, Fri, Sat; 9am-midnight Thur; closed Sun. **Admission** 5 pesos. **Map** p312 D11.
Right near the border of Vedado, La Madriguera is the headquarters of the Asociación Hermanos Saíz, the youth wing of the UNEAC (Union of Writers and Artists of Cuba). Its main aim is to provide institutional support for and promotion of young artistic talent, but it also organises concerts, exhibitions, conferences and festivals. La Madriguera is located

Cabaret

More Vegas than Berlin, Havana's *cabaret-espectáculos* are song and dance variety shows performed by G-stringed *mulatas*. Aware of their huge popularity with foreign visitors, their primary function these days seems to be to fleece tourists. Performances are often staged in hotels, making this easier for them.

Attempts to subvert the state's monopoly have met with little success. Transvestite shows enjoyed a boom after the success of the film *Strawberry and Chocolate*, but official attitudes to homosexuality vacillate, with clubs often being shut down or forced underground. For local information on transvestite venues, ask around the **Fiat Bar** on the corner of the Malecón and Calle 25, Vedado.

Dress regulations apply in most cabarets: avoid shorts, sleeveless T-shirts and sandals.

Cabaret Nacional

Paseo de Martí (Prado), esquina a San Rafael, Centro Habana (632361). **Open** 10pm-4am daily (show starts at midnight). **Tickets** $3. **Map** p313 D14.
Two shows, one a musical review, the other a band playing popular Cuban music. It's dark, low-ceilinged and full of ladies of the night.

Cabaret Parisien

Hotel Nacional, Calle O, esquina a 21, Vedado (333564). **Open** *Box office from 9am daily. Cabaret 9pm-3am daily (show starts at 10pm).* **Tickets** $30; $50 incl dinner (video cameras permitted). **Map** p312 B12.
Sinatra once sang here for his mafia mates and molls. There may be no Meyer Lanskys or 'Lucky' Lucianos in the audience nowadays, but Kate Moss and Naomi Campbell popped in recently to watch *Ajíaco Cubano*, a musical review with circus acts and a troupe of feathered dancers. After midnight the DJs take over. In addition, water ballet, complete with son-et-lumière, takes place around the swimming pool on Fridays and on either Monday or Wednesday. Call to confirm.

Cabaret Turquino

Hotel Habana Libre, Calle L, entre 23 y 25, Vedado (334011). **Open** 10pm-3am daily (shows start at 11.15pm & 1am). **Tickets** $11. **Map** p312 B11.
There's a panoramic view of the cityscape from the 25th floor of the Hotel Habana Libre. You can dine here, watch the 60-minute show, then bob to Euro-pop in the club.

La Cecilia

Avenida 5ta #11010, entre 110 y 112, Miramar (241562). **Open** phone for details. **Tickets** phone for details.
Named after *Cecilia Valdés*, Villaverde's 19th-century novel, this open-air club is set among palms and tropical plants, next to a pagoda-covered restaurant. Due to reopen in 2001.

Copa Room

Hotel Riviera, Malecón, esquina a Paseo, Vedado (334051). **Open** 8.30pm-3.30am Mon, Wed-Sun (show starts at 10.30pm); closed Tue. **Tickets** $25 incl one drink; $40 incl 2-course meal & drink. **Map** p312 A9.
Eat, drink and watch a 95-minute variety show directed by former Tropicana frontman Tomás Morales, with traditional Cuban music, then dance to the band in front of the stage.

Habana Café

Hotel Meliá Cohiba, Paseo, entre 1ra y 3ra, Vedado (333636). **Open** *Habana Café* noon-4am daily (show starts at 9.30pm). **Tickets** $11 drink minimum Mon-Sat; $10-$30 Sun. **Map** p312 A9.
Old movie cameras and posters line the walls, mobile phone-touting *jineteras* strut around, and a 1950s Buick honks its horn to start the variety show. The show includes magicians, contortionists, a big band, *bolero* singers and a *salsa* band.

Salón Rojo

Hotel Capri, Calle 21, entre N y O, Vedado (333747). **Open** 10.30pm-3.30am Tue-Sun (show starts at 11.30pm); closed Mon. **Tickets** $10 incl one drink. **Map** p312 B12.
Inaugurated in 1957 as a casino and cabaret, the Red Room has hosted shows by Tito Gómez and Omara Portuondo. Its present show is *Salsa y Sabor*, at the end of which the audience gets up and boogies. The atmosphere is Cuban, edgy and hot.

Sociedad Cultural Rosalia de Castro

Avenida de Bélgica (Egido) #504 altos, entre Máximo Gómez (Monte) y Dragones, Centro Habana (623193). **Open** 9pm-2am daily (show starts at 10pm). **Tickets** $1. **Map** p313 E14.
A variety show with the emphasis on full-on transvestite performances. Thanks to the state's renewed clampdown on the gay scene, its existence remains precarious.

Arts & Entertainment

The Tropicana

It is a typical Cuban perversity that one of the greatest examples of pre-Revolutionary decadence should have remained a cornerstone of Fidel's drive to promote tourism. Opened in 1931 and hailed as the biggest nightclub in the world, the Tropicana has played host to Benny Moré, Nat King Cole, Carmen Miranda, 'Lucky' Luciano, Maurice Chevalier, Josephine Baker, Ernest Hemingway, Jack Nicholson, Robert de Niro, Gary Glitter and – wait for it – Ken Livingstone.

Tucked away in the western neighbourhood of Marianao, Tropicana is reached by a drive lined with fountains and statues of naked women. Known as the *Paraíso Bajo Las Estrellas* (Paradise Under the Stars) because of its open-air setting, Tropicana's semi-circular stage is surrounded by tables with space for up to 1,400 people. The venue includes two places to eat and drink: **Los Jardines**, in the middle of the woods, and the snack bar **Rodney**, designed by the painter Nelson Domínguez. There is also an after-show nightclub, **Arcos de Cristal**.

The show, which is periodically re-choreographed, is *La Gloria Eres Tú* (*You Are the Glory*) and is directed by Santiago Alfonso. Make up your own mind as to whether the show is tackily sexist or infectiously sexy. The 20-piece band provides a mighty cue for the procession of dancers wearing sequinned dental-floss bikinis and chandelier-like headresses. Some 200 performers sashay through the full range of Cuban popular dance music – from *boleros* to *salsa*, *rumba* to *danzón*, and the dances of the main *orishas* (deities) of *santería* are performed.

Harvey Goldsmith took Tropicana over to the Royal Albert Hall in London in 1998 to mixed reviews. There are plans to tour the USA in 2001, a project devised by Raúl Castro (Fidel's bro) and Roger Clinton (Bill's bro). The show would open at Madison Square Gardens, travel throughout the USA, then play six months at Caesar's Palace, Las Vegas. A fitting finale, perhaps.

Tickets for the Tropicana can be booked through hotel tour desks or Havanatur. Bookings are refunded or exchanged in case of rain. Note that video cameras are prohibited.

The Tropicana

Calle 72 #4504, entre 41 y 45, Marianao (271717/ 270110). **Open** *Box office 10am-6pm daily. Tropicana 8pm-1am daily (show 10pm).* **Tickets** $65-$85 incl snack and wine; $75-$95 incl dinner; $25 bar seats (when available); $5 supplement for cameras. **Map** p310 F3.

Arts & Entertainment

in the beautiful park of La Quinta de los Molinos, where you'll find individual musicians and groups rehearsing at all times of the day. Stop by to find out about upcoming concerts or just hang out and listen to some great tunes. La Rockoteca disco is held here every Thursday (8pm to midnight).

Oasis
Paseo de Martí (Prado) #256, entre Ánimas y Trocadero (633829). **Open** 9pm-3am daily. **Admission** $3 drink minimum. **Map** p313 D14.
Lots of *salsa* and Cuban rhythms are played at this relaxed and very Cuban club. Some people have dinner at Basora, the Arab-Cuban restaurant upstairs, before coming down to Oasis to dance. There is a live show at 11pm.

El Palermo
Calle San Miguel #252, esquina a Amistad (619745). **Open** 10pm-4am daily. **Admission** $2. **Map** p313 D14.
This place is a favourite with Afro-Cuban youth due to the rap and other black music genres that dominate here. It's run-down, but recommended for a totally different kind of night out in Havana. Shows start at midnight.

La Peña de Yoya
San Lázaro #667 apt 9, entre Padre Varela (Belascoaín) y Gervasio (second entrance on the right of Casa de la Trova; no phone). **Open** 10pm-1am Fri only. **Admission** free. **Map** p313 C13.
Sadly, the almost-legendary Yoya died recently, but after 20 years of success her *peña* is still going strong. Every Friday night a loyal group of *filin* musicians and fans meet at the home of Yoya's sister Lucy to play and listen to old and new tunes in an intimate and very welcoming atmosphere. Highly recommended if you like romantic ballads and guitar music.

Rumba del Callejón de Hamel
Callejón de Hamel, esquina a Hospital (707338). **Open** 11am-3pm Sun only. **Admission** free. **Map** p312 C12.
Although slightly touristy, this weekly street *rumba* is still a must. The event takes place every Sunday in the picturesque Callejón de Hamel, one block south of Calle San Lázaro. Local artist Salvador has converted this little pedestrian lane into an Afro-Cuban world of its own, with brightly coloured murals, sculptures and installations. During the Sunday *rumbas* (*see p86*) the orishas are called (*see p29*) and the whole place comes to life.

Teatro América
Avenida de Italia (Galiano) #253, entre Concordia y Neptuno (625416). **Open** Box office 10am-4pm Tue-Sun; closed Mon. **Admission** $5. **Map** p313 D14.
Modelled after New York's Radio City Music Hall, the América hosts all kinds of concerts, but especially rock, rap and reggae. Check the theatre billboards for concert information. *See also p204.*

La Terraza
Hotel Lincoln, Avenida de Italia (Galiano) #164, esquina a Virtudes (338209). **Open** 10am-midnight Mon-Thur, Sun; 10am-2am Fri, Sat. **Admission** $1. **Map** p313 D14.
This open-air, roof-top disco is a little dilapidated, but it does have a great view of the ocean and the city. It's geared towards both foreigners and nationals – it tends to get packed with Cubans, especially on Saturdays – and prices are very reasonable. There's a mixed music policy (everything from *salsa* to techno) and a live show at 10pm from Friday to Sunday.

Los Tres Chinitos
Dragones, entre Manrique y Campanario (no phone). **Open** 11pm-6am daily. **Admission** $3. **Map** p313 D13.
Come prepared for some serious dancing and a lot of *jineteras* at Los Tres Chinitos in *barrio chino* (Chinatown). If you need to refuel or the late-night munchies suddenly hit you, pop next door for the best pizza in town (open 24hrs).

Vedado

Atelier
Calle 17, esquina a 6 (306808). **Open** 10pm-4am daily. **Admission** $5. **Map** p313 B9.
This cosy basement club has been recently refurbished and now boasts decent air-conditioning. Shows start at 11.30pm, and there's a Cuban disco afterwards.

La Azotea de Elda
Calle 23 #759, entre B y C (38150). **Open** 2-6pm 1st Sun of every month. **Admission** free (donations welcome). **Map** p312 C10.
If you happen to be in town on the first Sunday of the month make sure not to miss this wonderful *peña* in the heart of Vedado. Elda, who owns the Paladar del Amor downstairs (*see p134*), opens up her rooftop (*azotea*) to anyone interested in good Cuban music. This is a great opportunity to mingle with Cubans of all ages and listen to both well-known and amateur groups playing everything from rap to *son*. Complimentary rum and wine are served, or you can bring a bottle to add to the party spirit. The event is free, but people are encouraged to make a donation to the local cancer research hospital. An absolute gem.

Las Bulerías
Calle L, entre 23 y 25 (323283). **Open** *Café* 24hrs daily. *Restaurant* 10am-4am daily. **Admission** free. **Map** p312 B11.
By night, this Spanish-style tavern is no longer the wild disco it once was, but it still features live traditional Cuban dance music after midnight.

Café Cantante Mi Habana
Teatro Nacional, Paseo, esquina a 39 (335713). **Open** 10.30pm-5am Mon; 4-7pm, 10.30pm-5am Tue-Sun. **Admission** $10. **Map** p312 D10.
Relatively unknown, but nonetheless good bands play in the café of the National Theatre every night.

Arts & Entertainment

Weekends are especially recommended. The Café Cantante Mi Habana also offers matinée peso performances (*salsa* and *son* music), which are usually filled with Cubans and are fun and lively, if you're in the mood for a late-afternoon dancing sesh. For a more tranquil after-hours venue, check out the upstairs Delirio Habanero bar (*see below*). Dress code: no shorts.

Cafeteria Sofía

Calle 23 #202, esquina a O (320740). **Open** 24hrs daily. **Admission** free. **Map** p312 B12.
This airy cafeteria on La Rampa (the name for this end of Calle 23) has live music from 2pm to 6pm and from 8pm to 2am daily.

Casa de las Américas

Calle 3ra, esquina a Presidentes (G) (552706). **Open** 8am-4.30pm Mon-Fri; closed Sat, Sun. **Admission** 5 pesos. **Map** p312 A10.
Apart from organising conferences and exhibitions relating to Latin American and Caribbean literature, art and music, this cultural centre also hosts performances in a wide variety of contemporary and traditional musical forms. Concerts usually take place in the early evening on weekdays.

Casa de la Amistad

Paseo #406, entre 17 y 19 (302468). **Open** 11am-midnight Mon-Fri; 11am-2am Sat; 11am-6pm Sun. **Admission** $5 Tue, Sat only. **Map** p312 B9.
This elegant Tuscan-style villa used to be the headquarters of the House of Friendship between Cuba and the former Soviet Union. With the collapse of the Soviet bloc it has been converted into a tourist complex, featuring a restaurant, cigar shop and café.

Musical performances, mostly *son*, take place every night in the gorgeous garden and patio area. Tuesday night is *la Peña del Chan Chan* and sometimes features Compay Segundo when he is in town. On Saturdays various *son* and *bolero* groups play an extended show. *See also p93*.

Casa de la cultura de Plaza

Calzada #909, entre 6 y 8 (312023/38815). **Open** 9am-10pm Mon-Sat; closed Sun. **Admission** $3-$5. **Map** p311 A8.
This *casa*, named after the official municipality in which it's located, has a fantastic outside stage and patio with a lovely mural by artists Ariel Diaz and Fiona Murphy dedicated to different art forms. Havana's famous jazz festival takes place here (*see chapter* **By Season**), as do many other concerts and smaller-scale gigs. Live *son*, *bolero* and jazz usually feature on Saturday nights at around 9pm.

Club Imágenes

Calle Calzada #602, esquina a C (333606). **Open** noon-3am daily. **Admission** free. **Map** p312 A10.
A perfect post-theatre, -movie or -cabaret venue. Live traditional and *bolero* music is played from 11pm onwards and light snacks and drinks are offered in the bar area. More substantial meals are also available in the restaurant.

Club Tikoa

Calle 23 #177, entre N y O (309973). **Open** 10pm-4am daily. **Admission** $2. **Map** p312 B12.
Located on La Rampa (the name for this end of Calle 23), Club Tikoa is very popular with young Cubans, who dance the night away to mostly Latin tunes, *salsa* and *merengue*.

Rumba from the Conjunto Folclórico Nacional de Cuba at **Teatro Mella**. *See p197*.

Arts & Entertainment

All that jazz at **La Zorra y el Cuervo**. *See p197.*

El Gato Tuerto

Calle O #14, entre 17 y 19 (662224). **Open** noon-6am daily. **Admission** $5 drink minimum. **Map** p312 B12.

The One-Eyed Cat used to be the place where young intellectuals and artists hung out in the 1970s and early '80s. It reopened recently after 12 years of closure, restored, revamped and redollared with pleasant, post-modern decor. *Filin* and *bolero* are still the main genres to be heard here, with near-legends such as Elena Bunke (Friday nights) and César Portillo de la Luz playing on an almost weekly basis. There's also a restaurant upstairs.

El Gran Palenque

Calle 4 #103, entre Calzada y 5ta (339075). **Open** 10am-10pm daily. **Admission** $5. **Map** p312 A/B9.

Every Saturday at 3pm the Gran Palenque outdoor bar/café hosts a live *rumba* show on Saturdays (*Sábado de la Rumba*) by the fantastic Conjunto Folclórico Nacional de Cuba (*see p208*). If you're into Afro-Cuban rhythms and dance, this is an event not to be missed. The Conjunto also offers dance and percussion classes.

Habana Café

Hotel Meliá Cohiba, Paseo, entre 1ra y 3ra (333636). **Open** noon-4am daily. **Admission** $11 drink minimum Mon-Sat; $10-$30 Sun. **Map** p312 A9.

The café has a 1950s wannabe air to it. It's decorated with American classic cars (a Chevy, a Pontiac and a Buick), pictures of Hemingway and loads of pre-Revolutionary memorabilia. Live traditional music is played here on and off all day long and there's a show at 10pm from Monday to Saturday. Sunday nights feature first-rate bands such as Azur Negra, NG La Banda and Los Van Van. (These concerts usually start around 11pm.) Due to the high cover charge, this is pretty much a non-Cuban environment. The food is trying to be Hard Rock.

Hurón Azul/UNEAC

Calle 17 #351, entre Presidentes (G) y H (324152). **Open** 5pm-2am daily. **Admission** $5. **Map** p312 B10/11.

The Unión de Escritores y Artistas de Cuba (UNEAC) hosts various weekly cultural events in the patio and garden of its beautiful mansion headquarters. (The name, incidentally, means 'blue ferret'.) Saturday is *bolero* night (9pm-2am); Wednesdays (5-8pm) alternate between *nueva trova* and *rumba*; and Sundays (from 5pm) feature *son* or *rumba*. All events can be highly recommended, although the *rumba* seems to be the most popular. Quite apart from the music, you might want to check out the scene in the Hurón Azul's bar, which attracts an eclectic mix of local artists, intellectuals, tourists and *jineteros*.

Jazz Café

Galerias del Paseo, Paseo, esquina a 1ra (553475). **Open** 11am-3am daily. **Admission** $10 drink minimum. **Map** p312 A9.

This is Chuchó Valdés' turf. His group Irakere and other famous Cuban jazz bands often play here in

Arts & Entertainment

two sets starting at 8pm and 11pm. Afterwards the place turns into a lively disco. The atmosphere is mellow and sophisticated. The café also operates as a restaurant, so come early to nab a good table.

El Karachi
Calle K, entre 15 y 17 (no phone). **Open** 10pm-5am daily. **Admission** $3. **Map** p312 B11.
El Karachi is well known for playing a variety of rhythms from pop to rap. There is a daily midnight show while on Sundays there's a techno matinée from 4pm to 9pm.

Pabellón Cuba
Calle N #266, esquina a 23 (324921/329056). **Open** 9am-5pm daily. **Admission** $1. **Map** p312 B12.
Apparently this 1960s creation used to be quite attractive, with its many waterfalls, lotus flowers and pools of tropical fish. Nowadays the Pabellón looks more like a decaying monster. Located on the corner of La Rampa, it is one of the UJC's (Union of Young Communists) main cultural venues. All sorts of events take place here, including live concerts during the cultural festivals. *Salsa*, rap, rock and reggae gigs all feature; there's also a disco. Check outside billboards or call for further information.

Patio de María
Calle 37, entre Paseo y 2 (810722). **Open** usually 7.30am-11pm daily. **Admission** 5 pesos. **Map** p312 D9.
Director María Gattorno turned this former *casa de la cultura* into a thriving and totally unpretentious community centre for Havana's counter-cultural and specifically *roquero* youth. During one of Cuba's bleakest periods, the early 1990s, the Patio performed a major social function by giving these youngsters a space to express themselves, and over the years has also been very involved in AIDS prevention educational work. As the time of going to press, the Patio was in the process of restoration but is still offering an important, if reduced, programme of activities. Look out for notices around Coppelia (*see p132* **Scream for ice-cream**), the university (*see p88*) and other social hubs. Note that the venue is officially called the Casa de Cultura Roberto Branly, but is more commonly known by its address.

Piano Bar Delirio Habanero
Teatro Nacional, Paseo, esquina a 39 (335713). **Open** noon-4am daily. **Admission** $5 drink minimum. **Map** p312 D10.
A great multi-theatre, -show or -dinner place. Live *bolero* and *son* are played in a cosy and intimate setting with an impressive night-time view on to the Plaza de la Revolución.

El Pico Blanco
Hotel St John's, Calle O #206, entre 23 y 25 (333740). **Open** 10pm-4am daily. **Admission** $5. **Map** p312 B12.
Known as the 'Rincón del filin' (*filin* corner), this is very much *the* place for live *filin* and *bolero* music.

Performances start at 11pm and go on till at least 1am, after which the place turns into a disco. Located on the top floor of the Hotel St John's, this club has an amazing view of the bay and the city. It's the perfect place for a tranquil evening.

La Red
Calle 19 #151, esquina a L (325415). **Open** *Sept-June* 10pm-4am daily. *July, Aug* 3-9pm, 10pm-4am daily. **Admission** $1 Mon-Thur; $2 Fri-Sun. **Map** p312 B11.
A charmingly dilapidated, pre-Revolutionary basement club with fishing motifs and retro decor. There's good seating and dancing space and, wait for it, air-conditioning that works. A show with live music – usually *salsa*, reggae or rap – takes place at midnight every night. Afterwards the place turns into a regular disco. Snacks are available.

Teatro Mella
Línea #657, entre A y B (38696/35651). **Open** *Box office* 10am-5pm daily. **Admission** $5-$10. **Map** p312 B9.
The Teatro Mella is home of the Conjunto Folclórico Nacional de Cuba (*see p208*) and is mainly used for dance performances. However, rock and *trova* concerts are also often held here.

Teatro Nacional de Cuba
Paseo, esquina a 39 (796011/704655/785590). **Open** *Box office* 10am-6pm Tue-Sun; closed Mon. **Admission** $2-$10. **Map** p312 D10.
The Teatro Nacional is a theatre/concert hall/nightclub complex, containing the Sala Covarrubia and Sala Avellaneda, the Café Cantante (*see above*), as well as the Delirio Habanero piano bar (*see above*). The two salas frequently host the National Symphony Orchestra as well as other big names from the *nueva trova*, rock and *son* scene. *See also p203*.

Las Vegas
Calzada de Infanta #104, esquina a 25 (707939). **Open** 10pm-5am daily. **Admission** $5. **Map** p312 C12.
This bar with a separate dance area is popular with Afro-Cuban youth. There's a show at 11.30pm and light snacks are served.

La Zorra y el Cuervo
Calle 23, entre N y O (662402). **Open** 9.30pm-4am daily. **Admission** $5. **Map** p312 B12.
Named after a well-known Spanish fable ('The Fox and the Crow'), this near-legendary jazz basement on La Rampa hosts well-known local and foreign musicians every night. The first set begins at 10.30pm, the second at midnight. Freezing air-conditioning.

Along Río Almendares

El Chevere
Club Almendares, Calle 28A, esquina a 49c, Kohly (244990). **Open** 5pm-midnight daily (see also below). **Admission** $3-20. **Map** p311 D7.
Open-air disco nestling between vine-clad rocks and

Arts & Entertainment

the River Almendares, in the middle of the Bosque de La Habana. Live bands (usually *salsa*) play around 7pm and again at 9pm. The admission price varies according to profile of artists – for Los Van Van expect to pay $20. Very Cuban clientele, which dwindles in the cooler months, so check to see which nights they are open. The Club Almendares poolside bar next door stays open after the disco, but you'll have to pay another $8 (drinks included) to get in.

Miramar & the western suburbs

El Bolero
Complejo Dos Gardenias, Avenida 7ma, esquina a 26 (242353/249662). **Open** 10pm-3am daily. **Admission** $10. **Map** p311 B5.
Havana's main *bolero* club hosts different groups and singers in two shows every night (from 10pm to midnight and from 12.15am to 3am).

Los Caneyes del Papa
Marina Hemingway, Calle 248 esquina a 5ta, Barlovento (241150). **Open** 10.30pm-4am daily. **Admission** $10.
Standard nightclub with a live *salsa* band at 12.30am on Friday and Saturday nights. It's only worth a visit if you are staying at or close to the Marina.

Casa de la Música
Calle 20 #3308, esquina a 35 (240447). **Open** 4-7pm Mon; 4-7pm, 10pm-2.30am Tue-Sun. **Admission** 10 pesos-30 pesos afternoon performances; $10-$20 evening performances. **Map** p311 C6.
If you're looking for a really good place for live *salsa* and money is not a factor, then this is the place to come. Situated in a beautiful mansion in Miramar,

the Casa de la Música hosts all the well-known groups in the evening, plus less-famous bands playing *salsa* and traditional music in the afternoons. Food and drinks are served.

La Cecilia
Avenida 5ta #11010, entre 110 y 112 (241562). **Open** currently closed for renovation. **Admission** phone for details.
The cabaret area of this tourist complex was closed for renovation at the time of going to press. When it reopens in 2001, La Cecilia is expected to host big-name *salsa* bands on Thursday to Sunday nights. There will probably be no cover charge, but a $10 drinks minimum is likely to be enforced.

Club Ipanema
Hotel Copacabana, Avenida 1ra, entre 44 y 46 (241037). **Open** 10pm-4am daily. **Admission** $5 Tue-Sun; $8 with free drinks Mon. **Map** p310 B3.
If you're looking for a standard club with good air-conditioning, a reasonable cover, decently priced drinks and a good mix of Cuban and other beats, this is where you want to be.

Havana Club
Hotel Comodoro, Avenida 3ra, esquina a 84 (242902). **Open** 10pm-5am daily. **Admission** $5. **Map** p310 B1.
This crowded Western-style disco is a favourite *jinetera* haunt. There's good music though, especially for *salsa* and techno aficionados.

La Maison
Calle 16 #701, esquina a 7ma (241546). **Open** 9.30pm-1am daily. **Admission** $10. **Map** p311 B6.
This tourist entertainment and shopping complex has a nightly show (10.15pm to 12.30pm) followed by an outdoor disco (*see also p139*).

Festivals

Festivals are all the rage in Cuba, not least because they attract foreigners and therefore plenty of greenbacks. The most popular (and populist) musical fest by far is the annual carnival (**Carnaval de la Habana**), which takes place from late July to mid-August, but there are plenty of other musical events throughout the year – from the renowned **Festival Internacional de Jazz** to the more obscure **Festival de Música Electroacústica**. All of them feature excellent music and are worth checking out. Even rap has made it to Havana (*see p168* **A load of rap**).

Festival tickets are usually sold in dollars and prices normally depend on whether you buy a pass for the entire festival (usually around $100-$150) or just attend individual

concerts ($5-$20). If you are going to be in Havana for the duration of one of the festivals listed, apply to the festivals department of the **Instituto Cubano de la Música** (ICM) for 20 per cent off the price of a festival pass. The ICM office is located on Calle 15, esquina a F, Vedado (328298/323503/icm@cubarte.cult.cu).

Festival dates often change from year to year and most festivals take place at venues all over town. We have listed the month of the festival, the most common venues, and the name of the festival organiser from whom you can get more detailed information. For listings information and more detailed reviews of these and other festivals, *see* chapter **By Season**.

Arts & Entertainment

Chuchó Valdés and Irakere sometimes play the **Jazz Café**. *See p196.*

Arts & Entertainment

Piano Bar Piel Canela

La Maison, Calle 16, esquina a 7ma (241543).
Open 10pm-4am daily. **Admission** $5 drink minimum. **Map** p311 B6.
This late-night bar features live *bolero* music and a comedy show from 10 to 11.30pm. The clientele is mainly Cuban.

Salón Rosado Beny Moré

Avenida 41, esquina a 46, Playa (235322).
Open 24hrs daily. **Admission** $10. **Map** p311 D5.
This is where *habaneros* come for serious dancing. It's a huge venue (very packed, very sweaty and loads of fun) hosting big-name *salsa* bands, especially at the weekend. (To give you an idea, Los Van Van tend to play here on a Monday when they're in town.) There's cabaret from 9pm Tuesday to Thursday and a dance band from 9pm till 2am Friday to Sunday. Sunday matinées for an older crowd run from 1 to 6pm. Until recently, the Rosado was best known for the fights that regularly broke out here, but the heavy police presence seems to have quietened things down. Phone Luís Duvalón for details of the concert schedule. Note that there are separate areas for Cubans and foreigners.

Teatro Karl Marx

Avenida 1ra, esquina a 8 (230801). **Open** *Box office* 9am-6pm Mon-Sat; closed Sun. **Admission** $10; peso price varies. **Map** p311 A6.
Better known as 'el Carlos Marx', this is Havana's largest theatre, with a seating capacity of almost 5,000. As tickets are still in pesos, this is where Cubans come to see big names such as Isaac Delgado, Silvio Rodríguez and Los Van Van. Recently, Buena Vista Social Club held its first Cuban concert here. Tourist tickets are priced in dollars, but you can often pay in pesos.

The eastern bay & coast

Casa de la cultura de Alamar

Calle 164, esquina a 5ta B, Zona 7, Alamar (650624). **Open** 8am-8pm daily.
Alamar is the home of Cuba's hip hop and other youth cultures and is best known for its disco nights and annual rap festival (*see p168* **A load of rap**). However, it also offers a wide range of other musical activities, and, although it's a little bit out of the way, is definitely worth the trip.

Casa de la trova de Guanabacoa

Calle Martí #111, entre Versalles y San Antonio, Guanabacoa (977687). **Open** 9am-11pm Tue-Sun; closed Mon. **Admission** 1 peso.
Further from the city centre, but just as wonderful, the *casa de la trova* at Guanabacoa also tends to be somewhat less touristy. *Trova* performances are held here from 8pm till late, Thursday to Sunday, as well as on Saturday and Sunday afternoons at 4pm. Children's musical events take place at 2pm every Tuesday and Wednesday.

Performing Arts

Havana doesn't let shortages that would cripple other countries get in its way. Instead, it puts on the performance of its life.

Havana is one of the hottest crucibles of dance, theatre and cabaret in the world. Performing artists have broken down barriers between different disciplines, overcoming acute material shortages and applying an eclectic range of techniques – classical and contemporary, local and international – to create a vibrant performance culture.

Dance throbs through Havana's veins. Cubans even walk as if they are dancing, using fluid movements of shoulders, wrists, hips and neck. Conversations are punctuated by flamboyant gestures. Cuba has one of the most distinguished ballet companies in the world, and is the birthplace of many popular dances, including *son, timba, danzón, cha-cha-chá, rumba, mambo, songa, mozambique*; and the Afro-Cuban religious dances of *santería, palo monte* and *abakuá*. At the same time, Cuba has assimilated international influences, from classical ballet to the contemporary choreography of Martha Graham, Pina Bausch and Merce Cunningham.

Havana also provides the stage for challenging and original drama. The Revolution triggered a boom in playwriting and new companies. While only 40 Cuban plays were performed in Havana between 1952 and 1958, 281 were staged in 1967 alone. Following a period of excessively socio-political theatre in the 1970s, many companies refused to accept the idea that theatre was a 'tool of the Revolution'. A series of workshops given by Eugenio Barba in the 1990s inspired many theatre groups to reject naturalism and focus their attentions on the body rather than the mind, the image rather than the idea, the voice rather than the word. This has led to a physically energetic theatre that is accessible beyond language barriers, as demonstrated by the great success that companies such as **Teatro Buendía** have had across the world. However, if you don't speak Spanish, try to do some homework on the style of a production beforehand. The vast majority of productions are in Cuban Spanish, where consonants and the final syllables of words tend to be omitted. English-language productions are rare; the last staging in English was in 1992 with a production of Carlos Fuentes' *Orchids in the Moonlight* at the **Teatro Nacional**.

Cuban companies have drawn their textual inspiration from both Cuban and international sources. Havana's reality has been reflected back to audiences through Spanish versions of plays as diverse as *Waiting for Godot, The Tempest, The Crucible* and *The Good Person of Szechuan*. Local playwrights have also flourished. Look out for works by Virgilio Piñera, Antón Arrufat and Senel Paz, whose play *La Catedral del Helado (Cathedral of Ice-cream)* was later turned into the hit film *Fresa y Chocolate (Strawberry and Chocolate)*.

Cuba's achievements in the performing arts are even more impressive when you take working conditions into account. Salaries for performing artists and technicians, as with most other Cubans, fluctuate between $100-$200 per year. As a result, many performers take second jobs, or rely on remittances from families abroad. Nor can performers escape the other hardships the rest of the country faces: public transport shortages mean that an actor can spend six hours a day travelling between home and rehearsal room; supplies of material and technical resources, such as costume fabrics, dance shoes and music, are scarce. Then there's the Caribbean heat, compounded by a lack of air-conditioning, which drains energy quickly. And, as if all this weren't enough, restrictions on foreign travel have limited artists' horizons.

The intrusion of ideology into the arts also poses problems. Live performing arts are given more artistic freedom than recorded media such as film and literature, but artists must still heed Fidel's warning of 'within the Revolution everything; outside nothing.' To be allowed to work professionally, artists must have successfully completed their college training, which includes a course in Marxist aesthetics. There is a definite 'white list' of writers (José Martí, José Lezama Lima, Che Guevara) and a greyish-black list, made up of anyone critical of the Revolution (Reinaldo Arenas, Octavio Paz, Mario Vargas Llosa and, until the government finally gave up trying to repress

▶ For cabaret, clubs and popular dance music venues, *see chapter* **Music & Nightlife**.

him in 1999, Antón Arrufat, one of Cuba's finest playwrights). When in doubt about whether material might offend the Revolution, artists tend to censor their own work. Sometimes, the enforced restrictions become intolerable, with the unfortunate result that artists emigrate to develop their careers in Europe or the Americas. Emigrés have included the playwrights Joel Cano and José Triana.

TICKETS & INFORMATION

Phone numbers are provided for all the theatres and companies listed below, but box office operators are unlikely to speak English, and you should not rely on telephone reservations. Few theatres have advance booking facilities, and credit cards (never US ones) are only accepted in major venues such as **The Tropicana** (*see p193*). The best way to acquire reliable information and guaranteed seats is to go to the theatre beforehand (even on the day). Tickets for non-residents (ie, mainly non-Cubans) are usually paid for in US dollars, while residents/Cubans normally pay around five pesos for tickets. Where venues officially give prices in both dollars and pesos, we have listed both.

Events listings can be found in the free and well-known English and Spanish weekly paper, *Cartelera*, though it's pretty flimsy and unreliable. Available in the major hotels, it is supposed to come out on Thursdays, but often doesn't appear until the following

Wednesday, the day it ceases to be useful. Better listings can usually be found in *Juventud Rebelde*. Information on performances is also given on the Cubavisión TV programme *Hurón Azul* on Thursday evenings at 10.30pm (unless *el Comandante* is speaking), or on *Cartelera* on Saturdays at midday; radio information is provided on *Buenos Días, Ciudad* on Radio Ciudad Habana; or in *Granma*, the daily rag. Otherwise, enquire in hotel tourist offices, or ask a dancer or actor, or at a hotel concierge desk. Cuban and Latin American performances are also covered by *Tablas* and *Conjunto*, both quarterly magazines available from UNEAC (*see p196*) and, sporadically, at some bookshops and kiosks.

Generally speaking, your best bet is to see what's on when you get here rather than plan your entire trip around one performance (major festivals excluded): even basic information in Cuba is notoriously hard to get hold of and consequently box office and performance times and ticket prices given in this chapter should be taken as a guideline only. Note too that not all venues have air-conditioning.

Major venues

Gran Teatro de La Habana

Paseo de Martí (Prado) #458, entre San Rafael y San Martín (San José), Centro Habana (613077/613078/613079). **Open** *Box office*

Teatro Amadeo Roldán, restored to its former glory. *See p204.*

Arts & Entertainment

The **Conjunto Folclórico Nacional de Cuba** putting on a colourful performance....

9am-5pm Tue-Sun; closed Mon. *Performances* 8.30pm Thur-Sat; 5pm Sun; no performances Mon-Wed. **Tickets** $3-$10 performances; $2 tour of theatre. **Map** p313 D13.

Havana's beautiful, baroque Grand Theatre was built in the early 19th century by the megalomaniac Spanish Governor Tacón. His intention was to build the largest theatre in Latin America, funded by levying a hefty tax on slaves imported to the island. The eponymous theatre, which seated 4,000 people and had 150 boxes, opened in 1846 with a season of Verdi operas. Between 1907 and 1914 it was remodelled by Belgian architect Paul Belau. The completed neo-baroque wedding cake of a building was named the Centro Gallego (Galician Centre) because Galicians financed the project, and opened with a spectacular production of *Aïda*.

The theatre now has various performance spaces, most importantly the 2,000-seater Sala García Lorca, named after the Spanish poet and playwright who visited and fell in love with Havana in 1930. Performers here have included the actresses Sarah Bernhardt and Eleonora Duse, the tenor Enrico Caruso, and musicians Arthur Rubinstein and Sergei Rachmaninov. This is the performance space for the Ballet Nacional de Cuba (*see p210* **Pointes mean prizes**), the Ballet Español

de La Habana, directed by Eduardo Veitia; and the Teatro Lírico de España. It is also the base for the Centro Pro Arte Lírico, formed in 1995 to fuse the companies producing opera and *zarzuelas* (comic operettas; *see p205*). The institution often stages co-productions with Spanish or Italian companies, and its most popular works in repertory are the Cuban *zarzuelas Cecilia Valdés*, *María la O* and *El Batey*, the Spanish *zarzuelas Luisa Fernanda* and *Las Aceituna*; and the operas *La Traviata*, *Rigoletto* and *Tosca*. Many opera fans bring their own scores and follow the music, singing along to arias, tapping their feet and giving standing ovations after each act. The 120-seater Sala Antonín Artaud stages experimental works, while the 509-seater Sala Alejo Carpentier puts on drama of all kinds.

Live musical performances (mostly classical, opera and *zarzuela*) are held on most evenings, but especially at weekends (there's often a Sunday matinée). Call or check the large billboards outside the theatre for upcoming events. *See also p80.*

Teatro Nacional de Cuba

Paseo, esquina a 39, Vedado (796011/704655/ 785590/Café Cantante 335713). **Open** *Box office* 10am-6pm Tue-Sun; closed Mon. *Performances* times vary. **Tickets** $2-$10; 2-10 pesos. **Map** p312 D10.

...and a strange one. See p208.

Arts & Entertainment

Opened in June 1959, the National Theatre was the first major building to be inaugurated after the Revolution. The layout is reminiscent of London's Royal Festival Hall, and its brutalist use of concrete and glass makes it similarly ugly from the outside. It has been described as a theatre waiting for its first season. Performances are sometimes cancelled because of official functions such as an emergency police force convention.

On the positive side, some of Cuba's best theatre and dance is rehearsed and performed here. There are five performance spaces, the largest of which is the 2,500-seater Sala Avellaneda, named after the 19th-century poet and playwright Gertrudis Gómez de Avellaneda, whose 20 plays show a mastery of both the tragic and the comic forms. This impersonal and dilapidated space, often dark, is used for large-scale dance and theatre productions.

The 800-seater Sala Covarrubias was named after the playwright Francisco Covarrubias, hailed as the founder of modern Cuban theatre. He became famous as the pioneer of the *negrito* (the white actor with a black face), even before Thomas Rice in the USA. The space was renovated in 1998 and is popular with a range of theatre companies.

The Noveno Piso (Ninth Floor) is a warehouse-like flexible space that has become a centre for avant-garde productions of theatre and dance. It is managed by the Fundación Ludwig, which was set up to support Cuban arts by a German chocolate manufacturer and art collector, Peter Ludwig, who died in 1996.

The third-floor piano bar, Delirio Habanero (*see p197*), overlooks the Plaza de la Revolución, and was renovated in 2000. In the basement is the Café Cantante Mi Habana (*see p194*), which has comedy shows in the afternoons and evenings. In addition, the tropical vegetation surrounding the theatre is sometimes used for children's shows, and there are facilities for rehearsals, workshops and classes.

Classical music venues

Basílica Menor de San Francisco de Asís

Calle Oficios, entre Brasil (Teniente Rey) y Amargura, La Habana Vieja (629683). **Open** *Box office* 9am-6pm daily. **Tickets** $3-$10. **Map** p316 E15.
This beautiful church with great acoustics provides an excellent setting for classical concerts. Performances usually take place at 6 or 7pm and often feature visiting foreign musicians. If you get the chance, catch a performance here of Renaissance Spanish court music by Ars Longa.

Teatro Amadeo Roldán

Calzada #512, esquina a D, Vedado (321168/ 324521/324522). **Open** *Box office* 9am-8pm Tue-Sun; closed Mon. **Tickets** $5-$10. **Map** p310 A10.
After a serious fire laid waste to the theatre in the 1980s, it was gradually restored and only re-opened in 1998. Named after the famous Cuban composer and musician, the theatre hosts mainly classical con-

certs, although occasionally jazz and *trova* can also be heard here. The acoustics in both concert halls are fantastic and there is an in-house bar.

Other venues

Casa de la Comedia

Calle Justiz #18, entre Baratillo y Oficios, La Habana Vieja (639282). **Open** *Box office* 1hr before performance. *Performances* times vary. **Tickets** $2. **Map** p315 E15.
The mission statement of the House of Comedy is to promote new Cuban plays. Also known as the Salón Ensayo (Rehearsal Room), it is the base for the company El Taller, directed by Dima Rolando. Afro-Cuban rituals are often held on its patio, and stand-up comedy shows are staged some Saturdays and Sundays at 7pm (*see also p206* **Havana laugh**).

Centro Cultural Bertolt Brecht

Calle 13, entre I y J, Vedado (329359). **Open** *Box office* 2hrs before performance. *Performances* children's show 10am Sat, Sun; others vary. **Tickets** $5; $3 concessions. **Map** p312 B11.
Founded in 1968, with a range of work from classics to comedy (*see p206* **Havana laugh**), this cultural centre is home to a 300-seater café theatre and a smaller 150-seater space. Three companies work here: Teatro Caribeño, Pequeño Teatro de La Habana and Teatro Mío.

Gaia

Calle Brasil (Teniente Rey), entre Cuba y Aguiar, La Habana Vieja (information 620401/ www.gaiacuba.com). **Open** phone for details. **Map** p316 E15.
Gaia is a theatre space project currently in development. Plans are underway to provide rehearsal, workshop and exhibition space, with particular focus on theatre projects or collaborations from the English-speaking world. The redevelopement project was inaugurated on 1 January 2000 with *A Millennium Night's Dream*, a party-spectacle. In collaboration with the British Council, Gaia recently staged *Cooking with Elvis* in the Teatro Nacional (*see p203*), the first new British play performed in Cuba since *An Inspector Calls* opened in 1947. The organisers welcome suggested projects and/or partnerships.

Teatro América

Avenida de Italia (Galiano) #253, entre Concordia y Neptuno, Centro Habana (625416). **Open** *Box office* 10am-4pm Tue-Sun; closed Mon. *Performances* times vary. **Tickets** $5. **Map** p313 D14.
Vaudeville and variety shows are staged in this imposing art deco building at weekends.

Teatro Fausto

Paseo de Martí (Prado) #201, esquina a Colón, Centro Habana (631173). **Open** *Box office* 2-8pm Tue-Sun; closed Mon. *Performances* 8.30pm Fri; 10am (children's show), 8.30pm Sat; 10am (children's show), 5pm Sun; no performances Mon-Thur. **Tickets** $3-$5; $2.50-$3 concessions. **Map** p316 D14.

Directed by Armando Suárez del Villar, the Fausto offers variety and comedy shows (*see p206* **Havana laugh**), as well as children's theatre. Flamboyant writer, director and actor Hector Quintero sometimes stages works here.

Teatro Hubert de Blanck
Calzada #654, entre A y B, Vedado (301011). **Open** *Box office* 3-6pm Wed-Fri; 3-5pm Sat, Sun; closed Mon, Tue. *Performances* 8.30pm Fri, Sat; 5pm Sun; no performances Mon-Thur. **Tickets** $5; 5 pesos. **Map** p312 A9.
The former home of the 19th-century Belgian musician Hubert de Blanck, who founded Havana's first music conservatory, was remodelled as a theatre in 1955 by his family. Director Bertha Martínez works here, recently staging Lorca's *La Zapatera Prodigiosa*. It is also the production house for Abelardo Estorino, who is Cuba's most frequently performed living playwright. Past productions of note include *Morir del Cuento* and *El Robo del Cochino*.

Teatro Mella
Calle Línea #657, entre A y B, Vedado (38696/ 35651). **Open** *Box office* 2hrs before performance Fri-Sun; closed Mon-Thur. *Performances* times vary. **Tickets** $5-$10. **Map** p312 B9.
Recently refurbished, this 1,500-seater theatre is used for dance, folklore, circus and variety shows, as well as seasons of dance and comedy (*see p206* **Havana laugh**).

Teatro Nacional de Guiñol
Calle M, entre 17 y 19, Vedado (326262). **Open** *Box office* 1hr before performance. *Performances* 3pm Fri; 5pm Sat; 10.30am, 5pm Sun; no performances Mon-Thur. **Tickets** $2; $1 concessions. **Map** p312 B11.
Founded in 1963, this is Cuba's leading children's theatre and puppetry company. It has staged 120 productions, 30 of which remain in repertory, and under the artistic directorship of Roberto Fernández has served as a school for puppeteers and children's writers. Joel Cano's *La Fábula del Insomnio* has featured here in the past. *See also p176.*

Teatro el Sótano
Calle K #514, entre 25 y 27, Vedado (320630/ 320833). **Open** *Box office* 5-8.30pm Wed-Sat; 3-5pm Sun; closed Mon, Tue. *Performances* times vary. **Tickets** $3-$5. **Map** p312 C11.
Home of the recently stagnant Grupo Teatro Rita Montaner, the repertory of the Basement Theatre (confusingly, not in a basement) includes work by Valle-Inclán. It also presents tacky comedy shows on Thursday evenings.

Teatro Trianón
Calle Línea #706, entre Paseo y A, Vedado (309648). **Open** *Box office* 2hrs before performance. *Performances* times vary. **Tickets** 5 pesos. **Map** p312 B9.
Teatro Trianón is home to the company Teatro el Público, directed by the highly talented Carlos Diaz,

Zarzuela

Zarzuela is a popular form of opera that first appeared in Spain in the 17th century. It wasn't until the 19th century, however, that this musical-style theatre became widely known and liked. Its growing popularity brought it to Cuba in the 1920s. There the genre was adapted to incorporate local musical styles like the rumba, *danzón* and *contradanza* and to deal with typical, everyday Cuban issues. Among the great Cuban *zarzuela* composers, Ernesto Lecuona (1896-1963) stands out. Some of his best-known pieces are *María La O, Rosa la China* and *El Cafetal*. Other respected names include Gonzalo Roig (1890-1970), author of *Cecilia Valdés*, which later became Cuba's most famous *zarzuela*, and Rodrigo Prats (1909-1980), the composer of *María Belén Chacón, Amalia Batista* and *Soledad*.

who in the past has produced non-Cuban works such as Tennessee Williams' *The Glass Menagerie*, Arthur Miller's *The Crucible* and *Tea and Sympathy* by Maxwell Anderson.

Theatre companies

Argos Teatro
Information: Calzada de Ayestarán #507a, esquina a 20 de Mayo, Vedado (785551/781883/620401). **Map** p312 E10.
Argos was formed in 1996 by graduates of Buendia (*see below*) with the intention of creating innovative, must-see theatre from old stories. Celdrán is one of the most exciting young directors working in Cuba, and widely considered a leader of the theatrical avant-garde. Argos's work is based on image and action. Its most recent production is a dynamic revision of Calderón's *La Vida es Sueño*, and the company's repertory includes versions of Brecht's *Boal* and *The Good Person of Szechuan*; and *La Pequeña Oresteia*, based on Euripides' *Oresteia* and Sartre's *Flies*. Argos normally performs in the Noveno Piso at the Teatro Nacional (*see p203*), although plans are afoot for productions to take place in the former masonic lodge where the troupe rehearses.

Teatro Buendía
Calle Loma, esquina a 39, Nuevo Vedado (816689). **Open** *Box office* 2hrs before performance. *Performances* 8.30pm Fri-Sun; no performances Mon-Thur. **Tickets** 4 pesos. **Map** p311 D8.
Formed in 1985 under the directorship of Flora Lauten (the last Miss Cuba before the Revolution), Buendía was named after the epic family in García

Arts & Entertainment

Havana laugh

Comedy in Havana is no joking matter. Visitors just don't find it funny. For starters, there's the language problem. You need an excellent grasp of Spanish to understand Cuban comedy, and you need a complex vocabulary of sub-textual references, the most common being gestures indicating a beard to portray Fidel.

Then there's the politically correct problem. Jokes are often sexist (about all women being whores or unfaithful wives), racist (about stupid, thieving *negritos*) or homophobic (about mincing fags – *maricones*, and devilish dykes – *tortilleras*).

If decoded and tolerated, however, humour in Havana is both funny and sophisticated. The best live comedy, mime, and clown shows can be found at the **Casa de la Comedia** (*see p204*), **Teatro Nacional** (*see p203*), **Teatro Mella** (*see p205*) and the **Teatro Fausto** (*see p204*). The only real taboo is jokes about José Martí. The most popular jokes for stand-up comedians are about *el caballo* (the horse – Fidel), sex, Raúl Castro, the Special Period, gays, blacks, foreigners, exile, religion and Pepito, the archetypal man in the street. They provide both laughter and a crucial safety valve for real frustrations about daily life. (For this very reason, Fidel probably invented the wittiest anti-Fidelista jokes himself.)

Here is a selection of Havana's naughtiest gags. But be warned: tell them to your average Cuban and you'll make a friend; tell them to a Minister of State and you may end up on the phone to your consulate.

Q: What proof is there that Adam and Eve were Cuban?

A: Because they didn't have any clothes, went around bare-footed, weren't allowed to eat apples and were still told they were living in paradise.

Q: What do you call a Cuban orchestra after an international tour?

A: A quartet.

A foreign correspondent stops a Cuban in the street for an interview.
'Tell me, how did you used to live before the Revolution?'
'On the verge of an abyss.
'And what happened after the Revolution?'
'We took a step forward.'

Márquez's *One Hundred Years of Solitude*, and was arguably the most innovative, courageous and internationally successful Cuban theatre company of the 1990s. Committed to finding an autonomous voice, the company has benefited from contact with international masters such as Peter Brook, Enrique Buenaventura, Jerzy Grotowski and Eugenio Barba. Its production of *Innocent Eréndira*, Gabriel Garcia Márquez's tale of prostitution and rebellion, toured the world for five years to great acclaim. Its version of *The Tempest, Otra Tempestad*, was staged in London's Globe Theatre in 1998 following more than two years of rehearsals. Buendia has been a school for some of Cuba's top emerging directors such as Carlos Celdrán, Esther Cardoso, Antonia Fernández and Nelda Castillo, and has provided superb training for young actors. The company performs in a Greek Orthodox church that the actors converted themselves. The audience sits on hard, steeply raked benches, so remember to bring a cushion.

Teatro de la Luna

c/o Teatro Nacional, Paseo, esquina a 39, Vedado (796011/704655/785590). **Map** p312 D10.
Led by versatile young director, choreographer and actor Raúl Martin, the Theatre of the Moon tends to perform in the Teatro Nacional (*see p203*). Martin has directed Marianela Boan as Blanche Dubois

and in *Ultimos días de una casa*, a monologue based on a poem by Dulce María Loynaz. He has also adapted works by Virgilio Piñera such as *Los Siervos*, which have strong socio-political references and require an excellent knowledge of Cuban Spanish to understand.

Dance companies

Así Somos

Information: Calle A #310, Apt 7b, entre 3ra y 3ra A, Miramar (234276/lorna@cubarte.cult.cu). **Map** p311 A7.
Así Somos (The Way We Are) was founded in 1981 by Lorna Burdsall. US-born Burdsall trained at the Julliard in New York under Alfredo Corvino, Merce Cunningham, Martha Graham and Anthony Tudor. She fell in love with a Cuban Bacardí rum executive in New York and in 1955 moved back with him to Havana. After the Revolution, Burdsall was a founder member of Danza Nacional (now Danza Contemporánea de Cuba; *see p208*) and helped introduce new techniques into Cuban modern dance.

Lorna is best described as an artistic magpie, assembling her work out of theatre, music, dance, masks and contemporary folklore. To give you an idea of her eclecticism, she uses flashlights for lighting, shammy leathers for costumes, Soviet army-

Arts & Entertainment

Another hot and sweaty session for
Danza Contemporánea de Cuba. *See p208.*

surplus silk parachutes for backdrops, poetry by Lorca and Martí, musical sources ranging from Astor Piazzola to Chopin; her young granddaughter is the principal dancer. Lorna also holds dance classes for children and adults in her house; see p209).

El Ciervo Encantado
The Enchanted Stag is directed by Nelda Castillo, former Buendía director. She has no fixed address, but is red-headed, and can sometimes be found round the park of Línea and K, in Vedado. Nelda is a gutsy challenger of the status quo, and has unflinchingly resisted the 'ideologisation' of art. The State has refused to give her a theatre, so she must work underground. Seek out her *De dónde son los cantantes?*, which uses text from a cousin *enfant terrible* of dissidence, Guillermo Cabrera Infante.

Codanza
Information: Calle Fomento #202, entre Arias y Agramonte, 8010, Holguín, Cuba (024 42234/ fax 024 425179).
Catch this company, which is based in Holguín, eastern Cuba, if you can. Founded in 1992 and directed by Marisel Godoy, the company's work uses a ballet base to build a style that mixes popular rhythms with theatre and comedy. It successfully toured Spain in 2000 and performs during dance festivals in Havana.

Conjunto Folclórico Nacional de Cuba
Calle 4 #103, entre Calzada y 5ta, Vedado (34560/ 303939/303060). **Open** *Box office* from 2pm on days of performance. **Map** p312 A9.
One of Cuba's most internationally famed dance companies, the Conjunto Folclórico Nacional de Cuba enjoyed a successful run in London in early 2000. Founded way back in 1962, it is directed by Teresa Gonzales, a dancer, choreographer and teacher. She has worked to fuse the European roots of Cuban dance with its African origins, especially those of the Yoruba, Locumi, Bantu and Congo cultures. The company has a repertoire of over 70 productions and usually performs in the Teatro Mella (see p205). The Conjunto plays excellent *rumba* on the patio of the central café/bar area every Saturday (see p196) and also offers dance classes through Folcuba (see p209).

DanzAbierta
Information: Conjunto Folclórico Nacional de Cuba, Calle 4 #103, entre Calzada y 5ta, Vedado (information 334387). **Map** p312 A9.
Under the direction of Marianela Boán, a former dancer in Danza Contemporánea de Cuba (see p208), DanzAbierta creates what could be described as Cubanised post-modernism. Boán is regarded as the grande dame of contemporary dance and innovatively mixes the gestures of everyday life with social and political comment and techniques reminiscent of Pina Bausch. Her best pieces of recent years are *El Pez en el Asfalto*, a witty reflec-

tion on the absurdities of the Special Period; and *El Árbol y el Camino*, in which five naked dancers use coat-hangers like branches to portray the tree of life. The company rehearses at the Conjunto Folclórico Nacional building (see *above*) and performs in the Gran Teatro (see p201), Teatro Mella (see p205) and Teatro Nacional (see p203). The company made its UK debut at the Edinburgh Fringe Festival in August 2000, where its production of *El Pez en el Asfalto* gained a huge amount of critical acclaim.

Danza Combinatoria
Information: Calzada de Infanta (Menocal), esquina a Arroyo (Manglar), edificio 20 plantas, piso 6, Apto 65, Centro Habana (no phone/aljm@artsoft.cult.cu). **Map** p312 E11.
This well-established, nine-member company stages performances of sensual, sculptural surrealism, directed by the highly creative Rosario Cardenas. Within the troupe of dancers, look out for the amazingly elastic Eruadyé Muñiz. Cardenas' best work to date, based on a poem by Virgilio Piñera about a woman who is dying of tuberculosis, is *María Viván*, a breathtaking fantasy tour of anarchically arranged images.

Danza Contemporánea de Cuba
Information: Teatro Nacional, Paseo, esquina a 39, (information 792728/796410). **Map** p312 D10.
The powerhouse of Cuban contemporary dance was founded in 1959 by Ramiro Guerra and Lorna Burdsall (see p206 **Así Somos** and p209). The company of 30 young performers is now directed by former dancer Miguel Iglesias and combines classical ballet with Cuban popular dance and international contemporary influences. It performs in the Gran Teatro (see p201), the Teatro Nacional (see p203) and Teatro Mella (see p205) and on regular national and international tours. The company's leading choreographers are Lidice Núñez, Isidro Rolando, Esteban Delgado (who choreographed the exuberant cabaret *Havana Night*), Jorge Abril and Luz María Collazo (see p210). Núñez is considered one of the most exciting ambassadors of a new generation of cosmopolitan choreographers. Her work is performed in the repertory of Danza Contemporánea, usually in the Sala García Lorca of the Gran Teatro (see p201), and has toured in Europe and the Americas. One of Núñez's best-choreographed pieces is the magical *Terriblemente Inocente*.

Danza Teatro Retazos
Information: Calle 82 #1317, entre 13 y 15, Miramar (tel/fax 249986/www.retazosdance.com). **Map** p310 D2.
Ecuadorean choreographer Isabel Bustos leads a sensual, disciplined chaos of unusual physicalities. She describes her work as 'intimist', that's to say founded on an aesthetic of intimacy and emotion, with imaginative choices of both performance spaces and music, which ranges from Algerian to Lenny Kravitz.

Arts & Entertainment

Dance classes & courses

Unless you enjoy being sniggered at as a rhythmless tourist, you'd do well to take some dance lessons, preferably before you go to Havana. At least try and learn the basic one-two-three of *salsa* and *son*. There has been a boom in Latin dance tuition across the world over recent years, so you shouldn't have any difficulty finding a class. Alternatively, get in touch with one of the following places/teachers when you get to Cuba.

If it's tango you'd like to learn, several of the venues mentioned in chapter **Music & Nightlife** (*pp186-199*), in particular the **Caserón del Tango** (*see p191*), should be able to recommend teachers.

State tuition

Cátedra de Danza

Information: Calle 5ta #253, entre D y E, Vedado (324625/www.balletcuba.cu). **Map** p312 A10.
Established by Alicia Alonso in March 1999 and attached to the Ballet Nacional de Cuba (BNC, *see p210* **Pointes mean prizes**), this centre seeks to train teachers and students in the Cuban school of ballet, and its roots in Caribbean, Latin American and European dance. Classes are offered in ballet, pointes, variations, classical duets, modern dance, physical preparation and the history of dance. Courses are taught by leading choreographers at the BNC and other experts, and are tailor-made according to an individual's or group's needs. A basic 30-day course of ballet, pointes, and physical preparation costs $250. If required, three-week International Dance Workshops can be arranged outside Cuba, for which a contract must be signed between the interested educational establishment and BNC. In addition, the school offers a *taller vocacional* (vocational workshop) for five- to 16-year-olds, to encourage enthusiasm for ballet. For further details contact Cátedra de Danza at the above address or check out the website.

Cuballet/Prodanza

Information: Avenida 51 #11805, entre 118 y 120, Marianao (208610).
Cuballet offers a 30-day general course in pointes, classical repertory, history of dance, modern dance and folklore. The courses commence at the beginning of January and August every year, and cost $350 per person. Longer courses can also be arranged, tailored to students' requirements. Based in the same building, Prodanza provides training in classical ballet and modern dance for eight- to 25-year-olds. The school is formally known as the Escuela Vocacional del Centro de Promoción de Danza, and is under the general direction of Laura Alonso, Alicia Alonso's daughter. Specific courses are offered in pointes, physical efficiency, modern dance and folklore. A 30-day course costs $250.

Classes usually take place in the Gran Teatro (*see p201*). Prodanza has also staged some notable productions in the past, among them a ballet of Dracula.

Folcuba

Information: Calle 4 #103 entre Calzada y 5ta, Vedado (tel/fax 553823). **Map** p312 A9.
Tuition is given in all kinds of popular Cuban dance: *son, mambo, cha-cha-chá, casino, salsa, rumba, arará* and *santería* dances. Classes are given by the best teachers from the Conjunto Folclórico Nacional de Cuba (*see p208*). Lectures are also given on Cuban culture and music. Courses are open to all ages and start on the first Monday in January and July. An initial test separates students into three levels. The cost of the courses ranges from $250 to $350.

Instituto Superior de Artes (ISA)

Calle 120 #1110, esquina a 9na, Cubanacán (enquiries 288075/isa@cubarte.cult.cu).
ISA's faculty of dance and theatre offers post-graduate courses to Cubans and non-Cubans in music, theatre, dance and the visual arts. Interested students must validate their degree certificate in the Cuban embassy in the country where they live. Students taking a year off as part of their degree are also eligible, with the support of their university. Matriculation takes place on 1 August, following an initial examination to assess skill levels. A one-year course in theatre costs $2,500, and encompasses acrobatics, voice and diction, history of theatre, history of art, philosophy and psychology. Other options, by enquiry, include stage-fighting, contemporary dance and ballet. Prospective students are warned that, whilst the ISA offers some of the best teachers in the country, staff morale is low, which affects punctuality and general discipline. Former foreign students recommend hiring ISA's teachers for private lessons.

Private tuition

Private classes in dance and drama can be arranged through **Gaia** (*see p204*) or directly with one of the following.

Hilda Rosa Barrera

Information: Calle Habana Park #114, entre Sánchez y Manila, Cerro (709273). **Rates** vary. **Map** p311 F8.
Former contemporary dancer, Hilda Rosa is now a choreographer and teacher at the ISA (*see above*). She offers classes in contemporary dance, folklore and popular Cuban dance (especially *salsa, merengue* and *rumba*). She speaks only basic English and prefers out classes. Her rates depend on the level of each dancer.

Lorna Burdsall

Information 234276/lorna@cubarte.cult.cu.
Rates free (donations welcome).
Founder of the Danza Contemporánea de Cuba (*see p208*), Lorna Burdsall offers classes for adults and

Pointes mean prizes

A highlight of any trip to Havana is a performance by the Ballet Nacional de Cuba. The company's fusion of tropical passion with Soviet discipline has arguably made it as technically accomplished as its cousins in St Petersburg, New York, Paris, Milan and London, and, given their healthy diet of little fast food and plenty of sex, its dancers are probably even more physically powerful.

Ballet in Cuba was entirely European until the mid 20th century. It first arrived in 1842 when the ballerina Fanny Elssler danced in the Teatro Tacón (now the Gran Teatro; see p201). (Cuban audiences were treated to another European star in 1917 when Anna Pavlova performed in Havana.) Home-grown ballet was encouraged by the Sociedad Pro-Arte Música, founded in 1931, three of whose students made ballet history: Alicia Martínez Hoyo (pictured), the first Cuban dancer to be given her pointes; and the Alonso brothers, Alberto and Fernando. Alicia and Fernando fell in love, travelled to the USA together to study at the School of American Ballet, and married in the Cuban consulate in Washington in 1937.

Born on 21 December 1920, Alicia Alonso became Cuba's most important ballerina and choreographer. For her professional debut in 1938, she performed in the New York musicals Great Lady and Stars in Your Eyes. The following year she joined the American Ballet Caravan, forerunner of today's New York City Ballet, and then moved to Ballet Theatre in 1940, the year it was founded. Her career nearly ended in 1941 when she suffered a detached retina. Although her eyesight was permanently damaged, she returned to dance for the company two years later. In New York, she caught the attention of contemporary choreographer Anthony Tudor, who directed her in Undertow (1945), and George Balanchine, who directed her in Theme and Variations (1947). In 1948 she teamed up with both Alonso brothers to set up a company in Havana, the Ballet Alicia Alonso, and in 1950 they established a ballet school. In 1955 the company was renamed the Ballet de Cuba, and in 1961 became the Ballet Nacional de Cuba.

As well as producing in Cuba, Alicia has worked extensively abroad. She danced with the Bolshoi, most notably in a production of Carmen (1967) that was directed by her brother-in-law, Alberto. It is still performed regularly in Havana, with its Picasso-inspired costumes and a haunting opening tableau of a red and black shape that is both a womb and a bull's head. Most celebrated for her role as Giselle, Alicia Alonso left her mark in many of the great theatres of the world: as Sleeping Beauty at the Opéra in Paris and Milan's Scala; and as La Fille mal gardée in Prague. Like Margot Fonteyn, she continued to dance into old age, performing for the last time in 1995, aged 75, in En Medio de la Tarde, a ballet composed specially for her, and again directed by Alberto Alonso.

---

children, which she calls *felicicios* (happy exercises). The classes take place in her home and there is no formal charge, although donations are welcome. Phone or email for more information.

Luz María Collazo

Information: Calle 40 #157, Apto 25, entre 36 y Zoológico, Nuevo Vedado (810729). **Rates** $7 per hr. **Map** p311 E6.

Actress and dancer who shot to fame in Cuba for her role in the movie *Cuba Sí*, Luz María is now a choreographer at Danza Contemporánea (see p208), and combines patience with rigour in the heroic task of trying to convert rigid Anglo-Saxon torsos into lithe machines of sensuality. She teaches all forms of popular Latin dance and folklore and speaks reasonable English. Out classes are preferred.

Mayra Varona

Information: Apto 9, Calle Concordia #151, entre San Nicolás y Manrique, Centro (631075).

Rates $5 per hr one-to-one tuition; other rates negotiable. **Map** p313 D14.

Well known in Cuba as a TV dancer and choreographer for over 30 years, Mayra Varona teaches and choreographs all kinds of Latin American popular dance forms for both amateurs and professionals in theatre, television, cabaret and musicals. Classes are held at her home and elsewhere.

Festivals

April is the best month for performing arts festivals. The annual week-long street dance festival **La Habana Vieja: Ciudad en Movimiento**, directed by Isabel Bustos, is sponsored by the feudal lord of Old Havana, Eusebio Leal. Every day, over 500 artists from various countries perform in inner courts of colonial museum-houses like the Casa Guayasamín and the Casa Bolívar, or in

Arts & Entertainment

Over the years Alicia has bewitched Fidel Castro into personally supporting the ballet. He was so enchanted on his first visit in 1959 that he awarded the company four times the grant it had asked for. He has also backed its international forays, including a tour of the USA in 1978, and another one planned for 2001. In 1999, UNESCO awarded Alicia the prestigious Pablo Picasso medal for her outstanding contribution to dance.

In late 2000, the Ballet Nacional had a whopping 87 works in repertory, of which around 12 were choreographed by Alicia Alonso. Various European companies now use her adapted versions of the classics in their repertory. The company has commissioned a number of new ballets, including Alberto Alonso's *Un Retablo para Romeo y Julieta* and José Parés' *Un Concierto en Blanco*. Numerous other choreographers have worked with the Ballet Nacional. Look out for the smoldering *Tierra y Luna*, choreographed by Spaniard María Rovira, and inspired by Lorca's poetry.

As a venue, the **Gran Teatro** (*see p201*) has an interior that can compete with the world's great ballet stages, although the orchestra pit resembles the *Marie Celeste* because of a decision to cut costs by using recorded music. Ballet performances are probably the only events that start punctually in Cuba, so turn up on time unless you want to be stranded at the back until the interval. It is also possible to watch rehearsals during the week (for details, contact the Ballet Nacional directly).

Ballet Nacional de Cuba

Information: Calzada #510, entre D y E, Vedado (552952/552953/ www.balletcuba.cu). **Map** p312 A10.

the Plaza Vieja, or in processions through the old town. Also starting in April is the dance festival **Los Días de la Danza** in the Teatro Mella (*see p205*); the **Festival de Academias de Ballet**, including shows by students at the international ballet school; and the **Festival Elsinore**, with theatre and dance productions by students from the national arts school ISA (*see p209*). **La Huella de España**, organised by the Ballet Nacional, is a festival of Spanish ballet every March/April.

Summer festivals include the **Festival Nacional del Humor** in July, an annual comedy season, based in the Teatro Mella (*see p205*), and **Cuba Danza**, a biennial festival of modern dance classes, workshops and performances organised by Danza Contemporánea (*see p208*), which is held every even-numbered year in August. International ballet and theatre festivals take place in Havana in alternate years; the **Festival Internacional de Teatro** happens in September in odd-numbered years, and the **Festival Internacional de Ballet** kicks off at the end of October in even-numbered years.

Carnaval de La Habana takes place on the last two weekends of July and the first two weekends of August. There's a procession (*comparsa*) down Paseo de Martí (Prado) and the Malecón, made up of floats of musicians, singers and dancers who represent their own neighbourhood or local school. The *comparsa* is lead by a standard-bearer and people carrying *farolas* (lanterns). They are followed by dancers, singers and musicians playing drums, *congas*, maracas, square bells, truck wheels, trumpets, trombones and saxophones. As at any popular event, take care of your personal belongings.

For further details on these and other festivals, *see chapter* **By Season**.

Arts & Entertainment

Sport & Fitness

Though the heat in Havana can sap energy quickly, there's a whole kitbag of activities to keep you busy should you want to partake.

Despite its relatively small population, Cuba has produced an impressive number of world-class athletes over the years. The country's extraordinary prowess in baseball and boxing is well known, but there's plenty of action across a range of other sporting disciplines, too.

Since the Revolution, all sport in Cuba has been government supported and exclusively amateur. Money has been poured into the promotion of amateur sport, creating a level of participation and achievement in the last 40 years that Cubans are understandably very proud of. The National Institute for Sport and Recreation, or INDER, was formed in 1961 and today some 1.2 million Cubans of all ages practise sports at all levels. In total there are almost 40 accredited disciplines, each with a governing federation affiliated to the INDER.

The achievements of Cuba's amateur athletes in the Olympic Games are a measure of the success of the country's sports policies. Aside from the Games in Los Angeles in 1984 and in Seoul four years later, Cuba has made an appearance at every Olympics for more than a century. The first gold came from fencer Ramón

Fonst way back in 1900. (Fonst simultaneously became the first athlete from Latin America ever to win an Olympic gold). Despite severe economic hardship (especially during the Special Period, starting in the 1990s) and the introduction of professionals into the Olympics (since the Barcelona Olympics in 1992), the national team continues to impress. Cuba came ninth in the final medal table at the 2000 Sydney Olympics, with 11 gold, 11 silver and seven bronze medals.

Cuba has also been hugely successful in the Pan-American Games (which are held every four years, in the year before the Olympics), finally knocking the USA from the top spot during the 1991 Games in Havana. The **Panamericano** complex to the east of the city was constructed to host the 1991 Games and is still the largest sports centre in the city (*see p114*). The surroundings are now rather dilapidated, but the facilities include the Estadio Panamericano for athletics, the Velodromo Reinaldo Paseiro for cycling, the Baragua pool complex and the Panamericano tennis complex.

Stunning but underused
Estadio José Martí in Vedado.

Arts & Entertainment

INFORMATION

For official information about a particular sport, contact the following federations: **athletics** (972101); **baseball** (797980/781662/786882); **basketball** (577156); **boxing** (577047); **cycling** (633776/683661); **judo** (411732); **tae kwon do** (545000/04/20 ext. 184); **tennis** (972121); **volleyball** (413557); **wrestling** (577344). Although the person answering the phone often won't be able to speak English, they will do their best to help. You can also contact the press and information department of INDER on 577084.

Cubadeportes (Calle 20 #705, entre 7 y 9, Miramar; 240945) publishes an annual list of sporting events, but is not geared to take queries from tourists.

Note that, while as much specific information about sporting events and venues as possible is given in this chapter, such details are not always particularly reliable in Cuba – therefore, you're always advised to check with the venue in question or at a hotel tourist desk before going out of your way to attend a match or participate in a sport. Unless otherwise stated, hours given below are opening hours for offices at the venues, rather than match times.

For information about sports hot-spots outside Havana, in particular fishing, diving and golf, *see chapter* **Beyond Havana**.

Spectator sports

For general information and help with obtaining tickets for events, the tourist desks or PR department of major hotels are useful places to start. *Cartelera*, the weekly listings paper, generally includes details of forthcoming events for 'major' sports such as baseball and volleyball, but better sources of information are *Juventud Rebelde*, *Granma* and the sports TV news at 6pm. In terms of prices of tickets, foreigners normally pay in dollars the peso amount at a one-to-one rate, which is still remarkably cheap.

Baseball

When you hear locals in Havana talking passionately about Los Azules ('the Blues'), they're actually referring to the **Industriales**, the city's long-standing baseball team, founded in 1963, and the most successful team in the national league (Serie Nacional de Béisbol). It's the team to beat and the team that everyone – even the fans of its die-hard rivals – wants to watch in action.

The city's other team is the less well-known **Metropolitanos**, more commonly referred to as the Metros. Its players are generally young

and newly arrived to the national league. Founded in the late 1970s, the Metros don't get as much attention or arouse as much fervour as the Industriales. Despite the fact that the team improved a great deal in past years – even making it as far as the post-season play-offs (first in 1981, then again in 1998, 1999 and 2000 after a period in the doldrums) – it's still the Blues that people are really passionate about.

Both teams play home games at 'El Latino' stadium, formally the **Estadio Latinamericano**, the most important baseball stage in Cuba. It is the goal of every Cuban ballplayer to succeed within the hallowed confines of this 50-year-old stadium. During the season, check the back pages of *Granma* or ask at your hotel for details of upcoming matches. Due to the sheer number of games, tickets are usually easy to get hold of either directly from the stadium or if by asking your hotel tour desk. With the exception of some stadium seats that officials try to reserve for foreign visitors, tickets are generally sold on a first come, first served basis. For more on Cuban baseball, *see p215* **Playing the field**.

Estadio Latinamericano

Zequeira #312, Cerro (5706526/706576/786882). **Matches** 7.30pm Tue-Thur; 1.30pm, 7.30pm Sat; 1.30pm Sun. **Tickets** 3 pesos. **Map** p312 F10.

Basketball

The national basketball league (Liga Superior de Baloncesto – LSB) runs from September to November and consists of just four teams. The Havana team is the Capitalinos; they are often one of the main title contenders and can be seen in action at the **Sala Polivalente Ramón Fonst** and the **Coliseo de la Ciudad Deportiva**. Although basketball does not inspire the same mass following as baseball, the games can be intensely fought and great fun to watch. In recent years, LSB games have attracted increasing public attention, though in 1999 several of Cuba's best basketball players defected, and it may take a couple of years for the sport to recover.

Coliseo de la Ciudad Deportiva

Vía Blanca, esquina a Avenida Boyeros (545000/boxing department 577047). **Open** 8am-5pm Mon-Fri; closed Sat, Sun. **Tickets** $1-$3. **Map** p311 F7.

Sala Polivalente Ramón Fonst

Avenida de la Independencia, esquina a Bruzón, Plaza de la Revolución (820000). **Matches** 8.30pm Mon-Fri, Sat; 3pm Sun. **Tickets** $1-$3.

Boxing

Cuba has proved to be a fertile ground for producing great boxers, both during the professional years before 1962 and since the adoption of amateur rules thereafter. Cuba has been the overall champion of the boxing competition at every Olympic Games since Munich in 1972 and continued its impressive record by picking up four golds and two bronzes at the 2000 games in Sydney. The resolutely amateur nature of the sport in Cuba means that, despite their brilliance, Cuban boxers are not well-known on the international stage. Within Cuba, however, former and current stars of the ring, such as Kid Chocolate, Maikro Romero, Roberto Balado (all from Havana), Teofilo Stevenson and Felix Savon are national heroes. The Girardo Córdova Cardín Tournament is the most prestigious national competition and is held in a different Cuban city every April.

In Havana, the **Sala Polivalente 'Kid Chocolate'**, a multi-purpose sports facility opposite the Capitolio, stages local and national boxing matches. International championships are held at the much bigger **Coliseo de la Ciudad Deportiva** (*see p213*), home of the Federación Cubana de Boxeo. For a glimpse behind the scenes, you can see budding Stevensons training and fighting at the Arena Trejo, Cuba's oldest boxing gym and arena. Note that you might be charged a couple of dollars for the privilege. *See also p216* **Lords of the ring**.

Arena Trejo
Calle Cuba #815, entre Merced y Leonor Pérez (Paula), La Habana Vieja (620266). **Open** 8am-5pm Mon-Fri; closed Sat, Sun. **Tickets** $1. **Map** p316 F15.

Sala Polivalente 'Kid Chocolate'
Paseo de Martí (Prado), entre San Martín y Brasil, Centro Habana (628634). **Open** varies. **Tickets** $1-$3. **Map** p313 E14.

Cycling

Those who are into cycling but can't face taking to the roads themselves might like to go for the safer option of watching the national race team train at the **Velodromo Reinaldo Paseiro**, a purpose-built facility to the east of the city constructed for the Pan-American Games in 1991. The velodrome is home to the Escuela de Ciclismo de las Américas (Cycling School of the Americas), where beginners and advanced cyclists from all over the American continent come to upgrade their skills.

Major events held in 2000 included the Tour of Cuba; ask at your hotel or call the cycling federation (*see p217*) or the velodrome for forthcoming events.

Cubans are bats about baseball. *See p215.*

Velodromo Reinaldo Paseiro
Avenida Monumental Km 4, Villa Panamericana, Habana del Este (information 973776). **Open** 8am-6pm Mon-Fri; closed Sat, Sun. **Tickets** usually $1.

Martial arts

In addition to its success in boxing, Cuba has achieved impressive results in the martial arts, taking home six judo medals, five wrestling medals and two tae kwon do medals from the Sydney Olympic Games in 2000.

In Havana, you can watch martial arts at the **Sala Polivalente 'Kid Chocolate'** (*see above*) or the **Sala Polivalente Ramón Fonst** (*see p213*). Recent events, though, have taken place at the **Sala San Isidro**.

Sala San Isidro
Calle San Isidro, La Habana Vieja (676069). **Open** 8am-6pm Mon-Fri; closed Sat, Sun. **Tickets** $1. **Map** p316 F14/15.

Rodeo

Rodeos are held twice a month on Sundays at the stadium in **Parque Lenin** throughout the year. There are also fairs featuring rodeo action in the park in July, November and February.

The lively **Feria Agropecuaria de Boyeros** (Boyero Cattle Fair), very close to Havana's José Martí Airport, holds rodeos once a month. There are no fixed dates, so call and ask for Beatriz Sosa (who speaks English) to find out when the next one is on. Parking can be tricky but there is always space at the Mexican-style school across the road. The highlight of the year is the International Cattle Fair in February, when the place buzzes with business and entertainment (*see p122*).

Arts & Entertainment

Playing the field

Baseball is widely acknowledged to be Cuba's national pastime, but in practice, it amounts to a national obsession. For those fed up with the current noisome pro sports' commercialism, a visit to a Cuban ballpark during the Cuban league (Serie Nacional de Béisbol) in mid-winter or for the post-season series in late April and May represents a relaxing escape into baseball's innocent past.

Forget the usual scene: here there's no luxury box opulence, no mammoth electronic scoreboards, no pricey parking lots and no plastic-grass outfields. And definitely no spoiled-rotten, poorly motivated million-dollar ballplayers.

Anywhere you go in Cuba, you'll find that the diamond action remains astonishingly pure. The off-the-field distractions are minimal, leaving the game to thrive at its own pace and move to its own rhythms. Ballplayers still compete because of their bold passion for the game rather than any craving for the lucre. Teams in the national league represent geographic regions; players play for the province in which they live and are never sold to another team (Havana province is unusual, though, in having two teams, both under the same baseball commission).

Baseball was introduced to Cuba in the 1860s when American sailors used to tantalise Cuban longshoremen in Matanzas with the new sport. It was at this time that Nemesio and Ernesto Guillot brought back Alexander Cartwright's rules to the game after a trip to America.

However, it was Steve Bellan, Latin America's first ballplayer in the Major Leagues in the USA in the 19th century, who arranged the first official game in Cuba, on 27 December, 1874, between teams from Matanzas and Havana. The game took place on a field known as Palmar de Junco in Matanzas, which had been hastily fixed up for the occasion, and Bellan's Havana team overpowered its neighbours 51-9. There's still an old, battered ballpark on the site of this fateful game, still in use today, and the Matanzas local authorities are pushing to build a Cuban Baseball Hall of Fame here, though not without a fight from the Havana authorities.

For the moment though, the huge **Estadio Latinoamericano** (see p213) is the pride of the city and the field on which all Cuban ballplayers aspire to play. Ardent fans allege that players who succeed in the intense, pressure-boiling atmosphere of the 55,000-seater 'Latino' can play anywhere else in the world. And they're right. Nonetheless, there have been several defections to the USA by Cuban ballplayers, such as the internationally renowned Orlando 'El Duque' Hernández, pitching for the New York yankees, and his brother Livan Hernández (San Francisco Giants).

The Serie Nacional season lasts from late October until May, during which time 16 teams play 90 league matches followed by the play-offs. Matches usually take place all over Cuba on Tuesday, Wednesday, Thursday and Saturday at 7.35pm and Sunday at 1.30pm, with a week's recess for the New Year and another before the all-star game (a two-day friendly) between East and West in the middle of the season. Tickets for all matches cost between one and three pesos, and the same in dollars for foreigners.

Feria Agropecuaria
Avenida de la Independencia (Rancho Boyeros) #31108, Boyeros (06 834536). **Open** 10am-10pm daily. **Admission** $5. **Tickets** vary.

Parque Lenin
Calle 100, esquina a Cortina de la Presa, Arroyo Naranjo (443026). **Open** 9am-5.30pm Wed-Sun; closed Mon, Tue except in summer. **Tickets** vary.

Soccer

Football, the most universal of sports, is not a strong discipline in Cuba. The national team doesn't compare favourably with other Caribbean teams, let alone with the South American masters of the game, and has never made it past the preliminary qualifying matches of the World Cup. This lack of success is frustrating for a demanding Cuban public, eager to see their 11 do better. Nevertheless, fans follow every major international tournament on TV, regardless of whether the national team is taking part.

The Havana team, Ciudad Habana, nicknamed Los Rojos ('the Reds'), has improved over the years and in the 2000 season it faced Pinar del Río at home. Though the Reds lost, the fans had been given a taster of high-level football and can only expect more in the future. Games in Havana are held at the **Estadio Pedro Marrero**.

Lords of the ring

Of the 57 gold medals Cuba has won at the Olympic Games in the last century, nearly half of them have come from the boxing ring. If this statistic does not pack enough of a punch, consider that apart from in 1984 and 1988, when it did not compete, Cuba has been the overall champion of the Olympic boxing competition at every Games since 1972 – a super-heavyweight achievement by anyone's standards.

Boxing came to Cuba via the USA at the turn of the 19th century and in 1910 it became a national sport with the creation of a boxing commission. The same year saw the birth of Eligio Sardiñas, better known as 'Kid Chocolate', who became one of Cuba's sporting heroes. Sardiñas won two world titles during his ten-year career (1928-1938) and was instrumental in the promotion of boxing at home and abroad. He is still considered the greatest Cuban boxer of all time.

Sardiñas' achievements were followed by the success of other Cubans such as Gerardo 'Kid Gavilan' González, Urtiminio Ramos, Benny 'Kid' Paret and 'Mantequilla' Napoles, who all won professional world titles in their respective weights during the 1940s and '50s.

After the abolition of professional sport on the island in 1961, Cuba concentrated its attention on amateur boxing, starting a period of development that would see its fighters

dominate all International Amateur Boxing Association tournaments. Cuban boxers made their Olympic debut in Rome in 1960, but their first success didn't come until Mexico '68, when Enrique Regüeiferos and Rolando Garbey won silver medals in their respective categories.

Four years later in Munich, Cuba won the overall boxing competition for the first time, with golds for Orlando Martínez, Emilio Correa and the legendary Teófilo Stevenson. Stevenson went on to win three successive Olympic crowns, by repeating his unbeatable performance in Montreal and Moscow in '76 and '82. He also won the world titles in Havana (1974), Belgrade (1978) and Reno (1986).

But the Cuban boxing hall of fame doesn't end there – it includes many other impressive names, not least five-times world champion and three-times Olympic gold medallist Felix Savón and three-times super-heavyweight world champion and Olympic gold medallist Roberto Balado. And other names you might recognise are José Gómez, Ariel Hernández, Jorge Hernández, Juan Bautista Hernández, Angel Herrera, Juan Carlos Lemus, Rogelio Marcelo, Armando Martínez, Maikro Romero and Hector Vinent. And Cuban boxing's glory days aren't over yet – as recently as 1998, nine Cubans topped the world's best list.

Estadio Pedro Marrero

Avenida 41 #4409 Marianao, Playa (234698/ 235551/236935). **Matches** 3pm. **Tickets** $1.

Volleyball

Volleyball was quick to develop in Cuba. The national male team rose from nowhere to win the bronze medal at the Olympic Games in Montreal in 1976, while the women's team were crowned world champions two years later, and

have enjoyed continued international success ever since. Called Las Morenas del Caribe (a rough translation: the Wonderful Caribbean Brown Sugars), the women's team is considered by many to be the world's all-time best. It holds every major international title and won the Olympic title for the fourth time at the 2000 Games in Sydney.

Unfortunately, except during an international tournament, Cubans very rarely get to see such a prodigious team play at

Arts & Entertainment

home, but they do pack the **Coliseo de la Ciudad Deportiva** (*see p213*) to admire the men's team in action in the Liga Mundial de Voleibol (World Volleyball League), held every year in spring. For details of the schedule, and for information on tickets, contact the Coliseo or ask at your hotel tourist desk. Sometimes matches are held at the **Sala Polivalente Ramón Fonst** (*see p213*); for details call the Sala or the **Volleyball Federation** (*see p213*).

Active sports

Although they are not up to North American or European standards, public sports facilities in Havana are plentiful. The largest is the **Panamericano** complex to the east of the city (*see p114*). Visitors can also pay to use **Club Habana**, a private members' club on the coast to the west of the city, where facilities include tennis courts, a driving range for golf practice, a large swimming pool, a lovely beach, yacht hire, scuba diving excursions and other watersport facilities. *See also p104*. In addition, many upscale hotels offer a variety of sports and fitness facilities, some of which can be used by non guests.

Club Habana
Avenida 5ta, entre 188 y 192 (245700). **Open** 7.30am-10pm Mon-Sat; closed Sun. **Admission** *non-members* $10 Mon-Fri; $15 Sat, Sun; free under-13s.

Bowling

You won't find many ten-pin bowling facilities in Havana. Hit by the economic crisis of the 1990s, the main centre, constructed for the Pan-American Games, is in a distressingly run-down state. If you're desperate for some bowling action, you can pay $2.50 per game for use of the three ten-pin lanes at the **Havana Golf Club** (*see p218*) or take shots at the pins at bowling alleys in several hotels, such as **El Bosque** and **Kohly**. The Kohly charges $2 per person per game and also has billiard tables (billar) for $5 per hour. More demanding bowling lovers, however, should forget about Havana altogether and head straight for the far more upscale facilities at the **Bolera Varadero**.

Cycling

During the petrol shortages of the worst days of the Special Period, bikes became a necessity in Cuba and today Havana's streets are full of cyclists. Cycling is promoted by some companies as the most ecologically sound method of transport, by others simply as a

healthy way of getting around. If you fancy getting out of the city, contact the **Club Nacional de Cicloturismo Gran Caribe**, which organises cycling trips in the surrounding countryside, and also promotes ecological bike tours. For more information on cycling in Havana, including details of bicycle hire and repair services, *see p277*.

Club Nacional de Cicloturismo Gran Caribe
Information: Rumbos, Lonja del Comercio, Calle Amargura #2, esquina a Oficios, La Habana Vieja (669954/669908). **Open** 9am-5pm Mon-Fri; closed Sat, Sun. **Map** p316 E15.

Fishing

Want to follow in the footsteps of Ernest Hemingway? Sport fishing fanatics flock to Cuba to try their luck with the huge number of game fish that swim the Gulf Stream just off the coast of Havana. The country hosts numerous major fishing competitions, the most famous of which is the Ernest Hemingway International Marlin Tournament held annually in May or June, when marlin are running close to the shore. In 2000, more than 200 competitors from various nations entered the tournament. Other important international competitions include the Currican Tournament in April and the Blue Marlin Tournament in August or September.

For information, contact Commodore Escrich at his office at the Club Náutico Internacional Hemingway at Marina Hemingway either in person or by phone (246653/241689).

You can charter a boat for sport fishing at all times of year from **Marina Hemingway** (*see p219*) and **Marina Puertosol Tarará** (*see p219*), both of which also offer many other facilities.

If you prefer to fish in the peaceful waters of lakes, reservoirs or rivers, the **Agencia de Viajes Horizontes** tourist agency or at the tourist desk of a major hotel; they should be able to give you details of excursions to rich inland fishing spots such as Maspotón in Pinar del Rio province; the Laguna del Tesoro (Treasure Pond) in Ciénega de Zapata, and Yarigua in Cienfuegos.

However, the most typical way to fish *habanero* style is to bring your rod, line and hooks; arm yourself with bait and find yourself a spot on the Malecón for hours of fishing side by side with the locals.

Agencia Viajes Horizontes
Calle 23 #156, entre N y O, Vedado (662161/ 662160/662004/www.horizontes.cu). **Open** 8am-5.30pm Mon-Fri; closed Sat, Sun. **Map** p312 B12.

Arts & Entertainment

Go-karting

Although there's no Formula One or Indy Car racing tracks in Havana, budding Schumachers can satisfy their need for speed at the Kartadromo Cocomar, 25 kilometres (15 miles) west of downtown. It's the country's top karting circuit, and the place where top international drivers from Europe can be seen in action.

Kartadromo Cocomar

Villa Cocomar, Carretera Panamericana Km 23. Caimito (no phone). **Open** 9am-5pm Mon-Fri; closed Sat, Sun.

Golf

Cuba boasts one excellent golf course and two good ones. The best is the 18-hole **Varadero Golf Club**; two others within reach of Havana are the **Havana Golf Club**, a 20-minute drive from downtown, near Boyeros. The club consists of a nine-hole course (a second set of holes is due to open in 2001), plus tennis courts (*see p220*), a pool, bowling alley (*see p217*), bar and restaurant. There is also a practice range at the **Club Habana** complex (*see p104*), which can be used by visitors on payment of the daily admission charge.

Havana Golf Club

Calzada de Vento Km 8, Capdevila, Boyeros (558746/558747/338918/338919). **Open** 8.30am-8pm daily. **Fees** *Non-members* $20 for 9 holes; $30 for 18 holes. *Club hire* $10. *Caddie hire* $3 for 9 holes. *Lessons* $5 per 30mins.

Horseriding

The **Centro Ecuestre**, also known as the Club Hipico, offers riding lessons and pony rides in the expansive, grassy surroundings of Parque Lenin. Riding lessons are also available at the **Feria Agropecuaria de Boyeros** (*see p122*). If you're in Playas del Este, ask at the Hotel Club Atlántico (*see p59*) about hiring a horse.

If you've got small kids in tow, then more leisurely riding is available at **Parque de Anfiteatro** (*see p74*) in La Habana Vieja; alternatively, you can travel in style by hiring a horse and carriage from the rank nearby.

Centro Ecuestre

Parque Lenin, southern Havana (441058). **Open** June-Aug 9am-5pm daily. Sept-July 9am-5pm Wed-Sun; closed Mon, Tue. **Rides** $15 1hr.

Pool/*billares*

You won't find many bars with pool tables in Havana. In fact, the only stand-alone one we know of is the Kasalta sports bar at the corner

Heated discussion of the day's sports events.

of Avenida 5ta and Calle 4 in Miramar (tel. 240403). However, many hotels have now started to install pool tables in their bars and swimming pool snack areas. Rates are generally around $1 per game.

Running

The Comisión Marabana organises a schedule of road races and other competitive events throughout the year to celebrate special occasions in the Cuban national calendar. Key running events include the International Terry Fox Race (five kilometres/three miles) every February, which raises funds for cancer research; the Ultra Marabana (98 kilometres/62 miles in April); the Mother's Day Race (five kilometres) and the Clásico Internacional Hemingway race (ten kilometres/six miles) in May; the Olympic Day Mini Marathon (four kilometres/2.5 miles) in June; and the Marabana (Havana Marathon) in November. Contact the Comisión Marabana for more information about these events.

Serious runners can use the track at the **Estadio Panamericano**, but a far more pleasant way to stretch your legs is to follow the Malecón around the bay for a scenic early-morning or early-evening jog, when the heat is more bearable and the sea breezes offer some comfort (watch out for the potholes). **Parque Lenin** (*see p121*) to the south of the city is another attractive place for jogging.

Comisión Marabana

Ciudad Deportiva, Vía Blanca, esquina a Avenida Boyeros, Apartado 5130 (545022).

Estadio Panamericano
Carretera Vieja de Cojímar, esquina a Doble Vía,
Habana del Este (974140). **Open** 8.30am-5.30pm
Mon-Sat; closed Sun. **Admission** $1.

Sailing & boating

Marina Hemingway is Cuba's most established
marina and offers mooring for up to 100 yachts
in four parallel, six-metre-deep, specially
designed waterways that are protected against
strong waves and currents. Services include
electricity hook-ups, weather reports and boat
repairs. Boat-owners who are planning to
moor their vessels at the Marina needn't make
reservations (though it's always best to do so
because, occasionally, the Marina is too packed
to accept any more boats). Arriving vessels
should call the Marina's control tower on
VHF16 or VHF72 to announce their arrival.
The Marina authorities organise an
international sailing regatta, the Regata
Corona Internacional, which is usually held
in June . Yachts and motorboats can be rented
out from Náutica Puerto y Marlin at the
marina; rates range from $260 to $340
according to the type of boat hired.

There are also other services available,
such as sailing and boat rides along the
shore (these cost around $22 an hour), and
trips out on the *Gitana* boat, for $60 including
snorkelling, swimming and fishing, with
lunch included (a similar deal on a smaller
boat will cost $45).

To the east of the city, **Marina Puertosol
Tarará** has 50 berths (1.5 metres deep) each
with water and electricity hook-ups. Although
the facilities are not as good as those at the
Marina Hemingway, the surroundings are
nicer. Radio your arrival on VHF77. The
Marina Puertosol is the headquarters of the
international **Puertosol** tourism group,
whose administrative offices are located in
the Edificio Focsa (Calle 17, esquina a M,
Vedado; 334705), and provides a variety of
vessels for hire, including live-in motorboats
(from $2,100 per week).

Yachts can be rented by the day ($250) and
there are Hobiecat dinghies and pedal boats
available for exploring the marina and the
beach ($4 for 30mins). Guided yacht 'seafaris'
depart from the Marina at 9.30am and cost $50
each for a minimum of four passengers,
including fishing, snorkelling and lunch.

Marina Hemingway
*Calle 248, esquina a 5ta, Santa Fe (241149/Náutico
Puerto y Marlin 246848/297928/297270).*

Marina Puertosol Tarará
Vía Blanca Km 19, Playa Tarará (971462).

Scuba diving

Cuba's crystal blue waters and beautiful coral
reefs are among its main attractions, enticing
divers from across the world to explore a
kaleidoscopic world of wonderful colours
and abundant marine life. Among the tour
operators, **Puertosol** and **Horizontes**
offer attractive packages at good prices. Try
also **Club Habana** (*see p104*). However, most
deals involve excursions to sites a good distance
from Havana, such as Pinar del Rio province
and the Isla de la Juventud, in particular El
Colony, where world diving champion Deborah
Andollo practises.

Luckily for visitors based in Havana, there
are also some diving opportunities close to the
city itself. Shipwrecks can be explored off the
Barlovento shore to the west of Havana, where
the Atlantic and Gulf Stream currents intersect,
or at a series of dive sites known as the 'Blue
Circuit' (Circuito Azul), which extends east from
Bacuranao to the Playas del Este. (The western
beach at Tarará is a particularly worthwhile
spot for diving and snorkelling.) This section of
coastline boasts deliciously warm water and
rich marine life (*see pp114-115*).

Depending on which package you opt for,
excursions can include two daylight dives, boat
hire, tanks, weights and a diving instructor.
Equipment is good quality and instructors are
trained to international standards. To take part
in a diving trip, all divers require an
international scuba licence. Lessons and
initiation dives for beginners are also available.

Centro de Buceo 'La Aguja'
Avenida 5ta, esquina a 248, Santa Fé (246848).
Open 10am-4pm daily; dives at 10.30am and some
afternoons. **Rates** vary.

Buceo Marina Puertosol
*Calle 7ma, entre 3ra y Cobre, Tarará, Habana del
Este (971501 ext.239/971462/971414).* **Open** 9am-
5pm Mon-Fri; closed Sat, Sun.

Swimming

In the blistering heat and exhausting humidity
of a Havana day, you'll be glad that some hotels
have swimming pools that are open to the
public as well as hotel guests. For a list of the
best, *see p60* **Best hotel pools**.

Visitors can also make use of the facilities at
Club Habana (*see p104*). The large, well-
maintained pool and stretch of beautiful beach
at this private members' club offer some of the
best swimming in the city. Other alternatives
include the Centro Turístico La Giraldilla,
which has an attractive pool and a good café,
and the pool at Marina Hemingway.

If you prefer salt water to chlorine head, east to Playa Bacuranao and the Playas del Este (see pp114-115), where you'll find white sand, warm water and plenty of facilities at Marina Puertosol Tarará (see p219). This is also a good place for snorkelling and a wide variety of other watersports, but watch out for strong currents.

A word of warning: do not be tempted to join the local kids who swim in the sea off the Malecón; the water is badly polluted here and there are sharp rocks beneath the surface.

Centro Turístico La Giraldilla

Calle 222, esquina a 39, La Coronela, La Lisa (246062). **Open** 11am-7pm daily. **Admission** $5; $2 concessions; free under-6s.

Tennis & squash

Cuba is now pushing to develop tennis at a professional level, with national players entering the America group of the Davis Cup circuit. The Cuban tennis team train at the six tennis courts (*canchas del tenis*) at the Complejo Panamericano in eastern Havana, built for the Pan-Am Games in '91. These courts are also available for hire and provide training lessons and arrange exchange matches between Cuban players and foreign tennis clubs. The **Tennis Federation** (see p212) can also help coordinate accommodation and transportation at decent rates.

Club Habana (see p104) has tennis and squash courts, which can be used by non-members on payment of the daily admission fee. Alternatively, head out to the the **Havana Golf Club**), which has five tennis courts and hosts the second leg of the Torneo Satélite Cuba-México (Cuba-Mexico Satellite Tennis Tournament) each February. The courts can be hired between 8.30am and 8pm daily for $2 per hour. (Rackets and balls are not available.)

The following hotels have tennis and/or squash courts that can be used by non-guests; contact the hotels directly for details of rates: **Copacabana** (squash; see p59); **Meliá Habana** (tennis; see p58); **Nacional** (tennis; see p56); **Novotel Miramar** (squash & tennis; see p59); **Copacabana** (squash and tennis); Kohly (tennis); **Canchas del Tenis del Complejo Panamericano** (contact Julito or Lugo at the Tennis Federation; see p212).

Watersports

In addition to sailing, diving and snorkelling, the coast near Havana has facilities for other watersports such as jetskiing, kayaking and water-skiing. Try **Club Habana** (see p104), **Marina Hemingway** (see p219), **Marina Puertosol Tarará** (see p219) and the hotels in Playas del Este.

Fitness

To find out whether a hotel has a gym and health club on the premises, contact the hotel directly or check the list of hotel services given for every hotel in our **Accommodation** chapter (see pp48-60).

Outside the newer tourist hotels, Havana has plenty of gyms and sports centres that offer fitness classes at reasonable rates. Cuban fitness instructors are generally highly trained and the facilities are usually well equipped, although they may not have the most modern, state-of-the-art gear. Try to take a tour of the gym and get a free work-out before you sign up.

Club Habana

listings p104.
Gym, sauna, jacuzzi.

Gimnasio Integral Bioamérica

Calle 17, esquina a E, Vedado (329087). **Open** 8am-1pm, 2pm-8pm Mon-Sat; closed Sun. **Map** p312 B10.
Gym, aerobics, massages and facials.

Gimnasio Monte

Calle Monte, entre Suárez y Revillagigedo, Centro Habana (617748). **Open** 8am-8pm daily. **Map** p313 E13.
Gym, massage and a range of beauty services.

Gimnasio de la Villa Panamericana

Calle Central, Edificio #20 (972967). **Open** 8am-8pm daily.
Gym, massage and a range of beauty services.

Hotel Golden Tulip Parque Central

Calle Neptuno, entre Martí (Prado) y Agramonte, Centro Habana (606627/606628/606629). **Open** 8am-8pm daily. **Map** p313 D14.
One of the best-equipped gyms in Havana. As well as gym apparatus, fitness instruction and a jacuzzi are available. Use is restricted to hotel guests and members only. *See p53.*

Hotel Kohly

Hotel Kohly, Avenida 49, esquina a 36A, Playa (240240/241474/241619). **Open** 8am-8pm daily. **Map** p311 D6.
Gym, sauna, massage, aerobics, swimming pool and a tennis court.

Hotel Meliá Cohiba

Paseo, esquina a 1ra, Vedado (333636/333952/333956). **Open** 7am-7pm daily. **Map** p312 A9.
The excellent facilities here include a gym, fitness classes, sauna and massage. *See p56.*

Hotel Meliá Habana

Avenida 3ra esquina a 70, Playa (248500). **Open** hours vary. **Map** p310 B1.
Gym, aerobics, massage, sauna, tennis and pool. For hotel guests and members only. *See p58.*

Arts & Entertainment

Beyond Havana

Getting Started

If you need a change of pace from the frenetic streets of Havana, there are many other exciting destinations on the island to discover.

Havana is Cuba's capital city, the seat of government, the urban hub. It has the greatest number of people, music, sports and cultural events, museums, educational and arts centres, recreational activities… but it isn't all of Cuba. In fact, it is nothing like the rest of Cuba. So if you travel to the island and stay only in its capital, you will have seen Havana, but you won't have seen Cuba. For that reason, we urge you to make every effort, after delving into the historic, architectural, political, artistic and natural wonders of Havana, to make sure to also spend some time in the other provinces of the island.

When newcomers to the island venture outside of Havana, they most frequently head west, to the lovely Viñales Valley in Pinar del Río province, or east, to the world-famous Varadero Beach in Matanzas province. While these two are, indeed, significant sights, there are many more, off-the-beaten-track destinations to be discovered.

PRACTICAL INFORMATION

Note that, while we have given phone numbers, opening times and rates for museums, hotels and other places of interest, such information is subject to change. Accommodation at the more popular hotels and lodges can be booked in advance, though it's often worth asking locals for tips on good places to stay and eat once you get there. Tour groups such as Horizontes and Rumbos (see p223 **The chain gang**) are also useful resources.

As with everything else in Cuba, expect the unexpected when it comes to public transport. Petrol shortages can create problems at the last minute, though the Viazul buses, comfortable, air-conditioned and aimed specifically at tourists, are generally more reliable.

Note that Cubans often refer to (for example) Pinar del Río when they mean the province rather than the city.

Travelling around Cuba

By rail

There are daily departures from the central train station in Havana (see p273) to all the major towns in the country. Tickets can be bought in dollars in person at least an hour before your train goes, or before 7pm if you're

leaving at night. Tickets are also available in pesos, but must be booked days (or even weeks) in advance. For details of the electric train between Havana and Matanzas, see p111 **Chocolate choo-choo**.

Estación Central de Ferrocarriles

Avenida de Bélgica (Egido), esquina a Arsenal (information 614259). **Open** *Ticket office* 8am-7pm daily. **Map** p313 F14.

By bus

Tourists are encouraged to use the big **Viazul** coaches which are kitted out with air-conditioning, video screens and refreshments. You pay in dollars but prices are reasonable (eg $5 to Matanzas, $10 to Varadero, $51 to Santiago). The **Astro** company serves the same destinations and will always sell a few dollar seats to foreigners for half to two-thirds of the price, but the old buses are pretty uncomfortable and inclined to break down. You can also pick up Viazul buses where they originate at the terminal in Nuevo Vedado (Avenida 26, esquina a Zoológico, 811413/815652/811108; ticket office open 7am-7pm daily) before going on to the main terminal. For details of Havana's bus station, see p273.

Terminal de Omnibus Nacionales

Avenida de la Independencia (Rancho Boyeros) #101, Plaza de la Revolución (switchboard 709401/Viazul 792456/Astro 703397). **Open** 24hrs daily.

By air

Most domestic flights within Cuba leave from Terminal 1 of José Martí International Airport. **Cubana** (officially Cubana de Aviación) covers many destinations within Cuba, including Cienfuegos, Santiago de Cuba and Varadero. However, its flights, while usually the cheapest available, are prone to delays, and don't provide much in the way of comfort. Its most central office is on La Rampa in Vedado, at Calle 23 #64, esquina a Infanta (334949/334950/4446/9). A generally more expensive but more comfortable option is **Aero Caribbean**, which leaves from Terminal 5, covers Holguín; Santiago de Cuba; Trinidad and Varadero. Its office is at Calle 23, esquina a P, Vedado (797524/797525).

The chain gang

The following state-run tourism companies offer excursions and activities around Cuba, as well as within Havana. In the capital it's generally easy to get around on your own, but for farther-flung destinations such as Ciénaga de Zapata you'd do well to arrange a trip in advance. Many are bookable from Havana.

Asistur

248835/245278/ventas@asistur.get.cma.net.
Asistur was set up in 1991 with the aim of providing assistance to travellers. Among the services it offers are medical care, financial aid, legal help, the issue of new travel documents, airplane and hotel reservations.

Cubamar

662523/4/cubamar@cubamar.mit.cma.net.
Cubamar's objective is to promote youth and nature tourism, providing campsites and specialised villas and nature trails.

Cubanacán

*242976/242974/241656/
secrext@presid.cha.cyt.cu.*
This corporation, founded in 1987, covers 55 hotels, 63 restaurants and coffee shops, three marinas, 13 scuba centres, health tourism facilities and a travel agency.

Gaviota

*66677378/339780/1/
geren_prom@nwgaviot.ga.*
Gaviota runs 2,000 rooms for international tourism, along with marinas, restaurants, coffee shops and recreation centres, and owns a travel agency, a transportation company and a network of shops.

Gran Caribe

240575-82/karinaj@grancaribe.cma.net.
This hotel group, founded in 1994, has 35 hotels, most of which are four- or five-star. It also runs three well-known establishments: the Tropicana cabaret, and La Bodeguita del Medio and El Floridita restaurants.

Habaguanex

*338693/4/gerencia.comercial@
habaguanex.ohch.cu.*
This tourism company belongs to the Havana City Historian's Office, and is charged with promoting this industry in Old Havana. It runs five hotels and inns, as well as a large number of restaurants, coffee shops and stores, plus a travel agency.

Horizontes

334041-2/www.horizontes.cu.
Founded in 1994, Horizontes has 54 hotels (with more than 7,000 rooms) distributed throughout the island, in cities, beach resorts and beautiful natural settings. It also has a travel agency.

Islazul

325152.
Catering largely to the Cuban market (though its facilities also include quotas for foreign visitors), Islazul has 51 hotels and a chain of gastronomic establishments.

Puertosol

245923-6/comerc@psol.cma.net.
This chain of marinas was set up to promote the establishment of watersports, providing docks, yachting and recreation centres. It has six marinas, nine international scuba centres and a floating hotel in the Jardines de la Reina archipelago, south of the main island.

Rumbos

*332694/330669/662113/
presiden@rumnac.rumb.cma.net.*
Has the basic mission of increasing tourism options that aren't administered by the hotels. It operates a large network of restaurants and food services, as well as golf facilities in Cuba. It also has a small number of hotels, the Vaivén tourist buses and a travel agency.

Transtur

338384/webmaster@transtur.com.cu.
The largest tourism transportation company on the island, Transtur offers car rentals, buses and taxis, for which it possesses a broad and diverse fleet of vehicles, including luxury cars, economy cars and family cars. It has reservation centres and sales offices all over the country, as well as in the large hotels.

Pinar del Río Province

Waterfalls, orchid gardens, large mouth bass, limestone *mogotes* and giant murals – the province of the 'pine forest by the river' has got the lot.

The *autopista* A4 runs from Havana through the lush green countryside of Havana province (the area outside the city is designated as a separate province) and into Pinar del Río province, passing fields of growing sugar cane, bananas and corn interspersed with sapphire-blue artificial lakes created by Cuba's new system of irrigation dams and reservoirs. (Some of the lakes are excellent for bass fishing.) Once inside Pinar del Río province (literally 'pine forest by the river'), the first hills and mountains of Sierra del Rosario begin to rise up in the distance, often covered with light cloud. It is not unusual to get caught in a quick rain shower and see a double rainbow when driving through this area.

South of the motorway, in western Havana province you will pass the historic city of **Artemisa**, many of whose citizens gave their lives in the famous attack on the Moncada Barracks (*see p15*). Their spirit still lingers on at the **Museo de Historia** and the **Mausoleo de los Mártires**. Cuban culture abounds here, at the local *casa de la cultura*. While you're here, you might want to stop off at the **Centro Ecuestre** for a spot of horse-riding. If you decide to spend a night here, the town has several small hotels, and there are plenty of restaurants and *paladares* for those who just want to stop and eat.

GETTING THERE BY CAR
The easiest way to get to Pinar del Río province is along the six-lane *autopista* (A4) which ends at the provincial capital, **Pinar del Río**. A more scenic, but less direct route is via the Carretera Central (CC), which heads in the same general direction, but continues beyond Pinar del Río to the **Península de Guanahacabibes**. **Las Terrazas**, **Soroa**, **San Diego de los Baños** and **Viñales** can be reached by turnings off the motorway and the Carretera Central. You can also go on one-day or overnight excursion to **Viñales** and the tobacco areas of Pinar del Río on one of the many tour buses from Havana – ask at your hotel information desk or contact the Havanatur, Rumbos or Cubatur agencies (*see p223*). The Circuito Norte (CN) runs inland along the coast west of Havana. This is the best route to coastal destinations and is an alternative way of getting to Viñales.

Las Terrazas

For those who love the peaceful beauty of natural surroundings, one of the most enchanting spots on the island is just a short distance further along the *autopista*. The community of **Las Terrazas**, nestled in a valley of the Sierra Rosario mountains, takes its livelihood and its name from the terraces that were dug into the hills in a massive reforestation effort in the late 1960s.

The community is of special significance to nature lovers and to those interested in the social and political history of Cuba. It still represents the essence of the Revolution's original ideology to ensure that the social and economic benefits the rebels had fought for reached the poor *campesinos* in the remotest corners of the country. The idea was to convince these small peasant farmers, who usually lived in dirt-floor, thatched-roof *bohíos* with no electricity or indoor plumbing, and no access to education and healthcare, to move closer together, to form small villages or farm cooperatives, so that all these services could be developed.

In the Sierra del Rosario area there was an additional factor at play. Like much of the rest of the island, centuries of tree-cutting by wealthy French colonialist coffee growers and poor peasants eking out a living from the soil had left the area ecologically devastated. To turn this around, the governmental environmentalists proposed terracing the mountainsides and engaging in major reforestation efforts to stop the erosion and restore the ecosystem.

Homes were built for the *campesino* families and also for the workers who came in from other areas to help build the terraces and take part in the reforestation programme. Las Terrazas is now a picturesque village winding along the terraces bordering an artificial lake formed by damming the San Juan River. The community of nearly 1,000 residents is still primarily engaged in reforestation, but for the past decade, the people who came together three decades ago to bring the forests back to life are also running the best and most developed ecotourism project in Cuba. The project

Beyond Havana

is centred around the lovely, elegant **Hotel Moka**, a high-class ecolodge surrounded by the forest overlooking the village.

At the open-air front desk of Moka – where a tree grows right through the roof – you can book hikes and nature walks through the surrounding mountains guided by environmental professionals from the Ecology Resource Centre. The area is now part of a natural park designated as a Biosphere Reserve by UNESCO in 1985.

Here endemic species of flora and fauna prevail in one of the world's few remaining tropical mountain rainforests. The world's smallest frog –about the size of a thumbnail – and the world's smallest hummingbird can be seen here, along with Cuba's national bird, the red, white and blue Cuban trogon (*tocororo* in Spanish), and an abundance of ferns, flowers and trees.

Alternatively, you may prefer to go on bike or horseback, both of which you can also arrange at the desk. Other organised excursions include visiting the nearby resort of **Soroa** (*see below*), or taking a guided tour of **Viñales** (*see p228*) or **Cayo Levisa** (*see p229*), off the Pinar del Río coast. But you don't have to wander far from Moka to enjoy one of Pinar del Río's greatest delights: bathing in the cascades of **Río San Juan**, where the water rushing over the rocks provides a hydro-massage for those who swim in the natural pools carved out by the river.

When they are not tramping through the landscape, visitors can enjoy a number of tourist-oriented home enterprises that have sprung up in Las Terrazas recently, including *paladares* (*see below*), painting and silk screen studios; and wood, ceramics and recycled papercraft workshops.

A worthwhile side trip from Las Terrazas (via the road near the entrance to the protected areas of the Biosphere Reserve) takes you to **Buena Vista**, restored from the ruins of one of the many coffee plantations built and later abandoned by French colonists. The manor house is located on the highest point of the narrowest stretch of the island, and offers breathtaking views across 51 kilometres (32 miles) of forested hills north to the Atlantic Ocean and south to the Caribbean Sea.

The panorama more than justifies the name of the plantation Buena Vista, or 'good view'. History buffs will relish the chance to see what life was like in these old plantations; everything from the old-fashioned kitchen to the walls of the slave quarters, and the old coffee grinding and drying areas, have been carefully preserved and restored.

Where to stay & eat

The accommodation of choice in Las Terrazas is **Hotel Moka** (082 335516/240553/comercial @terraz.get.cma.net). Advance reservations and tour bookings can be made by telephone or email. The hotel also provides meals. Alternatively, the community has several excellent eateries (ask for recommendations when you get here), which charge about $10 to $13 for a full meal. **La Fondita de Mercedes**, is perhaps the pick of the bunch, dishing up typical Cuban meals of fish, pork or chicken. The food is served on the patio, which affords a lovely view over the green hills and red-tiled rooftops of the Las Terrazas. The hotel can make reservations for you, or you can stop by during the day to choose your meal and tell Mercedes what time you want to eat.

Nearby **Casa del Campesino** provides a more elaborate version of Mercedes' home-cooked meal in an original country setting, with animals wandering in the yard. At the foot of the stone stairway leading down from the Hotel Moka is the **Café de María**. Although it only serves coffee, it is well worth a visit to hear the tales of the tiny, smiling grey-haired proprietress, who remembers lugging buckets of water for miles over the hillsides to cook and clean for her family in the old days.

At **Buena Vista**, one of the colonial buildings has been restored and converted into a restaurant. It only serves lunch, and you must make reservations through Hotel Moka.

Soroa

Eighty kilometres (50 miles) west of Havana and a short distance from Las Terrazas is Cuba's well-known Soroa resort. Long famed for its scenic waterfall and extensive orchid gardens, Soroa has always been high on the list for those who like to get away from the city without having to go too far. As well as the chance to stay in the wonderful surroundings of hills, forests and brooks, the resort offers guided walks in the area.

From the resort, a trail leads over the narrow river and winds down to the base of the **Arco Iris** (rainbow) waterfall. The trail passes the nesting areas of the *tocororo*, Cuba's national bird, and offers impressive views of the valley and sea beyond. The steepest part of the descent has stone steps dug into the hillside; once you get to the bottom you can swim in the natural pools at the base of the waterfall. Other walks lead to the village of Soroa, the ruins of a French colonial coffee plantation, a lookout point with a breathtaking view of the valley, and to a

Beyond Havana

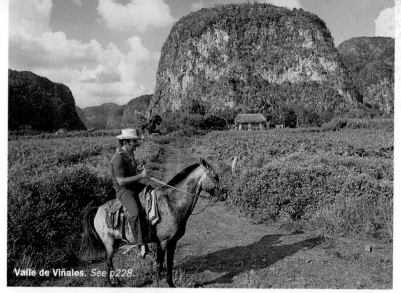
Valle de Viñales. See p228.

hidden pool in the woods known as Pocetas del amor (lovers' pool). You can also go on guided birdwatching tours, or horseback riding to a local *campesino* community.

Legend has it that the **orchid garden** at Soroa was started by Tomás Camacho, who constructed a hillside house and garden for his young daughter. Later, Camacho enlarged the garden, dedicating it to the memory of his wife and/or daughter (depending which version of the story you believe), and began importing hundreds of varieties of orchids from all over the world. The garden now shelters 700 varieties of orchid, 200 of which are indigenous.

The settlement itself was founded by Jean Pierre (or possibly Jean-Paul) Soroa. He was one of the many French coffee growers who fled the 19th-century rebellion in Haiti to settle in Pinar del Río, believing this wooded, mountainous region would provide a safe haven for the lucrative coffee trade. Several of the elegant old homes in this cluster of wooded hills, including the original Soroa mansion, are now rented out to tourists.

Where to stay & eat

Visitors to the **Soroa** resort stay in more-than-comfortable, air-conditioned cabins with a fresh-water swimming pool. Other accommodation is provided in converted colonial houses and in more conventional motel-like singles and duplexes on grassy slopes that surround the pool. Facilities include a money-changing service, fax, medical post and a well-stocked, air-conditioned store that sells packaged food and beverages, snacks, rum and

cigars, as well as clothes, shoes, toiletries and sundries. There is also a campsite, **La Caridad**, in the woods nearby. Protection from the often wet elements is provided by small concrete cabins spread among the trees.

For more information on the resort and community of Soroa, contact **Horizontes** in Havana (*see p223*) or locally (tel. 085 2122/085 2040/085 78218).

Further west

Further into Pinar del Río, 130 kilometres (80 miles) west of Havana, is **San Diego de los Baños**. For generations, Cubans have visited the healing thermal waters of this natural spa to ease the pain of arthritis and rheumatism and cure various skin diseases. The story goes that a slave who had been driven out of his master's plantation because he had leprosy happened to bathe in the mineral springs here and was cured. People began seeking the curative effects of the water, and a small town grew up around the springs. In 1891 the Spanish set up a spa under medical supervision.

In the 1980s, Servimed, which promotes health tourism in Cuba, took over the spa and developed it into a health tourism resort. The waters, with temperatures between 30 and 40 degrees Celsius (86° to 104° Farenheit), contain calcium, sulphides, sulphates, magnesium and fluoride. The mud at the mouth of the rivers is used for both medicinal and beauty treatments at the Spa. Other treatments include massage, hydromassage, acupuncture and healing walks through the natural beauty of the surrounding forests.

Heading west from San Diego is **Parque La Güira**, formerly part of a colonial estate belonging to a wealthy attorney named José Manuel Cortina. His mansion and sculpted garden have been preserved as a public museum containing original tapestries, statues, porcelain and other furnishings. Surrounding the mansion are a Japanese garden, a formal sculpted garden, and a Cuban garden filled with butterfly jasmine. The garden attracts a variety of birds and the small native deer, while the stream, ponds and lakes contain large mouth bass and carp.

At the northern edge of the park, 16 kilometres (ten miles) from Carretera Central, you can visit the **Cueva de Los Portales**, a cave that acted as the headquarters for Cuba's western army under the command of Che Guevara during the 1962 Missile Crisis (known in Cuba as the *Crisis de Octubre*; *see p236*). While Los Portales is the most visited cave, others in the area are believed to have provided shelter for the *cimarrones* (escaped slaves) during the colonial era.

Where to stay & eat

Balneario San Diego (tel. 37812), has air-conditioned rooms with satellite TV, a buffet-style restaurant, snack bar and cafeteria. There is modest accommodation at **La Güira** and at **Cueva de los Portales**. Other small hotels in the area are reserved for Cubans.

Pinar del Río

Although Las Terrazas and the Valle de Viñales are the best-known attractions of Pinar del Río province, the capital does have its own points of interest. Despite being only 186 kilometres (100 miles) south-west of Havana, Pinar del Río still seems more like a sleepy provincial town than a bustling provincial capital with a population of over 124,000. One of the last of the major cities founded in Cuba (1669), it still bears the marks of colonial architecture and Spanish design. Efforts to modernise the city in the last 40 years have resulted in a number of new schools, a university, sporting facilities, and modern medical services. The town also has a post office, book stores, a library, theatre and a number of museums.

The **Museo de Ciencias Naturales Sandalio de Noda** (Calle Martí Este #202, esquina a Avenida Pinares) features natural history exhibits ranging from replicas of dinosaurs to examples of local flora and fauna. The **Museo de Historia Provincial** further down the same street, at #58 (between Colón and Isabel Rubío) displays the history of the province from the indigenous period to the present, with paintings, furniture and other objects typical of distinctive periods. The **Casa de Antonio Guiteras Holmes**, at Calle Maceo Oeste #52 serves as a mini-museum, highlighting the life of this revolutionary figure from the 1930s.

Dos Hermanas mural. *See p228.*

Beyond Havana

Getting there

The quickest way to reach Pinar del Río is by **car**. If you don't have your own transport, a private driver from Havana (check first he has the correct insurance) will take you for around $25 one way.

The **bus** journey from Havana takes three hours 30 minutes with Astro and costs $7 (three departures daily). Viazul buses make the journey once a day and charge $11. The bus station in Pinar del Río is on Calle Adela Azcuy (082 3891), one block north of Calle José Martí.

Pinar del Río **train** station (tel. 082 5734) is at the corner of Calle Ferrocarril and Avenida Pinares Sur. There are trains from Havana every other day; the journey takes five to six hours and costs $6.50.

Where to stay & eat

The imaginatively named **Hotel Pinar del Río** offers accommodation and restaurant meals. If you're not staying there, your best bet for food is **Rumayor**, one kilometre north of the city, just off the main road to Viñales (241). *Paladares* abound, but they come and go, so it's best to ask the local population for recommendations when you are there.

Valle de Viñales

The stunning landscape around the Valle de Viñales is characterised by unique tree-covered limestone hillocks called *mogotes*, and fields of tobacco plants (called *vegas*) dotted with large, tent-shaped thatched sheds for curing tobacco. If you decide to stop for a closer look, most of the local tobacco growers will be happy to show you around, explain the process of growing and curing the various leaves that form the inner and outer parts of Cuba's world-famous cigars. If you hope to buy some cut-rate cigars, however, you will probably be out of luck. These farmers all have iron-clad contracts with the major cigar companies and, although you may get a puff or a gift of a cigar, you are unlikely to walk away with a whole box. Luckily, discount cigars can be picked up at the tobacco drying point (*secadero*) near the roadside restaurant **La Casa del Veguero**. Visitors are welcome for lunch at the restaurant and to visit the *secadero*. (*See also below.*)

The town and valley of Viñales are set amidst the **Sierra de los Órganos**, the mountain range just west of Sierra del Rosario. Created about a hundred million years ago, the limestone bedrock has been carved out over the millennia by underground rivers to create vast caverns. Although the vast limestone *mogotes* look solid from a distance, they are often riddled with rivers and caverns, which intrepid travellers can explore.

The valley itself is most often portrayed as it is seen from the high lookout point at **Hotel Los Jazmines**, and that is probably where a tour bus will first take you. While the view from Los Jazmines is undeniably breathtaking, and provides excellent photo opportunities, it has become quite touristy. The roofed lookout point is now filled with tables selling souvenirs, ranging from wood carvings to T-shirts and CDs of Cuban music.

A drive or hike through the valley itself is recommended for those who are really interested in communing with nature here. Good walking and climbing shoes are recommended, especially if you decide to scale one of the limestone *mogotes*. The most famous *mogote* in the area is **Dos Hermanas**, located five kilometres (three miles) west of Viñales town.

The cliff face is painted with a vast mural (**Mural de la Prehistoria**) tracing the evolutionary process of the region. The mural depicts prehistoric ammonites, a marine monster, the huge mammary rodent known as *Megalocnus rodens*, and an image of the early Guyano Indians who first inhabited this area. The mural was commissioned by Che Guevara and created in 1961 by Cuban painter Leovigildo González, a disciple of the great Mexican muralist Diego Rivera. The original was largely washed away by rain and faded by the sun, and was finally restored in lurid colours by scientists and painters from the National Academy of Sciences. Unfortunately the strident paintwork of the new mural jars with the beauty of the natural surroundings. A small restaurant is located opposite the mural, and guides and horses are available for those who want to explore the area.

There are more painted decorations in the **Cueva de los Indios**, five kilometres (three miles) north of the town. This fascinating cave takes its name from the remains of the indigenous inhabitants that were found here. The first part of the cave with its vaulted interior can be explored on foot, but for three kilometres you are guided in a boat along the subterranean river, past intriguing rock formations – a truly atmospheric, underworld experience.

Nearby, the **Cueva de San Miguel** has been converted into the extraordinary **Disco-bar Cuevas de Viñales**, which features a small bar and a nightly show. Before the bright lights and big beats, however, the cave supported both an indigenous population

Beyond Havana

and an escaped slave community. Guided visits can be arranged during the day.

Often forgotten in a tour of Viñales is the town itself, which is a shame, since the settlement, founded in 1875, is a charming place. The **Museo Municipale** (municipal museum) at Calle Salvador Cisneros #115, is housed in the former home of independence heroine Adela Azcuy (1861-1914). An old mansion next to the colonial-style church on one side of the small town square is now the village's *casa de la cultura*, where a variety of free cultural activities take place throughout the year.

Getting there

By **car** from Pinar del Río, take the 241 to Viñales. If you're travelling directly from Havana, Astro and Viazul both run a daily **bus** service to Viñales ($8 and $12 respectively). There is no bus station in Viñales, but the ticket office is at Calle Salvador Cisneros #63A in the main square.

Where to stay & eat

Hotel Los Jazmines (tel. 08 93205/93206) is the best known accommodation in the area and therefore the most touristy. Set above the valley, it offers a picture-postcard view of the *mogotes* and the distant surrounding mountains, which can be seen from the outdoor swimming pool and most of the rooms. Walking tours and horseback riding are available from the hotel.

Hotel La Ermita (tel. 08 93204) is located on another hilltop to the east of the valley. The view from here is broader and becomes breathtaking at sunrise and sunset, when mist covers the mountain peaks and settles in the valley. This modern hotel has tennis courts, and is within easy walking distance of the town.

Seven kilometres (4.5 miles) north of Viñales town, near the Cueva de los Indios is the **Hotel Rancho San Vicente** (tel. 08 93201), which offers small cabins surrounding a large lawn. The five individual thermal pools with sulphurous water and on-site massage treatments provide an additional attraction.

Close to Dos Hermanas is a campsite run by Cubamar (tel. 089 3223), which has two- and four-bed cabins, a swimming pool and restaurant, and offers horseback riding, trekking and guided tours.

Cayo Levisa

The road north of Viñales takes you through lush landscapes and beautiful vistas out to the coastal fishing village of **La Esperanza**. From here you can catch the ferry to **Cayo Levisa**, a

small island some 40 minutes off the coast. (If you're coming from Havana, follow the Circuit Norte through Bahia Honda and La Palma, before turning off towards the coast. There is another boat to Cayo Levisa from the coastguard station at Palma Rubia.) With some of the best beaches in Pinar del Río, and a lobster lunch provided as an additional enticement, Cayo Levisa is in great demand even by those who aren't after the snorkelling and scuba diving. For those interested in taking greater advantage of this small coral key in the Gulf of Mexico, the island has a small hotel of the same name, run by **Horizontes** (tel. 666075). Contact Horizontes in Havana for reservations (*see p223* **The chain gang**).

Península Guanahacabibes & the keys

At the western tip of the island, the Guanahacabibes nature area has been designated as one of Cuba's six Biosphere Reserves by UNESCO. The area has an abundance of birds and other wildlife (including zillions of mosquitos), and there is excellent snorkelling and scuba diving at several points along the coast. Boat trips out to the keys offer visitors the chance to see crocodiles, tortoises and other creatures. Just watch out for fast-appearing cloudbursts in the late afternoon.

María La Gorda, on the far western tip of the island, has often been described as a divers' paradise. At the opposite end of the scale from Varadero's bustling beaches, Maria La Gorda is sought after not only because of the amazing diversity of sea life in the surrounding reefs, but also for its quiet isolation. It is small and relatively untouristed – and the locals intend to keep it that way. Divers have no hesitation in driving the five hours from Havana to reach this pristine destination, and enjoy the informal, relaxed atmosphere and the warm climate.

If there are non-divers in your group, or you want to diversify your activities, you can take guided walks through the area (all part of the biosphere reserve) with very friendly *campesino* guides and tour workers, all of whom are from the local area. Many only speak Spanish, but their warmth will overcome any language barriers. Watch out for the crocodiles and biting insects, though.

Where to stay & eat

There are 35 modest single-room *cabanas* on the beach at **María del Gorda**. If you arrive and there are none available, you can rent a tent or sleep in a hammock on the beach.

Matanzas Province

An area of exceptional natural beauty, home to lagoons, turtles, white sand beaches, the Bay of Pigs and the all-conquering tourist dollar.

Varadero

After Havana, the most visited spot in Cuba is the world-class **Varadero Beach**. And with good cause. This sunny peninsula has 22 kilometres of fine white sand beaches and crystal-clear aquamarine waters, a variety of hotels, restaurants and entertainment to please everyone's taste, and a range of prices to meet everyone's wallet.

Many people spend their entire holiday in Varadero. If your main stay is in Havana, you can visit Varadero on a one-day excursion (it's two hours from the capital), but two or three days would give you a better chance to enjoy all of its attractions. And both sunrise and sunset on the peninsula are spectacular enough to be worth staying one night just to see them.

Sightseeing

If lounging on a beach isn't your idea of fun, there are plenty of other things to see and do. For $10 per person you can ride in a horsedrawn coach all over Varadero, with the coachman pointing out spots of interest and regaling you with historical tales. You can also wander around on foot, bicycle or motor scooter.

Long a favourite resting and eating spot for local residents and visitors, **Parque Josones**, at the corner of Primera Avenida and Calle 56, gained new fame in 1999 as the workplace of Juan Miguel González, the man who waged a seven-month battle to bring his son Elián back home to Cuba after the child's mother and ten others lost their lives at sea in an abortive attempt to sneak into Florida by boat at the end of 1999. The little lad can sometimes be spotted here with his parents and grandparents – all of whom became celebrities during the long struggle with Miami Cubans who were attempting to keep the child there against his father's wishes.

But the Park itself is well worth the visit even without seeing the famous family – and maybe he's earned some privacy. Here you can take a quiet walk along tree-shaded paths, sit and read a book, or feed and watch the ducks, geese and other seabirds which often land here to beg a meal. There is an artificial lake for boating (only 50 US cents per person an hour), and a large swimming pool ($3 entrance fee, which includes $2 worth of food or drinks). Some excellent restaurants, cafés and bars dot the park (*see p235*).

Casa Villa Abreu (05 613189), the historical museum of Varadero, is small but charming. Set in an old woodframe house that was newly painted white and blue, its architecture is typical of the Southern United States in the 19th century and it has been beautifully restored. On the first floor the dining room has been furnished with pieces from that era. In the history section, drawings, photos and artifacts range from the aboriginal period to the present. It also has an interesting

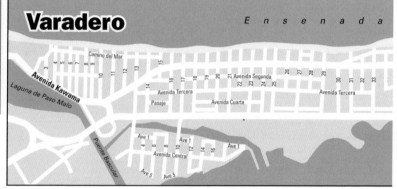

display of local sports, including fencing champions of the early 1900s and famous baseball figures of the last century. Set back near the beach on Calle Playa, the house is most easily spotted by the beautiful yellow flowering acacia tree in the yard of the house in front.

For those interested in the normal social life of this beach community, and Cuba in general, an interesting spot to visit is a beachfront house called **La Casa de Cariño** (The Home of Loving Care) on Calle Playa on the corner of 51st. Here, the local Presbyterian Church provides Varadero beach holidays for Cubans with special needs who would not ordinarily have this opportunity: elderly citizens and children with leukemia and chronic diseases. You can drop by the house, talk with the residents and their current visitors, or join them for lunch or dinner. (They do not have a restaurant, but the excellent, home-cooked meals are regularly offered to visitors, and donations to the programme are accepted.)

Further east is a terrace at the highest point in Varadero, overlooking the sea, ten metres above sea level. This is where smugglers in the 18th century hid their sugar, liquor and meats. They had a rock wall built around it, and from that point they could see the north and south coasts of the peninsula. On the outskirts of town, the **Delfinario** holds several dolphin shows a day. Cubans pride themselves on having trained the dolphins with loving care, and they are kept in a natural setting (not like the concrete 'sea world' theme parks found in other countries). Varying admissions prices will let you watch the show or even swim with the dolphins – who seem to enjoy it as much as the humans do.

VARAHICACOS ECOLOGY RESERVE

One of the most unusual and enjoyable excursions from Varadero is to the easternmost end of the Hicacos Peninsula, known as Punto

Frances, or **Varahicacos**. The local authorities have set aside this area of 295 hectares for an ecological reserve, and from ancient cave writings to 500 year old cactus trees, what they have preserved is a national treasure. The various trails through the reserve are well marked, but you will need the help of multilingual guides to really get the most out of your visit. For those with an interest in native plants, birds and reptiles the guided walking tours ($5) make an interesting morning or afternoon activity. If you go early in the morning or just before sunset, you can see a variety of birds during your walk. As well as the endemic species, in the winter months visitors can see numerous migratory birds from Canada, the United States and Cuba's northern cays.

There are four nature trails, some through coastal vegetation, others through caves. The first, and one of the best, includes a walk through the **Cueva Ambrosia**. Its walls are covered with pictographs from the aboriginal people of this area, believed to be more than 2,000 years old. Another trail leads to the **Cuevas de los Musulmanes**, where an aboriginal burial ground was found. Guides show visitors a replica of an ancient cadaver, indicating the foetal position in which people were buried. Another cave, with distinctive geological formations, presumably once housed people. Today it is filled with hundreds of bats. (none of which are considered dangerous)

Varahicacos lays claim to having the oldest cactus tree in Cuba – perhaps in Latin America. Called 'the patriarch', it is over 500 years old, and was probably here when Columbus arrived. It also boasts the only completely natural **beach** in Varadero. The sand along this 900-metre long stretch is brought in by the currents and is a light golden colour. (All the other beaches are made of fine white sand brought in

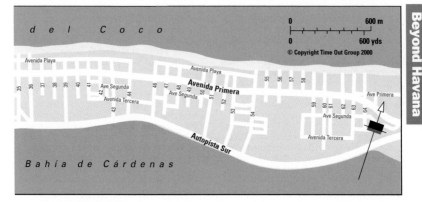

Beyond Havana

from nearby cays.) Caretakers of the eco-reserve put up beach umbrellas made from palm leaves; everything else is kept in a carefully preserved natural state. Close to the beach are the lagoon and salt flats, where the first salt mine in Latin America was founded in 1552. It remained in operation until 1959. You can see flamingos and other seabirds in the lagoon, and then spend the rest of the day resting on the beach and swimming in the clear seawater nearby. No hotels, stands, or other man-made constructions mar the area, so bring your own picnic lunch, if you plan to spend the day here.

Getting there

The **Vía Blanca** goes directly from Havana and the airport to Varadero. **Buses** arrive at the small Terminal de Omnibuses on calle 36 and Autopista Sur (Viazul 05 614886; Astro 05 612626). **Astro** buses to Havana ($5.50) leave once a day and take about three hours; **Viazul** buses to Havana ($10) leave three times a day and take two hours and 45 minutes.

The nearest **railway stations** are in Cárdenas, 18km to the south-east, and Matanzas, 42km to the west. This makes train connections with Havana and the rest of the country highly impractical.

All international and the majority of national **flights** arrive at the Juan Gualberto Gómez airport (05 613016), 25km to the west of Varadero. Cubana and Aero Caribbean serve a number of domestic destinations. The flight to Havana from here costs just $36, although overall it's a lot less convenient than the bus. Cars can be hired at the terminal.

Where to stay

Varadero Peninsula has more than 30 hotels and choosing the right one is key to getting the most out of your stay. Hotels range from small, homey and inexpensive to large, modern five-star extravaganzas. Some of the latter are billed as 'all-inclusive', but it's best to check beforehand to find out what this actually includes, besides room, meals, beach and pool privileges. For example, some include all nautical sports, while others only include the non-motorised ones. Most include a wide variety of entertainment, sports and other activities. Some even include excursions outside of the hotel. It is always best to book your hotels in advance, since tour-operators can get you better prices. The **Gran Caribe** and **Meliá** hotels tend to be large, elegant and expensive. But not all are equally high-priced, so it is worth asking your travel agent or the tourism bureau in Havana. All of the hotels

mentioned here provide ample shopping opportunities. They also offer transportation and guides for excursions around the peninsula and for seafaris, fishing and scuba-diving trips (*see pxx* **Sport in Varadero**). Note that, because they receive large numbers of European guests, many hotels in Varadero use 220-voltage current.

All but four of Varadero's hotels are on the northern coast (where the Atlantic is so calm and green you could swear it was the Caribbean). **Gaviota Coral** (05 668288) and **Mar del Sur** (tel/fax 05 612246) are on the Cárdenas Bay side of the peninsula; and **Punta Blanca** (05 668050-3) is halfway between the two. The northern shore hotels literally line the entire coast from the westernmost tip of the peninsula to the edge of the ecology reserve. Most hotels have natural barriers of seagrape, oleander, palm and other coastal plants that protect the dunes, provide some shade, and keep the ocean from washing the beaches away.

Some of the most exclusive hotels include **SuperClub** (05 667720/1) and **Club Med Varadero** (05 668288) – in fact, the latter is so 'inclusive' that it will not allow anyone in to visit guests. But there are also some hotels and restaurants used by both Cubans and visitors. One such hotel is the **Villa La Mar** (05 613910), part of the Islazul chain, which normally caters to domestic (Cuban) tourism. Each year 100,000 Cubans win a free holiday here by being selected as the best all-round workers at their workplace. You can spend your time alongside Cuban families who are enjoying the same beach, pool, meals and entertainment. The hotel has 264 rooms (with decor by Cuban artists), swimming pools for adults and children, and is only 150 metres from the beach. Its central location means it is close to Varadero's urban and commercial area and to the southern beach across the narrow peninsula known as **Mar del Sur**. Villa La Mar offers yachting trips and other excursions, including visits to the new dolphinarium; *see p231.*

The mid-range Horizontes hotel in Varadero is **Club Tropical** (05 667145-7), centrally placed at the corner of Calle 21 and Avenida 1ra (one of the main streets that traverses the island lengthwise). It has 114 comfortable and well-decorated rooms in the main building and 109 more in four separate buildings, all with private bath, cable TV, phones, balconies and a nice view of the pool and the beach. On the plus side, the hotel is attractive, small and with a homely feel, with a restaurant bordering a swimming pool. The hotel also has apartments in four separate buildings nearby which rent for as low as $50 a night. Prices include breakfast, or you can go all inclusive to make the most of the

Beyond Havana

This sporting life

WATERSPORTS

Many of the hotels in Varadero offer their own aquatic sports, boats, equipment and instructors. But if yours doesn't, or you're just visiting Varadero for the day, you might want to check out **Barracuda Diving Centre** (run by Marlin, as most aquatic sports centres on the island are) at the corner of Primera Avenida and Calle 58; tel. 05 613481). The centre offers scuba diving, snorkelling, trips on catamarans, fishing excursions and paragliding. For the more active, it can lay on half-day or full-day scuba-diving excursions to nearby coral reefs. It's usually $35 per dive ($30 if you have your own equipment), or $50 for cave or night diving. You can also arrange packages for multiple dives. In a group trip, those who want only to snorkel pay $25. Barracuda conducts introductory courses for $US70 and ACUC open water certification courses for US$365. It also offers advanced scuba courses. There is a bar and restaurant on the grounds to relax in afterwards or for those who decide to wait onshore.

PARAGLIDING AND SKYDIVING

A delightful experience for those who don't want to plunge under the sea is to go up in a parachute (firmly fastened by cable to the boat that takes you out) and get a bird's-eye view of Varadero. It sounds alarming, but is really a very relaxing experience with no danger at all, since the Barracuda crew reels you out from and back onto the deck of the boat. Your feet should never touch water. The more extreme sport of skydiving is offered at the **Centro Internacional de Paracaidismo** (tel. 05 667256).

BOAT EXCURSIONS

Seafaris, trips to the nearby cays, fishing, snorkelling, sailing, catamaranning and other sea activities can be found in a number of spots. **Marina Gaviota** (tel. 05 667755) at the east end of Autopista Sur, **Marina Chapelin** (tel. 05 667550) and Puertosol's **Acua Diving Centre** (tel. 05 668064) all provide more or less the same activities for the same prices.

Boat trips include the **Marina Chapelin**'s *Jolly Roger* catamaran safari to Cayo Blanco, an all-day excursion, which costs $60 but includes open bar, buffet lunch served aboard, snorkelling gear and transfers to and from your hotel. They sometimes offer a sunset cruise too. Or you can make the same trip to Cayo Blanco on yacht for $65 with lunch served on the key.

GOLF

Golfers and fans will have to go to Varadero to **Varadero Golf Club**, an 18-hole/par 72 course on Carretera de las Américas, in La Torre district, designed by the Canadian architect Les Furber, a disciple of master golf course builder Robert Trent Jones. It's in a delightful location, next to Varadero's beautiful white beaches. Shortly after it opened, in October 1999, the Varadero Golf Club hosted the 1st PGA European Challenge Tour. It also welcomes other tournaments around the year, including, in June, the International Amateur Open Golf Week. The driving range school offers a selection of beginner and advanced classes for locals and foreigners.

hotel's entertainment and sports facilities, including massage, acupuncture or acupressure, mud therapy and beauty treatments at amazingly low prices. (A 45-minute full-body massage costs only $10). On the downside, the three-storey hotel doesn't have lifts, and all rooms are above ground-level floor, so it is not wheelchair accessible. As in many of the lower-priced hotels, there are sometimes minor plumbing problems, but overall, Club Tropical is an exceptionally good buy for the price.

At the upper end of the scale, the newly remodelled **Cuatro Palmas** (05 667040) boasts attractive Spanish colonial decor. Its sister hotel, **Playa de Oro**, at the other tip of the peninsula, is stunningly modern in sweeping architectural design and earthtone colours. The high-roofed, open-air lobby has a bar. Its 385 rooms wind around a large, curving pool, with pool bar and a daytime poolside snackbar that converts into an open-air Italian restaurant in the evenings. Making your way behind the buildings to the beach (which is protected by a line of seagrape trees and other local plants), you will also find a *ranchón*, a typical, open-air barbecue-type restaurant. Service has recently improved, and the wide array of organised activities is complemented by a full gym with sauna, jacuzzi, exercise equipment and masseuse. The hotel is all-inclusive, but only non-motorised water sports are included among the free activities (catamarans, snorkelling).

Beyond Havana

The **Gran Hotel Varadero** (05 668243) and **Riu Turquesa Hotel** (05 668471-5) are among the newer, large hotels, situated at the far eastern end of the strip bordering the **Varahicacos Ecology Reserve** (*see p231*). .

Where to eat

Except for the all-inclusives, almost all the hotels have excellent restaurants, cafeterias and snack bars open to the public. The town is also sprinkled with fine restaurants and fast food places. The main restaurants are located around the Parque Josones (*see p230*). **El Retiro** (05 667316), once the home of the family which built the park in the 1940s, is an elegant restaurant for anyone who wants to get dressed up and eat out in style. Be warned: weddings and banquets are often held here (groups from Europe or Japan come here for this purpose), but the casual visitor can also drop in for a meal. **La Campana** (05 667224), an old stone building which was once a guest house, serves typical Cuban food in a more relaxed atmosphere. The food is well prepared and the service good. **Dante** (05 667738) is considered the best Italian restaurant in Varadero (some say the best in Cuba) and has a lovely, outdoor setting on a little piece of land jutting into and surrounded on three sides by the lake.

Shops & entertainment

As well as checking out the complexes within the hotels, shoppers can trawl the boutiques at the **International Conference Centre** or try to find unique items at the **crafts fare** outside the Coppelia ice-cream parlour on Calle Playa, esquina a 46.

Away from the glitzy and tourist-dominated hotels, the town has a miniature golf course, public beaches, nightclubs and cabarets, all of which are open to the local population.

For details of sporting activities, *see p233* **This sporting life**.

Ciénaga de Zapata

For those interested in nature and wildlife, Cuban history, scuba diving and snorkelling, or just a more unusual holiday spot, it is well worth spending at least two or three days in the Wetlands National Park and Biosphere Reserve, the **Ciénaga de Zapata** sometimes known as the Parque Nacional Montemar.

Rumbos has recently become the major player in terms of tourism groups in the area (previously it was Horizontes), which is a bonus for nature-lovers, because Rumbos staff in Ciénaga are very ecologically conscious, and

work closely with the environment ministry (CITMA). You can book hotels, tours or other park activities from the Rumbos office just before the turn-off (*see below*). For suggestions of activities while you are there, contact Mario Diaz, Rumbos director for the area, who can be found in his office next to the Australia sugar mill, at the end of the road that turns south into the wetlands area.

To see most of the environmental attractions of the biosphere reserve, you'll need at least two nights in Ciénaga de Zapata. A day trip is possible, but it doesn't give you enough time for the nature excursions, by boat or by land (which take between four and seven hours), which let you observe and enjoy a vast array of typical wetlands flora and fauna.

Guamá & around

At the entrance to the park is the **Fiesta del Campesino** restaurant where many tour buses stop. Although it's very touristy, and some visitors might be saddened by the sight of the animals in cages around the grounds (not to mention the large horned bull, which is made to get down on the ground so tourists can mount and ride him), but if you have no other chance to see this aspect of rural life in a more natural setting, it might be worth a stop. The food's better than it needs to be.

The first real point of interest, however, is further on at **Boca de Guamá**. This is the site of a tourist shopping centre and the **Criadero de Cocodrilos** (Crocodile Breeding Farm), where Cuban environmentalists successfully brought the Cuban and American varieties of crocodiles back from near extinction. A visit to the farm is great at any time, although greatly enhanced when its founder and former caretaker, Toby, is around to give you a guided tour. If you can't find him here, check at the Environmental Education Centre (*see p239* **Nature by numbers**). Be sure to wear long sleeves and a lot of mosquito repellent.

From Boca de Guamá you can take a ride in a launch ($10) across the **Laguna del Tesoro** (Treasure Lake) to the replica Taino fishing village and the historic (and touristy) **Hotel Guamá** (05 2979; $20 per person per night, negotiable for large groups). On the way, turtles can be seen sunning themselves on half-submerged logs, and there is an amazing variety of birds, especially in migratory season. On a typical trip you will encounter everything from the tiny bee-hummingbird to giant osprey and turkey vultures, egrets and cormorants, among others.

The 'hotel' is actually made up of cabins, on stilts over the water, which are designed to look

Beyond Havana

like *caneyes* (the round, wooden, thatched-roof dwellings of the original inhabitants of the area). Inside, they are fairly rustic, but have TV, air-conditioning, modern bathrooms, plus a small kitchenette in the two-bedroom family-style cabins. It's worth staying in them at least one night just for the ride out there through the canals on launches, and for waking up surrounded by the incredible natural beauty and abundant wildlife of the lagoons.

Spending the night at Guamá, however, does have a couple of disadvantages. One is mosquitoes and other insects, common to the entire wetlands area, and is minimal if you use enough repellent. Another is the distances. The cabins are set at a slight distance from each other throughout the lagoon, connected by high arching wooden bridges or reached by boat. This means it can take some time to get to and from the restaurant, reception area, and the swimming pool/bar-grill area. It also poses something of a problem if there happens to be a heavy thunderstorm (not at all uncommon during the summer months). Still, the beauty and plentiful (non-bloodsucking) wildlife more than make up for it.

Cueva de los Peces

A great spot for lunch is Cueva de los Peces (Fish Cave), where you can spend time swimming, snorkelling or scuba diving among multi-coloured ocean fish in the water-filled caves and fissures. The mixture of fresh- and seawater here is so clear that you can see the fish simply by standing on the bank, but gliding in and out of the ancient coral and limestone formations that form the *cenote* (limestone sinkhole) is even more astounding. At 75 metres, Cueva de los Peces is the deepest of the more than 82 *cenotes* in the wetlands area. (The fissures themselves may very well go much, much deeper, since they are the result of old earthquakes and movements.)

The Cueva de los Peces has a restaurant in a typical wood and stucco house among the trees near the entrance to this small park area, but it is much more interesting to eat at the outdoor *ranchón* bar-cafeteria skirting the water of the *cenote* (food is cooked in the kitchen of the main restaurant and brought down to the *ranchón*, so the quality is the same). The restaurant has a good variety of well-prepared food, including fish, chicken, rice and desserts (average from $4.50 to $10; lobster costs a little more, about $15). Equipment for snorkelling or diving can be rented at the restaurant or bar-cafeteria, though it's quite inexpensive.

Between the *ranchón* and the water – just a few yards over limestone rock – there is an old

Yanilla tree, with large hollows in its branches inhabited by iguanas and owls.

Continuing down the main road, you will come to **Punta Perdiz** (Pheasant Point), a small cafeteria-restaurant built to look like a steamship. You could easily drive right by it, as the main attractions are hidden from the road. Behind the restaurant (which costs $1 to enter) is a beach area in development. Natural beach umbrellas made from poles and palm leaves provide shade over plastic lounge chairs; docks and ladders are provided to ease access into the surf over the jagged coral and limestone rocks. Punta Perdiz also rents snorkelling equipment, as well as games including chess, checkers and volleyball. Off to the right, about a kilometre of fine sandy beach curves along the coast.

Rumbos is in the process of building a barbecue grill near the beach to provide additional refreshments without having to leave your beach chair and umbrella. It has also been working with environmental officials to replant sea grapes behind the dunes to protect the beach from the invading marabu, which is so pervasive in this area. From the beach you can look through the crystalline waters to see the sealife below, gaze across the bay at the far side of the park, or just sit back lazily and watch the large brown pelicans swooping down for their fish dinners.

The Bay of Pigs

Another ten kilometres down the road you come to the town, beach and museum of **Playa Girón** – a tiny fishing village on the Bahía de Cochinos or the Bay of Pigs. This seaside hamlet would have remained unknown to the outside world had US-based Cuban exiles not mistakenly chosen this spot and the adjacent Playa Larga for their abortive invasion in 1961, a US-backed attempt to set up a counter-Revolutionary force in the area. Cubans refer to the famous invasion as 'the victory of Playa Girón'. The attack was a dismal failure for the invaders: local militias and Cuban troops repelled the attack in 72 hours, but not without leaving a painful toll of civilian as well as military casualties.

The museum in the village recounts this history, primarily through black and white photos. Museum guides speak only Spanish, and being able to understand the language will help you make the best of the museum, but nevertheless you can still learn a great deal about what happened here four decades ago. Probably most poignant are the photos of young militiamen who died in the battle when they were barely into their teens, and the tales of the local inhabitants killed by the bombing,

Isn't it time you wrote home?

strafing and bullets of the invading forces. The museum has two small souvenir counters, and there are a handful of stores across the street offering food, drinks and snacks as well as clothing, music and souvenirs.

Both Playa Larga and Playa Girón also have major diving centres but if you continue down the road you'll reach **Caleta Buena** (Good Cove) one of the best snorkelling spots on the Zapata Peninsula (and a great place for beginners at scuba diving). Here the natural cove formed by the coral and limestone rocks provides a calm transparent sea with a great abundance of multi-coloured fish to contemplate in a safe and comfortable setting. The semi-circle of the cove rim has been prepared with

It's a busy life on the **Varadero** beaches.

Nature by numbers

If you're not travelling on an organised tour from Havana to the Ciénaga de Zapata, one of the first places you could stop at is the **Centro de Educación Ambiental** (Environmental Education Centre). By following the main road into the park area, you will come to the small buildings marked by a sign for the centre. Here a tiny, two-room museum provides an anthropological history of the region dating back to the Pleistocene era, with stark black-and-white photos showing what life was like for the men, women and children who barely eked out a living making charcoal, hunting and fishing and growing what they could in the years prior to 1959.

But the main attraction is a large scale model of the entire park and peninsula, along with the displays of birds, fish, mammals, plants and even soils. Most of the displays are movable, touchable and/or interactive, since this is primarily an education centre for children. But printed signs in Spanish and English make it a worthwhile educational opportunity for adults (and non Spanish speakers) as well.

Alongside the museum, classrooms are set up for the ongoing environmental education for the residents of local communities and the increasing numbers of tourism agents, guides, managers and employees in the area. Interesting data includes the fact that Ciénaga de Zapata wetlands park and beaches covers 4,520 sq kilometres and that it contains at least 900 species of endemic plants (and local researchers, who double as tour guides three days of the week, are still discovering new ones all the time). There are five animals that can only be found in this area, two of them birds endemic to the Zapata Swamp (the Zapata Wren or *Ferminia cerverai*, and the Zapata Rail, or *Yanolimnas ceverai*). In total, there are 12 known mammals, 160 birds, 31 reptiles, four types of fresh-water fish, five amphibians, and a great number of insects and other invertebrates that make the Zapata peninsula their home. In addition, at least 65 migratory birds have been spotted here. A bird-watcher's paradise! The people of the area live off of forestry, fishing, beekeeping, tourism and crafts.

thatched-roofed areas and lounge chairs and tables, each with its own small dock and ladder for descending into the water.

This area has a marlin snorkel and diving rental centre and instructors, as well as kayaks, catamarans and sail boats. Scuba diving lessons are $10 for a beginner's lesson in the Cove; if you want to take a boat out for deep-sea diving, the cost goes up to $25 for your lesson (compared to as much as $60 in other places). Other features include crafts fairs by local artisans, and an open-air massage parlour, with rates from $10.

Entrance to Caleta Buena is $12 for the whole day, including buffet lunch and all drinks (half price for children). If you arrive after 3pm you pay just $6.

For those who like a more rugged and natural environment, a virtually unknown cove called **Caleta del Toro** lies six kilometres beyond Caleta Buena. Entrance to this is still free, since it is in a completely natural state – but the road out there is rough and full of rocks and potholes, making it risky driving if you are in your own vehicle. Other diving centres can be found along the entire strip, from Punta Perdiz to Playa Girón.

Other activities

West of the Bay of Pigs are two excellent bird and wildlife refuges that can each be visited on a guided walking tour. The tour leaves early, so make sure you have accommodation booked for the previous night. The tour of **Santo Tomás** takes you through thinly wooded forests, while **Las Salinas** presents a starkly different view of salt flats.

For both, you have to skirt the thick marabu plants that cover the peninsula and compete with other local vegetation. Less hardy enthusiasts, or those worried about the wear and tear on their car, can arrange for Rumbos to drive them out to either of these sites in a jeep or small truck. Most excursions cost from $12-$15 per person.

Rumbos can organise boat trips along the **Río Hatiguanico**. The River flows along the western edge of the park and can only be reached by driving 40 kilometres back west along the *autopista* in the direction of Havana. If you're planning to include this in your trip to Ciénaga de Zapata, it makes sense to do it on either the first or the last day.

Getting there

There's virtually nothing in the way of public transport in this region, but there are regular one-day excursions to this area with **Rumbos**

or **Havanatur** in Havana (for details of both, *see p223* **The chain gang**).

Alternatively, if you don't want to stay in the area, you can usually drive here in under two hours in a rented car from Havana. Taking the main *autopista* east towards Matanzas and the central provinces, you really shouldn't be able to miss the turn-off for Playa Girón and the Ciénaga de Zapata reserve. At the junction, a giant-sized boat is flanked by an Oro Negro petrol station and a Rumbos tourist office on the right-hand side of the road, and crowds of people stand waiting for buses or hoping to hitch a ride.

Where to stay

For those who just want to stay close to a sandy beach, both Playa Larga and Playa Girón have simple, stucco tourism facilities very near the sand. But anyone interested in the incredible diversity of the park and wetlands should try to stay at **Hotel Guamá** (*see p235*) or **Finca Don Pedro**.

Hotel Playa Larga (tel. 059 7219) has 57 reasonable rooms (cabins or bungalows), all with air-conditioning, radio, fridge and TV. It also has three restaurants and three bars, plus a tennis court and a swimming pool. Cars can be hired here. **Hotel Playa Girón** (tel. 52594118) boasts 292 air-conditioned rooms with TV and radio, refrigerator, pool, a choice of five restaurants, three bars, a nightclub, tennis court, shop and car rental. Both hotels are part of the Horizontes chain and you can make reservations at the Horizontes office in Havana (*see p223*). Otherwise, there are various *casas particulares* to choose from in the area.

Just inside the entrance to the park is Finca Don Pedro. Much newer than other accommodation in the park, the ten wood cabins surrounding an old farmhouse are both more rustic and much nicer than the ones in Guamá (although we're told that the latter will be renovated in 2001). Built like typical Cuban *bohíos* (thatched-roof, rectangular wood cabins with small front porches), they have screened windows open on all sides to present a view of the surrounding countryside.

There's no air-conditioning or television in these cabins (although they do have lights and modern refrigerators), and they're cheaper than those at Guamá, costing $28 a night for a cabin for two in low season, or $38 for a four-person cabin with a beautifully finished, polished wood upper loft. The latter is favoured by sports fishermen who come to seek bass, small tarpon and other fish that abound in the Ciénaga lagoons and canals.

The Central Provinces

With historic towns and stunning natural scenery, the island's central provinces are truly at the heart of Cuba.

Villa Clara Province

Santa Clara & around

The most important town in Villa Clara province is its capital city, Santa Clara, known as 'Che's city'. Ernesto 'Che' Guevara was the leader of the rebel column that took the city in 1958. This key event effectively spelled the end of Batista's rule in Cuba.

A huge statue of the guerrilla leader, the **Monumento a Che Guevara**, towers over the entrance to the city at Avenida de los Desfiles on Plaza de la Revolución (0422 205878). Below the statue is the hero's mausoleum, which also houses the remains of the other Latin American guerrillas who died with him. This is where most visitors to the Santa Clara come to pay tribute to Guevara, or just to learn a little of the history of the Revolution. Note that the mausoleum is closed on Sundays. You will come across other shrines to Che as you walk around the city. For a photo of the monument and an account of Guevara's life and Revolutionary career, *see p242* **Guerrilla in the midst**.

Like most colonial-era cities, Santa Clara's municipal life is centred around a public square. The **Parque Leoncio Vidal** is named after a hero of the 19th-century independence war against Spain. It is edged by Calles Vidal and Abreu; the latter is named after one of the heroines of that same struggle, Marta Abreu. The park is bordered by buildings housing governmental offices, the public library and cultural centres, as well as the **Hotel Santa Clara Libre** (*see p244*). However, in contrast to the squares in most cities of the period, this park is not overlooked by a church.

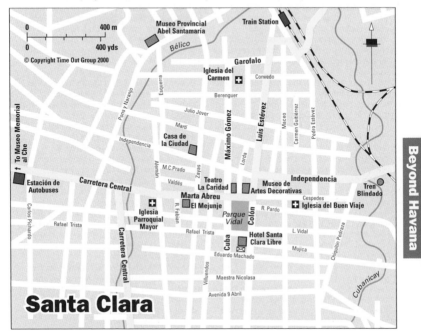

Guerrilla in the midst

Ernesto 'Che' Guevara de la Serna was born on 14 June 1928 in Rosario, Argentina. He was a sickly child who developed asthma at the age of two, a condition from which he suffered for the rest of his life. Consequently, most of his primary schooling was provided by his mother and by the extensive library his parents kept at home. According to some biographers, it was from this library that he gained the exposure to Marx, Engels and Freud that was to form the foundation of his later political thought. Che's secondary schooling was more conventional, and he was a fairly average student, excelling only in literature and sports. Nevertheless, his performance was sufficient for him to gain admittance to Buenos Aires University in 1947, to study medicine. He emerged a qualified doctor, with a speciality in dermatology, in early 1953.

During his time at university, Che was not notably politically active. Instead, he embarked on a number of extended journeys around Latin America. What he saw appalled him. Everywhere there was grinding poverty, corruption and government incompetence.

Che's political consciousness was awakened further when he returned home and saw a series of similarly corrupt and incompetent regimes in control of Argentina. The young Che developed a healthy contempt for the charade of parliamentary democracy as it was practised throughout Latin America, and a deep distrust of the army. His greatest hatred was for capitalism and imperialism, however, particularly the US form. It was these twin demons, Che felt, that were responsible for all the misery he had seen.

After his graduation from university in 1953, Che's life entered a period of profound transition. He could no longer be content to live the life of a prosperous family doctor now that he had witnessed the poverty and misery of the Latin world. He spent the next several years travelling extensively. While working at the General Hospital in Mexico City, he was introduced by mutual friends to the brothers Raúl and Fidel Castro.

Che was immediately swept up by the Revolutionary zeal of the Castros and their followers. When the time came to board the *Granma* for its date with destiny, Che was there. He had been brought along principally to serve as the Revolutionaries' doctor, but quickly distinguished himself as an inspired guerrilla leader. Che was quickly promoted to *Comandante*, in charge of a large part of the Revolutionary army.

At the end of the Revolution, Che was Castro's most trusted confidant. He was instrumental in transforming Castro from a liberal socialist into a committed communist. Che's communism, however, was not that of Moscow or Beijing. He was determined that Cuba would not replace the US with yet another foreign master. Che wanted Cuba to tread a new path, independent and free of political baggage and corruption, governed on Leninist lines. During the remaining years of his life, Che's thinking moved even further away from orthodox communism, towards a kind of idealised anarchism.

Che occupied a number of key posts in the Cuban government during the years following the Revolution. His growing idealism, however, was increasingly at odds with the grim political realities facing the government. Castro felt it necessary to ally his country more and more with the USSR as US hostility to his government grew during the 1960s. Che was opposed to this move and the two formerly close friends grew distant. In 1965, feeling that he could contribute no more to Cuba, Che wrote Castro a letter of farewell and took himself off to the Congo and finally to Bolivia to advance the cause of international revolution in those countries.

Bolivia was a revolution too far for Che. The government had only recently instituted significant land reforms, which benefited peasant farmers significantly. Consequently, when Che began recruiting the peasant soldiers he needed for his revolution, he received only a lukewarm response. He persisted throughout 1967, however, but this time his gamble failed to pay off. He was captured by Bolivian troops after a fierce battle in Quebrada del Yuro near Vallegrande, in which he was badly wounded. Fearing the international publicity a trial would focus on the regime, the Bolivian government ordered his immediate execution and disposal. Early the following morning, on 9 October 1967, the order was carried out.

In July 1997, Che's remains were found buried in an unmarked grave near a Bolivian airstrip and returned to Cuba. In October, he received a state funeral and was reinterred in his mausoleum at Santa Clara (*see p241*).

Following in Che's footsteps? The little rebels of **Santa Clara**.

Getting there

Astro and Viazul **buses** arrive at the Terminal
de Omnibuses Nacionales (0422 292114), which
is located on the corner of Carretera Central and
Oquendo, in the west of the city. Astro buses
($12) to Havana leave twice a day and take over
four hours. Viazul buses ($18), which take the
same length of time, go once a day.

The **railway station** (0422 22895) is on the
Parque de los Mártires but you have to go
across the park to Calle Luis Estévez Norte
#323 to book. There are two departures a day
for Havana ($10). Santa Clara has no airport.

Where to stay & eat

Although the old **Hotel Santa Clara Libre**
(0422 207548-51) is right on the central *plaza*
and convenient for anyone who wants to walk
around the town and soak up the atmosphere of
this colonial city, the most popular places to
stay are on the outskirts of the city.

Los Caneyes (0422 4512-5) is a motel in
a woody area just outside of town, run by the
Horizontes chain. All of its buildings are made
to look like Indian wood and thatch round-
houses on the outside, but inside they are
comfortable modern hotel rooms, with cable
TV and hot water in the bathrooms. The dining
area and other buildings follow suit. A modern
twist comes in the form of a swimming pool and
jacuzzi, an outdoor disco, a well-stocked shop

and another that sells crafts, and a recreation
area. For many repeat visitors, though, the
main attraction is Eunice, the on-site masseuse,
who combines traditional, modern, herbal and
alternative methods to relax and heal your body
and your mind. Los Caneyes is just a short way
from the Che Guevara memorial.

Another attractive place a little further out
of town is Cubanacán's **Villa La Granjita**
(0422 206051-53), with 75 rooms. It is also set
in a wooded area and combines natural-looking
cabins with modern indoor conveniences. If
you're looking for quiet and privacy, this is a
nice place to stay, and still within easy reach
of the city.

Elsewhere in the province, there are two
other very special places to stay. One is the
Elguea Spa (042 686298), to the north-west,
and the second is **Hotel Hanabanilla** (042
491125) on the mountain lake of the same name.
Elguea has a long tradition of providing cures
for a variety of illnesses through its sulphuric
waters and mud baths, and has a staff of
medical professionals to assist you. Hanabanilla
offers breathtaking views and excellent fishing.

Remedios

North-east of Santa Clara is the fascinating
historical town of San Juan de los Remedios.
Founded in 1513 as Santa Cruz de la Sabana,
it was the second Spanish town to be settled
by the newly arrived Spanish conquistadors.

and was maintained as a feudal fiefdom by Spanish nobleman Vasco Porcallo de Figueroa (whose principal claim to fame was to have reputedly fathered 300 children during his lifetime). Despite his reported cruelty to the indigenous population (the wanton rape of its women and slaughter and subjugation of its men), Porcallo de Figueroa was named mayor of the new 'Villa' of Remedios in 1545.

Piracy, which was the bane of many Spanish settlements in Cuba, was for Remedios the main form of economic sustenance. Its inhabitants earned their living from smuggling, and actual raids by the pirates were infrequent. Far from the two earliest Spanish capitals (Santiago and Havana), the territories of Remedios, Sancti Spíritus and Trinidad in the central regions lay outside the jurisdiction of Spanish governors.

But even more than its early friendly links with the pirates, Remedios owes its mystique to legends about devils and exorcisms. In 1682, the story goes, a priest was called upon to exorcise the devil from a local woman. The devil threatened to unleash his evil legions on the people unless they abandoned their village. Eighteen families (comprising some 200 people) decided to heed the devil's warning, and left Remedios. It was these 18 families who founded the city of Santa Clara, on 15 July 1689.

Two years later the inhabitants of Santa Clara set fire to Remedios to rid the area of the devil's curse; this 'holy war' was only ended in 1694 by order of the Spanish government. (Other accounts say the inhabitants of Santa Clara were angry at the collaboration of the local citizens with the pirates who continued to plague Cuba). In any case, under the Crown's protection, Remedios continued to grow. It is now a relatively large town, with a population of 18,000, although if you wander around its streets, you may well feel you have gone back several centuries in time. It has all the colonial charm of Trinidad with very little of its tourism.

Some of the area's history is marked in annual events held in Remedios. The **Parrandas** festival, held in the last week of December, features colourful floats and fireworks, traditional dancing, and plenty of beer and rum to create an exciting end-of-year ritual. Since 1820 the parishes of San Salvador and del Carmen have taken part in these festivals. If you happen to be in town during the festival, look out for San Salvador's symbol, the rooster, and Carmen's, the sparrowhawk. The **Museo de las Parrandas**, on Calle Máximo Gómez #71, gives a glimpse of the history of the festivals, which are unique to this central region of the country. Flags, banners and costumes are preserved here along with samples of homemade fireworks and floats.

Many visitors find that wandering around the back streets of Remedios is interesting enough in itself, but if you're looking for sights, you may want to seek out the **Plaza Martí**. This typically Spanish central park is shaded by royal palm trees and dotted with marble and wrought-iron benches. One side is dominated by the **Iglesia de San Juan Bautista**, which was built in 1692, and is one of Cuba's oldest churches. The church has recently been restored, revealing some of the ornate splendour inside. The carved cedar altar is inlaid with gold leaf, and the Moorish-style ceiling is made of mahogany. Various statues of Jesus and the Virgin Mary – including one of the Virgin of Charity of El Cobre (Cuba's patron saint; *see p260* **Virgin on the fanatical**), and one of the Virgin of the Immaculate Conception – look down over the pews. Overhead, a bell tower rises three storeys, with a bell on each level.

If you like colonial architecture and furnishings, visit the equally pretty church of **Nuestra Señora del Buen Viaje** at Alejandro del Río #66 and the **Teatro Rubén M Villena** at Cienfuegos #30.

Near Plaza Martí, in a smaller park, is the 'liberty statue', carved by an Italian sculptor in 1920, and dedicated by the people of Remedios to 'the martyrs of the homeland'.

Also worth visiting is the **Museo de Música Alejandro García Caturla** on the north side of the *plaza*. Caturla was one of Cuba's foremost composers. In addition to period furniture and decorations typical of the early 1900s, when the composer lived and wrote his music, the museum includes some of his manuscripts. Caturla was only 14 when he began writing music in 1920, and was influenced by both the sounds of Africa and the classical music of Stravinsky. Although born into a wealthy family, his memory is cherished by Revolutionary Cubans today because of his identification with the poor and oppressed. Caturla defied the traditions of the Spanish ruling class in many ways, particularly by his marriage to a black woman. Although interracial relationships were not unheard of at the time, black women were generally regarded as mistresses for upper class gentlemen, rather than suitable wives.

As well as being a musical composer, García Caturla studied the law, and eventually became a municipal judge, with a reputation for incorruptibility. In 1940 he was assassinated by a policeman, who was due in court the next day accused of beating a woman to death. However, many supporters of the composer suspected that the murder was orchestrated by wealthy right-wing rulers who found Caturla's liberal, honest conduct inconvenient.

Beyond Havana

A few minutes' walk from Plaza Martí (at Calle Antonio Maceo #56, entre Carilla y Ariosa), is a beautiful colonial home housing the **Museo de Historia Local**. The museum traces the history of the area and can best be appreciated on a guided tour.

Once viewed as just a place to visit from Santa Clara, Remedios has become increasingly popular as a stopping-off point in its own right. Visitors who want to spend more time in the town can stay at the **Hotel Mascotte** (0422 395481) on Parque Martí, which has very inexpensive rooms (from just $9) with lovely 19th-century decor.

Cienfuegos Province

Cienfuegos

Founded in 1819, the city of Cienfuegos is a whole tourism resort in itself, according to its inhabitants at least. Set on a beautiful bay, the city was subject to pirate attacks and periodic battles for dominance among the European powers of the 17th and 18th centuries and, unlike the rest of the island, it was founded by French settlers rather than Spanish conquistadors or their British competitors. Its French background, combined with direct influence from the United States, gives Cienfuegos its unique characteristics.

In terms of architecture, French influence has left the city with attractive neo-classical buildings. Wander around the beautiful downtown area, centred around **Parque Martí**. Bordering the *plaza* are numerous important buildings, among them the **Catedral de la Concepción Inmaculada**. Founded in 1869, the Cathedral boasts lovely stained-glass windows, which were brought over from France during the time of the Paris Commune. Also on the square are the **Teatro Tomás Terry** (one of the city's cultural landmarks), the **Casino Español**, the **Museo Histórico**, the **Ayuntamiento** (City Hall), the **Casa de la cultura** and the **Fondo de Bienes Culturales**, which displays and sells art.

Other places of interest in the city include the gardens of UNEAC (the Union of Writers and Artists) and two unique cemeteries: the **Tomás Acea** and **La Reina**. The cemeteries can be visited independently or on a guided tour. Whatever its multicultural past might suggest, Cienfuegos wouldn't be a Cuban city if it didn't have a cigar factory. One-hour visits to the **Habanos** factory can be arranged on request.

Some 15 kilometres from the city centre is Cienfuegos' famed **Jardín Botánico**. The garden covers an area of nine square kilometres and contains more than 2,000 species of plants, some of which date back to prehistoric times. Tours of the garden, lasting two and a half hours, are offered daily.

Another favourite for visitors to Cienfuegos is the **Castillo de Jagua**, located at the mouth of the Bahía de Cienfuegos. The 17th-century fortress can be reached by ferry from the wharf in Cienfuegos at Calle 25, esquina a 46. Many tours to the castle include lunch at its restaurant, where you can sample the house cocktail, the Dama Azul (Blue Lady).

If you've enjoyed your trip to the castle by boat, Rumbos can provide a one-hour boat trip around the bay and past several of the keys, where you could also go swimming and snorkelling. A longer six-hour excursion by boat across the bay will take you to the **Casa del Pescador** (Fisherman's House), for a 'pirate fiesta', complete with music, dancing and competitions.

Inland is **Finca La Isabela**, a *campesino* farm serving typical Creole dishes. While on the farm you can choose to go horseback riding, listen to country music and watch *campesino* dances. Bus tours to the *finca* are usually on Thursdays, but it's best to check with Rumbos.

Getting there

All **buses** arrive at the Terminal de Omnibuses on Calle 49, entre 56 y 58 (0432 5270). Astro buses to Havana ($14) leave five times a day and take five hours. Viazul buses ($20) leave twice a day and take about four hours.

The **railway station** is across the road (0432 5495). In theory the service to Havana ($16) runs once a day, but it's not very reliable.

There are no domestic flights in or out of **Aeropuerto Jaime González**.

Where to stay & eat

Hotel Pasacaballos (Carretera Rancho Luna, km.22; 096212) comprises 188 air-conditioned rooms with radio, TV and private bath. There's also a restaurant, bar, swimming pool, game room, disco, medical services, shop, parking, garden, currency exchange, post office and tourism bureau. Pasacaballos overlooks the entrance to the Cienfuegos Bay and provides easy access to the city.

Hotel Jagua (Paseo del Prado, entre 0 y 2; 432 3021/5) has 140 air-conditioned rooms (with private bath, TV, radio, telephone and room service), and 13 poolside cabanas. Other facilities include a cabaret, bars and an adjacent

Beyond Havana

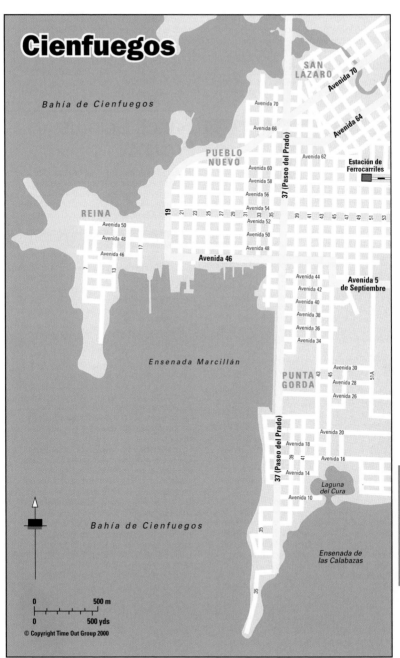

Cienfuegos

Bahía de Cienfuegos

SAN
LÁZARO

Avenida 70

Avenida 70

Avenida 64

Avenida 66

Avenida 62

Estación de
Ferrocarriles

PUEBLO
NUEVO

37 (Paseo del Prado)

Avenida 60

Avenida 58

Avenida 56

REINA

Avenida 54

Avenida 50

19

21

23

25

27

29

31

33

35

39

41

43

45

47

49

51

53

Avenida 52

Avenida 48

17

Avenida 50

Avenida 46

7

13

Avenida 48

Avenida 46

Avenida 44

Avenida 5
de Septiembre

Avenida 42

Avenida 40

Avenida 38

Avenida 36

Avenida 34

Ensenada Marcillán

Avenida 30

PUNTA
GORDA

43

45

51A

Avenida 28

Avenida 26

37 (Paseo del Prado)

Avenida 20

Avenida 18

39

41

Avenida 16

Avenida 14

Laguna
del Cura

Avenida 10

Bahía de Cienfuegos

35

Ensenada de
las Calabazas

35

0   500 m

0   500 yds

© Copyright Time Out Group 2000

Beyond Havana

restaurant specialising in seafood. Its tourism bureau offers trips and excursions to many of the sights in the area.

Tourist information

The **Rumbos** office in Cienfuegos is at Calle 20 #3905, entre 39 y 41, Punta Gorda (0432 9651/51937495).

The rest of the province

For all its unique cultural, artistic and historical attractions, the city of Cienfuegos actually pales in comparison to the lush beauty of the province that surrounds it. For those who like the outdoors, excursions into the countryside and up into the mountains, with their caves, waterfalls, lakes and hiking trails will be the most delightful aspect of a visit to this area.

Cubamar provides an energetic way of seeing the province of Cienfuegos. Its guides are primarily young naturalists, and it has rustic but very comfortable air-conditioned rooms in scenic **Guajimico**, 42 kilometres from the city on the way to Trinidad. The road to Guajimico passes through varied landscapes, bordered by the La Jutia River, which empties into the Caribbean. Vegetation ranges from coastal bush and mangroves to ceiba and palm trees, evergreen forests and cactuses.

It's hard to choose between the province's many spectacular sites, but if you have time for only one, try to visit **El Nicho** in the Escambray mountain range. (Cubamar or Rumbos can arrange this for you, or if you have a sturdy car and a good map, you can try it yourself. A guide helps.) The trek around El Nicho is outstanding, taking in babbling brooks and streams, cascades and waterholes that you can swim in, and a pristine cave (**El Calvo**), surrounded by dense green foliage that you can wander through. (A typical tour here will last a good eight or nine hours. Cubamar arranges overnight excursions.)

A shorter, half-day excursion from Cienfuegos will take you to the village of **Yaguanabo Arriba**, where you can visit a dairy farm and go horseback riding through the mountains, observing the local flora and fauna. The trail ends at **Pozo Lindo** (pretty pool), from where you walk to **Pozo Escondido** (hidden pool) for a dip in the cool mountain waters. If you want to make a full day of it, you can also go on from Yaguanabo by mountain bus to **El Colorado**, a typical mountain hamlet. Continue on horseback to **Las Guasimas**, then on foot to **Cueva de Martin Infierno**, where you can see the largest stalagmite in the Americas.

For a taste of the coast, head 20 kilometres south of Cienfuegos to **Playa Rancho Luna**, one of the most beautiful beaches in the province. Buses to the beach depart several times a day from the main bus station in Cienfuegos. Alternatively, Rumbos can arrange excursions, fishing trips, 'seafaris' and outings to the southern keys.

Sancti Spíritus Province

Heading south-east from the central provinces you will be greeted by an array of scenery, ranging from seascapes to mountains. The Escambray range, which starts in Cienfuegos and Santa Clara, extends to Sancti Spíritus.

Trinidad

Trinidad was founded as the Villa de la Santísima Trinidad on the site of a small Indian settlement in 1514. The city, with its red tile roofs, cobblestone streets, stained-glass arches and intricately designed wrought-iron grated windows, was declared a World Heritage site by UNESCO in 1988.

There are disputes over whether the first mass here was celebrated by Franciscan Father Juan de Tesin, or by the equally renowned Father Bartolomé de las Casas, who was a great defender of the indigenous peoples on the island. The cross, however, was frequently accompanied by the gun, and the area also served as a recruiting ground for Hernán Cortez, when he set out on his expedition to conquer Mexico, gathering horses, men and supplies here.

For the next two centuries Trinidad was mostly a quiet valley where Spanish settlers raised cattle and grew tobacco. But its proximity to the sea also made it a home for smugglers and *contrabandistas*, including slave traders from the British-controlled isles of the Caribbean. It wasn't until the 19th century that sugar cane became an important crop here. The slave rebellion in Haiti had a marked impact on the region, as French colonial settlers fled to Cuba in droves. By 1827 they had set up more than 50 small sugar mills in the valley near Trinidad, thus earning it the name **Valle de los Ingenios** (Valley of the Sugar Mills), and making Trinidad one of the most prosperous cities on the island. Sugar soon became its most important product and the commercial boom this created enabled the newly wealthy landholders to build the fine homes that have lasted to this day.

A view over tiled and tranquil **Trinidad**.

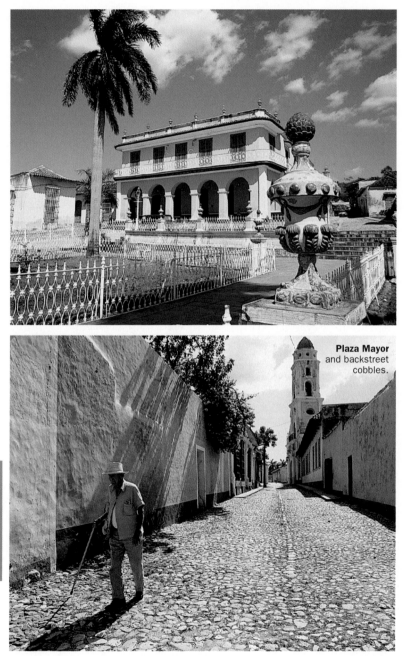

Plaza Mayor and backstreet cobbles.

The Wars of Independence against Spain took a heavy toll on this area, and by the time they were over, neighbouring Cienfuegos and Matanzas provinces had become the hub of the sugar trade. Trinidad remained in a time warp. No longer a bustling commercial centre, it maintained its Old World charm and elegance through the centuries.

The city's museums and churches are concentrated around the delightful **Plaza Mayor**. As well as being as a major tourist attraction, this central square is a popular meeting point for locals. Here you can sit on one of the park benches, in the shade provided by a canopy of bougainvillea, and watch the hustle and bustle of daily life in the town. During the day the area surrounding the park is very lively, with local vendors selling ice-cream, cold drinks and sweets made from tamarind to the local children.

The **Iglesia Parroquial de la Santísima Trinidad** (Holy Trinity Church) on the north-east side of Plaza Mayor was the main parochial church of Trinidad until 1814, when it was destroyed by a storm. The church was rebuilt in 1892 and resumed its former role. Today it is worthing for the ancient sacred relics it contains, such as the 1713 Cristo de la Vera Cruz (Christ of the True Cross).

As befits a historical city, Trinidad has a number of museums, housed in the former homes of the landed aristocracy. On Plaza Mayor itself, the Palacio del Conde Brunet (Calle del Cristo at the corner of Desengaño) is now the **Museo Romántico**, and the former home of Sánchez Iznaga has become the **Museo de Arquitectura Colonial**. The mansions of Alderman Ortiz and Don Juan Andrés Padrón have been combined as the **Museo de Arqueología Guamuhaya** and the **Museo de Ciencias Naturales Alexander von Humboldt**. (People may refer to them by either name.) Within the museums you can still see the opulence with which the sugar barons and traders lived off the sweat of their African slaves. The collection of furniture, arranged in beautifully restored rooms at the Museo Romántico, is particularly stunning.

The **Museo Histórico Municipal** is located nearby, at Calle Simón Bolívar (Desengaño) #423, on the corner of Callejón de Peña, in a mansion that once belonged to the Borrell family. In 1830 it passed into the hands of an unscrupulous German, known locally as Justo Cantero. Allegedly, Cantero acquired his vast sugar estates by poisoning an old slave trader named Pedro Iznaga and marrying his widow, then killing her as well.

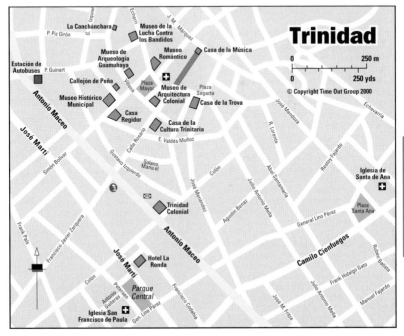

Beyond Havana

Streetfinder

Navigating Trinidad can be rather confusing, because the street names found in current guide books and on street signs are not the same as the old names used by the locals. The following list will help you find your way around town:

Old name	New name
Calle de la Gloria	Gustavo Izquierdo
Calle Desengaño	Simon Bolívar
Calle Gutiérrez	Antonio Maceo
Calle Rosario	Francisco J Zerquera
Calle Encarnación	Vicente Suyama
Calle Guaurabo	Pablo Pichs Girón
Calle del Cristo	Fernando Hernández Echerri
Calle Jesús María	José Martí
Calle Real del Jigue	Ruben Martinez Villena
Calle de la Media Luna	Ernesto Valdes Múñoz
Calle San Procopio	Lino Pérez
Calle Reforma	Anastasio Cardenas
Calle Boca	Piro Ginart
Calle San José	Ciro Redondo
Calle Alameda	Jesús Menéndez
Calle Santa Ana	José Mendoza
Calle Santo Domingo	Camilo Cienfuegos
Calle Lirio	Abel Santamaría
Calle Guasima	Julio A Mella

The **Museo Nacional de la Lucha Contra los Bandidos** portrays the history of the five-year-long battles between local rebel forces and counter-Revolutionary insurgents (*bandidos*) hiding out in the surrounding Escambray mountains after 1959. Exhibits include photos, authentic objects and parts of a US U-2 spy plane that was shot down in the area. The museum is housed in the former **San Francisco de Asís** convent, a block north of Plaza Mayor. The bell tower of the convent, which rises over the roofs of the city, is sometimes open to the public (or the friendly guard may let you climb to the top). From here you will have a breathtaking view over Trinidad, taking in the city's oldest church, **Nuestra Señora de la Candelaria de la Popa**. While you're at the top, have a good look at the bells and the machinery that operates them. Close inspection will reveal that they were made in Boston.

Another interesting square is the **Plaza Santa Ana** at the corner of Calles Santo Domingo and Santa Ana. In addition to the remains of the Iglesia Santa Ana, the *plaza* is the location of the former **Cárcel Real** (Royal Prison). This walled fortress-like structure is now home to the city's most important cultural centre. In its broad, sun-drenched courtyard (you can stay in the shade of the roman-arched passageways that surround it), the Trinidad Folk Ensemble perform Afro-Cuban dances and music for visitors. Inside the building is an art gallery exhibiting the best work by local artists, a handicrafts bazaar, a ceramics shop and a shop run by the Fondo de Bienes Culturales, whose headquarters is at the corner of Calle Desengaño and Media Luna. There is also a bar, cafeteria, coffee shop and restaurant.

Getting there

Buses from other provinces arrive at the bus terminal (0419 2597/3737) on Calle Piro Guinart #224, between Maceo and Izquierda. Astro buses leave every other day for Havana ($21) and take six hours. Viazul buses go twice a day ($25) and take around five hours.

The **train station** is located on the south-western edge of town, although it only serves destinations in the nearby area, such as the Valle de los Ingenios.

Aeropuerto Alberto Delgado (0419 2296) is two kilometres south-west of the city centre. There is one **flight** in from Havana every Tuesday ($82), but strangely there are no flights back to the capital.

Visitors might also like to make use of the **Compañía de Turismo y Recreación** in Trinidad, which offers a range of tours and visits in the city, as well as coach trips and rental of scooters and bicycles.

Where to stay & eat

Although the tiny city of Trinidad has no hotels, it is littered with *casas particulares*. It is worth taking the time to visit a few of these private homes before taking your pick. Make sure you choose one with a blue and white emblem, which means it's official and declared to the authorities. Be aware that visitors arriving on their own at the bus station may be met by a somewhat intimidating wall of eager hosts and *jineteros* (hustlers).

If you book a trip to Trinidad through a tour company in Havana, it will usually include accommodation at the Topes de Collantes health spa (*see p254*), or at one of the hotels on the Ancón peninsula (*see p255*).

There are several fine restaurants in Trinidad, with beautiful decor and a variety of tasty dishes. One of these is **El Jigue**, on the corner of Calles Real and Boca. Nearby,

Major marble in the **Plaza Mayor**. *See p251.*

Taberna La Chanchánchara, also on Calle Real between Boca and San José, is one of the oldest buildings in Trinidad, combining architectural styles from the 18th, 19th and 20th centuries. It is an active place, with music and dancing, and serves a speciality cocktail made of rum, honey, lemon and water, which is named after the tavern.

The **Trinidad Colonial** restaurant on the corner of Calles Gutiérrez and Colón is a more formal eatery, with an international haute-cuisine menu. The restaurant is trying to imitate the rich elegance of the 19th century; it contains a bar that blends with the decorative style of the surroundings, and a boutique that sells antiques and reproductions of masterpieces. The **Ristorante Allegro**, on Calle Real between Boca and Guaurabo, has Italian cuisine, also served in an atmosphere reminiscent of colonial times, while **Las Begonias** restaurant, nearby on the corner of Calles Gutiérrez and Desengaño, is named after the flower prevalent in most Trinidad gardens. Las Begonias serves light meals, and service is unusually fast.

Better prices – and sometimes even better cuisine – can often be found in the city's *paladares*, and if you stay in a *casa particular*, your hostess may very well prepare meals for you for very reasonable prices. In terms of snacks, every street has at least one stall selling a variety of flavoured drinks, as well as small stands selling sandwiches or pizzas for around three pesos.

Around Trinidad

Although this colonial city has more than enough attractions to keep a visitor busy, it would be a shame to travel all the way to Trinidad and not take advantage of the other attractions in the area. If you're short of time, choose between the deserted sugar mills of the **Valle de los Ingenios**, the beaches of the **Península de Ancón** peninsula, with their excellent snorkelling and scuba-diving sites, and the forested mountains that shelter the deeply relaxing **Topes de Collantes** natural health spa and hotel.

Just two kilometres from Trinidad, **Mirador Cerro de la Vigía** provides a rare view of the entire city of Trinidad, with its labyrinth of streets. The red tiled roofs of its mansions and the wrought iron of doors and balconies glitter brilliantly in the sunshine. The look-out at the top of a 180-metre ascent is best reached on horseback. Moving higher up into the clouds, **Mirador La Loma del Puerto**, at 192 metres, provides a panoramic view of the entire valley and surrounding hills.

Valle de los Ingenios

Sweeping through the hills north-east of Trinidad, towards Sancti Spíritus, the Valle de los Ingenios (Valley of the Sugar Mills) was the most important sugar-producing area in colonial Cuba. Today, the valley can be regarded as a museum of the sugar industry and has been declared a UNESCO cultural heritage site. Its 65 archeological plots include the remains of numerous mills, with parts of their machinery and a great many tools and utensils still intact. You will also find the remains of 15 manor houses, a slave hamlet, warehouses, infirmaries, a bell tower and other buildings.

A key site within the Valley is the **Manaca Iznaga**, one of the most important sugar mills during the 19th century. The best-preserved parts of the old mill are the slaves' quarters; the buildings that served as warehouses; and the 43.5-metre Manaca Iznaga tower, from which you can see the entire valley. The old mansion of the Iznaga family has been fitted out with a bar and restaurant that serves typical dishes of the region. Nearby is **Casa Cuachinango**, an old house on the banks of the Río Ay. The *casa* was built for rest and contemplation and is surrounded by fruit trees, wild flowers and several natural swimming holes. Visitors are encouraged to ride horses, milk cows and 'steal' honey from the beehives. There is a bar built around a large tree trunk on the grounds and a restaurant on the veranda.

Further along the Sancti Spíritus road, **Hacienda Los Molinos** is a working cattle ranch that organises horseback rides through the surrounding fields. The Hacienda's restaurant specialises in Cuban food; it also has a bar, grill, juice fountain and four lovely rooms with radio, TV and fans, for those who want to spend the night.

The most interesting way to see the Valley is on the delightful tourist train that runs between Trinidad and Guachinango. The old railway carriages have the capacity to seat 70 people. The train stops at the ruins of the Magua mill, and again for lunch at Manaca Iznaga. Reservations should be made through Rumbos in Trinidad.

Topes de Collantes

Twenty kilometres (12.5 miles) north of Trinidad, and surrounded by a totally different type of landscape that is filled with giant ferns, moss, lichens, pine and eucalyptus trees, the road winds up the mountains of the Escambray to **Topes de Collantes**. It is not the highest peak of the Escambray range; Pico San Juan

(1,156 metres) and Pico de Potrerillo (931 metres) both beat the 771-metre elevation of this resort, but it certainly has the most interesting history in the area.

Construction of the main building at Topes de Collantes was started in 1937 by then-dictator Fulgencio Batista. Building work was interrupted when he lost the 1944 elections, but was eventually completed after the coup that brought Batista back to power again, in 1953. Topes de Collantes opened as a tuberculosis sanatorium in 1954.

During the fighting against the counter-Revolutionaries in the Escambray in the early 1960s the building served briefly to house local militia, but was converted into a teacher-training school in 1966. The prevailing theory at the time was that the country needed teachers who were willing and able to trek through rugged terrain in order to teach pupils living in the most outlying rural and mountain areas. Later, the building was used as a hotel and temporary residence for local families needing housing.

The main structure was rebuilt in 1984, with additional, smaller buildings among the towering trees and ferns, and was taken over by the Gaviota chain, which began using it as a health spa. When it first opened the spa catered primarily to Cubans, who had been referred here by their doctors or hospitals for specific treatments or rehabilitation, for everything from injured limbs to obesity.

Today, the **Kurhotel** (tel. 042 40304, reservations through Gaviota) uses natural therapies on its clients. It relies chiefly on remedies made from local herbs and plants, complemented by exercise regimes that make use of the surrounding countryside. It also offers massage and beauty treatments.

Treks, which are available to non-residents for a $3 fee, include visiting the 62-metre waterfall known as **Salto del Caburni**, or the **Salto de Vegas Grandes**. On some trips, tour groups have lunch at the **Hacienda Codina**, where attractions include orchid and bamboo gardens, nature trails, and swimming and mud baths. As a tourist adventure, Topes can also arrange a trip to **Parque la Represa** on the Vega Grande river. As well as providing a habitat for a larger variety of endemic ferns than most people knew existed, this park also houses the largest caoba tree in Cuba and a swimming cave called the **Cueva La Batata**. The park restaurant is housed in a villa built by Fulgencio Bastista's wife.

Guides are recommended for all these excursions; most are more accessible by jeep or horseback than on foot, unless you're an experienced trekker.

Península de Ancón & the keys

South of Trinidad, the Península de Ancón is caressed by the warm blue-green waters of the Caribbean, and is a paradise for those who love sun and watersports. The name Ancón literally means the hind leg of a horse; some say the it refers to the shape of the peninsula, others that it refers to the large rock rising over the María Aguilar peninsula that was originally used as a landmark for sailors.

The **Hotel Ancón** on the peninsula has the advantage of the best private beach on the south coast of Cuba. The hotel, built in the 1980s and run by the upmarket **Gran Caribe** hotel group (05 4194011/3155), is certainly the nicest accommodation near Trinidad. It provides all sorts of watersports, including sailing, snorkelling and scuba diving around the sunken ships along the coast. The hotel has 279 air-conditioned rooms, a swimming pool, massage room, unisex hairdresser, two tennis courts and various restaurants and bars. There are several shops on site, as well as handicraft displays and sales, and mopeds, bikes and cars can also be hired. Evening entertainment includes cabaret and floor shows. The hotel tourism bureau offers trips and excursions to Trinidad, Topes de Collantes, and other areas, as well as air tours, yacht trips to Cayo Blanco and Cayo Macho, and deep-sea fishing.

Alternative accommodation can be found next door at the new **Hotel Trinidad del Mar** or at Horizontes' **Hotel Costasur** (0419 6100/6190) on Playa Maria Aguilar, further down the coast. Built in 1975, it has 111 rooms in the main building and two newer extensions, plus 20 rooms in duplex bungalows. There is a hexagonal swimming pool, and a sandy beach off to the right, where guests can go scuba diving or horseback riding. The hotel has a buffet dining room, but if you're looking for a good seafood meal, try the **Grill Caribe**, on the beach just past the hotel.

Off the white sand beaches of Playa Ancón is **Cayo Blanco de Casilda**, with its own beautiful beach and reefs that are perfect for snorkelling. Just off its western tip, at a depth of 18 to 40 metres, scuba divers can view the largest black coral grove in Cuba. At the edge of the island shelf, you can swim among red snappers, bass, turtles, lobsters and a variety of multi-coloured tropical fish. The marina provides catamarans, water scooters, surf boards and water bikes, plus all the gear needed for scuba diving and snorkelling. Boats visit nearby islets as well as venturing out to remote keys, such as the archipelago Jardines de la Reina. A 45-foot yacht moored here offers a live show and restaurant.

Beyond Havana

Santiago de Cuba Province

Cuba's second largest city, some gorgeous pine forests, a world-famous religious shrine and a rich ethnic blend of inhabitants all distinguish this corner of Cuba.

The city and province of Santiago de Cuba is bordered by Holguín to the north, Guantánamo to the east, the Caribbean Sea to the south and Granma to the west. Almost the whole of the province is mountainous and clad in the beautiful pine forests of the **Sierra Maestra**. It is home to the highest mountain in Cuba, the **Pico Real del Turquino** (1,974 metres/6,476 feet), usually referred to simply as Pico Turquino, and the largest rock in Cuba, the **Gran Piedra** (*see p263*). The province incorporates several national parks, the largest of which, **Baconao**, is a UNESCO Biosphere Reserve. The main agricultural activities in the region are sugar, citrus, banana, cocoa and coffee. It is also the country's richest mining zone for copper, iron and manganese.

The province was the site of key battles during both the 19th century wars of independence and the 1953-59 Revolutionary war, and this is reflected in numerous museums and monuments throughout the area. This historical resonance, along with the province's natural beauty, attracts many visitors, who come to visit the provincial capital, **Santiago de Cuba** – the third oldest city on the island – and to explore the rural and mountain areas. In addition to its justly famous capital city, Santiago is also the home of the popular religious shrine to La Virgen de la Caridad, Cuba's patron saint (*see p260* **Virgin on the fanatical**), located in the small mining town of **El Cobre**, half an hour's drive west of the capital city.

Santiago de Cuba

The city of Santiago de Cuba, 970 kilometres (603 miles) south-east of Havana, is Cuba's second largest city, with more than a million inhabitants. The city is located in a horseshoe-shaped valley and protected from the sea by an attractive bay surrounded by mountains. Although there is some heavy industry around the edges, this is supported by a well-deserved and growing tourist industry.

The city started life in 1515 at the mouth of the Río Paradas, as the third *villa* built by Diego Velázquez (*see p7*). The settlement soon moved to its present location and became Cuba's capital city, until it was officially replaced by Havana in 1607. During the 17th century, Santiago was besieged by pirates from France and England, leading to the construction of the **Castillo del Morro**, still intact and now housing the piracy museum (*see p259*). Because of its location at the extreme south-east of the island, Santiago was the recipient of various waves of migration. The first African slaves in Cuba were brought here; French colonists fleeing from neighbouring Haiti settled here; and Jamaicans also frequently made the short trip between the islands. As a result, the population of Santiago de Cuba is more of a truly ethnic blend than the inhabitants of many other parts of Cuba.

The city played a major role in the early days of the Revolution, earning it the title of *ciudad héroe* (heroic city). It is seen to represent the soul of Revolutionary struggle and boasts two major landmarks: the **Cuartel Moncada**, where Fidel Castro first attacked the Batista regime in 1953 (*see p258; see also p15*); and **La Granjita Siboney** (on the road to Playa Siboney), the farmhouse where more than one hundred Revolutionaries gathered on the night before the attack. Both sites are now museums.

Sightseeing

Santiago experienced various growth spurts over the centuries, resulting in an eclectic range of architectural styles from colonial to art deco. The city centre is marked by its red tiled roofs and narrow streets hemmed in by old, but often beautiful, pastel-coloured buildings.

Parque Céspedes & around

Parque Céspedes is in the centre of town and everything revolves around it, with most of the main museums within easy walking distance. The **Hotel Casa Granda** (*see p262*) covers the entire east side of the park, and the

Cathedral, **Santa Iglesia Basílica Metropolitana**, is on the south side, with the entrance on Calle Félix Peña. The first church on the site was completed in 1524, but four subsequent disasters, ranging from earthquakes to pirate attacks, forced the cathedral to be rebuilt four times. The edifice now standing was restored in 1818, with new decoration added in the early 20th century. On the north side, the **Casa del Gobierno** features a strong Moorish influence, particularly in the patio.

On the west side of the park, and unfortunately flanked by a drab bank building, is the beautiful 16th-century Casa de Velázquez, housing the **Museo de Ambiente Histórico Cubano**. The house, which was started in 1516 and completed 1530 is the oldest in Cuba and is now one of the best places to visit for a complete immersion in the colonial period. Velázquez lived on the top floor, while the ground floor was used as a contracting house and smelting room for gold. Each room depicts a particular period from the 16th and 18th centuries, demonstrating the development of Cuban material culture, with furniture, china, porcelain and crystal; there is also a 19th-century extension. Visitors are permitted to wander in and out of the rooms freely.

Two blocks east of the park, opposite the Palacio Provincial, is the **Museo Emilio Bacardí**, the second oldest museum in Cuba. The museum is named after the industrialist Emilio Bacardi Moreau, who was its main benefactor and who collected many of the items now displayed here. Exhibits on Cuba from prehistory to the Revolution are held downstairs, while the first floor has one of the most important collections of Cuban colonial paintings.

Outside, there is a reconstruction of a typical colonial street front and courtyard. The archaeology hall has mummies from Egypt and South America, including a Peruvian specimen over 1,000 years old and an 2,000-year-old Egyptian mummy from the 18th dynasty that was personally acquired by Emilio Bacardí and brought back to Cuba. Alongside these exhibits, here are also exhibits of ancient art, ethnology, documents on the history of Santiago and a hand-made torpedo that was used by the rebels during the first War of Independence.

A short walk east along Calle Aguilera is the delightful **Plaza de Dolores**, also known as the *Bulevar*. This pretty square has a coffeehouse, **La Isabelica**, on the corner. A little further along is **Plaza de Marte**, a pick-up and drop-off point for most urban transport.

© Copyright Time Out Group 2000

Calle Heredia & south

Calle Heredia runs along the southern side of Parque Céspedes behind the Cathedral. The most visited of numerous cultural sites on the street is the **Casa de la Trova** at #208. A long-standing symbol of Santiago's musical culture, the *casa* remains one of the most popular stopping points for visitors, who can enjoy light refreshments while listening to the excellent music of the local *trovadores*. There is a small music museum upstairs. On the opposite side of the street, the **Museo del Carnaval** exhibits a collection of instruments, drums and costumes from Santiago's famous July carnival. Photographs trace the history of the carnival and the cultures that influenced it.

Nearby, on the corner of Calle San Felix, is the **Casa Natal de José María Heredia**. Santiago's most famous poet was born in this house on 31 December 1803, after his parents had fled to the city from Santo Domingo in 1801. In his short but eventful life, Heredia created a poetic cannon which transformed the form and content of Latin American poetry, prompting José Martí to claim him as 'the first poet in America'. Colonial rulers in the 19th century tried to have his birthplace demolished, but influential people in the city, including Emilio Bacardí, succeeded in buying it. They handed the house over to the municipal government for restoration in 1902. Today the house is regarded as a national monument; it is home to a museum dedicated to the poet's life, as well as a cultural centre and a meeting point for current local poets.

Also on Calle Heredia is **Galería de Confronta**, a contemporary art gallery, while nearby on the corner of Pío Rosado is the small church, **Iglesia de Santa Lucía**. The surrounding streets have plenty of interesting architecture.

South-east of Parque Cespedes, on picturesque Calle Padre Pico, is a beautiful yellow building with a nice courtyard that has been restored as the **Museo de la Lucha Clandestina**. The museum was founded to mark the 20th anniversary of the armed uprising in Santiago, Central Ermita and other parts of Oriente in 1956. The purpose of the museum is to highlight the support given by the local urban population during the battle in the Sierra Maestra, with an exhibition of the citizen's underground struggle against dictatorship. Housed on two floors, exhibits revolve around Frank País, from his early attempts to foment a Revolutionary consciousness to his integration into the Movimiento 26 de Julio under Fidel Castro.

Three blocks south of the museum on Calle General T Padros is **Iglesia de los Desamparados**.

North of Parque Céspedes

Seven blocks north of the park is the birthplace of the Revolutionary heroes José and Frank País (Avenida Gen. Banderas #266, entre Trinidad y Habana). Frank was the leader of the underground movement in Santiago that provided support for Fidel and the 26th of July rebels (as detailed in the Museo de la Lucha Clandestina; *see above*). He was killed by the police in 1957 and is buried in the Santa Ifigenia cemetery (*see p259*). The house is now the **Museo Hermanos País**.

An earlier independence hero was born nearby at Calle Maseo #207 on 14 June 1845. The **Casa Natal de Antonio Maceo** contains biographical information about the great military commander of the 1868 and 1895 wars of independence and details of his 32 years' devotion to the struggle.

There are several worthwhile 18th-century churches in the surrounding streets, including **Iglesia de la Santísima Trinidad** (Calle Félix Peña, esquina a San Jerónimo); **Iglesia de San Francisco** (Calle San Francisco) and **Iglesia de Santo Tomás** (Calle Habana, esquina a Félix Peña).

Cuartel Moncada & around

More than any other single site in Santiago, the **Cuartel Moncada** (Moncada Barracks) symbolises Fidel Castro's Revolution. As the second largest military installation of the Batista dictatorship, it was attacked (unsuccessfully) by Castro and his Revolutionaries on 26 July 1953. When the Revolution triumphed in 1959, the rebels fulfilled one of their early promises by turning the fortress into a school. To mark the tenth anniversary of the attack, one of the buildings was converted to the **Museo Histórico 26 de Julio**, featuring photos, mementos, plans and drawings of the battle. All commentaries are in Spanish but English-speaking guides will take you through the exhibits. The outside walls of the garrison have been repainted, but bullet holes marking the original ones produced in the battle with Batista's troops have been faithfully reconstructed to produce a more vivid impression of the battle that took place there.

Just west of the barracks is the **Parque Histórico Abel Santamaría**, a small square commemorating one of the young men who took part in the assault. Santamaria was captured and had his eyes gouged out by Batista's

Beyond Havana

troops, and was later killed in prison when he refused to betray his comrades. Santamaría and other rebels were occupying a hospital at the time of his capture, and since then all eye hospitals in Cuba have been named after him.

Further north

General Antonio Maceo, one of the foremost revolutionaries of the 19th-century independence wars, is honoured in the **Plaza de la Revolución** at the junction of Avenida de los Libertadores and Avenida de las Américas, to the north of the city centre. The monument consists of a gargantuan bronze statue of the general on horseback, surrounded by huge iron machetes rising from the ground at different angles.The **Museo de Holografía** is housed below the monument, and features an eternal flame and holograms of artefacts from the war of Independence and the Revolutionary war.

To commune with Santiago's heroes, you shouldn't miss visiting the **Cementerio Santa Ifigenia**, on Avenida Crombet in the Juan Gualberto Gómez district, north-west of the city. The highlight of this impressive cemetery is José Martí's mausoleum, a huge structure with a statue of Martí inside, built in a circular design so shafts of sunlight enter all day from different directions. Martí is surrounded by six statues of women, representing the six Cuban provinces of the 19th century. Along the path leading to the mausoleum are signposts commemorating successful independence battles, each with a quote by Martí. Also in the cemetery are the graves of Frank País, Carlos Manuel Céspedes and Emilio Bacardí.

East of the centre

One of Santiago's most acclaimed painters, **Miguel Angel Botelín**, has a studio open to the public at Calle Nunez de Balboa #8, entre 10 y Pedro Alvarado in the Terrazas district. Beautiful renditions of the colonial city, its streets, rooftops and population, can be purchased here in original or reproduction.

Further east, the former high-class neighbourhood of Visa Alegre has a number of interesting sights, including the **Centro Cultural Africano Fernando Ortíz** (Avenida Mandulay #106). This excellent cultural centre displays items reflecting Cuba's African heritage and also doubles as a research centre for Afro-Cuban history. Its backyard patio offers drinks and Afro-Cuban music and dance. **Casa del Caribe** (Calle 13 #154) is devoted to the study of Caribbean life. The *casa* serves as a mini-museum primarily for Afro-Cuban religious artefacts, and as a research

centre for the history and culture of the region. Nearby at Calle 13 #206 is the **Museo de la Religión**, displaying religious items particularly concerning *santería*. Also in the area, the **Museo de la Imágen** (Calle 5, esquina a Calle 8) has displays of cameras, photographs, cine (film) and television clips.

Further south, on Avenida Raúl Pujol, is the **Parque Zoológico Santiago** and the **Loma San Juan**. Spain signed the surrender of Santiago to the United States on this hill on 16 July 1898. An ancient Ceiba tree symbolises the end of Spanish dominion in the Americas, while nearby are other monuments of the Spanish-Cuban-American war, with plaques to the soldiers of all three nationalities who died.

Castillo de Morro & Cayo Granma

Fourteen kilometres (8.5 miles) south of the city along the Carretera Túristica is the clifftop fort of **Castillo del Morro**. It offers a breathtaking view of the entrance to the Bay as the colonial defenders of the city must have seen it. The Morro houses the **Museo de la Piratería**, which charts the pirate attacks made on Santiago during the 16th century by pirates such as the Frenchman Jacques de Sores and the Englishman Henry Morgan. Exhibits include many of the weapons used in both the attack and defence of the city. You can wander around the fort for a $3 entrance fee, with or without a guide. As you enter the fascinating stone rooms, including the prison cells, the chapel and the cannon-loading bay, you will be surrounded by the building's history. From the roof you can admire the view of the Bay of Santiago and imagine the old tall-masted sailing ships entering its harbour and the fierce battles waged there. Alternatively, follow some 16th-century steps almost down to the waterline.

Traffic on the Carretera Túristica passes through **Ciudadmar**, from where you can catch a ferry to the island of **Cayo Granma** in the estuary. Cayo Granma was originally known as Cayo Smith after its wealthy owner and was a resort for rich Santiago families. Now most of its 600 inhabitants travel to Santiago to work. There are no vehicles on the island, but three *paladares* serve seafood in an idyllic setting looking across the bay.

Entertainment

Santiago de Cuba is overflowing with musical talent. The city is often considered the heart and soul of Cuban music and is the undisputed spiritual home of the *son* (*see p45*). At the **Casa de la trova** on Calle Heredia images of old

Beyond Havana

Virgin on the fanatical

The small mining town of El Cobre, named for the copper mines that once flourished here, would probably never have made it into the tour guides and history books were it not for a religious miracle that took place on the coast nearby in 1628.

Almost all Cubans know the legend of how the Virgin of Charity appeared in the Bay of Nipe near Santiago to brothers Rodrigo and Juan de Hoyos, mulattos of mixed white and black heritage, and Juan Moreno, a black boy of about ten. Other versions of the legend say that all three witnesses were named Juan and that one was white, one was mulatto and one was black, reflecting Cuba's racial makeup, but all versions agree that as the young men were clinging for their lives in a storm-tossed boat, they heard a voice declare: 'I am the Virgin of Charity.'

Across the waves they saw a wooden board inscribed with the words 'I am the Virgin of Charity', and a statue of the Virgin Mary, dressed in a yellow gown and depicted as a mulatta. On her left arm she carried a brown-skinned baby Jesus. In her right hand, she held a cross. The story of the vision rapidly gained popularity, leading local Catholics to erect a shrine to the Virgin in El Cobre. She is now the patron saint of Cuba and worshipped by Cubans all over the island and abroad. Although the faithful in Cuba today have their own distinct and divergent religious practices, based on an amalgam of Catholicism and African religions (see p28), they all honour the Virgin of Charity of El Cobre.

It is said that in the years after the 1959 Revolution, even Fidel Castro wore a medallion engraved with the Virgin of Charity that was given him by a little girl. When religious belief later became outlawed in Cuba, Fidel stopped wearing the medallion, but his mother, Lina Ruz, nevertheless offered thanks at the shrine of the Virgin of Charity for keeping her son safe during his time in the Sierra Maestra mountains.

The board bearing the image of the virgin is now framed and displayed on the first floor of the basilica In El Cobre. The statue, about a metre tall, is in a small chapel on the second floor, where Cubans light candles and pray and after leaving their offerings.

According to the Reverend Jorge Palma, who oversees the shrine, hundreds of Cubans from around the country and from Miami, Europe and elsewhere travel here each month to thank the Virgin for miracles. Anywhere from 20 to 100 people make the pilgrimage each day, and as a result, El Cobre has also become a significant tourist attraction. Cuban girls traditionally offer thanks here on their 15th birthday (see p172 **Sweet 15**) and Cubans living abroad pay homage here on return visits.

Throughout the rest of the year, other offerings are left behind by visitors as expressions of love and thanks: neatly folded uniforms of officers of the Revolutionary Armed Forces; the official red book of the Union of Young Communists; the yellow pencils of students who passed their exams; and a kidney stone the size of an egg, successfully removed from a woman from Havana. Most moving of all is a recent letter from a young man describing his harrowing journey by raft to reach the 'promised land' of southern Florida. Although he arrived safely, the young man describes seeing other rafts that arrived with no one aboard. In retrospect, he says that he probably should not have made such a dangerous voyage. 'Don't do it,' says the note, 'life is worth so much more.'

soneros look down on the musicians, as elegant santiagüeros lose themselves in the dance and the rum flows free. There is also a regular rumba on Sunday mornings at the **Museo del Carnaval**. For a calmer session you can enjoy choral, orchestral and chamber music at the **Sala Dolores** (on Plaza Dolores). An international choir festival is held here every year in December.

In early July, the **Festival del Caribe** (the Caribbean Festival, also known as the Fiesta of Fire) brings groups from all over the Caribbean for street shows, theatre events and a parade. This is followed by **Carnival**, when comparsas and paseos parade their congas around the streets in spectacular style, past stages set up for bands and kiosks selling beer and frituras.

Getting there

Interprovincial buses arrive at the **Astro** terminal (0226 23050) on Avenida de los Libertadores, near Plaza de la Revolución. Tourist buses pull into the **Viazul** bus depot (0226 28484) next door. Both companies run daily services to and from Havana. The journey takes about 15 hours and costs $47 with Astro or $51 with Viazul.

The **railway station** (0226 2836) is located on Avenida Jesús Menéndez, north-west of the city centre. Standard trains to and from Havana run every other day ($30). There is also a deluxe train, Locura Azul, with one departure a day for $42. The journey takes approximately 14 hours.

Both international and national flights come into **Aeropuerto Internacional Antonio Maceo** (0226 91014/91830), located eight kilometres (five miles) south of the city. There are 17 flights a week to Havana ($100); the journey usually takes around two and a quarter hours. There is a car rental desk in the airport.

Where to stay

Visitors with specific tastes will not have a problem in Santiago, since the city's eclecticism means there is accommodation to suit just about anyone. If you like all the advantages of modern, first class hotels, the **Hotel Santiago** (0226 87070, reserva@hotstgo.scu.cyt.cu, rates from $90), run by the Meliá chain, will meet your needs. Towering over the city in a red, white and blue structure on Avenida de las Américas (esquina a Manduley), the hotel offers everything modern travellers could desire, including a variety of restaurants, shops and

Dance to the music at **Festival del Caribe**. *See p260.*

services, a large swimming pool complex and spa where you can indulge in a hydro-massage, a telecommunications network that allows you to email all over the world and a well-equipped business centre. The hotel also has its own rum and cigar tasting rooms and was in the process of converting its disco into a Habana Café-style cabaret in 2000.

For those who want a feel for the history and culture of Santiago, the **Hotel Casa Granda** (0226 86600, reserva@casagran.gca.cma.net, rates from $73), at the corner of Calle Heredia and Parque Céspedes, is ideal. From its open-air rooftop bar you can look out over the city and the bay and when you walk out of its doors you are in the heart of the city. The hotel restaurant offers some of the finest cuisine in Cuba.

Looking for a more relaxed, suburban atmosphere with a touch of history thrown in? The low buildings and duplexes of the **Horizontes Hotel San Juan** (0226 87200, rates from $42) in Vista Alegre are spread out among trees, ferns and giant plants, next to San Juan Hill. If you've come with children, the swimming pool offers a shallow section for tots and a volleyball net for teens, and Santiago zoo is just a block away. The hotel has cars and motorbikes for hire.

For a good view overlooking the entire city of Santiago, the bay and the distant mountains of the Sierra Maestra, no place equals the **Hotel Versalles** (Altura de Versalles s/n, km 1, Carretera del Morro, 0226 91504,

gerente@versall.scu.cyt.cu, rates from $53). Set on a hilltop just minutes from the airport, it is still the favourite of many frequent visitors and tour groups to Santiago and it's easy to understand why. The sun glinting off the stained-glass windows of the Versalles Restaurant catch your eye as you drive down the airport road into the city. There's also a swimming pool, disco, tennis courts and a small shop. Rooms are tastefully decorated and comfortable, with cable TV, phones and modern bathrooms.

Also on the south side of the city is the less expensive Isla Azul's **Balcón del Caribe** (Carretera al Morro, 0226 91011, rates from $31), which has rooms along open-air-connecting hallways and separate bungalows lining the edge of the cliffs. A large saltwater pool makes up for the fact that you can't get to the sea from here. The hotel offers a large dining area, poolside snackbar and evening entertainment. It's a relatively short drive from Castillo de Morro, but rather far from everything else.

Beyond the City

Parque Baconao

The Baconao Biosphere Reserve stretches from the eastern edge of Santiago de Cuba as far as the border with Guantánamo province. Despite deforestation, it is an area of great natural diversity that encompasses mountains, dense forests and beaches.

To reach this area take the main road east out of Havana, via Siboney. Guided tours and excursions can also be arranged by tourist agencies in Santiago.

Gran Piedra

A visit to the **Gran Piedra** is a pleasant one-day excursion from Santiago. This vast boulder sits on top of a mountain in the Baconao reserve, at the tip of the Cordillera de Gran Piedra mountain range. From its summit, 1,214 metres above sea level, there are great views of the valley below and the Caribbean Sea beyond. To reach the top, visitors must climb dozens of steps carved into the rock. Bring sturdy shoes and warm clothes, as it can get chilly at this altitude.

The access road to Gran Piedra is about 15 kilometres (ten miles) east of Santiago, close to a sculpture park. The road winds its way steadily upwards, passing through several microclimates from tropical vegetation to pine forest on its way to the summit. Before reaching Gran Piedra, it passes the **Jardín Botánico**, a luscious garden created from a former coffee plantation.

For those interested in more exploration of this lush mountain area, **Hotel Gran Piedra** (0226 86395) provides 22 rooms at the base of the rock (rates from $29).

The coast

Two kilometres south of the turning to Gran Piedra is the **Granjita Siboney**, a historic farmhouse, where Fidel Castro and other rebels gathered before launching their attack on the Cuartel Moncada in 1956. The farmhouse is now a museum with Revolutionary exhibits from the time, while he road leading to it is lined with monuments commemorating the attack.

South of here is **Playa Siboney**, a small village with a beach that's popular with locals. Further east **Club Bucanero** (0226 86363, reserva@bucaner.scu.cyt.cu) overlooks its own beautiful cove, which is ideal for swimming and snorkelling. This high-class resort also offers other activities such as sailing, guided walks and climbing tours in the Baconao reserve. All-inclusive double room rates range from $116 in low season to $175 in high season. The food is nothing to write home about, but for those staying in Santiago, a day trip out here is still worthwhile. Admission costs around $15 including lunch, or $25 including dinner, a show and drinks. You can drive out there yourself or make reservations via Gran Caribe or Havanatur.

Continue east along the coast to reach **Playa Daiquirí** (the unappealing home of the famous cocktail), beautiful **Playa Bacajagua**, and the **Reserva El Indio**, a former hunting area turned eco-reserve that's great for walking and

Listen to the *trovadores* at the renowned **Casa de la Trova**. *See p258.*

Beyond Havana

Shoppers overflow onto the road on Calle José Antonio Saco, aka Enramada, and the main

cycling. Accommodation in the reserve (0226 86213; rates from $30) is attractive and secluded, consisting of 20 surprisingly well-decorated rooms, plus a fine dining area, a pool and a small beach.

Further east, a series of beaches and minor attractions lead towards Guantánamo province; a tourist agency in Havana or Santiago will be able to provide details of accommodation in the area.

North & west of the city

El Saltón

North-west of El Cobre (see p260 **Virgin on the fanatical**), the hills of the Sierra Maestra were the location of the third front during the Revolutionary war. Yet despite the area's violent past, it is here that you'll find a dream

mountain retreat. **Hotel Saltón** (Carretera a Filé, Contramaestre; no phone) was created as an anti-stress health spa, and provides 22 rooms hidden among wooded hills, with a bubbling brook that runs from a quiet pond at the foot of a lovely waterfall. The spa still offers therapists, psychologists, masseuses, a jacuzzi and other modern anti-stress aids. But visitors say the best anti-stress activity is just floating on your back in the natural pool, looking at the rainbows forming from the spray of the waterfall. Good food is available at the open-air bar and restaurant overlooking the stream. Local guides can identify every bird, plant and creature for miles around, as paths from the spa lead to look-out points or deep into the landscape of the Sierra Maestra. To reach El Saltón head north-west of El Cobre as far as Cruce de los Baños and then south-west through the village of Filé.

commercial drag of Santiago de Cuba.

The coast

Driving along the coast road west from Santiago is an exhilarating experience; the road hugs the shoreline tightly as far as the western end of the province and beyond, with the great wall of the Sierra Maestra mountains bearing down on it from the north. Dotted along the coast are exquisite coves and basic fishing villages, plus the wrecks of two Spanish ships with their gun turrets poking suggestively out of the water.

Playa Sevilla (60 kilometres/35 miles) west of Santiago is overlooked by the majestic **Hotel Sierra Mar** (022 26319, sierramar@smar.scu.cyt.cu). The hotel has 200 rooms lined up on terraces, which form steps down to the pretty beach, with its offshore coral reef. The family-oriented hotel includes a lovely swimming pool, a games

room, and plenty of entertainment and activities for children and adults. For a little more privacy in a similar locale, **Los Galeones** (022 26160, galeones@smar.scu.cyt.cu) is a secluded lodging shaded with trees. This lovely hideaway is located on top of a hill and has views of both the mountains and the sea. The rooms surround a small swimming pool, and there is a restaurant, but guests also have access to all of the services and entertainment at the Sierra Mar. Transportation is provided between the two hotels.

Below Los Galeones is the town of **Chivirico** (80 kilometres/50 miles west of Santiago), which boasts beautiful Caribbean beaches and a perfect climate. Continue west of here to reach Las Cuevas and the trail head of the **Ruta al Pico Real del Turquino** to the summit of Cuba's highest mountain.

Isla de la Juventud

It might seem a paradise island today, with its nature trails and palms, but it wasn't always this way, as a visit to the Presidio Modelo will show.

The Isla de la Juventud (Island of Youth) has had several names over its long history. It was once known as the Isla de los Pinos (Isle of Pines) for its vast forests of pine trees, but also as Parrot Island, Treasure Island and Pirates Island. Coves, bays and caves provided tempting hiding places for pirates trawling the Caribbean Sea, and numerous sea battles took place in the waters surrounding the island.

With visions of pirates' ships, sunken treasure, black-sand beaches and ancient forests, this little 'island off an island' has long captured the imagination of foreign visitors. It bears the imprint of English, American, Japanese and other settlers who made a home here over the years. Japanese settlers are today concentrated around the village of **La Fe**, south of Nueva Gerona. The community is supported by the Japanese embassy in Havana and many of its older members still speak Japanese.

Until 1926, Americans made up the largest foreign community on the island, with their own businesses, newspapers, banks, shipping companies, post office and import-export businesses. They were primarily vegetable farmers, who exported their produce to mainland USA, and were forced to leave the island in 1926 after bad weather and hurricanes wiped out their crops. Some were also reacting against the repressive policies of the Machado dictatorship. Machado was a frequent visitor to the island and built his infamous **Presidio Modelo** (*see p269*) here in the same year. Many of the original American settlements on the island, such as San Pedro, have virtually disappeared.

After the 1959 Revolution the government tried to help develop the underpopulated island, by sending in students and teams of workers who planted citrus orchards and built schools. Although they were only obliged to stay for three years, many of these young people married and settled on the island.

The Isla has long been known for its ceramics and pottery factory, marble production and rich sea life. All of these have now become attractions for its growing tourism industry. But it is still relatively untouched, and visitors who delight in meeting people and discovering places in their natural state will find much to enjoy here.

Sightseeing & activities

There are many things to do on the Isle of Youth. You can dive for sunken treasure and marvel at the natural underwater beauty in the **Ensenada de Siguanea**; visit the fantastic **Cueva de Punta del Este**, with its well-preserved aboriginal drawings; or recapture the history of the Cuban Revolution in the round buildings of the **Presidio Modelo**, where Fidel Castro and other rebels were imprisoned after their 1953 attempt to unseat the dictatorship of Fulgencio Batista.

Nueva Gerona

The heart of the town lies around a central *plaza*, bordered on four sides by Calles 28, 37, 30 and 39. Formerly known as Lacret Park, it is now named after the Guerrillero Heróico (heroic guerrilla, referring to Che Guevara). The *plaza* contains the **Museo Histórico Municipal** (Calle 30, entre 37 y 39), which was rebuilt recently to mark the 45th anniversary of Fidel's release from prison. (Most public buildings are closed on Sundays, so it is best to visit during the week.) A more modern movie house – breaking up the architectural aesthetic of the square – sits on the corner of Calles 37 and 28, and a pretty, old Spanish-style church, built in 1831, is on the corner of Calles 28 and 39.

Calle 39 – officially named after José Martí – is the town's main pedestrian street. As you walk along it from the *plaza*, you pass the local government offices and the Café D'Prisa, followed by the **Galería de Arte Marta Machado** (Calle 39, esquina a 26), where local artists display their work. Also on Calle Martí is the **InfoCaribe** telecommunications centre, which offers email and other services, and a **Rumbos** office, which houses a tourist information desk, a small dollar shop and an outdoor café. Nearby is the Chinese **El Dragón** restaurant and the Cuban **El Cochinto**, which unsurprisingly serves mainly pork. Around the corner is the **Patio** disco cabaret for salsa music and dancing (Calle 24, entre 37 y 39). Elsewhere in the town is a large, atypical wooden house surrounded by a covered porch, which was once known as 'Mister Kellerman's house'. The wealthy

Chill out in the glorious surroundings of **Ensenada de Siguanea**. *See p268.*

Beyond Havana

Isla de la Juventud

Islas de Mangles

0   10 miles
0   10 km
© Copyright Time Out Group 2000

Golfo de Batabanó

Cayos de los Inglesitos

Nueva Gerona

El Abra ▨
Presidio Modelo ▨

Embalse del Medio

Santa Ana ○

La Demajagua ○

○ Júcaro

Cayos los Indios

Embalse Viet Nam Heróico

Cayo San Juan

Melvis ○

La Victoria ○

○ La Fé

Ensenada de la Siguanea

○ Argelia Libre

○ La Reforma

Siguanea ○

Julio Antonio Mella ○

Hotel Colony

Cayo Piedra ○

○ Punta del Este

Parque Nacional ▨

○ Cocodrilo

○ Carapachibey

CARIBBEAN SEA

white American was known and liked for the assistance he gave to the poor population of former slaves on the island.

Heading south on the way out of town you pass a small **cemetery** for those who fell in battle. Although there are no street names here, you can locate it by asking for the hospital or bus station that border it. You will also pass the **Abel Santamaría housing project**, which contains the island's only nine-storey building. The housing project is similar in design to the Soviet-style pre-fab buildings put up all over the mainland in the '60s and '70s. These were constructed to meet the severe housing shortage and to get people out of dirt-floored, thatch-roofed *bohíos*, but became exceedingly ugly once their original coats of paint had worn off. In contrast, by using crushed stone instead of pure concrete, the Abel buildings have maintained their interesting colours and textures, despite the aggressive wear and tear of the elements.

Just outside Nueva Gerona, on the road towards El Colony and Punta Francés, is the **Planetarium** (km. 41 Carretera Siguanea), which in fact houses a small natural history museum. Nearby is the **El Abra** farming cooperative, which runs a small restaurant on the edge of the irrigation reservoir. The

restaurant is a popular lunch spot for tourists and local residents. From here you can also go on a 45-minute trek up the wooded hill to a lookout point at 500 metres (1,600 feet) for a breathtaking view of the island. No guide is needed.

Ensenada de Siguanea

Siguanea bay on the south-west coast is the location of the island's primary resort, **El Colony** (Carretera Siguanea Km.41, 061 98181, reservas@colony.gerona.inf.cu), run by the Puertosol Marina chain. In Cuba's pre-Revolutionary heyday, this was where North Americans and others came for gambling, women and, allegedly, drugs. There were rumoured to be close links between the Miami-based Mafia and the dictator Fulgencio Batista in running this vice haven. Since 1959, however, El Colony's chief attraction has been its association with the Puertosol diving centre and its proximity to 56 world-class diving sites.

The **Ensenada de Siguanea** is home to an abundance of colourful fish, corals, sponges and other sea life, which can all be explored on excursions from the diving centre. Well-trained, internationally accredited diving instructors will give patient, thorough classes to beginners, and advanced instruction to licensed divers. The centre also offers special diving experiences, such as night diving and sunken ships, to more advanced sub-aqua enthusiasts.

Fishermen also seek out this area. Trolling, bottom fishing and fly-fishing can be arranged from El Colony with appropriate vessels and equipment, weather and season permitting. The Caribbean is home to jewfish, snappers and groupers for bottom fishing; bonefish and tarpon for fly fishing; and shark and marlin for those with the patience and skill for trolling. If you're a beginner, experienced fishermen are on hand to help you.

Despite El Colony's fame, the two-storey main hotel and its adjacent bungalows have been badly in need of a face-lift for some time. Puertosol Marina hopes to have all necessary reconstruction work completed by the end of 2001, but in the meantime, the ongoing demand for accommodation means that the hotel stays open, despite deficiencies that range from old and inadequate plumbing fixtures to unsightly signs of aging. The scuba divers, for the most part, don't care, as they spend all day in the water. Besides, the place is clean, comfortable and friendly, with rooms that face the lovely, palm-dotted beach.

As the morning mists rise you can see the outlines of the wharf and the wooden frame of El Mojito bar emerging out of the sea. The shallow waters near the beach make this an ideal place for children, while adults can sun themselves in between swimming and snorkelling in the deeper water at the end of the wharf. The resort also has an inviting swimming pool and a small gallery, which displays local art, from ceramics to painting. At night El Mojito bar serves up a potent mixture of salsa music and rum or beer. Moped rental is available for those who want to see the island on their own, plus kayaks, paddle-boats and catamarans for exploring the bay, and the hotel's multilingual guides offer numerous excursions and nature trails.

Other sights

The **Presidio Modelo**, five kilometres (three miles) east of Nueva Gerona, is still a forbidding sight. Built in the late 1920s, the five-storey circular buildings of the former prison have come to represent the harsh repression of the Machado regime. Between 1953 and 1955 Fidel Castro and others were incarcerated in a section of the complex that is now a small museum. Enemy prisoners were also held here during World War II.

For a complete contrast, visit the **Cueva de Punta Este**, on the south-east coast of the island. The cave, which was discovered in 1910, features indigenous art and is considered one of the most significant examples of cave painting in the Caribbean. Although the cave lies in a prohibitied area of the island, south of Cayo Piedra, you can visit it by means of a tour from El Colony. Independent travellers will need to obtain a permit to explore this part of the island.

Also within the restricted zone, just south of the Ensenada de Siguanea, is the settlement of **El Cocodrilo**. The original community, known as Jacksonville, was settled by immigrants from the Caiman Islands. The old wooden houses are built in a typical Caiman style and many of the residents still speak English. El Crocodilo is surrounded by jungle-like vegetation with stunning untouched beaches nearby. Boats from Punta Francés at the tip of the bay, often make the five-minute trip by sea to visit here.

In addition to excursions to the sights detailed here, El Colony organises tours to the island's **Criadero Cocodrilo** (crocodile breeding station), and **Jones' Jungle**. An American woman named Jones, who lived on the island, imported numerous trees from all over the world for planting on her estate. The trees have since grown to create an area of wild vegetation and fascinating nature trails.

Getting there

There are several flights a day to Nueva Gerona, the island's main town, but they are often booked up far in advance. If you know you want to include a visit to La Isla in your Cuban itinerary, it's a good idea to organise it before you arrive in Cuba. Otherwise, your best chance of getting a ticket is through your hotel tour desk in Havana or through Cubanacán (see p223).

If you can't get a flight, there are also maritime routes to the island from the southern coastal city of Batabanó. The slow ferry takes five hours (on average); the 'fast' boat takes only two hours, but doesn't go every day. Both ferries are dependent on weather conditions, but then again, so are the planes; a heavy fog or storm can stop all flights to the island and keep you overnight wherever you are.

If you have booked accommodation at **El Colony**, **Villa Isla** or **Rancho de Tesoro**, you can arrange to be picked up from the airport when you arrive. Otherwise a very short cab ride will get you to Villa Isla and Rancho de Tesoro, and $15 will cover the journey to the Colony, which is about 45 minutes away. You can also rent a car at the airport, which is a good idea if you plan to explore the island rather than stay in just one place.

Beyond Havana

The Isla de la Juventud is one place where you'll feel as free as a bird – in this case a **turkey vulture.**

Where to stay

The most famous place to stay on the island is **El Colony** on the Ensenada de Siguanea (see p268), however, if your main interest is exploring the Isle of Youth itself rather than just its waters, you may want to try one of three other hotel-motels: Villa Isla, Rancho de Tesoro or Los Codornices. None has beach access, and they are all some distance from the diving spots, but all are close to the airport and the town of Nueva Gerona.

The most upscale of the three modest hotels is the **Villa Isla de la Juventud** (tel. 061 3290/3256/3278), located just over two kilometres from Nueva Gerona towards the airport. It is still locally known by its former name of Villa Gaviota, despite now being run by the Isla Azul chain. There are 20 rooms in modern duplex bungalow style, with hot water, air-conditioning, cable TV, and small refrigerators. Decorations, curtains and paintings in the rooms were created by the hotel workers themselves. There's also a large, clean swimming pool, a small, pretty dining room and a Caracol shop. A raised lookout point over the pool offers a view of the surrounding wooded hills. A local salsa group performs in the afternoons and evenings, and the warmth and friendliness of Cuban hospitality is evident everywhere.

One kilometre further south, **Rancho del Tesoro** (Autopista de Santa Fe km3, 061 23035/23657) is an extremely attractive complex in a mock-colonial architectural style. The rooms form a rectangle around a central courtyard where there's stone statuary, a fountain, and flowering vines hanging from overhead beams. The Rancho is currently undergoing construction work to add a swimming pool to the complex in 2001 and to allow for hot water in the rooms. Nevertheless, this is a comfortable place with air-conditioning, cable TV, and a shop and restaurant. Pretty sculpted replicas of aboriginal cave drawings and hand-painted ceramic decorations add to the attractiveness of the decor.

Otherwise, **Los Codornices** (tel. 061 24947) is OK at a pinch. It has the advantage of being slightly cheaper than the others, and even closer to the airport, but it is predominantly geared towards local Cuban tourism and has few facilities. The separate bungalows are attractive enough from the outside (white with red roofs), but very spartan inside. They have air-conditioning, TV, and a private bathroom with a shower, but no hot water, and although each has a small refrigerator and cooking area, this does not include a stove. The small swimming pool is not always clean, and is surrounded by speakers blaring very loud music. The very small dining room serves a limited menu.

Directory

Directory

Getting Around

Arriving & leaving

By air

Flights to Havana arrive at **Aeropuerto Internacional José Martí** (switchboard 264644/335777). The airport is 25 kilometres (16 miles) south-west of central Havana and consists of five terminals, with no interconnecting transport between them, apart from taxis. Domestic flights use Terminal 1 (*see p223*); charter flights from Miami and New York arrive at Terminal 2; most other international flights arrive at the relatively flashy Terminal 3 (flight information 264133/335786/335753); Terminal 4 serves the military; and Aero Caribbean flights come into Terminal 5. Terminal 3 has a 24-hour tourist information desk (666101/666112), a bureau de change and several car rental desks (*see p276*).

There is no public transport from the international terminals but taxis can be found right outside the terminal buildings. The journey into town takes 30 minutes and costs about $12. Some tourist agencies run minibuses to downtown for tour groups, which independent travellers can also use for a charge. Public buses (*see p273*) run from the domestic terminal to Vedado and Parque Central but, due to the distances between terminals, this service is useful only if you have arrived on a domestic flight at Terminal 1.

There are direct flights to Havana from Europe, Canada, the Caribbean and Central and South America, many of which are run by the national airline **Cubana de Aviación**. Cubana flights tend to be the cheapest available, but they are also notoriously unreliable.

Direct scheduled flights to Havana on Cubana depart from London Gatwick one to three times a week, depending on the season. **British Airways** (in the UK 0345 222111/www.british-airways.com) also has a direct service from London Gatwick twice a week. As alternatives, try **Iberia** (in the UK 020 7830 0011/www.iberia.com) and **Air France** (in the UK 0845 0845 111/www.airfrance.fr).

There are no direct flights from the USA (the planes coming in from Miami and New York are not for tourists), Australia or New Zealand to Cuba. Cubana runs scheduled services from Toronto and Montréal in Canada; from Cancún and Mexico City in Mexico; and from several Caribbean, Central and South American airports. Nassau in the Bahamas is a handy stopover for people connecting from the US. From Canada charter flights are provided by **Air Transat** (www.airtransat.com), **Royal Airlines** (www.royalairlines.com), and **Skyservice** (www.skyservice.com). From the Caribbean, try **Air Jamaica** (www.airjamaica.com) or **AeroCaribbean**; and from Mexico, try **Aerocaribe** (www.aerocaribe.com.mx) or **Mexicana de Aviación** (www.mexicana.com.mx).

Foreign visitors departing from Cuba on international flights are charged $20 departure tax. This must be paid at either of the designated counters between the check-in areas and passport control. For details of customs regulations in and out of Cuba, *see 279*.

Cubana de Aviación
Calle 23 #64, esquina a Infanta (Menocal), Vedado (334446/334447/334448/334449/fax 333082/www.cubana.com). **Open** 8.30am-4pm Mon-Fri; 8.30am-noon Sat; closed Sun.

Cubana de Aviación (UK)
49 Conduit Street, London W1R 9FB (020 7734 1165/fax 020 7437 0681). **Open** 9.30am-5.30pm Mon-Fri; closed Sat, Sun.

By sea

There are no international scheduled ferry services to Havana and, due to the US embargo, few cruise ships dare to visit Cuba as part of their itinerary. Cruise ships dock at the **Terminal Sierra Maestra** (Avenida San Pedro, Habana Vieja, 336607), a beautiful, ultra-modern conversion of the former colonial customs building.

For information on international cruise companies currently operating to Havana, contact a specialist tour operator or travel agent.

By rail

There are daily departures from the central train station in Havana to all the major towns in the country. Tickets can be bought in dollars in person at least an hour before your train goes or before 7pm if you're leaving during the night. Tickets are also available in pesos, but must be booked days (or sometimes even weeks) in advance. For details of the national rail network and specific services, *see p222*. For information on the electric train that runs between Havana and Matanzas, *see p111* **Chocolate choo-choo**.

Estación Central de Ferrocarriles
Avenida de Bélgica (Egido), esquina a Arsenal (information 614259). **Open** *Ticket office* 8am-7pm daily. **Map** p313 F14.

By bus

Well-equipped, long-distance **Viazul** buses (and the older, less reliable **Astro** buses) depart from the national bus station (*listings below*) and the terminal in Nuevo Vedado (Avenida 26, esquina a Zoológico, 811413) for destinations around the country. For general information on bus travel in Cuba, *see p222*.

Terminal de Omnibus Nacionales
Avenida de la Independencia (Rancho Boyeros) #101, Vedado (709401/792456). **Open** 24hrs daily. **Map** p312 D10.

Getting around Havana

Buses

Before the Special Period, Havana's buses (*guaguas*, pronounced wa-was) efficiently served the whole city but fuel shortages, lack of equipment and general inefficiency during the 1990s left the whole system on the brink of collapse. The situation has improved in the last couple of years, with two agencies controlling the service but buses are still subject to massive overcrowding, making even the shortest journey a daunting undertaking. During rush hours (7-9am and 4-6pm) the crush of passengers becomes unbearable and,

unless you're travelling long distances, it is usually quicker and more pleasant to walk

Transmetro rents out charter buses to companies to ferry their employees, although they do sometimes pick up individuals. **Omnibus Metropolitanos** is the main provider with its *ruteros* (standard city buses, 40 centavos flat rate) and *taxibuses* (1 peso), which run non-stop services between the city, the airport, and bus and train stations. Much of the overload in the system is carried by metrobuses known as *camellos* (camels). These are converted articulated trucks that carry up to 300 passengers and cover marginally longer distances.

Contary to appearances, queues (*colas*) do operate at bus stops (*paradas*) so it is important to ask for *'el último'* (the last in the queue) and board the bus directly after that person. At metrobus

Package Cuba

Travel agents

United Kingdom

Regent Holidays (UK) Ltd
15 John Street, Bristol BS1 2HR (0117 921 1711/fax 0117 925 4866/www.regent-holidays.co.uk.
Regent Holidays promotes itself as offering 'holidays for thinking people'. It specialises in travel to less frequented destinations in Central Asia and the former Soviet bloc, and currently offers two package deals to Cuba. Regent will also create bespoke itineraries for independent travellers.

Journey Latin America
12 & 13 Heathfield Terrace, Chiswick, London W4 4JE (tours 020 8747 8315/flights 020 8747 3108/fax 020 8742 1312/www.journeylatinamerica.co.uk).
The well-respected JLA offers a wide range of packages to numerous destinations in Latin

America, including Cuba. The website has details of its current offers.
Branch: 2nd Floor Barton Arcade, 51 - 63 Deansgate, Manchester M3 2BH (0161 832 1441/fax 0161 832 1551/man@journeylatin america.co.uk).

United States
See p275 **Travel by US citizens to Cuba**.

Canada

Friendship Tours
Joyce Holmes, 12883 98th Avenue, Surrey, British Columbia V3T 1B1 (604 581 4065/fax 604 581 0785/friendship@ home.com)
A small Canadian outfit, Friendship Tours organises educational and leisure trips to Cuba, focusing on authentic cultural experiences rather than the standard tour-and-beach combination.

Directory

terminuses there are often two queues: one for passengers who want a seat and one for those who are prepared to stand. Once in the bus, keep a close eye on your belongings (crowded buses are fertile ground for pick-pockets) and make your way to the exit as soon as possible to avoid missing your stop.

Most buses run at least hourly during the day and slightly less often between 11pm and 5am. There are no route maps for Havana but the front of each bus normally displays the route number and destination. (Metrobus routes are prefixed by the letter 'M'.) Many of them converge on **Parque de la Fraternidad** in La Habana Vieja. Other useful places to pick up buses are **Parque Central** in Centro Habana and **La Rampa** (Calle 23) in Vedado.

Tourist buses

The useful but under-publicised **Vaivén Bus Turístico** run by Rumbos was suspended in 2000 for a complete revision of the service. It ran in a loop between Miramar and La Habana Vieja and, at $4 for a day pass, was an attractive alternative to taxis or buses. Call Agencia de Viajes Rumbos (243688/243689) to find out whether it has been reinstated.

Taxis

Although much of Havana (and especially La Habana Vieja) is best explored on foot, taxis are useful for travel between neighbourhoods. There are plenty to choose from, although they are harder to find in less-visited areas.

Official tourist taxis (*turistaxis*) are modern cars with the usual taxi signs on the roof. The cheapest rates are offered by **Panataxi** (555555), but their taxis are not often found cruising the streets, so you'll need to phone for one. Rates within the city are not negotiable and meters start at $1, with each kilometre charged at 60¢-80¢ (night-time rates are about 20 per cent higher). Prices for long distances can be negotiated, and, depending on the type and size of car, can compare favourably to the cost of renting.

Cheaper than the tourist taxis are the black and yellow Ladas of the **Empresa Provincial de Taxi**. These vehicles are state-owned but privately operated and they are not supposed to take foreigners. You might be able to flag one down, but phone bookings are only accepted for Cubans getting to and from hospital. Meters start at 1 peso, with each kilometre charged at 25 centavos. Non-Cubans are often charged in dollars, but even so the rate still works out at half the price of a tourist taxi.

Drivers of private cars with a windscreen sticker saying '*Pasaje*' only have a permit to carry Cubans, but may be willing to take foreign passengers who pay in dollars. Look out for the additional cardboard 'taxi' sign on the dashboard. There are also numerous illegal taxis, often driven by underpaid Cuban professionals, trawling the streets and hanging around tourist hotels. Both permit-holding and illegal drivers can usually be hired for half a day for about $20. Drivers are fined if they are caught with a foreigner in the back of their car, but most Cubans are usually very keen to take the risk for a dollar fare. The only liability for the passenger is that the vehicle may break down, though they may also get drawn into bureaucratic hassle. With any non-metered taxi always agree the price before you get in and don't be afraid to bargain.

The cost of a *colectivo* (collective taxi) is shared among all the passengers, even if their destinations vary. They are found at specific places (such as bus terminals) and set off only once they have a full load; for this reason, they are not particularly practical for tourists.

For a uniquely Cuban experience look out for the pre-Revolution classic American cars used as official and unofficial taxis throughout the city. **Gran Caribe** (577338) has a fleet of period models in tip-top condition. The cars can be hired either as taxis for specific short runs in the city, or with a driver by the hour ($15) or the day ($90), with fixed prices for trips out of town ($260 return to Viñales, for example).

Taxi companies
Fénix 639720/639680
Habanataxi 539085/6
Micar 242715
Rex (limousine service) 339160
Taxis OK 249518/19
Transgaviota 272727
Transtur/Turistaxi 336666

Other forms of transport

Rickshaw-style tricycles, known as *bicitaxis*, are a pleasant way of roving the streets of La Habana Vieja and Centro. They are cheaper than tourist taxis and a far more relaxing way of covering short distances. Expect to pay a dollar per ride within the old city. Alternatively, hail a *cocotaxi* – a three-wheeled scooter with a bright orange cab. These are now found as far out as Miramar and can be hired for about $5 per hour by up to three people. Horse-drawn carriages can be picked up at various tourist spots in La Habana Vieja for a 50-minute tour of the all the key sights for $5 per all person. The *cochero* (driver) will also provide a normal taxi service to wherever you want to go.

Travel by US citizens to Cuba

The real problems for US travellers to Cuba began in 1962 when President John F Kennedy, reeling froom the effects of the Bay of Pigs fiasco and the Cuban Missile Crisis, imposed an economic embargo on the island and prohibited US citizens from spending money in Cuba. This restriction effectively prevented all but a few 'licensed' US citizens from travelling legally to Cuba and has remained in force ever since, embellished by subsequent guidelines and amendments. Despite the government's interminable rules, however, there are now more US citizens visiting Cuba than at any point since the Revolution. (Figures from the Cuban tourist ministry suggest that over 165,000 Americans visited the island in the year 2000.)

In January 1999, President Bill Clinton expanded the category of those permitted to travel to Cuba by promulgating a 'people-to-people' policy, designed to streamline licensing and encourage the expansion of educational, cultural and humanitarian exchange. Great you might think; but, in October 2000, as a final flourish before leaving office, he turned the policy into law (hidden in the depths of a complicated agricultural bill). Those in the know suspect that this codification will make the issue of travel licences subject to stricter scrutiny.

Applying for a licence

Today, in order to set foot on the island and legally engage in a financial transaction US citizens (with a valid passport) must travel under either a 'genéral' or a 'specific' licence issued by the **Office of Foreign Assets and Control** (OFAC), a division of the US Treasury Department. OFAC's 'general' licenses are primarily for government officials, journalists, and Cuban-Americans travelling to Cuba once a year to visit close family relatives. 'Specific' licences are issued on a case-by-case basis for humanitarian purposes, educational exchanges and travel in connection with professional research. Applications for a licence that hint of a business or vacationing purpose will almost certainly get a thumbs down. Applications should be sent in writing to the Licensing Division, OFAC, US Department of Treasury, 1500 Pennsylvania Avenue NW, Treasury Annex, Washington, DC 20220. For information call 202 622 2480 or consult the website: www.treas.gov/ofac. The Cuban government requires US citizens to have a visa to visit the island, so you'll also have to contact the **Cuban Interests Office** in Washington, DC (*see p289*).

Organised trips

The least bureaucratic way for a US passport holder to travel to Cuba (and perhaps the most educational option) is to hop on board a trip sponsored by one of the following well-known licensed organisations, or ask them to custom-design one for you.

Center for Cuban Studies

124 West 23rd Street, New York, NY 10011 (212 242 0559/fax 212 242 1937).

Cross-Cultural Solutions

47 Potter Avenue, New Rochelle, NY 10801 (1-800 380 4777/914 632 0022/fax 914 632 8494/info@cross culturalsolutions.org).

Cuba Now

1244 South Fourth Street, Louisville, Kentucky 40203 (502 479 3666/www.cuba now.org).

Spending money in Cuba

You are permitted to spend $185 per day while in Cuba and to bring back only $100 worth of goods, with exceptions for artwork. Also, remember that credit cards, travellers' cheques and personal cheques issued in the United States cannot be used in Cuba.

Illegal travel to Cuba

Of course you could forget about the legal issues and fly to the island from a third country destination (*see p272*). As far as Cuban officials are concerned it is not illegal for US visitors to enter Cuba. However, if upon your return to the United States a US customs official knows you have been to Cuba without a licence, you could be subject to a prison sentence and a hefty fine of up to $500,000. Customs officers at Havana's José Martí airport know the score to this extent, and are usually willing not to stamp US passports to prevent the passport holder from getting into trouble back home.

Directory

Driving

Traffic travels on the right. Speed limits, which are rigorously enforced, are 20kph (12.5mph) in driveways and car-parks; 40kph (25mph) around schools; 50kph (31mph) in urban areas; 60kph (37mph) in rural areas; 90kph (56mph) on paved highways; and 100kph (62mph) on the motorway. Any traffic fines you incur ($10) must not be paid directly to the police, but will be deducted from your car rental deposit.

Driving can be useful for venturing out of the city, but is not recommended in Havana itself. As well as missing out on the pleasure of walking the streets or being driven in the back of a classic American car, visiting drivers are likely to find themselves horribly confused by the city's warren of one-way streets. The volume of traffic is increasing every month and Havana now has noticeable rush-hour traffic.

Some *habaneros* drive quite recklessly and are inclined to make unpredictable moves. The use of indicators is not particularly widespread, so watch out for surprise stops, often in the middle of the road, and unannounced turns in fast-moving traffic. Cyclists present a further hazard as they observe few rules of the road and often ride two abreast. Avoid driving around La Habana Vieja (much of which is pedestrian-only anyway) and keep away from the busy and poorly maintained Vía Blanca.

Breakdown services

Your car hire company should deal with all breakdowns. In addition to this, repair services are provided by a branch of **Oro Negro** at Avenida 5ta, esquina a 120, in Playa (286149) between 8am and 7pm Monday to Saturday. There are other branches at Avenida 7ma, esquina a 2, in Miramar (241906) and Avenida 13, esquina a 84, in Playa (241938).

If your broken-down car needs towing, call **Agencia Peugeot** (577533), which will charge 75¢ per kilometre to get to the car and $1 per kilometre to tow it to wherever you want to go.

Fuel stations

Servi-Cupet and **Oro Negro** petrol stations (*servicentros*) sell super (*especial*) at 90¢, regular at 75¢ and diesel at $45¢ per litre. Both companies have several 24-hour petrol stations in the city. Note that the pump attendants in Havana are under instructions to sell only *especial* to drivers of hired cars and you will have difficulty persuading them to let you put anything else in your tank. Local petrol stations, which require special vouchers and charge in pesos, often run out of fuel and do not carry *especial*. Avoid buying black-market fuel from individuals on the street.

Parking

There are no parking meters on the streets of Havana and, although you have to avoid places where the pavement is painted yellow, it is unusual to have difficulties finding a parking space. However, car theft is a problem in the city, so it's often safer to use designated car parks (*parqueos*) with a guard (*custodio*). These charge $1 to $2 overnight and can be found opposite **Hotel Sevilla**; at the **Hotel Nacional**, and at **Parque El Curita**. **Hotel Habana Libre** charges $4 a day for use of its underground car park. For all these hotels, *see chapter* **Accommodation**. Illegally parked cars are subject to fines and may be towed away.

Car hire

None of the international car rental companies have offices in Cuba so visitors are reliant on the national providers (*listings below*). With the rise in tourism, the demand for hire cars in Cuba often outstrips the supply. In high season (December to April) it may be wise to reserve a car before you arrive although this can only be done 15 days in advance and doesn't necessarily ensure that your car will be ready and waiting when you get to Cuba. Once in Havana, most hotels have a car rental desk or can at least help you make arrangements. The main car rental companies have offices all over the city and also in the arrivals area of airport Terminal 3. Some of these are open 24 hours daily.

To rent a car, you must be at least 21 years old, with one year's driving experience, and must hold a valid national driving licence or an international driving permit.

Renting a car is the easiest way to see the country, but it is not cheap. Unless you are looking for a long-term contract prices do not vary much, most companies charging around $45 to $100 per day, plus a deposit of $200 to $300. The fee and deposit must be paid in advance by cash, credit card (not issued by a US bank) or travellers' cheques. Rates include unlimited mileage, but insurance, fuel and parking are extra. On hiring the car you will be charged 90¢ a litre (cash) for a tank of petrol (check it's full) but don't expect a refund for any fuel remaining in the tank when the car is returned. You will be offered insurance (payable in cash) either covering accidents but not theft (policy A; $10-$12) or covering all risks except loss of radio and spare tire (policy B; $15). Any additional drivers

Directory

are charged a flat fee of $10-$15 each or $3 per day. If you don't fancy driving yourself, some companies can also provide chauffeurs, for which you will pay a daily rate, plus room and board if you are away overnight. Keep your rental agreement with you until you return the car or you will be charged a $50 penalty.

If you are involved in an accident or have something stolen from your car you will need to obtain a police report (*denuncia*) in order to make an insurance claim. Rental cars are often poorly maintained, so try to get a new vehicle and always check it carefully – a test drive is a good idea. Make it clear if you want seat belts in the back as many cars do not have them.

Rental companies

Cubacar 332277
Havanautos 240647/
www.havanautos.cubaweb.cu
Micar 242444
Panautos 663286
Transtur 244057
Vía Rent a Car 243606

Cycling

Cycling became a necessity due to the fuel shortages during the Special Period and remains a popular mode of transport despite widespread potholes, copious bus fumes, and the perils of sharing the road with the average *habanero* motorist. Most Cubans use clunky Chinese bikes, although road bikes are becoming more common. Puncture repairs – a quotidian problem given the state of the roads – are available all over Havana, wherever you see the sign '*ponchera.*' There are scores of bicycle parking places (*parqueos*) where you pay one or two pesos to leave your bike in the charge of an attendant. These *parqueos* are a much safer alternative to leaving your bike on the street, although you still should secure frame and wheels with a strong lock. Spare parts and tools are scarce so bring whatever you might need with you if you are travelling with your own bike. Contact the **Federación Cubana de Ciclismo** in Habana del Este (973776/951286) for further information.

Bicycle hire

There are currently no bike rental outlets in Havana (as far as we know), but you can easily arrange to borrow one from a Cuban for a few dollars. Alternatively, pick up a second-hand bike from the **Cuatro Caminos** market (*see p160*) for about $20.

The **Club Nacional de Cicloturismo Gran Caribe** will provide bikes for those taking part in one of its cycling tours (*see p217*).

Walking

As a pedestrian, keep on the lookout for *bici-* and *cocotaxis* when you cross the street as they tend to come whizzing out of nowhere.

Resources A-Z

Addresses

In Cuba (and in this guide), addresses state first the street name, then the number (often designated by a # sign), followed by the two cross street (*entrecalles*) between which the building is situated. Thus, the restaurant La Mina, Calle Oficios #6, entre Obispo y Obrapía will be found on Calle Oficios, between Calle Obispo and Calle Obrapía. If a building is right on the corner (*esquina*) of two streets, both streets are given, but the street where the entrance is located tends to be given first. So the Museo del Automóvil, Calle Oficios #13, esquina a Jústiz will be on Calle Oficios at the corner of Calle Jústiz. (Note that this address could also be given in a shorter form, as Calle Oficios y Jústiz). A street name follow by 's/n' indicates that the building has no street number. Residential addresses sometimes specify *altos* (upper floor), *bajos* (ground floor) or *sótano* (basement) in their address, or use *primero piso* (first floor), *segundo piso* (second floor) and so on.

Some street names in the city centre were changed after the Revolution, but *habaneros* are inclined to use the old and new names indiscriminately, which can be very confusing for the unsuspecting visitor. To make matters worse, the words *calle* (street) and *avenida* (avenue) are often omitted entirely in directions or an address; even *habaneros* sometimes confuse the two, and in some cases even they do not know if a street is officially a *calle* or *avenida*. Cubans are likely to give directions that refer to well-known landmarks rather than streets, and may invent directions if they're not sure of an exact location.

In this book we have given the official/new name of each street with the old name in brackets. Most maps also follow this practice. For a list of new and old street names, *see p278* **Streets of Havana**.

Attitude & etiquette

Cubans are generally friendly people and intensely family-orientated. They are also usually well disposed towards

Streets of Havana

The streets below have a new (official) name and an old (popular) name, both of which are used on maps and in speech. For further information *see p277*.

New name	Old name
Agramonte	Zulueta
Aponte	Someruelos
Avenida Antonio Maceo	Malecón
Avenida de las Misiones (northern half)	Monserrate
Avenida de Bélgica (southern half)	Egido
Avenida Carlos Manuel de Céspedes	Avenida del Puerto
Avenida de España	Vives
Avenida de Italia	Galiano
Avenida Salvador Allende	Carlos III
Avenida Simón Bolívar	Reina
Brasil	Teniente Rey
Capdevila	Cárcel
Leonor Pérez	Paula
Máximo Gómez	Monte
Padre Varela	Belascoaín
Paseo de Martí	Paseo del Prado
San Martín	San José

tourists. As a foreigner you will be expected to pay for Cuban friends when you go out with them, regardless of the occasion. (It is assumed that all foreigners are rich, which, relatively they are.)

While Cubans usually address those whom they don't know as *Compañero/Compañera* (comrade) it is more appropriate for foreigners to use *Señor/Señora/Señorita* with strangers. Women are inclined to greet everyone, even those they do not know well, with one kiss on the cheek and men are prone to shaking hands more than their counterparts in Britain or in the US.

Everyday life for a Cuban demands a lot of patience so if things get frustrating for you, do not expect much sympathy. It pays to be firm, but losing your temper is likely to make things worse. Cubans are known for their laid-back attitude, so unless you want to end up having a heart attack (and the heat doesn't help),

your best bet is just to adapt and go with the flow.

Note that people of darker complexions are more likely to suffer harassment from the police than are white tourists. Visitors who are black or of Latin appearance might be asked to show their passports to gain access to hotels or other places where Cuban citizens might not normally be allowed.

Business

Cuba remains, politically at least, firmly committed to socialism, and the state continues to control all but some very small businesses. However, opportunities in Cuba abound and increasing numbers of suppliers and investors come to do business here every year. Joint ventures have meant the development of big business, especially in the fields of tourism, mining, power generation, and biotechnology.

In the past many business visitors have entered Cuba on

tourist visas, but now the authorities are attempting to put a stop to this, so anyone entering the country with a laptop and without the usual holiday-maker's paraphernalia risks arousing some suspicion. On the other hand, it takes at least six weeks to get a business visa and you can apply only with sponsorship from an appropriate Cuban government organisation. Also bear in mind that visa regulations can change at short notice, so it's wise to check with the Cuban Consulate in your home country before setting off. Those visiting Havana for any purpose should remember that annual trade fairs and international summit meetings, as well as the usual peak tourist season, can make it hard to book flights and hotels. *See p290* **When to go**.

Business services & facilities

There are now several hotels offering adequate facilities for the business visitor, including meeting rooms, fax and Internet facilities and some secretarial or translation services. First-timers tend to use the Hotels **Meliá Cohiba**, **Nacional**, **Golden Tulip Parque Central**, or **Meliá Habana** (*see chapter* **Accommodation**). These hotels are also likely to carry copies of *Business Tips on Cuba*, targeted at foreign investors. Representatives at your embassy can usually advise on commercial services available locally and, if you are unable to use the fax at your hotel, these may be available at the embassy for a small fee. If you require Spanish language support during your stay, **ESTI** (Cuban Centre for Translation and Interpretation) can provide a translation and/or interpretation service (323603/fax 327395).

For courier services, *see p285*; for further information on sending faxes, *see p288*; and for more on Internet access, *see p282*.

Customs

Incoming visitors over the age of 18 are permitted to bring the following items into Cuba: personal effects; gifts worth up to $100; 10 kilogrammes of medication; two litres of alcoholic drink; 200 cigarettes or 50 cigars or 250 grammes of tobacco. The import of food, plant and animal products, telecommunications equipment and firearms is subject to restrictions. Banned items include narcotics, obscene publications, explosives and pre-recorded video cassettes.

Departing visitors may export cigars up to the value of $2,000 (with a sales invoice); 50 cigars (without a sales invoice); six bottles of rum and up to $5,000 in cash. For restrictions on the export of art and antiques, *see p150*, and for allowances for US citizens, *see page 275* **Travel by US citizens to Cuba**.

Disabled

Havana is not a great place for disabled travellers. There are very few amenities or services for people with physical disabilities, and the potholed streets make it very hard for travellers in wheelchairs to get around.

A few hotels (the most expensive ones) claim to have proper facilities, maybe even a room or two adapted for disabled guests, however, these may not meet international standards. Disabled travellers are strongly advised to make their needs clear to their travel agent or tour operator, who should then make a special booking for appropriate accommodation.

Drugs

There are plenty of 'recreational' drugs around in Havana. However, you should resist all temptation to buy or use drugs during your stay, as the penalties for illegal drug use are ferocious. Most foreigners in Cuban jails are there for drug-related offences. Only a very foolhardy visitor would even consider bringing drugs into the country.

Electricity

The national grid operates on 110-volt, 60AC, as in the USA and Canada, although newer, European-managed hotels may have a 220-volt system, or even a combination of both. Two-pin plugs of the American flat pin type and screw-type light fittings are used. Visitors from the UK and the rest of Europe will require an adaptor to run any British electrical appliances in Cuba, but keep such items to a minimum because they could be confiscated at the airport.

Despite some recent improvements in the electricity supply, Havana is still subject to unexpected electricity blackouts (*apagones*), so it's a good idea to pack a pocket torch along with some spare batteries. Also, bear in mind that faulty wiring and dodgy sockets are common.

Embassies & consulates

Australia and New Zealand do not have diplomatic or consular representatives in Cuba, so the interests of those countries are represented by the Canadian and British embassies respectively. In the absence of an embassy, the USA is officially represented by the US Interests Section in Havana, under the protection of the Swiss Embassy.

British Embassy
Calle 34 #702 & #704, entre 7ma y 17, Miramar (241771/consular fax 248104/commercial fax 249214/ embrit@ceniai.inf.cu). **Open** 8am-3.30pm Mon-Fri; closed Sat, Sun. **Map** p310 C4.

Canadian Embassy
Calle 30 #518, esquina a 7ma, Miramar (242516/fax 332044). **Open** 8.30am-5pm Mon-Thur; 8.30am-2pm Fri; closed Sat, Sun. **Map** p311 B5.

United States Interests Section
Calzada, entre L y M, Vedado (333551/333552/333553/333554). **Open** 8.30am-5pm Mon-Fri; closed Sat, Sun. **Map** p312 A11.

Emergencies

In emergencies, **Asistur**, the 24-hour assistance agency for tourists, is a good first contact. In serious cases contact your embassy (*see above*).

Asistur
Casa del Científico, Paseo de Martí (Prado) #212, esquina a Trocadero, Centro Habana (338339/338920/ 338527). **Open** *Office* 8.30am-5.30pm daily. *Phone lines* 24hrs daily. **Map** p313 D14.
Deals with insurance claims, arranges replacement documents and helps with financial problems.

Emergency phone numbers
Ambulance (Asistur) 671315.
Ambulance (Clínica Cira García) 242811-4.
Ambulance (Red Cross) 405093/405094.
Fire brigade 811115.
Police 820116.

Health

The public health system is held up as one of the Revolution's greatest achievements. Statistically the number of doctors, dentists, clinics and hospital beds per capita is impressive, although the condition of equipment and facilities has been deteriorating in recent years.

At 73 years for men and 78 years for women, life expectancy in Cuba is on a par with that of the US. Many

Directory

tropical diseases have been eradicated, including, typhoid, diphtheria, tetanus, polio, and hepatitis A. Mosquitoes are not malarial but can be a nuisance, so bring plenty of repellent with you. There have also been occasional outbreaks of mosquito-carried dengue fever in Cuba, the last in 1996.

Random checks carried out by the embassies confirm that the city's water supply is safe to drink. However, diarrhoea may still be a problem, so tourists are advised to stick to bottled water, which is available in restaurants, *paladares* and shops. Avoid eating food bought from street vendors (especially anything with ice in it, like ice-cream) and carry water-purifying tablets in remote areas of the country, where you may come into contact with Giardia and other waterborne parasites.

Accident & emergency

In a medical emergency, call all the ambulance numbers, as emergency services have been known not to answer at all (*see p279*). Minor accidents can be dealt with at the city hospitals that cater for foreigners (*see p281-2*). In the event of possible poisoning, contact the **Poison control centre** (201230/208751).

Before you go

You're required to have a yellow fever vaccination if you're arriving in Cuba directly from South America. Otherwise, no other vaccinations are strictly required for travel to Cuba, but might be worth considering, especially if you're going off the beaten track. The UK Department of Health recommends vaccinations for hepatitis A, polio and typhoid. You might also want to consider a hepatitis B

vaccination if you are a frequent traveller or intend to stay overseas for a long period. All travellers should have had booster injections for tetanus and diptheria within the last ten years, and ensure that their measles, mumps and rubella immunisation is complete. Tuberculosis is rare in Cuba; however, children under 12 shoul be immunised as a precaution; check with your doctor before you go. Pregnant women should check with their doctors which vaccines are safe before being immunised.

Note that some vaccinations require you to have an initial injection, followed by a follow-up injection a few weeks later, so make sure you leave enough time for both injections before your trip; a course of injections should be started no later than six weeks before travel.

This information applies to travellers from the UK, the US and most other developed countries. For further information, consult the **Travel Doctor** website, www.traveldoctor.com.au.

Complementary medicine

The impact of the US blockade on medical supplies together with the sudden end to Soviet aid in 1990 meant that Cuba was practically forced to develop alternative medicine (*medicina alternativa*) and complementary techniques. These are now used in practically all health centres and hospitals and are hugely popular with local people. There is particular interest in acupuncture, acupressure, massage and suction treatment, as well as the so-called *medicinas verdes*: herbalism; homeopathy; and honey remedies. Ozone therapy is also being pioneered here.

Alternative remedies are available from **Farmacia Ciren**, Calle 216, esquina a

11B, Playa (215044) and **Farmacia Las Praderas**, Calle 230, entre 15a y 17, Siboney (337473/337474). These outlets also provide information on practitioners of complementary therapy. There are also two homeopathic pharmacies in Vedado; on the corner of Calle 23 and Calle M, and on the corner of Línea and Calle 14, and the international pharmacies listed below all carry a modest selection of herbal remedies. Every neighbourhood has a herb shop (*yerbero*), which sells a wide variety of herbs for medicinal and religious use.

Contraception & abortion

Sadly, in Cuba, abortion is commonly used as 'contraception'. Condoms (*preservativos*) are widely available, but they're Chinese in origin, unreliable and about as sensual as a rubber glove. Visitors should bring with them any forms of contraception they may need during their stay. For a discussion of sex and sexuality in Cuba, *see p183*.

Dentists

Dental treatment at any of the hospitals for foreigners (*see below*) is good and certainly no more expensive than it would be in the private system in Britain.

Doctors

In addition to the doctors at the international hospitals, many of the bigger hotels have a doctor on site who can be consulted for around $20.

Hospitals & clinics

Havana has a large number of hospitals, mostly reserved for Cubans, although some will see foreign patients. The last

Directory

Jockeying for attention

Jineterismo is a quintessential Cuban phenomenon. The term *jinetero*, and its female version, *jinetera*, literally means 'jockey' and is derived from the fact that such people 'ride' off the backs of tourists, that is, make a living out of squeezing dollars out of them. By extension, and because of the way some of these people earn their living, the term can also mean prostitute – even Cubans disagree as to whether or not and to what extent the boundaries are blurred.

JINETEROS

A male *jinetero* is not usually a prostitute (although you never know). Instead his main objective is to make a quick buck and he will have no qualms about selling you anything. *Jineteros* hover around waiting for the right moment to approach, and then greet foreigners with a friendly 'hi, my frien'.' Cigars are a *jinetero*'s main bread and butter, but 'guiding' tourists to paladares for the 'best meal in Havana' has also become a lucrative business. *Jineteros* operating in this way will have made a previous arrangement with the *paladar* owners (often their relations), in return for commission. You may get a surprisingly good meal in this way, but if you do decide to risk it, always agree on prices first; many an innocent tourist has parted with $40 per person for rice and beans in granny's kitchen. Use your common sense and you may even grow quite

fond of these unique Havana characters, as – God bless 'em – they are the worst salesmen in the world.

JINETERAS

Jineteras (literally, 'jockeys' – the Cubans have surpassed themselves with this sickeningly apt name) are small-scale prostitutes out to make a few precious dollars by ensnaring gullible or seedy foreign visitors. These (often very young) girls will follow foreign men around, hassling them and trying all the tricks in the book to make them feel special. All this attention may be endearing and flattering, but remember they'll be cornering the next guy an hour later.

More seriously, Cuba's enviably low level of sexually transmitted disease is being endangered by the rise in both prostitution and unsafe sexual practices. (It is common now for prostitutes to be offered $10 extra not to use a condom.) The government has tightened up on soliciting since the International Trade Fair in 1996, but still the numbers of young girls prowling the streets are disturbing. Unfortunately, there is no practicable way for foreign men to avoid this unlooked-for attention; wherever you are in Havana and whatever you look like, you will be chatted up. The best policy is to ignore it. (Saying a particular *jinetera* is not your type, will only encourage a harem of girls to gather around you so you can take your pick.)

---

ten years have also seen the development of a network of hospitals and clinics catering exclusively to foreigners and charging in dollars. Most of these are concentrated in and around Havana. In addition to emergency care, they also offer advanced treatment in practically every sphere of health: orthopaedic surgery, neuro-rehabilitation, dentistry, cancer treatment, cardiology, hypertension, basic and comprehensive medical check-ups, eye surgery (short-sightedness, glaucoma and cataracts), geriatric conditions and plastic surgery. Of particular interest are those that have achieved

international recognition, such as **CIREN**, for its work on Parkinson's disease, nervous system conditions and spinal injuries affecting both adults and children.

As well as offering emergency and specialist treatment, some clinics are aimed at relatively healthy (and wealthy) people who simply want to improve their quality of life. The four-star **La Pradera**, for example, is specifically promoted as a hotel-cum-health resort.

English-speaking staff are available at most institutions dealing with foreigners. Nevertheless, Cubanacán acknowledges that language

can sometimes be a barrier, and a smattering of Spanish or a fluent friend with you will always help.

Centro Internacional de Salud La Pradera

Calle 230, entre 15A y 17, Siboney, (337473/337474/ fax 337198/337199/www.softcal. cubaweb.cu/praderas.
This clinic offers a wide-ranging health and beauty programme, including aerobics, massage, laser therapy, anti-cellulite treatment, anti-stress therapy, general medical check-ups, dentistry and specialist care for multiple sclerosis, neurological and orthopaedic conditions. In 2000 its most famous patient was Diego 'Hand of God' Maradona, who checked in to recover from his cocaine addiction.

Centro Internacional de Restauracion Neurologica (CIREN)

Avenida 25 # 15805, entre 158 y 160, Cubanacán (216999/336028/ fax 332420/336302/ www. ciren.cubaweb.cu).
The International Centre for Neurological Recovery treats patients with multiple sclerosis, Parkinson's disease and other injuries or conditions affecting the nervous system. Additionally, it offers dental services and a full range of plastic surgery, together with holistic treatments, such as ozone-based therapy, acupuncture, Chinese massage and 'creative visualisation'.

Clínica Cira García

Calle 20 #4101, esquina a Avenida 41, Miramar (242811/242814/fax 241633/www.infomed.sld.cu/cira/ www.ciracubanacan.cu). Map p311 B6.
Exclusively for foreigners, this state-of-the-art clinic is a well designed and, in many respects, luxurious building. It is one of the jewels in the crown of Cuba's health system and offers a broad programme of treatment that includes some 41 types of plastic surgery. Reports are of generally speedy, efficient and attentive treatment.

Hospital Cimeq

Avenida 216, esquina a 11B, Siboney (215022/336497/ 336499).
This slightly grim place out in the suburbs is where Fidel and other Cubans and some foreigners get treated.

Hospital Hermanos Ameijeiras

Padre Varela (Belascoaín), esquina a San Lázaro, Centro Habana (577077/576053). Map p313 C13.
This hospital is for Cubans, but has designated areas for dollar-paying patients.

Pharmacies

Local pharmacies open either on *turnos regulares* (8am to 6pm Mon-Fri; 8am-noon Sat, closed Sun) or *turnos permanentes* (24 hours daily). You'll find these all over Havana but unless you have a very simple complaint their poorly stocked shelves may not be of much use. There are also several *farmacías internacionales* in Havana (listed below), which supply a comprehensive range of medication in dollars to foreign visitors. Cubans are not allowed to use these outlets. Note that the **Hotel Comodoro** (*see p59*) also has a small pharmacy. For complementary medicine stockists, *see p280*.

Centro International Oftalmológica Camilo Cienfuegos

Calle 13, entre L y M, Vedado (333599). **Open** 8am-8pm daily. Map p312 A/B11.

Clínica Cira García

Calle 20 #4101, esquina Avenida 41, Miramar (242880/242811). **Open** 24hrs daily. Map p311 B6.

Farmacia Internacional

Avenida 41, esquina a Calle 20, Miramar (242051). **Open** 9am-9pm daily. Map p311 C6.

Plaza Hotel

Calle Agramonte (Zulueta) #267, esquina a Neptuno, Centro Habana (615703). **Open** 24hrs daily. Map p313 D14.

Prescriptions

Due to the relative difficulty in getting hold of medication in Cuba, be sure to bring with you any prescription drugs you may need during your stay

STDs, HIV & AIDs

STDs such as herpes and gonorrhea are fairly common in Cuba, but syphilis and AIDS are rare. Visitors who have sex while they are in Cuba should always use condoms they have brought with them from home. *See also p31 and p281* **Jockeying for attention**. For general information on HIV and AIDs in Cuba, *see p185* **Positive attitudes**.

Lineayuda

303156. **Open** *Phoneline* 9am-9pm Mon-Fri; closed Sat, Sun.
This anonymous helpline is an important source of information about sexually transmitted diseases and especially AIDS. It was set up under a grant from Medicins sans Frontières and is under the jurisdiction of the Ministry of Public Health.

ID

Visitors should carry a photocopy of their passport around with them at all times. You will only need the passport itself when you want to change money, use a travellers' cheque, draw out cash using a credit card, or pay for something with a $50 or $100 bill.

Insurance

Visitors are highly recommended to take out private travel insurance for their trip to Cuba. A good policy should cover flight cancellation, theft, loss of life and medical costs. Health insurance is particularly advised, since the cost of medical services adds up quickly, even in Cuba. Make sure you are covered for hospitalisation, nursing services, doctors' fees and repatriation.

Internet

Although still in their infancy in Cuba, Internet facilities are becoming more widely available, both to resident business people and to visitors. Reliable access has been a problem, but a modernisation programme to install new phone lines and digital exchanges by the state telecommunications company, **Etecsa**, has improved the service a lot. Etecsa has two subsidiary Internet service providers: **Ceniai** (626565/ 635209) and **Infocom** (244444).

Internet access

To date, **Cibercafé Capitolio** is the only place offering public Internet access in the whole of Havana, although there are plans for more in the very near future. The better business hotels also have email

Directory

and Internet facilities, available to non-residents, including the **Meliá Cohiba**, **Nacional**, **Golden Tulip Parque Central** and **Meliá Habana** (*see chapter* **Accommodation**). If you use these places you avoid the Capitolio's queues, but you pay for the privilege. For example, Internet access at the Golden Tulip costs $4.50 for 15 minutes, or $12 for an hour. Strangely, email starts at the same price, but costs $17.50 for an hour; however, it's generally reliable, if slow. The cheapest option for sending and receiving email is an **Infotur** tourist office (*see p288*); they charge $1 per page to send or receive an email, plus 25¢ per page for print outs. For a review of useful websites, *see p294*.

Cibercafé Capitolio

Capitolio, Calle Industria, esquina a San Martín (San José), Centro Habana (626565/635209). **Open** 9.30am-6pm daily. **Rates** $5 per hr. **Map** p313 D/E14.
There are seven PCs available, but, due to heavy demand, it's usually necessary to queue.

Language

For Cuban-Spanish words and phrases, *see p293*.

Legal assistance

As a first point of call, visitors should contact **Asistur** or their consulate (*for both, see p279*). **Consultoria Juridica Internacional** specialises in legal help for foreigners.

Consultoria Jurídica Internacional

Calle 16 #314, entre 3ra y 5ta (242490/fax 242303). **Open** 8.30am-noon, 1.30-5.30pm Mon-Fri; closed Sat, Sun. **Map** p311 .

Libraries

If you're hoping to improve your knowledge of Cuba by visiting one of the local libraries, you're likely to be

disappointed. You won't have difficulty locating a library in Havana, but finding any quality texts in them is a different story. Most of the libraries are poorly stocked with international books thin on the ground.

Biblioteca del Instituto de Literatura y Lingüística

Avenida Salvador Allende (Carlos III) #710, entre Castillejo y Soledad, Centro Habana (754505/785405). **Open** 8am-4pm Mon-Fri; 8am-1.30pm Sat; closed Sun.
Probably the best source of novels and non-Spanish texts in Havana. But it is not a lending library and you need to hand over your passport if you want to consult the books.

Biblioteca Nacional

Avenida de la Independencia (Rancho Boyeros) s/n, entre Aranguren y 20 de Mayo, Plaza (555442). **Open** 8am-9pm Mon-Fri; 8am-6pm Sat; closed Sun.
Havana's main library occupies 16 floors of books, magazines and books and some exhibition space. Again, this is not a lending library and even consulting a book is a complicated business. Bring as many documents as you can in the way of diplomas, certificates, proof of educational qualifications etc in order to improve your chances of seeing the book you actually want.

Biblioteca Pública Provincial Rubén Martínez Villena

Calle Obispo #59, entre Oficios y Baratillo, La Habana Vieja (629035). **Open** 8am-8.45pm Mon-Fri; 8am-4.30pm Sat; closed Sun. **Admission** free. **Map** p316 E16.
This library has recently been renovated; it seems to be easier to look at the books, but there is still no public access to the shelves. A passport is required.

Lost property

Lost property is '*objetos perdidos*' in Spanish.
Airport Terminal 3 has a '*reclamaciones*' counter open 24 hours daily.
If you leave something in a taxi call the taxi office as soon as possible and ask staff to try and track it down (though it's unlikely they'll be able to).

Money

To keep foreign visitors on their toes, Cuba has three currencies in circulation: the US dollar; the Cuban peso; and the *peso convertible*. However, despite this triple currency system, dollars rule, and virtually every transaction you make in Cuba will be in dollars. The US dollar became legal tender in Cuba in 1993, and since then it has flooded the market. Every Cuban is keen to get his or her hands on the mighty greenback, as it is the only means of buying luxury consumer goods and of achieving a more comfortable standard of living.

Cuba, in particular Havana, is not the bargain destination that most visitors imagine. Although peso prices are often dirt cheap, foreign visitors paying in dollars are surprised by how much money they end up spending here. Moreover, unlike many Latin American countries, Cuba is not really a bargaining culture; you may be able to negotiate on long-distance taxi fares, or the price of objects sold in crafts markets (although these are usually excellent value), but elsewhere you will be expected to pay the quoted price.

Recently, European suppliers operating in a business context in Cuba have started to quote prices in Euros. Use of the currency is limited at present, but is likely to become more widespread.

Dollar currency

Each dollar is divided into 100 cents (¢). Coins range from copper pennies (1¢) to silver nickels (5¢), dimes (10¢) and quarters (25¢), plus rarer half-dollar and one-dollar coins. Notes come in denominations of $1, $5, $10, $20 and $50. In Cuba, dollars are known as *dolares*, or *divisa* (slang terms include *barro* and *fula*).

Directory

However, many people say pesos when they mean dollars – if in doubt, double check whether they are referring to *pesos cubanos* or *dolares* – and, to add to the confusion, the dollar symbol ($) is often used to denote the peso and the *peso convertible* (as well as the dollar). In these instances, the context should tell you whether a price is in dollars or pesos. When a peso price is quoted, non-Cubans paying in dollars will sometimes receive preferential treatment, such as being able to jump the queue.

Carry dollars in low denominations, as many places will not be able to give change, and take your passport (or a photocopy) if you intend to pay with a $50 or $100 note in all but the most upmarket places.

Pesos cubanos

The Cuban peso, known as the peso, or *moneda nacional* (national currency), has an exchange rate of 20 to a dollar. Each peso is divided into 100 centavos. Notes are available in denominations of one, three, five, ten, 20 and 50 pesos; coins start at one centavo, followed by five centavos, ten centavos, 20 centavos, one peso and three pesos.

Although you'll pay for nearly everything in the city in dollars, it is useful to have a handful of pesos for use on buses, in taxis and at street stalls, *agromercados*, peso restaurants, cinemas and concerts. You will probably use pesos more if you spend time outside Havana. Note that the export of Cuban pesos is prohibited (although customs officials are unlikely to be bothered by a few coins).

Pesos convertibles

The convertible peso was introduced in 1995. Nominally it has the same value as the dollar, but in practice dollars are still the currency with clout. You may get given *pesos convertibles* in change, even if you've paid in dollars; you are not being ripped off, but spend them before you leave as they cannot be taken out of Cuba.

The currency circulates as notes of one, five, ten, 25, 50 and 100 pesos, and coins of five, ten, 25 and 50 centavos.

ATMs

There are now cash machines in Havana at the **Hotel Golden Tulip Parque Central** (*see p53*), the **Plaza de Carlos III** (*see p150*), the **Banco Metropolitano** on Avenida 5ta, esquina a 112, in Miramar, and the **Banco Internacional de Comercio** on Avenida 3ra, esquina a 78, also in Miramar. However, they only take Visa cards and allow a maximum withdrawal of just $300. It is unwise to rely on ATMs for your cash as they don't always work, although it is clear that the banks are trying to improve the system

Banks

Banks in Havana will exchange foreign currency into dollars and cash travellers' cheques. Branches of the **Banco Financiero Internacional**, **Banco Internacional de Comercio** and **Banco Metropolitano** may also let you withdraw cash against a credit card (as long as the card was not issued by a US bank).

Bureaux de change

Cadeca (short for *casa de cambio*) exchange offices are found throughout Cuba, in tourist areas and also next to the *agromercados*. The rates are usually in line with those at the banks, service is pretty reliable, and, because there are so many branches, the queues are often shorter. Use the *cadecas* to buy or sell dollars,

to break larger dollars bills so that you have smaller cash for tipping and to cash travellers' cheques. Some hotels will also change your money, even if you are not a guest, but note that it's best to complete the transaction before 6pm when most hotels cash up.

Credit cards

Credit cards issued by US or affiliated banks are not accepted anywhere in Cuba. In theory non-US credit cards are accepted in a few shops and restaurants and in almost all tourist hotels; however, you should not rely on one credit card, since it sometimes seems quite arbitrary which ones are rejected. Even if your card is accepted, be prepared to wait ages for the staff to phone for the authorisation code.

If you don't mind queuing, credit-card withdrawals can be made at some banks (*see above*), and at the **Hotel Habana Libre** (*see p55*) between 9am and 7pm Monday to Saturday. Alternatively, the bank office at the **Hotel Nacional de Cuba** (*see p56*) is open 8am to 8pm daily and you seldom have to wait.

Natural hazards

Heat

Havana's hot and humid climate can take some time to get used to. Try not to go out in the midday sun, and drink plenty of water or soft drinks throughout the day to avoid dehydration. You should also increase your intake of salt. These measures are especially important if you have diarrhoea.

Hurricanes & storms

Hurricanes occasionally occur between September and November, but are usually well forecasted. They are characterised by very strong winds and torrential rains, but do not present a substantial risk to human life, as long as sensible precautions are taken. *See also p290*. If an electrical storm brews up while you are out – most likely during the summer months – keep away from royal palm trees, which tend to attract lightning.

Jellyfish

Jellyfish are sometimes found at some of the beaches near Havana. Their stings are not lethal, but they can be pretty uncomfortable if you have the misfortune to swim through a crowd of them. Stings are best relieved with calamine lotion or an antihistamine cream.

Sun

Don't underestimate the strength of the sun; use sun-cream (at least SPF15) and wear a sun-hat with a brim and sunglasses whenever you go outdoors. This applies particularly to children.

Opening hours

Like everything else in Havana, opening hours are very variable; the times given below are only intended as guidelines. As a basic rule, if you have to get something done, do it in the morning, and allow plenty of time.

Banks

Open 8.30am-3pm Mon-Fri; closed Sat, Sun.

Government offices

Open 8.30am-12.30pm, 1.30-5.30pm Mon-Fri; closed Sat, Sun.

Markets

Open 8am-6pm Tue-Sat; 8am-noon Sun; closed Mon.

Shops

Open 10am-5.30pm Mon-Sat; closed Sun. However, many shops have extended hours and some are also open on Sundays.

Police stations

All crimes should be reported immediately, in person, to the **Policia Nacional Revolucionaria** (PNR). There is a police station in every district and, it sometimes seems, a policeman on every street corner. The General Command of the PNR is on Calle Tacón, opposite the Parque Arqueológico, in La Habana Vieja, but if you need the address of your nearest police station, call 820116.

Postal services

Cuba's postal service (*Correos de Cuba*) is slow and unreliable, and petty theft within the postal service is rife. If you want to send a postcard home and you do not mind it arriving many weeks after you return from your holiday (or not at all) your best bet is to send it from one of the big hotels, where you can usually buy the stamps you need. Otherwise you will have to rely on people you know travelling in and out of Cuba to carry letters and parcels for you. This also the safest way to receive mail, as there are no reliable poste restante (general delivery) services.

Urgent communications should be sent as faxes – usually possible from a hotel (*see p288*). Larger items can be sent by the costly but largely reliable **DHL** courier service (Avenida 1ra s/n, esquina a 26, Miramar; tel. 241578/241876/244093/fax 240999).

Religion

Since the early 1990s, freedom of religion has been part of the Cuban constitution. Notionally, the majority of those who practise religion in Cuba are Roman Catholics; in practice, however, many are followers of the Afro-Cuban religion *santería*, which combines

Catholicism with Yoruba beliefs. The Pope's celebrated visit in 1998 was a massive boost for Cuban Catholicism and led to a rise in church attendance on the island. Havana has no shortage of Catholic churches from the colonial era, but you will also find an Episcopalian and a Presbyterian church, two synagogues and a mosque. For further information on religion, *see p28* **Religious life**.

Islam

Casa de los Árabes

Calle Oficios #16, entre Obispo y Obrapía, La Habana Vieja (615868). Open 9am-4.30pm Tue-Sat; 9am-1pm Sun; closed Mon.

Judaism

Casa de la Comunidad Hebrea

Calle I #241, entre 13 y 15, Vedado (328953). Open 9.30am-5pm Mon-Sat; closed Sun. *Services* May-Sept 7pm Fri; 10am Sat; Oct-Apr 6pm Fri; 10am Sat.

Sinagoga Adath Israel de Cuba

Calle Acosta, esquina a Picota, La Habana Vieja (613495). Open 8am-noon, 5pm-8pm daily. *Services* 8am, 6pm Mon-Fri 9am, 6pm Sat; 9am Sun.

Protestant

Iglesia Episcopal

Calle 13 #876, esquina a 6, Vedado (35656). Open phone to check. Map p312 B9.

Iglesia Presbiteriana-Reformada en Cuba

Calle Salud #222, entre Campanaria y Lealtad, Centro Habana (621219). Open phone to check.

Safety & security

Until fairly recently La Habana Vieja was notorious for petty theft from tourists, but the presence of police on many street corners (in much of this area as well as in Vedado and some of Centro Habana) has greatly diminished the

Directory

problem. Nevertheless, pickpockets are still about; don't flash cameras, jewellery or wallets around. Violent crime against tourists is rare, though not unheard of.

If you are the victim of a robbery, you should contact the police immediately. Although it is highly unlikely they will recover your property, you will need a police statement in order to make an insurance claim (see p285).

Smoking

Smoking is tolerated in most public places and no-smoking areas are rare.

Study

Just as Cuba is becoming a hip holiday destination, so studying there is also a growing market. However, the bureaucracy of arranging to study in Cuba is a nightmare – in fact, once you've managed to enrol, filled out the endless forms and solved the visa mysteries, the exams may seem like a piece of cake. In most cases the red tape is best left to specialist organisations.

If you do choose to enrol directly while you're in Cuba, the choice of courses on offer can be wider and, in some cases, cheaper than at home. However, the process of enrolment will be far more complicated than if you make arrangements from your home country. Your first stop should be the **Mercadu** agency, which organises courses at Cuban universities ranging from dance to Spanish language. Mercadu can also organise accommodation for foreign students, although be aware that the organisation takes $5 per day for booking them into a *casa particular*.

Agencia Mercadu
Calle 13, #951, esquina a 8, Vedado (333087/662998/333028/agencia@ mercadu.get.tur.cu). **Map** p311 B8.

Student visas

Study in Cuba is possible with a tourist visa (*see p289*), but you will have to leave the country every two months. If you wish to stay in Cuba for longer, you will need to apply for a student visa. If you are exceedingly organised and enrol on a course at a well-established institution (such as ISA; *see p287*) before you arrive in Cuba, the school will do the paperwork for you and you will be able to apply for a student visa from the Cuban consulate in your country. More often than not, however, students will have to do all the paper-pushing themselves once they are in Cuba, before their tourist visa runs out.

Student visas are issued by the educational institution in question via their department of International Relations, or by the Dirección de Posgrado in the case of the University of Havana. For your application you will require six passport photos, $80, a valid tourist card, a valid passport and a copy of the licence certificate of your residence in Havana. As of February 2000, to obtain a student visa, foreign students must live either in University accommodation (restricted) or in an official *casa particular*. They will also need bucketloads of patience.

Once you have obtained your student visa, remember that you must give two weeks' notice and pay a fee of $30-$45 before leaving the country. In an emergency it may be possible to leave at shorter notice, but this will involve more cash and more hassle.

Long-term study

If you'd rather save your time and brainpower for academic rather than bureaucratic challenges, the easiest route is to enrol at a university in your home country that offers a year in Cuba as part of the study programme. For some years, universities such as Essex, Wolverhampton and North London (in the UK) and Ohio Wesleyan University (in the USA) have offered interesting study programmes in Cuba in the fields of language, business and culture. For further information, ask at the Latin American department of the university of your choice.

Cuba has also become a popular destination for medical students. Despite the constant shortage of medicines, students are attracted to Cuba due to its excellent healthcare reputation and the hands-on teaching methods – Cuban medical students are thrown right into the deep end from the second year of their course, in contrast to most European medical students who aren't allowed to administer so much as a Band-Aid until they've done their finals. Note that anyone who's thinking of studying medicine in Cuba should have an excellent command of Spanish.

Language courses

International organisations offering language courses in Cuba are few and far between. However, two institutions currently doing a good job of marketing themselves are **Idiomas y Aventuras**, which is based in Lucerne, Switzerland (Hirschengraben 41, Postfach 7419, Lucerne 7; www.idiomas.ch), and Scottish company **Caledonian Languages Abroad** (The Clock House, Bonnington Mill, 72 Newhaven Road, Edinburgh, EH6 5QG (within the UK 0131 621 7721/ fax 0131 621 7723/www. caledonia languages.co.uk) offers all types of courses, from salsa to language classes.

University of Havana

One of the more popular ways to study Spanish in Cuba is to enrol at the University of Havana, which offers language and grammar courses for all levels, plus classes on Cuban culture and film. To enrol, simply turn up at the Dirección de Posgrado on Calle J, entre 25 y 27 in Vedado at 9am on the first Monday of the month. You will need to do an introductory test. Courses run for two to four weeks ($200/$250 respectively), with classes daily from Monday to Friday. *See also p88.*

Universidad de La Habana
Main entrance: Avenida de la Universidad, esquina a J, Vedado (783231/International Relations 781506/334163). **Open** 8am-5.30pm Mon-Fri; closed Sat, Sun. Closed Aug.

Instituto Superior de Artes

If you're after more flexible schedules, try the Instituto Superior de Artes (*see p106*). This music and art college has a very dedicated Spanish language faculty and will do its utmost to find a course to suit the language needs and length of stay of every potential student. Prices average about $9 per three-hour class.

For art students, ISA is also the logical place to land. The college is very prestigious and only the best of Cuba's artistic talent is accepted, but on a short-term basis, ISA welcomes foreign students to study music, art, drama and dance at all levels. Foreign students interested in a full-time course ($2,500 per year) must sit an entrance examination.

Instituto Superior de Artes
Calle 120 #1, entre 9na y 13, Cubanacán (288075/ isa@cubarte.cult.cu).

Film study

Many South Americans – and the odd North American and European – come to Cuba to study filmmaking at the prestigious **Escuela Internacional de Cine, Televisión y Video** in San Antonio de los Baños, southwest of Havana. This is a really fun school with highly talented teachers and students. The school charges about $2,500 per year for its filmmaking courses, and Spanish classes are offered too. For further information, contact the school directly at Apartado Aeroeo 4041, San Antonio de los Baños, Provincia de La Habana (0650 3152/fax 335341).

Telephones

The phone system is gradually improving in Havana, but the incidence of wrong numbers, crossed lines (usually when it rains), phones being out of order and other problems is still frustratingly high. Many *habaneros* do not have a phone, but in these cases it is customary to take instead the number of a neighbour who will either yell for the person you want or take a message. Foreigners living in a *casa particular* often share the phone line with the owners even if they are in a separate part of the house. The landlord fields all calls and will ask incoming callers to hang up and call again straightaway (*'repite la llamada, por favor'*) to get through to the tenants.

Dialling & codes

To call Havana from overseas, first dial your international access code (0011 from Australia; 011 from Canada; 00 from New Zealand; 00 from the UK; 011 from the USA), followed by 53 (for Cuba), 7 (for Havana), and finally the five- or six-digit number.

The state telephone company **Etecsa** recently changed some (but not all) phone numbers starting with 57 to 67 and those starting with 66 to 60, and readers should be aware that, although the numbers listed throughout this guide were correct at press time, they are prone to change suddenly. Etecsa normally provides a recorded message for three months after a number change.

Making a call

To call another part of Cuba from Havana, first dial 0, followed by the city code. City codes are included in the listings in this guide for all venues outside Havana.

To make an international call from Cuba dial 119, followed by the country code, the area code and then the number. Useful international codes are: Australia 61; Canada 1; New Zealand 64; UK 44 (drop the initial zero of the area code); USA 1. The cost of international calls is high, starting at around $2.50 per minute to North America and going up $6 per minute for much of the rest of the world. Charges can be higher still from hotels, so you should consider using a phone card at a public phone (*see below*). Foreign charge cards can not be used in Cuba.

Cuban area codes
Holguín 24.
Matanzas 52.
Pinar del Río 82.
Sancti Spíritus 41.
Santa Clara 422.
Santiago de Cuba 226.
Trinidad 419.
Varadero 5.
Viñales 8.

Cuban operator services
Directory enquiries 113.
International enquiries 09.
National operator 00.
Repairs 114.
Wake-up call 702511.

Public phones

There are three kinds of public telephones in Havana (dollar phones, peso phones and card phones) and they are found all over the city. The most widespread are dollar phones, which charge 15¢ for three minutes. Peso phones charge just five centavos for three minutes, but are not common in tourist areas and don't work for international calls. Card phones accept only pre-paid telephone cards, sold at many hotels and dollar shops in denominations of $10, $25 and $45.

Telephone directories

The Havana phone directory is updated every year, although numbers change so rapidly that it is still only of limited use. Many entries are only listed by category (à la *Yellow Pages*), which can make looking for individual venues problematic. You may look for an eatery under *restaurante*, for example, when it's actually been classed as a *cafetería*. Note too that while private domestic numbers are listed in the directory, private enterprises, such as *paladares*, are not.

Mobile phones

Mobile phones can be hired from **Cubacel**, which has an office at José Martí airport (Terminal 3) and two in Miramar. (The head office is at Calle 28 #510, entre 5ta y 7ma, Miramar; 802222.) Be warned, though, that the cost of using a mobile phone in Cuba is phenomenally high, starting with a flat fee of $120 to activate the phone, followed by a monthly fee of $40. Calls are charged on top of this at a rate of 40¢ per minute within Cuba, $2.40 per minute to North America, and around $5 per minute to Europe. Incoming

calls are also charged. All calls are pre-paid in person at the Cubacel office. If you run out of credit on your phone (which may happen surprisingly quickly), you'll have to call the office to arrange for more before they'll reconnect you.

Cubacel, the local service provider, has a reciprocal agreement with some Canadian companies (only). Nationals of other countries will not be able to use their own phone.

Faxes

Faxes can received and sent from larger hotels (about $6 per page to Europe).

Time

Cuba is five hours behind Greenwich Mean Time and therefore equivalent to Eastern Standard Time (New York and Miami). Daylight saving time runs from May to October.

Tipping

All tourists are relatively wealthy compared to the average Cuban, so if you get good service, tip accordingly. Tip five to ten per cent in restaurants and cafés. In hotels leave a dollar on the pillow every morning, or, if you are in a *casa particular*, hand over a few extra dollars when you leave. Alternatively, you can leave hard-to-come-by items such as toiletries, soap and so on, though cash is always preferred. Porters and taxi drivers should get a dollar.

Toilets

Finding a public toilet in Havana can be a troublesome and time-consuming task, but fortunately, most hotels and restaurants will let you use their facilities. Some toilets have attendants who should be tipped up to 25 cents before you leave. Try to carry some

tissues or toilet roll with you; although toilet paper is now readily available in the shops, it is still a rare commodity in Cuban public toilets.

Tourist information

Before you go

Tourism in Cuba is governed by the **Ministerio de Turismo** (Calle 19 #710, Vedado; tel. 334202/330545/ www.cubatravel.cu). A number of state tourist agencies – **Cubanacán**, **Cubatur** and **Havanatur** – represent Cuba abroad. US citizens should contact the Canadian representatives of these organisations in Toronto or Montréal.

Cuban Tourist Board

154 Shaftesbury Avenue, London WC2H 8JT (020 7240 6655/fax 020 7836 9265/cubatouristboard.london @virgin.net). **Open** 10am-7pm Mon-Fri; closed Sat, Sun.

Bureau de Tourisme de Cuba

Suite 1105, 440 Boulevard Rene Levesque Ouest, Montréal H2Z 1V7 (514 875 8004/fax 514 875 8006).

Cuban Tourist Board

Suite 705, 55 Queen Street East, Toronto M5C 2R6 (416 362 0700/fax 416 362 6799).

In Havana

The government tourist bureau, **Infotur**, runs tours in Havana and to elsewhere in Cuba. It has four information offices in the city, the main one being in La Habana Vieja. In addition, most hotels have a tourist information desk where staff arrange package tours and provide information and maps. The desk in the lobby of the **Hotel Habana Libre** (*see p55*) is particularly good. In general it can be difficult to get clear, definitive information on events and venues in Cuba.

Infotur

Calle Obispo 521, entre Bernaza y Villegas, La Habana Vieja (333333/636095). **Open** 9am-8.30pm daily.
Branches: Terminal 3, Aeropuerto Internacional José Martí (666112/666101); Avenida 5ta, esquina a 112, Miramar (247036/fax 243977); Avenida de las Terrazas, entre 10 y 11, Habana del Este (961111/971261).

Visas & immigration

Tourist cards & visas

All foreign visitors to Cuba require a passport (valid for at least six months beyond their departure from Cuba), an onward or return air ticket and a tourist card (*tarjeta de turista*). Tourist cards will be issued automatically if you book a package tour; independent travellers can buy tourist cards from the travel agent or airline when they purchase their ticket or at the check-in desk before they board the plane to Cuba. The **Cuban Consulate** in London will also issue a tourist card for £15 on presentation of a photocopy of your passport and booking confirmation from a travel agent. As a last resort you can buy the card when you land at José Martí Airport, although this is not recommended because you are likely to be charged twice as much. Some airlines will not allow passengers without a tourist card to board the plane in the first place.

On arrival, immigration officials will stamp your tourist card with the date of your arrival. It is valid for four weeks from that date.

Hang on to your tourist card throughout your stay in Cuba; you will need it to leave the country and a replacement costs $25. You are expected to give details on the tourist card of your intended address for at least the first two nights of your stay in Cuba. To avoid

hassle it is best to enter the name of a state hotel rather than a *casa particular*, and certainly do not leave this section blank, otherwise you could have your passport confiscated until you have booked approved hotel accommodation at the airport tour desk. For further information on this, *see chapter* **Accommodation**.

If you intend to stay in Cuba for a longer period, or you are travelling on business or for journalistic purposes, you will require a visa. Applications should be made through a Cuban consulate at least three weeks in advance of your trip.

Cuban Consulate General (Australia)

PO Box 1412, Marouba NSW 2035 (612 9311 4611/fax 61 2 9311 1255).

Cuban Embassy (Canada)

338 Main Street, Ottawa, Ontario K1S 1E3 (613 563 0141/fax 613 563 0068).
Branches: Cuban Consulate General, Suite 401, 5353 Dundas Street West, Etobicoke, Ontario M9B 6H8 (416 234 8181/fax 416 234 2754); **Cuban Consulate General**, 1415 Avenue des Pins Ouest, Montréal, Québec H3B 1B2 (514 843 8897/fax 514 982 9034).

Cuban Embassy (UK)

167 High Holborn, London WC1V 6PA (020 7240 2488/fax 020 7836 2602).

Cuban Interests Office (USA)

2639 16th Street NW, Washington, DC 20009 (202 797 8609/202 797 8518/fax 202 986 7283).

Extending your stay

If you wish to extend your stay in Cuba beyond the four weeks designated on your tourist card, you have to go in person to the immigration office (*Control de Extranjeros*) with your passport and tourist card before your first tourist card runs out. (Ignore the out-of-date information about being able to get an extension

at the Hotel Habana Libre.) It is best to go to the office as near to 8.30am as you can. If you go later in the morning, expect a long queue. To save time, it is recommended to tell the visa officials that you'll be travelling around the island staying in state hotels. If you mention that you are staying in a *casa particular* they may request more information. You will rarely encounter any problems getting an extension, although it will cost you $25 and must be paid using stamps of the same value. The stamps are available from branches of **Banco de Comercio** or **Banco Financiero Internacional**. These banks can be found all over Havana, but the nearest branches to the immigration office are opposite each other on Calle 42, on the corner of Avenida 29, and Avenida 31.

Control de Extranjeros

Ministerio del Interior, Calle 20, entre 3 y 5, Miramar. **Open** 8.30am-3pm Mon-Fri; closed Sat, Sun.

Cubans & naturalised citizens

As far as the Cuban government is concerned, anyone who was born in Cuba is Cuban, even if they have since become a naturalised citizen of another country. Visitors who fall into this category require an entry permit (*autorización de entrada*) to reenter the country and can also apply to the nearest Cuban diplomatic office (*see p279*) for a *Vigencia de Viaje*, which allows them to visit Cuba as often as they like within a two-year period.

US visitors

For details of regulations governing US visitors to Cuba, *see p275* **Travel by US citizens to Cuba**.

Weights & measures

The metric system (kilometres, metres and centimetres; kilogrammes and grammes) is compulsory in Cuba. However, produce is sold by the pound in *agromercados*. Temperature is given in Celsius (˚C).

What to take

Clothes

Light-weight, loose-fitting clothes, preferably made of cotton, will help to keep you cool and fresh in the heat and humidity. Don't forget, though, that the temperature can drop in the winter, so pack a warm jumper and/or light jacket too. (You may find you end up wearing warm clothes indoors to combat the ferocious air-con in Havana's hotels.) Pack a sun-hat to protect you from the strong sun and a brolly for those unexpected downpours.

Medical supplies

Many day-to-day medical supplies are not readily available in Cuba. In addition to prescription medicines, you should consider bringing the following:
antihistamine tablets/cream
antiseptic wipes and cream
aspirin/paracetamol
bandages/Band-Aids
contraceptive pill
diahorrea preparation
multi-vitamins
rehydration salts

Other essentials

adaptor if necessary
condoms
locks for luggage
money belt
mosquito repellent
photocopies of documents
sun-cream (SPF15)
tampons
torch and spare batteries

Useful extras

candles
cigarette papers/rolling tobacco
dictionary (English-Spanish)
envelopes
pens and pencils
pen-knife (bury it in your hold luggage or you may be taken for a terrorist)
cotton buds
sanitary towels (these are available, but you won't be able to choose which brand you buy)
teaspoon
toiletries (lipsticks, emery boards)
umbrella
water-purifying tablets

When to go

High season in Cuba lasts from November to April and July to August. During this time hotels are at their busiest and most expensive, with most places fully booked at Christmas, New Year and Easter. Room rates tend to be 20 to 40 per cent lower at other times of year, but as most Cubans take their holidays in July and August, beaches are packed in high summer. Many hotels in Havana are fully booked for the **Día de Rebeldía Nacional** around the 25 to the 27 July; and also during trade shows such as the **Feria Internacional de La Habana** (FIHAV) in early November. If you want to visit the city at these times, book flights and hotels as early as possible.

Public holidays

On the following days most shops, museums and businesses are closed.
Día de la Liberación (Liberation Day) 1 Jan
Día de los Trabajadores (Labour Day) 1 May
Día de Rebeldía Nacional (Celebration of the National Rebellion) 25-27 July
Inicio de la Guerra de Independecia (Anniversary of the First War of Independence) 10 Oct
Navidad (Christmas) 25 Dec

Climate

Cuba is located in the tropics and has two distinct seasons: summer (May to October), which is hot and wet, and winter (November to April), which is slightly cooler and drier. Gulf Stream currents warm the waters around the island, while the north-east trade wind known as *la brisa* cools the city throughout the year. Humidity rarely falls below 70 per cent and can reach an enervating 90 per cent. Two-thirds of the annual rainfall (132cm; 52in) falls between May and November, usually as short, sharp showers but also during occasional heavy and prolonged storms. In some years, Cuba is subjected to a dry period (*la seca*) lasting three to five months. Otherwise December, February, March and April are the driest months of the year. The mean annual temperature is 25.2°C (77°F) with an average of eight hours' sunshine per day. The warmest months are July and August, when the average temperature is 28°C (82.4°F); the average temperature during the coldest month (January) is a pleasant 22°C (71.6°F), although severe cold fronts from the north can cause winter temperatures to drop as low as 10°C (50°F).

Cuba lies within the hurricane belt. August to October is hurricane season, but severe weather can also hit at other times of year.

For weather information, pick up a copy of *Granma* (*see page 292*), which prints a daily weather forecast. There are also regular weather reports in Spanish on Cuban TV.

Women

Although it's a macho country, Cuba is, on the whole, much safer for women than many other Caribbean countries. However, a woman

Directory

travelling on her own should be prepared to cope with stares, *piropos* (comments) and even proposals of marriage. Many Cubans want to escape the harsh conditions of the island and would marry a foreigner in order to do so. If it bothers you, wear a ring on your wedding finger and invent a fictional husband.

Although Cuban women wear short skirts and a lot of lycra, foreign females may prefer to wear less revealing clothes in order to avoid unwanted attention. If you are hassled by a Cuban man, make it clear that you're not interested and he will usually get the message.

If you need help or advice, contact the **Federación de Mujeres de Cuba**. For more on the position of women in Cuban society, *see p30*.

Federación de Mujeres de Cuba (FMC)

Paseo #260, esquina a 13, Vedado (552771). **Map** p312 B9.
Originally set up to implement the equality laws of the Revolution, the Federación now promotes the interests of women.

Working in Havana

If you plan to work in Cuba, you should apply for a visa from the Cuban consulate in your home country (*see p289*). You will need to know the name and details of the business or organisation that is sponsoring your stay; allow at least three weeks for your application to be processed. Journalists and students (*see p286*) require special visas to enter the country; these are also available from the local consulate.

Media

One of the first subjects to come up in a discussion of Cuba is the freedom of the press – or the lack of it. The mass media is sponsored and subsidised by the government. It is therefore rigidly in alignment with the policies advocated by the Revolution. Supporters argue that the Revolution is in turn responding to the interests of the Cuban people, however, this is a naïve interpretation of and excuse for the total lack of political and social debate in the country's media.

Admittedly, there is no place in the press for journalism that is denigrating to a section of society; racism, sexism, bigotry, xenophobia, and child or adult pornography are all outlawed. Nor, however, is there room for criticism of the government.

Some Cubans blame the lack of political debate in the media on the economic siege by the United States, arguing that certain subjects cannot be openly discussed while the country is involved in desperate battle to stave off economic crisis. In their view, it is not until the country becomes 'normal' again that press restraints can be lifted. In the meantime, it must broadcast the truth about the country's reality and the lives of the Cuban people.

This argument may sound persuasive, but it is not sufficient. The US economic war on the island undoubtedly plays its part in restricting freedom of information, but nevertheless it can be argued that 'broadcasting the truth about the country's reality' is precisely what the Cuban media fails to do.

Newspapers

You'll find three national newspapers at newsstands, but due to paper shortages, they are sometimes hard to come by and sell out quickly in the mornings. All three are also available on the Internet. In addition, there are some 15 other local newspapers across the nation, the most important being *Tribuna de La Habana* and *Opciones*. Some of the most radical journalism in the country has come from the Catholic Church, in trailblazing parish magazines such as *Palabra Nueva* in Havana and particularly *Vitral* in Piñar Rios. Foreign-language newspapers and magazines can be purchased at the newsstand in the **Hotel Habana Libre** (*see p55*).

National newspapers

Granma

www.granma.com.
Printed by the Communist Party, this is the island's newspaper of record and its best-known publication. It's as dry and humourless as you'd expect, and sometimes appears to be talking about life on another planet. *Granma* does carry good cultural information, though, and some of its articles are well written, if a little pompous. A weekly international edition is available in English, Portuguese, German and French – but it's no livelier.

Juventud Rebelde

www.jrebelde.cubaweb.cu.
Far superior to *Granma* is *Juventud Rebelde*, with well-written articles, an excellent theatre and arts section, and a more analytical approach to domestic and international news.

Trabajadores

www.trabajadores.cubaweb.cu.
The island's other mainstream rag is a mix of the other two.

Local newspapers

Tribuna de La Habana

www.tribuna.islagrande.cu.
Havana's newspaper covers everything that's happening in the city. The paper's webpage is replete with information, too.

Opciones

www.opciones.cubaweb.cu.
A weekly financial, trade and tourist publication focusing on investment opportunities in Cuba.

Magazines

Now that the economic crisis has eased somewhat and paper is once more available, albeit in limited amounts, many more magazines and journals are flooding the country. Hardly any of the island's publications carry adverts, which makes a refreshing change for Western readers. In addition to those detailed below, try also *Revolución y Cultural*, a monthly cultural magazine; *Temas*, a heavyweight socio-political quarterly publication; *Tablas*, a quarterly magazine devoted to theatre in Cuba; and tourist publications such as *Opus* and *Habanero*.

Bohemia

The doyen of Cuban magazines, this monthly has been running for some 70 years. It carries articles on culture, literature, science, economics, sports and politics. Although a little drab, it has good in-depth reporting on domestic violence, street crime (low in Cuba), delinquency and other social issues.

Cartelera

www.cartelera.com.
A weekly tourist publication in English and Spanish that contains information on theatre, ballet, cinema, bookshops, museums, galleries, sports and music, both in Havana and Varadero. Note that only state-run venues are listed. It's available for free in major hotels, though it can be hard to get hold of a copy. Alternatively, you can get it from *Cartelera*'s office at Calle 21 #459, entre E y F, Vedado (553840/553693). Although *Cartelera* is often touted as a listings magazine, it's pretty flimsy and information is not always up to date. That said, it's one of the few sources of listings for tourists – or anyone – in Cuba.

La Gaceta de Cuba

This bi-monthly magazine complements *Unión* (*see below*) with coverage of theatre, photography, cinema and other arts.

Música Cubana

Published by the Cuban Union of Writers and Artists (UNEAC), this quarterly is a must for fans of Cuban music, both past and present. There are articles on Silvio Rodríguez, Beny Moré, Juan Formell, Pablo Milanés, Bola de Nieve, Rita Montaner et al.

Tricontinental

www.granma.cu/tricontinental/.
This well-written quarterly offers academic, socio-political analysis in Spanish and English. It is produced by the Organisation in Solidarity with the Peoples of Africa, Asia and Latin America (OSPAAAL).

Unión

Published by UNEAC, this bi-monthly art and literature magazine has in-depth reporting on Cuban and foreign artists, writers and poets.

Television

With only two television channels available, viewing in Cuba is limited. Nevertheless, almost the entire population watches TV every day – invariably with the volume turned up very high. Some 70 per cent of the content relates to Cuba, and if you seek to change channels to avoid soporific details of the sugar harvest, forget it. If it's of national significance – and especially if Fidel is speaking – both channels will likely be airing it at the same time. (Cubans call Fidel Castro the 'test card' or 'screensaver' because his speeches are so long.) Nevertheless, Cuban documentaries are usually very informative and intelligent, and children's programming is less violent than in Europe and the US.

If you want to remain on good terms with Cubans never, we repeat never, call them between 9.30 and 10.15pm on a weeknight. This is when the nightly soap opera succeeds in transfixing most of the country. In fact, such is the influence of the soap opera genre on Cuban life that it is responsible for introducing words like '*paladar*' (from a Brazilian soap) to the language. It is said that most burglaries in Cuba take place during this hour when everyone – man, woman and child – is glued to the box.

One of the interesting contradictions evident in Cuba is that the TV ceaselessly – and with reason – reminds the population of the violent nature of life in US inner cities, and then proceeds to show films on Saturday night that glorify the same violence.

Most hotels carry CNN (in both Spanish and English), a watered-down version of HBO and a number of other Italian, Spanish and German channels.

Radio

Radio has historically played a very important role in Cuba. A shortage of newsprint and reduced TV air time during the mid-1990s economic crisis added millions of listeners to the airwaves. There are 62 stations across the island today, of which **Radio Metropolitano** broadcasts in the capital only and focuses on Havana's cultural life. For a non-Cuban perspective on international news, the **BBC World Service** (www.bbc.co.uk/worldservice) is a godsend, but you'll need a shortwave radio. Tune into 5975, 6195, 15220 or 17840 mHz. Cuba also has a short-wave international station, **Radio Habana Cuba** (www.radiohc.cu), which broadcasts news, current affairs, cultural programmes, sports and music in nine languages. Frequencies are posted on the website.

National radio stations

Radio Enciclopedia a mix of cultural programming.
Radio Musical Nacional Classical music.
Radio Progreso Music and light talk.
Radio Rebelde Launched by Che Guevara in the mountains of the Sierra Maestra during the war against Batista, it now broadcasts news and current affairs.
Radio Reloj News and the time 24 hours a day, with the irritating sound of a clock tick-tocking permanently in the background.
Radio Taíno 24-hour music and news station that identifies itself as 'your tourist station in Cuba' and also broadcasts in English.

Directory

Essential Vocabulary

Like other Latin languages, Spanish has different familiar and polite forms of the second person (you). Many young people now use the familiar *tú* form most of the time; for foreigners, though, it's always advisable to use the more polite *usted* with people you do not know, and certainly with anyone over 50. In the phrases listed here all verbs are given in the *usted* form. While it will certainly help to know some Castillian Spanish, Cuban Spanish is notably different in some of its vocabulary (such as *carro* rather than *coche* for car), and also in its tendency to drop final letters of words and also the 'd' from the final '*ado*' of words. It's rare to come across a Cuban who speaks fluent English, though many, in Havana at least, speak a few words.

For food- and drink-related vocabulary, *see p145*.

Pronunciation

c before an **i** or an **e** is soft, like **s** in **s**it.
c in all other cases is as in **c**at.
g, before an **i** or an **e**, and **j** are pronounced with a guttural **h**-sound that does not exist in English – like ch in Scottish lo**ch**, but much harder.
g in all other cases is pronounced as in **g**et.
h at the beginning of a word is normally silent.
ll is pronounced almost like a **y**.
ñ is like **ny** in ca**ny**on.
z is always the same as a soft **c**, like **s** as in **s**it
A single **r** at the beginning of a word and **rr** elsewhere are heavily rolled.

Basics

hello *hola*; hello (when answering the phone) *hola, diga*
good morning, good day *buenos días*; good afternoon, good evening *buenas tardes*; good evening (after dark), good night *buenas noches*
goodbye/see you later *adiós/hasta luego*
please *por favor*; thank you (very much) *(muchas) gracias*
you're welcome *de nada*
do you speak English? *¿habla inglés?*

I don't speak Spanish *no hablo español*
I don't understand *no entiendo*
what's your name? *¿cómo se llama?*
speak more slowly, please *hable más despacio, por favor*
wait a moment *espere un momento*
Sir/Mr *señor (sr)*; Madam/Mrs *señora (sra)*; Miss *señorita (srta)*
excuse me/sorry *perdón*
excuse me, please *oiga* (to attract attention; literally 'hear me')
OK/fine/(or to a waiter) that's enough *vale*
where is... *¿dónde está...?*
why? *¿porqué?*; when? *¿cuándo?*; who? *¿quién?*; what? *¿qué?*; where? *¿dónde?*; how? *¿cómo?*
is/are there any... *¿hay...?*
very *muy*; and *y*; or *o*
with *con*; without *sin*
open *abierto*; closed *cerrado*
what time does it open/close? *¿a qué hora abre/cierra?*
pull (on signs) *tirar*; push *empujar*
I would like... *quiero...* (literally, 'I want...'); how many would you like? *¿cuántos quiere?*
I like me *gusta*
I don't like *no me gusta*
good *bueno/a*; bad *malo/a*; well/badly *bien/mal*; small *pequeño/a*; big *gran, grande*; expensive *caro/a*; cheap *barato/a*; hot (food, drink) *caliente*; cold *frío/a*
something *algo*; nothing *nada*
more/less *más/menos*
the bill/check, please *la cuenta, por favor*
how much is it? *¿cuánto es?*
do you have any change? *¿tiene cambio?*
price *precio*; free *gratis*
discount *descuento*
bank *banco*; to rent *alquilar*; (for) rent, rental *(en) alquiler*; post office *correos*; stamp *sello*; postcard *postal*; toilet *los servicios*

Getting around

airport *aeropuerto*; railway station *estación de ferrocarriles*; car *carro* or *coche*; bus *guagua* or *rutero* (general terms for a city bus); autobús (air-conditioned tourist bus); *camello* (pink articulated bus); train *tren*
a ticket *un billete*; return *de ida y vuelta*; bus stop *parada de autobús*; the next stop *la próxima parada*
excuse me, do you know the way to...? *por favor, ¿sabe como llegar a...?*
left *izquierda*; right *derecha*; here *aquí* or *acá*; there *allí*
straight on *recto*; to the end of the street *al final de la calle*; as far as *hasta*; towards *hacia*
near *cerca*; far *lejos*

Accommodation

do you have a double/single room for tonight/one week? *¿tiene una habitación doble/para una persona para esta noche/una semana?*
where is the car park? *¿dónde está el parking?*
we have a reservation *tenemos reserva*
an inside/outside room *una habitación interior/exterior*
with/without bathroom *con/sin baño*; shower *ducha*
double bed *cama de matrimonio*; with twin beds *con dos camas*
breakfast included *desayuno incluído*
air-conditioning *aire acondicionado*; lift *ascensor*; swimming pool *piscina*

Time

morning *la mañana*; midday *mediodía*; afternoon/evening *la tarde*; night *la noche*; late night/early morning (roughly 1-6am) *la madrugada*
now *ahora*; later *más tarde*; yesterday *ayer*; today *hoy*; tomorrow *mañana*; tomorrow morning *mañana por la mañana*
early *temprano*; late *tarde*
delay *retraso*; delayed *retrasado*
at what time...? *¿a qué hora...?*
in an hour *en una hora*
the bus will take 2 hours *el autobús tardará dos horas*
at 2 *a las dos*; at 8pm *a las ocho de la tarde*; at 1.30 *a la una y media*
at 5.15 *a las cinco y cuarto*; at 22.30 *a veintidós treinta*
Monday *lunes*; Tuesday *martes*; Wednesday *miércoles*; Thursday *jueves*; Friday *viernes*; Saturday *sábado*; Sunday *domingo*
January *enero*; February *febrero*; March *marzo*; April *abril*; May *mayo*; June *junio*; July *julio*; August *agosto*; September *septiembre*; October *octubre*; November *noviembre*; December *diciembre*
spring *primavera*; summer *verano*; autumn/fall *otoño*; winter *invierno*

Numbers

0 *cero*; 1 *un, uno, una*; 2 *dos*; 3 *tres*; 4 *cuatro*; 5 *cinco*; 6 *seis*; 7 *siete*; 8 *ocho*; 9 *nueve*; 10 *diez*; 11 *once*; 12 *doce*; 13 *trece*; 14 *catorce*; 15 *quince*; 16 *dieciséis*; 17 *diecisiete*; 18 *dieciocho*; 19 *diecinueve*; 20 *veinte*; 21 *veintiuno*; 22 *veintidós*; 30 *treinta*; 40 *cuarenta*; 50 *cincuenta*; 60 *sesenta*; 70 *setenta*; 80 *ochenta*; 90 *noventa*; 100 *cien*; 1,000 *mil*; 1,000,000 *un millón*

Further Reference

Books

Fiction & literature

Bush, Peter (editor) *The Voice of the Turtle: a collection of Cuban short stories translated into English.* The short story is a strong genre in Cuba and this collection gives a good overall picture, spanning over a century.

Cabrera Infante, Guillermo *Tres Tristes Tigres* (*Three Trapped Tigers*). A sharply comic novel of pre-Revolutionary Havana in which the hedonistic city itself is a protagonist.

Carpentier, Alejo *Los pasos perdidos* (*The Lost Steps*). It is in this novel that the great Cuban writer develops his theory of Magic Realism.

Garcia, Cristina *Dreaming in Cuban* (1992). The young Cuban-American writer explores the theme of families divided by politics and the Florida Straits through three generations.

Greene, Graham *Our Man in Havana* (1958). Set on the very eve of Castro's Revolution, the darkly comic novel evokes Havana in the 1950s through the misadventures of a vacuum-cleaner salesman turned reluctant spy.

Guillen, Nicolas
Guillen was the Revolution's official poet and has been widely translated. Apart from his political poems, Guillen is best known for his very rhythmical Afro-Cuban works, which have often been set to music.

Hemingway, Ernest *The Old Man and the Sea* (1952). This tale of a local fisherman's epic struggle won Hemingway the Nobel Prize for Literature in 1954. Hemingway lived in Cuba for many years and donated the prize to the Virgen de la Caridad del Cobre, Cuba's patron saint. Try also *Islands in the Stream* (1970), based on the author's experiences hunting Nazi

submarines during World War II, and *To Have and Have Not* (1937), an exciting account of illegal trade between Havana and Florida.

Hijuelos, Oscar *The Mambo Kings Play Songs of Love.* This Cuban-American novel describes the world of Cuban musicians playing in New York in the 1950s.

Iyer, Pico *Cuba and the Night* (1995). An ambivalent love story set in the dark days of 1980s Havana.

Lezama Lima, Jose *Paradiso* (*Paradise*). Lezama Lima is the giant of 20th-century Cuban literature. This, his only novel, gives a richly detailed picture of Havana through the eyes of a sensitive young protagonist growing up in the city.

Piñera, Virgilio
Best known as a playwright, particularly of absurdist drama, Piñera is one of Cuba's most important writers, although though not much of his work has been translated.

Sarduy, Pedro and Stubbs, Jean (editors) *AfroCuba: an anthology of Cuban writing on race, politics and culture.*

Sarduy, Severo *De Donde son los Cantantes?* (*From Cuba with a Song*). This patchwork novel explores Cuba's identity through Spanish, African and Chinese roots. Sarduy left Cuba and lived in Paris for many years before he died of AIDS in 1993.

Non-fiction

Arenas, Reinaldo *Antes que anochezca* (*Before Night Falls*). The autobiography of the Cuban dissident and homosexual. Arenas was persecuted and imprisoned in Cuba and finally abandoned the island in 1980 for New York. Suffering from AIDS, Arenas committed suicide in 1990.

Anderson, John Lee *Che Guevara: A Revolutionary Life*

(1997). A weighty and exhaustive biography of the Revolutionary hero.

Cabrera Infante, Guillermo *Mea Cuba.* Banned in Cuba for its strong condemnation of Castro, this collection of essays and memoirs presents a personalised account of the literary/political scene during the early years of the Revolution.

Fuentes, Norberto *Hemingway in Cuba* (1984). A key account of the author's life in Cuba, with ample illustrations.

González-Wippler, Migene *Santería: The Religion* (1994). Loads of interesting information on Afro-Cuban religion.

LaFray, Joyce *¡Cuba Cocina!* (1994). Cuban cooking served up in all its glory.

Martí, José
Anyone hoping to understand Cuba must have some knowledge of Martí's poems, essays and letters. Martí wrote prolifically and his works are collected in over 30 volumes, most of which have been translated into English.

Matthews, Herbert *Revolution in Cuba* (1975). A sympathetic analysis by the *New York Times* journalist.

Miller, Tom *Trading with the Enemy: A Yankee travels through Castro's Cuba* (1992). Part travelogue, part social analysis, Tom Miller's astute comments on Cuba in the 1990s is one of the best recent books about the island.

Smith, Stephen *The Land of Miracles* (1998). Tales of touring Cuba in an American car.

Szulc, Tad *Fidel: A Critical Portrait* (1986). An excellent, revealing biography of the Revolutionary leader.

Thomas, Hugh *Cuba, or the Pursuit of Freedom 1726-1969* (1971). Historian Hugh Thomas's scholarly history of the island is 30 years old now, but is still probably the standard work on

The word on Cuba

Traditionally, literature in Cuba includes essayists, philosophers and biographers, as well as poets and novelists. Literature has also always been closely connected to the political life of the island. The combination of independence movements and harsh Spanish censorship meant that most literature of quality was written and published in exile and was rebellious in sentiment.

19TH CENTURY

Father Félix Varela (1787-1853) was one of the earliest and most significant figures of the time. Varela was a philosophy teacher who influenced a whole generation of Cuban intellectuals. He became a vociferous believer in independence and was exiled to New York where he produced a publication dedicated to the freedom struggle: *El Habanero*.

Cuba's great romantic poet-patriot, **José María Herédia** (1801-1836) died in Mexico, having spent much of his short life in exile. He wrote impassioned, nationalistic verse that inspired several generations of Cuban patriots. Poems like 'Niágara' and 'A Emilia' are still part of every school anthology.

Gertrudis Gómez de Avellaneda (1814-1873), prolific poet, novelist and playwright, was born in Cuba, but is claimed by Spain where she spent most of her life. De Avellaneda was not a political exile but her seminal abolitionist novel *Sab* was banned in Cuba when it was published.

The great 19th-century Cuban novel is *Cecilia Valdés* by **Cirilo Villaverde** (1812-94). Set in Havana in the 1820s, the novel was not published until after abolition, but the story of the hopes and downfall of the beautiful mulatta in Colonial Havana society has become a beloved classic.

As well as being the apostle of the nation, **José Martí** (1853-95) is Cuba's most important 19th-century literary figure. Martí's works are full of the exile's poignant love for the lost homeland. His prolific writings are collected in over 30 volumes and his words are everywhere in Cuba. You may not be aware as you sip your *mojito* that the words of 'Guantanamera' are from a poem by Martí.

20TH CENTURY

In 1971 **Herberto Padilla** (1932-) was arrested and forced to make a Stalinesque public confession concerning a published anthology of mildly subversive poems, which had won him the Casa de las Americas prize. Padilla's arrest shocked the world and alerted intellectuals in Cuba to the repressive climate that was to dominate for the next ten years. Ultimately, the Padilla affair precipitated the emigration of numerous Cuban writers, including Reinaldo Arenas, Severo Sarduy and Lydia Cabrera.

In contrast, **José Lezama Lima** (1910-1976) never left Cuba. He was passionate about Havana and no political upheaval could remove him. The central figure in the city's literary life, Lezama Lima is best known for his monumental, baroque novel *Paradiso* (1966), which traces the development of a sensitive boy in the macho society of Havana.

Alejo Carpentier (1904-1980) lived in Venezuela for years but returned to Cuba in 1959 and was made UNESCO ambassador to Paris. His novels include *El Reino de este mundo* (*The Kingdom of this World*), *El Siglo de las Luces* (translated as *Explosion in the Cathedral*) and *Los Pasos Perdidos* (*The Lost Steps*) in which he develops his theory of Magic Realism, which influenced a generation of Latin American writers.

Guillermo Cabrera Infante (1929-) left Cuba in 1966. Probably the best Cuban writer working today, Cabrera Infante is officially anathema on the island for his vilification of Castro, particularly in his collection of essays on the literary/political scene, *Mea Cuba*. Cabrera Infante's works include *Tres Tristes Tigres* (*Three Trapped Tigers*) and, directly in English, 'Holy Smoke', an essay on tobacco.

Mulatto poet **Nicolás Guillén** (1902-1989) became the offical poet of the Revolution. Known mainly for his Afro-Cuban rhythms, his poems often contain Yoruba refrains. Guillén is the most translated and anthologised of all Cuban writers.

Apart from writers who left the island in their maturity, a generation of Cuban-Americans have produced a hybrid literature that straddles two cultures. **Oscar Hijuelos** was born in New York in 1951 to Cuban parents. His novel *The Mambo Kings Play Songs of Love* about two Cuban musician brothers gives a detailed picture of Cuban-American life. **Christina García** was born in Cuba in 1958 but left when she was a young child. Her novel *Dreaming in Cuban* deals with the division of a family between Castro's Cuba and the United States.

Directory

Cuba's history. Try also Thomas's more recent and equally definitive *The Cuban Revolution* (1986).

Film

See *p179* **Cuban films**.

Music

Antología del Bolero – Collecion Tributo

This CD provides an excellent introduction to the complexities and variety of bolero music.

Fiesta Cubana: El Bolero

Another compilation CD, this one contains some of the giants of Cuban bolero music, including Beny Moré, Frank Domínguez and Bola de Nieve.

Rapsodia Rumbera

This compilation of rumba music includes works in all the major styles (yambú, guaguancó, rumba-columbia). Many of the great rumba musicians are featured on the CD, including Chano Pozo, Malanga, Nieve Fresneda and Tio Tom.

Cantos de Santería

A fascinating and mystical CD, this is one of the only recordings available dedicated to the religious music of Regla de Ocha or Santeria, the Christian/African synthesis religion still practised in Cuba and South America.

Vivencias – Charanga Típica de Guillermo Rubalcaba

A rich and complex recording of the music of the piano virtuoso Guillermo Rubalcaba, this CD combines internationally known orchestral works with waltz classics and a selection of more intimate pieces.

Websites

Afro-Cuba Web

www.afrocubaweb.com.
This site draws together a vast array information on themes

such as culture, politics, literature, music, dance, theatre and racial identity to celebrate the influence of African culture on Cuban life.

CubaNet

www.cubanet.org.
Based in Florida and run by Cuban expatriates, CubaNet neverthless describes itself as 'a tax-exempt, non partisan and non-profit organisation that... informs the world about Cuba's reality'. The somewhat strident tone of much of the editorial content leaves the reader in no doubt as to just where the site's sympathies lie, and they sure as hell ain't with Fidel. The site delivers its message in English, Spanish, German and French.

The Cuban Experience

http://library.thinkquest.org/18355/index.shtml
An award-winning student-produced site, which offers a wealth of resources on Cuban history and politics, culture, travel, personalities, events and attractions.

Cuban Music Shop

www.discuba.caribbeansources.com.
The website for the Cuban Music Shop offers a wealth of information on all styles of Cuban music and discographies of the major artists. The site has experienced some technical difficulties in the past and has had to suspend its online shopping service, but it remains an excellent way to learn more about Cuban music.

Cubarte

www.cult.cu.
The Cubarte site, in English and Spanish, is a key resource for the traveller interested in the cultural and artistic life of the island. It contains extensive information on upcoming events, performances and concerts as well as information on cinema and video releases.

Cubaweb

www.cubaweb.cu.
A good general portal for

information and links to resources relating to Havana and Cuba, Cubaweb covers topics including news, tourism, business, the Internet, government, trade, culture and events. The site is produced in both English and Spanish – so doubles as a study aid.

Granma

www.granma.cu.
The website for the official newspaper of the Cuban Communist Party, Granma provides state-approved news in five languages: Spanish, English, French, German and Portuguese.

Guía Turística de La Habana

www.prensa-latina.cu/Pubs/prisma/guia.
Presented with a charming abundance of substance over style, this single (long) page offers contact information for a wide range of hotels, shops, restaurants and music venues in Havana.

La Habana

www.lahabana.com.
This site makes an excellent introduction to Havana, with resources covering all the major social and cultural attractions, as well as good background information on Cuban history and government.

US-Cuba Commission

www.uscubacommission.org.
For the traveller who likes their holidays to be liberally laced with politics, the US-Cuba Commission's site gives up-to-the-minute information on the latest developments in US-Cuba relations.

VRFabulous

www.vrfabulous.com/education/havana11a.html.
Semi-virtual-reality 360° panoramic views of Havana. You can scroll around the photographs to get a real feeling of what its like to stand on a typical Havana street corner on a sunny afternoon. While the site could do with a few more photographs, it still makes a great taster of the Havana experience.

Index

Place of Interest and/or Entertainment	▨
Railway Station	▨
Park	▨
College/Hospital	▨
Beach	▨
Steps	▨▨▨▨
Area Name	**VEDADO**
Church	✚
Information	i
Post Office	✉

Maps

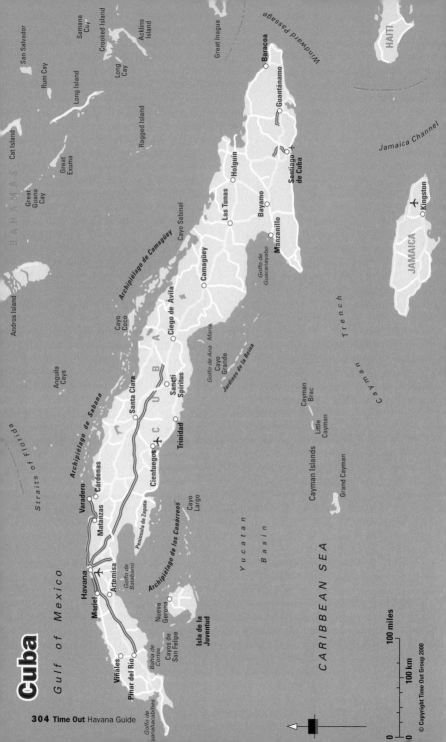

Cuba

Gulf of Mexico

Straits of Florida

BAHAMAS

San Salvador
Cat Island
Rum Cay
Long Island
Great Exuma
Great Guana Cay
Andros Island
Anguila Cays
Samana Cay
Crooked Island
Acklins Island
Long Cay
Ragged Island
Great Inagua

Windward Passage

HAITI

Baracoa
Guantánamo
Holguín
Santiago de Cuba
Bayamo
Manzanillo
Las Tunas
Camagüey
Ciego de Ávila
Sancti Spíritus
Santa Clara
Trinidad
Cienfuegos
Cárdenas
Varadero
Matanzas
Havana
Artemisa
Mariel
Viñales
Pinar del Río
Nueva Gerona
Isla de la Juventud

Archipiélago de Camagüey
Archipiélago de Sabana
Archipiélago de los Canárreos
Cayo Sabinal
Cayo Coco
Cayo Largo
Cayo de Ana Maria
Cayo Grande
Golfo de Guacanayabo
Golfo de Ana Maria
Golfo de Batabanó
Jardines de la Reina
Península de Zapata
Bahía de Cortés
Cayos de San Felipe
Golfo de Guanahacabibes

C U B A

Yucatan Basin

CARIBBEAN SEA

Cayman Trench

Cayman Brac
Little Cayman
Cayman Islands
Grand Cayman

JAMAICA
Kingston

Jamaica Channel

100 miles

100 km

0

© Copyright Time Out Group 2000

Havana Overview

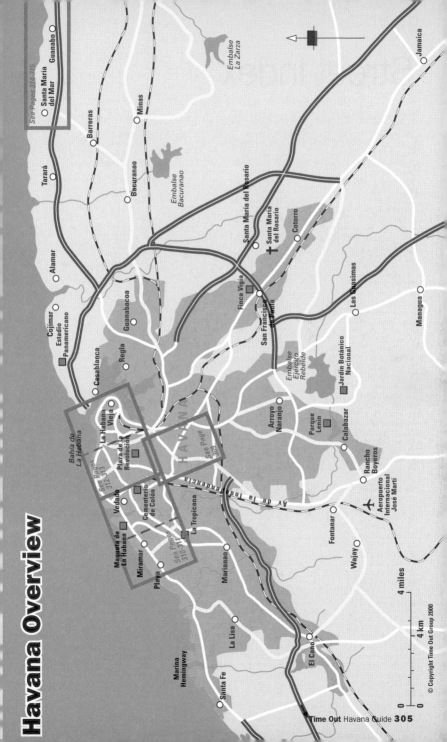

Santa María del Mar   Guanabo

Barreras

Minas

Tarará

Bacuranao

Embalse La Zarza

Alamar

Cojímar   Estadio Panamericano

Guanabacoa

Casablanca

Regla

Embalse Bacuranao

Santa María del Rosario

Santa María del Rosario

Cotorro

Finca Vigía

San Francisco de Paula

Las Guasimas

Managua

Embalse Ejército Rebelde

Jardín Botánico Nacional

Bahía de La Habana

La Habana Vieja

Plaza de la Revolución

Arroyo Naranjo

Parque Lenin

Calabazar

Maqueta de La Habana

Vedado

Cementerio de Colón

La Tropicana

AV de la Independencia

Rancho Boyeros

Miramar

Playa

Marianao

Fontanar

Aeropuerto Internacional José Martí

Wajay

Marina Hemingway

La Lisa

El Cano

Santa Fe

See page 312-313

See page 310-311

Jamaica

HAVANA

4 miles

4 km

0

0

© Copyright Time Out Group 2000

Street Index

Acosta - p313 E14-15/F15
Acosta, Avenida de - p309 J8/
K9-10/L11
Agramonte - p313 D14/E14
Agua Dulce - p309 G10-11
Aguacate - p313 D15/E15
Aguiar - p313 D15/E15
Aguila - p313 D14/E13/F13
Agusitina - p309 K9
Almendares - p312 D11
Altarriba - p309 J11
Amargura - p313 E15
Amenidad - p309 E11
- p312 E11
Amistad - p313 D14
Andrés (San Miguel) - p309 K8-9
Angeles - p313 D13/E13
Ánimas - p313 C13/D14
Apodaca - p313 E14
Aramburú - p312 C12/D12
Aranguren - p312 D10
Árbol Seco - p312 D12/E12
Armas - p309 K10-11
Armas, Plaza de - p313 E16
Armonia - p309 G8-9
Arroyo - p312 E11-12
Auditor - p309 E10/F10
- p312 E10/F10
Avellaneda - p309 K9
Ayestarán, Calzada de - p312 E10
Ayuntamiento - p312 E9
B - p311 A7
B - p312 A9/B9-10/C10
Barcelona - p313 D14
Bejucal, Calzada de - p309 K9/L9
Bélgica, Avenida de - p313 D14/E14
Bellavista - p309 G9
Benjumeda - p312 D11/E11-12
Bernal - p313 D14
Bernaza - p313 D14/E14
Blanquizal - p309 J11
Borrego - p309 E10
- p312 F11
Brasil (Teniente Rey) - p313 E15
Bruzón - p312 D11
Buenaventura - p309 K10
Buenos Aires - p309 G9-10
Buenos Aires, Calzada de -
p309 F10-11/G10
C - p311 A7
C - p312 A10-C10
C. Protestantes - p312 D9
Cádiz - p309 F8
- p311 F8
Cádiz - p312 F11
Calzada del Cerro - p311 F8
Camilo Cienfuegos, Avenida - p309
K11
Campanario - p313 C14/D13/E13
Cárcel - p313 D15
Cárdenas - p313 E14
Carlos Manuel de Céspedes, Avenida -
p312 D9-10/E9
Carlos Manuel de Céspedes, Avenida -
p313 D15
Carmen - p309 J8-9/K10
Carmen - p312 E12
Castillejo - p312 D12
Castillo - p312 F12
Catedral, Plaza de La - p313 D15

Cerezo - p309 G9
Cerro, Calzada del - p309 F8-10; p312
F9-10
Cervantes - p309 K8
Chacón - p313 D15
Chaple - p309 G8-9
Chávez - p313 D13
Churruca - p309 F8
- p311 F8
Churruca - p313 E15
Cienfuegos - p313 E14
Clavel - p309 E9/F9
Clavel - p312 E11-12
Clavel - p312 E9-10
Coco - p309 H10/J11
Colina - p309 J11
Colón - p309 F8
- p311 F8
Colón - p313 D14-15
Colón, Avenida de - p311 D8
- p312 D9
Compostela - p313 D15/E15
Concepción - p309 K11
Concepción de La Valla - p312 E12
Concordia - p312 C12
- p313 C13/D13-14
Condesa - p313 E13
Consulado - p313 D14
Continental - p309 K8
Conuco - p309 K8
Corrales - p313 E13-14
Correa - p309 H10-11
Cristo - p313 E14
Cuarteles - p313 D15
Cuba - p313 D15/E15
Cuchillo - p313 D13
D - p312 A10-C10
D'strampes - p309 H9/J9
Delicias - p309 H11/J10-11/K10
Desagüe - p312 D11/E12
Desamparado - p313 E14-15
Diaria - p313 F13-14
Diez de Octubre, Calzada de - p309
G11/H11
Dragones - p313 E14
Durege - p309 G10/H10
E - p312 A10-C10
Economia - p313 E14
Egido - p313 E14/F14
Empirio - p311 E7
Enamorados - p309 G10-11/H11
Encarnacion - p309 H10
Enrique Barnet (Estrella) -
p312 D11-12
Ermita - p312 E9-10
Escobar - p312 E12
- p313 C13/D13
Espada - p312 C12
España, Avenida de - p313 F13
Esperanza - p309 G8-9
Esperanza - p313 F13
Estancia - p312 E9
Este - p311 E8
Estévez - p312 F11-12
Estrada Palma - p309 H9/J9-10
F - p312 A10-C10
Fábrica - p313 F13
Factor - p311 E8
Factoria - p313 E14/F14
Falgueras - p309 F9-10

Falgueras - p312 F9-10
Felipe Poey - p309 J10/K9-10
Fernandina - p312 F11-12
Figueroa - p309 H9/J9
Figuras - p312 E12
Florencia - p309 G9
Flores - p309 G10/H10
Franco - p312 D12/E12
Fretre de Andrade - p309 J8/K8
Gelabert - p309 K9
General E. Núnez - p312 E10
General Lacret - p309 H9-10/J10
Genios - p313 D15
Gertrudis Este - p309 L9-10
Gertrudis Oeste - p309 K8
Gervasio - p313 C13/D13
Gloria - p313 E13-14
Goicuria - p309 H9/J8/K8
Gomez - p309 G9/H9
Gral Serrano - p309 G10/H10
H - p312 A10/B11
Habana - p313 D15/E15
Hamel - p312 C12
Heredia - p309 J9-10/K9
Hidalgo - p311 D8/E8
- p312 D9
Hornos - p312 C12
Hospital - p312 C12/D12
Humboldt - p312 B12
I - p312 A11/B11
Independencia, Avenida de La - p311
E8/F7-8
- p312 E9
Industria - p313 D14
Infanta - p309 F8
- p311 F8
Infanta, Calzada de - p312
C12/D11/E11
Italia, Avenida de (Galiano) - p313 D14
J - p312 A11-C11
Jesús María - p313 E14/F15
Jesús Peregrino - p312 D12
Jorge - p309 K8
José Antonio Cortina - p309 J9
Jose Antonio Saco - p309 J9-10/K9
Jose de La Luz y Caballero - p309 J9-
10/K9
Jovellar - p312 C12
Juan Bruno Zayas - p309 J9-10/K9
Juan Delgado - p309 H9/J8-9
Julia Borges - p312 D9
K - p312 A11/B11
L - p312 A11-C11
L. Ferrocarril - p312 E10
La Rosa - p309 F9
- p312 E9/F9
La Torre - p311 D7
Lagunas - p313 C13-14
Lamparilla - p313 E15
Lawton - p309 K10-11
Lealtad - p313 C13/D13/E13
Leonor Pérez (Paula) - p313 E14-15
Libertad - p309 H9/J9-10
Lindero - p312 E12
Linea - p311 B7-8
- p312 A9-10/B9/B11-12
Lombillo - p309 F9
- p311 D8/E8
- p312 E9/F9
Lugareño - p312 D11

Luis Estévez - p309 H9-10/J10
Luyano, Calzada de - p309 H11
Luz - p309 J11
Luz - p313 E14-15
M - p312 A11-C11
M. Abreu - p312 E10
Macedonia - p309 G9
Magnolia - p309 G9-10
Malecón (Ave de Maceo) - p311 A8
- p312 A9-11/B12
- p313 C13-15
Maloja - p313 E13
Manglar - p312 E12
Mangos - p309 H11
Manrique - p313 C14/D13-14/E13
Marcelino Champagnat - p309 H8/J9
Mariano - p309 E9-10/F9
Marianó - p312 E9-10/F9
Marino - p312 E9
Marqués de La Torre - p309 H11/J11
Marquéz González - p312 C13/D12/E12
Masón - p312 E10
Matadero - p312 F12
Máximo Gómez (Monte)
- p313 E13/14/F12
Mayia Rodríguez - p309 H9/J8
Merced - p313 F14-15
Milagros - p309 J9-10
Milagros Este - p309 K10-11
Misión - p313 E14
Misiones, Avenida de Las (Monserrate)
- p313 D15
Morro - p313 D15
N - p312 B12/C12
Neptuno - p312 C12
- p313 D13-14
Nueva del Pilar - p312 E12
O - p312 B12/C12
O'Farrill - p309 J8/K9
Obispo - p313 E15
Obrapía - p313 E15
Oficios - p313 E15-16
Omoa - p312 F12
Oquendo - p312 C12-E12
- p313 C13
O'Reilly - p313 D15/E15
P. Vidal - p312 E11
Padre Varela - p312 D12-E12
- p313 C13/D13
Palatimo, Calzada - p309 G8
Panchito Gómez - p312 E10
Panorama - p312 D9
Parque - p309 G9
Parraga - p309 J10/K9-10
Paseo - p312 A9-D9-10
Paseo de Martí (Prado) - p313 D14-15
Patria - p309 E10/F10
- p312 E10/F10
Patrocinio - p309 J8-9/K9|9-10
Paz - p309 G10/H10
Pedro Consuegra - p309 K9-10/L10
Pedro Pérez - p309 E10/F10
- p312 E10/F10
Pedroso - p309 E10-11
- p312 E10-11
Peña Pobre - p313 D15
Peñalver - p312 D11-12
- p313 E13
Perkins - p309 G8-9
Pezuela - p309 F8

Pezuela - p311 F8
Pila - p312 F12
Pinera - p309 F9
- p312 E9/F9
Pje. Vista Hermosa - p309 E10
- p312 E10
Plasencia - p312 D11-12
Pocito - p312 D12
Porvenir, Avenida - p309 K11/L10
Prensa - p309 F8
- p311 F8
Preseverancia - p313 C13/D13
Presidentes, Avenida de Los - p312
A10-C10
Primelles - p309 F8
- p311 F8
Príncipe - p312 C12
Puerta Cerrada - p313 F13
Puerto, Avenida del - p313 F13-14
Quiroga - p309 J11
Rabí - p309 G11/H11
Rancho Boyeros, Avenida - p312
D10/E9-10
Rastro - p312 E12
Rayo - p313 D13/E13
Recreo - p309 G8-9
Recurso - p311 E7
Refugie - p313 D15
Remedios - p309 H11/J11
Resguardo - p309 G9
Retiro - p312 D11-12
Revillagigedo - p313 E13/F13
Revolución - p309 K9
Revolución, Plaza de La - p312 D9-10
Reyes - p309 J11
Rodriguez - p309 G10-11
Romay - p309 E10
Romay - p312 F11
Salud - p312 D12
Salvador - p309 G9
Salvador Allende, Avenida - p312 D11-12
San Anastasio - p309 K10-11
San Anselimo - p309 G9-10
San Benigno - p309 G10/H10-11
San Bernardino - p309 H10-11
San Carlos - p312 D12/E12
San Catalina Este - p309 K10
San Cristobal - p309 F8
- p311 F8
San Francisco - p309 K10-11
San Francisco - p312 C12
San Ignacio - p313 D15/E15
San Indalecio - p309 G11/H10
San Isidro - p313 E14-15
San Joaquín - p309 E10
- p312 F11
San Juan de Dios - p313 D15
San Julio - p309 G10/H10
San Lázaro - p309 K10-11
San Lázaro - p312 C12
- p313 C13-14
San Leonardo - p309 G10-11
San Luis - p309 H11/J11
San Mariano Este - p309 K10
San Martin - p312 C12/D12/E11
San Miguel - p312 C12
- p313 D13-14
San Nicolás - p313 D13-14/E13
San Pablo - p309 E10/F10

- p312 E10/F10
San Pedro - p309 E9/F9
- p312 E9/F9
San Pedro - p313 E15
San Rafael - p312 C12/D12
- p313 D13-14
San Salvador - p309 F9/G9
Santa Catalina - p309 F9-10
- p312 F9-10
Santa Catalina, Avenida de - p309
H8/J9-10
Santa Emilia - p309 H10-11
Santa Irene - p309 H10-11
Santa María - p311 F7
Santa Marta - p312 E11-12
Santa Rosa - p309 E10
- p312 F11-12
Santa Teresa - p309 F8
- p311 F8
Santiago - p312 D12
Santo Suárez - p309 H10-11
Santo Tomas - p309 F9
Santo Tomás - p312 E11-12
Sevillano - p309 K8
Simón Bolivar, Avenida (Reina)
- p313 D13/E13
Sitio - p312 D12/E12
Sol - p313 E14-15
Soledad - p312 C12
Suarez - p313 E14/F14
Subirana - p312 D12/E12
Suzarte - p309 G9/H8
Tamarindo - p309 G10-11
Tenerife - p312 E12
- p313 E13
Territorial - p312 E10
Tres Palacios - p309 J11
Trocadero - p313 D14-15
Tulipán - p309 F9
- p311 D8/E8
Ulacia - p312 E9/F9
Unión y Ahorro - p309 F10-11
- p312 F10-11
Universidad Campos - p309 E10
- p312 F11
Ursula - p309 K8/L9
Valle - p312 C11-12/D12
Vapor - p312 C12
Velarde - p309 F8
Velazco - p313 E14-15
Vento, Calzada de - p309 H8
Via Blanca - p309 G8-11
Via Monumental - p313 B16
Villegas - p313 E14-15
Virtudes - p313 C13/D13-14
Vista Alegre - p309 J8-9
Vista Alegre Este - p309 K10
Vista Hermosa - p309 F9-10
- p312 F9-10
Washington - p309 G8
Washington, Avenida - p312 B12
Xifré - p312 D11
Zaldo - p312 E11
Zanja - p312 D12
Zapata, Calzada de - p312 C9-10
Zapote - p309 H10-11
Zequeira - p309 E10
- p312 F11
Zulueta - p313d14-15

Southern Havana

© Copyright Time Out Group 2000

Miramar & the Western Suburbs

A

0   500 m
0   500 yds
© Copyright Time Out Group 2000

B

Embajada Rusa

Iglesia de San
Antonia de Padua

40A 40 38 36A

42

36 34 32 30

5ta

5A

60

5B

7ma

7A

7B

QUEREJETA

7B

7C

11

13

15

17

19

C

9

11

13

15

17

76

74 72 70

68 66 64 62

21

23

25

27

29

84

86 82 80 78

19

ALMENDARES

31

D

21

23

25

74A 72A 70A

68A

68A 66A 64A 62A 60A

60

52 50

54

56

58

27

29

BUENAVISTA

31

33

35

E

29B

29C

29E

29F

29G

29H

LA CEIBA

Tropicana

25

74 41

31

76

78

80

82

F

41

84

86

88

35

47

Marina Hemingway

5 **6** **7** **8**

Malecón

Ave 1ra

Ave 3ra

Ave 5ta

Teatro
Karl Marx

Avenida 1ra

Maqueta de
La Habana

MIRAMAR

Avenida 3ra

Restaurant
1830

Linea

Museo del Ministerio
del Interior

Avenida 5ta

Avenida 7ma

Almendares

ICAIC

LA SIERRA

Cementerio
de Colón

Parque
Almendares

KOHLY

La Torre

Ave de Colón

NUEVO
VEDAO

Tulipán

Lombillo

Hidalgo

Estación de Ferrocarriles
19 de Noviembre

Este

Almendares

Factor

Empirio

Recurso

Santa María

Avenida de la Independencia

Calzada del Cerro

Colón

San Cristóbal

Prensa

Primelles

Pezuela

Churruca

Santa Teresa

Time Out Havana Guide **311**

Infanta

Cádiz

Ciudad
Deportiva

✔ To Southern Habana

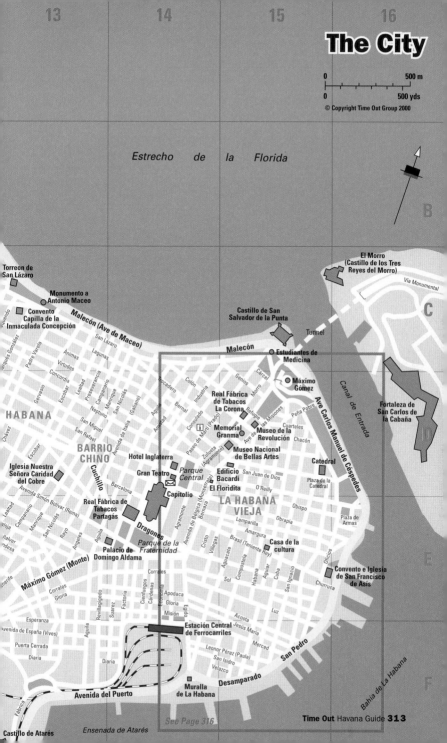

The City

0   500 m
0   500 yds

© Copyright Time Out Group 2000

Estrecho de la Florida

El Morro (Castillo de los Tres Reyes del Morro)

Vía Monumental

Torreón de San Lázaro

Monumento a Antonio Maceo

Convento Capilla de la Inmaculada Concepción

Malecón (Ave de Maceo)

Castillo de San Salvador de la Punta

Malecón

Tunnel

Estudiantes de Medicina

Máximo Gómez

Canal de Entrada

Fortaleza de San Carlos de la Cabaña

HABANA

Real Fábrica de Tabacos La Corona

Memorial Granma

Museo de la Revolución

Museo Nacional de Bellas Artes

BARRIO CHINO

Hotel Inglaterra

Iglesia Nuestra Señora Caridad del Cobre

Gran Teatro

Parque Central

Edificio Bacardí

El Floridita

Catedral

Plaza de la Catedral

Capitolio

LA HABANA VIEJA

Real Fábrica de Tabacos Partagás

Dragones

Parque de la Fraternidad

Palacio de Domingo Aldama

Plaza de Armas

Casa de la cultura

Máximo Gómez (Monte)

Convento e Iglesia de San Francisco de Asís

Estación Central de Ferrocarriles

Muralla de La Habana

Desamparado

San Pedro

Bahía de La Habana

Avenida del Puerto

See Page 316

Ensenada de Atarés

Castillo de Atarés

Playas del Este

SANTA MARÍA DEL MAR

Laguna Itabo

Mi Cayito

Vía Blanca

Playa Santa María del Mar

Avenida de las Terrazas

Avenida del Sur

Vía Blanca

Servicio Norte

Servicio Sud

Iglesia

Balcón

Playa Mégano

Avenida del Mar

Avenida Primera

Avenida 3

EL MÉGANO

Vía Blanca

SANTA MARÍA LOMA

Avenida7

Avenida 9

Avenida 11

Avenida 13

Oeste

Avenida de las Banderas

Balcón

▲ See page 315

500 m
500 yds

© Copyright Time Out Group 2000

La Habana Vieja

14 **15** **16**

Máximo Gómez

D

Real Fabricá de Tabacos La Corona
Museo de la Revolución
Memorial Granma
Museo Nacional de Bellas Artes

Hotel Inglaterra
Parque Central
Gran Teatro
Capitolio

Edificio Bacardí
El Floridita

Catedral

Castillo de la Real Fuerza

Museo de la Ciudad
Plaza de Armas

Iglesia del Santo Cristo del Buen Viaje

Casa de la Obra Pía

Casa de la cultura

E

Aquarium

Convento e Iglesia de San Francisco de Asís

Plaza Vieja

Convento de Santa Clara

Estación Central de Ferrocarriles

F

Muralla de La Habana

Bahía de La Habana

Canal de Entrada

Ave Carlos Manuel de Céspedes

Parque Céspedes

0   300 m

0   300 yds

© Copyright Time Out Group 2000